A HISTORY OF MOTOR VEHICLE REGISTRATION IN THE UNITED KINGDOM

(THIRD EDITION)

D1823329

L. H. NEWALL

With revisions edited by
John Harrison

Production of this edition was made possible with financial help from Frank Gillett, John Harrison, Adrian Hayward-Wills, Rod Lomax and Peter Robson.

First published 1999
Third edition 2008
Fourth impression with minor revisions 2017

Newby Books
Easingwold Town Hall Company Ltd
The Advertiser Office
Market Place
Easingwold
York YO61 3AB

Tel 01347 821329
www.newbybooks.co.uk

ISBN 978-1-872686-32-5

Printed by G H Smith & Son, Easingwold, York YO61 3AB
Telephone 01347 821329. Facsimile 01347 822576. www.ghsmith.com

CONTENTS

THE AUTHOR

This new edition affords the opportunity to include a few words about the author. Les Newall maintained a lifelong interest in vehicle registrations, right up until his death in 2000. He was an acknowledged expert on registration plates the world over, but those of the UK were his special interest, and he was the leading amateur authority on the subject.

UK registrations were not Les's only interest – he was a member for many years of Europlate, a worldwide group of number plate enthusiasts; for a number of years he was a committee member, and at one time was president. Les was an avid collector of licence plates and built up a substantial collection from all over the world.

His interest in registrations began in the 1930s, about the time the first three-letter issues appeared. Les pursued this hobby, involving the keeping of meticulous records, in addition to a career in municipal transport management. Through the Birmingham Locomotive Club he found several other people interested in registrations, and they frequently exchanged information. Such correspondence increased greatly with the advent of year letters and developed into the Registration Newsletter, which continues to this day, and which Les handed over to me in 1994 after the 100th issue.

This book reflects the painstaking detail of the records he kept of sightings of his own and from many correspondents, which set down our best knowledge of what combinations and range of numbers and letters have been issued, when, and by which office. In addition to sightings on the road, Les studied in detail the statutory instruments which at one time decided who issued what, and he and fellow hobbyists have spent many hours poring over what records survived from local authority issues of registrations prior to centralisation in 1974. Such studies have provided much of the detail in this book.

Whether your interest is hobby-wise or professional, I hope you find the book as useful and readable as I did.

Graham Cox

FOREWORD

Registration of motor vehicles in the United Kingdom commenced in 1903 and, with few exceptions, a registration mark issued at any time is still valid for use today. However, the system has been subject to modifications over the years.

Initially registration marks consisted of a one or two letter index mark followed by a number between 1 and 9999. This format sufficed until 1932, by which time certain authorities had exhausted all their available numbers. The solution was to issue three-letter index marks of which the first was a serial letter and the other two the existing two-letter marks of the authorities concerned. The three letters were followed by a number between 1 and 999. By 1953 a further modification was required and as they ran out of available marks authorities commenced the issue of their index marks in reverse order, i.e. from one to four numerals followed by one or two letters or one to three numerals followed by three letters.

The "year letter" system was commenced in 1963 by authorities which had exhausted all their available marks and by the new registering burgh of Kirkcaldy in Scotland. All other authorities gradually changed over to the new system by 1st January 1965. The format was now three letters, followed by one to three numerals, followed by a single letter which changed each year. Initially the letter change took place on 1st January. But in 1967 the switch to 1st August took place. I, O, Q and U were not used as year letters, the latter allegedly being omitted to avoid confusion with V. Year-letter Y was used for the year commencing 1st August 1982 and Z was not used, all combinations including Z being reserved for issue in Ireland. Accordingly, on 1st August 1983, the year prefix format was commenced. This is a reverse of the previous format and thus consists of the year-letter, followed by up to three numerals and a three-letter index mark. A further change occurred when it was decided, in 1998, that in future the age indicator would change every six months. Hence S prefix ran from 1st August 1998 to 28th February 1999 and the remaining prefixes T, V, W, X, and Y at six monthly intervals, Y suffix ending 31st August 2001. Thereafter a completely new system is due to come into operation and thus the system which provides the main subject matter of this book will come to an end after almost 98 years of operation.[1]

The successive formats adopted in both parts of Ireland have not followed strictly the same pattern as that in Great Britain. Registrations without year letter both in "forward" and "reverse" formats continued to be issued in the Republic of Ireland up till 31st December 1986 when a completely new system commenced, finally marking departure from the system used since 1903. In Northern Ireland, the use of registrations without year letters continues to this day, albeit with three letters followed by up to four numerals.

---

[1] Editor's note. This foreword was, of course, written in 1999 prior to the adoption of what is now the current system in September 2001. This system is described in more detail in the postscript at the end of the book.

ACKNOWLEDGMENTS

The compilation of this work would not have been possible without the co-operation of a considerable number of people. The help received may conveniently be divided into two categories. Firstly those people who, like me, have spent many hours poring over dusty tomes in various County Record Offices and similar locations up and down the country in order to extract information from the relatively small volume of Local Taxation Office records which survived the mass destruction following centralisation. I would like to thank especially David Hales, Jonathan Del Mar, Douglas Wilson, Alan Cain, David Carter and the late Jess Tawn. I also acknowledge the very considerable assistance of Peter Jaques of the Kithead Trust.

In the second category of helpers are the many correspondents, too numerous to mention by name, who have shared their observations of the registration scene over a very long period.

I would also like to thank the staff at the DVLA and at various VROs for their tolerance in dealing with the many questions that I have put to them over the years.

I am indebted to Reg Wilson for his help with the cover design.

Unfortunately it has not been possible for me or my colleagues to visit each and every location where records are held. The Appendix detailing registration marks issued by individual local authorities mentions information missing from my records which may still be available at the locations noted. If any readers of this book are able to visit any of the named locations and provide the missing details I shall be very pleased to hear from them.

OUTLINE OF THE LEGISLATION

BEFORE 1903

As early as 1681 it was required that carts licensed to ply for hire in the City of London should be marked with the City coat of arms and a number on a brass plate. The London Hackney Carriage Act of 1831 referred to "stage coaches......being duly licensed and having proper numbered plates" and before the end of the century London and probably other local authorities required hackney carriages to carry numbered plates. The Revenue Act of 1869, effective 1 January 1870, imposed a uniform system of taxation for horse-drawn carriages. The Locomotives Act of 1898 required county councils or county borough councils to register or license "heavy locomotives", (excluding those used for agricultural purposes), operating within their area. A "heavy locomotive" was one with an unladen weight of or exceeding 3 tons, (in practice almost exclusively steam powered vehicles).

THE MOTOR CAR ACT, 1903

This was the first legislation to require the universal registration of motor vehicles, and the requirement to carry number plates. Section 2 includes the following sub-sections :
(1) Every motor car shall be registered with the council of a county or county borough, and every such council shall assign a separate number to every car registered with them.
(2) A mark indicating the registered number of the car and the council with which the car is registered shall be fixed on the car or on a vehicle drawn by the car, or on both, in such manner as the council require in conformity with regulations of the Local Government Board made under this Act.
The Act came into force on 1st January 1904. "Heavy locomotives" were excluded from the registration provisions of the 1903 Act since they were already required to be registered or licensed under the Locomotives Act of 1898. The Heavy Motor Car Order of 1904 redefined the upper weight limit for a "motor car" from 3 tons to 5 tons and thus vehicles with unladen weights between these figures became regulated by the Motor Car Act of 1903 rather than the Locomotives Act of 1898. Tramcars were also excluded from the provisions of the Act.

THE REGULATIONS OF 1903

The regulations referred to in Section 2 of the 1903 Act duly appeared as :
The Motor Car (Registration & Licensing) Order, 1903. Statutory Rules and Orders 1903, No. 998.
The Motor Car Registration & Licensing (Scotland) Order 1903. SR&O 1903, No. 1001.
The Motor Car (Registration & Licensing) (Ireland) Order 1903. SR&O 1903, No. 1002.
The following is a summary of their main provisions :
Article I of Part I required that "The Council of every County and the Council of every County Borough shall establish and keep a Register (hereinafter referred to as "the Register of Motor Cars") for the registration of motor cars. The index mark distinguishing the Council of the County or County Borough with which a motor car is registered shall....be the letter or letters shown opposite to the name of that Council in Part I of the First Schedule to this Order". (The provisions of this schedule are dealt with in detail in the chapter "Allocation of Index Marks".) This article required that the register was to be kept in the form specified in the Second Schedule and provided that the Council may, if they thought fit, keep the Register in two parts, one relating to motor cars and the other to motor cycles.

Article II specified the fees for registration and Article III required that the Council, on receipt of an application for registration "shall forthwith assign a separate number to the motor car.....".

Article IV provided that on change of ownership "an application shall be made either to cancel the registration of the car or to continue the existing registration under the new ownership."

Article VI stated "If the Council are satisfied that a motor car which has been registered with them is destroyed, broken up, or permanently removed from the United Kingdom, or registered with another registering authority under the Act of 1903, or if the owner of a registered motor car....requests them to cancel the registration..... they shall cause the entries in the Register of Motor Cars .... to be cancelled and may, if they think fit, assign the registered number of the motor car to any other motor car belonging to the same or any other owner".

Article VII : "The mark to be carried by a registered motor car, in pursuance of section 2 of the Act of 1903, shall consist of two plates which must conform as to lettering, numbering and otherwise, with the provisions set out in the Fourth Schedule to this Order. Designs, painted or otherwise, shown upon the motor car may, if it is desired, be used instead of plates......" (The provisions of the Fourth Schedule are detailed below).

Article VIII Dealt with the positioning of plates, (one front, one rear, in an upright position), and provided for the use of double sided plates on the front of motor cycles or tricycles not exceeding 3 cwt. unladen. Article IX provided for the display of a duplicate plate on a trailer. Article X pemitted Councils, if they thought fit, to supply plates and make a charge for them. Article XI provided for the illumination of rear plates during hours of darkness.
Article XII dealt with the assignment to manufacturers or dealers of a general identification mark and specified the form such marks should take.

The First Schedule set out the initial allocation of index marks to the County Councils and County Borough Councils. (It should be mentioned that the local government structure in Scotland was different from that in the rest of Great Britain and, there being no County Boroughs in Scotland, registration authorities were defined as "the council of every county and the Council of every royal, parliamentary or police burgh, containing within its boundaries......a population... of, or exceeding 50,000."). It should be noted that throughout this study are used the official titles of counties, county boroughs and burghs, as set out in the SR&Os. In some cases these titles differ from the commonly used versions.
The Fourth Schedule specified that plates must be rectangular, but both "square" plates, (with letter(s) on the upper line and numerals on the lower), or oblong plates (with letters and numbers in one line), were permitted. "The ground of the plate must be black, the letters and figures must be white". Dimensions specified :
Height of letters and figures : 3½" Width (except figure 1) : 2½" Width of stroke : 5/8"
Top and bottom margin : ½" Space between adjoining letters and between adjoining numerals : ½" Side margin : 1" Between upper and lower lines on "square" plates : ¾"
Between letters and figures on oblong plates : 1½"
For motor cycles and tricycles not exceeding 3 cwt unladen, each of the above dimensions is halved and the shape of the plate need not be rectangular.
(The sketch incorporated in the Schedule shows a hyphen between letters and numerals on oblong plates, but this was never a statutory requirement).

STATUTORY RULES & ORDERS

Further Statutory Rules & Orders, (later known as Statutory Instruments), were issued as and when it became necessary to allot additional registration marks, both to newly created county boroughs and to those councils whose existing allocation of marks was nearing exhaustion. The Orders also regulated all other aspects of vehicle registration and licensing. A full listing of all the Statutory Rules and Orders and Statutory Instruments, listing their effect on the allocation of index marks, will be found in Appendix 6.

ROADS ACT, 1920

The main purpose of this Act was to make provision for the collection and application of the excise duties on mechanically propelled vehicles and on carriages. It came into operation on 1st January 1921.

The detailed procedure for registration and licensing was laid down in the Road Vehicles (Registration & Licensing) Regulations, 1921. The principal changes to the procedure under the Motor Car Act of 1903 relating to registration marks were :

1. A requirement that a vehicle should be registered with the Council within whose area it was ordinarily kept. (Under the 1903 Act an owner could register a vehicle with any Council of his choice).
2. The re-issue of void registration numbers was discontinued. (See Article VI of the 1903 Regulations).
3. "Heavy Locomotives" were brought into the general scheme of registration and the provisions for the separate registration of motorcycles and heavy goods vehicles were discontinued.

The relevant sections are as follow :

Part I, Regulation 2 : "A person who desires to obtain a licence for a mechanically propelled vehicle shall apply to the Council in whose area such vehicle is ordinarily kept....."

Regulation 3 : "A vehicle shall be deemed to be ordinarily kept in the area of the Council in which is situated the garage in which the vehicle is ordinarily kept, provided that where a person satisfies the Council of the area in which he declares his principal place of business to be situated that a vehicle is not ordinarily kept in any one area, application may be made to that Council..."

Regulation 9 sets out the conditions for the issue of general identification marks, (trade plates), to manufacturers and dealers.

Regulation 14 (1) "The index mark and registration number which has been declared to have been the index mark and registration number were at the 31st day of December 1920 shall be entered in the Register and on the licence, and shall thereafter attach to that vehicle until the same is broken up, destroyed or sent permanently out of the United Kingdom. (2) In the case of any other vehicle the Council shall assign to the vehicle an index mark and a registration number according to the index mark allotted under these Regulations to the Council, and shall enter such mark and number in the Register and upon the Licence."

The Second Schedule set out a consolidated list of the index marks allotted under the 1903 Regulations and those added by subsequent SR&Os. The Fourth Schedule laid down the specification of the plates, which was identical to that under the 1903 Act, except that natural aluminium colour is now specified as an alternative to white and that the hyphen is absent from the sketch of the oblong plate.

THE VEHICLES (EXCISE) ACTS 1949 & 1962

The Vehicles (Excise) Acts of 1949 of 1962 re-enacted the provisions of the Roads Act 1920 relating to vehicle licensing and registration with only minor changes.

THE VEHICLES AND DRIVING LICENCES ACT 1969

This Act presaged a major change in the system of registration and licensing since it foreshadowed the centralisation of vehicle licensing and the setting up of the Driver and Vehicle Licensing Centre. The Act provided that on the "transfer date", (to be specified by the Minister of Transport by Order), the functions conferred on local authorities by previous Acts would be transferred to the Minister of Transport.

THE VEHICLES (EXCISE) ACT 1971

This laid down the detailed changes in legislation resulting from the Vehicles and Driving Licences Act, 1969, and the Vehicles and Driving Licences (Transfer of Functions) order, 1971, including the new provision for the allocation of registration marks to dealers.

The "transfer date" was eventually specified as 1 April 1971, from which date the local authorities became agents of the Minister of Transport until such time as centralisation was completed, in practice until 1978.

Minor details of the registration and licensing system were regulated by means of circulars issued by the government bodies to local authorities. The various instruments of legislation will be dealt with in greater detail in subsequent chapters.

MINISTRY OF TRANSPORT CIRCULARS

After the passing of the Roads Act of 1920 Statutory Rules & Orders were supplemented by a series of Circulars issued by the Ministry of Transport to registration authorities, dealing with the minutiae of the system. The Circulars were numbered in a series commencing with RF 100 dated 4 October 1920. (RF = Road Fund). Of special interest was RF 182 of January 1925. This was the first edition of a booklet which became "Registration & Licensing Councils - Index Marks and Addresses". This was reprinted on numerous occasions up to 1979, (latterly as VE 182 - VE = Vehicles Excise.) A similar format was adopted for V 382 in 1974, this being the equivalent publication covering the index marks and addresses of the Local Vehicle Licensing Offices, (and later of the VROs). This publication has also been revised and reprinted at intervals.

There was also a set of Information Circulars, (No. 1 was dated January 1921). From time to time a consolidated version of the Information Circulars was issued in the form of "The Handbook", revised and reprinted at intervals until 1975.

ALLOTMENT OF INDEX MARKS TO COUNCILS

SINGLE AND TWO-LETTER INDEX MARKS PRECEDING NUMBERS

The Regulations of 1903 allotted only one index mark to each council. As these were exhausted further regulations were made, allotting additional index marks. In the early years it was usual for individual Orders to be made for each council as and when a new index mark was required; later on, however, with the increase in the number of vehicles, the number of new marks allotted by each Order tended to increase. From time to time, when amendments were made to the Registration & Licensing Regulations, the Schedules listing index marks have been set out in full, with or without the inclusion of new index marks. In this chapter an attempt is made to follow the various systems used for the allotment of index marks to councils, and while there was a vague overall plan, there are many exceptions to the general pattern, many of them inexplicable. One reason may be found in the fact that the expansion in motor traffic took place at a rate which could not possibly have been envisaged when the original plan was drawn up. Again, through the years there was doubtless a succession of officials concerned in the task of allotting index marks and this would also tend to militate against the adoption of an orderly system. The various stages of development are treated separately in order to make each step more easy to follow, but it must be borne in mind that the divisions which follow are purely arbitrary.

ENGLAND & WALES

Original allotment, 1903

Index marks were allotted to every administrative county and county borough then existing. Some geographical counties were divided into two or three administrative counties - Yorkshire was divided into its three Ridings, Lincolnshire into its three Parts, Suffolk and Sussex into East and West, whilst the Isle of Ely, the Soke of Peterborough and the Isle of Wight were administered separately from Cambridgeshire, Northamptonshire and Hampshire respectively. The apparently haphazard order of allocation of the original index marks is explained by the fact that councils were listed in descending order of population, according to the Census of 1901, but allowing for boundary changes in the intervening two years. The largest councils took the single letters, followed by AA, AB, AC etc., and the initial allocation extended from A (London C.C.) to FP (Rutland C.C.). The population figures used for the allocation are set out in Appendix 1. (The marks G and V for Glasgow B.C. and Lanark C.C. respectively were apparently also allotted on the population basis, but owing to the differing treatment of the Census figures in Scotland it has not been possible to arrive at a figure which would place them precisely in the table. However, Edinburgh does not fit into the population table and it seems likely that 'S' for Scotland was chosen for the capital city).

Combinations including the following letters were not used initially in England and Wales :

    G, S and V - reserved for Scotland.

    I and Z - reserved for Ireland.

    Q   - probably omitted to avoid confusion with O.

The following two-letter combinations were also omitted : DD, DT and ER.

The attitude of mind of the Edwardian era undoubtedly had a bearing on these omissions - anything relating to religion, the evils of drink or the Crown would be avoided.

DD and DT might have been taken as abbreviations of Doctor of Divinity and delirium tremens respectively, whilst ER was the then Royal Cipher. However, another more intriguing theory may be advanced for the initial omission of ER. Examination of the 1903 population figures shows that the Borough of Cambridge falls exactly between Montgomeryshire and Rotherham and, of course, ER was eventually allotted to Cambridgeshire. Was there, perhaps, an aborted proposal to elevate Cambridge to county borough status at the time when the 1903 legislation was being drafted ?

Subsequent Allotments

These fall into three categories :
(1)   Index marks for county boroughs created after 1903.
(2)   Index marks for councils having exhausted their first and subsequent marks.
(3)   Alteration of the original index marks allotted to Dorset C.C. (BF) and Northampton C.B.C. (DF) following objections from motorists in those areas to being labelled bloody fools or simply damned fools !

1904 - 1919
The first new marks required were for the newly constituted county boroughs of Blackpool and Tynemouth, which took the next available combinations, FR and FT.
Then followed an Order changing the original Dorset mark, BF. In place of this, FX was allotted, FU and FW being passed over at this stage for an unknown reason.
It is interesting to note that, at this stage, the substitution of FX for BF was not compulsory in the case of vehicles already registered, and a number of thick-skinned owners retained their BF numbers until they were obliged to change them in 1921.

The first council to require a second index mark was, of course, London, and even at this early stage it was recognised that the larger councils would require several index marks. London, therefore was not given FY, but LC, which, besides being well clear of any combinations hitherto allotted was phonetically apt - London County.   From now on "blocks" of letters were reserved for the largest councils, and, in two other cases, these took into account the "phonetic" element, viz : MX etc. for Middlesex, KT etc. for Kent. Where this was not possible, (e.g. Birmingham, Surrey - because the B-'s and S-'s were not available), the "blocks" followed on the appropriate single letter, viz : O, OA; P, PA etc.

The "phonetic" element was introduced in the case of some of the later issues, to which reference will be made later, and also appeared in the next mark to be allotted after LC. This was NH, allotted to Northampton C.B.C. in substitution for DF. The council minutes show that this mark was issued at the request of the council, the Local Government Board's original proposal being to allot FY.   This substitution was again permissive and not obligatory in the case of vehicles already registered. (It is of interest to observe that whilst the objection to DF had apparently been overcome by 1922, when it was re-allocated to Gloucester C.C., BF was never issued as such. the later allotment to Staffordshire being in three-letter combinations only.)

Following FY for the new county borough of Southport in 1905, subsequent issues in the normal alphabetical sequence continued from HA onwards, the G-'s being passed over, reserved for future Scottish requirements.
The allotments of 1904 - 1919 (actually to SR&O 146 of 2.1.20) may be summarised as follows :

(a) Alphabetical Sequence

FR, FT, FX, FY, HA to HF, HH, HJ to HP, HR, HT.

Of these HK was the first additional mark to be required by a council other than those having been allotted "block" issues. It is rather surprising that Essex was not considered to warrant a block allocation, though, of course, it would not have been possible to allot either a "phonetic" series or one following on its original F index mark, (but note that Lancashire, similarly placed, were later given a "block" issue in the T-'s). HO, HP, HR and HT were also second marks; the remainder, with the exception of FX, were for newly created county boroughs. After the promotion of Darlington to this status in 1915, only one further county borough (Doncaster in 1927) was created before the introduction of "year-letter" marks.

(b) "Block" Issues
(i) "Phonetic"

London : LC, LN, LB, LD, LA, LE, LF, LH, LK, LL, LM, LO, LP, LR, LT, LU, LW, LX and LY. Following LC (London County) came LN (LondoN).

The order of the next three is interesting - a possible explanation is that it was originally intended to reserve LA as a "block" issue for Glamorgan, but that it was released for London when it was seen that Glamorgan was making comparatively slow progress. Following LE strict alphabetical sequence was followed, but with the omission of LJ as well as LV. Although -J's were used in the initial issues and HJ followed in 1914, no further marks containing 'J' were allotted until 1926.

Middlesex : MX, MC, MD. After MX (MiddleseX)) came MC (Middlesex County), then MD, leaving MA and MB in reserve for Cheshire.

Kent : KT, KN and West Riding : WR - purely "phonetic".

(NH for Northampton C.B.C. also "phonetic", though not a "block" issue.)

(ii) Following initial letter

Birmingham : OA, OB, OE. No explanation can be offered for the curious omission of OC and OD; OC, in fact, is one of the oddest marks of all, as will be seen later.

Liverpool : KB, KC. (It seems certain that KA was passed over at this stage to avoid confusion with Liverpool's General Identification marks, which were in the format K-A and a number).

Others : PA, PB, NA, NB, MA, WA.

(iii) Others

Lancashire was given TB in 1919 - the first example of a "block" issue which followed neither the initial letter of the name of the council, nor the council's single letter mark, neither of which were available, of course. TA was left for Devon.

(During this period EH was taken over from Hanley C.B.C. by the new county borough of Stoke-on-Trent, into which it was incorporated, and DR was transferred to Plymouth when it absorbed Devonport.)

1920 - 1921

After HT, the next "alphabetical" issue was NK. It would appear that the remaining H-'s were "blocked" for Bristol; J-'s were not used at this stage and as the bulk of the K-'s, L-'s, M-'s, also the early N-'s, were earmarked for "block" issues, NK was the next available, following on NH. London, having completed the L-'s, received a new block in the X-'s.

Summary of allotments, January 1920 to July 1921 :

(a) Alphabetical sequence.
NK to NP, NR, NT, NU, NW, NX, NY.

The allotment of NU and NW to Derbyshire and Leeds respectively is rather odd, in view of the fact that RA and UA were available and, in fact, used later. The "phonetic" NL is thought to be purely coincidental.

(b) "Block" issues
London : XA to XF, XH, XK to XM - allotted in strict alphabetical sequence. (Also during this period came the first of the Q-'s, QQ, which were reserved for issue to foreign visitors).
Birmingham : OH and OK - again peculiar, since OF was available.
Kent : KE and West Riding : WY - purely "phonetic".
Others : ME, NC and PC - straightforward continuation of existing blocks;
TA and YA - following initial letter.

Others
RE for Staffordshire is interesting - it may have been intended at this stage to leave all the P-'s for Surrey and that RE was "alphabetical". However, the allotment of NU in the same SR&O suggests that at this stage the early R-'s were not "blocked". Note also that the next R- allotted was RK.

1921 - SR&O No. 1748
This Order allotted such a remarkable collection of oddments that it deserves a paragraph to itself. Firstly it gave three of the earlier omissions : DD, ER and FU. MO and MR are very odd - it must have been decided that Middlesex would not need all the M-'s, but no explanation can be offered as to why these two were picked out. KU and OR are in a similar category, representing invasions of the territories of Kent and Birmingham respectively; these two also commenced their own "blocks". (Note that both Middlesex and Birmingham were eventually given marks outside their own series).
HU followed HT for Bristol and KK completed the word "KENT" in the second letters of that county's marks. The remainder in this Order were quite straightforward "block" issues : MB, ND, TC, WB, XN, XO and XP.

1922 - 1924
(a) Alphabetical sequence
The next Order gave PM to East Sussex, it having apparently been decided that Surrey would not need to go beyond PL. Then followed, in alphabetical order, (except for TM) : PP, PR, PT, PU, PW, PX, PY, RK, RL, RM, RO, RP, RR, RT, RU, RW, RY, TM, TN, TO, TP, TR, TT, TU, TW, TX, TY, UD, UE, UF, UH, UK, UN, UO, UP, UR, UT, UX, UY, WF, WH, WK, WL, WM, WN, WO.
The starting point in each series was determined by the need to leave room for continuation of existing blocks. There were, as usual, many peculiar omissions :
PN, PO - both came in handy later for Sussex (East and West respectively), but it seems doubtful whether they were left open for this purpose.
RN - Royal Navy ?
RX, UL, UU and UW - no apparent reason.
The T-'s originally started at TN, TM appearing after UK - presumably it was thought that too many T-s had been "blocked". (Note that WP, the next available alphabetical mark, did not appear until the "tidying-up" of 1928.)

(b) Block issues

London : The X- series was completed quite normally with XR, XT, XU, XW, XX and XY, followed by YK, YL, YM, YN, YO, YP and YR, the earlier Y-'s being at this stage left for Somerset.

Liverpool : The missing KA appeared.

Birmingham : OC was belatedly allotted, but was followed not by OD and OF, but by OL, OM, ON and OP. However, although allotted, OC was ignored by Birmingham - before it was required, OL had been allotted and this was used next, OC being kept in "cold storage" until all their other marks had been used. There is no similar case, although some of London's later marks were not used strictly in order of allotment, e.g. GU and YY. One is tempted to think that officials in Birmingham overlooked the fact that OC had been allotted, (possibly because of its being out of alphabetical sequence), and called upon Whitehall for a new issue when OK was nearing completion. Support is lent to this theory by the fact that the SR&O (631 of 1923) which gave OL, included no other new marks, (being, indeed, the last such, apart from the special case of Doncaster in 1927 and the Staffordshire "emergency" of 1960), which suggests a "rush job". Note also that OO was omitted - either to avoid confusion between O's and noughts or between OO and QQ - although it had to be pressed into use in 1961.

Derbyshire : RA belatedly appeared to follow R in a new "block" for this county.

Leeds : UM, UA. UM calls for comment and was allotted at this stage to regularise an error. An M.o.T Circular to local authorities dated 4.8.22 stated "The mark UM has been allotted to certain vehicles by Leeds C.B.C. under a misapprehension. In view of the inconvenience and expense involved it has been decided that the identification marks already allotted should be allowed to stand, and that in the next Order relating to Index Marks the mark UM will be appropriated to the Leeds authority." (UM was used by Leeds prior to 1921 as a general identification mark and this fact probably has some connection with the error.)

Gloucestershire : DF, which had offended Northampton motorists in 1905, had apparently become respectable 19 years later and was given to Gloucestershire, presumably because of its proximity to their other "disinterred" mark, DD.

The remaining "block" issues of this period followed quite logically on former marks : KL, KM, KO; KW; MF, MH, MK, ML, MM; NE, NF; OT; PD, PE, PF, PH; RF; TD, TE; WT, WU, WW; YB, YC.

(c) "Phonetic" issue.

KH, having hitherto been reserved, presumably for Liverpool, made a most fortuitous "phonetic" mark for Kingston-opon-Hull.

1926

(a) Alphabetical sequence

By this date England's needs had become more pressing than Scotland's and the letter 'V', which had hitherto appeared only on Scottish plates, was appropriated for the next alphabetical series. Another hitherto Scottish letter, 'G', also appeared on an English plate for the first time with VG, while the series also included VJ, the first use of 'J' since 1914. The series allotted in 1926 was : VB, VC, VE, VF, VG, VH, VJ, VK, VL, VM, VN, VO, VP, VT, VW, VX and VY. Note that VD was omitted, only to be used in Scotland two years later. VR, VU and VV were also passed over temporarily. There is some evidence of an attempt at "phonetic" allocation in VC, VH, VL, VM, VN and VY, where the second letter of the index mark coincides with the initial of the council. This tendency was also marked in the 1928 to 1930 allotments containing 'G' and 'J'. It is noteworthy that two councils hitherto using "block" issues received marks in this series, viz : Manchester (VM) and Birmingham (VP). In the case of Manchester, this was unavoidable without using NG, and G-'s at this stage were not yet in general use in England. There were, however, several O-'s still available for Birmingham; indeed, OX was allotted in the same SR&O and this incursion into the V-'s seems quite unnecessary.

(b) "Block" issues

London received marks in three series :

(i) The remaining Y-'s following on from YR and including YV, and also YE, YF and YH, it being evident by now that Somerset would not need them : YE, YF, YH, YT, YU, YV, YW, YX and YY.

(ii)   XV, taking advantage of the newly released 'V' to fill the gap in the X- series.

(iii   The previously omitted U-'s (i.e. UL, UU and UW), together with UC, (hitherto "blocked" for Leeds), and UV.

Sheffield : WE   (WC omitted for obvious reasons, but omission of WD not so easily explained - possibly "War Department", but it appeared two years later.)

Middlesex : MP, MT and MY. Although the Isle of Man is not under the jurisdiction of Whitehall, MN, the Manx mark, was not surprisingly avoided. There does not appear to be any logical explanation, however, for the omission at this stage of MU. MW, like MO and MR, was for some mysterious reason, allotted elsewhere.

Bristol : HW. Although certain -V's appeared in 1926, it was not until 1928 that they became general and HV was then allotted elsewhere.

The following were quite logical : KD, KP, PK, WX.

(c) Others

Like SR&O 1748 of 1921, the 1926 Order called for some tidying-up :

FW - another example, like Gloucester C.C., of a council having two "resurrected" marks in proximity.

KX - No logical explanation why this could not have been reserved for Bradford, who later received KY.

MW - This should have gone to Middlesex (cf. MR).

PN - Conveniently following PM for East Sussex.

PO - Surely no coincidence that this went to West Sussex ?

RD - Not required by Derbyshire, made a convenient "phonetic" for Reading, (cf. KH).

RX - Another illogical omission from its proper sequence in 1923.

TH, TK and TL - Released, presumably, from Lancashire's block.

Mention must also be made here of DT, one of the 1903 omissions, which made a most appropriate mark for Doncaster upon its incorporation as a county borough in 1927.

1928 - 1932

By now there were so few available combinations left that all restrictions were abandoned and after the three SR&Os of this period, only three combinations remained, with the exception of those containing I, Q and Z.

The issues of this period may be summarised as follows :

(a) Alphabetical sequence.

One new series remained - the J-'s and all these, except for JJ, appeared in 1928. The "phonetic" element is referred to later. The remaining -G, -J and -V issues might also be considered "alphabetical", though many of these were incorporated into "block" issues as mentioned below.

"Alphabetical" allotments were, then :

JA, JB, JC, JD, JE, JF, JG, JH, JJ, JK, JL, JM, JN, JO, JP, JR, JT, JU, JV, JW, JX and JY.

BG, CG, EG, HG, KG, LG, NG, TG, XG, YG.

LJ, MJ, NJ, RJ, UJ, XJ.

BV, CV, DV, EV, FV, GV, HV, KV, LV, NV, PV, RV, TV, VV, WV.

It may be noted here that YJ went to Scotland - the only example of a Scottish two-letter mark not containing 'G', 'S' or 'V'.

(b) "Block" issues.

One new "block" appeared - the G- series for London, all of which were allotted in 1928, viz : GC, GF, GH, GJ, GK, GN, GO, GP, GT, GU, GW, GX, GY.

There are the usual anomalies :

GL and GR were missed, only to be allotted elsewhere in 1932.

GV was also allotted elsewhere, but a possible explanation is that this was treated as a -V, rather than a G-, and possibly earmarked, though not actually allotted, before the G-series proper. GG was given to Glasgow, in preference to GC or GF, and the explanation for this will be found in the section dealing with Scotland.

Many of the remaining "block" issues of this period were the -G's, -J' and -V's, simply because there was nothing else left. These were as follows : DG; KJ; MG, MV; OG, OJ, OV; PG, PJ; TJ; UG and WJ. (The two latter, although not "block" issues in the strict sense, fit in with the respective councils' first letter).

Others which could have been fitted into the "block"scheme were KG, LG and NG, instead of which the councils in question received LV (phonetic), JJ and XJ respectively. Note also that Lancashire received TJ rather than TG, but for Middlesex this position was reversed, receiving MG, not MJ.

Other "block" issues were :

KF, KR, KY, MU, OF, OU, PL, RB, TF, UB and YD, all quite logical, but Bristol's set was completed with HY, while HX went, quite illogically, to Middlesex.

(c) Others

The remaining "oddments" were dealt with as follows :

HX - to Middlesex, although MJ was available.

OW, RC - allotted, sensibly enough, to the county town to follow the block of the appropriate county.

OD, OY - unused marks from the "blocks" of Birmingham and Southampton C.C. respectively.

RH - possibly "blocked" for Staffordshire originally.

GC, GR, GV, RN, VR, VU, WD and WP - omissions previously commented upon.

The following are examples of the "phonetic" element in the late issues :

BG, BV, CV, EV, LV, NG, NV, WV - first letter is initial of council,

JB, JC, JE, JH, JO, JW - second letter is initial of council.

The only combinations now remaining were BF, OO and WC. They remained unused for almost 30 years until towards the end of the reversed format era, when the pressing needs of certain authorities caused them to be allotted, albeit BF and WC in certain three-letter combinations only, in 1960-61.

Q- SERIES

The special Q- series is reserved for issue to vehicles arriving from overseas without an International Circulation Permit. Until 1930, only the combination QQ was allotted for this purpose, being nominally allotted to London County Council, but in practice issued through the Automobile Association and The Royal Automobile Club, as well as by the L.C.C. directly. The SR&O of 1930 allotted further Q- series marks, nominally to London C.C. but in practice issued by the following motoring organisations:

QA – Automobile Association
QC – Royal Automobile Club
QS – Royal Scottish Automobile Club.

Further Q- series were allotted in 1946 (QB, QD & QE), 1951 (QF, QG, QH, QJ, QK, QL, QM, QN and QP) and 1971 (QR, QT, QU, QV, QW, QX and QY). Not surprisingly QO was not allotted; QU, QV and QW have not been used. QI and QZ were allocated for issue to vehicles imported direct into Northern Ireland, but there is no evidence they were brought into use.

SCOTLAND

Index marks were allotted to each county council and each "registering burgh" which was defined as a royal, parliamentary or police burgh with a population of, or exceeding, 50,000.

Original Allotments, 1903

The three largest councils received single-letter marks. Edinburgh was allotted S, as appropriate for the Scottish capital, whilst Glasgow and Lanarkshire received G and V respectively, as mentioned in the paragraph dealing with the original allotments in England and Wales. The remaining councils were listed in alphabetical order, county councils first, followed by the "registering burghs". The series commenced with SA for Aberdeenshire, then SB to SY, followed by AS, BS etc. to PS for Zetland. Then came RS for Aberdeen B.C. down to YS for Partick. The following counties were renamed after 1903, hence their position in the list:

SO – formerly Elginshire, renamed Morayshire
SR – formerly Forfarshire, renamed Angus
SS – formerly Haddingtonshire, renamed East Lothian
SX – formerly Linlithgowshire, renamed West Lothian.

The letters I, Q and Z were, of course, not used, nor at this stage were combinations including the letters C and F. As mentioned earlier, the letters G and V were used in Scotland and remained exclusively Scottish until 1926. It is all the more surprising, therefore, that the "double-Scottish" combinations GS and SG were passed over initially.

Subsequent issues

With one exception, all subsequent Scottish issues contained the letters G, S or V. It will be more convenient to deal with these under the respective councils, rather than in chronological order.

Glasgow

Used a "block" issue on the English pattern, following on its single-letter mark, but still avoiding the use of C and F, notwithstanding that elsewhere in Scotland these letters were used from 1923 onwards: GA, GB, GD, GE and GG. Glasgow also acquired the marks US and YS when its boundaries were extended in 1912 to embrace the burghs of Govan and Partick.

Lanarkshire

VA followed V, but by the time a third mark was required VB and VC had already been allotted in England, so Lanarkshire was allotted VD, which had been shunned south of the border.

Edinburgh

Following S, the unused S- combinations were allotted in the order SG, SF and SC. The final Edinburgh mark was FS; meanwhile WS had been taken over, with the burgh of Leith, in 1920.

Others

The amalgamation of the separate burghs of Motherwell and Wishaw into a single authority in 1920 created the new burgh of Motherwell & Wishaw with a population exceeding 50,000, which thus became a registering burgh, receiving the Scottish G with its own initial, i.e. GM. This "phonetic" element also occurs in FG - Fife, AG - Ayr and AV - Aberdeenshire, whilst Aberdeen burgh received RG to go with RS. Perth received GS. When Dundee required a second mark in 1930 it was allotted YJ, whilst at the same time marks containing 'G' were given to English councils. The remaining -S mark, CS, was one of the last of all to be allotted and went to Ayrshire in 1932.

(It may be mentioned here that after Motherwell and Wishaw, no new registering authorities came into being until 1963/4 when, as a result of their 1961 census figures being over 50,000, Kirkcaldy and Coatbridge became registering burghs, but by now no two-letter marks remained and these two councils adopted the "year-letter" scheme from the outset.)

IRELAND

Original Allotments, 1903

It must be borne in mind that until 1922 the whole of Ireland was part of the United Kingdom. Index marks were allotted to all county councils and county borough councils. Initial allotments for Ireland followed an alphabetical system like Scotland's, commencing at IA (for Antrim) to IZ, then AI to NI (for Wicklow), finally the county boroughs from OI (Belfast) to WI (Waterford).

Note that 'Z' was used and henceforward was exclusively used in Irish marks, as was 'I'. Combinations of G, Q, S and V were not used and another omission, for obvious reasons was II, but the almost equally ambiguous IO was used. Two counties were renamed after partition, Kings County becoming Offaly and Queens County becoming Laoighis, (formerly rendered as Leix).

Subsequent allotments

Only two new marks were required before partition, for Belfast and Dublin C.B.C., which took XI and YI respectively. After partition the system in the Irish Free State (later known as Eire and now as the Republic of Ireland) remained compatible with that in the United Kingdom until 31st January 1986, after which a completely new system was instituted for new registrations, though previously registered vehicles still retain their original registration marks. However there was a subtle change in the system for allocating new marks, Northern Ireland receiving combinations ending in Z and the Free State those commencing with Z. Each component part of Ireland henceforth commenced its own series of SR&Os.

Irish Free State/Eire/Republic of Ireland

After ZI for Dublin C.B.C. the single letter Z was allotted to Dublin C.C. The subsequent series ZA, ZB etc. were allotted in alphabetical order as required to councils having exhausted their first or subsequent index marks, reaching ZY by 1954, but omitting ZG, ZQ, ZS and ZV. ZZ was allotted out of sequence in 1925 to perform the same function as the English Q- series. After the allocation of ZY the Republic commenced the issue of three-letter marks, but when Dublin were running short of available marks in 1986 SI, ZG, ZS and ZV were allotted to them. (ZV in two-letter format was not required by Dublin before the commencement of the new system, but was allotted 1.1.92 to be used by any authority as an "age-related" mark for vehicles over 30 years old.) In the meantime (in 1981), three-letter combinations of GI, IS and IV had been allotted, but these three combinations were never used as two-letter marks, whilst IG* and VI were never allotted in any form.

Northern Ireland

After XI, the next new mark required was again for Belfast. This was AZ and the series BZ, CZ etc. was allotted in alphabetical sequence as required, including GZ, SZ (somewhat surprisingly) and VZ, but omitting QZ. The latter was later allotted for imports to Northern Ireland, along with QI, but there is no evidence that these two marks were ever brought into use.

THREE-LETTER INDEX MARKS PRECEDING NUMBERS

ENGLAND, WALES AND SCOTLAND

Three-letter Index Marks were first allotted by SR&O No. 332 of 1932, (dated 29 April 1932). Although there seems no good reason why all the three-letter marks could not have been allotted under a single SR&O, the policy until 1964 was to allot a few years' requirements at a time, further SR&Os having been issued at regular intervals meanwhile. The people responsible for allocation in the Ministry of Transport appear to have been poor forecasters of the rate of issue of various authorities; there are endless inconsistencies of which the following are extreme examples:

AHB was allotted as early as 1935, but not required until August 1958; in the same SR&O Rotherham is allotted only AET and BET, the latter being issued in December 1937. The 1959 Order gives ASJ and BSJ to Bute - never required, but Stirling only to SWG which was reached by May 1961.

Although in subsequent Orders complete blocks of Index Marks with the same initial letter(s) were allotted to each authority, the first two (1932 and 1935) allotted part-series only to some authorities, e.g. in 1932 Nottingham C.C. to CRR only and in 1935 Norfolk to DAH only. The letters I, Q and Z were not, of course, used as first letters.

The Ministry "allocaters" took care to exclude some marks to which exception might be taken on decency or other grounds, but some others were allotted of which the authorities concerned fought shy. In other cases the Ministry themselves had second thoughts and subsequently deleted a few marks which had been allotted but not yet used. In most cases the reasons for omissions are obvious, but an explanation is needed for two combinations which would be offensive in the Celtic languages, i.e. DUW (Welsh for God) and BAS

---

*Editor's note. IG was commenced, in three-letter combinations, by Enniskillen LVLO in 2004 on completion of their IL series.

(Gaelic for death). Nairn omitted BAS in the year-letter sequence and it was not even allocated to Inverness LVLO/VRO. Reflecting the relaxed standards of decency in the 1990s, many of the previously proscribed combinations were released, firstly from 15.2.96 for purchasers of "Select" registrations and, commencing with P-UBF in January 1997, for normal issues. Although allotted, AHO and BHO were not issued in the forward format to obviate confusion withy AH and BH numbers with zero prefix for heavy motor cars, some of which would still be in circulation in 1935/6. No reason can be offered for the omission of DWO – it has been suggested that it was omitted to avoid confusion with DW numbers with zero prefix, but there is no evidence that Newport ever employed lead zeros. RAF was initially omitted, to avoid confusion with vehicles belonging to the Royal Air Force, but released for issue when the Services adopted their post-war numbering system.

In two cases, three-letter combinations which would normally belong to other authorities were allotted to London County Council for special purposes. Firstly GPO, the whole of which was issued to the General Post Office and secondly USN, allotted to London in 1942 as a prefix for vehicles belonging to the United States Navy. However, such vehicles never became liable to civilian registration and, although they did carry plates with the letters USN followed by up to four numerals, such registrations did not properly form part of the British system.

The King's (and Queen's) printers have not been immune from making errors. Cheshire suffered badly in this respect. BTU and DMA were omitted in error in the 1932 SR&O and GMA was misprinted as GMR in the 1938 one. These errors were subsequently corrected, but account for the combinations in question being issued out of sequence. Later errors included the misprint of NSW for HSW in 1955 and the omission of XHH in 1959. The 1964 Order was a particularly disastrous one for the printers: HXB was misprinted as HXR; OEF, WDW, SAV and SSA were omitted, but in the case of the last two error was compounded upon error when they were incorrectly allotted to Aberdeen Burgh Council, instead of the County Council. All these errors were corrected in later Orders.

NORTHERN IRELAND

The practice in Northern Ireland differed from that on the mainland in two respects:
(1) Three-letter index marks were not used until all registration authorities had used their two-letter marks in the reverse format.
(2) Three-letter index marks were followed by up to four numerals.
Three-letter marks were allotted by the Orders of 1965 and 1970, after which centralisation took place and no further legislation was necessary for this purpose.
The three-letter, up to four numeral, format is still in use in the province.

REPUBLIC OF IRELAND

Allocations commenced in 1954 and followed the pattern of that adopted in Great Britain, the last allocation being made in 1981.

Appendix 6 lists all SR&)s and Sis concerned with the allocation of three-letter index marks in Great Britain and Ireland, together with a full analysis of the errors, omissions and exceptions.

EXTRACT FROM FIRST SCHEDULE OF THE MOTOR CAR

(REGISTRATION & LICENSING) ORDER 1903

Registering Council.	Index Mark.	Registering Council.	Index Mark.
1.	2.	1	2
London County Council.. ..	A.	County Council of East Sussex.	A F.
County Council of Lancaster ..	B.	County Council of Hertford ..	A.R.
County Council of the West Riding of Yorkshire.	C.	Council of the County Borough of Kingston-upon-Hull.	A.T.
County Council of Kent ..	D.	Council of the County Borough of Nottingham.	A.U.
County Council of Stafford ..	E.	County Council of Salop ..	A.W.
County Council of Essex ..	F.	County Council of Monmouth	A.X.
County Council of Middlesex..	H.	County Council of Leicester ..	A.Y.
County Council of Durham ..	J.	Council of the County Borough of Salford.	B.A.
Council of the County Borough of Liverpool.	K.	Council of the County Borough of Newcastle-upon-Tyne.	B.B.
County Council of Glamorgan	L.	Council of the County Borough of Leicester.	B.C.
County Council of Chester ..	M.	County Council of Northampton.	B.D.
Council of the County Borough of Manchester.	N.	County Council of the Parts of Lindsey.	B.E.
Council of the County Borough of Birmingham.	O.	County Council of Dorset ..	B.F.
County Council of Surrey ..	P.	County Council of Bucks ..	B.H.
County Council of Derby ..	R.	County Council of East Suffolk	B.J.
County Council of Devon ..	T.	Council of the County Borough of Portsmouth.	B.K.
Council of the County Borough of Leeds.	U.	County Council of Berks ..	B.L.
Council of the County Borough of Sheffield.	W.	County Council of Bedford ..	B.M.
County Council of Northumberland.	X.	Council of the County Borough of Bolton.	B.N.
County Council of Somerset ..	Y.	Council of the County Borough of Cardiff.	B.O.
County Council of Southampton.	A.A.	County Council of West Sussex	B.P.
County Council of Worcester..	A.B.	Council of the County Borough of Sunderland.	B.R.
County Council of Warwick ..	A.C.	County Council of the East Riding of Yorkshire.	B.T.
County Council of Gloucester..	A.D.	Council of the County Borough of Oldham.	B.U.
Council of the County Borough of Bristol.	A.E.	County Council of Oxford ..	B.W.
County Council of Cornwall ..	A.F.	County Council of Carmarthen	B X.
County Council of Norfolk ..	A.H.	Council of the County Borough of Croydon.	B.Y.
County Council of the North Riding of Yorkshire.	A.J.	County Council of Denbigh ..	C.A.
Council of the County Borough of Bradford (Yorkshire).	A.K.	Council of the County Borough of Blackburn.	C.B.
County Council of Nottingham	A.L.	County Council of Carnarvon..	C.C.
County Council of Wilts ..	A.M.	Council of the County Borough of Brighton.	C.D.
Council of the County Borough of West Ham.	A.N.	County Council of Cambridge	C.E.
County Council of Cumberland	A.O.	County Council of West Suffolk	C.F.

ORDER OF ISSUE OF INDEX MARKS

ONE AND TWO LETTER MARKS PRECEDING NUMBERS

Although the Act decreed that registration should be in effect from 1 January 1904, most authorities commenced registering vehicles in December 1903 and a few in November. The oft-repeated claim that A 1 was the first British registration is meaningless in this context – thousands of vehicles had already been registered before the operative date. Indeed the evidence is that A 1 was not allocated until December 1903, (the exact date is not available since all the LCC's records have been destroyed), whilst Buckinghamshire, Somerset and Hastings had commenced registering vehicles in November.

There was usually a time lag between the date of allotment of a mark by a SR&O and the date the mark was taken into use, but one and two-letter index marks were brought into use in the same order in which they were allotted by SR&O, with very few exceptions. The late issue of OC has already been referred to, and the only case where the order of allocation and the order of issue differed was that of some of the London County Council's later issues.

THREE-LETTER MARKS PRECEDING NUMBERS

Three-letter marks were not always issued in alphabetical sequence. Staffordshire's first three marks were ARF, (the very first three-letter issue in July 1932), BRF and CRF, because although RF was finished, RE was still in use for motorcycles only. Next after ARF was Middlesex with AMY, issued out of sequence to celebrate Amy Johnson's historic flight. Numerous authorities, (e.g. Bedfordshire, Birkenhead, Coventry, Southampton – see Appendix 1 for details), issued their three-letter marks in the same order in which their two-letter marks had been allotted, e.g. for Bedfordshire: ABM, ANM, ATM, AMJ – not ABM, AMJ, ANM, ATM, etc. Devon adopted a unique system. They took each two-letter mark in the order in which it had been allotted and issued it in as many three-letter combinations as had been allotted in the latest SR&O. Thus the initial order was ATA, BTA, ATT, BTT, AUO, BUO, ADV, BDV, AOD, BOD and this pattern continued to JOD. For a more detailed version of Devon's sequence , see page 97. Middlesex allocated certain combinations to major distributors and this led to irregularities in the order of issue, but a major departure from the normal order took place in late 1938 when RMX to RMY were specially allotted to the War Department, (normal Middlesex issues were then in the Kxx series), followed by PHX to PMY and SHX.

In general, three-letter index marks were used only when the authority in question had exhausted its two-letter series. There were a few exceptions, e.g. Staffordshire, who continued to issue RE for motorcycles until it reached 9999 in 1947, and Middlesex, who still had several incomplete two-letter series when they commenced issuing three-letter marks. Some of the smaller Scottish counties were still using two-letter marks until they commenced the year-letter system in 1964 or 1965.

Reserved Series

There are numerous instances of complete series being allotted to a single registrant. Mention has already been made of the fact that complete series were reserved for War Department vehicles by Middlesex, with whom almost all military vehicles had been registered since 1921. In the two-letter era blocks of up to 2000 numbers had been reserved, but with the onset of three-letter marks complete blocks of 999 were set aside, (although in the first few "War Department" series the numbers 1-20 were omitted from the block issue.) Several complete series and large blocks in other series were issued solely to armoured vehicles and when in the post-war years Middlesex were running short of available marks, many of these series and blocks were used again for normal issue. Since the possibility of armoured vehicles transferring to civilian use could be ignored the usual objections to the reissue of void numbers did not apply.

The largest recipient of complete series was, however, the General Post Office, almost all of whose vehicles were registered by the London County Council until 1 October 1969 when they commenced to be registered locally. Between 1939 and 1969 over 150 complete or near complete blocks were thus reserved. London also reserved complete series for other government departments.

Watford was the home of the L.M.S. Railway's road motor department and Hertfordshire allotted several complete series to the railway company and, later, to the London Midland Region of British Railways. Two cities (Birmingham with JOJ and Glasgow with SGD) reserved whole series for their municipal bus fleet and, in the latter case, other Corporation vehicles.

Another notable recipient of complete blocks was the vehicle distribution company, Stewart and Ardern, who for a long period had their own series issued by Middlesex, usually with separate series for private and commercial vehicles in use simultaneously.

When the Home Delivery Export Scheme commenced in 1953, London, Birmingham and Coventry reserved complete series for these issues.

Complete, or almost complete, series were also allotted to Claude Rye, motorcycle dealer (RYE) and Sir Alfred McAlpine, public works contractors (MCA).

Segregation of Vehicle Types

A few authorities, notably London, Middlesex and Birmingham registered commercial vehicles and/or motorcycles separately from cars.

Other variations from normal order of issue are noted in the pages of Appendix 3 and the sequences in the two parts of Ireland in Appendices 4 and 5.

ORDER OF ISSUE OF REGISTRATION NUMBERS

ONE AND TWO LETTER MARKS PRECEDING NUMBERS

1903 to 1920
It was initially envisaged that single and two-letter index marks would be followed by the numbers 1 to 999. The Local Government Board's circular to county and county borough councils dated 20th November 1903, which set out the minutiae of the operation of the Motor Car Act, contained this paragraph :

"The Board contemplate that Councils will usually assign consecutive numbers to cars registered with them. They think, however, that for purposes of ready identification, it is not desirable that numbers consisting of more than three figures should be assigned, and they will be prepared, if desired, to assign a fresh index mark to any Council who may require to start a fresh series of numbers under a new mark". However, it would appear that the Local Government Board very quickly had second thoughts, even before London exhausted its initial mark, since it must have become obvious that the increasing use of cars would require a system with a greater capacity than originally envisaged. Thus, all one and two-letter marks were followed by up to four numerals.

The commonest method of issue of registration numbers was, of course, to allot numbers sequentially from 1 to 9999, but there were numerous variations from this practice. Article IV of the 1903 Regulations stated "If the ownership of the car is changed, notice of the change shall be given either by the new, or the old owner to the Council with which the motor car is registered, and an application shall also be made either to cancel the registration of the car or to continue the existing registration under the new ownership". Article VI provided that "If the Council are satisfied that a motor car which has been registered with them is destroyed, broken up, permanently removed from the United Kingdom, or registered with another registering authority under the Act of 1903, or if the owner of a registered motor car by application in writing requests them to cancel the registration thereof (except where in the case of a change in ownership, there is an application to continue the existing registration) they shall cause the entries in the Register of Motor Cars with respect to the motor car to be cancelled, and may, if they think fit, assign the registered number of the motor car to any other motor car whether belonging to the same or any other owner" Thus, these two regulations authorised the re-issue of void numbers, and it was possible for a car to receive a new number on change of ownership, or for a new car to receive a void registration number. (The Roads Act of 1920 put an end to this practice). The 1903 Regulations further specified that "The Council of any County or County Borough may, if they think fit, keep the Register of Motor Cars in two parts, one relating to motor cars not being motor cycles, and the other part relating to motorcycles." In those early days motorcycles were, in some areas, as numerous as cars. As with much of the original legislation, there was no uniformity of practice between the various authorities. Many simply kept separate registers for the two categories, but used a common sequence of numbers issued in numerical order as and when required. At the other extreme were those authorities who not only kept separate registers. but also adopted a separate and duplicate sequence of numbers for motorcycles; in many cases the two series continued side by side until the end of 1920. Derbyshire, for example issued to the end of 1920 R 1-5395 for cars and R 1-5795 for cycles; from 1.1.21 a common series R 5796 up. (In a few cases there were three parallel series, in the case of those authorities using a separate sequence for Heavy Motor Cars). Other authorities, whilst using a common series of numbers, adopted numbering schemes by means of which motorcycles could readily be identified.

Two methods of differentiation were adopted : (1) the allocation of distinct blocks of numbers for motorcycles and (2) the "odds and evens" principle.

As an example of the "blocking" system, Preston may be cited. In CK motorcycles were allocated the blocks 50-400, 1001-1999, 5001-7999 and in RN 9001-9650. (Preston were rather unusual in continuing segregation after 1920). Two well known exponents of the "odds and evens" principle, since their use extended into the thirties and forties, were Eastbourne and Wallasey. In Eastbourne's HC odd numbers were used for four wheelers and even numbers for cycles. HC 9999 was reached in 12/28, whereupon JK was commenced for cars etc., but cycles continued in HC until 2/48, when JK was completed, and the remaining even HCs, (from 8056 up), were used for all classes. Wallasey was similar, cycles again taking even numbers, but when cars reached 9999 in 10/34, cycles were only at around 4400 and the remaining even numbers were used for all classes.

A further complication arose with the passage of the Heavy Motor Car Order of 1904, which came into operation on 1st January 1905. This required the keeping of a separate register for vehicles with an unladen weight of between 2 and 5 tons. Again, the majority of councils numbered heavy motor cars in a common series with other vehicles, but in other cases the duplicated number series or the use of number blocks like those outlined for motorcycles applied equally to heavy motor cars. Thus, at least two councils, (Hanley and Oldham), had three separate series numbered from EH 1 up and BU 1 up respectively. The following examples typify councils using a common series issued in number blocks to the various categories : London : The actual block pattern was not consistent in every series, but typical were LP, LR, LT and LU in which 1 to 4000 were motorcycles, 4001 to 8000 cars and vans and 8001 to 9999 heavy motor vehicles. Lancashire : B was mainly divided into blocks of 500, though there was one motorcycle block of 1000. Car blocks commenced at B 1, 1001, 3001, 4001, 5001, 6001, 7001 and 9001; cycles at B 501, 1501, 2501, 3501, 4501, 6501, 7501 and 9501; heavy motor cars at B 2001, 5501 and 8501. Not surprisingly Preston followed a similar pattern to that of the county in which it was situated, but the sizes of the blocks in CK were more varied. Glamorgan's blocks in L also segregated the same three categories but were even more inconsistent in size. Salford was a rather special case; although a common series of numbers was used for all categories of vehicle, the series having reached just over BA 1000 in 1914, a special block BA 2000 up was commenced for the Salford Fire Brigade. Thereafter, further special blocks were allocated ahead of the main series and it was not until BA 2300 up in 1920 that normal sequence was resumed.

A few councils used a zero prefix to denominate heavy motor cars, the most prolific use of this system being employed by Berkshire, Buckinghamshire, Norfolk and West Sussex, whose series reached BL 0366, BH 0522, AH 0824 and BP 0163. Smaller users of this practice included the Isle of Ely and Bath.

From 1921

The Regulations issued under the authority of the 1920 Act specified that the registration "shall .... attach to that vehicle until the same is broken up, destroyed or sent out of the United Kingdom". (Despite this provision, extra-statutory arrangements were brought in to enable an owner to retain a "cherished" registration mark, as will be seen later). The Heavy Motor Car Order was rescinded and vehicles weighing over 5 tons unladen became subject to normal registration. Large numbers of previously unregistered steam rollers and traction engines were registered in 1921. Although registrations issued under the Motor Car Act of 1903 were allowed to stand under the new legislation, councils were enjoined by Ministry of Transport circulars to cease the reissue of void numbers, the duplication of motor car and motorcycle numbers and the further issue of zero-prefixed numbers. However, the Ministry's instructions were not always heeded. Bath reissued some zero-prefixed FB numbers after 1920, Clackmannanshire's SL 0xx series continued until 1925 and Merionethshire even started a new series for motorcycles from FF 01 in January 1921, but this series was short-lived, terminating at FF 0112 in October 1921.

Another aberration, which was soon discontinued, concerned the first ever - albeit unauthorised - three-letter index mark. This was Aberdeen Burgh Council's brief use of the prefix RSX on heavy motor cars.

Motorcycle segregation continued under certain Councils and a unique instance was Staffordshire's use of RE for this purpose. This was brought into use immediately it was allotted in January 1921, before E was complete, and was used exclusively for motorcycles, not being completed until 1947.

From 1921 onwards almost every War Department vehicle was registered in Middlesex, who allocated large number blocks, up to 2000 in some cases, for such vehicles. Middlesex also issued certain other series irregularly in the late 1920s/early 1930s.

Finally, mention must be made of the series QM, QP and QT, issued through the Automobile Association in blocks dependent upon shape of plate, (i.e. whether two square, two oblong, one oblong and one square or a single motorcycle plate.)

THREE LETTER MARKS PRECEDING NUMBERS

The numbers 1 to 999 were usually issued in numerical order, but low numbers, even hundreds, triples and other "nice" numbers were frequently allotted early or held back for municipal vehicles, official bodies or other favoured registrants on request. In many instances this has resulted in odd examples of an index mark appearing a little time before the main series. These cases are too numerous to be mentioned individually, particularly with certain Councils, (e.g. Hertfordshire), and only notable examples are referred to in Appendix 1.

However, the most widespread departure from numerical issue came in the form of single numbers or blocks of numbers for fleet users, especially p.s.v. operators, who wished to have registration numbers coinciding with their vehicles' fleet numbers. The use of 999 for police and emergency vehicles was also a common practice.

Vehicles belonging to foreign embassies or high commissions, official civic cars and the like have frequently been given appropriate special registration numbers very much in advance of their due date of issue - known examples are referred to under the appropriate councils in Appendix 3.

In a very small number of cases the numeral '0' has been issued for mayoral or other civic vehicles, i.e. LM 0 for the Lord Mayor of London, G 0, S 0, and RG 0 for the Lord Provosts of Glasgow, Edinburgh and Aberdeen respectively, V 0, SY 0, HS 0 and VS 0 for the Chairmen of the appropriate county or burgh council.

REISSUE OF VOID NUMBERS

The reissue of numbers previously used was frowned upon after 1920 and the only noteworthy exceptions before 1955 were QQ 1000-9999 and the Middlesex blocks originally allocated to armoured vehicles of the War Department.

However, in response to a growing desire for "cherished" numbers, in 1955 the Ministry of Transport instructed local authorities that they could, on request and on payment of the then statutory fee of £5 for a cherished transfer, re-issue a registration mark and number if they were satisfied that the vehicle to which it had been originally issued had either been destroyed or permanently exported. This concession was discontinued in 1962.

Thereafter the reissue of used numbers was confined to the special marks for heads of diplomatic missions and to veteran and vintage vehicles of genuine historic interest; Bournemouth was prominent in reissuing a number of ELs for this purpose, especially in the EL 1xxx range. This practice ceased with the introduction of "Age-Related" marks in 1983.

It has been suggested by several Registration Authorities that in order to avoid the allotment of additional Index Marks, the proper course is for them to search the old registers, cancel registrations which appear to be dead, and reissue the numbers. The Minister, however, is not in favour of the adoption of this procedure - at any rate, for the present."   *Circular RF 150, 2.3.22*

The arrangement for the issue of void marks was discontinued by the Minister in 1962. No void mark should therefore be reissued by a Council unless they are expressly authorised to do so by the Driving and Motor Licences Division of the Ministry to certain exceptional circumstances, see Paragraphs 259 and 261. (*These paragraphs refer, respectively, to special registration marks for the Heads of Diplomatic Missions and Registration of Veteran Vehicles.*)

A reconditioned vehicle of this kind, (*i.e. a "Veteran" car*), would, of course be entitled to keep the original registration mark if it had been registered under the Motor Car Act of 1903, but where it is impossible to produce evidence to this effect or the vehicle is a "rebuild" it is allotted a registration mark from the current series. In view of the special Construction & Use arrangements it has been agreed that it would be desirable to allocate an index mark more appropriate to the vehicle's age. Councils are asked, therefore, to give sympathetic consideration to any requests for appropriate numbers for these vehicles. Because of the ban on the reissue of void marks imposed by the Minister in 1982 it will be desirable to refer any case to this Department where it is not possible to meet such a request from unused marks in an earlier series. Consideration will then be given to the reissue of a "void" mark to meet the exceptional circumstances. It cannot be too strongly emphasised that this should not be regarded as a relaxation of the ban on the reissue of "void" marks. Only a very small number of vehicles should fall to be dealt with under the foregoing paragraph. *M.o.T. "Handbook", 1965 edition.*

MARKS WITH NUMERALS PRECEDING LETTERS

By 1953 some authorities were running out of available marks and the adoption of marks in the "reverse" format, i.e. with numerals preceding letters, was authorised by Statutory Instrument 1953, No. 2321, dated 28.2.53.

As in 1932, Staffordshire was the first authority which needed to take advantage of this new format and between April and July 1953 issued 1000 E to 2500 E; followed, again as in 1932, by Middlesex, who issued 1000 H to 9999 H between June 1953 and March 1954. However, there followed a temporary suspension of the issue of the single letter series and from then until 1957 all further reverse issues were of three-letter marks. In that year, however, Essex and Leeds commenced issuing F and U respectively in reverse format and Sheffield broke new ground with the first reverse two-letter series, WB. Thereafter, one, two or three letter series were all in use, depending, it would seem, on the whim of the authority in question. Some issued their single and two-letter series first, others their three-letter ones. In a few cases where two-letter series were in use special arrangements were made for motorcycles in order to avoid their having four figure numbers and hence larger plates. Motorcycles were either allotted numbers below 1000 in single or two-letter series or were registered in three-letter series whilst other vehicles concurrently used single or two letter ones.

It will have been noted that reverse E and reverse H commenced not at 1, but at 1000 and thereafter very many reverse series commenced at numbers other than 1. The reason for this was to avoid conflict with numbers already issued for trade plates which, since 1921, had been in the form of up to four numerals (including lead zeros) followed by one or two letters. Normal issues for series which were already in use for trade plates started at numbers above the highest number used for the latter purpose and leaving room for anticipated future issues, but where a series had not been used for trade plates it could and did start at 1.

The Ministry of Transport instructed local authorities not to issue reverse format registrations with index marks commencing with the letter 'O', since there could obviously be confusion, for example, between 3210 AA and 321 OAA. All went well until December 1959 when, presumably because they had overlooked this instruction, Chester CBC issued OFM. Shortly afterwards Surrey, Derbyshire and Lancashire also transgressed. However, whereas Chester completed to 999 OFM, the other three either realised the error of their ways or had it pointed out to them. Surrey completed OPA and OPB but abandoned OPC after only a handful had been issued; Derbyshire completed ONU and ORA but did not start ORB; Lancashire completed OTB but curtailed OTC at 444. There was then a lull before further transgressions of what may be called "The 'O' Rule". Bristol were next, in 12/61, issuing all their Oxx combinations, as did Cornwall, from 3/62. However, Somerset, who also started OYA in 3/62, did not issue OYB, OYC or OYD. Finally, after a further lull, the last to transgress was West Sussex in 2/64, issuing OBP and OPO, but not OPX. Eventually Chester exhausted all their three-letter reverse marks and were forced to issue reverse FM. However, to avoid confusion, every number ending with 0 was omitted, (until, much later, when the series was in use for re-registrations and at least one example slipped through). Surrey never issued reverse PA, PB or PC, nor Lancashire TB or TC, whilst Bristol, Somerset, Cornwall issued no reverse two-letter marks. So it was that, in the end, the only pairs between which confusion may have been caused were NU/ONU, RA/ORA, BP/OBP and PO/OPO.

The introduction of reverse format marks led to the the explosion in the practice of motorcycle segregation in the fifties. Although a handful of authorities, mainly in Scotland, were still issuing two-letter/four numeral marks, in the greater part of the country dealers had for many years past become accustomed to providing rear two-line plates for motorcycles with no more than three characters per line and motorcycles had been designed accordingly. Alarmed at the prospect of having to provide larger plates representations were made which resulted in the MoT requesting councils to avoid, as far as possible, motorcycle registrations with four numerals.

There were two main ways in which this objective could be achieved by those authorities who wished, or who were in many cases forced, to use one- or two-letter reversed marks : (1) by reserving the numbers below 1000 in such series for cycles or (2) by reserving some three-letter series (either forward or reverse) for cycles. Both practices were quite widespread and in the case of some authorities at different times, both methods were used.

Manchester was one of a few authorities to anticipate the onset of four digit marks and accordingly, having reached the end of XXJ in June 1959, cars went into reverse N (from 1000), YNA to YXJ being reserved for cycles. When YXJ 999 was reached motorcycles then continued in the 100-999 blocks of NB, NE, NF and VM, these series having already been issued for cars from 1000 up. The authority with the most complicated situation was Essex, cars and cycles being split and rejoined no fewer than five times. This was due partly to the trade plate situation and partly to their rapidly diminishing stock of available marks. In the early fifties EV, HK, NO, PU, TW, VW and VX were in use on trade plates but it was then decided to concentrate issues in the last four of these. However, it took some time to call in the trade plates in the other three series, this being necessary in order that normal issues in reverse EV, HK and NO could start at 1 and not 1001. Reverse AEV to mid JVW were mixed; at this point cars started using reversed F, followed by HK and NO - motorcycles then used three-letter only marks until YVX; however cars joined motorcycles (a) in LPU to RNO, between the end of reverse NO and the start of reverse EV; (b) very briefly in SHK to SPU between EV and TW, (which was followed by VW and VX), (c) again very briefly in UEV between VX and PU and (d) in UPU on completion of PU, remaining with cycles until YVX. The latter was followed by (forward) OO, in which 1-999 were reserved for cycles, followed by AOO and BOO, cars rejoining in COO.

Sheffield's WB was the first two-letter reverse; this was followed by WE and WJ. All of these had commenced from 1, but there had been no attempt to segregate cycles. W was then commenced from 1000 and it was only when this was well established that cycles were segregated in AWA and half of AWB; cars had used WA (from 1001) before rejoining cycles in AWB. Norfolk was one of the authorities using both methods at different times; reverse issues commenced with AH, starting concurrently at 1 for motorcycles and 1000 for cars etc. Motorcycles reached 999 AH before cars reached 9999 AH and then went into 1-999 NG and similarly into 1-999 VF. When 999 VF was reached motorcycles went into AAH and onwards. Meanwhile cars used 1000-9999 NG, 1000-9999 VF and 1000-9999 PW. Cars then commenced BNG whilst cycles completed BAH; thereafter rejoining in late CNG or early CPW. When it was impossible to allocate three-numeral marks to cycles many authorities did the next best thing and gave them numbers containing a '1'. Uniquely Fife reserved 1-2000 for cycles in FG. Two authorities which did not use reverse four-digit marks, but which nevertheless segregated cycles for a while during this period were Devon, (between 11/55 and 3/58 with (forward) UTA, VTA, WTA, WOD and YTT) and West Bromwich (between 6/59 and 12/64 with XEA, reverse BEA, LEA and SEA).

ISSUE OF TWO- AND THREE-LETTER MARKS (WITHOUT YEAR-LETTER) AFTER 1964

(The comments which follow apply equally to registrations with numerals preceding index marks).

For all normal purposes, the issue of registration marks without a year letter ceased after 31 December 1964. However, the issue of such marks continued for certain purposes, mainly for the re-registration of vehicles previously bearing cherished marks. At first, with a few exceptions, such vehicles which were first registered before the authority in question commenced year-letter marks were allocated replacement marks in the last non-suffix series used. When it became necessary, many authorities commenced new "non-suffix" series long after 1964. Mainly these were either "forward" or "reverse" three-letter series, but Huddersfield broke new ground in 1967 when they commenced reverse CX for this purpose, (the few remaining numbers in their last normal series, YVH as prefix, having been used up). In some cases such numbers as were available were soon exhausted and the earliest available year-letter series was then used instead.

However, on 30 July 1976, following a dispute at the DVLC, the trade union placed a ban on further transfers of cherished numbers and when this ban was lifted on 10 January 1977 it was ordained that all replacement marks for vehicles registered in 1964 or earlier, except for vehicles of historic interest, should be 'A' or 'B' suffix marks. This was apparently due to the fact that non-suffix replacements were themselves becoming cherished, placing a burden on the staffs of the DVLC and LVLOs. Although the LVLOs had taken over responsibility for the allocation of new issues as from 1.10.74, the LTOs remained responsible for the issue of re-registrations until 1977. MoT Circular No. 132 of 1977 required all LTOs to submit to the appropriate LVLO a list of all unused numbers available for re-registrations and from mid-1977 this function was taken over by the LVLOs. The issue of odd examples of non year-letter marks for veteran and vintage vehicles continued.

Some new series brought into use for re-registrations after 1974 commenced at numbers other than 1 in order to prevent the issue of "cherishable" numbers for re-registrations and for the same reason "nice" numbers, such as even hundreds and "three-of-a-kind" were omitted.

Until 1979 and subject to the various minor aberrations described in these pages, the allocation of registration marks by the various authorities had progressed in a reasonably orderly sequence. However, during the next decade came three developments which caused the old order to fall apart and further issues of two and three-letter marks appeared in a quite unstructured manner. These development are described in the next three paragraphs.

From 1979 onwards there began to appear an increasing number of isolated marks in all formats which fell outside the normal sequence of issues of the LTOs and LVLOs. Setting aside the possibility of incorrect plates, (either by accident or design), there appear to be three possible explanations for these "irregular" marks :

(1)   Errors in transferring documentation on to the central computer.
(2)   Special issues by the DVLC to resolve disputes in cases where there were two claimants to the same   cherished mark.
(3)   Marks obtained by fraudulent means but subsequently accepted by the computer.

Next, from August 1983 came a complete overhaul of the treatment of vehicles requiring re-registration following the transfer of cherished marks and also of imported second-hand vehicles, ex Ministry of Defence vehicles and vehicles previously used only off-road or under trade plates. These changes are fully described in the section headed "Age Related Marks".

Finally, on 14 December 1989, the DVLA launched its "Classic Collection" scheme, under which previously unissued marks were offered for sale at auctions held periodically in different parts of the country. At first the registrations offered were in series which had not previously been issued at all, but later unused numbers in part-issued series were also offered.

It is understood that, at the present time, owing to the incompleteness of the registers of motor cars kept under the Motor Car Act 1903, there are in existence many duplicate marks, and that some vehicles carrying identification marks on the 31st December last were not properly registered.

A Council may learn, (Form RF 16/1), that a vehicle bearing one of its numbers is carried on the register of another Council although another vehicle has already been recorded since January 1921 as bearing the same mark and number. In such a case it will be the duty of the Council whose mark the vehicle bears, to prosecute enquiries to ascertain which of the owners of the vehicles bearing the mark was entitled to use it on his vehicle at the 31st December last and in the case of those not so entitled to inform the Council with whom the vehicles bearing these marks are re-registered. The latter will thereupon allot one of its own series of numbers, recall the licence and registration book issued under the wrong number and require the licencee (sic) to obtain fresh number plates.

The above remarks do not, of course, apply to the rare cases where a Council has in the past issued duplicate numbers and a motor car and a motor cycle have both been properly registered before 31st December last under the same number; in such cases both vehicles should retain their numbers.

Circular RF 114, 27.1.21

PHASING IN OF YEAR-LETTER SYSTEM

By 1963 several authorities were nearing the exhaustion of all their available marks under both the "forward" and "reverse" formats. Furthermore new registration authorities were to be created for which no marks were available under the current system. Accordingly the "year-letter" system was introduced, the format being a three-letter index mark, a number of up to three digits and a single letter to denote the year of registration.The new authorities were to be allotted the basic index marks XA, XB, XC etc., which were not to be used by London County Council in the new format. Originally the year-letters covered a calendar year; A = 1963, B = 1964, C = 1965 and D = 1966. In 1967, however, it was decided that the year-letter would in future change on 1 August; accordingly E ran from 1 January to 31 July 1967 and F started 1 August 1967. I, O, Q, U and Z were not used as year-letters. In 1983 the format was reversed so that the year-letter became a prefix, starting again with A, followed by a number of up to three digits and a three-letter index mark. In June 1998 it was announced that a completely new registration system would commence on 1 September 2001. As an interim measure to avoid the problems caused by the peaking of car sales in August, the year letter would change every six months. S ran from 1 August 1998 to 28 February 1999 and thereafter the remaining prefixes T, V, W, X and Y would each last for six months, ending 31 August 2001.

The first authority to commence using the year-letter system was Middlesex who, having exhausted all their available marks under the old system, commenced with AHX-A in February 1963. Next came Kirkcaldy, the first new Scottish registration authority for 43 years, from 2 April 1963. It was then decided that, rather than commence the issue of reverse issues, any further authority exhausting their forward marks would commence the year-letter system. Accordingly, the remaining 12 authorities converting during 1963 fell into three categories :

1. Those who had exhausted all their available marks under the old system, (Staffordshire, Lancashire and Essex).

2. Those who had exhausted all their "forward" marks, (Huddersfield, Plymouth, Northumberland, Stockport, Oxfordshire, Salford, Bolton and Aberdeenshire).

3. Motherwell & Wishaw, who had exhausted all their available marks then allotted to them by Statutory Instrument, i.e. up to FGM, since GGM to YGM were not allotted to them until 1 April 1964.

The remaining authorities were scheduled in an apparently random manner to commence the new system in accordance with a predetermined timetable between January 1964 and January 1965. It is understood that this was done to enable number plate manufacturers gradually to increase the production and stocks of the new $3^1/_8$" characters. A few authorities changed over ahead of schedule, because they were running out of available marks (Holland, Kesteven, West Suffolk, Darlington, Grimsby and Ayr), or had reached their last allotted mark (Blackburn - SCB), whilst Doncaster switched early for an unknown reason and Worcester CBC changed later than scheduled. Three new registration authorities (Luton, Solihull and Coatbridge) started in April 1964.

The tabulation on the following page shows the scheduled and actual dates of adoption of the new system.

	Scheduled	Actual		Scheduled	Actual		Scheduled	Actual
Middlesex		18/2/63	Bucks	4/64	1/4/64	Berwick	7/64	1/7/64
Kirkcaldy		2/4/63	Isle of Ely	4/64	1/4/64	Clackmannan	7/64	1/7/64
Staffordshire		2/7/63	London CC	4/64	1/4/64	Dumfries	7/64	1/7/64
Huddersfield		28/8/63	Luton	4/64	1/4/64	Sutherland	7/64	1/7/64
Lancashire		1/9/63	Merthyr	4/64	1/4/64	Holland	9/64	10/7/64
Plymouth		12/9/63	St. Helens	4/64	1/4/64	Grimsby	8/64	24/7/64
Northumberland		1/10/63	Solihull	4/64	1/4/64	Caernarvon	8/64	4/8/64
Motherwell		10/63	Selkirk	4/64	1/4/64	Radnor	8/64	4/8/64
Essex		11/63	W. Lothian	4/64	1/4/64	Somerset	8/64	4/8/64
Salford		1/11/63	Coatbridge	4/64	1/4/64	Westmorland	8/64	4/8/64
Stockport		4/11/63	Greenock	4/64	1/4/64	Birkenhead	8/64	4/8/64
Oxfordshire		6/11/63	Glamorgan	5/64	1/5/64	Birmingham	8/64	4/8/64
Bolton		2/12/63	W. Sussex	5/64	1/5/64	Eastbourne	8/64	4/8/64
Aberdeen CC		2/12/63	Warwickshire	5/64	1/5/64	Ipswich	8/64	4/8/64
Cheshire	1/64	2/1/64	Yorks., N.R.	5/64	1/5/64	Oldham	8/64	4/8/64
Hereford	1/64	2/1/64	Bournemouth	5/64	1/5/64	Smethwick	8/64	4/8/64
Merioneth	1/64	2/1/64	Burton-on-T	5/64	1/5/64	Sunderland	8/64	4/8/64
Norfolk	1/64	2/1/64	East Ham	5/64	1/5/64	Tynemouth	8/64	4/8/64
Rutland	1/64	2/1/64	Kingston-u-Hull	5/64	1/5/64	Wakefield	8/64	4/8/64
Surrey	1/64	2/1/64	Liverpool	5/64	1/5/64	Wigan	8/64	4/8/64
Worcestershire	1/64	2/1/64	Southend	5/64	1/5/64	York CBC	8/64	4/8/64
Bath	1/64	2/1/64	Swansea	5/64	1/5/64	Caithness	8/64	4/8/64
Bootle	1/64	2/1/64	Wolverhampton	5/64	1/5/64	Dunbarton	8/64	4/8/64
Canterbury	1/64	2/1/64	Banff	5/64	1/5/64	Midlothian	8/64	4/8/64
Carlisle	1/64	2/1/64	Fife	5/64	1/5/64	Dundee	8/64	4/8/64
Newcastle	1/64	2/1/64	Kirkcudbright	5/64	1/5/64	West Suffolk	9/64	4/8/64
Bute	1/64	2/1/64	Aberdeen BC	5/64	1/5/64	Cardigan	9/64	1/9/64
Kinross	1/64	2/1/64	Doncaster	6/64	1/5/64	Cornwall	9/64	1/9/64
Glasgow	1/64	2/1/64	Denbigh	6/64	1/6/64	Kent	9/64	1/9/64
Blackburn	2/64	28/1/64	Derbyshire	6/64	1/6/64	Nottinghamshire	9/64	1/9/64
Berkshire	2/64	3/2/64	Lindsey	6/64	1/6/64	Barrow	9/64	1/9/64
Durham	2/64	3/2/64	Peterborough	6/64	1/6/64	Bristol	9/64	1/9/64
Gloucestershire	2/64	3/2/64	Wiltshire	6/64	1/6/64	Bury	9/64	1/9/64
Leicestershire	2/64	3/2/64	Yorks., E.	6/64	1/6/64	Dewsbury	9/64	1/9/64
Salop	2/64	3/2/64	Blackpool	6/64	1/6/64	Lincoln CBC	9/64	1/9/64
East Sussex	2/64	3/2/64	Bradford	6/64	1/6/64	Walsall	9/64	1/9/64
Isle of Wight	2/64	3/2/64	Chester	6/64	1/6/64	Warrington	9/64	1/9/64
Cardiff	2/64	3/2/64	Coventry	6/64	1/6/64	W. Hartlepool	9/64	1/9/64
Derby	2/64	3/2/64	Gloucester	6/64	1/6/64	Moray	9/64	1/9/64
Exeter	2/64	3/2/64	Halifax	6/64	1/6/64	Wigtown	9/64	1/9/64
Nottingham CBC	2/64	3/2/64	Hastings	6/64	1/6/64	Paisley	9/64	1/9/64
Sheffield	2/64	3/2/64	Reading	6/64	1/6/64	Darlington	1/65	1/1/65
Southport	2/64	3/2/64	Rochdale	6/64	1/6/64	Bedfordshire	1/65	1/1/65
Perth	2/64	3/2/64	Ayr	6/64	1/6/64	Brecknock	1/65	1/1/65
Stirling	2/64	3/2/64	Kincardine	6/64	1/6/64	Hampshire	1/65	1/1/65
Edinburgh	2/64	3/2/64	Lanark	6/64	1/6/64	Montgomery	1/65	1/1/65
Monmouth	3/64	27/2/64	Roxburgh	6/64	1/6/64	Pembroke	1/65	1/1/65
Cambridge	3/64	2/3/64	Kesteven	7/64	1/6/64	Croydon	1/65	1/1/65
Cumberland	3/64	2/3/64	Worcester	5/64	9/6/64	Leeds	1/65	1/1/65
Dorset	3/64	2/3/64	Carmarthen	7/64	1/7/64	Norwich	1/65	1/1/65
Flint	3/64	2/3/64	Devon	7/64	1/7/64	Oxford CBC	1/65	1/1/65
Hertford	3/64	2/3/64	Huntingdon	7/64	1/7/64	Rotherham	1/65	1/1/65
Northants CC	3/64	2/3/64	E. Suffolk	7/64	1/7/64	S. Shields	1/65	1/1/65
Yorks., W.R	3/64	2/3/64	Barnsley	7/64	1/7/64	Stoke	1/65	1/1/65
Burnley	3/64	2/3/64	Brighton	7/64	1/7/64	Wallasey	1/65	1/1/65
Gt Yarmouth	3/64	2/3/64	Dudley	7/64	1/7/64	W. Bromwich	1/65	1/1/65
Leicester CBC	3/64	2/3/64	Gateshead	7/64	1/7/64	West Ham	1/65	1/1/65
Middlesbrough	3/64	2/3/64	Manchester	7/64	1/7/64	Argyll	1/65	1/1/65
Portsmouth	3/64	2/3/64	Newport	7/64	1/7/64	Inverness	1/65	1/1/65
E. Lothian	3/64	2/3/64	Northampton CBC	7/64	1/7/64	Nairn	1/65	1/1/65
Renfrew	3/64	2/3/64	Preston	7/64	1/7/64	Orkney	1/65	1/1/65
Ross & Cromarty	3/64	2/3/64	Southampton CBC	7/64	1/7/64	Peebles	1/65	1/1/65
Anglesey	4/64	1/4/64	Angus	7/64	1/7/64	Zetland	1/65	1/1/65

SEQUENCE OF ISSUE - YEAR-LETTER MARKS

With two exceptions, all the LTOs commenced their year-letter issues with their three-letter index marks in alphabetical sequence; (or in the case of authorities like Devon, index marks in "chronological" sequence, with A multiples). The exceptions were two Scottish authorities and the inevitable conclusion is that they misunderstood instructions which had been issued by the Ministry of Transport for the commencement of the scheme. East Lothian had been issuing HSS in February 1964 and switched to JSS-B as from 1.3.64. Greenock, who had been issuing EVS in March 1964 merely continued this same series with the addition of the 'B' suffix. Furthermore, any numbers allocated, but not taken up, before 1.4.64, were allowed to stand but with the addition of 'B'. Thus there was an overlap between plain EVS numbers and those in EVS-B.

Instead of returning to Axx multiples at the start of each year authorities were instructed to continue through the alphabet, but from the outset it was evident that there were two schools of thought in relation to the precise method of achieving the transition from one year-letter to the next. On the one hand were the authorities who adopted a clear borderline, either by making a distinct break in the year-end series or by starting a completely new series for the new year-letter. Among the authorities issuing A suffix marks an example of the former is Lancashire, who finished 1963 with BTB-A and started 1964 with CTB-B, and of the latter, Huddersfield, with AVH-A reaching 2xx and restarting at AVH 401B. These authorities required that any numbers reserved, but not taken up, before the end of the year would be surrendered and replaced by completely new marks. On the other hand there were authorities who would allow a previously reserved number to stand for the new year by merely changing the suffix letter. Thus there would be overlaps between numbers with the old suffix and those with the new. As usual there was a maverick. Dundee started with ATS-B and moved into AYJ-B by the end of 1964. However, they started again with ATS for C suffix issues and reached BYJ 682C. D started with BYJ 745D but after 999 was reached they again reverted to the beginning with ATS-D. However, when only 40 numbers had been issued in this series they were pulled up short and switched to CTS-D.

In nearly all cases gaps were left at the end of the year to provide replacement marks, with the year-letter appropriate to the date of first registration, for vehicles from which cherished marks were transferred. In some cases this meant that the first new year series began at a number other than 1. There were a handful of authorities who left no gap and accommodated cherished mark replacements, (i.e. re-registrations), in whichever series was current at the time, but with the suffix letter appropriate to the age of the vehicle. This method was practised by Northumberland, the Isle of Wight, Bolton and Sutherland. As time went on many and varied were the devices employed for providing suitable re-registration marks, especially in cases where the original block became exhausted. A few set aside a block of numbers which could be used with a variety of year-letters. Exponents of this practice included Norfolk, Northumberland, Oxfordshire, Newport and, (in later days), Caithness. Aside from the "censored" combinations it was very unusual for any gaps in sequence to be left by local authorities; however, some complete series were omitted in the year-end gaps by a few authorities,(e.g. Essex, Surrey, West Sussex and Birmingham). Many authorities continued the practice of segregating motorcycles in order to keep down the plate size; usually the numbers 1-99 were reserved, or sometimes up to 199 and other numbers containing the numeral '1'.

THE 'N' RULE

The date for the takeover of first registration from the local authorities had been deferred two or three times before it actually took place on 1 October 1974. Earlier, 1 January 1974 had been planned and when this date was in prospect it was intended that all the LVLO registration trios would commence with Axx multiples. To this end the MoT issued a Memorandum (No.80) in June 1972 stating:

"In the year 1973/74, LTOs during the period they remain responsible for first registrations, i.e. between 1 August and 31 December 1973, will be confined to using registration marks containing a prefix letter in the range "N" and "Y" inclusive. LVLOs, for the remainder of the year, i.e. from 1 January to 31 July 1974, will use registration marks with prefix letters "A" to "M" inclusive only. Thus, if a council is issuing the prime mark AB say, then –
(a) if the last mark issued for the year ended 31 July 1973 is TAB 123L, there can be a straightforward continuation and the first mark for issue on or after 1 August 1973* would be TAB 124M;
(b) if the last mark issued is DAB 123L, issues on or after 1 August 1973* would jump forward to commence with NAB 1M;
(c) if the end of the series (YAB 999M) were reached before 31 December 1973, the next mark for issue would become NAB 1M or N- - 1M with a different prime mark.
[*in the actual text of the memorandum these two dates were misprinted as 1974!].
NB For the purpose of these examples it has been assumed that any reserve of unused marks for future cherished transfers etc. will have been set aside before the last mark for the year ended 31 July 1973 has been issued.
It will of course be necessary for LTOs to ensure that any advance allocations of marks with the suffix letter "M" which they may make to dealers are restricted to vehicles which are to be licensed not later than 31 December 1973. Advance allocations of marks for vehicles which are not to be licensed until January 1974 or later will be issued by LVLOs after 18 December 1973."

Not surprisingly this affected about half of the LTOs. The first manifestation of this policy came in November 1972, when Ayrshire jumped the gun and followed YSD-L by NAG-L. Others jumping to N multiples in advance of 1 August 1973 were Norwich, moving from YVG-L to NCL-L, Swansea from LWN-L to NCY-L and Worcester from GFK-L to NFK-L. Holland County Council ended L with YDO and could well have continued into YDO-M and YJL-M, but chose instead to commence M year with NDO. Two other authorities adopted the 'N' Rule in a non-standard manner, i.e. Nottingham CBC, who moved from FTV-L to NTO-M instead of the expected NAU-M, whilst Yorkshire (North Riding) commenced M issues not with NAJ-M but NPY-M, starting at 501. The reason is probably related to pre-printed documentation. All authorities not already mentioned followed the 'N' Rule as it was intended and all authorities reaching the end of the alphabet between August and October 1973 recommenced at Nxx-M.

As seems inevitable, there were some transgressors, mainly authorities which, as a matter of course, allowed registrations reserved in one year to be carried over to the next with merely a change in suffix letter. In terms of the number of vehicles concerned, Reading were the biggest offenders with many numbers in LDP and LRD and a few in KDP, KRD and MDP, originally allotted as 'L', being allowed to stand after 31 July 1973 with 'M' suffix. Berkshire also allowed a handful of 'M' overlaps to stand, (in KMO, KRX, LRX and MJB). Montgomery were not affected by the "N Rule" as far as their normal issues were concerned, since they were already on PEP at the end of 'L' year. However, their motorcycle block in KEP had lagged far behind and consideration of the 'N Rule' was probably overlooked, insofar as KEP continued into M suffix, (and, for that matter, into N). Liverpool, not normally an overlapping authority, allowed a batch of advance allocated bus registrations to stand and GKA 481 and 486-545 came out with M suffix. There was also an isolated example of KUT-M from Leicestershire. Later a few re-registrations came out with first letters A to M and suffix M, but probably not until the "N Rule" had been abandoned. The authorities concerned were Norfolk (MVF), Bolton (BWH), Newport (EDW) and Worcester (GFK).

In fact, the 1 January 1974 deadline for transfer of new registrations to LVLOs proved optimistic. Another abortive date of 1 April 1974 came and went and when, eventually, the final date of 1 October 1974 was established it was decided that LVLO issues would commence with Gxx multiples, with the LTOs' 'N' suffix marks being in the ranges Axx to Fxx and Nxx to Yxx. Accordingly the "N Rule" was abandoned insofar as it affected authorities reaching the end of the alphabet in or after December 1973. With hindsight it is difficult to see any logic in the abandonment of the "N Rule", rather than its modificaton to take account of the delay in the handover, since this only led in the end to the rather untidy system which did come in with N registrations whereby local authorities used A to F and N to Y prefixes and LVLOs G to M prefixes. Be that as it may, starting with Inverness and Manchester in December 1973, authorities reaching the end of the alphabet between then and August 1974 reverted to Axx-M or -N. As seems inevitable with any aspect of British registrations, there were exceptions - Greenock and Derby CBC were late adherants to the "N-Rule" with NVS-M and NCH-M in February and May 1974 respectively. Perhaps their stationery was already printed when the "N Rule" was relaxed ?   Even more strange, however, are the cases of Bath and Dunbarton, both of which unaccountably jumped to A prefix with N suffix when there was no good reason for them to do so, (TGL-M to AFB-N and SSN-M to ASN-N). Did they misinterpret the circular which announced the abandonment of the "N Rule" ? (Dunbarton had already faithfully followed the rule in moving from JSN-L to NSN-M).

The final anomaly to be mentioned was, by the standards of those days, potentially the most serious. At this period Ipswich and East Suffolk were alternating the marks of the two constituent authorities. GDX-L had been followed by OBJ-M to WRT-M - then followed GPV-M in 7/74 !   By this date, of course, the "N Rule" had been abandoned, but it had obviously not been envisaged by the DVLC that any authority would have got as far down the alphabet as Gxx. Thus we have both GPV-M (by Ipswich & East Suffolk) and GPV-N (by Ipswich LVLO). This chapter chronicles the extent of other such duplications as they were at the time, but numerous similar examples have since arisen through re-registrations.

It should be mentioned that when, much later, LVLOs issued new series for M and N suffix re-registrations, no regard was had either to the 'N' rule or the 'G' rule. (Please note that "'N' rule" and "'G' rule are not official terms).

<u>Summary of the Application of the "N Rule"</u>

The following authorities were not affected by the "N Rule" and did not reach the end of the alphabet during 'M' year. County Councils : Anglesey, Berks *, Brecknock, Caernarvon, Cardigan, Carmarthen, Dorset, Flint, Cardiff & Glamorgan, Greater London, Hampshire, Merioneth, Montgomery *, Somerset, Surrey, Warwick, Westmorland; County Boroughs : Barrow, Birkenhead, Bootle, Bristol, Burnley, Dewsbury, Dudley, Eastbourne, Gateshead, Halifax, Hartlepool, Hastings, Leeds, Lincoln, Newcastle, Oldham, Plymouth, Teesside, Torbay, Tynemouth, Wallasey, Wigan; Scottish Counties : Argyll, Banff, East Lothian, Lanark, Midlothian, Moray, Renfrew, Ross & Cromarty, Roxburgh, West Lothian; Scottish Burghs : Coatbridge, Dundee, Paisley.

The following applied the "N Rule" at the L/M changeover and did not reach the end of the alphabet during 'M' year : County Councils : Bedford, Cornwall, Cumberland, Denbigh, Derby, Devon, Durham, Essex, Gloucester, Hereford, Huntingdon & Peterborough *, Kent, Lancs, Leicester, Holland *, Kesteven, Lindsey, Monmouth, Norfolk *, Northants, Northumberland, Pembroke, Radnor, Rutland, Salop, West Suffolk, East Sussex, West Sussex, Isle of Wight, Wilts, East Riding, North Riding; County Boroughs : Barnsley, Birmingham, Blackpool, Bolton *, Bournemouth, Bradford, Brighton, Burton, Canterbury, Carlisle, Chester, Coventry, Grimsby, Huddersfield, Kingston-on-Hull, Leicester, Liverpool *, Merthyr, Newport, Nottingham, Rochdale, Rotherham, Salford, Solihull, Southampton, Southend, Stockport, Wakefield, Walsall, Warley, Warrington, York; Scottish counties : Angus, Berwick, Bute, Caithness, Clackmannan, Dumfries, Kincardine, Kinross, Kirkcudbright, Nairn, Orkney, Peebles, Selkirk, Stirling, Sutherland, Wigtown, Zetland; Scottish burghs : Edinburgh, Glasgow, Motherwell.

The following were not affected by the "N Rule" at the L/M changeover, but reached the end of the alphabet and switched to Nxx during M year : Counties : Buckingham, Cambridge, Nottingham, Oxford, West Riding; County boroughs : Derby, Northampton, Portsmouth, Stoke, Sunderland; Scottish county : Perth; Scottish burghs : Aberdeen, Greeock.

The following were not affected by the "N Rule" at the L/M changeover, but reached the end of the alphabet and switched to Axx during M or N year : Counties : Cheshire, Herts, Stafford, Worcester; County boroughs : Blackburn, Bury, Darlington, Doncaster, Gloucester, Great Yarmouth, Luton, Manchester, St. Helens, Sheffield, Southport, South Shields, West Bromwich, Wolverhampton; Scottish counties : Aberdeen, Fife, Inverness; Scottish burgh : Kirkcaldy.

The following adopted an anomalous position, explained in the foregoing text : Ipswich & East Suffolk; County boroughs : Bath, Norwich, Reading, Swansea, Worcester; Scottish counties : Ayr, Dunbarton.

[* see reference in text above]

CHANGES IN PRACTICE FOLLOWING CENTRALISATION

In general all LVLOs followed the established pattern of leaving gaps between the issues of one year and the next, although there was little consistency in the size of gaps. Some gaps were, for no apparent reason, inordinately large, whilst on the other hand some were so small that they were soon exhausted by re-registrations and the usual practice was then to continue the sequence, so that the same index mark trio came to be used with consecutive year-letters. At first this was practised only as a last resort, but by the mid-1990s it almost seemed deliberate policy, when a new re-registration mark was required, to jump over the gap and use the same trio which had commenced the following year's isues. In other cases, although marks were available "in the gap", completely random series were used instead.

Furthermore, it became quite commonplace for whole series, (other than "censored" ones and those in the year-end gaps), to be omitted, sometimes for no apparent reason, and as time went on the number of omitted series increased. The practice of segregating motorcycles was discontinued.

As for numbering, With few exceptions serials for suffix marks commenced at 1; however, some series, mainly those of the smaller LVLOs started at higher numbers in order to provide the re-registration gap, (e.g. JSS-P which commenced at 501 and LBR-P which commenced at 500. Examples of series split between two suffix letters also occurred, but these were much less common than was the case with the LTOs. Examples are GPS with N and P suffix and TJS with V and W.

As from the commencement of the year prefix A on 1 August 1983 the numbers 1-20 (1-22 in some years) were withheld from normal issues in all series and in the section on "Sale of Marks" is described the practice of omitting certain other numbers from the normal sequence in year-prefix series with a view to their sale as "Classic" or "Select" registrations. There were in addition, other omissions. These included xxG 1T, xxT 1 T, A55 xxx and A550-559 xxx, K15 Sxx and K155 xxx. As is commonplace in U.K. registration practice there were exceptions to the rule and certain of these numbers did escape the ban. From 15 January 1996 K15 Sxx combinations were released for use on "Select" registrations.

Reserved and Special Series

Specially reserved series for Home Delivery Exports were continued by Coventry LVLO (until late 1977 - S suffix) and London Central. Blocks exclusively for Vauxhall were allocated firstly by Luton and latterly by other LVLOs, whilst by the early 1990s it was not uncommon for large dealers and car hire companies to have complete series allocated for their use.

A completely new series of export marks was commenced as from 1 January 1993. These were for vehicles exported to countries within the European Community. Their format was (1) the year letter followed by the registration number then a three-letter trio consisting of a letter denoting the month running from A for January to M for December, (I omitted), and the letters XP. These registrations were issued by the following VROs : Birmingham, Chelmsford, Coventry, Leeds, London Central, Luton, Northampton, Norwich, Oxford and Stoke; also Coleraine in Northern Ireland.

CENTRALISATION OF VEHICLE REGISTRATION & LICENSING

The Ministry of Transport initiated discussions with interested parties as early as 1964 on the need for a new system of vehicle and driver licensing. The Vehicle and Driving Licences Act of 1969 marked the first legislative step along the road towards the centralisation of vehicle and driver licensing and the setting up of the Driver & Licensing Centre with its network of Local Vehicle Licensing Offices, which were to replace the county and county borough councils' Local Taxation Offices. Section 1 of the 1969 Act read as follows:

(1) The functions conferred on local authorities by the Vehicles (Excise) Act 1962 and of the Road Traffic Act 1960 (which provide for the levying of excise duty on vehicles, the licensing and registration of vehicles and the licensing of drivers) shall be transferred to the Minister of Transport by virtue of this section on the transfer date.

(2) In this Act "the transfer date" means such date as the Minister may by order appoint for the purposes of the foregoing subsection;......"

The provisions of the 1969 Act were supplemented by the Vehicles (Excise) Act of 1971, which its preamble described as "An Act to consolidate certain enactments relating to excise duties on mechanically propelled vehicles, and to the licensing and registration of such vehicles with amendments to give effect to recommendations of the Law Commission and the Scottish Law Commission." The "transfer date" referred to above, was eventually fixed at 1 April 1971, but it was to be another seven years before the transfer of functions was completed. In the meantime the Acts had made provision for the local authorities to become Agents of the Minister of Transport during the transitional period. Thus it was no longer necessary for Statutory Instruments to be made to authorise changes in registration and licensing provisions and the future allocation of index marks was made by administrative arrangements. One of the major functions to be undertaken by the DVLC and the LVLOs was the registration and first licensing of vehicles. The allocation of registration marks became a function of the LVLOs, of which there were originally 81 spaced at about 30 miles from each other throughout the country, (closer in the London area), whilst the DVLC at Swansea would house the central computer upon which the details of all vehicles would be recorded. The list of LVLOs originally proposed contained a few differences from the pattern eventually adopted.

In the main the LVLOs assumed the index marks of the LTOs in whose areas they were situated but there was some reallocation, intended to even out the anticipated consumption of marks. Most of the reallocated marks were those from Scottish LTOs. In the event, the forecasting which lay behind this reallocation proved to be faulty and in no time at all the first letters of the index marks of some LVLOs were racing ahead of the pack. There were some peculiar anomalies in the reallocation. It would seem that those responsible had but the foggiest idea of the geography of the Midlands – why else would the three Wolverhampton marks be transferred to Birmingham, whilst Dudley received three of the Warwickshire marks? Another anomaly was than an official list of the reallocation, dated 18.12.73, showed the allocation for a number of LVLOs in a non-alphabetical sequence and in most cases the order shown in this list had been used for the actual sequence of issue. After several postponements the LVLOs assumed responsibility for the first registration of vehicles as from 1 October 1974 and, as related in the paragraph on "the 'N' Rule", all LVLOs started with Gxx-N combinations. (There was a suggestion from the DVLC that P suffix issues would start with Axx, but this did not materialise and the sequence at changeover times continued much as before, but usually with enhanced provision for re-registrations.)

Between 1974 and 1978 the records of the local taxation offices were gradually transferred to the central computer, usually one year's issues at a time. Other functions of the LTOs were also transferred to the DVLC until by 1977 they were left with little but handling the issue of replacement marks for cherished mark transfers and the issue of trade plates and licences. The last of the LTOs shut their doors for good in March 1978.

Returning to the LVLOs, the St. Boswells office was relocated at Selkirk in March 1975 and there have been some local changes of office address, notably in the London area, where the following changes in location have taken place : North East from Stratford to Ilford (ca. 1982); North West from Ealing to Ruislip (ca. 1975) and again to Stanmore (ca. 1992), and South West from Wimbledon to Croydon (ca. 1990) and, following the merger with London Central, back to Wimbledon in 1997. However, the first major changes took place in 1980/81 when 28 of the original 81 LVLOs were closed. (31 closures were originally envisaged but Dudley, Haverfordwest and Inverness were reprieved and Durham was closed instead of Middlesbrough). The index marks of the closed offices were then reallocated to the nearest large office which remained open. Further closures took place commencing with London South East on 18 June 1993, (although this was later reopened).

It was originally intended that the index marks of the closed offices would lapse, but following an outcry from motorists who resented the loss of the local marks, provision was made for their continued issue by the VRO which had absorbed them. However, the application of this provision was very uneven. In many areas, particularly in Scotland, local marks were allocated as a matter of course to the dealers and operators who had formerly used them, so that there was no noticeable diminution in their rate of issue. At the other extreme Exeter set their face resolutely against any continuation in the marks of Plymouth and Barnstaple, (though it must be admitted that in the case of the latter there was no local tradition to be perpetuated). Maidstone was only slightly less resolute and after only half-a-dozen isolated examples, Canterbury issues ceased in 1983. The bulk of Warrington local issues by Liverpool have been confined to council-owned vehicles, together with a few issued to meet special requests from motorists, though RTB-Y was used as a general Liverpool area issue. Other areas where local marks have been issued, but not as a matter of course to all dealers, include Bolton and York. (Several Bolton series have been used for Manchester area re-registrations.) On the other hand, there have been a few cases, all in Wales, where local marks displaced in 1974 have been restored to their original areas. Thus when Aberystwyth LVLO was closed, EJ was reallocated to Haverfordwest and has since been issued in the former Cardiganshire area, whilst Bangor took over FF for the former Merionethshire area. Furthermore Haverfordwest adopted separate issues for the former Carmarthenshire and Pembrokeshire areas. Swansea, whilst not allocating EP exclusively to the Montgomeryshire area, do nevertheless endeavour to issue this combination to dealers in that area as far as possible. Finally, from 1987, FO was restored to the former Radnorshire area. Full details of the allocation of index marks to LVLOs/VROs will be found in Appendix 2.

As from 30 March 1987 Local Vehicle Licensing Offices were renamed Vehicle Registration Offices - this reflected the transfer to the Post Office of all routine licence renewals. The Driver and Vehicle Licensing Centre became the Driver and Vehicle Licensing Agency as from 2 April 1990. On 12 August 1994 the DVLA announced that a new scheme for first registration was to be brought in. In July 1994 a pilot scheme had begun with some Ford dealers in Bristol enabling new cars to be registered from dealers' premises by use of computer links between manufacturers, dealers and the DVLA's computers.

The scheme became known as "Automated First Registration and Licensing" - AFRL for short. It was originally envisaged that this system would be virtually universal by the end of 1995 and the need for an over the counter service would be unnecessary. (It is noteworthy that the following provision had been made in the 1969 and 1971 Acts : "The Minister may by regulations make such provision as he considers appropriate with respect to the allocation of registration marks for vehicles to motor dealers......" (In practice local authorities had, of course, for many years allotted blocks of numbers to dealers and other large users). Consequently it was envisaged that all the remaining VROs would be closed by 1997. Huddersfield closed on 30 December 1994 and Coventry on 15 March 1996. The Hull VRO moved to Beverley on 18 March 1996. However, despite the the formal introduction of AFRL, beginning with BMW dealers in 1996, there came another change of heart concerning the proposed closure of VROs. In April 1996 it was announced that a further nine offices would close by March 1997 and that London Central would merge with Croydon in a new location but this would leave 40 VROs open for the foreseeable future. Full implementation of the AFRL scheme took longer than originally anticipated, but further implementation took place at an increasing pace in 'P' and 'R' prefix years. Partly as a consequence of the spread of the AFRL system the traditional sequence of issue of index marks was abandoned and an almost random sequence ensued. A further consequence was that former "local marks" came to be increasingly used for the normal issues of the parent VRO.

CENTRALISATION IN NORTHERN IRELAND

The Motor Licensing Central Office, (later the Driver and Vehicle Licensing Centre, Northern Ireland, "DVLNI"), opened on 1 October 1973. All the existing county and county borough local taxation offices remained in use but became Local Vehicle Licensing Offices with effect from 1 January 1974 and later, Vehicle Registration Offices, with appropriate changes in nomenclature. Centralisation and computerisation of driver and vehicle licensing in Northern Ireland followed the mainland pattern and took effect as from October 1986, (Belfast had actually led the way in March of that year). Little evidence of the change in status was to be discerned in the allocation of registration marks. All that happened was that the series currently in use was abandoned and the next series commenced for each VRO in October 1986. Unused marks in the last "pre-computer" series were set aside for re-registrations.)

LOCAL VEHICLE LICENSING OFFICES/VEHICLE REGISTRATION OFFICES

There were originally 81, grouped into areas as indicated, each with an area office. The code numbers appear on computer generated tax discs issued by VROs as the first three digits in the second group of numbers.

No.	Office Name	Date Closed	Marks absorbed by :	
301	Aberdeen			
302	Ayr	16.06.81	Glasgow	
303	Dumfries	13.02.81	Carlisle (initially but briefly by Glasgow)	
304	Dundee			
305	Edinburgh			
306	Glasgow			
307	Inverness			
308	Keith	16.04.81	Aberdeen	
309	Kirkwall	12.12.80	Inverness	
310	Lerwick	12.12.80	Aberdeen	
311	Oban	14.11.80	Glasgow	
312	St. Boswells	14.11.80	Edinburgh	(Office moved to Selkirk March 1975)
313	Stirling	13.02.81	Edinburgh	
314	Stornoway	14.11.80	Inverness	
315	Stranraer	15.05.81	Glasgow	
316	Wick	13.02.81	Inverness	
320	Durham	13.02.81	Newcastle	
321	Middlesbrough			(Office moved to Stockton 20.3.00)
322	Newcastle			
324	Barrow	15.05.81	Preston	
325	Bolton	13.03.81	Manchester	
326	Carlisle			
327	Kendal	18.09.81	Preston	
328	Liverpool	13.09.96	Preston, Chester	
329	Manchester			
330	Preston			
331	Warrington	16.06.81	Liverpool	
333	Grimsby	14.11.80	Lincoln	
334	Huddersfield	30.12.94	Leeds	
335	Hull			(Office moved to Beverley 18.3.96)
336	Leeds			
337	Sheffield			
338	York	14.11.80	Leeds	
340	Boston	21.08.81	Lincoln	
341	Leicester	15.10.96	Nottingham, Birmingham, Northampton, Peterborough	
342	Lincoln			
343	Nottingham			
345	Cambridge	14.11.80	Peterborough	
346	Ipswich			
347	Norwich			
348	Peterborough			
350	London Central	18.04.97	London South West	
351	London North East *	29.11.96	Chelmsford	
352	London North West *			
353	London South West *			
354	London South East *	18.06.93	London South West	Reopened 17.03.97
355	London Central			(Office for postal applications, located in Dundee).

No.	Office Name	Date Closed	Marks absorbed by :
357	Brighton		
358	Canterbury	13.02.81	Maidstone
359	Chelmsford		
360	Guildford	07.03.97	Portsmouth, Reading, London South West
361	Hastings	14.11.80	Brighton
362	Luton		
363	Maidstone		
364	Newport, I.o.W.	13.02.81	Portsmouth
365	Northampton		
366	Oxford		
367	Portsmouth		
368	Reading		
370	Barnstaple	16.04.81	Exeter
371	Bournemouth		
372	Bristol		
373	Exeter		
374	Gloucester	07.03.97	Worcester, Bristol
375	Plymouth	12.12.80	Exeter
376	Salisbury	12.12.80	Bournemouth
377	Swindon	07.03.97	Bristol
378	Taunton	06.12.96	Exeter, Bristol
379	Truro		
381	Birmingham		
382	Coventry	15.03.96	Northampton, Birmingham, Worcester, Nottingham, Oxford
383	Dudley	15.10.93	Birmingham
384	Stoke-on-Trent	13.12.96	Birmngham, Shrewsbury
385	Worcester		
390	Aberystwyth	16.01.81	Bangor. EJ later transferred to Haverfordwest.
391	Bangor		
392	Cardiff		
393	Chester		
394	Haverfordwest	13.09.96	Swansea
395	Hereford	16.04.81	Gloucester
396	Shrewsbury		
397	Swansea		
399	DVLC (for duplicate licences etc.)		

* The suburban London LVLOs were originally officially known by the names listed but by 1991 they had become known by their locations, i.e. Ilford, Ruislip, Croydon and Sidcup respectively. The North East office was at Stratford until about 1982. North West office had originally been at Ealing until about 1975 and moved again from Ruislip to Stanmore about 1992. South West had been at Wimbledon until about 1990 and moved back to Wimbledon on 21st April 1997 following its merger with London Central. Selkirk, Beverley and Stockton adopted these names on moving from their previous locations.

INTERNATIONAL CIRCULATION

The United Kingdom was a party to the International Convention on Motor Traffic of 11 October 1909 and under the Provisional Regulations of 9/3/21 the special mark QQ was allotted for issue to vehicles arriving in this country without a valid International Travelling Pass issued under the Convention. The principal motoring organisations were appointed as registration authorities for the purpose of these temporary registrations and, although all 'Q' combinations were nominally allotted to the London County Council, (and subsequently to the Greater London Council and London Central VRO), by far the greater number of 'Q' registrations are, in fact, allocated through the Automobile Association and the Royal Automobile Club. Initially QQ 1-1000 were allotted to the County Council and the remainder to the motoring organisations.

Subsequently, in 1930, the Automobile Association, the Royal Automobile Club and the Royal Scottish Automobile Club were allotted their own index marks for this purpose, i.e. QA, QC and QS respectively, although there is no evidence that the latter organisation ever exercised its duties in this respect and the mark QS was later used by the RAC. When the LCC had reached QQ 1000 they re-issued QQ 1001-9999, (by this time long extinct), - apart from the re-use of certain Middlesex marks originally allotted to armoured vehicles this was the only instance of a mass re-use of registrations after 1921.

Further allotments of index marks were made to the three licensing agents through the Q series, up to QT, issued to the AA in 1976. After expiry of this series QX and then QY were used for all three agencies, the letters X and Y being year identifiers to coincide with the X and Y year suffix on normal issues. Additionally an allotment was made in these series to the Royal Air Force Base at Mildenhall, where registration of vehicles belonging to members of the United States Forces in the United Kingdom was undertaken. The format was then reversed with up to four numerals followed by QA, QB etc., the second letter again coinciding with the year prefix currently in use. It should also be mentioned here that the marks QI and QZ were allotted in 1963 to perform the same function in Northern Ireland, but in practice these marks were never brought into use. ZZ, introduced in 1925, performs a similar function in the Republic of Ireland.

[Numbers in the 'Q' series were not issued consecutively, especially by the AA, and there was considerable overlap between the commencement of a new series and the completion of the preceding one. The AA series QM, QP and QT were issued in distinct number blocks, dependent partly upon the make of vehicle and partly upon the shape of the plates, (i.e. whether two square, two oblong, one oblong and one square, or a single motorcycle plate.)]

AGE RELATED MARKS

Prior to the introduction of year-letter marks there was no obvious way of relating a registration number to the age of the vehicle on which it was borne and, with a few exceptions, authorities issued marks in a single sequence, irrespective of the age of the vehicle being registered. However, when the year-letter system was introduced it was decided that vehicles from which cherished marks had been transferred should receive a new mark commensurate with the date of original registration. Accordingly gaps were left at the end of each year's issues in order to accommodate these cases. However, little effort was made to give an appropriately dated registration to other classes of vehicles, other than new ones, being registered for the first time, i.e. imported vehicles, ex military vehicles, vehicles previously used only on trade plates or not on public roads, vehicles kit-built or rebuilt and incorporating parts of older vehicles and vehicles which had lost their original registration numbers, (e.g. through having been delicensed for more than three years). Lancashire was the only authority to make any conscious attempt to correctly date such vehicles. Marks without year suffix therefore continued to be issued for the re-registration of appropriately aged vehicles until 1977 when they were discontinued because the replacement numbers themselves had created an undesirable number of additional "cherishable" marks. Exceptions were made, however, in the case of veteran vehicles, even to the extent of reissuing void numbers for vehicles deemed to be of historical significance, a practice which had otherwise ceased in 1962. In particular a good many veteran and vintage vehicles received void EL numbers during this period, whilst WFX and reverse DEL were similarly used for vehicles manufactured between 1931 and *1955*. Although these were nominally Bournemouth LVLO series they were used almost nationwide. Unused numbers in high SL were also used in similar circumstances to those in EL.

With the introduction of marks with the year-letter first as from 1st August 1983 the opportunity was taken to date correctly the registration of all vehicles. From this date all used vehicles, (i.e. donor vehicles in cherished mark transfers, imported used vehicles, ex-military vehicles, those previously operated under trade plates or off-road etc.), were to receive appropriately dated marks. Where satisfactory evidence of the age of such a vehicle could not be produced it would receive a registration mark with a 'Q' prefix in place of a year letter. If satisfactory evidence of age could be produced at a later date a normal registration could be substituted for the "Q" plate. Special arrangements were put in place for vehicles dating from before 1964. The oldest, those built before 1931 were to receive unused numbers in certain Scottish two-letter series, BS for true "veteran" vehicles, and for the others DS and, when that was exhausted, SV. These registrations were allocated directly by the DVLA. Vehicles dating from 1.1.31 to 31.12.55 initially received numbers in unused Scottish three-letter series, commencing with ASV, BSV etc in the range 101-999. These numbers were allocated in blocks, usually of 100 or 200, to individual LVLOs. After YSV 999 a handful of marks in ASV and BSV with letters last were issued before the policy changed back to the obviously more appropriate letters first format. Subsequent series used have been CSU to YSU, (XSV was originally omitted, then issued after YSU), BSK to YSK, GVS to YVS, TYJ to YYJ. The next two series were former Welsh ones: KFF to YFF, and GFO to YFO (except UFO); then Scottish again with PSY to YSY, ASJ to YSJ and ASL to YSL. Vehicles first registered between *1.1.56* and 31.12.63 were to receive "A" suffix marks and to enable this to be done each LVLO commenced a new series of "A" suffix marks, most starting with their earliest (alphabetical) combinations, but in other cases starting with purely random series. (Neither East Suffolk nor Ipswich had previously issued "A" suffix marks and Ipswich LVLO seem to have anticipated the new arrangements by starting WDX-A in 1982).

There was a change in the system as from 2 December 1991 when the age range for the non-suffix age related marks was extended to 31.12.62. At the same time such marks, with few exceptions, were made non-transferable. Owners of pre 1963 vehicles with A suffix marks could apply for replacement non suffix marks.

Until 1983, the registration numbers of vehicles whose records had not been transferred to the computer, not having been licensed since 1974 or earlier, could nevertheless be resuscitated provided that satisfactory documentary evidence, such as the possession of an appropriate green registration book, was available. However, in 1983 the DVLA announced that any such numbers which were not recorded on the computer by 30 November 1983 would be cancelled. Subsequently the authorities relented and allowed the reinstatement of cancelled registrations in cases where the provenance of the vehicle could be authenticated, preferably by an appropriate owners' association. This concession was announced in October 1989; such reinstated numbers to be on a non transferable basis.

AGE-RELATED MARKS IN NORTHERN IRELAND

Although year-letters are not used in Northern Ireland it is possible to identify dates of issue and blocks of numbers are withheld in certain series so that re-registered series may receive appropriate marks. For the re-registration of vehicles whose correct age cannot be determined the special series QNI, followed by a serial number, was brought into use as from 1 January 1990. (This series corresponds to the mainland's Q prefix series).

SPECIAL MARKS FOR DIPLOMATIC CORPS

There were no special registration marks for foreign or commonwealth missions, nor for their diplomats until the special issue, (by arrangement with Londonderry C.C.), of the mark NZ 1 for the use of the New Zealand High Commissioner in April 1949. This was the first of very many marks specially allocated to the heads of diplomatic missions. Such marks usually consist of the number 1 followed or preceded by a two- or three-letter mark indicative of the name of the mission; exceptionally, Malaysia has the special mark 1 M. In a few cases year-letters are used, notably in the appropriate SPA 1N for Spain.These special marks were assigned originally by the London County Council, later the GLC and latterly by London Central VRO, in consultation with the authority to which the basic index mark in question is allotted. They may be marks which the original issuing authority has confirmed as void, or they may be marks outside the normal sequence of issue, including a few that would never be issued in the U.K. in normal way, for example marks containing the letters "I", "Q" and "Z". After NZ 1, the next special issue appears to have been PAK 1 for the High Commissioner of Pakistan and since Bradford at that date had not been allotted this combination, it was specially included in the allocation authorised in the next Statutory Instrument, (1949, No. 1618). However, this procedure was not repeated and none of the other specials outside the normal range of issue had any statutory status.

Few other Heads of Mission took advantage of this concession during the 1950s; most of those who did were the High Commissioners of Commonwealth countries, a notable exception being the Philippines, whose PHI 1 was the first to include the letter "I" in a U.K. mark. However, from the mid-1960's the practice took off and today there are few countries with missions in the U.K who have not taken advantage of the facility. Normally the issue of such special marks was limited to one per mission, but there were a few exceptions. In the cases of Australia and Canada, in addition to the mark issued to the High Commissioner, the Agent-General of each province or state has his own special mark. This was also the case during Nigeria's brief federal status, when there were separate issues for the Eastern and Western Regions, as well as the Federal Government. Special marks have also been allotted to the heads of some missions from International Organisations. From time to time some countries have dispensed with their special numbers for security reasons; in other cases marks were changed, either upon a change in the name of the country, or when a more appropriate mark became available. In a very few cases discontinued special marks have remained in use as normal issues.

In 1979 a completely new series of marks was introduced for vehicles belonging to foreign missions, supplementing but not displacing the "Heads of Missions" marks already described. The new series of marks comprised a three-digit number identifying the mission, a letter 'D' for official vehicles of diplomatic missions, 'X' for the vehicles of consular and other accredited non-diplomatic personnel, and then by a three-digit serial number, commencing at 101 for diplomats, 400 for non-diplomatic staff of International Organisations and 700 for consular or other non-diplomatic staff. There have, howvere, been some exceptions to this numbering scheme. (Not all embassies used X marks). In the initial allocation the numbers 101 to 282 inclusive were allocated to the then existing missions in alphabetical order, (Afghanistan to Zambia), the larger missions being allocated two or more prefix codes, up to a maximum of five. International Organisations were initially allotted prefix codes 900 to 919. These two series have since been extended following the creation of more independent countries, newly accredited missions and international organisations, (now extending to 319 and 941 respectively as at 4/98). A special series of codes in the 350-400 range, plus 600, 700 and 800 were brought into use mid-1984 for security reasons. There are a number of countries, mainly Francophone African countries, with which we have diplomatic relations but which have no embassy in the U.K.; such countries are allotted codes which have not been brought into use. The new system officially commenced on 1st January 1979, but replating had commenced as early as 9 October 1978.

In March 1984 the government introduced new measures to restrict the issue of X series marks to those having diplomatic immunity from parking and similar traffic offences. Thereafter there was a large reduction in the number of X plates in use and many embassies ceased to use them, though they continued to be commonly used by international organisations. In consequence the special series RXS, (in normal format marks), with the appropriate year suffix or prefix, (commencing for each year at 21), was introduced from 1st April 1984 for issue to the third and subsequent cars of diplomats. Such marks remain with the vehicle when sold, whereas vehicles with diplomatic format plates are reregistered on disposal. Little use was made of the RXS series - it seems unlikely that more than 30 were ever issued and they seem to have been discontinued in 1987.

CHERISHED REGISTRATION MARKS

Cherished registration marks, (though not the term itself), are almost as old as registrations themselves. As early as June 1904 the pages of The Autocar contained a letter from a reader, aggrieved because on changing his car the authorities had refused to transfer his number to his new vehicle. He wrote : "I am about selling my car, DA 6, and wish to retain my No. 6 on a new car. I am told I cannot do this; that the new car will have to be registered under an entirely new number. Will you kindly tell me whether what I have been told is correct ?......." The editor commented "There is no provision in the new Motor Car Act nor yet in the Local Government Board regulations which would enable you to carry out your wishes. The procedure to be followed is laid down by Article IV of the Local Government Board Regulations, 1903, which provides for the new owner of a car that has changed hands to retain the original registration mark if he so desires, but if he does not desire to do so the number is cancelled. There is no choice given to the original owner to retain the old number for any new car that he may become possessed of." The next issue contained letters from readers suggesting that a number could be retained on change of ownership if the owner cancelled his registration, then made a fresh application for registration of a new car and requesting that his original number, which would then be "void", be allotted to his new vehicle. The following is an extract from a typical letter "I wrote to the Clerk of the Council where I had got the number FN 25 for my Darracq, requesting him to cancel that registration, also pointing out that under the regulations the Council is empowered to allot any cancelled number to any other motor car - of course for a new fee of £1 and I requested the Clerk to obtain for me the registration of my new 16 h.p. Rochet-Schneider under the number FN 25. I have today obtained my certified copy of this registration, so I am still FN 25". This ruse appeared to satisfy all aspirants for cherished marks during the currency of the 1903 Act - certainly studies of the surviving registers show frequent instances of a number being reissued to a new vehicle in the ownership of the original holder of the number.

On a purely legal interpretation the Regulations issued under the 1920 Act put a stop to this practice. The wording was quite unequivocal "The index mark and registration number which is declared to have been the index mark and registration number at the 31st day of December 1920 shall be entered on the register and on the licence, and shall thereafter attach to that vehicle until the same is broken up, destroyed or sent permanently out of the United Kingdom." Not surprisingly, this new rule provoked howls of outrage from motorists who had retained their original numbers. "The Autocar" of 14 May 1921 contained a paragraph on the subject headed "Cherished Registration Numbers", the earliest use of this term that I have found. This was followed in the issue of 28 May 1921 by a whole page of letters from angry readers. No doubt many of the great and good were able to bend the ear of the Minister of Transport and Information Circular No. 5, addressed to local authorities on 19 July 1921 was the result. The following are extracts : "The scheme of registration and licensing prescribed under the Finance Act 1920 and Roads Act 1920 requires that a vehicle shall retain its identification mark and number irrespective of change of ownership etc., but strong representations have been made to the Minister by owners who, when disposing of a car, desire, usually from sentimental reasons, to transfer its identification mark and number to a new car.......While any substantial departure from the normal procedure would cause serious inconvenience to Councils, and involve material expense to the Road Fund, the Minister wishes, so far as practicable, to meet the expressed desire of a section of the motor owning community and will accordingly raise no objection to Councils acceding to a request for the transfer of an identification mark and registration number on payment of a fee of £5, subject to the conditions set out below.......The fee of £5 has been fixed in order to cover the additional work imposed on the Council concerned and to limit the number of these exceptional cases. It will be recognised that from an administrative standpoint the transfer of identification marks and numbers from one vehicle to another is undesirable, and any request for such transfer is presumably based upon sentimental or business grounds...........The Ministry recognises that these arrangements are extra-statutory and that it is not competent to him to direct Councils to accede to such requests for transfer, but he hopes that they will co-operate, so far as practicable, in meeting the wishes of motorists in this matter, especially as the fee of £5 will enure to the Road Fund and increase the amount available for road grants.....It should be noted that while the representations to the Minister have been in connection with private motor cars, the arrangements set out in these paragraphs may, if desired, be applied to motor vehicles of any class."

It will be noted that cherished numbers were permitted only as an extra-statutory concession and this remained the case until 1985. The privilege was used only to a limited extent in the pre-war years and in all except a very few cases the numbers cherished were those that had been in the family since the early years; the craze for initials, birth dates, model numbers and jokey mis-spaces had not yet materialised and the system as devised in 1921 remained unchanged until 1955. By this time the vogue for cherished numbers was beginning to burgeon and the Ministry conceded, in Circular No. 11 of 1955, that local authorities could, if they wished, re-issue any void numbers on payment of the statutory fee, which still remained at £5. The result was that a great many very early numbers were resuscitated until the Ministry ended the concession as from 5 March 1962. Thereafter cherished mark dealers began to flourish. There have been numerous changes in the detailed conditions relating to the transfer of marks, and there was a period in 1976-7 when they ceased to be handled owing to a trade dispute at the DVLC, except in cases where neither vehicle's records had been transferred to the DVLC computer, but these matters are outside the scope of the present study. Following the dispute, the transfer fee was increased to £50; later still it became £80.

At long last, in 1985, the "legality" of transferred marks was recognised, when SI No. 2089 added the phrase in italics to the existing regulations, which had by this time been incorporated in The Road Vehicles (Registration and Licensing) Regulations 1971 No. 450, Regulation 9 (3) : "The registration mark assigned to a vehicle shall remain the registration mark of that vehicle until the vehicle is broken up, destroyed or sent permanently out of Great Britain, *save when the mark is assigned to another vehicle or another mark is assigned to the vehicle by the Secretary of State.*"
The next major change came with the sale of marks by the DVLA.

TRANSFER OF IRISH MARKS

1. Republic of Ireland marks can no longer be transferred to U.K. registered vehicles.
2. Northern Ireland marks may be transferred (a) within Northern Ireland and (b) within Great Britain if the donor vehicle is brought to the mainland, registered with the DVLA and the mark transferred to another vehicle registered with the DVLA.
3. A mainland registration can be transferred within Northern Ireland if the vehicle is "exported" there and obtains Northern Ireland documentation.

SALE OF MARKS

The first intimation of the sale of marks directly by the Driver and Vehicle Licensing Agency came in 1983, with the introduction of marks with the year-letter first. The first 20 numbers of each series were withdrawn from normal issues, with a view to their possible sale by the DVLA at a later date, but it was another six years before the Sale of Marks scheme was introduced. There were initially to separate schemes:

1. "The Classic Collection". Sales by auction of "attractive" numbers which had not previously been issued. The first such auction was held at Christie's on 14 December 1989 and auctions have since been held at intervals of about two months at various venues throughout the country.

2. "Select Registrations". Originally announced towards the end of 1989 it was not until 1 October 1990 that the scheme was launched. "Select Registrations" comprise a mark with the current year-letter, (the scheme commenced with H), a number between 1 and 20, a two-digit number divisible by 10 or 11 or a three-digit number divisible by 100 or 111, and a three-letter combination of the applicant's choice. Additionally, in "H" year only, BMW car and motorcycle model numbers were included in the scheme. All such numbers were, of course, omitted from normal issues, as were the numbers 72, 147, 280, 560 and 747 in 'J' to 'P' prefix years. A different selection of numbers was omitted from normal issues in 'R' year, including the numbers 1 to 22 inclusive. From S prefix onwards the first 31 numbers were withheld from normal issues, together with 121, 123 and 321; these numbers being available as 'Select' marks (Some 121s were issued in error as normal marks during the 'S' year).

A third scheme was introduced in August 1991. Known originally as "Custom" marks they comprised the year-letters A, H or later, a number in the range 1-20 and a three-letter mark. The scheme was extended to cover J prefix marks when K became the current year-letter, and so on. B prefix marks were added to the scheme as from 15 January 1996 and C prefix from 6 April 1999. The "Custom" name was later dropped and such sales were included under the "Select" name. Originally the number 666 was excluded from those available under the "Select" and "Custom" schemes. The issue of the number had been discontinued in September 1989 following representations from motorists who identified it as "the mark of the Beast" in the Book of Revelations. However, this number became available under the schemes from 15 February 1996, but only from J prefix onwards. Initially the choice of letter combinations available under both the "Classic" and "Select" schemes was subject to the usual tabos on unacceptable trios, though from the outset some combinations which had never appeared as normal issues, (e.g. XXX, YTK), have been allowed. However, as from 15 February 1996, the following trios not authorised for normal issues were made available under the Sale of Marks schemes: ABF, APE, AWC, BAS, BBF, BOG, BUB, BUG, DWO, GPO, HOG, LAV, NBG, SOT, UBF and UWC; together with the following which, while authorised have been withheld from normal issues in recent years: FAG, FAT, GUT, MUG, SOW, VCK. The more objectionable combinations, however, remain banned. (Later some of the "released" trios also appeared on normal issues).

A variant of the "Select Scheme" is the special issue by the DVLA of marks in circumstances which would achieve publicity for the "Sale of Marks" scheme. Probably the first manifestation of this policy was the co-operation between the DVLA and HJ Heinz and Co., whereby the latter offered as competition prizes 100 Rover Metros, all of which had the registration H57 followed by a three-letter combination appropriate to the name of the prize-winner. The competition ran from September to December 1990. Also at around this time the number H70 PAR was awarded in a competition in "Golfing World". In similar vein, a suppliant in the "Jim'll Fix It" TV show was granted her wish for a "MUM" registration by the special issue by the DVLC of 937 MUM. Later came the practice of selling blocks of "Select" marks to manufacturers, including numbers not normally included in the scheme, again with publicity in view. The first such block identified was in J-MMC for Mitsubishi Motors, followed by K1-50 FMC for the Ford Motor Company.

SALE OF MARKS IN NORTHERN IRELAND

As a preliminary to the sale of marks in Northern Ireland the numbers 1-100 were withdrawn from normal issues in November 1985 and 1-999 in April 1989. Numbers 9501-999 were also withheld, being used mostly for security type re-registrations or similarly deserving vehicles. Further numbers were withheld on the eve of the first auction. Since February 1996 multiples of 1000 and 1111 have been withheld, together with some car model numbers and cubic capacities, e.g. 316, 318, 325,1100, 1200 and other attractive numbers like 1234. In addition in certain series the first 2,000 numbers have been withheld.

The first auction sale of marks took place on 28 February 1996. A new departure, not so far adopted in the rest of Great Britain, is the sale of marks by tender. In the first such exercise 328 numbers were on offer and the closing date for tenders was 20 June 1996.

Numbers offered under the DVLNI sales comprise (1) numbers below 1000, (2) numbers above 9500, (3) other "nice" numbers withheld from normal issues, like "four-of-a-kind" and palindromic numbers, (4) numbers unused in 1986 in the final series prior to computerisation.

The scheme of registration and licensing prescribed under the Finance Act 1920 and Roads Act 1920 requires that a vehicle shall retain its identification mark and number irrespective of change of ownership etc., but strong representations have been made to the Minister by owners who, when disposing of a car, desire, usually from sentimental reasons, to transfer its identification mark and number to a new car. While any substantial departure from the normal procedure would cause serious inconvenience to Councils, and involve material expense to the Road Fund, the Minister wishes, so far as practicable, to meet the expressed desire of a section of the motor owning community and will accordingly raise no objection to Councils acceding to a request for the transfer of an identification mark and registration number on payment of a fee of £5.........The fee of £5 has been fixed in order to cover the additional work imposed on the Council concerned and to limit the number of these exceptional cases. It will be recognised that from an administrative standpoint the transfer of identification marks and numbers from one vehicle to another is undesirable, and any request for such transfer is presumably based upon sentimental or business grounds. *Circular RF 134, 19.7.21*

GENERAL IDENTIFICATION MARKS AND TRADE PLATES

GENERAL IDENTIFICATION MARKS 1904 - 1920

Section 2 (4) (b) of The Motor Car Act of 1903 made provision for the issue of special plates for dealers and manufacturers in the following terms :

"The council of any county or county borough in which the business premises of any manufacturer of, or dealer in, motorcars are situated, may, on payment of such annual fee, not exceeding three pounds, as the council require, assign to that manufacturer or dealer a general identification mark which may be used for any car on trial after completion, or on trial by an intending purchaser....".   The Motor Car (Registration & Licensing) Order, 1903, (and its equivalents for Scotland and Ireland), laid down the specification of General Identification Marks in the following terms :-

"..... the mark shall be such as the Council directs in each case, provided that :

(a) it shall consist of two plates, each bearing the index mark of the Council and some other distinguishing letter or letters; and each having placed thereon or annexed thereto some distinguishing number; and

(b) The colouring of the plates shall be different from that used for the plates forming the ordinary identification mark; and

(c) The lettering and numbering of the plates shall, as far as possible, be similar to those required in the case of the plates forming the ordinary identification mark."

It will be observed that the wording of the regulations was delightfully vague and it is not surprising that they spawned a wide diversity in both colouring and format. With regard to the former, The Local Government Board's Circular to local authorities dated 20th November 1903 stated ".....it has been considered desirable that the colouring of the plates shall be different from those used on registered motor cars. It is suggested that white lettering on a red ground would be suitable and would make these plates readily distinguishable from those carried by registered cars."

Little information about the colours used by individual authorities has survived and much of the information on them derives from monochrome photographs, which can only indicate "light on dark" or "dark on light". From what little information is available it would appear that some notice was taken of the Local Government Board's recommendation. The Motor Car Journal of 13.2.04, in reply to a reader's query, stated "As a rule, white letters on a red ground seem to be favoured by the local authorities."   Certainly Cornwall, Dorset, Essex, Gloucestershire and Midlothian used this colouring. There were further comments on GIM colours in The Motor Car Journal of 20.2.04 : "In the County of Westmorland, each member (*of the motor trade*) .... can have the selection of three colours - red, green or blue. At Nottingham the mark is in black letters on a yellow ground". It is known that Birmingham's were white on blue and London's black on white - others using "dark on light", (which were probably either red or black on white) were Buckinghamshire, Norfolk, Middlesex and Wiltshire.

47

As for format, by far the commonest comprised three elements : (1) the index mark of the council; (2) a letter indicating the dealer; (3) a numeral from 1 upwards depending upon the number of plates required by each dealer. In London and Surrey the format was similar, but with the second and third elements reversed. At different times Coventry used both the aforementioned formats. The dealers' identification letters were usually issued in alphabetical sequence, often including the letters I, Q and Z, not found on ordinary plates. If all of A to Z were thus allocated the series might continue with AA, AB, AC etc., or with AA, BB, CC etc. It was not uncommon for authorities to meet dealers' wishes to have their initials as their distinguishing letters - in fact in the case of Birmingham and, to a lesser extent, London, this was more the norm than the exception. For example Birmingham allocated O-AY to Alldays, O-LR to Lanchester and O-WY to Wolseley, while London allocated (in the format A-8-DC etc) DC to the Daimler Company, B to Beaufort, N to Napier, O to Oldsmobile and EMC (note three letters) to the Eagle Motor Company.

Other authorities used a format comprising of (1) the index mark of the council, (2) a letter or letters which were the same on each plate, (3) a numeral. A notable user of this format was Kent, whose GIMs ranged from D.G.1 to D.G.1199. Other authorities using a similar format included the following, (first and second elements as shown) : Liverpool (K.A.); Manchester (N.MR); Leeds (U.M.), Westmorland (EC-W); Newcastle (BB-N); Bradford (AK-B); Burnley (CW-X).   Sheffield initially used W.A. and a number (sometimes rendered as Wa), but this was later altered.   We may speculate that Kent's 'G' stood for 'general', Manchester's 'MR' and Leeds' 'M' for 'manufacturer', but the choice of the indicators used by Westmorland, Newcastle and Essex is puzzling. (It is worthy of note that dashes or full points were often omitted, giving rise to some GIMs which looked suspiciously like normal registrations of a much later period). Essex's system was unique. The format was the letter F, followed by the letter E, a numeral indicating the dealer and a further progressive numeral, the various elements being separated by dashes. A typical example would be F-E-40-56, belonging to the AEC Company of Walthamstow. In practice most Essex GIMs were of two-line format with a horizontal divider - the letter F above the line and the other elements below.   Finally, a handful of authorities - Salford was one - merely issued dealers with a registration taken from the normal sequence, but with altered colouring. (In the case of Salford the letters MR were interposed between the index mark BA and the serial number).

GENERAL IDENTIFICATION MARKS, 1921-1922

Although continuing their former name, the dealer plates first issued under the 1920 Act were more akin to what later became known as "Trade Plates". They were regulated by The Motor Vehicles (Registration & Licensing) Regulations of 1921. The format was now standard. Plates had red characters on a white background and had a two-line format. The upper line comprised a numeral commencing at 0001, the lower a one- or two-letter index mark indicating the council. The front plate had a licence plate affixed. These plates, as well as all subsequent trade plates, were officially issued.

TRADE PLATES 1923-1969

Complaints were received from traders concerning the huge size of the 1921-2 plates, ($14\frac{1}{2}$" x $10^{27}/_{32}$"), ; furthermore it was considered that two different types of trade plate were desirable. "General" trade plates were to have white characters on a red ground, while "Limited" trade plates continued the colouring of the former "General Identification Plates". The former were hedged about with fewer restrictions than the latter.

The format of both types was identical : a serial number, (initially 001-099, increased later in 1923 to 001-0999 - altered in 1925 to 001-999), followed by a one- or two-letter index mark denoting the council. A few authorities have continued the issue of four-digit numbers, usually with lead zeros, but in other cases with numbers above 999. In the case of authorities having two or more index marks practice varied. Some used only one series for both "General" and "Limited" plates, whilst others used more than one, sometimes with separate series for each category; some even used separate series for motorcycle only plates. The extreme example was London County Council, who used each and every one of their two-letter marks with 001-099, (with separate series for "Limited" and "General") before using numbers 100 and above. Exceptionally Norfolk and West Bromwich used EVF and AEA for trade plates, whilst the creation of new registration authorities in 1963-7 demanded a new format. This comprised a letter (not a year letter as such, but the year-letter in current use when the new authority was created, i.e. A for Kirkcaldy, B for Coatbridge, Luton and Solihull and F for Torbay), then a number - officially 01-99, but Luton exceeded this - then a three-letter index mark indicating the council.

TRADE PLATES 1970 to date

A reversion to a single series of trade plates took place as from 1 January 1970; retaining the format and colouring of the former Limited trade plates. Centralisation of vehicle licensing has had no effect on the format of trade plates.

G.I.M. PLATES - GENERAL INSTRUCTIONS

The letters on each plate must be the index mark allotted to the Licensing Authority by whom the motor car or motor cycle G.I.M. is issued. The sizes of the letters and figures and the spacing must be as laid down in the Fourth Schedule of the Regulations, (Registration & Licensing Duty) issued under the Motor Car Acts 1896 and 1903, (paragraphs 4, 5, 6 & 7). The numbering of every G.I.M. will consist of four figures, the series running from 0001 to 0999, as follows :

 The first nine numbers : 0001, 0002, 0003 0009,
 the 2nd ten numbers : 0010, 0011 0019,
 and so on up to 0999.

Any numbering that has to be done after the above 999 numbers have been used will start again at 0001 but the second (or subsequent) index marks allotted to the Licensing Authority will be used.

The plates, as issued by the Licensing Authority, whether for motor car G.I.M. licence (£10), or for motorcycle G.I.M. licence (£1.10s) will consist of a pair of numbered plates, i.e. a front plate carrying the licence holder and containing the appropriate licence card, and a back plate. The numbers on each pair of plates to correspond.   *Circular RF 106, 11.12.20*

REGISTRATION OF MILITARY VEHICLES

PRIOR TO WORLD WAR I

The very earliest military vehicles carried normal civilian registrations issued by various local authorities, usually the ones in which the vehicle was based. Even from the outset, however, it would seem that each vehicle was allotted a military serial which may not necessarily have been displayed. Some vehicles had an Army Service Corps number painted on the side in white, e.g. ASC 1, ASC 75 etc., plus normal registration plate.

WORLD WAR I

With the onset of the Great War, civilian registration ceased for vehicles employed by the several expeditionary corps and various numbering systems were brought into use. It seems likely that different systems were used in different theatres of war. One such system employed a series letter, (which may have denoted vehicle type), followed by a broad arrow and a serial number. Whilst these various series were in use for vehicles serving overseas it would appear that civilian registration continued throughout the war for home-based army vehicles.

Towards the end of the war, in September 1918 the Local Government Board issued a circular to local authorities setting out the arrangements made by the military authorities in conjunction with the Home Office and the Police Authorities with regard to the temporary registration in this country of motor vehicles intended for use with the Expeditionary Forces, of military motor vehicles belonging to the Dominion Governments and to the Government of the United States of America and of certain other motor vehicles. The circular specified that -

"1. Each motor vehicle is to bear a number followed by an initial letter or letters indicating the particular service to which it belongs, as follows :
War Office Vehicles.   The letters B, or C, or CA, CB, CC etc.
Canadian Vehicles.   The letter K.
Australian Vehicles.   The letter A.
Vehicles belonging to the United States of America.   The letter U.
British Red Cross vehicles.   The letters RX.
French Red Cross vehicles.   The letters ZX.
Vehicles belonging to the British Ambulance Committee.   The letters BAC.

The numbers and letters are to be 5" in height and 1 inch in width and of a bright yellow colour and are to be placed in such a position that they can be seen from the front and rear of the vehicle".
(It would appear that the War Office 'C' suffix was allocated to vehicles of the Royal Air Force).

1921 to 1939

War Office vehicles again became subject to civilian registration under the Roads Act of 1920. From 1921 onwards all such vehicles were registered with Middlesex County Council. During the two-letter era blocks of numbers, usually at the end of a series, (e.g. MG 8001-9999), were allocated to the War Department but when the three-letter marks came in whole series were allocated.

1939 to 1949

Shortly after the outbreak of World War II civilian registration of military vehicles again ceased. Army vehicles were then identified by their military service serials. The allocation of such numbers had commenced in 1921 and they were carried on the sides of vehicles, but not used as registrations before 1939. There were two separate series, numbers running consecutively in each series, irrespective of prefix letters. The serial numbers, (known officially as "W.D. Numbers"), in each list were prefixed by a letter denoting the vehicle type:

'A' Vehicles

D	"Dragons"
F	Armoured Cars
R	"Rota Trailers"
S	S.P.M.s (i.e. Gun Carriers)
T	Tanks and Carriers

'B' Vehicles

A	Ambulances
C	Motorcycles
H	Tractors and articulated vehicles

L	Lorries (1 ton and upwards)
M	Cars and coaches
P	Amphibians
S	S.P.M.s (Note that S.P.M.S appear in both 'A' and 'B' lists)
V	Vans
X	Trailers
Z	Trucks (up to 15 cwt.)
No prefix	Miscellaneous, including road rollers, excavators, cranes, electric trucks, etc.

Vehicles allotted to the Canadian Forces had the type prefix preceded by the letter 'C', (e.g. CF, CS, CT). The serials of rebuilt vehicles carried a suffix letter to indicate the Royal Ordnance Factory carrying out the work.

Royal Air Force
The registration of Royal Air Force vehicles comprised the letters RAF followed by a serial number.

Royal Navy
The registration of Royal Navy vehicles comprised a serial number followed by the letters RN. The general series ran to 9999 RN, with trailers taking numbers 10000 RN up.

1949-1994

Military vehicles did not revert to civilian registration after World War II. Instead a completely new system was commenced in 1949. The format was two numerals, two letters and two further numerals. The serial letters AA to AY were allocated to the Royal Air Force and RN to the Royal Navy, but whereas all existing Army and Air Force vehicles were renumbered into the new system, existing Naval vehicles retained their old nnnn RN marks until withdrawn. Other serial letters covered the Army and government agencies like the Ministry of Public Buildings and Works for vehicles in overseas theatres. In contrast to civilian practice trailers belonging to the Army and Air Force carried their own distinctive registrations. The system was modified in 1982 when a unified series was introduced, with serials KA to KL inclusive, excepting only specialised vehicles of types exclusive to the Royal Air Force and Royal Navy, which continued to be registered in AY and RN respectively.

Royal Navy

Whereas all vehicles of the other services were renumbered in 1949 existing Royal Navy vehicles retained their nnnn RN serials until they were taken out of service. All new vehicles received nn RN nn numbers and, in contrast to the normal practice of the other services nn RN nn serials were continually recycled. The Royal Navy also showed a departure from the other services in their treatment of trailers. Each trailer had its own serial in the nnnnn RN series, but on the road displayed the registration of the towing vehicle. Another feature unique to the Navy's system was a handful of shunting locomotives at RN rail-served shore establishments also received nn RN nn serials.

Initially the series NA to NZ was reserved for the Royal Navy, but in the event this series was mainly used for other purposes.

Royal Air Force

Air Force vehicles were allocated the serial letters AA to AY inclusive, omitting only AI. (AO and AQ, which were added after the initial allocation, were the only example of a code including the letters O and Q). Serial letters were allocated in accordance with vehicle type.

Army

Initially vehicles existing in 1949 were allocated marks in the series YA to YZ, ZA to ZC and ZR to ZY, depending upon vehicle type, whilst vehicles rebuilt for extended service were numbered or renumbered in the series RA to RH.

New vehicles introduced from about 1950 onwards fell into one of three categories, i.e. A for armoured vehicles, B for general transport and C for engineers' vehicles. Later a fourth category was added for mechanical handling vehicles. Vehicles were ordered on an annual procurement and a separate series was allotted for each category in each year.

Other Agencies

Vehicles belonging to Government Agencies and Welfare Organisations used in overseas theatres were also numbered in the military series.

A listing of the serial letters used under the 1949-94 system follows.

The following is believed to be a complete list of serials used under the system :

AA to AY (including AO & AQ)	Royal Air Force vehicles
AZ	D.o.E. vehicles used at airfields, including overseas
BA, BB	Army 'A' vehicles
BC to BS	Army 'B' vehicles
BT	Transfers to Army from other services and locally purchased vehicles.
BX	Vehicles received from USA under Military Aid Development Programme.
BY	Army 'C' vehicles
CA, CC	Army 'A' vehicles (CC later used for "Chassis and Cab" – vehicles on deliveries)
CE, CL	Army 'B' vehicles
CP	Construction plant
CV	Captured vehicles in Falklands War
CW, CY	Army 'C' vehicles
DA, DC, DD	Army 'A' vehicles
DE, DL, DM	Army 'B' vehicles
DV	Army Engineers' vehicles, ex RAF airfield construction.
DW, DY, DZ	Army 'C' vehicles
EA to EE	Army 'A' vehicles
EK to ET	Army 'B' vehicles
EU to EW	Army 'C' vehicles
EX	Military Engineering Experimental Establishment
EY, EZ	Army 'C' vehicles
FA to FF	Army 'A' vehicles
FG to FM	Army 'B' vehicles
FU to FZ	Army 'C' vehicles
GB	Army 'B' vehicles
GC	Army 'A' vehicles
GD	Army 'C' vehicles
GE	Army 'A' vehicles
GF	Army 'B' vehicles
GG	Army 'C' vehicles
GH	Army 'A' vehicles
GJ	Army 'B' vehicles
GK	Army 'C' vehicles
GL	Army Mechanical Handling
GM	Army 'A' vehicles
GN	Army 'B' vehicles
GP	Army 'C' vehicles
GR	Army Mechanical Handling
GS	Army 'A' vehicles
GT	Army 'B' vehicles
GU	Army 'C' vehicles
GV	Army Mechanical Handling
GX	Army 'B' vehicles

HA, HB	Army 'A' vehicles
HD, HE	Army 'A' vehicles
HF to HJ	Army 'B' vehicles
HP	Army Mechanical Handling
HV to HY	Army 'C' vehicles
KA to KL	Unified Services
LV	Leased vehicles
MA	Military Attaches (allocated, perhaps unused)
MH	Materials Handling
MS	Military Sales (to foreign governments etc)
MW	Ministry of Works to overseas theatres
NA	NAAFI vehicles in overseas theatres
NC	"Non-census" vehicles purchased locally
NE	Royal Navy, forklift trucks
NK	Royal Navy, water trailers
NS	Vehicles supplied to other ministries. (Allocated, but perhaps unused).
NV	Royal Navy vehicles in Canada
PB	Ministry of Public Buildings and Works
RA to RH	Ex World War II vehicles rebuilt and renumbered
RN	Royal Navy
SP	Research and Development vehicles
TC	Transportable containers/cabins
TE	Trailers
TF	Trailer Fire Pumps
TG	Trailer guns
TH	Demountable containers
TM	Trailer-mounted equipment, mainly generators
TP	Temporary plates, (akin to civilian Trade Plates)
WA & WB	Trials vehicles
WH	"White Helmets" motorcycle display team
WL	Far East Land Forces Welfare Vehicles
WP	D.o.E. vehicles in overseas theatres
XA to XK	Vehicles in overseas theatres, mainly BAOR purchased locally and World War II vehicles renumbered
YA to YZ	Ex World War II vehicles renumbered
ZA to ZC	Ex World War II vehicles renumbered
ZE	Forklift trucks
ZF & ZG	Army mechanical handling
ZR to ZW	Ex World War II armoured vehicles renumbered.
ZX, ZY	Ex World War II Engineers' vehicles renumbered
ZZ	Commonwealth vehicles operated in the U.K.

1994 to date

A new "reversed" format was introduced in 1994, comprising two letters, two numerals and two letters. The series began with AA 00 AA and the first two letters progressed first, so that AA 99 AA was followed by AB 00 AA until ZZ 99 AA which was then followed by AA 00 AB. However, the Royal Air Force and Royal Navy continued the use of AY and RN (in the older format) respectively.

SPECIFICATION AND EXHIBITION
OF REGISTRATION PLATES

Regulations for the exhibition of registration plates were contained in the Motor Car (Registration & Licensing) Orders of 1903. Article VII read "The mark to be carried by a registered motor vehicle.......shall consist of two plates which must conform as to lettering, numbering or otherwise, with the provisions set out in the Fourth Schedule to this Order. Designs, painted or otherwise, shown upon the motor car may, if it is desired, be used instead of plates...." Article VIII continued : "The plates forming the identification mark shall be fixed, one on the front of, and the other on the back of, the motor car, in an upright position, so that every letter or figure on the plate is upright and easily distinguishable, in the case of the plate placed on the front of the motor car, from in front of the car, and in the case of the plate placed on the back of the motor car, from behind the car. In the case of a motor tricycle or motor bicycle of a weight not exceeding three hundredweights, the plate fixed on the front of the cycle may, if it is a plate having duplicate faces, ... be fixed so that from whichever side the cycle is viewed the letters or figures on one or other face of the plate are easily distinguishable, though they may not be distinguishable from the front of the cycle...."

Article XI provided for the carrying of trailer plates : "When another vehicle is attached to a motor car, either in front or behind, the plate required to be fixed on the front or back of the motor car, or a duplicate of such plate, shall be fixed on the front or on the back of the vehicle attached, as the case requires, in the same manner as the plate is required to be fixed on the motor car." Article X provided that "A Council with whom a motor car is registered may, if they think fit, supply to the owner of the car, if he so desires, the plates forming the identification mark on the car, and make a charge for them." It is not known whether any Council exercised its powers under this Article.

The detailed specification of registration plates was laid down in an Appendix to the Orders of 1903 and various subsequent SR&Os and SIs. The appendix was illustrated by sketches showing 'AB 242' in both one-line and two-line formats. All characters were to be 3½" in height, the stroke of characters $^5/_8$", width of characters (except figure 1) 2½", space between characters and top and bottom margins ½", side margins 1" and between top and bottom lines on two-line plates ¾", space between letters and numerals 1½". Each of the dimensions for plates for motorcycles not exceeding 3cwt. unladen was halved and the plate need not be rectangular as long as the minimum margins were preserved. It has been stated that the 1903 regulations required hyphens between letters and numerals and it is true that the sketch for the one line plate does show 'AB-242'. However, there is no mention of hyphens in the very detailed specifications and the 1921 Regulations, which are otherwise identical to the 1903 ones, no longer show the hyphen in the sketch. In the 1949 Regulations there was a separate specification for the rear plates of motorcycles - the height of letters and numerals was specified as 2½", with correspondingly reduced figures for stroke width ($^9/_{16}$") and margins. Front plates could still be half normal dimensions. The 1953 Regulations (SI 231), which provided for reverse format registrations, included four sketches, showing 'AB 242' and '242 AB' in two-line format and 'ABC 242' and '242 ABC' in one-line but the specifications were otherwise unchanged, except that certain dimensions for spaces and margins were more precisely delineated for plates "....where the registration mark consists either of a single plate with letters and figures embossed or pressed thereon or with separate letters and figures attached thereto or of separate plates each with a single letter or figure embossed or pressed thereon or attached thereto..."

S.I. 1610 of 1962, which introduced year-letter formats, permitted characters of reduced size so that seven digits could be accommodated on the same size plates as used hitherto. The new height was $3\frac{1}{8}$" and other dimensions were reduced proportionately, i.e. stroke $\frac{9}{16}$", width $2\frac{1}{4}$", space between characters and top and bottom and side margins $\frac{7}{16}$", between top and bottom lines on two-line plates $\frac{3}{4}$", between letters and numerals $1\frac{5}{16}$". The old specifications remained valid alongside the new. There were now 12 sketches showing various formats (including three-line plates for the rear of motorcycles and year prefix formats, which were not to appear for another 21 years !)

The 1903 Regulations required merely that "The ground of the plates must be black, the letters and figures must be white". This was unchanged in the Provisional Regulations of 1921, but SR&O 1462 of 1924 included the following "If they (i.e. the letters and figures) are exhibited on a flat rectangular plate the plate may be constructed of cast or pressed aluminium having raised letters and figures". (Prior to this most plates had been hand-painted). The proviso in the 1903 Regulations permitting the registration mark to be painted directly on the vehicle was absent from the Provisional Regulations of 1921, but the substantive Regulations, SR&O 1924, No. 1462 allowed it to be shown ".....on a flat unbroken rectangular surface forming part of the vehicle."

In the early post-war years there was a vogue, particularly on public service vehicles, for rear plates which could be illuminated from behind, showing white by day and red when illuminated. This type of plate was belatedly authorised by SI 1618 of 1949 in these terms : "If the identification mark is so constructed and used that it is illuminated by transparency or translucency, the letters and figures must all, when so illuminated dring the hours of darkness......appear, in the case of the front identification mark, white, and in the case of the rear identification mark either white or red....."

Minor changes in specifications were provided by SI 1951 No. 1381. The regulations applying to motorcycles were applied also to pedestrian controlled vehicles exceeding 8 cwt unladen weight; works trucks were permitted to have plates either on both sides or at the rear only, instead of front and rear as hitherto. The corners of motorcycle rear plates were permitted to have rounded corners. SI 1953 No. 1753 authorised the use of silver or light grey as well as white letters and figures. This was a belated recognition of aluminium plates with unpainted characters which had, in fact, been in use for a considerable time before 1953.

When the "Home Delivery Export Scheme" became established the plates for vehicles registered under the scheme were provided with a yellow border, though there was never any statutory provision for this. On reflective plates, the yellow border was replaced by a red one but the coloured borders were discontinued as from 1 October 1989. (Other coloured borders had been used for decorative purposes but all such were banned by the MoT in 1990).

The Ministry of Transport was party to an experiment with reflective plates, (initially front plates in black on white only), in 1964 which, strictly speaking, were illegal. These experiments led to the authorisation of the optional fitting of reflective plates, black on white at the front, black on yellow at the rear, the reflective backing complying with British Standard AU 145 of 1967. The enabling Statutory Instrument was No. 1844 of 1967, coming into operation on 20 December 1967.

SI 1865 of 1972 made reflective plates compulsory for all vehicles first registered on or after 1 January 1973 with the exception of (a) a vehicle with an unladen weight of or exceeding 3 tons bearing compulsory "Long Vehicle" markings, (b) a vehicle used wholly or mainly as a stage carriage, (c) a bicycle, invalid carriage, pedestrian-controlled vehicle, works truck or agricultural machine. The BS number was now AU 145a. The requirement for bicycles and invalid vehicles to carry front plates was discontinued as from 1 August 1975, by virtue of SI 1975 No. 1809. When reflective plates were introduced in the Republic of Ireland, rear plates had black lettering on a red ground, but with the introduction of the new system from 1 January 1987 both front and rear plates became black on reflective white.

Although the regulations lay down precise requirements for the dimensions of plates, it seems odd that the actual character font of letters and numerals has never been specified, as in Germany for example, where the regulations include an accurately drawn alphabet, with which plate manufacturers must comply. A proposed new British Standard (AU 145b) was put forward for consultation in October 1988 and this did, in fact, include a standard character font. However, beyond the experimental use of this font on diplomatic plates and on plates supplied by one large dealer in Cardiff, no action was taken on the proposed Standard. Thus in Britain there have been many different styles of "typography". The authorities have, on the whole, taken a tolerant view of such varieties. However, in 1978 the Serck Company commenced the manufacture of a "modern" style of plate with characters modelled on "computer" numerals and such was the confusion between A and R, D and O, S and 5 that the authorities were forced to act and Serck was persuaded to modify their characters to obviate the confusion. Other fads which the authorities have ruled against was one for "3D-style" plates, incorporating shading to the characters and "rainbow" plates which showed the colours of the spectrum when viewed from certain angles.

Similarly there has been much variety in the materials used in plate manufacture. Prior to World War II almost all plates were one of three types, i.e. hand painted, cast aluminium or die-pressed aluminium. In the post-war years a wide variety of plate types came onto the market, which was dominated by firms like Bluemels and Hills. The die-pressed aluminium type remained popular, but other types emerged which could be more easily made up on the premises of car dealers, rather than being factory-made as hitherto. These had separate characters, initially of aluminium, but later increasingly of plastic, which were either riveted to the plate or fastened in pre-drilled holes by metal spring clips. The backing plates remained of metal during this period. Early reflective plates continued the same styles of manufacture but by the 1980s came the style which is almost universal today, i.e. a plate entirely of acrylic plastic, made up as a three-layer "sandwich", with the characters encased in plastic sheets exhibiting a flush surface. Again there are varieties, including some with "engraved" characters. Over the years a substantial proportion of manufacture red plates have featured a raised border, but this has never been a legal requirement.

Note for third edition: Following a consultation paper issued in August 1999 an optional EU-style plate was introduced and a standard font was made compulsory. The specification for the plate is set out in BS AU 145d. More details are included on page 298.

RECORDS KEPT BY LOCAL TAXATION OFFICES

The Regulations of 1903 specified that, *inter alia* :-

"The Council of every County and the Council of every County Borough shall establish and keep a Register (herein-after referred to as "the Register of Motor Cars") for the registration of motor cars......"

"The Council.....may, if they think fit, keep the Register of Motor Cars in two parts, one part relating to motor cars not being motor cycles, and the other part relating to motor cycles."

"The Council, on the registration of a motor car, shall forthwith furnish the owner of a motor car with a copy of the entries in the Register relating to the motor car."

Registers usually comprised heavy bound ledgers, the standard form having 4 to 6 entries per page and showing, in respect of each vehicle, the index mark and number, name and address of owner, description or type of car, type and colour of body, unladen weight, whether intended for (a) private use, (b) use for trade purposes or (c) as public conveyance, date of registration. Note that no chassis number was entered, so that it might have proved difficult to establish the exact identity of any vehicle in case of doubt. The records required were, therefore, fairly simple. These pre-1921 registers were almost invariably neatly written up in copperplate handwriting, although, since void numbers were reissued, entries were frequently crossed through and over-written, leading to some untidyness. Each register typically held entries for between 300 and 700 vehicles. Almost invariably pre-printed and handsomely bound ledgers were used, supplied by a firm of commercial stationers. The only document that the owner held was a copy of the registration particulars. Many Councils did keep a separate register for motorcycles, even where these were numbered in a common series with cars. Later, the Heavy Motor Car Order of 1904 required the keeping of a separate register for Heavy Motor Cars. This unsophisticated system was set to change with the passing of the Roads Act of 1920.

The 1903 Act required simply that "Every motor car shall be registered with the Council of a County or County Borough..." which meant in practice that an owner could choose any Council with which to register his vehicle. There was, however, an important change in the 1920 Act, which combined the registration and first licensing of a vehicle in one transaction. The Provisional Regulations of 9.3.21 read :

"2. A person who desires to obtain a licence for a mechanically propelled vehicle shall apply to the Council in whose area such vehicle is ordinarily kept by means of a declaration in such one of the prescribed forms as shall be applicable.

3. A vehicle shall be deemed to be ordinarily kept in the area of the Council in which is situated the garage in which the vehicle is ordinarily kept.

Provided that where a person satisfies the Council of the area in which he declares his principal place of business or permanent postal address to be situated that a vehicle is not ordinarily kept in any one area, application for a licence may be made to that Council and a licence issued by them." (It may be noted in passing that with the introduction of centralised licensing there was a reversion to the pre-1921 practice, in that a vehicle may be first registered at the VRO of the applicant's choice.)

These new conditions dictated the form of record keeping under the 1920 Act. The principal document was now the vehicle file, of which there was one for each vehicle registered, containing the original declaration, subsequent applications for renewal of licences, changes of ownership, changes in vehicle details (e.g. colour, type of body etc.) and any other relevant documents. There was no longer a statutory requirement to keep a register although most Councils kept a modified form of the register, more properly an allocation book, in which were recorded the names of the dealer and/or owner to which each registration number was originally allotted, together with the class of vehicle, with or without such other details as each Council thought fit to record, and, usually, the dates of (a) allocation and (b) first registration. In the case of a small minority of Councils, such details were recorded on specially designed cards, (not to be confused with RF 16s described below), instead of the more usual bound books or loose leaf ledgers. In very few cases were these allocation books compiled as meticulously as the old registers.

The vehicle file was always held by the Council with which the vehicle was currently registered. Thus, if the owner of a vehicle moved his place of residence to another Council's area, or if he disposed of the vehicle to an owner in another area, then the vehicle file was transferred **to** the Council in which the vehicle was now kept. However, the Council which originally registered the vehicle had to keep track of where it was currently registered and to that end a card index system was devised. The basic card was the RF16, which subsequently had several variants, on which were recorded the registration number, the taxation class and the make, together with the names of the Council from which or to which the vehicle was transferred and a date stamp to show the date of the latest transfer. When a Council first licensed a vehicle registered in another area an RF16 was sent to the registering authority requesting the vehicle file; the card was then retained by the registering authority to indicate the present location of the vehicle. This information was used, *inter alia,* for dealing with Police enquiries. When a vehicle had been notified as broken up, permanently exported or not licensed for three years or more the RF16/1 was replaced by a 'Last Owner' card, (RF *16/1B),* on which were recorded various details of the vehicle; the vehicle file would then be destroyed. The code numbers of all documents required by the 1920 Act were at first prefixed RF (Road Fund), being later amended to VE (Vehicle Excise). When, in the run-up to centralisation, a vehicle's records were transferred to the central computer at Swansea, the fact was recorded on a computer-generated Form VC2, which replaced the RF16/VE16.

As for the vehicle owner, (or, more properly, keeper), his basic document was the Registration Book, (RF 60), colloquially known as the 'Log Book'. This showed the registration number, vehicle particulars, the name and address of the keeper, date of first registration and a record of licences issued. The book had to be transferred to the new owner on change of ownership. There was space for seven changes of ownership and if these were all used a replacement registration book was issued. (Upon centralisation the VE 60 was replaced by *V5,* but this no longer gave details of previous owners.)

Upon completion of centralisation and the approaching closure of the LTOs, an edict went out from the DVLA that all the old Local Taxation Office records were to be destroyed. Fortunately for posterity, some persons holding these records could not bear to see them destroyed and in many cases they were able to persuade the local Record Offices to take on at least a representative selection of records and in some cases a virtually complete collection of registers/allocation books. In many other cases the more recent records were taken under the wing of the local Police, who found them of great use in checking details of stolen vehicles. In most cases these records also found their way to the Record Offices after they ceased to be of use to the Police. Later, the DVLA revoked their instruction, but this change of heart came too late to save the records of many larger authorities, like the Greater London Council, Birmingham, Manchester, Liverpool, etc. Details of surviving records may be found in the booklet by Philip Riden, "How to Trace the History of Your Car". The author has also compiled a list of the known surviving records, set out in somewhat greater detail.

TAX DISCS

The Roads Act of 1920 prescribed annual duties payable on motor vehicles and Regulations issued thereunder laid down the form of the licence disc, to be carried on the vehicle as evidence that the appropriate duty had been paid. The licence disc, (or tax disc as it became more popularly known), was a partially pre-printed circular document, 3" (76mm) in diameter, which was to be affixed to the windscreen or elsewhere on the nearside of the vehicle in a weatherproof holder. Details of the vehicle class and make, its registration number, horse power or seating capacity or unladen weight, (depending on the taxation class) and a date stamp showing the name of the issuing authority were added manually. The 3" diameter of the tax disc remains unchanged to this day, but over the years there have been various alterations to the format and colouring of the disc and of the licensing periods.

Initially a vehicle could be taxed for a calendar year, or for one of four quarters ending on 24 March, 30 June, 30 September or 31 December. In 1961 four monthly licensing was substituted for quarterly and licensing periods ceased to be tied to the calendar year, so that a vehicle could be licensed for any consecutive period of 12 months or 4 months. In 1981 there was a further change, since when the only options have been for annual or six-monthly licensing.

For the first two years, all tax discs were printed in black on a plain background, but thereafter annual discs were printed on white paper and had a bold coloured overprint in the form of either a vertical band, a diagonal band or an upright cross, (all with irregular edges to avoid the areas with handwritten particulars.) The colours changed , generally on a three-year cycle, to aid identification of a current disc. The format was changed to two horizontal bands of colour for the period 1957-1960. Throughout the whole of this period quarterly discs were printed on coloured paper, without the overprint, and again with the paper colour varying from period to period. Since 1961 discs for all periods have had a deep coloured band, in the upper half; between 1961 and 1986 inclusive a four-yearly cycle of blue, brown, green and red bands was used, but this system broke down in 1987 and since then turquoise and purple have been added to the cycle. A Welsh language version of the disc is issued in Wales and there are minor differences on Northern Ireland discs.

This brief review has described only the licences for most ordinary classes, such as private car, motorcycle, light goods and public service vehicle, but over the years there have been special licence discs for other categories, such as agricultural and heavy goods vehicles. All these have been the usual 3" diameter circular discs, but over the years the various classes of trade plates have used oblong, triangular, trapezoidal and diamond shaped discs.

APPENDIX 1

TABLE SHOWING HOW THE INITIAL ALLOCATION OF INDEX MARKS
WAS MADE IN ACCORDANCE WITH THE 1901 CENSUS FIGURES

TABLE SHOWING HOW THE INITIAL ALLOCATION OF INDEX MARKS WAS MADE IN ACCORDANCE WITH THE 1901 CENSUS FIGURES

(Note : The figures shown are those given in "Summary Tables - Area, Houses and Population" published in 1903, amended to allow for boundary changes between 1901 and 1903). The figures for the county councils exclude, of course, the populations of the county boroughs lying within their boundaries.

A	London CC	4,536,541		CF	West Suffolk CC	117,553
B	Lancaster CC	1,799,807		CH	Derby CBC	114,848
C	W. Riding of Yks. CC	1,389,176		CJ	Hereford CC	114,125
D	Kent CC	936,240		CK	Preston CBC	112,989
E	Stafford CC	879,142		CL	Norwich CBC	111,733
F	Essex CC	816,640		CM	Birkenhead CBC	110,915
G	Glasgow BC approx.	796,000		CN	Gateshead CBC	109,888
H	Middlesex CC	792,314		CO	Plymouth CBC	107,636
J	Durham CC	768,024		CP	Halifax CBC	104,944
K	Liverpool CBC	702,247		CR	Southampton CBC	104,824
L	Glamorgan CC	601,061		CT	Kesteven CC	103,962
M	Chester CC	593,885		CU	South Shields CBC	100,858
N	Manchester CBC	543,872		CW	Burnley CBC	97,043
O	Birmingham CBC	522,204		CX	Huddersfield CBC	95,047
P	Surrey CC	519,654		CY	Swansea CBC	94,537
R	Derby CC	484,846		DA	Wolverhampton CBC	94,187
T	Devon CC	436,938		DB	Stockport CBC	92,832
U	Leeds CBC	428,968		DC	Middlesbrough CBC	91,302
V	Lanark CC approx.	411,000		DE	Pembroke CC	87,894
W	Sheffield CBC	409,070		DF	Northampton CBC	87,021
X	Northumberland CC	387,791		DH	Walsall CBC	86,430
Y	Somerset CC	385,111		DJ	St. Helens CBC	84,410
AA	Southampton CC	364,445		DK	Rochdale CBC	83,114
AB	Worcester CC	358,377		DL	Isle of Wight CC	82,418
AC	Warwick CC	347,722		DM	Flint CC	81,485
AD	Gloucester CC	331,118		DN	York CBC	77,914
AE	Bristol CBC	329,366		DO	Holland CC	77,610
AF	Cornwall CC	322,334		DP	Reading CBC	72,217
AH	Norfolk CC	313,504		DR	Devonport CBC	70,437
AJ	N. Riding of Yks. CC	286,036		DU	Coventry CBC	69,978
AK	Bradford CBC	279,767		DW	Newport (Mon.) CBC	67,270
AL	Nottingham CC	274,716		DX	Ipswich CBC	66,630
AM	Wilts CC	271,394		DY	Hastings CBC	65,528
AN	West Ham CBC	267,358		EA	West Bromwich CBC	65,175
AO	Cumberland CC	266,933		EB	Isle of Ely CC	64,495
AP	East Sussex CC	261,696		EC	Westmorland CC	64,409
AR	Hertford CC	258,423		ED	Warrington CBC	64,242
AT	Kingston-upon-Hull CBC	240,259		EE	Grimsby CBC	63,138
AU	Nottingham CBC	239,743		EF	West Hartlepool CBC	62,267
AW	Salop CC	239,783		EH	Hanley CBC	61,559
AX	Monmouth CC	230,806		EJ	Cardigan CC	61,078
AY	Leicester CC	225,911		EK	Wigan CBC	60,674
BA	Salford CBC	220,957		EL	Bournemouth CBC	59,762
BB	Newcastle-u-Tyne CBC	215,328		EM	Bootle CBC	58,556
BC	Leicester CBC	211,579		EN	Bury CBC	58,029
BD	Northampton CC	207,485		EO	Barrow-in-Furness CBC	57,586
BE	Lindsey CC	206,528		EP	Montgomery CC	54,901
BF	Dorset CC	202,063		ET	Rotherham CBC	54,349
BH	Buckingham CC	197,046		EU	Brecknock CC	54,213
BJ	East Suffolk CC	189,170		EW	Huntingdon CC	54,125
BK	Portsmouth CBC	188,133		EX	Great Yarmouth CBC	51,316
BL	Berks CC	180,354		EY	Anglesey CC	50,606
BM	Bedford CC	171,707		FA	Burton-upon-Trent CBC	50,386
BN	Bolton CBC	168,215		FB	Bath CBC	49,839
BO	Cardiff CBC	164,333		FC	Oxford CBC	49,336
BP	West Sussex CC	151,553		FD	Dudley CBC	48,733
BR	Sunderland CBC	146,077		FE	Lincoln CBC	48,784
BT	E. Riding of Yks. CC	144,748		FF	Merioneth CC	48,852
BU	Oldham CBC	137,246		FH	Gloucester CBC	47,955
BW	Oxford CC	137,124		FJ	Exeter CBC	47,185
BX	Carmarthen CC	135,328		FK	Worcester CBC	46,624
BY	Croydon CBC	133,895		FL	Soke of Peterboro' CC	41,122
CA	Denbigh CC	131,582		FM	Chester CBC	38,309
CB	Blackburn CBC	129,216		FN	Canterbury CBC	24,899
CC	Caernarvon CC	125,649		FO	Radnor CC	23,281
CD	Brighton CBC	123,478		FP	Rutland CC	19,709
CE	Cambridge CC	120,264				

APPENDIX 2

ALLOCATION OF INDEX MARKS

The left-hand section shows the local authority or authorities to which the index mark was allotted prior to centralisation. In the period 1971-74 the following pairs of authorities set up Joint Motor Taxation Offices: Berks CC and Reading CBC, Devon CC and Exeter CBC, Glamorgan CC and Cardiff CBC, Lancaster CC and Preston CBC, Lindsey CC and Lincoln CBC, Oxford CC and Oxford CBC, East Suffolk CC and Ipswich CBC, Inverness CC and Ross and Crmarty CC. For further details see Appendix 7, which also shows changes in organisation and nomenclature of local authorities from 1.4.74. In the Republic of Ireland, joint offices were set up between Dublin CC and CBC (1952) and Cork CC and CBC (1974). The right-hand section shows the Local Vehicle Licensing Office or Vehicle Registration Office to which each index mark is or was allotted. Latterly the remaining London offices have become generally known as Stanmore (London NW), Sidcup (London SE) and Wimbledon (London SW) The dates shown are those of allocation, not necessarily the dates of issue.

Note for third edition: In March 2000 Middlesbrough Vehicle Registration Office moved to Stockton and changed its name to Stockton. From 1 January 2001 Vehicle Registration Offices became known as Local Offices. In January 2006 Stanmore Local Office moved to Borehamwood and changed its name to Borehamwood. In July 2007 the Reading Local Office relocated to Theale and similarly changed its name. Luton Local Office is scheduled to close in March 2008.

A	London CC	1903-1965			
	Greater London	1965-1974			
AA	Southampton CC *	1903-1974	Salisbury	1974-1980
			Bournemouth	1980-
AB	Worcester CC	1903-1974	Worcester	1974-
AC	Warwick CC	1903-1974	Coventry	1974-1996
			Northampton, Birmingham,	1996-
			Nottingham, Worcester or Oxford	
AD	Gloucester CC	1903-1974	Gloucester	1974-1997
			Worcester or Bristol	1997-
AE	Bristol CBC	1903-1974	Bristol	1974-
AF	Cornwall CC	1903-1974	Truro	1974-
AG	Ayr CC	1924-1974	Hull	1974-1996
			Beverley	1996-
AH	Norfolk CC	1903-1974	Norwich	1974-
AI	Meath CC	1903-1986		
AJ	Yorks. (NR) CC	1903-1974	Middlesbrough	1974-
AK	Bradford CBC	1903-1974	Sheffield	1974-
AL	Nottingham CC	1903-1974	Nottingham	1974-
AM	Wilts CC	1903-1974	Swindon	1974-1997
			Bristol	1997-
AN	West Ham CBC	1903-1965	Reading	1974-
	Greater London	1965-1974		
AO	Cumberland CC	1903-1974	Carlisle	1974-
AP	East Sussex CC	1903-1974	Brighton	1974-
AR	Hertford CC	1903-1974	Chelmsford	1974-
AS	Nairn CC	1903-1974	Inverness	1974-
AT	Kingston-u-Hull CBC	1903-1974	Hull	1974-1996
			Beverley	1996-
AU	Nottingham CBC	1903-1974	Nottingham	1974-
AV	Aberdeen CC	1924-1974	Peterborough	1974-
AW	Salop CC	1903-1974	Shrewsbury	1974-
AX	Monmouth CC	1903-1974	Cardiff	1974-
AY	Leicester CC	1903-1974	Leicester	1974-1996
			Birmingham, Northampton,	1996-
			Peterborough or Nottingham	
AZ	Belfast CBC	1927-1974	Belfast	1974-
B	Lancaster CC	1903-1974		
BA	Salford CBC	1903-1974	Manchester	1974-
BB	Newcastle CBC	1903-1974	Newcastle	1974-
BC	Leicester CBC	1903-1974	Leicester	1974-1996
			Birmingham, Northampton,	1996-
			Peterborough or Nottingham	
BD	Northampton CC	1903-1974	Northampton	1974-
BE	Lindsey CC	1903-1974	Grimsby	1974-1980
			Lincoln	1980-
BF	Dorset CC	1903-1920	Stoke-on-Trent	1974-1996
	Stafford CC #	1960-1974	Birmingham or Shrewsbury	1996-
BG	Birkenhead CBC	1928-1974	Liverpool	1974-1996
	Wirral MBC	1974-1974	Preston or Chester	1996-

*   The County Council of Southampton changed its name officially to The County Council of
Hampshire in 1959.

\# Allocated in three-letter combinations only.

BH	Buckingham CC	1903-1974	Luton	1974-
BI	Monaghan CC	1903-1986		
BJ	East Suffolk CC	1903-1974	Ipswich	1974-
BK	Portsmouth CBC	1903-1974	Portsmouth	1974-
BL	Berks CC	1903-1974	Reading	1974-
BM	Bedford CC	1903-1974	Luton	1974-
BN	Bolton CBC	1903-1974	Bolton	1974-1981
			Manchester	1981-
BO	Cardiff CBC	1903-1974	Cardiff	1974-
BP	West Sussex CC	1903-1974	Portsmouth	1974-
BR	Sunderland CC	1903-1974	Durham	1974-1981
			Newcastle	1981-
BS	Orkney CC	1903-1974	Kirkwall	1974-1980
			Inverness	1980-
BT	Yorks, (ER) CC	1903-1974	York	1974-1980
			Leeds	1980
BU	Oldham CBC	1903-1974	Manchester	1974-
BV	Blackburn CBC	1928-1974	Preston	1974-
BW	Oxford CC	1903-1974	Oxford	1974-
BX	Carmarthen CC	1903-1974	Haverfordwest	1974-1996
			Swansea	1996-
BY	Croydon CBC	1903-1965	London NW	1974-
	Greater London	1965-1974		
BZ	Down CC	1929-1974	Downpatrick	1974-
C	Yorks (WR) CC	1903-1974		
CA	Denbigh CC	1903-1974	Chester	1974-
CB	Blackburn CBC	1903-1974	Bolton	1974-1981
			Manchester	1981-
CC	Caernarvon CC	1903-1974	Bangor	1974-
CD	Brighton CBC	1903-1974	Brighton	1974-
CE	Cambridge CC	1903-1965	Cambridge	1974-1980
	Cambridgeshire &		Peterborough	1980-
	Isle of Ely CC	1965-1974		
CF	West Suffolk CC	1903-1974	Reading	1974-
CG	Southampton CC *	1930-1974	Salisbury	1974-1980
			Bournemouth	1980-
CH	Derby CBC	1903-1974	Nottingham	1974-
CI	Queens County	1903-1921		
	Laoighis CC **	1921-1986		
CJ	Hereford CC	1903-1974	Hereford	1974-1981
			Gloucester	1981-1997
			Worcester or Bristol	1997-
CK	Preston CBC	1903-1974	Preston	1974-
CL	Norwich CBC	1903-1974	Norwich	1974-
CM	Birkenhead CBC	1903-1974	Liverpool	1974-1996
	Wirral MBC	1974-1974	Preston or Chester	1996-
CN	Gateshead CBC	1903-1974	Newcastle	1974-
CO	Plymouth CBC	1903-1974	Plymouth	1974-1980
			Exeter (never used)	1980-
CP	Halifax CBC	1903-1974	Huddersfield	1974-1994
			Leeds	1994-
CR	Southampton CBC	1903-1974	Portsmouth	1974-

* The County Council of Southampton changed its name officially to the County Council of Hampshire in 1959.
** Spelling rendered as Laois CC from ca. 1975.

Code	Name	Years	Location	Years
CS	Ayr CC	1932-1974	Ayr	1974-1981
			Glasgow	1981-
CT	Kesteven CC	1903-1974	Boston	1974-1981
			Lincoln	1981-
CU	South Shields CBC	1903-1974	Newcastle	1974-
CV	Cornwall CC	1928-1974	Truro	1974-
CW	Burnley CBC	1903-1974	Preston	1974-
CX	Huddersfield CBC	1903-1974	Huddersfield	1974-1994
			Leeds	1994-
CY	Swansea CBC *	1903-1974	Swansea	1974-
CZ	Belfast CBC	1932-1974	Belfast	1974-
D	Kent CC	1903-1974		
DA	Wolverhampton CC	1903-1974	Birmingham	1974-
DB	Stockport CBC	1903-1974	Manchester	1974-
DC	Middlesbrough CBC	1903-1968	Middlesbrough	1974-
	Teesside CBC	1968-1974		
DD	Gloucester CC	1921-1974	Gloucester	1974-1997
			Worcester or Bristol	1997-
DE	Pembroke CC	1903-1974	Haverfordwest	1974-1996
			Swansea	1996-
DF	Northampton CBC	1903-1920	Gloucester	1974-1997
	Gloucester CC	1924-1974	Worcester or Bristol	1997-
DG	Gloucester CC	1928-1974	Gloucester	1974-1997
			Worcester or Bristol	1997-
DH	Walsall CBC	1903-1974	Dudley	1974-1993
			Birmingham	1993-
DI	Roscommon CC	1903-1986		
DJ	St. Helens CBC	1903-1974	Warrington	1974-1981
			Liverpool	1981-1996
			Preston or Chester	1996-
DK	Rochdale CBC	1903-1974	Bolton	1974-1981
			Manchester	1981
DL	Isle of Wight CC	1903-1974	Newport I.o.W.	1974-1981
			Portsmouth	1981-
DM	Flint CC	1903-1974	Chester	1974-
DN	York CBC	1903-1974	York	1974-1980
			Leeds	1980-
DO	Holland CC	1903-1974	Boston	1974-1981
			Lincoln	1981
DP	Reading CBC	1903-1974	Reading	1974-
DR	Devonport CBC	1903-1914	Plymouth	1974-1980
	Plymouth CBC	1914-1974	Exeter (not used)	1981-
DS	Peebles CC	1903-1974	Glasgow	1974-
DT	Doncaster CBC	1927-1974	Sheffield	1974-
DU	Coventry CBC	1903-1974	Coventry	1974-1996
			Northampton, Birmingham,	1996-
			Nottingham, Worcester or Oxford	
DV	Devon CC	1928-1974	Exeter	1974-
DW	Newport CBC	1903-1974	Cardiff	1974-
DX	Ipswich CBC	1903-1974	Ipswich	1974-
DY	Hastings CBC	1903-1974	Hastings	1974-1980
			Brighton	1980-
DZ	Antrim CC	1932-1974	Ballymena	1974-

* SCY with year letter suffix J onward transferred to Cornwall CC for Isles of Scilly 1971.

E	Stafford CC	1903-1974			
EA	West Bromwich CBC	1903-1974	Dudley	1974-1993	
			Birmingham	1993-	
EB	Isle of Ely CC	1903-1965	Cambridge	1974-1980	
	Cambridgeshire &		Peterborough	1980-	
	Isle of Ely CC	1965-1974			
EC	Westmorland CC	1903-1974	Kendal	1974-1981	
			Preston	1981-	
ED	Warrington CBC	1903-1974	Warrington	1974-1981	
			Liverpool	1981-1996	
			Preston or Chester	1996-	
EE	Grimsby CBC	1903-1974	Grimsby	1974-1980	
			Lincoln	1980-	
EF	West Hartlepool CBC	1903-1967	Middlesbrough	1974-	
	Hartlepool CBC	1967-1974			
EG	Soke of Peterboro' CC	1930-1965	Peterborough	1974-	
	Huntingdon	1965-1974			
	& Peterborough CC				
EH	Hanley CBC	1903-1910	Stoke-on-Trent	1974-1996	
	Stoke-on-Trent CBC	1910-1974	Birmingham or Shrewsbury	1996-	
EI	Sligo CC	1903-1986			
EJ	Cardigan CC	1903-1974	Aberystwyth	1974-1981	
			Bangor	1981-1983	
			Haverfordwest	1983-1996	
			Swansea	1996-	
EK	Wigan CBC	1903-1974	Warrington	1974-1981	
			Liverpool	1981-1996	
			Preston or Chester	1996-	
EL	Bournemouth CBC	1903-1974	Bournemouth	1974-	
EM	Bootle CBC	1903-1974	Liverpool	1974-1996	
			Preston or Chester	1996-	
EN	Bury CBC	1903-1974	Bolton	1974-1981	
			Manchester	1981-	
EO	Barrow-in-Furness CBC	1903-1974	Barrow-in-Furness	1974-1981	
			Preston	1981-	
EP	Montgomery CC	1903-1974	Swansea	1974-	
ER	Cambridge CC	1921-1965	Cambridge	1974-1980	
	Cambridgeshire &		Peterborough	1980-	
	Isle of Ely CC	1965-1974			
ES	Perth CC	1903-1974	Dundee	1974-	
ET	Rotherham CBC	1903-1974	Sheffield	1974-	
EU	Brecon CC	1903-1974	Bristol	1974-	
EV	Essex CC	1928-1974	Chelmsford	1974-	
EW	Huntingdon CC	1903-1965	Peterborough	1974-	
	Huntingdon				
	& Peterborough CC	1965-1974			
EX	Great Yarmouth CBC	1903-1974	Norwich	1974-	
EY	Anglesey CC	1903-1974	Bangor	1974-	
EZ	Belfast CBC	1935-1974	Belfast	1974-	
F	Essex CC	1903-1974			
FA	Burton-on-Trent CBC	1903-1974	Stoke-on-Trent	1974-1996	
			Birmingham or Shrewsbury	1996-	
FB	Bath CBC	1903-1974	Bristol	1974-	

FC	Oxford CBC	1903-1974	Oxford	1974-
FD	Dudley CBC	1903-1974	Dudley	1974-1993
			Birmingham	1993-
FE	Lincoln CBC	1903-1974	Lincoln	1974-
FF	Merioneth CC	1903-1974	Aberystwyth	1974-1981
			Bangor	1981-
FG	Fife CC	1923-1974	Brighton	1974-
FH	Gloucester CBC	1903-1974	Gloucester	1974-1997
			Worcester or Bristol	1997-
FI	Tipperary N.R. CC	1903-1986		
FJ	Exeter CBC	1903-1974	Exeter	1974-
FK	Worcester CBC	1903-1974	Dudley	1974-1993
			Birmingham	1993-
FL	Soke of Peterboro' CC	1903-1965	Peterborough	1974-
	Huntingdon &			
	Peterboro' CC	1965-1974		
FM	Chester CBC	1903-1974	Chester	1974-
FN	Canterbury CBC	1903-1974	Canterbury	1974-1981
			Maidstone	1981-
			(Not used since 1981)	
FO	Radnor CC	1903-1974	Hereford	1974-1981
			Gloucester	1981-1997
			Worcester or Bristol	1997-
FP	Rutland CC	1903-1974	Leicester	1974-1996
			Birmingham, Northampton,	1996-
			Peterborough or Nottingham	
FR	Blackpool CBC	1904-1974	Preston	1974-
FS	Edinburgh BC	1928-1974	Edinburgh	1974-
FT	Tynemouth CBC	1904-1974	Newcastle	1974-
FU	Lindsey CC	1921-1974	Grimsby	1974-1980
			Lincoln	1980-
FV	Blackpool CBC	1928-1974	Preston	1974-
FW	Lindsey CC	1926-1974	Lincoln	1974-
FX	Dorset CC	1904-1974	Bournemouth	1974-
FY	Southport CBC	1904-1974	Liverpool	1974-1996
			Preston or Chester	1996-
FZ	Belfast CBC	1937-1974	Belfast	1974-
G	Glasgow BC	1903-1974		
GA	Glasgow BC	1917-1974	Glasgow	1974-
GB	Glasgow BC	1921-1974	Glasgow	1974-
GC	London CC	1928-1965	London SW	1974-
	Greater London	1965-1974		
GD	Glasgow BC	1924-1974	Glasgow	1974-
GE	Glasgow BC	1926-1974	Glasgow	1974-
GF	London CC	1928-1965	London SW	1974-
	Greater London	1965-1974		
GG	Glasgow BC	1928-1974	Glasgow	1974-
GH	London CC	1928-1965	London SW	1974-
	Greater London	1965-1974		
GI *	Tipperary S.R.	1981-1986		
GJ	London CC	1928-1965	London SW	1974-
	Greater London	1965-1974		
GK	London CC	1928-1965	London SW	1974-
	Greater London	1965-1974		

* Allotted in 3-letter combinations only.

GL	Bath CBC	1930-1974	Truro	1974-
GM	Motherwell & Wishaw BC	1920-1974	Reading	1974-
GN	London CC	1928-1965	London SW	1974-
	Greater London	1965-1974		
GO	London CC	1928-1965	London SW	1974-
	Greater London	1965-1974		
GP	London CC	1928-1965	London SW	1974-
	Greater London	1965-1974		
GR	Sunderland CBC	1930-1974	Durham	1974-1981
			Newcastle	1981-
GS	Perth CC	1924-1974	Luton	1974-
GT	London CC	1928-1965	London SW	1974-
	Greater London	1965-1974		
GU	London CC	1928-1965	London SE	1974-
	Greater London	1965-1974		
GV	West Suffolk CC	1928-1974	Ipswich	1974-
GW	London CC	1928-1965	London SE	1974-
	Greater London	1965-1974		
GX	London CC	1928-1965	London SE	1974-
	Greater London	1965-1974		
GY	London CC	1928-1965	London SE	1974-
	Greater London	1965-1974		
GZ	Belfast CBC	1942-1974	Belfast	1974-
H	Middlesex CC	1903-1965		
	Greater London	1965-1974		
HA	Smethwick CBC	1907-1966	Dudley	1974-1993
	Warley CBC	1966-1974	Birmingham	1993-
HB	Merthyr Tydfil CBC	1908-1974	Cardiff	1974-
HC	Eastbourne CBC	1910-1974	Hastings	1974-1980
			Brighton	1980-
HD	Dewsbury CBC	1912-1974	Huddersfield	1974-1994
			Leeds	1994-
HE	Barnsley CBC	1912-1974	Sheffield	1974-
HF	Wallasey CBC	1912-1974	Liverpool	1974-1996
	Wirral MBC	1974-1974	Preston or Chester	1996
HG	Burnley CBC	1928-1974	Preston	1974-
HH	Carlisle CBC	1914-1974	Carlisle	1974-
HI	Tipperary S.R. CC	1903-1986		
HJ	Southend-on-Sea CBC	1914-1974	Chelmsford	1974-
HK	Essex CC	1914-1974	Chelmsford	1974-
HL	Wakefield CBC	1915-1974	Sheffield	1974-
HM	East Ham CBC	1915-1965	London Central	1974-1997
	Greater London	1965-1974	London SW	1997-
HN	Darlington CBC	1915-1974	Middlesbrough	1974-
HO	Southampton CC *	1916-1974	Salisbury	1974-1980
			Bournemouth	1980-
HP	Coventry CBC	1919-1974	Coventry	1974-1996
			Northampton, Birmingham,	1996-
			Nottingham, Worcester or Oxford	
HR	Wilts CC	1919-1974	Swindon	1974-1997
			Bristol	1997-
HS	Renfrew CC	1903-1974	Glasgow	1974-

*   The County Council of Southampton changed its name officially to the County Council of Hampshire in 1959

HT	Bristol CBC	1920-1974	Bristol	1974-
HU	Bristol CBC	1921-1974	Bristol	1974-
HV	East Ham CBC	1928-1965	London Central	1974-1997
	Greater London	1965-1974	London SW	1997-
HW	Bristol CBC	1926-1974	Bristol	1974-
HX	Middlesex CC	1928-1965	London Central	1974-1997
	Greater London	1965-1974	London SW	1997-
HY	Bristol CBC	1928-1974	Bristol	1974-
HZ	Tyrone CC	1943-1974	Omagh	1974-
IA	Antrim CC	1903-1974	Ballymena	1974-
IB	Armagh CC	1903-1974	Armagh	1974-
IC	Carlow CC	1903-1986		
ID	Cavan CC	1903-1986		
IE	Clare CC	1903-1986		
IF	Cork CC	1903-1986		
IH	Donegal CC	1903-1986		
IJ	Down CC	1903-1974	Downpatrick	1974-
IK	Dublin CC	1903-1952		
IL	Fermanagh CC	1903-1974	Enniskillen	1974-
IM	Galway CC	1903-1986		
IN	Kerry CC	1903-1986		
IO	Kildare CC	1903-1986		
IP	Kilkenny CC	1903-1986		
IR	Kings County CC	1903-1921		
	Offaly CC	1921-1986		
IS *	Mayo CC	1981-1986		
IT	Leitrim CC	1903-1986		
IU	Limerick CC	1903-1986		
IV *	Limerick CC	1981-1986		
IW	Londonderry CC	1903-1974	Coleraine	1974-
IX	Longford CC	1903-1986		
IY	Louth CC	1903-1986		
IZ	Mayo CC	1903-1986		
J	Durham CC	1903-1974		
JA	Stockport CBC	1928-1974	Manchester	1974-
JB	Berks CC	1928-1974	Reading	1974-
JC	Caernarvon CC	1928-1974	Bangor	1974-
JD	West Ham CBC	1928-1965	London Central	1974-1997
	Greater London	1965-1974	London SW	1997-
JE	Isle of Ely CC	1928-1965	Cambridge	1974-1980
	Cambridgeshire & Isle of Ely CC	1965-1974	Peterborough	1980-
JF	Leicester CBC	1928-1974	Leicester	1974-1996
			Birmingham, Northampton, Peterborough or Nottingham	1996-
JG	Canterbury CBC	1928-1974	Canterbury	1974-1981
			Maidstone (not used since 1981)	1981-
JH	Hertford CC	1928-1974	Reading	1974-
JI	Tyrone CC	1903-1974	Omagh	1974-
JJ	London CC	1932-1965	Canterbury	1974-1981
	Greater London	1965-1974	Maidstone (not used since 1983)	1981-

* Allotted in three-letter combinations only.

Code	Authority	Years	Place	Years
JK	Eastbourne CBC	1928-1974	Hastings	1974-1980
			Brighton	1980-
JL	Holland CC	1928-1974	Boston	1974-1981
			Lincoln	1981-
JM	Westmorland CC	1928-1974	Reading	1974-
JN	Southend-on-Sea CC	1928-1974	Chelmsford	1974-
JO	Oxford CBC	1928-1974	Oxford	1974-
JP	Wigan CBC	1928-1974	Warrington	1974-1981
			Liverpool	1981-1996
			Preston or Chester	1996-
JR	Northumberland CC	1928-1974	Newcastle	1974-
JS	Ross & Cromarty CC	1903-1974	Stornoway	1974-1980
			Inverness	1980-
JT	Dorset CC	1928-1974	Bournemouth	1974-
JU	Leicester CC	1928-1974	Leicester	1974-1996
			Birmingham, Northampton, Peterborough or Nottingham	1996-
JV	Grimsby CBC	1928-1974	Grimsby	1974-1980
			Lincoln	1980-
JW	Wolverhampton CBC	1928-1974	Birmingham	1974-
JX	Halifax CBC	1928-1974	Huddersfield	1974-1994
			Leeds	1994-
JY	Plymouth CBC	1928-1974	Plymouth	1974-1980
			Exeter (not used)	1980-
JZ	Down CC	1946-1974	Downpatrick	1974-
K	Liverpool CBC	1903-1974		
KA	Liverpool CBC	1922-1974	Liverpool	1974-1996
			Preston or Chester	1996
KB	Liverpool CBC	1914-1974	Liverpool	1974-1996
			Preston or Chester	1996
KC	Liverpool CBC	1920-1974	Liverpool	1974-1996
			Preston or Chester	1996-
KD	Liverpool CBC	1926-1974	Liverpool	1974-1996
			Preston or Chester	1996-
KE	Kent CC	1920-1974	Maidstone	1974-
KF	Liverpool CBC	1928-1974	Liverpool	1974-1996
			Preston or Chester	1996-
KG	Cardiff CBC	1928-1974	Cardiff	1974-
KH	Kingston-u-Hull CBC	1923-1974	Hull	1974-1996
			Beverley	1996
KI	Waterford CC	1903-1986		
KJ	Kent CC	1930-1974	Maidstone	1974-
KK	Kent CC	1921-1974	Maidstone	1974-
KL	Kent CC	1923-1974	Maidstone	1974-
KM	Kent CC	1924-1974	Maidstone	1974-
KN	Kent CC	1917-1974	Maidstone	1974-
KO	Kent CC	1924-1974	Maidstone	1974-
KP	Kent CC	1926-1974	Maidstone	1974-
KR	Kent CC	1928-1974	Maidstone	1974-
KS	Roxburgh CC	1903-1974	St. Boswells	1974-1975
			Selkirk	1975-1980
			Edinburgh	1980-
KT	Kent CC	1913-1974	Canterbury	1974-1981
			Maidstone (not used)	1981-

KU	Bradford CBC	1921-1974	Sheffield	1974-
KV	Coventry CBC	1928-1974	Coventry	1974-1996
			Northampton, Birmingham,	1996-
			Nottingham, Worcester or Oxford	
KW	Bradford CBC	1924-1974	Sheffield	1974-
KX	Buckingham CC	1926-1974	Luton	1974-
KY	Bradford CBC	1928-1974	Sheffield	1974-
KZ	Antrim CC	1946-1974	Ballymena	1974-
L	Glamorgan CC	1903-1974		
LA	London CC	1910-1965	London N.W.	1974-
	Greater London	1965-1974		
LB	London CC	1907-1965	London N.W.	1974-
	Greater London	1965-1974		
LC	London CC	1905-1965	London N.W.	1974-
	Greater London	1965-1974		
LD	London CC	1909-1965	London N.W.	1974-
	Greater London	1965-1974		
LE	London CC	1911-1965	London N.W.	1974-
	Greater London	1965-1974		
LF	London CC	1912-1965	London N.W.	1974-
	Greater London	1965-1974		
LG	Chester CC	1928-1974	Chester	1974-
LH	London CC	1912-1965	London N.W.	1974-
	Greater London	1965-1974		
LI	Westmeath CC	1903-1986		
LJ	Bournemouth CBC	1928-1974	Bournemouth	1974-
LK	London CC	1913-1965	London N.W.	1974-
	Greater London	1965-1974		
LL	London CC	1914-1965	London N.W.	1974-
	Greater London	1965-1974		
LM	London CC	1914-1965	London N.W.	1974-
	Greater London	1965-1974		
LN	London CC	1906-1965	London N.W.	1974-
	Greater London	1965-1974		
LO	London CC	1914-1965	London N.W.	1974-
	Greater London	1965-1974		
LP	London CC	1915-1965	London N.W.	1974-
	Greater London	1965-1974		
LR	London CC	1916-1965	London N.W.	1974-
	Greater London	1965-1974		
LS	Selkirk CC	1903-1974	Stirling	1974-1981
			Edinburgh	1981-
LT	London CC	1917-1965	London N.W.	1974-
	Greater London	1965-1974		
LU	London CC	1918-1965	London N.W.	1974-
	Greater London	1965-1974		
LV	Liverpool CBC	1930-1974	Liverpool	1974-1996
			Preston or Chester	1996-
LW	London CC	1919-1965	London N.W.	1974-
	Greater London	1965-1974		
LX	London CC	1919-1965	London N.W.	1974-
	Greater London	1965-1974		
LY	London CC	1919-1965	London N.W.	1974-
	Greater London	1965-1974		
LZ	Armagh CC	1946-1974	Armagh	1974-

M	Chester CC	1903-1974		
MA	Chester CC	1918-1974	Chester	1974-
MB	Chester CC	1921-1974	Chester	1974-
MC	Middlesex CC	1916-1965	London NE	1974-1996
	Greater London	1965-1974	Chelmsford	1996-
MD	Middlesex CC	1919-1965	London NE	1974-1996
	Greater London	1965-1974	Chelmsford	1996-
ME	Middlesex CC	1920-1965	London NE	1974-1996
	Greater London	1965-1974	Chelmsford	1996-
MF	Middlesex CC	1922-1965	London NE	1974-1996
	Greater London	1965-1974	Chelmsford	1996-
MG	Middlesex CC	1928-1965	London NE	1974-1996
	Greater London	1965-1974	Chelmsford	1996-
MH	Middlesex CC	1923-1965	London NE	1974-1996
	Greater London	1965-1974	Chelmsford	1996-
MI	Wexford CC	1903-1986		
MJ	Bedford CC	1928-1974	Luton	1974-
MK	Middlesex CC	1924-1965	London NE	1974-1996
	Greater London	1965-1974	Chelmsford	1996-
ML	Middlesex CC	1924-1965	London NE	1974-1996
	Greater London	1965-1974	Chelmsford	1996-
MM	Middlesex CC	1924-1965	London NE	1974-1996
	Greater London	1965-1974	Chelmsford	1996-
(MN reserved for Isle of Man)				
MO	Berks CC	1921-1974	Reading	1974-
MP	London CC	1926-1965	London NE	1974-1996
	Greater London	1965-1974	Chelmsford	1996-
MR	Wilts CC	1921-1974	Swindon	1974-1997
			Bristol	1997-
MS	Stirling CC	1903-1974	Stirling	1974-1981
			Edinburgh	1981-
MT	Middlesex CC	1926-1965	London NE	1974-1996
	Greater London	1965-1974	Chelmsford	1996-
MU	Middlesex CC	1928-1965	London NE	1974-1996
	Greater London	1965-1974	Chelmsford	1996-
MV	Middlesex CC	1928-1965	London SE	1974-
	Greater London	1965-1974		
MW	Wilts CC	1926-1974	Swindon	1974-1997
			Bristol	1997-
MX	Middlesex CC	1912-1965	London S.E.	1974-
	Greater London	1965-1974		
MY	Middlesex CC	1926-1965	London S.E.	1974-
	Greater London	1965-1974		
MZ	Belfast CBC	1947-1974	Belfast	1974-
N	Manchester CBC	1903-1974		
NA	Manchester CBC	1913-1974	Manchester	1974-
NB	Manchester CBC	1919-1974	Manchester	1974-
NC	Manchester CBC	1920-1974	Manchester	1974-
ND	Manchester CBC	1921-1974	Manchester	1974-
NE	Manchester CBC	1923-1974	Manchester	1974-
NF	Manchester CBC	1924-1974	Manchester	1974-
NG	Norfolk CC	1928-1974	Norwich	1974-
NH	Northampton CBC	1905-1974	Northampton	1974-

NI #	Wicklow CC	1903-1986			
NJ	East Sussex CC	1930-1974	Brighton	1974-	
NK	Hertford CC	1920-1974	Luton	1974-	
NL	Northumberland CC	1920-1974	Newcastle	1974-	
NM	Bedford CC	1920-1974	Luton	1974-	
NN	Nottingham CC	1920-1974	Nottingham	1974-	
NO	Essex CC	1920-1974	Chelmsford	1974-	
NP	Worcester CC	1921-1974	Worcester	1974-	
NR	Leicester CC	1921-1974	Leicester	1974-1996	
			Birmingham, Northampton,	1996-	
			Peterborough or Nottingham		
NS	Sutherland CC	1903-1974	Glasgow	1974-	
NT	Salop CC	1921-1974	Shrewsbury	1974-	
NU	Derby CC	1921-1974	Nottingham	1974-	
NV	Northampton CC	1928-1974	Northampton	1974-	
NW	Leeds CBC	1921-1974	Leeds	1974-	
NX	Warwick CC	1921-1974	Dudley	1974-1993	
			Birmingham	1993-	
NY	Glamorgan CC	1921-1974	Cardiff	1974-	
NZ	Londonderry CC	1948-1974	Coleraine	1974-	
O	Birmingham CBC	1903-1974			
OA	Birmingham CBC	1912-1974	Birmingham	1974-	
OB	Birmingham CBC	1915-1974	Birmingham	1974-	
OC	Birmingham CBC	1922-1974	Birmingham	1974-	
OD	Devon CC	1930-1974	Exeter	1974-	
OE	Birmingham CBC	1919-1974	Birmingham	1974-	
OF	Birmingham CBC	1928-1974	Birmingham	1974-	
OG	Birmingham CBC	1928-1974	Birmingham	1974-	
OH	Birmingham CBC	1920-1974	Birmingham	1974-	
OI	Belfast CBC	1903-1974	Belfast	1974-	
OJ	Birmingham CBC	1930-1974	Birmingham	1974-	
OK	Birmingham CBC	1921-1974	Birmingham	1974-	
OL	Birmingham CBC	1923-1974	Birmingham	1974-	
OM	Birmingham CBC	1923-1974	Birmingham	1974-	
ON	Birmingham CBC	1924-1974	Birmingham	1974-	
OO	Essex CC	1961-1974	Chelmsford	1974-	
OP	Birmingham CBC	1924-1974	Birmingham	1974-	
OR	Southampton CC *	1921-1974	Portsmouth	1974-	
OS	Wigtown CC	1903-1974	Stranraer	1974-1981	
			Glasgow	1981-	
OT	Southampton CC *	1924-1974	Portsmouth	1974-	
OU	Southampton CC *	1928-1974	Bristol	1974-	
OV	Birmingham CBC	1928-1974	Birmingham	1974-	
OW	Southampton CBC	1928-1974	Portsmouth	1974-	
OX	Birmingham CBC	1926-1974	Birmingham	1974-	
OY	Croydon CBC	1928-1965	London NW	1974-	
	Greater London	1965-1974			
OZ	Belfast CBC	1950-1974	Belfast	1974-	
P	Surrey CC	1903-1974			
PA	Surrey CC	1913-1974	Guildford	1974-1997	
			Portsmouth, Reading or London SW	1997-	

*   The County Council of Southampton changed its name officially to The County Council of Hampshire in 1959.

\#   QNI issued in Northern Ireland for vehicles of indeterminate age, from 1990.

PB	Surrey CC	1919-1974	Guildford	1974-1997
			Portsmouth, Reading or London SW	1997-
PC	Surrey CC	1921-1974	Guildford	1974-1997
			Portsmouth, Reading or London SW	1997-
PD	Surrey CC	1922-1974	Guildford	1974-1997
			Portsmouth, Reading or London SW	1997-
PE	Surrey CC	1923-1974	Guildford	1974-1997
			Portsmouth, Reading or London SW	1997-
PF	Surrey CC	1924-1974	Guildford	1974-1997
			Portsmouth, Reading or London SW	1997-
PG	Surrey CC	1928-1974	Guildford	1974-1997
			Portsmouth, Reading or London SW	1997-
PH	Surrey CC	1924-1974	Guildford	1974-1997
			Portsmouth, Reading or London SW	1997-
PI	Cork CBC	1903-1986		
PJ	Surrey CC	1930-1974	Guildford	1974-1997
			Portsmouth, Reading or London SW	1997-
PK	Surrey CC	1926-1974	Guildford	1974-1997
			Portsmouth, Reading or London SW	1997-
PL	Surrey CC	1928-1974	Guildford	1974-1997
			Portsmouth, Reading or London SW	1997-
PM	East Sussex CC	1922-1974	Guildford	1974-1997
			Portsmouth, Reading or London SW	1997-
PN	East Sussex CC	1926-1974	Brighton	1974-
PO*	West Sussex CC	1926-1974	Portsmouth	1974-
PP	Buckingham CC	1922-1974	Luton	1974-
PR	Dorset CC	1922-1974	Bournemouth	1974-
PS	Zetland CC	1903-1974	Lerwick	1974-1980
			Aberdeen	1980-
PT	Durham CC	1922-1974	Durham	1974-1981
			Newcastle	1981-
PU	Essex CC	1922-1974	Chelmsford	1974-
PV	Ipswich CBC	1928-1974	Ipswich	1974-
PW	Norfolk CC	1922-1974	Norwich	1974-
PX	West Sussex CC	1922-1974	Portsmouth	1974-
PY	Yorks. (NR) CC	1922-1974	Middlesbrough	1974-
PZ	Belfast CBC	1952-1974	Belfast	1974-

'Q' Series for temporary imports. All except QI & QZ nominally allocated to London County Council, (up to 1965), Greater London Council (1965-1974), London Central VRO (1974-1997) and London SW VRO from 1997, but actually issued by the authorities shown on page 119. QI and QZ allotted by Northern Ireland S.I. in 1963 but never, apparently, brought into use.

R	Derby CC	1903-1974		
RA	Derby CC	1924-1974	Nottingham	1974-
RB	Derby CC	1928-1974	Nottingham	1974-
RC	Derby CBC	1928-1974	Nottingham	1974-
RD	Reading CBC	1926-1974	Reading	1974-
RE	Stafford CC	1921-1974	Stoke-on-Trent	1974-1996
			Birmingham or Shrewsbury	1996-
RF	Stafford CC	1924-1974	Stoke-on-Trent	1974-1996
			Birmingham or Shrewsbury	1996-
RG	Aberdeen BC	1926-1974	Newcastle	1974-

* GPO allocated to London County Council 1936-1965; Greater London Council 1965-1974.

RH	Kingston-u-Hull CBC	1928-1974	Hull	1974-1996
			Beverley	1996-
RI	Dublin CBC	1903-1986		
RJ	Salford CBC	1930-1974	Manchester	1974-
RK	Croydon CBC	1922-1965	London NW	1974-
	Greater London	1965-1974		
RL	Cornwall CC	1923-1974	Truro	1974-
RM	Cumberland CC	1923-1974	Carlisle	1974-
RN	Preston CBC	1928-1974	Preston	1974-
RO	Hertford CC	1923-1974	Luton	1975-
RP	Northampton CC	1923-1974	Northampton	1974-
RR	Nottingham CC	1923-1974	Nottingham	1974-
RS	Aberdeen BC	1903-1974	Aberdeen	1974-
RT	East Suffolk CC	1923-1974	Ipswich	1974-
RU	Bournemouth CBC	1923-1974	Bournemouth	1974-
RV	Portsmouth CBC	1928-1974	Portsmouth	1974-
RW	Coventry CBC	1923-1974	Coventry	1974-1996
			Northampton, Birmingham, Nottingham, Worcester or Oxford	1996-
RX	Berks CC	1926-1974	Reading	1974-
RY	Leicester CBC	1923-1974	Leicester	1974-1996
			Birmingham, Northampton, Peterborough or Nottingham	1996-
RZ	Antrim CC	1954-1974	Ballymena	1974-
S	Edinburgh BC	1903-1974		
SA	Aberdeen CC	1903-1974	Aberdeen	1974-
SB	Argyll CC	1903-1974	Oban	1974-1980
			Glasgow	1980-
SC	Edinburgh BC	1926-1974	Edinburgh	1974-
SD	Ayr CC	1903-1974	Ayr	1974-1981
			Glasgow	1981-
SE	Banff CC	1903-1974	Keith	1974-1981
			Aberdeen	1981-
SF	Edinburgh BC	1923-1974	Edinburgh	1974-
SG	Edinburgh BC	1919-1974	Edinburgh	1974-
SH	Berwick CC	1903-1974	St. Boswells	1974-1975
			Selkirk	1975-1980
			Edinburgh	1980-
SI	Dublin CC & CBC	1981-1986		
SJ	Bute CC	1903-1974	Ayr	1974-1981
			Glasgow	1981-
SK	Caithness CC	1903-1974	Wick	1974-1981
			Inverness	1981-
SL	Clackmannan CC	1903-1974	Dundee	1974-
SM	Dumfries CC	1903-1974	Dumfries	1974-1981
			Glasgow	1981-1981
			Carlisle	1981-
SN*	Dunbarton CC	1903-1974	Dundee	1974
SO	Elgin CC	1903-1919	Aberdeen	1974-
	Moray CC	1919-1974		
SP	Fife CC	1903-1974	Dundee	1974-
SR	Forfar CC	1903-1928	Dundee	1974-
	Angus CC	1928-1974		

* USN allocated to London County Council but never used for civilian registrations.

SS	Haddington CC	1903-1921	Aberdeen	1974-
	East Lothian CC	1921-1974		
ST	Inverness CC	1903-1974	Inverness	1974-
SU	Kincardine CC	1903-1974	Glasgow	1974-
SV	Kinross CC	1903-1974	(Not allocated)	
SW	Kirkcudbright CC	1903-1974	Dumfries	1974-1981
			Glasgow	1981-1981
			Carlisle	1981-
SX	Linlithgowshire CC	1903-1921	Edinburgh	1974-
	West Lothian CC	1921-1974		
SY	Midlothian CC	1903-1974	(Not allocated)	
SZ	Down CC	1954-1974	Downpatrick	1974-
T	Devon CC	1903-1974		
TA	Devon CC	1920-1974	Exeter	1974-
TB	Lancaster CC	1919-1974	Warrington	1974-1981
			Liverpool	1981-1996
			Preston or Chester	1996-
TC	Lancaster CC	1921-1974	Bristol	1974-
TD	Lancaster CC	1923-1974	Bolton	1974-1981
			Manchester	1981-
TE	Lancaster CC	1924-1974	Bolton	1974-1981
			Manchester	1981-
TF	Lancaster CC	1928-1974	Reading	1974-
TG	Glamorgan CC	1928-1974	Cardiff	1974-
TH	Carmarthen CC	1926-1974	Swansea	1974-
TI	Limerick CBC	1903-1986		
TJ	Lancaster CC	1930-1974	Liverpool	1974-1996
			Preston or Chester	1996-
TK	Dorset CC	1926-1974	Plymouth	1974-1980
			Exeter (not used)	1980-
TL	Kesteven CC	1926-1974	Lincoln	1974-
TM	Bedford CC	1924-1974	Luton	1974-
TN	Newcastle CBC	1923-1974	Newcastle	1974-
TO	Nottingham CBC	1923-1974	Nottingham	1974-
TP	Portsmouth CBC	1923-1974	Portsmouth	1974-
TR	Southampton CBC	1923-1974	Portsmouth	1974-
TS	Dundee BC	1903-1974	Dundee	1974-
TT	Devon CC	1923-1974	Exeter	1974-
TU	Chester CC	1924-1974	Chester	1974-
TV	Nottingham CBC	1928-1974	Nottingham	1974-
TW	Essex CC	1924-1974	Chelmsford	1974-
TX	Glamorgan CC	1924-1974	Cardiff	1974-
TY	Northumberland CC	1924-1974	Newcastle	1974-
TZ	Belfast CBC	1954-1974	Belfast	1974-
U	Leeds CBC	1903-1974		
UA	Leeds CBC	1923-1974	Leeds	1974-
UB	Leeds CBC	1928-1974	Leeds	1974-
UC	London CC	1926-1965	London Central	1974-1997
	Greater London	1965-1974	London SW	1997-
UD	Oxford CC	1924-1974	Oxford	1974-
UE	Warwick CC	1924-1974	Dudley	1974-1993
			Birmingham	1993-

Code	Authority	Years	Location	Years
UF	Brighton CBC	1924-1974	Brighton	1974-
UG	Leeds CBC	1930-1974	Leeds	1974-
UH	Cardiff CBC	1924-1974	Cardiff	1974-
UI	Londonderry CBC	1903-1974	Londonderry	1974-
UJ	Salop CC	1930-1974	Shrewsbury	1974-
UK	Wolverhampton CBC	1924-1974	Birmingham	1974-
UL	London CC	1926-1965	London Central	1974-1997
	Greater London	1965-1974	London SW	1997-
UM	Leeds CBC	1922-1974	Leeds	1974-
UN	Denbigh CC	1924-1974	Barnstaple	1974-1981
			Exeter (not used)	1981-
UO	Devon CC	1924-1974	Barnstaple	1974-1981
			Exeter (not used)	1981-
UP	Durham CC	1924-1974	Durham	1974-1981
			Newcastle	1981-
UR	Hertford CC	1924-1974	Luton	1974-
US	Govan BC	1903-1912	Glasgow	1974-
	Glasgow BC	1912-1974		
UT	Leicester CC	1924-1974	Leicester	1974-1996
			Birmingham, Northampton, Peterborough or Nottingham	1996-
UU	London CC	1926-1965	London Central	1974-1997
	Greater London	1965-1974	London SW	1997-
UV	London CC	1926-1965	London Central	1974-1997
	Greater London	1965-1974	London SW	1997-
UW	London CC	1926-1965	London Central	1974-1997
	Greater London	1965-1974	London SW	1997-
UX	Salop CC	1924-1974	Shrewsbury	1974-
UY	Worcester CC	1924-1974	Worcester	1974-
UZ	Belfast CBC	1955-1974	Belfast	1974-
V	Lanark CC	1903-1974		
VA	Lanark CC	1921-1974	Cambridge	1974-1980
			Peterborough	1980-
VB	Croydon CBC	1926-1965	Canterbury	1974-1981
	Greater London	1965-1974	Maidstone (not used)	1981-
VC	Coventry CBC	1926-1974	Coventry	1974-1996
			Northampton, Birmingham, Nottingham, Worcester or Oxford	1996-
VD	Lanark CC	1928-1974	Luton	1974-1977
			(No longer allocated)	
VE	Cambridge CC	1926-1965	Cambridge	1974-1980
	Cambridgeshire & Isle of Ely CC	1965-1974	Peterborough	1981-
VF	Norfolk CC	1926-1974	Norwich	1974-
VG	Norwich CBC	1926-1974	Norwich	1974-
VH	Huddersfield CBC	1926-1974	Huddersfield	1974-1994
			Leeds	1994-
VJ	Hereford CC	1926-1974	Hereford	1974-1981
			Gloucester	1981-1997
			Worcester or Bristol	1997-

VK	Newcastle CBC	1926-1974	Newcastle	1974-
VL	Lincoln CBC	1926-1974	Lincoln	1974-
VM	Manchester CBC	1926-1974	Manchester	1974-
VN	Yorks (NR) CC	1926-1974	Middlesbrough	1974-
VO	Nottingham CC	1926-1974	Nottingham	1974-
VP	Birmingham CBC	1926-1974	Birmingham	1974-
VR	Manchester CBC	1928-1974	Manchester	1974-
VS	Greenock BC	1903-1974	Luton	1974-
VT	Stoke-on-Trent CBC	1926-1974	Stoke-on-Trent	1974-1996
			Birmingham or Shrewsbury	1996-
VU	Manchester CBC	1928-1974	Manchester	1974-
VV	Nortampton CBC	1928-1974	Northampton	1974-
VW	Essex CC	1926-1974	Chelmsford	1974-
VX	Essex CC	1926-1974	Chelmsford	1974-
VY	York CBC	1926-1974	York	1974-1980
			Leeds	1980
VZ	Tyrone CC	1956-1974	Omagh	1974-
W	Sheffield CBC	1903-1974		
WA	Sheffield CBC	1919-1974	Sheffield	1974-
WB	Sheffield CBC	1921-1974	Sheffield	1974-
WC	Essex CC *	1961-1974	Chelmsford	1974-
WD	Warwick CC	1928-1974	Dudley	1974-1993
			Birmingham	1993-
WE	Sheffield CBC	1926-1974	Sheffield	1974-
WF	Yorks (ER) CC	1924-1974	Sheffield	1974-
WG	Stirling CC	1928-1974	Sheffield	1974-
WH	Bolton CBC	1924-1974	Bolton	1974-1981
			Manchester	1981-
WI	Waterford CBC	1903-1986		
WJ	Sheffield CBC	1928-1974	Sheffield	1974-
WK	Coventry CBC	1924-1974	Coventry	1974-1996
			Northampton, Birmingham,	1996-
			Nottingham, Worcester or Oxford	
WL	Oxford CBC	1924-1974	Oxford	1974-
WM	Southport CBC	1924-1974	Liverpool	1974-1996
			Preston or Chester	1996-
WN	Swansea CBC	1924-1974	Swansea	1974-
WO	Monmouth CC	1924-1974	Cardiff	1974-
WP	Worcester CC	1928-1974	Worcester	1974-
WR	Yorks (WR) CC	1915-1974	Leeds	1974-
WS	Leith BC	1903-1920	Bristol	1974-
	Edinburgh BC	1920-1974		
WT	Yorks (WR) CC	1922-1974	Leeds	1974-
WU	Yorks (WR) CC	1923-1974	Leeds	1974-
WV	Wilts CC	1928-1974	Brighton	1974-
WW	Yorks (WR) CC	1924-1974	Leeds	1974
WX	Yorks (WR) CC	1926-1974	Leeds	1974
WY	Yorks (WR) CC	1921-1974	Leeds	1974
WZ	Belfast CBC	1956-1974	Belfast	1974-

* Allocated in three-letter combinations only.

X	Northumberland CC	1903-1974		
XA	London CC	1920-1965 *	(Not allocated)	
	Greater London	1965-1974 *		
	Kirkcaldy BC	1963-1974 #		
XB	London CC	1920-1965 *	(Not allocated)	
	Greater London	1965-1974 *		
	Coatbridge BC	1964-1974 #		
XC	London CC	1920-1965 *	(Not allocated)	
	Greater London	1965-1974 *		
	Solihull CBC	1964-1974 #		
XD	London CC	1920-1965 *	(Not allocated)	
	Greater London	1965-1974 *		
	Luton CBC	1964-1974 #		
XE	London CC	1920-1965 *	(Not allocated)	
	Greater London	1965-1974 *		
	Luton CBC	1964-1974 #		
XF	London CC	1920-1965 *	(Not allocated)	
	Greater London	1965-1974 *		
	Torbay CBC	1968-1974 #		
XG	Middlesbrough CBC	1928-1968	(Not allocated)	
	Teesside CBC	1968-1974		
XH	London CC	1920-1965 *	(Not allocated)	
	Greater London	1965-1974 *		
XI	Belfast CBC	1921-1974	Belfast	1974-
XJ	Manchester CBC	1930-1974	(Not allocated)	
XK	London CC	1921-1965 *	(Not allocated)	
	Greater London	1965-1974 *		
XL	London CC	1921-1965 *	(Not allocated)	
	Greater London	1965-1974 *		
XM	London CC	1921-1965 *	(Not allocated)	
	Greater London	1965-1974 *		
XN	London CC	1921-1965 *	(Not allocated)	
	Greater London	1965-1974 *		
XO	London CC	1921-1965 *	(Not allocated)	
	Greater London	1965-1974 *		
XP	London CC	1921-1965 *	Various VROs @	1993-
	Greater London	1965-1974 *		
XR	London CC	1923-1965 *	(Not allocated)	
	Greater London	1965-1974 *		
XS	Paisley BC	1903-1974	London Central	1974- $
XT	London CC	1923-1965 *	(Not allocated)	
	Greater London	1965-1974 *		
XU	London CC	1923-1965 *	(Not allocated)	
	Greater London	1965-1974 *		
XV	London CC	1926-1965 *	(Not allocated)	
	Greater London	1965-1974 *		
XW	London CC	1924-1965 *	(Not allocated)	
	Greater London	1965-1974 *		

*   Not used with year-letter.
#   Not used without year-letter.
@   Issued for tax-free exports to European Community.
$ RXS (only) issued for private vehicles of diplomats, apparently discontinued 1987

XX	London CC	1924-1965 *	(Not allocated)		
	Greater London	1965-1974 *			
XY	London CC	1924-1965 *	(Not allocated)		
	Greater London	1965-1974 *			
XZ	Armagh CC	1957-1974	Armagh	1974-	
Y	Somerset CC	1903-1974			
YA	Somerset CC	1921-1974	Taunton	1974-1996	
			Exeter or Bristol	1996-	
YB	Somerset CC	1923-1974	Taunton	1974-1996	
			Exeter or Bristol	1996-	
YC	Somerset CC	1924-1974	Taunton	1974-1996	
			Exeter or Bristol	1996-	
YD	Somerset CC	1928-1974	Taunton	1974-1996	
			Exeter or Bristol	1996-	
YE	London CC	1926-1965	London Central	1974-1997	
	Greater London	1965-1974	London SW	1997-	
YF	London CC	1926-1965	London Central	1974-1997	
	Greater London	1965-1974	London SW	1997-	
YG	Yorks (WR) CC	1928-1974	Leeds	1974-	
YH	London CC	1926-1965	London Central	1974-1997	
	Greater London	1965-1974	London SW	1997-	
YI	Dublin CBC	1921-1986			
YJ	Dundee BC	1930-1974	Brighton	1974-	
YK	London CC	1924-1965	London Central	1974-1997	
	Greater London	1965-1974	London SW	1997-	
YL	London CC	1924-1965	London Central	1974-1997	
	Greater London	1965-1974	London SW	1997-	
YM	London CC	1924-1965	London Central	1974-1997	
	Greater London	1965-1974	London SW	1997-	
YN	London CC	1924-1965	London Central	1974-1997	
	Greater London	1965-1974	London SW	1997-	
YO	London CC	1924-1965	London Central	1974-1997	
	Greater London	1965-1974	London SW	1997-	
YP	London CC	1924-1965	London Central	1974-1997	
	Greater London	1965-1974	London SW	1997-	
YR	London CC	1924-1965	London Central	1974-1997	
	Greater London	1965-1974	London SW	1997-	
YS	Partick BC	1903-1912	Glasgow	1974	
	Glasgow BC	1912-1974			
YT	London CC	1926-1965	London Central	1974-1997	
	Greater London	1965-1974	London SW	1997-	
YU	London CC	1926-1965	London Central	1974-1997	
	Greater London	1965-1974	London SW	1997-	
YV	London CC	1926-1965	London Central	1974-1997	
	Greater London	1965-1974	London SW	1997-	
YW	London CC	1926-1965	London Central	1974-1997	
	Greater London	1965-1974	London SW	1997-	
YX	London CC	1926-1965	London Central	1974-1997	
	Greater London	1965-1974	London SW	1997-	
YY	London CC	1926-1965	London Central	1974-1997	
	Greater London	1965-1974	London SW	1997-	
YZ	Londonderry CC	1957-1974	Coleraine	1974-	

*   Not used with a year-letter.

Z	Dublin CC	1926-1986
ZA	Dublin CBC	1932-1986
ZB	Cork CC	1935-1986
ZC	Dublin CBC	1937-1986
ZD	Dublin CBC	1939-1986
ZE	Dublin CC	1939-1986
ZF	Cork CBC	1946-1986
ZG	Dublin CC & CBC	1981-1986
ZH	Dublin CBC	1947-1986
ZI	Dublin CBC	1926-1986
ZJ	Dublin CBC	1948-1986
ZK	Cork CC	1949-1986
ZL	Dublin CBC	1950-1986
ZM	Galway CC	1950-1986
ZN	Meath CC	1951-1986
ZO	Dublin CC & CBC	1951-1986
ZP	Donegal CC	1951-1986
ZR	Wexford CC	1951-1986
ZS	Dublin CC & CBC	1981-1986
ZT	Cork CC & CBC	1953-1986
ZU	Dublin CC & CBC	1953-1986
ZV*	Dublin CC & CBC	1981-1986
ZW	Kildare CC	1953-1986
ZX	Kerry CC	1953-1986
ZY	Louth CC	1954-1986
ZZ	Dublin CBC #	1925-

\#   Issued by Dublin CC & CBC, The Royal Irish Automobile Club. the Automobile Association or the council of any county adjoining Northern Ireland for temporary imports. The issue of this series continued after 1986, now followed by five numerals.

*   Issued by Dublin CC & CBC in three-letter combinations only. From 1992 ZV (alone) used by all authorities in the Republic for vehicles over 30 years old.

APPENDIX 3

REGISTRATION MARKS

WITHOUT YEAR LETTER

LISTED BY AUTHORITY AND DATE

All marks issued by Local Taxation Offices prior to the introduction of the year-letter system, together with all non-suffix/prefix marks issued subsequently by LTOs, VROs and the DVLA.

The Appendix includes all regular issues by each Local Taxation Office prior to the introduction of the year-letter system in 1963-5, together with non-suffix/prefix series commenced subsequently for re-registrations and "Age-Related" marks allocated through the DVLA. It also includes special marks allocated in LTO sequences by London County Council, the Greater London Council and London Central VRO for issue to the vehicles of the heads of diplomatic missions. It does not, however, include any mark issued under the Sale of Marks scheme, nor any "irregular" mark issued by the DVLA to resolve disputes or otherwise recognised by the DVLA.

The figures shown for first numbers issued each year and the dates of issue of three-letter series are, in many cases, approximations. This is because there was often a time lag between the allocation of a registration number and the date the vehicle was first licensed. The latter date is the official date of first registration. Thus it was possible for a vehicle to have an earlier date of registration than one with a lower registration number. Low numbers were frequently allocated a little ahead of the main series, but the commencement dates shown are those upon which the series was taken into general use. Completion dates are shown only in those cases where they do not coincide with the month of commencement of the next mark in the series, except that differences of only one month are ignored.

Details of issues in the reverse format, i.e. with numerals preceding letters, are shown in italic type.

In the compilation of this appendix I am particularly indebted to David Hales, Jonathan Del Mar, Douglas Wilson, Alan Cain, David Carter, the late Jess Tawn and others who have kindly provided me with the results of their examination of the records of various Local Taxation Offices. There are, however, certain records remaining in County Record Offices and similar locations which neither I nor my colleagues have yet been able to peruse. Such locations are indicated in the text and I shall be pleased to hear from any reader who may be able to provide any of the missing details.

In the pages which follow marks are listed by issuing authority in alphabetical order in each of the following groups, (this being the order used by the Local Government Board and the Ministry of Transport in all legislative and official documentation) :

1 County Councils, England & Wales.
2 County Borough Councils, England & Wales.
3 County Councils, Scotland.
4 Burgh Councils, Scotland.

The registration authorities newly created in 1963-1968, (i.e. Luton, Solihull, Torbay, Coatbridge and Kirkcaldy), are excluded, since they did not issue any marks without a suffix letter.

COUNTY COUNCIL OF ANGLESEY

A common sequence for all vehicles.

EY   12/03-9/51

First issues each year :

1904	17	1912	257	1920	953		1928	3234	*	1936	5431	1944	7590
1905	54	1913	342	1921	1307	*	1929	3490		1937	5854	1945	7686
1906	73	1914	440	1922	1494	*	1930	3757		1938	6282	1946	7815
1907	100	1915	557	1923	1621	*	1931	4018		1939	6625	1947	8092
1908	118	1916	670	1924	1966	*	1932	4271		1940	6960	1948	8553
1909	137	1917	746	1925	2319	*	1933	4490		1941	7103	1949	8977
1910	160	1918	771	1926	2673	*	1934	4790		1942	7248	1950	9430
1911	195	1919	810	1927	2996	*	1935	5036		1943	7410	1951	9780

* approximate only.

AEY	6/51	DEY	3/56	GEY	4/59	KEY	3/61	NEY	2/63
BEY	11/53	EEY	8/57	HEY	1/60	LEY	10/61	OEY	8/63
CEY	1/55 #	FEY	6/58	JEY	7/60	MEY	6/62	PEY	3/64

Last normal issue PEY 112; re-registrations PEY 113-436. Because of objections to issue of non-suffix marks for re-registrations, series continued as PEY 437B up.

\#   CEY 1 special early issue ca. 4/52 for diplomatic mark.
    SEY 1 special diplomatic mark, ca. 11/77, replaced by *1 SEY* 3/96..

Commenced suffix marks 1.4.64

Superstition as to the ill luck attaching to the number 13 has made itself apparent. A Shropshire journal reports that in that county this number fell in the ordinary course to a lady motorist. She promptly had it sent back and said she would prefer a change. The request was acceded to. This, however, was not the end of the difficulty. A driver sent to register his master's car accepted the discarded No. 13, but came back next day with the message that his master's daughter would be better satisfied with another number ! "Thirteen" after this was not tried again with cars and it is now cancelled so far as the county of Salop is concerned. *The Motor Car Journal, 9.1.04*

COUNTY COUNCIL OF BEDFORD

A common sequence for all vehicles; first registration 18.12.03

BM	12/03		NM	12/20		TM	1/27		MJ	3/32

First issues each year :

1904	BM	61	1910	BM	1168	1916	BM	4681	1922	NM	1462	1928	TM	1955	1934	MJ	3323
1905	BM	336	1911	BM	1430	1917	BM	5628	1923	NM	2626	1929	TM	3996	1935	MJ	5921
1906	BM	493	1912	BM	1794	1918	BM	6472	1924	NM	4038	1930	TM	6131	1936	MJ	9561
1907	BM	681	1913	BM	2401	1919	BM	6851	1925	NM	5789	1931	TM	8085			
1908	BM	817	1914	BM	3003	1920	BM	8294	1926	NM	7905	1932	TM	9756			
1909	BM	964	1915	BM	3639	1921	NM	22	1927	NM	9933	1933	MJ	1431			

Three-letter marks, both in forward and reverse sequences, were issued in the same order as the two-letter marks, except that UNM preceded UBM, reverse *DMJ* followed *DBM* and reverse *Fxx* were in the order : *FBM, FNM, FMJ, FTM.*

Between 5/57 and 5/64 it was the usual practice to issue two series simultaneously; hence completion dates are shown for this period.

ABM	3/36	EBM	2/46	JBM	6/50	NBM	4/54	SBM	9/56	WBM	11/58- 2/59
ANM	5/36	ENM	6/46	JNM	10/50	NNM	6/54	SNM	11/56	WNM	11/58- 2/59
ATM	8/36	ETM	9/46	JTM	1/51	NTM	8/54	STM	2/57	WTM	2/59- 4/59
AMJ	12/36	EMJ	11/46	JMJ	4/51	NMJ	10/54	SMJ	4/57	WMJ	2/59- 4/59
BBM	3/37	FBM	2/47	KBM	7/51	OBM	12/54	TBM	5/57- 5/57	XBM	4/59- 6/59
BNM	7/37	FNM	5/47	KNM	11/51	ONM	2/55	TNM	5/57- 7/57	XNM	4/59- 7/59
BTM	9/37	FTM	7/47	KTM	1/52	OTM	3/55	TTM	8/57- 9/57	XTM	6/59- 8/59
BMJ	1/38	FMJ	10/47	KMJ	5/52	OMJ	5/55	TMJ	9/57-11/57	XMJ	7/59- 9/59
CBM	4/38	GBM	3/48	LBM	7/52	PBM	6/55	UBM	12/57- 3/58	YBM	8/59-10/59
CNM	8/38	GNM	7/48	LNM	10/52	PNM	8/55	UNM	11/57- 3/58	YNM	9/59-11/59
CTM	1/39	GTM	10/48	LTM	2/53	PTM	10/55	UTM	3/58- 5/58	YTM	10/59-11/59
CMJ	4/39	GMJ	2/49	LMJ	5/53	PMJ	11/55	UMJ	3/58- 6/58	YMJ	11/59- 1/60
DBM	7/39	HBM	5/49	MBM	7/53	RBM	1/56	VBM	5/58- 8/58		
DNM	5/40	HNM	8/49	MNM	10/53	RNM	4/56	VNM	6/58- 9/58		
DTM	1/42	HTM	12/49	MTM	12/53	RTM	5/56	VTM	8/58-11/58		
DMJ	4/44	HMJ	3/50	MMJ	2/54	RMJ	6/56	VMJ	9/58-11/58		

ABM	12/59- 2/60	DBM	1/61- 3/61	GBM	3/62- 5/62	KBM	4/63- 6/63	NBM	3/64- 4/64
ANM	12/59- 3/60	DNM	3/61- 5/61	GNM	4/62- 6/62	KNM	5/63- 7/63	NNM	3/64- 5/64
ATM	3/60- 4/60	DTM	3/61- 5/61	GTM	5/62- 7/62	KTM	6/63- 7/63	NTM	5/64- 5/64
AMJ	3/60- 4/60	DMJ	1/61- 3/61	GMJ	6/62- 9/62	KMJ	7/63- 9/63	NMJ	5/64- 7/64
BBM	4/60- 5/60	EBM	5/61- 7/61	HBM	7/62- 9/62	LBM	7/63- 9/63	PBM	7/64
BNM	4/60- 6/60	ENM	6/61- 8/61	HNM	9/62-12/62	LNM	9/63-10/63	PNM	8/64
BTM	5/60- 7/60	ETM	7/61- 9/61	HTM	9/62-11/62	LTM	9/63-11/63	PTM	9/64
BMJ	6/60- 8/60	EMJ	8/61-11/61	HMJ	11/62- 2/63	LMJ	10/63-12/63	PMJ	10/64
CBM	7/60-10/60	FBM	9/61-12/61	JBM	12/62- 2/63	MBM	11/63- 1/64	RBM	12/64
CNM	8/50-10/60	FNM	11/61- 2/62	JNM	2/63- 4/63	MNM	12/63- 1/64	RNM	**
CTM	10/60- 1/61	FTM	2/62- 4/62	JTM	3/63- 4/63	MTM	1/64- 3/64		
CMJ	10/60- 1/61	FMJ	12/61- 3/62	JMJ	4/63- 5/63	MMJ	1/64- 3/64		

** Only 1 RNM issued by Bedford C.C.; further issues for re-registrations by Luton LVLO.

Suffix Marks commenced 1.1.65

COUNTY COUNCIL OF BERKS

A common sequence for cars and cycles; heavy motor cars in separate series BL 01 up commencing 31.08.05; (BL 01 to 10 renumbered from main series). Series reached BL 0366 by end of 1920. In 1921 heavy motor cars still licensed in Berkshire were renumbered in main series, (from BL 88xx), but those transferred to some other authorities retained their BL 0xxx for many years after 1921.

| BL 1/04 | MO 5/22 | RX 5/27 | JB 3/32 |

First issues each year :

1905	BL 546	1911	BL 1974	1917	BL 5234	1923	MO 800*	1929	RX 3522	1935	JB 5497
1906	BL 791	1912	BL 2323	1918	BL 5545	1924	MO 2471*	1930	RX 5813	1936	JB 8138
1907	BL 1000	1913	BL 2802	1919	BL 5820	1925	MO 4421*	1931	RX 7992		
1908	BL 1183	1914	BL 3364	1920	BL 6758	1926	MO 6744*	1932	RX 9683		
1909	BL 1405	1915	BL 4041	1921	BL 8160	1927	MO 9101	1933	JB 1433		
1910	BL 1662	1916	BL 4698	1922	BL 9430*	1928	RX 1384	1934	JB 3338		

* approximate.

ABL	8/36	EBL	7/47	JBL	6/53	NBL	8/56	SBL	2/59	WBL	8/60
AJB	12/36	EJB	12/47	JJB	9/53	NJB	11/56	SJB	3/59	WJB	9/60
AMO	4/37	EMO	5/48	JMO	12/53	NMO	1/57	SMO	4/59	WMO	10/60
ARX	8/37	ERX	9/48	JRX	3/54	NRX	3/57	SRX	5/59	WRX	12/60
BBL	1/38	FBL	2/49	KBL	6/54	OBL	5/57	TBL	7/59	XBL	1/61
BJB	5/38	FJB	7/49	KJB	9/54	OJB	7/57	TJB	8/59	XJB	2/61
BMO	10/38	FMO	11/49	KMO	11/54	OMO	9/57	TMO	9/59	XMO	3/61
BRX	3/39	FRX	3/50	KRX	1/55	ORX	11/57	TRX	10/59	XRX	4/61
CBL	7/39	GBL	8/50	LBL	3/55	PBL	1/58	UBL	12/59	YBL	5/61
CJB	4/40	GJB	1/51	LJB	6/55	PJB	3/58	UJB	1/60	YJB	6/61
CMO	11/41	GMO	5/51	LMO	8/55	PMO	5/58	UMO	2/60	YMO	7/61
CRX	12/43	GRX	10/51	LRX	10/55	PRX	6/58	URX	3/60	YRX	8/61
DBL	2/46	HBL	3/52	MBL	12/55	RBL	8/58	VBL	4/60		
DJB	7/46	HJB	7/52	MJB	2/56	RJB	10/58	VJB	5/60		
DMO	11/46	HMO	11/52	MMO	4/56	RMO	11/58	VMO	6/60		
DRX	3/47	HRX	2/53	MRX	6/56	RRX	1/59	VRX	7/60		

ABL	10/61	CBL	8/62	DBL	1/63	EBL	5/63	FBL	8/63	GBL	1/64
AJB	12/61	CJB	9/62	DJB	2/63	EJB	5/63	FJB	9/63	GJB	8/68 *
AMO	2/62	CMO	11/62	DMO	3/63	EMO	6/63	FMO	10/63	GMO	ca.12/75 *
ARX	3/62	CRX	12/62	DRX	4/63	ERX	7/63	FRX	11/63		
BBL	4/62										
BJB	5/62										
BMO	6/62										
BRX	7/62										

* re-registrations only; (1 and 2 GMO early, 8/66, 2/67 respectively).

Special mark for Diplomatic Corps : *1 MO* ca. 6/82.

Suffix Marks commenced 3.2.64.

COUNTY COUNCIL OF BRECKNOCK

EU 12/03

First issues each year : (Surviving records show no dates before 1927)

1928	3540	1932	4729	1936	5873	1940	7159	1944	7744	1948	8907
1929	3847	1933	4940	1937	6205	1941	7282	1945	7875	1949	9490
1930	4192	1934	5189	1938	6601	1942	7440	1946	7968	(9999	issued
1931	4484	1935	5520	1939	6878	1943	7600	1947	8350	27.10.49)	

AEU	10/49	DEU	10/54	GEU	2/58	KEU	7/60	MEU	4/62	OEU	11/63
BEU	9/51	EEU	9/55	HEU	1/59	LEU	5/61	NEU	2/63	PEU	7/64
CEU	6/53	FEU	11/56	JEU	11/59						

WEU 1 special diplomatic issue 6/61.

Commenced suffix marks 1.1.65

6 (a). Licensing and registration to be combined in one act. Every vehicle in use, whether previously registered or not, to be registered or re-registered as the case may be, (on a new form of declaration), as on 1st January 1921.
6 (d). Every vehicle, at all times when on the road, to display in a conspicuous position its licence, which will be a distinctive coloured card indicating thereby its date of expiry.
7. It is desired to bring every mechanically-propelled road vehicle under contribution and to obtain accurate registers with regard to them showing, so far as possible, where they are located. With this object in view every such vehicle must be registered afresh at the beginning of the year 1921 and the applicant, in the declaration which he will be required to make, must furnish full registration particulars of the vehicle.
8. In cases where the vehicle has not previously been registered, or where it is registered, but not with the Local Authority in whose area it is kept, a new identification mark and number will probably require to be allotted.
9. In cases where the vehicle is already registered with the Local Authority in whose area it is kept, fresh registration particulars will be required, but a new identification mark and number will probably not require to be allotted.

Circular RF 100, 4.10.20

COUNTY COUNCIL OF BUCKINGHAM

A common sequence for cars and cycles; separate series BH 01 to BH 0522 for heavy motor cars 1905-1921.

BH	11/03	PP	3/23	KX	3/28

First issues each year : (No records survive in respect of the years not listed).

1904	BH	118	1907	BH	706	1915	BH 3003	1925	PP 3052*	1928	PP 9528	1931	KX 6233
1905	BH	429	1913	BH 1888			1920	BH 5033	1926	PP 5266*	1929	KX 1658	1932	KX 7906
1906	BH	572	1914	BH 2362			1921	BH 6685	1927	PP 7345*	1930	KX 3950	1933	KX 9619

* approximate.

Random dates in Heavy Motor Car series :

1905	BH 01-05	1914	BH 041-045	1916	BH 070	1919	BH 0142-0305
1906	BH 013-015	1915	BH 054-069+077	1917	BH 078-092	1920	BH 0306-0519
(BH 01 issued 24.3.05)						1921	BH 0520-0522

ABH	3/33	EBH	7/37	JBH	7/46	NBH	2/50-1/51 *	SBH	7/53	WBH	6/55
AKX	10/33	EKX	11/37	JKX	10/46	NKX	2/50-7/50	SKX	9/53	WKX	7/55
APP	3/34	EPP	3/38	JPP	1/47	NPP	7/50-1/51	SPP	12/53	WPP	9/55
BBH	7/34	FBH	7/38	KBH	4/47	OBH	1/51	TBH	2/54	XBH	11/55
BKX	1/35	FKX	12/38	KKX	7/47	OKX	5/51	TKX	4/54	XKX	12/55
BPP	5/35	FPP	4/39	KPP	10/47	OPP	7/51	TPP	6/54	XPP	2/56
CBH	9/35	GBH	7/39	LBH	3/48	PBH	12/51	UBH	8/54	YBH	3/56
CKX	1/36	GKX	5/40	LKX	6/48	PKX	4/52	UKX	10/54	YKX	5/56
CPP	5/36	GPP	12/41	LPP	10/48	PPP	7/52	UPP	12/54	YPP	7/56
DBH	9/36	HBH	5/43	MBH	2/49	RBH	10/52	VBH	2/55		
DKX	12/36	HKX	3/45	MKX	6/49	RKX	1/53	VKX	3/55		
DPP	3/37	HPP	4/46	MPP	10/49	RPP	4/53	VPP	4/55		

* NBH was reserved for goods, tractors and hackneys and issued simultaneously with NKX and NPP. No other series was similarly segregated.

ABH	9/56	EBH	4/58	JBH	6/59	NBH	5/60	TBH	4/61	XBH	4/62
AKX	11/56	EKX	5/58	JKX	7/59	NKX	6/60	TKX	5/61	XKX	5/62
APP	1/57	EPP	7/58	JPP	8/59	NPP	6/60	TPP	5/61	XPP	5/62
BBH	3/57	FBH	8/58	KBH	9/59	PBH	7/60	UBH	6/61	YBH	6/62
BKX	4/57	FKX	9/58	KKX	10/59	PKX	9/60	UKX	7/61	YKX	7/62
BPP	6/57	FPP	11/58	KPP	11/59	PPP	9/60	UPP	8/61	YPP	8/62
CBH	7/57	GBH	12/58	LBH	12/59	RBH	10/60	VBH	9/61		
CKX	9/57	GKX	1/59	LKX	1/60	RKX	11/60	VKX	11/61		
CPP	10/57	GPP	2/59	LPP	2/60	RPP	1/61	VPP	12/61		
DBH	12/57	HBH	3/59	MBH	3/60	SBH	1/61	WBH	1/62		
DKX	2/58	HKX	4/59	MKX	3/60	SKX	2/61	WKX	2/62		
DPP	3/58	HPP	5/59	MPP	4/60	SPP	3/61	WPP	3/62		

There was no segregation of motorcycles in the reverse two-letter series.

BH (from 2001)	9/62	KX (from 1)	4/63	PP (from 1)	11/63

Suffix marks commenced 1.4.64

COUNTY COUNCIL OF CAERNARVON

A common sequence for all vehicles.

CC 1/04   JC 3/31

First issues each year : (No dates of issue available from official records for 1922-28.)

1905	CC 102	1912	CC 504	1919	CC 1675	1933	JC 995	1940	JC 6710	1947	JC 8251
1906	CC 137	1913	CC 686	1920	CC 2008	1934	JC 1598	1941	JC 6864	1948	JC 8931
1907	CC 198	1914	CC 902	1921	CC 2675	1935	JC 2340	1942	JC 6996	1949	JC 9737
1908	CC 239	1915	CC 1177	1929	CC 8242	1936	JC 3270	1943	JC 7141		
1909	CC 279	1916	CC 1425	1930	CC 9184	1937	JC 4240	1944	JC 7318		
1910	CC 329	1917	CC 1564	1931	CC 9941	1938	JC 5187	1945	JC 7480		
1911	CC 391	1918	CC 1604	1932	JC 439	1939	JC 6011	1946	JC 7646		

(Although ACC commenced 2/49, JC was not completed until 4/49.)

ACC	2/49	DCC	5/55	GCC	12/58	KCC	5/61	NCC	8/63
AJC	8/50	DJC	1/56	GJC	6/59	KJC	10/61	NJC	12/63
BCC	2/52	ECC	8/56	HCC	11/59	LCC	3/62	OCC	3/64
BJC	5/53	EJC	5/57	HJC	4/60	LJC	7/62	OJC	6/64
CCC	3/54	FCC	12/57	JCC	8/60	MCC	12/62		
CJC	10/54	FJC	6/58	JJC	1/61	MJC	4/63		

Suffix marks commenced 4.8.64.

The official name of the authority was The County Council of Carnarvon until altered to Caernarvon
as a result of a motion to the Council's Parliamentary Committee on 19 December 1925.

COUNTY COUNCIL OF CAMBRIDGE

CE   1/04   ER   7/22   VE   9/28

No records available on dates of first issues each year.

ACE	2/34	ECE	8/41	JCE	5/50	NCE	9/54	SCE	9/57	WCE	2/60
AER	8/34	EER	1/44	JER	11/50	NER	1/55	SER	12/57	WER	4/60
AVE	3/35	EVE	1/46	JVE	3/51	NVE	3/55 *	SVE	3/58	WVE	5/60
BCE	8/35	FCE	7/46	KCE	7/51	OCE	6/55	TCE	5/58	XCE	7/60
BER	2/36	FER	11/46	KER	1/52	OER	9/55	TER	8/58	XER	9/60
BVE	8/36	FVE	3/47	KVE	6/52	OVE	11/55	TVE	11/58	XVE	12/60
CCE	1/37	GCE	8/47	LCE	10/52	PCE	3/56	UCE	1/59	YCE	2/61
CER	7/37	GER	2/48	LER	3/53	PER	5/56	UER	4/59	YER	4/61
CVE	2/38	GVE	7/48	LVE	7/53	PVE	8/56	UVE	5/59	YVE	5/61
DCE	9/38	HCE	1/49	MCE	11/53	RCE	12/56	VCE	7/59		
DER	4/39	HER	7/49	MER	3/54	RER	3/57	VER	10/59		
DVE	12/39	HVE	12/49	MVE	6/54	RVE	6/57	VVE	12/59		

* NVE 1 was an early issue, 9/54, for Commercial Motor Show.

ACE	8/61	BCE	4/62	CCE	11/62	DCE	5/63	ECE	10/63	FCE	7/76 #
AER	11/61	BER	6/62	CER	1/63	DER	7/63	EER	1/64		
AVE	1/62	BVE	8/62	CVE	3/63	DVE	9/63	EVE	2/64		

re-registrations only.

Special marks for Diplomatic Corps : *1 GER* c. 4/63, *1 PER* c. 4/65, *1 SVE* 5/63.

Commenced suffix marks 2.3.64

As from 1 April 1965 this authority was merged with the County Council of the Isle of Ely to form the new County
Council of Cambridgeshire and The Isle of Ely.

COUNTY COUNCIL OF CARDIGAN

A separate and duplicate series for cycles maintained, unusually, until November 1925.

EJ   12/03

First issues each year :

	Cars	Cycles		Cars	Cycles				
1904	6	5	1915	205	188	1926	1557	1937	5056
1905	20	28	1916	268	264	1927	1922	1938	5498
1906	25	42	1917	319	301	1928	2197	1939	6004
1907	36	52	1918	332	316	1929	2444	1940	6463
1908	50	56	1919	354	326	1930	2721	1941	6647
1909	61	61	1920	430	362	1931	3010	1942	6860
1910	72	69	1921	649	449	1932	3278	1943	7101
1911	88	75	1922	800	565	1933	3531	1944	7302
1912	103	92	1923	973	664	1934	3802	1945	7441
1913	135	114	1924	1176	780	1935	4140	1946	7619
1914	165	141	1925	1379	908 *	1936	4594	1947	7993
								1948	8685

* Highest number in motorcycle series - EJ 1037.

AEJ	5/49	DEJ	2/54	GEJ	4/57	KEJ	6/59	NEJ	7/71	REJ	9/63
BEJ	2/51	EEJ	3/55	HEJ	2/58	LEJ	3/60	OEJ	4/62	SEJ	4/64
CEJ	12/52	FEJ	1/56	JEJ	10/58	MEJ	10/60	PEJ	1/63		

Commenced suffix marks 1.9.64

COUNTY COUNCIL OF CARMARTHEN

Duplicated series for cars and motorcycles until the end of 1920.

BX   12/03   TH   7/29

First issues each year, (no records survive for 1922-3).

	Cars	Cycles			Cars	Cycles			Cars		Cars
1905	BX 35	BX 65		1914	BX 342	BX 532		1925	BX 5191	1933	TH 3035
1906	BX 50	BX 93		1915	BX 487	BX 718		1926	BX 6445	1934	TH 3901
1907	BX 69	BX 112		1916	BX 666	BX 893		1927	BX 7429	1935	TH 4999
1908	BX 87	BX 127		1917	BX 792	BX 961		1928	BX 8383	1936	TH 6441
1909	BX 115	BX 148		1918	BX 828			1929	BX 9249	1937	TH 7961
1910	BX 132	BX 181		1919	BX 849	BX 1001		1930	TH 284	1938	TH 9600
1911	BX 167	BX 219		1920	BX 1089	BX 1199*		1931	TH 1322		
1912	BX 196	BX 289		1921	BX 1628						

* Highest in motorcycle series BX 1659.

ABX	3/38	EBX	3/48	JBX	7/53	NBX	4/56	SBX	9/58	WBX	6/60
ATH	11/38	ETH	10/48	JTH	12/53	NTH	8/56	STH	12/58	WTH	9/60
BBX	6/39	FBX	5/49	KBX	4/54	OBX	1/57	TBX	3/59	XBX	1/61
BTH	3/41	FTH	1/50	KTH	9/54	OTH	5/57	TTH	6/59	XTH	3/61
CBX	5/43	GBX	10/50	LBX	1/55	PBX	8/57	UBX	9/59	YBX	5/61
CTH	3/46	GTH	6/51	LTH	5/55	PTH	12/57	UTH	11/59	YTH	8/61
DBX	1/47	HBX	3/52	MBX	8/55	RBX	3/58	VBX	2/60		
DTH	8/47	HTH	12/52	MTH	12/55	RTH	6/58	VTH	5/60		

ABX	1/62	BBX	6/62	CBX	1/63	DBX	6/63	EBX	1/64	FBX	5/64
ATH	4/62	BTH	9/62	CTH	4/63	DTH	10/63	ETH	3/64		

Suffix marks commenced 1.7.64

91

COUNTY COUNCIL OF CHESTER

A common sequence for all vehicles.

M   12/03   MA   1/19   MB   7/22   TU   8/25   LG   12/28

First issues each year :

1904	M 202	1909	M 2161	1914	M 5824	1919	M 9979	1924	MB 4001*	1929	LG 167
1905	M 671	1910	M 2573	1915	M 7198	1920	MA 2112	1925	MB 7354	1930	LG 3180
1906	M 1023	1911	M 3000	1916	M 8260	1921	MA 5043	1926	TU 868	1931	LG 5913
1907	M 1423	1912	M 3659	1917	M 9143	1922	MA 8485	1927	TU 4103	1932	LG 8033
1908	M 1796	1913	M 4658	1918	M 9558	1923	MB 1036	1928	TU 7256		

* approximate

ALG	11/32	ELG	6/37	GMA	10/46*	NLG	9/50	SLG	10/53	WLG	9/55
AMA	3/33	EMA	9/37	JMA	1/47	NMA	11/50	SMA	12/53	WMA	11/55
AMB	8/33	EMB	1/38	JMB	4/47	NMB	1/51	SMB	2/54	WMB	12/55
ATU	1/34	ETU	3/38	JTU	7/47	NTU	4/51	STU	3/54	WTU	1/56
BLG	4/34	FLG	7/38	KLG	10/47	OLG	7/51	TLG	5/54	XLG	3/56
BMA	8/34	FMA	11/38	KMA	1/48	OMA	10/51	TMA	6/54	XMA	4/56
BMB	12/34	FMB	2/39	KMB	4/48	OMB	1/52	TMB	8/54	XMB	5/56
CLG	3/35	FTU	4/39	KTU	7/48	OTU	3/52	TTU	10/54	XTU	6/56
CMA	6/35	GLG	7/39	LLG	10/48	PLG	5/52	ULG	11/54	YLG	8/56
CMB	10/35	GMB	12/39	LMA	2/49	PMA	8/52	UMA	1/55	YMA	10/56
BTU	1/36*	GTU	7/40	LMB	4/49	PMB	10/52	UMB	2/55	YMB	11/56
CTU	3/36	HLG	1/42	LTU	7/49	PTU	12/52	UTU	3/55	YTU	1/57
DLG	6/36	HMA	5/43	MLG	10/49	RLG	3/53	VLG	4/55		
DMA	10/36	HMB	5/45	MMA	1/50	RMA	4/53	VMA	6/55		
DMB	1/37	HTU	3/46	MMB	4/50	RMB	6/53	VMB	7/55		
DTU	3/37	JLG	7/46	MTU	6/50	RTU	8/53	VTU	8/55		

* In SR&O 1932 No. 332 BTU and DMA were omitted in error from Cheshire's allocation, hence the initial omission of BTU. Both these marks were included in SR&O 1935 No. 581 and BTU was issued after CMB with DMA in its correct position. In SR&O 1938 No. 6 GMA was misprinted as GMR - the latter was, of course, ignored by Cheshire but GMA was not issued until after the error was corrected in SR&O 1941 No. 1149 - it then followed JLG.

ALG	2/57	ELG	8/58	JLG	10/59	NLG	9/60	TLG	8/61	XLG	9/62
AMA	3/57	EMA	9/58	JMA	11/59	NMA	10/60	TMA	9/61	XMA	10/62
AMB	5/57	EMB	10/58	JMB	12/59	NMB	11/60	TMB	10/61	XMB	10/62
ATU	5/57	ETU	11/58	JTU	1/60	NTU	12/60	TTU	11/61	XTU	11/62
BLG	7/57	FLG	12/58	KLG	2/60	PLG	1/61	ULG	12/61	YLG	12/62
BMA	8/57	FMA	1/59	KMA	2/60	PMA	1/61	UMA	1/62	YMA	1/63
BMB	9/57	FMB	2/59	KMB	3/60	PMB	2/61	UMB	2/62	YMB	2/63
BTU	10/57	FTU	3/59	KTU	3/60	PTU	3/61	UTU	3/62	YTU	2/63
CLG	12/57	GLG	4/59	LLG	3/60	RLG	3/61	VLG	3/62		
CMA	1/58	GMA	4/59	LMA	5/60	RMA	4/61	VMA	4/62		
CMB	2/58	GMB	5/59	LMB	5/60	RMB	4/61	VMB	5/62		
CTU	3/58	GTU	6/59	LTU	6/60	RTU	5/61	VTU	5/62		
DLG	4/58	HLG	7/59	MLG	6/60	SLG	6/61	WLG	6/62		
DMA	5/58	HMA	7/59	MMA	7/60	SMA	6/61	WMA	6/62		
DMB	6/58	HMB	9/59	MMB	8/60	SMB	7/61	WMB	7/62		
DTU	7/58	HTU	10/59	MTU	9/60	STU	7/61	WTU	8/62		

There was no segregation of motorcycles in reverse two-letter series.

LG (from 1) 3/63   TU (from 1) 8/63

Special mark for Diplomatic Corps : 1 M 12/63

Commenced suffix marks 2.1.64

COUNTY COUNCIL OF CORNWALL

Registrations commenced 7.12.03.
Duplicate series for cars and motorcycles until 1920..

AF 12/03   RL   11/24   CV   5/29

First issues each year :

	Cars	Cycles			Cars	Cycles			All Vehicles	
	AF	AF			AF	AF				
1904	40	22		1913	938	767		1929	RL	9042
1905	112	149		1914	1189	998		1930	CV	1426
1906	176	211		1915	1458	*		1931	CV	3915
1907	231	270		1916	1737	1603		1932	CV	5802
1908	311	300		1917	1913	1753		1933	CV	7654
1909	391	336		1918	1976	1820		1934	CV	9534
1910	488	384		1919	2067	1874				
1911	616	462		1920	2432	2270				
1912	760	594		1921	3252					

* no information available; (nor on last motorcycle number in separate series nor first issues for 1922-1928 inclusive.)

AAF	3/34	EAF	1/38	JAF	10/46	NAF	5/50	SAF	1/54	WAF	1/56
ACV	7/34	ECV	5/38	JCV	1/47	NCV	9/50	SCV	3/54	WCV	4/56
ARL	12/34	ERL	10/38	JRL	5/47	NRL	2/51	SRL	5/54	WRL	6/56
BAF	4/35	FAF	2/39	KAF	8/47	OAF	5/51	TAF	7/54	XAF	8/56
BCV	8/35	FCV	6/39	KCV	12/47	OCV	9/51	TCV	10/54	XCV	11/56
BRL	12/35	FRL	1/40	KRL	4/48	ORL	2/52	TRL	12/54	XRL	1/57
CAF	3/36	GAF	5/41	LAF	7/48	PAF	5/52	UAF	2/55	YAF	4/57
CCV	7/36	GCV	7/42	LCV	11/48	PCV	9/52	UCV	4/55	YCV	5/57
CRL	11/36	GRL	11/43	LRL	3/49	PRL	1/53	URL	6/55	YRL	7/57
DAF	2/37	HAF	3/45	MAF	6/49	RAF	5/53	VAF	7/55		
DCV	5/37	HCV	2/46	MCV	10/49	RCV	7/53	VCV	9/55		
DRL	9/37	HRL	6/46	MRL	2/50	RRL	10/53	VRL	11/55		

Cornwall was one of the authorities which overlooked the M.o.T.'s instruction not to issue reverse Oxx combinations.

AAF	9/57	EAF	4/59	JAF	7/60	NAF	11/61	SAF	3/63	WAF	5/64	
ACV	11/57	ECV	5/59	JCV	8/60	NCV	12/61	SCV	5/63	WCV	6/64	
ARL	1/58	ERL	7/59	JRL	9/60	NRL	2/62	SRL	6/63	WRL	7/64	
BAF	3/58	FAF	8/59	KAF	11/60	OAF	3/62	TAF	7/63	XAF	9/64	**
BCV	5/58	FCV	10/59	KCV	1/61	OCV	5/62	TCV	8/63			
BRL	6/58	FRL	11/59	KRL	2/61	ORL	6/62	TRL	9/63			
CAF	7/58	GAF	12/59	LAF	3/61	PAF	7/62	UAF	10/63			
CCV	9/58	GCV	2/60	LCV	4/61	PCV	9/62	UCV	12/63			
CRL	10/58	GRL	3/60	LRL	5/61	PRL	10/62	URL	1/64			
DAF	12/58	HAF	4/60	MAF	6/61	RAF	12/62	VAF	2/64			
DCV	1/59	HCV	5/60	MCV	7/61	RCV	1/63	VCV	3/64			
DRL	3/59	HRL	6/60	MRL	9/61	RRL	3/63	VRL	4/64			

** Re-registrations only

Special issues for Diplomatic Corps :   IRL 1 3/58   1 RL /84

Commenced suffix marks 1.9.64

COUNTY COUNCIL OF CUMBERLAND

Registrations commenced 4 December 1903.

A common sequence for all vehicles.

AO 12/03   RM 4/24

First issues each year :

	AO		AO		AO		RM		RM
1904	98*	1911	1056	1918	3835	1925	776	1932	8390
1905	283*	1912	1338	1919	3905	1926	2175	1933	9192
1906	378*	1913	1707	1920	4665	1927	3378		
1907	486*	1914	2201	1921	6110	1928	4593		
1908	593	1915	2745	1922	7252	1929	5610		
1909	723*	1916	3279	1923	8276	1930	6688		
1910	854	1917	3696	1924	9490	1931	7615		

* approximate, exact figure not available due to missing motorcycle register, but maximum inaccuracy is 3.

AAO	1/34	BAO	8/39	JAO	3/49	NAO	9/53	SAO	3/56	WAO	7/58
ARM	11/34	ERM	8/41	JRM	9/49	NRM	1/54	SRM	7/56	WRM	9/58
BAO	7/35	FAO	7/43	KAO	4/50	OAO	5/54	TAO	11/56	XAO	12/58
BRM	4/36	FRM	11/45	KRM	1/51	ORM	9/54	TRM	4/57	XRM	3/59
CAO	12/36	GAO	10/46	LAO	8/51	PAO	1/55	UAO	7/57	YAO	5/59
CRM	7/37	GRM	5/47	LRM	4/52	PRM	5/55	URM	11/57	YRM	7/59
DAO	4/38	HAO	1/48	MAO	11/52	RAO	8/55	VAO	2/58		
DRM	1/39	HRM	8/48	MRM	4/53	RRM	12/55	VRM	4/58		

AAO	10/59	DAO	11/60	GAO	1/62	KAO	3/63	NAO	11/74**
ARM	12/59	DRM	1/61	GRM	3/62	KRM	4/63		
BAO	3/60	EAO	3/61	HAO	5/62	LAO	6/63		
BRM	4/60	ERM	5/61	HRM	7/62	LRM	8/63		
CAO	6/60	FAO	7/61	JAO	10/62	MAO	10/63		
CRM	8/60	FRM	9/61	JRM	12/62	MRM	1/64		

** re-registrations only.

Commenced suffix marks 2.3.64

COUNTY COUNCIL OF DENBIGH

A common sequence for all vehicles.

Registrations commenced 15/12/03.

CA 12/03   UN 3/27

First issues each year :

	CA		CA		CA		UN		UN
1904	32	1912	597	1920	2671	1928	996	1936	9291
1905	124	1913	767	1921	3748 *	1929	2186		
1906	173	1914	1014 #	1922	4692	1930	3409		
1907	215	1915	1356	1923	5441	1931	4455		
1908	273	1916	1714	1924	6248	1932	5409		
1909	343	1917	1917	1925	7283	1933	6275		
1910	401	1918	2012	1926	8565	1934	7124		
1911	482	1919	2081	1927	9730	1935	8139		

CA 1000 late issue in July 1914.
* CA 5873 early issue 1921, (issued in error but allowed to stand).
There was considerable overlapping at year ends after 1921 and the figures shown for subsequent
years are actually one higher than the last number issued in the previous year.

ACA	7/36	BCA	1/47	JCA	8/52	NCA	10/55	SCA	7/58	WCA	6/60
AUN	4/37	BUN	10/47	JUN	5/53	NUN	2/56	SUN	11/58	WUN	8/60
BCA	2/38	FCA	4/48	KCA	10/53	OCA	6/56	TCA	3/59	XCA	11/60
BUN	12/38	FUN	1/49	KUN	4/54	OUN	12/56	TUN	5/59	XUN	3/61
CCA	9/39	GCA	8/49	LCA	8/54	PCA	5/57	UCA	8/59	YCA	5/61
CUN	7/41	GUN	5/50	LUN	2/55	PUN	9/57	UUN	11/59	YUN	7/61
DCA	10/43	HCA	2/51	MCA *	2/53	RCA	2/58	VCA	2/60		
DUN	5/46	HUN	12/51	MUN	5/55	RUN	5/58	VUN	4/60		

* MCA was a special issue for the McAlpine group of construction companies and continued in issue until the
commencement of year letters.

After YUN, reverse *UN* was issued simultaneously from 1 up for motorcycles and 1000 up for other vehicles.
After *9999 UN* cars etc. used *ACA, AUN* and *BCA*, while motorcycles continued in the *1-999 UN* block.

UN	*10/61*	*ACA*	*12/63*	*AUN*	*3/64*	*BCA*	*5/64*

Special mark for Diplomatic Corps : 1 HUN ca. 3/82

Commenced suffix marks 1.6.64

COUNTY COUNCIL OF DERBY

R 12/03   NU 3/23   RA 7/26   RB 11/29

A separate and duplicated series for cars and motorcycles up to the end of 1920: Cars: R 1 – 5394; motorcycles R 1 – 5795. There was also a third parallel series for Heavy Motor Cars which reached at least R 51, but was apparently abandoned in 1914 or 1915.
As from 1.1.21 a common series R 5796 up.

First numbers issued each year are not available before 1929, but the following numbers were issued in January (1922-8) or February (1921) of the years shown.

1921	R 5979	1923	R 9861	1925	NU 4893	1927	RA 1337
1922	R 7953	1924	NU 1972	1926	NU 8066	1928	RA 4623

First issues each year :

1929	RA 7373	1930	RB 296	1931	RB 3062	1932	RB 5289	1933	RB 7260	1934	RB 9722
ANU	1/34	ENU	6/37	JNU	9/44	NNU	1/49	SNU	5/52	WNU	8/54
ARA	5/34	ERA	11/37	JRA	11/45	NRA	4/49	SRA	9/52	WRA	10/54
ARB	9/34	ERB	2/38	JRB	4/46	NRB	7/49	SRB	11/52	WRB	11/54
BNU	1/35	FNU	5/38	KNU	7/46	ONU	10/49	TNU	2/53	XNU	1/55
BRA	4/35	FRA	8/38	KRA	10/46	ORA	2/50	TRA	4/53	XRA	3/55
BRB	7/35	FRB	12/38	KRB	1/47	ORB	5/50	TRB	6/53	XRB	4/55
CNU	12/35	GNU	3/39	LNU	5/47	PNU	9/50	UNU	8/53	YNU	5/55
CRA	3/36	GRA	6/39*	LRA	7/47	PRA	1/51	URA	11/53	YRA	6/55
CRB	6/36	GRB	9/39	LRB	10/47	PRB	4/51	URB	1/54	YRB	8/55
DNU	10/36	HNU	7/40	MNU	2/48	RNU	7/51	VNU	3/54		
DRA	1/37	HRA	12/41	MRA	5/48	RRA	10/51	VRA	4/54		
DRB	4/37	HRB	3/43	MRB	9/48	RRB	2/52	VRB	6/54		

GRA 1 - 37 were issued early, commencing 6/38, for the Greyhound Racing Association. General issue from 6/39.

Derbyshire commenced reverse issues with three-letter marks and was one of the authorities to overlook the instruction that reverse Oxx combinations should not be issued. However, the error was realised after the issue of reverse ONU and ORA. ORB was not issued. After YRB the following were issued : R from 1; NU from 1000 and RA from 1000. Numbers ending in '0' in NU and RA were issued, resulting in near duplication as between, e.g. 735 ONU and 7350 NU. Motorcycles were not segregated in reverse series.

ANU	9/55	ENU	5/57	JNU	11/58	NNU	1/60	SNU	12/60	WNU	2/62
ARA	10/55	ERA	6/57	JRA	12/58	NRA	2/60	SRA	2/61	WRA	3/62
ARB	12/55	ERB	7/57	JRB	1/59	NRB	3/60	SRB	3/61	WRB	4/62
BNU	2/56	FNU	9/57	KNU	3/59	ONU	4/60	TNU	4/61	XNU	5/62
BRA	3/56	FRA	11/57	KRA	4/59	ORA	5/60	TRA	5/61	XRA	5/62
BRB	5/56	FRB	1/58	KRB	5/59	ORB	not issued	TRB	5/61	XRB	6/62
CNU	6/56	GNU	2/58	LNU	6/59	PNU	5/60	UNU	6/61	YNU	7/62
CRA	7/56	GRA	3/58	LRA	7/59	PRA	6/60	URA	7/61	YRA	8/62
CRB	10/56	GRB	5/58	LRB	8/59	PRB	7/60	URB	8/61	YRB	10/62
DNU	12/56	HNU	6/58	MNU	9/59	RNU	8/60	VNU	9/61		
DRA	2/57	HRA	7/58	MRA	10/59	RRA	10/60	VRA	11/61		
DRB	4/57	HRB	9/58	MRB	12/59	RRB	11/60	VRB	1/62		

R (from 1)   11/62   NU (from 1000)   7/63   RA (from 1000)   4/64

Commenced suffix marks 1.6.64

COUNTY COUNCIL OF DEVON

T 12/03-12/20   TA 7/20 *   TT 6/24   UO 10/26   DV 3/29   OD 8/31

Registration commenced 2.12.03. Cars and motorcycles were segregated in a common series until the end of 1920. Originally the segregation was on an "odds and evens" principle; later on a "block" principle. Heavy motor cars were included with motor cars. Motorcycle blocks were : T 1 to T 1699 (odd numbers only); T 2301 to T 2499 (odds and evens); T 2501 to T 9999 (odd numbers only). However, cars reached T 9998 in 10/20 while motorcycles were still in T 93xx and whilst the remaining odd numbers were used mainly for cycles, the following odd numbers were used for other vehicles : T 9315-9413, 9467, 9471, 9473 and 9601-9899. Early TA issues were sequential, but there was a very brief resumption of the "odds and evens" principle with TA 71-89 (odds only) being motorcycles; segregation abandoned thereafter.

* Only TA 1 to TA 5 issued before 11/20.

First issues each year (no records survive for 1923-8) :

	Cars	Cycles		Cars	Cycles		All Vehicles	
	T			T				
1904	170	125	1913	2790	2673	1921	TA	90
1905	406	457	1914	3644	3367	1922	TA	2643
1906	632	587	1915	4620	4309			
1907	952	717	1916	5554	5121	1929	UO	9070
1908	1240	807	1917	6070	5481	1930	DV	3454
1909	1526	931	1918	6264	5633	1931	DV	7742
1910	1783	1089	1919	6470	5781	1932	OD	1072
1911	1956	1271	1920	7688	7215	1933	OD	4482
1912	2169	1591				1934	OD	7973

At the outset Devon adopted a unique sequence for the issue of their three-letter marks. From ATA to JOD the prime marks were taken in chronological order and issued in as many combinations as had been allotted by the latest SR&O before proceeding to the next prime mark. From KTA to YOD and for all reverse issues simple "chronological" order was followed.

ATA	6/34	DDV	12/38	JDV	10/47	NTA	7/51	STA	12/54	WTA	1/57-7/57 *
BTA	10/34	EDV	2/39	FOD	12/47	NTT	10/51	STT	2/55	WTT	3/57
ATT	12/34	COD	5/39	(GOD not alloc.)		NUO	1/52	SUO	3/55	WUO	5/57
BTT	3/35	DOD	8/39	HOD	3/48	NDV	4/52	SDV	4/55	WDV	6/57
AUO	5/35	EOD	12/39	JOD	5/48	NOD	7/52	(SOD not alloc.)		WOD	7/57-3/58 *
BUO	8/35	FTA	7/40	KTA	7/48	OTA	9/52	TTA	5/55	XTA	8/57
ADV	11/35	GTA	7/41	KTT	9/48	OTT	11/52	TTT	6/55	XTT	9/57
BDV	1/36	HTA	4/42	KUO	12/48	OUO	2/53	TUO	7/55	XUO	11/57
AOD	3/36	JTA	1/43	KDV	2/49	ODV	4/53	TDV	9/55	XDV	1/58
BOD	6/36	FTT	10/43	KOD	5/49	OOD	6/53	TOD	10/55	XOD	2/58
CTA	9/36	GTT	11/44	LTA	7/49	PTA	8/53	UTA	11/55-5/56#	YTA	3/58
DTA	11/36	HTT	11/45	LTT	8/49	PTT	10/53	UTT	11/55	YTT	3/58-9/58 @
ETA	1/37	JTT	3/46	LUO	11/49	PUO	12/53	UUO	1/56	YUO	4/58
CTT	4/37	FUO	6/46	LDV	1/50	PDV	2/54	UDV	3/56	YDV	6/58
DTT	6/37	GUO	9/46	LOD	4/50	POD	3/54	UOD	5/56	YOD	7/58
ETT	9/37	HUO	11/46	MTA	6/50	RTA	4/54	VTA	5/56-1/57 *		
CUO	12/37	JUO	1/47	MTT	9/50	RTT	6/54	VTT	6/56		
DUO	3/38	FDV	3/47	MUO	12/50	RUO	8/54	VUO	8/56		
EUO	5/38	GDV	5/47	MDV	2/51	RDV	9/54	VDV	10/56		
CDV	9/38	HDV	7/47	MOD	5/51	ROD	11/54	VOD	1/57		

Mainly motorcycles from ca. 250 up.   * mainly motorcycles.   @ mainly motorcycles from 12 up.

COUNTY COUNCIL OF DEVON (continued)

ATA	8/58	DTA	10/59	GTA	11/60	KTA	11/61	NTA	1/63	STA	1/64
ATT	9/58	DTT	11/59	GTT	12/60	KTT	12/61	NTT	2/63	STT	1/64
AUO	10/58	DUO	12/59	GUO	1/61	KUO	1/62	NUO	3/63	SUO	2/64
ADV	11/58	DDV	1/60	GDV	2/61	KDV	2/62	NDV	3/63	SDV	3/64
AOD	12/58	DOD	2/60	(GOD not alloc.)		KOD	3/62	NOD	4/63	(SOD not alloc.)	
BTA	1/59	ETA	3/60	HTA	2/61	LTA	4/62	PTA	5/63	TTA	3/64
BTT	2/59	ETT	3/60	HTT	3/61	LTT	5/62	PTT	5/63	TTT	4/64
BUO	3/59	EUO	4/60	HUO	4/61	LUO	5/62	PUO	6/63	TUO	5/64
BDV	4/59	EDV	5/60	HDV	5/61	LDV	6/62	PDV	7/63	TDV	5/64
BOD	5/59	EOD	5/60	HOD	5/61	LOD	7/62	POD	8/63	TOD	6/64
CTA	6/59	FTA	6/60	HTA	6/61	MTA	8/62	RTA	9/63		
CTT	6/59	FTT	7/60	JTT	7/61	MTT	9/62	RTT	9/63	UTA 6/76 **	
CUO	7/59	FUO	8/60	JUO	7/61	MUO	10/62	RUO	10/63		
CDV	9/59	FDV	9/60	JDV	9/61	MDV	11/62	RDV	11/63		
COD	9/59	FOD	10/60	JOD	10/61	MOD	12/62	ROD	12/63		

** Re-registrations only.

Special marks for Diplomatic Corps :   ITA 1 ca. 3/63.   1 TT ca. 5/65

Commenced suffix marks 1.7.64

10.   Paragraphs 8 and 9 of the Circular Letter (RF 100) of 4th October referred to the question of identification marks and registration numbers. It has now been decided that all vehicles which are already registered at 31st December next shall at any rate during 1921 retain the mark and number allotted to them. At a subsequent date it may be found necessary to revise the system of numbering, but in view of the amount of work necessarily falling upon Local Authorities next year the Minister has postponed consideration of this matter.   *Circular RF 105 29.11.20*

COUNTY COUNCIL OF DORSET

BF 12/03   FX 12/04 *   PR 1/23   TK 12/27   JT 11/33

Until September 1910 there was a separate and duplicate series for motorcycles. Thereafter all vehicles were numbered in a common sequence. Motorists raised strong objection to Dorset's initial issue, BF, and accordingly the Local Government Board agreed to substitute FX. However, for existing registrants it was optional whether or not they changed their registration from BF to FX. Those who did retained the same serial numbers, which had reached BF 162 for cars and BF 150 for motorcycles. 42 car owners and 41 motorcycle owners chose not to change.

* only FX 163 (car) issued before 1/05.

First issues each year :

	Cars	Cycles								
1904	BF 80	BF 38	1911	FX 740	1918	FX 4059	1925	PR 3750	1932	TK 7248
1905	FX 164	FX 151	1912	FX 1061	1919	FX 4289	1926	PR 6010	1933	TK 8741
1906	FX 235	FX 197	1913	FX 1468	1920	FX 5201	1927	PR 8055	1934	JT 357
1907	FX 313	FX 254	1914	FX 1980	1921	no record	1928	TK 74	1935	JT 2073
1908	FX 410	FX 315	1915	FX 2606	1922	no record	1929	TK 1898	1936	JT 4068
1909	FX 494	FX 356	1916	FX 3366	1923	no record	1930	TK 3855	1937	JT 6355
1910	FX 594	FX 410 *	1917	FX 3803	1924	PR 1710	1931	TK 5724	1938	JT 8549

* Last in separate motorcycle series = FX 473;   first motorcycle in general series = FX 694.

AFX	10/38	EFX	5/50	JFX	10/55	NFX	4/59	SFX	7/61	WFX	8/74 *
AJT	3/39	EJT	10/50	JJT	1/56	NJT	6/59	SJT	10/61		
APR	10/39	EPR	3/51	JPR	4/56	NPR	7/59	SPR	12/61		
ATK	4/41	ETK	8/51	JTK	7/56	NTK	9/59	STK	3/62		
BFX	3/43	FFX	1/52	KFX	10/56	OFX	10/59	TFX	5/62		
BJT	6/45	FJT	6/52	KJT	1/57	OJT	12/59	TJT	6/62		
BPR	5/46	FPR	11/52	KPR	4/57	OPR	2/60	TPR	8/62		
BTK	10/46	FTK	5/53	KTK	6/57	OTK	4/60	TTK	11/62		
CFX	3/47	GFX	7/53	LFX	9/57	PFX	5/60	UFX	1/63		
CJT	8/47	GJT	12/53	LJT	12/57	PJT	6/60	UJT	3/63		
CPR	1/48	GPR	3/54	LPR	3/58	PPR	8/60	UPR	5/63		
CTK	6/48	GTK	7/54	LTK	5/58	PTK	10/60	UTK	6/63		
DFX	11/48	HFX	11/54	MFX	7/58	RFX	1/61	VFX	8/63		
DJT	4/49	HJT	2/55	MJT	10/58	RJT	3/61	VJT	10/63		
DPR	8/49	HPR	5/55	MPR	1/59	RPR	4/61	VPR	12/63		
DTK	1/50	HTK	7/55	MTK	2/59	RTK	6/61	VTK	1/64		

* re-registrations only.

Commenced suffix marks 2.3.64

COUNTY COUNCIL OF DURHAM

A common sequence for all vehicles.

J 12/03   PT 11/22   UP 7/27

No information is available on first issues each year before 1929 :

| 1929 | UP 2151 | 1931 | UP 5136 | 1933 | UP 7426 | 1935 | UP 9921 |
| 1930 | UP 3718 | 1932 | UP 6360 | 1934 | UP 8618 |

Three-letter issues started with the sequence APT, BPT, AUP, BUP but thereafter were alphabetical.

APT	12/34	EPT	6/39	JPT	3/48	NPT	6/52	SPT	5/55	WPT	4/57
BPT	7/35	EUP	7/40	JUP	8/48	NUP	1/53	SUP	8/55	WUP	6/57
AUP	3/36	FPT	9/42	KPT	2/49	OPT	5/53	TPT	11/55	XPT	8/57
BUP	10/36	FUP	1/45	KUP	7/49	OUP	10/53	TUP	2/56	XUP	10/57
CPT	4/37	GPT	5/46	LPT	1/50	PPT	3/54	UPT	4/56	YPT	12/57
CUP	10/37	GUP	11/46	LUP	8/50	PUP	6/54	UUP	6/56	YUP	3/58
DPT	4/38	HPT	3/47	MPT	3/51	RPT	11/54	VPT	9/56		
DUP	12/38	HUP	8/47	MUP	11/51	RUP	2/55	VUP	1/57		

Reverse issues started with *APT* and continued in three letters for all vehicles to and including *JUP*. Then *PT* (from 1) for cars etc. and three-letter marks commencing *KPT* for motorcycles starting simultaneously.   *9999 PT* was followed by *UP* (from 1).   When *UP* was completed cars re-joined the three-letter sequence from *726 LUP.*

(PT was in use for trade plates from 001-099 only so there was no duplication if the cipher is taken into account. Durham LTO wrote : "No provision is made by this authority to avoid duplication of plates since it is considered that the colouration of trade plates is a sufficient safeguard".)

	All Vehicles			Cars etc.		M/ycles		All Vehicles	
APT	5/58	DPT	4/59	GPT	1/60	PT	8/60	KPT	8/60	MPT	9/63
AUP	7/58	DUP	5/59	GUP	3/60	UP	3/62-8/63	KUP	5/61	MUP	1/64
BPT	9/58	EPT	7/59	HPT	4/60			LPT	2/62	NPT ca.8/74 *
BUP	11/58	EUP	8/59	HUP	5/60			LUP	5/63 #
CPT	1/59	FPT	10/59	JPT	6/60
CUP	3/59	FUP	11/59	JUP	7/60

\# All vehicles from *726 LUP.*
* Re-registrations only.

Commenced suffix marks 2.2.64

COUNTY COUNCIL OF THE ISLE OF ELY

Registration commenced 22.12.03.

A common sequence for cars and motorcycles, but heavy motor cars in a separate series, (EB 01 to 076), 12/09-11/20

EB 12/03   JE 1/33

First issues each year, (records for 1923-1928 not available) :

1904	EB 19	1911	378	1918	1613	1929	7771	1936	2061	1943	6711
1905	117	1912	476	1919	1691	1930	8390	1937	3050	1944	6982
1906	158	1913	655	1920	2016	1931	8951	1938	4000	1945	7346
1907	193	1914	884	1921	2642	1932	9476	1939	4723	1946	7800
1908	238	1915	1137	1922	3504	1933	9975	1940	5440	1947	9100
1909	282	1916	1235			1934	JE 468	1941	5948		
1910	324	1917	1512			1935	1200	1942	6294		

Heavy Motor Car series :

1909	EB 01	1912	EB 03	1914	EB 08	1916	EB 010	1918	EB 018	1920	EB 052
1911	EB 02	1913	EB 06	1915	EB 09	1917	EB 012	1919	EB 023		

AEB	8/47	DEB	1/53	GEB	12/56	KEB	10/59	NEB	11/61	REB	12/63
AJE	5/48	DJE	11/53	GJE	7/57	KJE	2/60	NJE	4/62	RJE	3/64
BEB	2/49	EEB	8/54	HEB	2/58	LEB	5/60	OEB	8/62		
BJE	12/49	EJE	3/55	HJE	7/58	LJE	9/60	OJE	12/62		
CEB	1/51	FEB	10/55	JEB	1/59	MEB	2/61	PEB	5/63		
CJE	2/52	FJE	4/56	JJE	5/59	MJE	6/61	PJE	9/63		

Special mark for Diplomatic Corps : *1 LEB* c. 6/91

Suffix marks commenced 1.4.64

COUNTY COUNCIL OF ESSEX

Registration commenced 1.1.04.

F 1/04   HK 3/15   NO 1/21   PU 7/23   TW 9/25   VW 6/27   VX 5/29   EV 3/31

A common sequence for all vehicles, but in the early days motorcycles were segregated in distinct blocks. There were a few motorcycles with isolated numbers in the first 100 of F, but generally, commencing with F 41 - 56 they were segregated in blocks, usually of between 10 and 40 below F 1000, then blocks of 100 or 200 until from F 2201 - 9999 motorcycles took alternate blocks of 200, commencing F 2201, 2601, 3001 etc.   In HK the blocks were of varying sizes between 50 and 400.

HK 1-11 were issued out of sequence between 10/15 and 12/20.   HK 9971-9999 may have been unused.

First issues each year :

	Cars	Cycles		Cars	Cycles		All Vehicles
1905	F 1263	F 1161	1917	HK 2578	HK 2672	1922	NO 4235
1906	F 1647	F 1773	1918	HK 3193	HK 3273	1923	NO 7452
1907	F 2158	F 2224	1919	HK 3950	HK 3865	1924	PU 1334
1908	F 2548	F 2648	1920	HK 6468	HK 6606	1925	PU 5772
1909	F 2950	F 3098	1921	HK 9777	HK 9860	1926	TW 1076
1910	F 3666	F 3556				1927	TW 6556
1911	F 4191	F 4275				1928	VW 2256
1912	F 4977	F 5050				1929	VW 7588
1913	F 6402	F 6312				1930	VX 3050
1914	F 8078	F 7894				1931	VX 8505
1915	F 9692	F 9916				1932	EV 3848
1916	HK 1501	HK 1477				1933	EV 8730

AEV	3/33	EEV	10/36	JEV	2/40	NEV	3/48	SEV	12/50	WEV	4/53
AHK	4/33	EHK	11/36	JHK	7/40	NHK	4/48	SHK	2/51	WHK	5/53
ANO	6/33	ENO	12/36	JNO	7/41	NNO	5/48	SNO	3/51	WNO	5/53
APU	8/33	EPU	1/37	JPU	1/42	NPU	6/48	SPU	4/51	WPU	6/53
ATW	10/33	ETW	3/37	JTW	9/42	NTW	8/48	STW	4/51	WTW	7/53
AVW	12/33	EVW	3/37	JVW	8/43	NVW	9/48	SVW	5/51	WVW	7/53
AVX	2/34	EVX	4/37	JVX	7/44	NVX	11/48	SVX	6/51	WVX	8/53
BEV	3/34	FEV	6/37	KEV	5/45	OEV	12/48	TEV	7/51	XEV	9/53
BHK	5/34	FHK	6/37	KHK	11/45	OHK	1/49	THK	8/51	XHK	9/53
BNO	6/34	FNO	8/37	KNO	2/46	ONO	3/49	TNO	9/51	XNO	10/53
BPU	8/34	FPU	9/37	KPU	5/46	OPU	4/49	TPU	10/51	XPU	11/53
BTW	10/34	FTW	11/37	KTW	5/46	OTW	5/49	TTW	11/51	XTW	12/53
BVW	12/34	FVW	12/37	KVW	7/46	OVW	6/49	TVW	1/52	XVW	12/53
BVX	1/35	FVX	1/38	KVX	9/46	OVX	7/49	TVX	2/52	XVX	1/54
CEV	3/35	GEV	3/38	LEV	9/46	PEV	9/49	UEV	3/52	YEV	2/54
CHK	4/35	GHK	4/38	LHK	10/46	PHK	10/49	UHK	4/52	YHK	3/54
CNO	5/35	GNO	5/38	LNO	11/46	PNO	11/49	UNO	5/52	YNO	3/54
CPU	7/35	GPU	6/38	LPU	1/47	PPU	12/49	UPU	6/52	YPU	4/54
CTW	9/35	GTW	8/38	LTW	2/47	PTW	1/50	UTW	7/52	YTW	4/54
CVW	10/35	GVW	10/38	LVW	3/47	PVW	3/50	UVW	8/52	YVW	5/54
CVX	12/35	GVX	11/38	LVX	4/47	PVX	4/50	UVX	9/52	YVX	5/54
DEV	1/36	HEV	1/39	MEV	5/47	REV	5/50	VEV	9/52		
DHK	2/36	HHK	2/39	MHK	6/47	RHK	6/50	VHK	10/52		
DNO	3/36	HNO	3/39	MNO	7/47	RNO	7/50	VNO	11/52		
DPU	4/36	HPU	4/39	MPU	8/47	RPU	8/50	VPU	12/52		
DTW	5/36	HTW	5/39	MTW	10/47	RTW	9/50	VTW	1/53		
DVW	6/36	HVW	7/39	MVW	12/47	RVW	10/50	VVW	2/53		
DVX	8/36	HVX	8/39	MVX	1/48	RVX	11/50	VVX	3/53		

Essex commenced reverse issues with three-letter marks for all vehicles, from *AEV* to *JVW*. It was then decided to use the one- and two-letter series, commencing with *F* (from 1) for cars, whilst motorcycles continued in the three-letter sequence. All of Essex's two-letter series had been used at some time for trade plates, but those in *HK* and *NO* had been discontinued and these were the next two series used for cars, each commencing at 1. Then followed *EV*, from 1, after a delay during which remaining EV trade plates were called in. Since the remaining series were still in use on trade plates they all commenced at 1001, in the order *TW, VW, VX, PU*. There were gaps between the completion of *NO* and the commencement of *EV*, between *EV* and *TW* and between *VX* and *PU*. During these periods and after the completion of *PU* cars rejoined cycles in the three-letter series. (It should be noted that there were exceptions to the segregation system).

Mark	Date	Mark	Date	Mark	Date	Mark	Date	Notes	
AEV	6/54	GEV	3/56	NEV	1/59	VEV	2/61	F	2/57
AHK	7/54	GHK	3/56	NHK	2/59	VHK	2/61	HK	9/57
ANO	7/54	GNO	4/56	NNO	2/59	VNO	2/61	NO	3/58 then to LPU-RNO
APU	8/54	GPU	4/56	NPU	2/59	VPU	3/61		
ATW	8/54	GTW	5/56	NTW	3/59	VTW	3/61	EV	6/59 then to SHK-SPU
AVW	9/54	GVW	5/56	NVW	3/59	VVW	3/61		
AVX	10/54	GVX	5/56	NVX	3/59	VVX	3/61	TW	11/59
BEV	10/54	HEV	6/56	PEV	3/59	WEV	3/61	VW	3/60
BHK	10/54	HHK	6/56	PHK	4/59	WHK	4/61	VX	5/60 then briefly to UEV
BNO	10/54	HNO	7/56	PNO	4/59	WNO	4/61		
BPU	12/54	HPU	7/56	PPU	4/59	WPU	4/61	PU	8/60 then to UPU-YVX
BTW	12/54	HTW	8/56	PTW	4/59	WTW	5/61		
BVW	1/55	HVW	9/56	PVW	5/59	WVW	5/61		
BVX	1/55	HVX	10/56	PVX	5/59	WVX	5/61		
CEV	2/55	JEV	10/56	REV	5/59	XEV	5/61		
CHK	2/55	JHK	11/56	RHK	6/59	XHK	5/61		
CNO	3/55	JNO	12/56	RNO	6/59	XNO	6/61		
CPU	3/55	JPU	1/57	RPU	6/59	XPU	6/61		
CTW	4/55	JTW	1/57	RTW	7/59	XTW	6/61		
CVW	4/55	JVW	2/57	RVW	7/59	XVW	6/61		
CVX	4/55	JVX	3/57	RVX	8/59	XVX	6/61		
DEV	5/55	KEV	4/57	SEV	9/59	YEV	7/61		
DHK	6/55	KHK	5/57	SHK	10/59	YHK	7/61		
DNO	6/55	KNO	6/57	SNO	11/59	YNO	7/61		
DPU	6/55	KPU	7/57	SPU	11/59	YPU	7/61		
DTW	6/55	KTW	9/57	STW	12/59	YTW	8/61		
DVW	7/55	KVW	11/57	SVW	1/60	YVW	8/61		
DVX	8/55	KVX	2/58	SVX	2/60	YVX	8/61		
EEV	8/55	LEV	4/58	TEV	3/60				
EHK	8/55	LHK	5/58	THK	3/60				
ENO	9/55	LNO	7/58	TNO	4/60				
EPU	9/55	LPU	8/58	TPU	5/60				
ETW	10/55	LTW	9/58	TTW	5/60				
EVW	10/55	LVW	10/58	TVW	6/60				
EVX	11/55	LVX	10/58	TVX	7/60				
FEV	11/55	MEV	10/58	UEV	8/60				
FHK	12/55	MHK	11/58	UHK	10/60				
FNO	12/55	MNO	11/58	UNO	10/60				
FPU	1/56	MPU	12/58	UPU	1/61				
FTW	1/56	MTW	12/58	UTW	1/61				
FVW	2/56	MVW	12/58	UVW	1/61				
FVX	2/56	MVX	1/59	UVX	1/61				

COUNTY COUNCIL OF ESSEX (continued)

Since they were rapidly running out of available marks Essex were allotted the previously unused combinations OO and WC, (the latter allocated only in three-letter combinations), by Statutory Instrument dated 1.6.61. These additional marks were used in the sequence OO, AOO to YOO, BWC to YWC (all forward), AOO to YOO, BWC to YWC (reverse). Motorcycles used OO 1-999 then AOO and BOO, while cars were in OO 1000-9999. From COO all vehicles were in a common sequence.

OO   9/61

AOO	10/61	JOO	3/62	SOO	5/62	(AWC not alloc.)		JWC	9/62	SWC	12/62
BOO	11/61	KOO	3/62	TOO	5/62	BWC	7/62	KWC	10/62	TWC	12/62
COO	1/62	LOO	4/62	UOO	6/62	CWC	7/62	LWC	10/62	(UWC not alloc.)	
DOO	2/62	MOO	4/62	VOO	6/62	DWC	8/62	MWC	10/62	VWC	1/63
EOO	2/62	NOO	4/62	WOO	6/62	EWC	8/62	NWC	10/62	WWC	1/63
FOO	2/62	OOO	4/62	XOO	6/62	FWC	8/62	OWC	11/62	XWC	1/63
GOO	3/62	POO	5/62	YOO	7/62	GWC	9/62	PWC	11/62	YWC	2/63
HOO	3/62	ROO	5/62			HWC	9/62	RWC	12/62		

AOO	*2/63*	*JOO*	*4/63*	*SOO*	*5/63*	*(AWC not alloc.)*		*JWC*	*8/63*	*SWC*	*10/63*
BOO	*2/63*	*KOO*	*4/63*	*TOO*	*5/63*	*BWC*	*6/63*	*KWC*	*8/63*	*TWC*	*10/63*
COO	*2/63*	*LOO*	*4/63*	*UOO*	*5/63*	*CWC*	*7/63*	*LWC*	*9/63*	*(UWC not alloc.)*	
DOO	*3/63*	*MOO*	*4/63*	*VOO*	*5/63*	*DWC*	*7/63*	*MWC*	*9/63*	*VWC*	*10/63*
EOO	*3/63*	*NOO*	*4/63*	*WOO*	*6/63*	*EWC*	*7/63*	*NWC*	*9/63*	*WWC*	*10/63*
FOO	*3/63*	*(OOO not issued)*		*XOO*	*6/63*	*FWC*	*7/63*	*(OWC not issued)*		*XWC*	*11/63*
GOO	*3/63*	*POO*	*4/63*	*YOO*	*6/63*	*GWC*	*8/63*	*PWC*	*9/63*	*YWC*	*11/63*
HOO	*3/63*	*ROO*	*5/63*			*HWC*	*8/63*	*RWC*	*10/63*		

Commenced suffix marks 11/63

COUNTY COUNCIL OF FLINT

A common sequence for all vehicles.

DM 12/03

First issues each year (no records are available for 1913-1928

1904	30	1909	249		1929	6283	1933	8088
1905	90	1910	285		1930	6827	1934	8482
1906	142	1911	333		1931	7294	1935	9052
1907	172	1912	402		1932	7699	1936	9606
1908	215							

ADM	7/36	EDM	5/47	JDM	5/52	NDM	12/55	SDM	9/58	WDM	5/60
BDM	2/38	FDM	7/48	KDM	7/53	ODM	9/56	TDM	3/59	XDM	10/60
CDM	9/39	GDM	10/49	LDM	6/54	PDM	6/57	UDM	9/59	YDM	3/61
DDM	12/44	HDM	2/51	MDM	4/55	RDM	2/58	VDM	2/60		

ADM	*6/61*	*CDM*	*3/62*	*EDM*	*11/62*	*GDM*	*7/63*	*JDM*	*2/64*
BDM	*11/61*	*DDM*	*7/62*	*FDM*	*3/63*	*HDM*	*10/63*		

Commenced suffix marks 2.3.64

COUNTY COUNCIL OF GLAMORGAN

Registration commenced 22.12.03.

L 12/03   NY 8/21   TX 1/26   TG 7/30

Originally a common sequence for all vehicles, but when a separate register for Heavy Motor Cars was set up in 6/05 they were allotted L 500 to 600. However, in 5/08 L 521-600 were reallocated to motorcycles and thereafter there were distinct number blocks for motor cars, motorcycles and heavy motor cars.   Motorcycle blocks were L 521-600, 1400-1499, 1700-1899, 2000-2199, 2400-2699, 2800-2999, 3200-3599, 3800-3999, 4100-4300, 4401-4700, 4901-5000, 5101-5400, 5501-5800, 6101-6300, 6701-7000, 7201-7500, 7701-7900, 8301-8400, 8601-8639; the heavy motor car blocks were L 500-520, 1100-1199, 5001-5100, 6301-6500, 8101-8162.   (There is some evidence of segregation in TX and TG, but on the "odds and evens" principle - details are lacking).

First issues each year (no information available for 1922 - 1928) :

L

	All Vehicles	HMCs	Cycles		Motor Cars	HMCs	Cycles
1904	52 *			1913	1946	1115	2006
1905	400			1914	2358	1126	2532
	Motor Cars			1915	3139	1138	3315
1906	665	506		1916	4017	1148	3948
1907	868	512		1917	4530	1175	4268
1908	1020	520		1918	4530 **	1188	4496
1909	1214	1102	556	1919	4701	1199	4540
1910	1306	1103	1400	1920	5963	6348	5790
1911	1500	1107	1441	1921	8587 #	8163 #	8640 #
1912	1601	1108	1700	(NY 5453 issued 1/24)			

* L 1, 2 and 9 were late issues, 10/08, 4/05 and 5/05 respectively; L100-3, 105 and 111 were allocated 1903.
** All new cars during 1917 appear to have received reissued void numbers.
# These numbers are actually one higher than the last 1920 numbers; it is believed that the unused portions of the three blocks were used from 1.1.21 for all vehicles.

1929	TX 6537	1931	TG 897	1933	TG 4555	1935	TG 9120
1930	TX 8701	1932	TG 2667	1934	TG 6631		

Three-letter marks commenced in the order ANY, ATX, ATG, but thereafter were alphabetical.

ANY	4/35	ENY	3/39	JNY	1/49	NNY	5/53	SNY	7/55	WNY	6/57
ATX	7/35	ETG	6/39	JTG	5/49	NTG	8/53	STG	9/55	WTG	8/57
ATG	12/35	ETX	3/40	JTX	10/49	NTX	11/53	STX	11/55	WTX	10/57
BNY	4/36	FNY	8/42	KNY	3/50	ONY	2/54	TNY	1/56	XNY	11/57
BTG	7/36	FTG	2/45	KTG	7/50	OTG	4/54	TTG	3/56	XTG	1/58
BTX	12/36	FTX	5/46	KTX	1/51	OTX	6/54	TTX	4/56	XTX	3/58
CNY	3/37	GNY	10/46	LNY	5/51	PNY	8/54	UNY	6/56	YNY	4/58
CTG	6/37	GTG	2/47	LTG	10/51	PTG	10/54	UTG	8/56	YTG	6/58
CTX	10/37	GTX	6/47	LTX	3/52	PTX	12/54	UTX	11/56	YTX	7/58
DNY	3/38	HNY	10/47	MNY	7/52	RNY	3/55	VNY	2/57		
DTG	7/38	HTG	4/48	MTG	11/52	RTG	4/55	VTG	3/57		
DTX	12/38	HTX	8/48	MTX	3/53	RTX	5/55	VTX	5/57		

COUNTY COUNCIL OF GLAMORGAN (continued)

ANY	9/58	ENY	11/59	JNY	11/60	NNY	1/62	TNY	3/63	XNY	2/64
ATG	10/58	ETG	12/59	JTG	12/60	NTG	2/62	TTG	4/63	XTG	3/64
ATX	11/58	ETX	1/60	JTX	1/61	NTX	4/62	TTX	5/63	XTX	4/64
BNY	1/59	FNY	2/60	KNY	3/61	PNY	5/62	UNY	5/63	YNY	9/65 *
BTG	2/59	FTG	3/60	KTG	3/61	PTG	5/62	UTG	6/63	YTG	ca/78 *#
BTX	3/59	FTX	4/60	KTX	4/61	PTX	6/62	UTX	7/63		
CNY	4/59	GNY	4/60	LNY	5/61	RNY	7/62	VNY	8/63		
CTG	5/59	GTG	5/60	LTG	6/61	RTG	9/62	VTG	9/63		
CTX	6/59	GTX	6/60	LTX	7/61	RTX	10/62	VTX	10/63		
DNY	7/59	HNY	7/60	MNY	8/61	SNY	11/62	WNY	11/63		
DTG	9/59	HTG	8/60	MTG	10/61	STG	1/63	WTG	12/63		
DTX	10/59	HTX	9/60	MTX	11/61	STX	2/63	WTX	1/64		

* Re-registrations only.   # Commenced by Cardiff LVLO.

Commenced suffix marks 1.5.64

COUNTY COUNCIL OF GLOUCESTER

A common sequence for all vehicles.

AD 12/03   DD 9/21   DF 6/26   DG 4/30 (DG 1 early, 12/29)

First issues each year :

1904	AD	148	1911	AD	1710	1918	AD	5083	1925	DD	6008	1932	DG 3740
1905	AD	424	1912	AD	2134	1919	AD	5401	1926	DD	8659	1933	DG 5840
1906	AD	622	1913	AD	2800	1920	AD	6472	1927	DF	1433	1934	DG 8184
1907	AD	820	1914	AD	3507	1921	AD	8461	1928	DF	4131		
1908	AD	1040	1915	AD	4209	1922	DD	236	1929	DF	6613		
1909	AD	1247	1916	AD	4481	1923	no record		1930	DF	9260		
1910	AD	1471	1917	AD	4818	1924	DD	3679	1931	DG	1749		

AAD	9/34	EAD	7/39	JAD	11/48	NAD	8/53	SAD	4/56	WAD	9/58
ADD	1/35	EDD	1/40	JDD	3/49	NDD	10/53	SDD	6/56	WDD	11/58
ADF	5/35	EDF	1/41	JDF	7/49	NDF	1/54	SDF	8/56	WDF	12/58
ADG	9/35	EDG	2/42	JDG	10/49	NDG	3/54	SDG	10/56	WDG	2/59
BAD	12/35	FAD	2/43	KAD	3/50	OAD	5/54	TAD	1/57	XAD	3/59
BDD	3/36	FDD	9/44	KDD	6/50	ODD	7/54	TDD	3/57	XDD	4/59
BDF	7/36	FDF	1/46	KDF	10/50	ODF	10/54	TDF	5/57	XDF	6/59
BDG	11/36	FDG	6/46	KDG	2/51	ODG	12/54	TDG	7/57	XDG	7/59
CAD	2/37	GAD	9/46	LAD	5/51	PAD	2/55	UAD	9/57	YAD	8/59
CDD	4/37	GDD	12/46	LDD	9/51	PDD	4/55	UDD	11/57	YDD	9/59
CDF	9/37	GDF	3/47	LDF	1/52	PDF	5/55	UDF	1/58	YDF	11/59
CDG	12/37	GDG	5/47	LDG	5/52	PDG	7/55	UDG	3/58	YDG	12/59
DAD	4/38	HAD	8/47	MAD	8/52	RAD	8/55	VAD	4/58		
DDD	8/38	HDD	12/47	MDD	11/52	RDD	10/55	VDD	6/58		
DDF	12/38	HDF	4/48	MDF	2/53	RDF	12/55	VDF	7/58		
DDG	4/39	HDG	7/48	MDG	5/53	RDG	2/56	VDG not issued *			

* allotted by S.I., but omitted at request of motor traders.

In the early years of three-letter marks low numbers were frequently issued ahead of the main series. Examples are : ADG 1 (8/35), BDG 1 (6/36), CDF 1 (3/37), DDD 1 (3/38), EDD 2 (5/39).

COUNTY COUNCIL OF GLOUCESTER (continued)

In the reverse series *AD* for cars and *AAD* for motorcycles were issued simultaneously; thereafter cars continued in two-letter series and motorcycles in three letters.

AD (from 100)	1/60	AAD	1/60	BAD	7/62
DD (from 100)	4/61	ADD	6/60	BDD	7/63
DF (from 601)	7/62	ADF	2/61		
DG (from 601)	8/63	ADG	8/61		

Commenced suffix marks 3.2.64

COUNTY COUNCIL OF HEREFORD

A common sequence for all vehicles.

Registration commenced 1.1.04.

CJ   1/04   VJ   6/27

First issues each year :

1905	CJ	172	1917	CJ	2483	1929	VJ	1423
1906	CJ	251	1918	CJ	2567	1930	VJ	2386
1907	CJ	348	1919	CJ	2635	1931	VJ	3320
1908	CJ	455	1920	CJ	3158	1932	VJ	4124
1909	CJ	560	1921	CJ	4052	1933	VJ	4912
1910	CJ	668	1922	CJ	4845	1934	VJ	5799
1911	CJ	814	1923	CJ	5524	1935	VJ	6880
1912	CJ	1005	1924	CJ	6401	1936	VJ	8223
1913	CJ	1232	1925	CJ	7447	1937	VJ	9569
1914	CJ	1584	1926	CJ	8547			
1915	CJ	1966	1927	CJ	9467			
1916	CJ	2288	1928	VJ	528			

ACJ	4/37	ECJ	11/46	JCJ	7/51	NCJ	7/55	SCJ	7/58	WCJ	5/60
AVJ	1/38	EVJ	5/47	JVJ	4/52	NVJ	11/55	SVJ	10/58	WVJ	7/60
BCJ	10/38	FCJ	12/47	KCJ	11/52	OCJ	4/56	TCJ	1/59	XCJ	10/60
BVJ	7/39	FVJ	6/48	KVJ	6/53	OVJ	9/56	TVJ	4/59	XVJ	2/61
CCJ	1/41	GCJ	1/49	LCJ	1/54	PCJ	3/57	UCJ	6/59	YCJ	4/61
CVJ	8/42	GVJ	8/49	LVJ	5/54	PVJ	7/57	UVJ	9/59	YVJ	6/61
DCJ	7/44	HCJ	4/50	MCJ	10/54	RCJ	11/57	VCJ	12/59		
DVJ	4/46	HVJ	11/50	MVJ	3/55	RVJ	3/58	VVJ	3/60		

ACJ	9/61	BCJ	4/62	CCJ	10/62	DCJ	4/63	ECJ	9/63
AVJ	1/62	BVJ	6/62	CVJ	2/63	DVJ	6/63	EVJ	12/63

Commenced suffix marks 2.1.64

COUNTY COUNCIL OF HERTFORD

Registration commenced 16.12.03.

A common sequence for all vehicles.

AR 12/03   NK 1/21   RO 4/25   UR 3/28   JH 6/31

First issues each year : (no information available 1911-1928).

1904	AR 130	1929	UR 1878
1905	AR 684	1930	UR 5395
1906	AR 961	1931	UR 8443
1907	AR 1227	1932	JH 1069
1908	AR 1446	1933	JH 3734
1909	AR 1636	1934	JH 6719
1910	AR 1903		

Hertfordshire registered large numbers of vehicles belonging to the London, Midland and Scottish Railway and their successors, British Railways, (London Midland Region), whose road motor headquarters was at Watford. During the three-letter era it was the practice to allocate complete series to the railway company, starting with ANK which was commenced while JH was still current for normal issues.

											LMS/BR	
AAR	12/34	FAR	6/39	(LAR = BR)		RAR	11/53	WAR	12/55		ANK	6/34
AJH	3/35	FJH	9/39	LJH	8/49	RJH	12/53	WJH	1/56		BNK	3/36
(ANK = LMS)		FNK	5/40	LNK	11/49	(RNK = BR)		WNK	2/56		CNK	5/38
ARO	5/35	FRO	11/41	LRO	1/50	RRO	2/54	WRO	2/56		GAR	4/40
AUR	8/35	FUR	3/43	LUR	4/50	RUR	3/54	WUR	3/56		GRO	6/45
BAR	11/35	(GAR = LMS)		MAR	6/50	SAR	4/54	XAR	4/56		JJH	7/47
BJH	2/36	GJH	3/45	MJH	10/50	SJH	5/54	XJH	5/56		LAR	8/49
(BNK = LMS)		GNK	2/46	MNK	12/50	SNK	6/54	XNK	6/56		OAR	7/51
BRO	4/36	(GRO = LMS)		MRO	2/51	SRO	7/54	XRO	7/56		RNK	2/53
BUR	6/36	GUR	6/46	MUR	5/51	SUR	2/54	XUR	8/56		SUR	2/54
CAR	8/36	HAR	9/46	NAR	7/51	TAR	9/54	YAR	9/56		WRO	2/56
CJH	11/36	HJH	11/46	NJH	9/51	TJH	10/54	YJH	10/56			
(CNK = LMS)		HNK	1/47	NNK	11/51	TNK	11/54	YNK	12/56			
CRO	1/37	HRO	4/47	NRO	2/52	TRO	12/54	YRO	1/57			
CUR	3/37	HUR	6/47	NUR	4/52	TUR	2/55	YUR	2/57			
DAR	5/37	JAR	8/47	(OAR = BR)		UAR	3/55					
DJH	7/37	(JJH = BR)		OJH	6/52	UJH	3/55					
DNK	10/37	JNK	11/47	ONK	9/52	UNK	4/55					
DRO	1/38	JRO	2/48	ORO	11/52	URO	5/55					
DUR	3/38	JUR	5/48	OUR	1/53	UUR	6/55					
EAR	5/38	KAR	7/48	PAR	3/53	VAR	7/55					
EJH	8/38	KJH	11/48	PJH	4/53	VJH	8/55					
ENK	11/38	KNK	2/49	PNK	6/53	VNK	9/55					
ERO	2/39	KRO	4/49	PRO	7/53	VRO	10/55					
EUR	4/39	KUR	7/49	PUR	9/53	VUR	11/55					

Commenced reverse issues with three-letter marks for all vehicles, AAR to HNK. (HRO issued early for BR). Then cars etc, used two-letter marks AR, JH, NK, RO and UR while motorcycles continued in three-letter marks from HUR onward. After completion of UR cars rejoined cycles in late KUR.
(There were exceptions to the segregation system, e.g. JH contains motorcycles below 1000).

COUNTY COUNCIL OF HERTFORD (continued)

All Vehicles		Motorcycles		Cars etc.		All Vehicles		B.R.	
AAR	3/57	HUR	8/59	AR (from 1000)	8/59	LAR	5/62	HRO	7/58
AJH	4/57	JAR	11/59	JH (from 1)	3/60	LJH	5/62	PRO	2/61
ANK	5/57	JJH	3/60	NK (from 1000)	9/60	LNK	6/62		
ARO	6/57	JNK	5/60	RO (from 1000)	2/61	LRO	6/62		
AUR	7/57	JRO	7/60	UR (from 500)	9/61	LUR	6/62		
BAR	8/57	JUR	10/60			MAR	7/62		
BJH	9/57	KAR	2/61			MJH	7/62		
BNK	10/57	KJH	5/61			MNK	9/62		
BRO	11/57	KNK	6/61			MRO	10/62		
BUR	12/57	KRO	9/61			MUR	10/62		
CAR	1/58	KUR	2/62			NAR	10/62		
CJH	2/58					NJH	11/62		
CNK	3/58					NNK	11/62		
CRO	4/58					NRO	12/62		
CUR	4/58					NUR	12/62		
DAR	5/58					PAR	2/63		
DJH	6/58					PJH	3/63		
DNK	6/58					PNK	3/63		
DRO	7/58					(PRO = BR)			
DUR	8/58					PUR	3/63		
EAR	9/58					RAR	4/63		
EJH	10/58					RJH	4/63		
ENK	11/58					RNK	4/63		
ERO	11/58					RRO	5/63		
EUR	11/58					RUR	5/63		
FAR	12/58					SAR	5/63		
FJH	1/59					SJH	6/63		
FNK	2/59					SNK	6/63		
FRO	3/59					SRO	6/63		
FUR	3/59					SUR	6/63		
GAR	4/59					TAR	7/63		
GJH	5/59					TJH	7/63		
GNK	5/59					TNK	8/63		
GRO	5/59					TRO	8/63		
GUR	6/59					TUR	9/63		
HAR	7/59					UAR	9/63		
HJH	7/59					UJH	10/63		
HNK	7/59					UNK	10/63		
						URO	11/63		
						UUR	11/63		
						VAR	12/63		
						VJH	12/63		
						VNK	1/64		
						VRO	1/64		
						VUR	2/64		
						WAR	2/64		
						WJH	2/64 #		
						WNK	1/67 *		
						XAR	3/71 **		

\# Mainly re-registrations.

* Re-registrations only; mainly from 12/74, but 1 and 2 early (1/67, 11/68 respectively).

** Re-registrations only; only 1 and 2 XAR issued.

Commenced suffix marks 2.3.64

COUNTY COUNCIL OF HUNTINGDON

EW   1/04

Approximate first issues each year : (no information prior to 1929) :

1929	5800	1931	6800	1933	7600	1935	8565	1936	9100	1937	9900
1930	6300	1932	7200	1934	8050						

AEW	3/37	EEW	7/46	(JEW not alloc.)		NEW	3/54	SEW	1/57	WEW	5/59
BEW	5/38	FEW	7/47	KEW	3/51	OEW	1/55	TEW	9/57	XEW	11/59
CEW	1/40	GEW	9/48	LEW	5/52	PEW	9/55	UEW	5/58	YEW	3/60
DEW	3/43	HEW	1/50	MEW	5/53	REW	4/56	VEW	1/59		

AEW	7/60	CEW	4/61	EEW	3/62	GEW	1/63	(JEW not alloc.)		LEW	1/64
BEW	11/60	DEW	9/61	FEW	8/62	HEW	5/63	KEW	9/63	MEW	5/64

Suffix marks commenced 1.7.64

I am directed by the Minister of Transport to state that it is understood that considerable numbers of vehicles are being released by the Army for other Government and civilian use. Where such vehicles were registered in the ordinary way before the Army took them over this information will be specified when the vehicle is released by the Army and the registration book, if available, handed over. This should obviate difficulty when the vehicles are relicensed with a local taxation office; the original identification mark should of course again be carried, (except where a department such as the Air Ministry allots its own mark on taking over a vehicles.) If difficulty should arise owing to missing particulars of previous registration; enquiry may be made, specifying the War Department number of the vehicle and its make and type to the War Office.   There may be a few cases where a previous registration cannot be traced, in which event a new registration will be necessary; duplicate books may be required where the old book cannot be obtained and may be issued free of charge. New registration will of course be required for vehicles which had not been registered before being taken over by the Army".   *Circular RVL 10/33, 22.3.41.*

COUNTY COUNCIL OF KENT

A common sequence for all vehicles.

D 12/03	KN 8/17	KK 6/22	KM 9/25	KP 5/28	KJ 3/31
KT 6/13	KE 7/20	KL 5/24	KO 2/27	KR 10/29	

First issues each year :

1904	D 481	1910	D 4900	1916	KT 7206	1922	KE 7619	1928	KO 6576
1905	D 1677	1911	D 5851	1917	KT 9135	1923	KK 2289	1929	KP 3846
1906	D 2281	1912	D 7091	1918	KN 585	1924	KK 7713	1930	KR 1274
1907	D 2936	1913	D 8805	1919	KN 1776	1925	KL 4026	1931	KR 8437
1908	D 3579	1914	KT 1023	1920	KN 6097	1926	KM 1473	1932	KJ 4530
1909	D 4173	1915	KT 3915	1921	KE 1901 *	1927	KM 8946		

* 1920 finished at KE 1827; 1828-1900 not issued.

AKE	11/32	AKN	7/33	BKE	4/34	BKN	12/34
AKJ	1/33	AKO	10/33	BKJ	5/34	BKO	1/35
AKK	3/33	AKP	12/33	BKK	6/34	BKP	2/35
AKL	4/33	AKR	1/34	BKL	8/34		
AKM	6/33	AKT	3/34	BKM	10/34		

From 3/35 three separate sequences were in use concurrently, described as "Reserve Numbers", "Private Cars" and "Other than Private Cars". (The precise definition of "Reserve Numbers" is obscure). Note that EKJ preceded EKE and that the Gxx combinations were issued out of sequence.

Reserve Numbers (Any type of Vehicle)		Not Reserved (Private Cars only)		Not Reserved (other than Cars)	
CKE	3/35	BKR	3/35	BKT	3/35
CKJ	6/35	CKK	7/35	CKL	8/35
CKM	10/35	CKN	11/35	CKP	3/36
CKO	12/35	CKR	3/36	DKK	7/36
CKT	3/36	DKJ	6/36	DKP	1/37
DKE	5/36	DKM	10/36	EKK	6/37
DKL	8/36	DKR	2/37	EKP	12/37
DKN	10/36	EKE	6/37	FKK	6/38
DKO	12/36	EKN	10/37	FKR	3/39
DKT	3/37	FKE	3/38	GKO	8/39
EKJ	4/37	FKM	9/38	GKM	5/40
EKL	6/37	FKP	2/39		
EKM	9/37	GKJ	6/39 (fin. 11/42)	(GKM completed 5/41 - this	
EKO	11/37			group then joined column 2	
EKR	1/38			in GKJ)	
EKT	3/38				
FKJ	6/38				
FKL	8/38				
FKN	11/38				
FKO	1/39				
FKT	3/39				
GKE	4/39				
GKK	6/39				
GKL	9/39				
GKR	6/41				
GKT	2/42				

(GKT completed 10/42 - this group then joined column 2 in GKJ.)

COUNTY COUNCIL OF KENT (continued)

From 11/42 there was a reversion to a single sequence; then from 1/46 a resumption of segregation, but this time into only two categories : "Reserve Block" and "Not Reserved", both groups encompassing any type of vehicle. This continued until 9/48; thereafter a single sequence was resumed.

Single Sequence		Reserved		Not Reserved	
GKN	11/42	HKL	1/46	HKM	1/46
GKP	9/43	HKN	3/46	HKP	5/46
HKE	7/44	HKO	6/46	HKT	8/46
HKJ	4/45	HKR	8/46	JKJ	10/46
HKK	10/45	JKE	10/46	JKL	12/46
		JKK	12/46	JKN	2/47
		JKM	2/47	JKP	5/47
		JKO	4/47	JKT	7/47
		JKR	6/47	KKJ	9/47
		KKE	8/47	KKL	12/47
		KKK	11/47	KKN	3/48
		KKM	1/48	KKP	5/48
		KKO	4/48	KKT	7/48 (Fin. 9/48)
		KKR	6/48		

(KKR completed 31.8.48, then joined "Not Reserved" in KKT.)

Single Sequence

LKE	9/48	NKN	2/51	RKE	3/53	TKN	9/54	WKE	10/55	YKN	12/56
LKJ	11/48	NKO	3/51	RKJ	4/53	TKO	10/54	WKJ	10/55	YKO	1/57
LKK	12/48	NKP	4/51	RKK	5/53	TKP	10/54	WKK	10/55	YKP	2/57
LKL	1/49	NKR	5/51	RKL	6/53	TKR	11/54	WKL	11/55	YKR	2/57
LKM	3/49	NKT	6/51	RKM	6/53	TKT	11/54	WKM	12/55	YKT	3/57
LKN	4/49	OKE	7/51	RKN	7/53	UKE	12/54	WKN	12/55		
LKO	5/49	OKJ	8/51	RKO	8/53	UKJ	1/55	WKO	1/56		
LKP	6/49	OKK	9/51	RKP	9/53	UKK	1/55	WKP	1/56		
LKR	7/49	OKL	10/51	RKR	10/53	UKL	2/55	WKR	2/56		
LKT	8/49	OKM	11/51	RKT	10/53	UKM	2/55	WKT	3/56		
MKE	9/49	OKN	1/52	SKE	11/53	UKN	3/55	XKE	3/56		
MKJ	10/49	OKO	2/52	SKJ	12/53	UKO	3/55	XKJ	3/56		
MKK	11/49	OKP	3/52	SKK	1/54	UKP	4/55	XKK	4/56		
MKL	1/50	OKR	4/52	SKL	1/54	UKR	4/55	XKL	5/56		
MKM	2/50	OKT	5/52	SKM	2/54	UKT	5/55	XKM	5/56		
MKN	3/50	PKE	6/52	SKN	3/54	VKE	5/55	XKN	5/56		
MKO	4/50	PKJ	7/52	SKO	3/54	VKJ	5/55	XKO	6/56		
MKP	5/50	PKK	8/52	SKP	4/54	VKK	6/55	XKP	7/56		
MKR	6/50	PKL	9/52	SKR	4/54	VKL	6/55	XKR	7/56		
MKT	7/50	PKM	10/52	SKT	5/54	VKM	7/55	XKT	8/56		
NKE	8/50	PKN	11/52	TKE	6/54	VKN	7/55	YKE	9/56		
NKJ	9/50	PKO	12/52	TKJ	6/54	VKO	8/55	YKJ	9/56		
NKK	10/50	PKP	1/53	TKK	7/54	VKP	8/55	YKK	10/56		
NKL	11/50	PKR	2/53	TKL	7/54	VKR	9/55	YKL	11/56		
NKM	1/51	PKT	3/53	TKM	8/54	VKT	9/55	YKM	11/56		

COUNTY COUNCIL OF KENT (continued)

AKE	3/57	EKE	10/58	JKE	12/59	NKE	1/61	TKE	3/62	XKE	4/63
AKJ	4/57	EKJ	11/58	JKJ	12/59	NKJ	2/61	TKJ	3/62	XKJ	4/63
AKK	4/57	EKK	11/58	JKK	1/60	NKK	2/61	TKK	4/62	XKK	5/63
AKL	4/57	EKL	11/58	JKL	1/60	NKL	2/61	TKL	4/62	XKL	5/63
AKM	5/57	EKM	12/58	JKM	1/60	NKM	3/61	TKM	4/62	XKM	5/63
AKN	5/57	EKN	12/58	JKN	2/60	NKN	3/61	TKN	4/62	XKN	5/63
AKO	6/57	EKO	1/59	JKO	2/60	NKO	3/61	TKO	5/62	XKO	5/63
AKP	6/57	EKP	1/59	JKP	2/60	NKP	3/61	TKP	5/62	XKP	6/63
AKR	7/57	EKR	2/59	JKR	3/60	NKR	4/61	TKR	5/62	XKR	6/63
AKT	7/57	EKT	2/59	JKT	3/60	NKT	4/61	TKT	6/62	XKT	6/63
BKE	8/57	FKE	3/59	KKE	3/60	PKE	4/61	UKE	6/62	YKE	6/63
BKJ	8/57	FKJ	3/59	KKJ	3/60	PKJ	5/61	UKJ	6/62	YKJ	7/63
BKK	9/57	FKK	3/59	KKK	4/60	PKK	5/61	UKK	7/62	YKK	7/63
BKL	9/57	FKL	3/59	KKL	4/60	PKL	5/61	UKL	7/62	YKL	7/63
BKM	10/57	FKM	4/59	KKM	4/60	PKM	5/61	UKM	7/62	YKM	7/63
BKN	10/57	FKN	4/59	KKN	4/60	PKN	6/61	UKN	8/62	YKN	8/63
BKO	11/57	FKO	4/59	KKO	5/60	PKO	6/61	UKO	8/62	YKO	8/63
BKP	12/57	FKP	4/59	KKP	5/60	PKP	6/61	UKP	8/62	YKP	8/63
BKR	12/57	FKR	5/59	KKR	5/60	PKR	6/61	UKR	9/62	YKR	9/63
BKT	1/58	FKT	5/59	KKT	5/60	PKT	7/61	UKT	9/62	YKT	9/63
CKE	2/58	GKE	5/59	LKE	6/60	RKE	7/61	VKE	10/62		
CKJ	2/58	GKJ	6/59	LKJ	6/60	RKJ	7/61	VKJ	10/62		
CKK	3/58	GKK	6/59	LKK	6/60	RKK	7/61	VKK	10/62		
CKL	3/58	GKL	6/59	LKL	7/60	RKL	8/61	VKL	11/62		
CKM	3/58	GKM	6/59	LKM	7/60	RKM	8/61	VKM	11/62		
CKN	4/58	GKN	7/59	LKN	7/60	RKN	9/61	VKN	11/62		
CKO	4/58	GKO	7/59	LKO	8/60	RKO	9/61	VKO	12/62		
CKP	5/58	GKP	7/59	LKP	8/60	RKP	9/61	VKP	12/62		
CKR	5/58	GKR	8/59	LKR	8/60	RKR	10/61	VKR	1/63		
CKT	5/58	GKT	8/59	LKT	9/60	RKT	10/61	VKT	1/63		
DKE	6/58	HKE	9/59	MKE	9/60	SKE	11/61	WKE	1/63		
DKJ	6/58	HKJ	9/59	MKJ	9/60	SKJ	11/61	WKJ	2/63		
DKK	7/58	HKK	9/59	MKK	10/60	SKK	12/61	WKK	2/63		
DKL	7/58	HKL	10/59	MKL	10/60	SKL	12/61	WKL	2/63		
DKM	7/58	HKM	10/59	MKM	11/60	SKM	1/62	WKM	3/63		
DKN	8/58	HKN	10/59	MKN	11/60	SKN	1/62	WKN	3/63		
DKO	9/58	HKO	11/59	MKO	11/60	SKO	1/62	WKO	3/63		
DKP	9/58	HKP	11/59	MKP	12/60	SKP	2/62	WKP	3/63		
DKR	10/58	HKR	11/59	MKR	12/60	SKR	2/62	WKR	4/63		
DKT	10/58	HKT	12/59	MKT	1/61	SKT	3/62	WKT	4/63		

There was no segregation of motorcycles in two-letter reverse marks. (All commencing at 1, but 1 D was cancelled after allocation and not issued).

KM	9/63	KO	12/63	KP	3/64	KR	5/64	D	7/64

Commenced suffix marks 1.9.64

COUNTY COUNCIL OF LANCASTER

B 12/03   TB 11/19   TC 5/22   TD 12/24   TE 4/27   TF 12/29   TJ 11/32

Until 1921 separate blocks of numbers were allotted to (a) motor cars, (b) motorcycles and (c) heavy motor cars.

Motorcycle blocks were B 501-1000, 1501-2000, 2501-3000, 3501-4000, 4501-5000, 6501-7000, 7501-8500, 9501-9999, TB 501-1000, 1501-2000, 3501 up.

Heavy motor cars were B 2001-2500, 5501-6000, 8501-9000, TB 1001-1500, TB 2501 up.

The remaining numbers being used for motor cars. From ca. TB 2680 and 3656 remaining numbers in the heavy motor car and motorcycle blocks were used for all classes from early 1921.

Last issues in 1920 were ca. TB 2630, 3300 and 3530.

First issues each year : (no information available prior to 1921). [There was considerable overlapping at year ends and this was further complicated by the fact that from TF onwards two separate blocks were in simultaneous use. The list therefore actually shows the next number after the highest issued in the previous year.]

1921	TB 3530	1924	TC 6044	1927	TD 8453	1930	TF 325	1933	TJ 469
1922	TB 8003	1925	TD 264	1928	TE 2417	1931	TF 3924	1934	TJ 3873
1923	TC 1919	1926	TD 4394	1929	TE 6206	1932	TF 7330	1935	TJ 8435

ATB	5/35	ETB	4/39	JTB	11/47	NTB	4/51	STB	12/53	WTB	6/55
ATC	7/35	ETC	5/39	JTC	1/48	NTC	5/51	STC	1/54	WTC	7/55
ATD	10/35	ETD	7/39	JTD	3/48	NTD	7/51	STD	2/54	WTD	8/55
ATE	12/35	ETE	9/39	JTE	5/48	NTE	9/51	STE	3/54	WTE	9/55
ATF	2/36	ETF	3/40	JTF	7/48	NTF	11/51	STF	4/54	WTF	9/55
ATJ	4/36	ETJ	7/40	JTJ	9/48	NTJ	1/52	STJ	4/54	WTJ	10/55
BTB	6/36	FTB	9/41	KTB	11/48	OTB	3/52	TTB	5/54	XTB	10/55
BTC	7/36	FTC	5/42	KTC	12/48	OTC	4/52	TTC	6/54	XTC	11/55
BTD	10/36	FTD	3/43	KTD	2/49	OTD	5/52	TTD	7/54	XTD	12/55
BTE	12/36	FTE	2/44	KTE	4/49	OTE	7/52	TTE	8/54	XTE	1/56
BTF	2/37	FTF	2/45	KTF	5/49	OTF	9/52	TTF	8/54	XTF	2/56
BTJ	3/37	FTJ	10/45	KTJ	7/49	OTJ	10/52	TTJ	9/54	XTJ	2/56
CTB	5/37	GTB	2/46	LTB	9/49	PTB	12/52	UTB	10/54	YTB	3/56
CTC	7/37	GTC	5/46	LTC	10/49	PTC	1/53	UTC	11/54	YTC	4/56
CTD	9/37	GTD	7/46	LTD	12/49	PTD	3/53	UTD	12/54	YTD	4/56
CTE	11/37	GTE	9/46	LTE	2/50	PTE	4/53	UTE	1/55	YTE	5/56
CTF	1/38	GTF	10/46	LTF	3/50	PTF	5/53	UTF	2/55	YTF	6/56
CTJ	3/38	GTJ	12/46	LTJ	5/50	PTJ	5/53	UTJ	2/55	YTJ	6/56
DTB	4/38	HTB	1/47	MTB	6/50	RTB	6/53	VTB	3/55		
DTC	6/38	HTC	3/47	MTC	8/50	RTC	7/53	VTC	3/55		
DTD	8/38	HTD	5/47	MTD	9/50	RTD	8/53	VTD	4/55		
DTE	11/38	HTE	6/47	MTE	11/50	RTE	9/53	VTE	5/55		
DTF	1/39	HTF	8/47	MTF	1/51	RTF	10/53	VTF	5/55		
DTJ	3/39	HTJ	10/47	MTJ	2/51	RTJ	11/53	VTJ	6/55		

Lancashire was one of the authorities which overlooked the MoT's instruction that reverse Oxx combinations should not be issued. The error was acknowledged after OTB had been completed and OTC had reached 444.

COUNTY COUNCIL OF LANCASTER

ATB	7/56	ETB	1/58	JTB	3/59	NTB	3/60	STB	10/60	WTB	8/61
ATC	8/56	ETC	2/58	JTC	4/59	NTC	3/60	STC	11/60	WTC	9/61
ATD	9/56	ETD	3/58	JTD	4/59	NTD	3/60	STD	12/60	WTD	9/61
ATE	10/56	ETE	3/58	JTE	5/59	NTE	4/60	STE	12/60	WTE	10/61
ATF	11/56	ETF	4/58	JTF	5/59	NTF	4/60	STF	1/61	WTF	10/61
ATJ	12/56	ETJ	4/58	JTJ	5/59	NTJ	4/60	STJ	1/61	WTJ	11/61
BTB	1/57	FTB	5/58	KTB	6/59	OTB	5/60	TTB	2/61	XTB	11/61
BTC	2/57	FTC	5/58	KTC	6/59	OTC	5/60	TTC	2/61	XTC	12/61
BTD	3/57	FTD	6/58	KTD	7/59			TTD	2/61	XTD	1/62
BTE	3/57	FTE	6/58	KTE	7/59			TTE	3/61	XTE	1/62
BTF	4/57	FTF	7/58	KTF	8/59			TTF	3/61	XTF	2/62
BTJ	4/57	FTJ	8/58	KTJ	8/59			TTJ	3/61	XTJ	2/62
CTB	5/57	GTB	8/58	LTB	9/59	PTB	5/60	UTB	4/61	YTB	3/62
CTC	5/57	GTC	9/58	LTC	9/59	PTC	5/60	UTC	4/61	YTC	3/62
CTD	6/57	GTD	10/58	LTD	10/59	PTD	6/60	UTD	4/61	YTD	3/62
CTE	7/57	GTE	10/58	LTE	10/59	PTE	6/60	UTE	5/61	YTE	4/62
CTF	7/57	GTF	11/58	LTF	11/59	PTF	7/60	UTF	5/61	YTF	4/62
CTJ	8/57	GTJ	11/58	LTJ	11/59	PTJ	7/60	UTJ	5/61	YTJ	5/62
DTB	9/57	HTB	12/58	MTB	12/59	RTB	7/60	VTB	6/61		
DTC	9/57	HTC	1/59	MTC	12/59	RTC	8/60	VTC	6/61		
DTD	10/57	HTD	1/59	MTD	1/60	RTD	8/60	VTD	6/61 ·		
DTE	11/57	HTE	2/59	MTE	1/60	RTE	9/60	VTE	7/61		
DTF	12/57	HTF	3/59	MTF	2/60	RTF	9/60	VTF	7/61		
DTJ	12/57	HTJ	3/59	MTJ	2/60	RTJ	10/60	VTJ	7/61		

There was no segregation of motorcycles in reverse two-letter series and all commenced from 1.

TD 5/62   TE 10/62   TF 2/63   TJ 5/63

Commenced suffix marks 1.9.63

115

COUNTY COUNCIL OF LEICESTER

A common sequence for all vehicles.

AY 12/03   NR 3/21   UT 1/27   JU 1/32

In AY motorcycles took odd numbers and cars etc. even numbers. AY 9998 was reached 3/21 and NR started for cars, but motorcycles did not reach AY 9999 until 3/22

First issues each year :

	Cars		Cycles			Cars		Cycles			All Vehicles	
1904	AY	98	AY	109		1914	AY 3186	AY 2635		1929	UT 4217	
1905	AY	222	AY	381		1915	AY 3988	AY 3517		1930	UT 6290	
1906	AY	380	AY	551		1916	AY 4976	AY 4349		1931	UT 8186	
1907	AY	526	AY	643		1917	AY 5530	AY 4791		1932	UT 9945	
1908	AY	742	AY	731		1918	AY 5852	AY 4937		1933	JU 1635	
1909	AY	968	AY	861		1919	AY 6054	AY 5011		1934	JU 3451	
1910	AY 1226		AY	951		1920	AY 7156	AY 6379		1935	JU 5288	
1911	AY 1550		AY 1161			1921	AY 9402	AY 8333		1936	JU 7796	
1912	AY 1952		AY 1509			1922	NR 678	AY 9491				
1913	AY 2438		AY 2071									

Annual issue dates for 1923-1928 are not known to writer, (but information available in Leicestershire County Archives). Blocks commencing with the following numbers commenced in the months shown :

NR 1001	5/22		NR 4501	5/24		UT 2001	12/27
NR 2001	2/23		NR 6001	3/25		UT 4001	11/28
NR 3001	7/23		NR 8001	2/26			

AAY	12/36	EAY	4/47	JAY	10/52	NAY	1/56	SAY	11/58	WAY	7/60
AJU	3/37	EJU	8/47	JJU	2/53	NJU	3/56	SJU	1/59	WJU	9/60
ANR	7/37	ENR	1/48	JNR	5/53	NNR	5/56	SNR	2/59	WNR	10/60
AUT	1/38	EUT	5/48	JUT	8/53	NUT	8/56	SUT	4/59	WUT	12/60
BAY	6/38	FAY	10/48	KAY	11/53	OAY	10/56	TAY	5/59	XAY	1/61
BJU	11/38	FJU	2/49	KJU	2/54	OJU	1/57	TJU	6/59	XJU	3/61
BNR	3/39	FNR	7/49	KNR	4/54	ONR	3/57	TNR	7/59	XNR	4/61
BUT	8/39	FUT	10/49	KUT	6/54	OUT	5/57	TUT	9/59	XUT	5/61
CAY	4/40	GAY	3/50	LAY	9/54	PAY	7/57	UAY	10/59	YAY	6/61
CJU	6/41	GJU	6/50	LJU	11/54	PJU	9/57	UJU	11/59	YJU	7/61
CNR	6/42	GNR	10/50	LNR	1/55	PNR	11/57	UNR	1/60	YNR	8/61
CUT	10/43	GUT	2/51	LUT	3/55	PUT	3/58	UUT	2/60	YUT	10/61
DAY	5/45	HAY	6/51	MAY	5/55	RAY	4/58	VAY	3/60		
DJU	4/46	HJU	10/51	MJU	7/55	RJU	5/58	VJU	4/60		
DNR	8/46	HNR	3/52	MNR	9/55	RNR	7/58	VNR	5/60		
DUT	12/46	HUT	7/52	MUT	11/55	RUT	9/58	VUT	6/60		
AAY	12/61	BAY	6/62	CAY	12/62	DAY	5/63	EAY	9/63	FAY	4/70 *
AJU	2/62	BJU	7/62	CJU	2/63	DJU	6/63	EJU	10/63	* re-regist-	
ANR	3/62	BNR	8/62	CNR	3/63	DNR	7/63	ENR	11/63	rations only.	
AUT	5/62	BUT	10/62	CUT	4/63	DUT	8/63	EUT	1/64		

Commenced suffix marks 3.2.64

LINCOLNSHIRE – COUNTY COUNCIL OF HOLLAND

Separate series for cars, motorcycles and heavy motor cars prior to 1921. The motorcycle series reached DO 1673. Known heavy motor car issues are DO 4 (1912), DO 7 (1913) and DO 9 (1914).

DO   12/03   JL   4/32

First issues for each year :

	Cars	Motorcycles			Cars	Motorcycles
1904	DO 21	No information		1913	DO 401	DO 457
1905	DO 41	"		1914	DO 491	DO 591
1906	DO 59	"		1915	DO 588	DO 731
1907	DO 78	"		1916	DO 712	DO 871
1908	DO 114	"		1917	DO 836	DO 947
1909	DO 167	"		1918	DO 936	DO 978
1910	DO 217	DO 292		1919	DO 1025	DO 1001
1911	DO 251	DO 330		1920	DO 1305	DO 1254
1912	DO 330	DO 368		1921	ca DO 19xx (all vehicles)	

No information for 1922-1928 but details may be available in Lincolnshire Archives.

1929	DO 7883	1934	JL 1112	1939	JL 6113	1944	JL 9007
1930	DO 8590	1935	JL 1878	1940	JL 7025	1945	JL 9459
1931	DO 9195	1936	JL 2823	1941	JL 7558		
1932	DO 9849	1937	JL 4036	1942	JL 8072		
1933	JL 515	1938	JL 5198	1943	JL 8651		

ADO	10/45	FDO	9/52	LDO	6/57	RDO	6/60	WDO	3/63
AJL	8/46	FJL	4/53	LJL	10/57	RJL	9/60	WJL	6/63
BDO	3/47	GDO	11/53	MDO	3/58	SDO	2/61	XDO	9/63
BJL	9/47	GJL	5/54	MJL	7/58	SJL	5/61	XJL	11/63
CDO	5/48	HDO	11/54	NDO	11/58	TDO	7/61	YDO	2/64
CJL	12/48	HJL	4/55	NJL	3/59	TJL	11/61	YJL	4/64
DDO	8/49	JDO	9/55	ODO	6/59	UDO	3/62		
DJL	4/50	JJL	2/56	OJL	9/59	UJL	6/62		
EDO	1/51	KDO	6/56	PDO	1/60	VDO	9/62		
EJL	11/51	KJL	12/56	PJL	3/60	VJL	1/63		

No reverse issues. Commenced suffix marks (ahead of original schedule), 10.7.64.

LINCOLNSHIRE - COUNTY COUNCIL OF KESTEVEN

CT   12/03   TL   9/28

First issues for each year before 1929 are not known to writer, but information for early 1920s is available in Lincolnshire Archives. 1921 issues commenced CT 38xx.

1929	TL 157	1933	TL 2693	1937	TL 6080	1941	TL 9549
1930	TL 907	1934	TL 3264	1938	TL 7224		
1931	TL 1594	1935	TL 4047	1939	TL 8110		
1932	TL 2118	1936	TL 5010	1940	TL 9035		

ACT	1/42	FCT	11/50	LCT	4/56	RCT	3/60	WCT	2/63
ATL	10/43	FTL	6/51	LTL	11/56	RTL	6/60	WTL	4/63
BCT	1/46	GCT	3/52	MCT	4/57	SCT	9/60	XCT	7/63
BTL	9/46	GTL	12/52	MTL	10/57	STL	1/61	XTL	10/63
CCT	3/47	HCT	7/53	NCT	2/58	TCT	4/61	YCT	1/64
CTL	9/47	HTL	2/54	NTL	8/58	TTL	7/61	YTL	4/64
DCT	5/48	JCT	7/54	OCT	1/59	UCT	11/61		
DTL	12/48	JTL	2/55	OTL	4/59	UTL	3/62		
ECT	7/49	KCT	7/55	PCT	8/59	VCT	6/62		
ETL	4/50	KTL	11/55	PTL	12/59	VTL	9/62		

No reverse issues. Commenced suffix marks (ahead of original schedule), 1.6.64.

LINCOLNSHIRE - COUNTY COUNCIL OF LINDSEY

BE 12/03   FU 8/22   FW 6/29

First issues for each year. No information available for 1905-1908 nor 1922-1928 but some
information for the latter period may be available in Lincolnshire Archives.

1904	BE 53	1910	BE 830	1914	BE 1918	1918	BE 3889
		1911	BE 1003	1915	BE 2501	1919	BE 4088
		1912	BE 1233	1916	BE 3185	1920	BE 5248
1909	BE 671	1913	BE 1568	1917	BE 3551	1921	BE 7197

1929	FU 9358	1932	FW 2701	1935	FW 5615
1930	FW 700	1933	FW 3558	1936	FW 7032
1931	FW 1861	1934	FW 4438	1937	FW 8759

ABE	8/37	EBE	4/47	JBE	1/52	NBE	7/55	SBE	5/58	WBE	4/60
AFU	3/38	EFU	8/47	JFU	5/52	NFU	9/55	SFU	8/58	WFU	5/60
AFW	10/38	EFW	1/48	JFW	10/52	NFW	12/55	SFW	10/58	WFW	7/60
BBE	5/39	FBE	4/48	KBE	3/53	OBE	3/56	TBE	1/59	XBE	8/60
BFU	3/40	FFU	11/48	KFU	6/53	OFU	5/56	TFU	3/59	XFU	10/60
BFW	8/41	FFW	4/49	KFW	10/53	OFW	9/56	TFW	4/59	XFW	1/61
CBE	9/42	GBE	8/49	LBE	2/54	PBE	1/57	UBE	6/59	YBE	2/61
CFU	10/43	GFU	1/50	LFU	4/54	PFU	4/57	UFU	8/59	YFU	3/61
CFW	2/45	GFW	6/50	LFW	7/54	PFW	7/57	UFW	10/59	YFW	5/61
DBE	2/46	HBE	10/50	MBE	10/54	RBE	9/57	VBE	11/59		
DFU	7/46	HFU	3/51	MFU	2/55	RFU	1/58	VFU	1/60		
DFW	12/46	HFW	7/51	MFW	4/55	RFW	3/58	VFW	3/60		

ABE	6/61	CBE	5/62	EBE	3/63	GBE	11/63
AFU	7/61	CFU	6/62	EFU	4/63	GFU	1/64
AFW	9/61	CFW	8/62	EFW	6/63	GFW	3/64
BBE	11/61	DBE	10/62	FBE	7/63	HBE	4/64
BFU	2/62	DFU	12/62	FFU	8/63	HFU	5/64
BFW	3/62	DFW	2/63	FFW	10/63	HFW	9/75 *

* re-registrations only.

Special mark for Diplomatic Corps : *1 BE* c.3/67.

Commenced suffix marks 1.6.64

COUNTY COUNCIL OF LONDON

Absorbed into GREATER LONDON COUNCIL as from 1 April 1965.

In the first two series all vehicles were numbered in a common sequence; then from LN to XH inclusive (11/06 to 1/22) there were separate blocks in most series for (1) motorcycles, (2) cars and vans, (3) heavy motor cars.

		M/cycles	Cars & Vans	HMCs			M/cycles	Cars & Vans	HMCs
A	1/04				LP	9/15	1-4000	4001-8000	8001-9999
LC	5/05				LR	7/16	1-4000	4001-8000	8001-9999
LN	11/06	1-9700 [or 9750] mixed,			LT	7/18	1-4000	4001-8000	8001-9999
		9701 [or 9751] - 9999 mainly HMCs			LU	4/19	1-4000	4001-8000	8001-9999
LB	3/08	1-3000	3001-9999		LW	5/19	1-4000	4001-9999	
LD	5/09		1-9999		LX	7/19	1-4000	4001-8000	8001-9999
LA	4/10	1-3000	3001-9800	9801-9999	LY	9/19	1-4000	4001-8000	8001-9999
LE	7/11	1-3000	3001-9000	9001-9999	XA	1/20	4001-8000	1-4000	8001-9999
LF	5/12	1-3000	3001-8000	8001-9999	XB	4/20	1-4000	4001-8000	8001-9999
LH	2/13	1-3000	3001-8000	8001-9999	XC	6/20	1-4000	4001-8000	8001-9999*
LK	8/13	1-4000	4001-9999		XD	7/20	1-4000	4001-8000	8001-9999*
LL	3/14	8001-9999	1-8000		XE	9/20		1-9999	
LM	7/14	1-3000	3001-9999		XF	1/21	1-4000	4001-8000	8001-9999*
LO	3/15	1-4000	4001-9000		XH	3/21	1-1700	1701-3400 #	
		9001-9999 (exc. 9524/5)					3401-3500	3501-9999 #	

* these blocks also include cars and vans.   # No separate blocks for HMCs, (included with cars and vans).

From XK to YM inclusive (1/22 to 3/26) all vehicles were numbered in a common series.

XK	1/22	XN	2/23	XR	1/24	XW	10/24	YK	6/25
XL	5/22	XO	5/23	XT	4/24	XX	1/25	YL	7/25
XM	9/22	XP	8/23	XU	6/24	XY	4/25	YM	11/25

In most remaining two-letter series there was a separate block for commercial vehicles, as shown :

YN	3/26	4001-5000	YX	7/28	5001-5800	GK	9/30	9001-9600
YO	4/26	none	XV	10/28	5001-6000	GN	1/31	9001-9999
YP	6/26	6001-6500	UL	1/29	9001-9999	GO	3/31	9001-9700
YR	9/26	6001-7000	GU	3/29	9001-9999	GP	5/31	9001-9600
YE	1/27	5001-6000	UU	5/29	5001-5325 (appx)	GT	8/31	9001-9999
YF	3/27	none			9501-9999	GW	12/31	9001-9550
YH	5/27	7001-7600	UV	6/29	9001-9999	GX	3/32	9001-9550
YT	6/27	5001-5500	UW	9/29	9001-9999	GY	6/32	9001-9550
YU	9/27	5001-5500	GC	12/29	8701-9999	YY	9/32	9001-9600
		9001-9500	GF	3/30	9001-9400	JJ	11/32	9501-9999
UC	1/28	5001-6000			9501-9700			
YV	3/28	5001-5400	GJ	5/30	9301-9999			
YW	5/28	5001-5600	GH	7/30	none			

(LGOC buses did not normally conform with HMC or commercial blocks).

'Q' Marks for Temporary Imports

No official information is available to date exactly the commencement of marks in this series, (except for QX et seq.), but the years shown are believed to be accurate.

QQ	/21	*	QE	/51	AA	QL	/66	AA	QX	8/81	QE	8/87	QL	8/93
QA	/31	AA	QF	/54	AA	QM	/70	AA	QY	8/82	QF	8/88	QM	8/94
QC	/31	RAC	QG	/56	AA	QN	/71	RAC	QA	8/83	QG	8/89	QN	8/95
QS	/53	RAC #	QH	/57	RAC	QP	/71	AA	QB	8/84	QH	8/90	QP	8/96
QB	/47	AA	QJ	/57	AA	QR	/79	LC	QC	8/85	QJ	8/91	QR	8/97
QD	/49	RAC	QK	/60	AA	QT	/76	AA	QD	8/86	QK	8/92	QS	8/98

* Originally QQ 1-1000 direct issue by LCC, 1001-9999 by AA and RAC; GLC subsequently re-used 1001-9999.
# QS allotted 1930 to Royal Scottish Automobile Club, believed never used by them and rellocated to RAC.
LC = London Central VRO direct issue. (QT and all later marks also allocated through London Central VRO)

COUNTY COUNCIL OF LONDON (continued)

Three-letter Marks
Sequence of Issue

Although for ease of reference three-letter marks are shown in alphabetical order in the following tables, they were not always so issued. For the first six years marks were issued in fairly strict alphabetical sequence, no mark being more than two months earlier or later than its immediate neighbours. During this period the mark GPO was specially allocated to London instead of West Sussex and was reserved for issue to General Post Office vehicles. The first ordinary LCC mark specially allocated to the General Post Office was GGH in 10/39, five months ahead of GGF, and thereafter the sequence became somewhat less orderly - note especially GYN and GYO issued 9/43, earlier than any of GXV to GYM). The sequence of issue was further affected from HLA onward in early 1946, when the decision was made to segregate commercial vehicles, usually in groups of about 10 sequential marks. (During this period and after, the issue of a particular mark may have extended over a period of three years or more). The sequence became more orderly from the beginning of 1952 (MXA onwards), the separate marks for commercial vehicles being now allocated individually, rather than in groups. A year later, from the beginning of 1953, with NLP the segregation of commercial vehicles was abandoned, (to be revived very briefly at the start of the reverse format era). However, a further disruption to strict alphabetical sequence arose with the introduction of blocks of marks for vehicles supplied under the Home Delivery Export Scheme. Generally speaking, there were thereafter two sequences, each proceeding in fairly strict alphabetical order, until the end of non-suffix marks, (i.e. one for HDES and one for other issues). Because two or more series were usually in simultaneous use, and issue of a particular mark often spread over a long period, the tabulation which follows shows both start and finish dates for each series. Mention should also be made here of the mark USN, which was allocated to the LCC instead of Dunbartonshire in 1942 for vehicles of the United States Navy. However, this series was never brought into use on vehicles subject to civilian registration.

Special Series
General Post Office

Until 1.10.69, when they commenced to be registered locally, almost all GPO vehicles were registered by the LCC. From 1932 they had been allocated blocks, usually of 200 numbers, in various series from GX to BXT; then blocks of 300 in BXW, BYO, BYW, CGH, CGT and CLD. From January 1936, however, they were allocated complete series, (save that in the case of the first eleven the numbers 1 to 10 were excluded from the GPO allocation). An exceptional case was GLC, in which only 1-300 were allocated to the GPO, the remainder to other Government Departments. The full list of GPO marks was : CLP*, CXN*, CYW*, DGU*, DXK*, DYP*, EGU*, ELO*, EXD*, EXM*, FGN*, GGH, GGJ, GGY, GPO**, GLN, GLO, GLP, GUL, GUV, GUW, GXK, GXL, GYT, GYU, GYV, GYW, GYX, GYY, HGW, HGX, HGY, HLA, JLC, JLD, JLE, JUW, JXO, JXY, JYX, JYY, KGO, KYT, LUL, LUU, LYK, MLB, MLH, MYE, MYF, NGJ, NLW, NXO, NYH, OXN, OYF, PGO, PUL, PXX, RGJ, RGK, RLB, RXT, SGH, SLF, SLM, SLO, SXH, TGC, TUV, UXH, UXV, VUC, WLA, XXD, YLB, YLH, YXF.
* excluding 1-10.   ** GPO 1 & 2 issued 1937, 3 in 1961, 4-8 not issued, 9-999 in 1946. (Note that upon sale by the Post Office vehicles registered in GPO, (also in *GPO* and GPO-C), were required to be re-registered).

Other Government Departments

Special series were also allocated to Government Departments other than the General Post Office, (sometimes including London Transport and British Rail vehicles). As mentioned above, GLC was split between the Post Office (1-300) and other Government Departments. The following were exclusively Government : LYN, MLM, NGY, NYR, NYV, RGX, SXF, (also part only of : JXW, JXX. KYW, LYO (401-900), PGF, PGW (1-699), PLF (251-999), RGC (501-999), RXP (501-900), RYX (11-560) and SYH (101-550).

Commercial Vehicles

The following were allocated mainly to commercials, though there were exceptions, and some commercial vehicles received numbers in nominally "private" series, (e.g. some BRS vehicles in MUL) : HLW to HXA, HXW to HYU, JUV, JXA to JXN, JXP to JXV, KGH to KGN, KGP to KLC, KXT to KYK, LLT to LUC, LUV, LUW, LYE to LYH, LYL, LYM, LYO to LYR, MLA, MLC to MLF, MLK, MLL, MXB, MXD, MXL, MXU, MXV, MXX, MYV, NGF, NGX, NLB, NLL.

Home Delivery Export Scheme

The allocation of special marks commenced in 2/53 with NXC and the following blocks were allocated :
NXC to NXF, NXK, OGC to OGP, OUC to OXH, PLN to PLY, RUC to RXL, SYN to SYY, TXA to TXL, UGC to UGY, WGC to WGY, XGC to XGY, YGC to YGY. Some of these marks were exclusively allocated to Fords : SYW, TXA, TXB, TXE, UGC, WGO, WGX, YGC, YGJ, YGK, YGT, YGW. YGY.

Other

Two special series remain to be mentioned : LLA 1-400 were "allocated to Local Authority", presumably the LCC. (Some used on ambulances, but the block does not appear to have been fully issued).
RYE (excluding 1 - 9) was specially allocated to Claude Rye, motorcycle dealer.

Mark	Period	Mark	Period	Mark	Period	Mark	Period
AGC	3/33 - 3/33	AXP	1/34 - 3/34	BLO	12/34 - 3/35	CGC	8/35 - 10/35
AGF	3/33 - 3/33	AXR	2/34 - 2/34	BLP	11/34 - 12/34	CGF	8/35 - 9/35
AGH	3/33 - 3/33	AXT	3/34 - 4/34	BLR	12/34 - 1/35	CGH	8/35 - 10/35
AGJ	3/33 - 7/33	AXU	3/34 - 4/34	BLT	12/34 - 1/35	CGJ	8/35 - 9/35
AGK	3/33 - 4/33	AXV	2/34 - 3/34	BLU	12/34 - 1/35	CGK	9/35 - 11/35
AGN	3/33 - 5/33	AXW	2/34 - 4/34	BLW	12/34 - 2/35	CGN	8/35 - 1/36
AGO	3/33 - 1/34	AXX	4/34 - 5/34	BLX	1/35 - 1/35	CGO	9/35 - 10/35
AGP	4/33 - 7/33	AXY	2/34 - 3/34	BLY	1/35 - 2/35	CGP	10/35 - 11/35
AGT	4/33 - 4/33	AYE	3/34 - 3/34	BUC	2/35 - 2/35	CGT	9/35 - 11/35
AGU	4/33 - 5/33	AYF	3/34 - 4/34	BUL	1/35 - 3/35	CGU	9/35 - 11/35
AGW	4/33 - 6/33	AYH	5/34 - 5/34	BUU	1/35 - 2/35	CGW	10/35 - 11/35
AGX	5/33 - 5/33	AYK	3/34 - 4/34	BUV	1/35 - 2/35	CGX	10/35 - 12/35
AGY	5/33 - 7/33	AYL	4/34 - 4/34	BUW	3/35 - 3/35	CGY	11/35 - 11/35
AJJ	5/33 - 7/33	AYM	5/34 - 5/34	BXA	3/35 - 4/35	CJJ	10/35 - 11/35
ALA	5/33 - 6/33	AYN	4/34 - 5/34	BXB	2/35 - 3/35	CLA	11/35 - 12/35
ALB	5/33 - 6/33	AYO	4/34 - 5/34	BXC	2/35 - 3/35	CLB	11/35 - 12/35
ALC	6/33 - 7/33	AYP	4/34 - 5/34	BXD	2/35 - 3/35	CLC	11/35 - 12/35
ALD	5/33 - 6/33	AYR	4/34 - 5/34	BXE	3/35 - 4/35	CLD	11/35 - 12/35
ALE	6/33 - 7/33	AYT	6/34 - 6/34	BXF	3/35 - 3/35	CLE	11/35 - 12/35
ALF	6/33 - 8/33	AYU	5/34 - 6/34	BXH	3/35 - 4/35	CLF	12/35 - 1/36
ALH	6/33 - 8/33	AYV	5/34 - 7/34	BKX	3/35 - 4/35	CLH	12/35 - 1/36
ALK	7/33 - 9/33	AYW	5/34 - 7/34	BXL	3/35 - 3/35	CLK	12/35 - 3/36
ALL	7/33 - 11/33	AYX	6/34 - 7/34	BXM	3/35 - 4/35	CLL	12/35 - 2/36
ALM	7/33 - 9/33	AYY	6/34 - 7/34	BXN	3/35 - 4/35	CLM	12/35 - 1/36
ALN	7/33 - 8/33			BXO	4/35 - 5/35	CLN	1/36 - 2/36
ALO	8/33 - 9/33	BGC	6/34 - 7/34	BXP	3/35 - 4/35	CLO	12/35 - 1/36
ALP	8/33 - 9/33	BGF	6/34 - 7/34	BXR	4/35 - 4/35	CLP	1/36 - 7/36 PO*
ALR	8/33 - 9/33	BGH	6/34 - 9/34	BXT	4/35 - 4/35	CLR	1/36 - 2/36
ALT	9/33 - 9/33	BGJ	6/34 - 7/34	BXU	4/35 - 5/35	CLT	1/36 - 2/36
ALU	9/33 - 10/33	BGK	7/34 - 8/34	BXV	4/35 - 6/35	CLU	2/36 - 3/36
ALW	9/33 - 10/33	BGN	7/34 - 8/34	BXW	4/35 - 5/35	CLW	1/36 - 3/36
ALX	10/33 - 1/34	BGO	7/34 - 7/34	BXX	5/35 - 5/35	CLX	2/36 - 3/36
ALY	10/33 - 11/33	BGP	7/34 - 9/34	BXY	5/35 - 5/35	CLY	2/36 - 3/36
AUC	10/33 - 12/33	BGT	8/34 - 9/34	BYE	5/35 - 6/35	CUC	1/36 - 2/36
AUL	10/33 - 11/33	BGU	8/34 - 9/34	BYF	5/35 - 6/35	CUL	3/36 - 4/36
AUU	11/33 - 1/34	BGW	8/34 - 10/34	BYH	5/35 - 7/35	CUU	3/36 - 3/36
AUV	10/33 - 11/33	BGX	9/34 - 10/34	BYK	5/35 - 8/35	CUV	3/36 - 3/36
AUW	11/33 - 12/33	BGY	9/34 - 10/34	BYL	6/35 - 7/35	CUW	3/36 - 3/36
AXA	12/33 - 1/34	BJJ	8/34 - 11/34	BYM	6/35 - 7/35	CXA	3/36 - 4/36
AXB	11/33 - 1/34	BLA	9/34 - 11/34	BYN	6/35 - 7/35	CXB	3/36 - 5/36
AXC	11/33 - 12/33	BLB	10/34 - 11/34	BYO	6/35 - 7/35	CXC	3/36 - 3/36
AXD	12/33 - 2/34	BLC	9/34 - 10/34	BYP	6/35 - 7/35	CXD	3/36 - 5/36
AXE	12/33 - 3/34	BLD	10/34 - 12/34	BYR	6/35 - 7/35	CXE	3/36 - 4/36
AXF	12/33 - 2/34	BLE	10/34 - 11/34	BYT	7/35 - 8/35	CXF	3/36 - 4/36
AXH	1/34 - 4/34	BLF	10/34 - 12/34	BYU	7/35 - 9/35	CXH	4/36 - 4/36
AXK	1/34 - 2/34	BLH	11/34 - 1/35	BYV	8/35 - 9/35	CXK	4/36 - 5/36
AXL	1/34 - 3/34	BLK	11/34 - 12/34	BYW	7/35 - 8/35	CXL	3/36 - 4/36
AXM	1/34 - 2/34	BLL	11/34 - 2/35	BYX	7/35 - 7/35	CXM	4/36 - 5/36
AXN	1/34 - 3/34	BLM	11/34 - 1/35	BYY	7/35 - 9/35	CXN	4/36 - 7/36 PO*
AXO	3/34 - 3/34	BLN	11/34 - 1/35			CXO	4/36 - 5/36

PO* - Post Office, except 1-10.

CXP	4/36 - 5/36	DLO	12/36 - 2/37	EGC	7/37 - 2/38	EXP	3/38 - 5/38	
CXR	4/36 - 1/37	DLP	12/36 - 3/37	EGF	7/37 - 9/37	EXR	4/38 - 7/38	
CXT	4/36 - 5/36	DLR	12/36 - 1/37	EGH	7/37 - 10/37	EXT	4/38 - 7/38	
CXU	5/36 - 5/36	DLT	1/37 - 3/37	EGJ	7/37 - 11/37	EXU	3/38 - 6/38	
CXV	5/36 - 5/36	DLU	1/37 - 5/37	EGK	7/37 - 9/37	EXV	4/38 - 5/38	
CXW	5/36 - 5/36	DLW	1/37 - 2/37	EGN	7/37 - 9/37	EXW	4/38 - 4/38	
CXX	5/36 - 5/36	DLX	2/37 - 12/37	EGO	7/37 - 11/37	EXX	4/38 - 6/38	
CXY	5/35 - 8/36	DLY	12/36 - 1/37	EGP	8/37 - 9/37	EXY	4/38 - 5/38	
CYE	5/36 - 6/36	DUC	1/37 - 1/37	EGT	8/37 - 11/37	EYE	5/38 - 7/38	
CYF	5/36 - 6/36	DUL	2/37 - 3/37	EGU	8/37 - 4/38 PO*	EYF	5/38 - 6/38	
CYH	6/36 - 7/36	DUU	2/37 - 3/37	EGW	8/37 - 10/37	EYH	5/38 - 6/38	
CYK	6/36 - 9/36	DUV	1/37 - 2/37	EGX	8/37 - 1/38	EYK	5/38 - 7/38	
CYL	6/36 - 6/36	(DUW not allocated)		EGY	8/37 - 10/37	EYL	5/38 - 5/38	
CYM	6/36 - 8/36	DXA	2/37 - 3/37	EJJ	9/37 - 9/37	EYM	5/38 - 7/38	
CYN	6/36 - 7/36	DXB	2/37 - 5/37	ELA	9/37 - 12/37	EYN	6/38 - 10/38	
CYO	6/36 - 6/36	DXC	2/37 - 1/38	ELB	9/37 - 5/38	EYO	6/38 - 7/38	
CYP	6/36 - 7/36	DXD	3/37 - 3/37	ELC	9/37 - 10/37	EYP	6/38 - 7/38	
CYR	7/36 - 7/36	DXE	2/37 - 3/37	ELD	10/37 - 11/37	EYR	6/38 - 10/38	
CYT	7/36 - 9/36	DXF	2/37 - 4/37	ELE	10/37 - 4/38	EYT	6/38 - 8/38	
CYU	6/36 - 7/36	DXH	3/37 - 5/37	ELF	10/37 - 11/37	EYU	7/38 - 8/38	
CYV	7/36 - 10/36	DXK	3/37 - 7/37 PO*	ELH	10/37 - 11/37	EYV	7/38 - 9/38	
CYW	7/36 - 10/36 PO*	DXL	3/37 - 4/37	ELK	11/37 - 1/38	EYW	7/38 - 8/38	
CYX	7/36 - 9/36	DXM	3/37 - 4/37	ELL	11/37 - 7/38	EYX	8/38 - 8/38	
CYY	7/36 - 8/36	DXN	3/37 - 5/37	ELM	11/37 - 1/38	EYY	8/38 - 9/38	
		DXO	3/37 - 5/37	ELN	11/37 - 12/37			
DGC	8/36 - 12/36	DXP	3/37 - 4/37	ELO	11/37 - 3/38 PO*	FGC	6/38 - 9/38	
DGF	8/36 - 10/36	DXR	3/37 - 4/37	ELP	11/37 - 1/38	FGF	8/38 - 10/38	
DGH	8/36 - 11/36	DXT	4/37 - 7/37	ELR	12/37 - 12/37	FGH	9/38 - 12/38	
DGJ	8/36 - 9/36	DXU	4/37 - 6/37	ELT	12/37 - 1/38	FGJ	9/38 - 11/38	
DGK	9/36 - 9/36	DXV	4/37 - 5/37	ELU	12/37 - 1/38	FGK	9/38 - 3/39	
DGN	9/36 - 10/36	DXW	4/37 - 7/37	ELW	12/37 - 1/38	FGN	10/38 - 2/40 PO*
DGO	9/36 - 12/36	DXX	4/37 - 5/37	ELX	12/37 - 3/38	FGO	8/38 - 10/38	
DGP	9/36 - 12/36	DXY	4/37 - 6/37	ELY	12/37 - 1/38	FGP	10/38 - 11/38	
DGT	10/36 - 10/36	DYE	4/37 - 5/37	EUC	1/38 - 1/38	FGT	9/38 - 11/38	
DGU	10/36 - 5/37 PO*	DYF	5/37 - 6/37	EUL	12/37 - 2/38	FGU	9/38 - 9/38	
DGW	10/36 - 12/36	DYH	5/37 - 5/37	EUU	1/38 - 2/38	FGW	10/38 - 10/38	
DGX	10/36 - 11/36	DYK	5/37 - 7/37	EUV	1/38 - 2/38	FGX	11/38 - 11/38	
DGY	9/36 - 10/36	DYL	5/37 - 6/37	EUW	1/38 - 2/38	FGY	10/38 - 10/38	
DJJ	10/36 - 11/36	DYM	5/37 - 7/37	EXA	2/38 - 3/38	FJJ	11/38 - 11/38	
DLA	11/36 - 12/36	DYN	5/37 - 6/37	EXB	2/38 - 3/38	FLA	11/38 - 11/38	
DLB	11/36 - 12/36	DYO	6/37 - 6/37	EXC	2/38 - 3/38	FLB	11/38 - 11/38	
DLC	10/36 - 10/36	DYP	5/37 - 10/37 PO*	EXD	2/38 - 3/38 PO*	FLC	11/38 - 11/38
DLD	10/36 - 11/36	DYR	5/37 - 12/37	EXE	2/38 - 3/38	FLD	12/38 - 12/38	
DLE	11/36 - 3/37	DYT	6/37 - 7/37	EXF	3/38 - 3/38	FLE	12/38 - 12/38	
DLF	11/36 - 1/37	DYU	6/37 - 8/37	EXH	3/38 - 4/38	FLF	12/38 - 12/38	
DLH	11/36 - 11/36	DYV	6/37 - 8/37	EXK	3/38 - 4/38	FLH	12/38 - 12/38	
DLK	12/36 - 1/37	DYW	6/37 - 9/37	EXL	3/38 - 4/38	FLK	12/38 - 12/38	
DLL	12/36 - 1/37	DYX	6/37 - 7/37	EXM	3/38 - 4/38 PO*	FLL	12/38 - 12/38
DLM	11/36 - 12/37	DYY	6/37 - 7/37	EXN	3/38 - 4/38	FLM	2/39 - 3/39	
DLN	12/36 - 2/37			EXO	3/38 - 4/38	FLN	12/38 - 1/39	

PO* - Post Office, except 1-10.

FLO 1/39 – 3/39	GGC 2/40 – 2/40	GXP 7/43 – 1/44	HLO 4/46 – 5/47
FLP 1/39 – 2/39	GGF 3/40 – 7/40	GXR 7/43 – 8/44	HLP 5/46 – 5/48
FLR 3/39 – 5/39	GGH 10/39 – 1/40 PO	GXT 7/43 – 7/44	HLR 5/46 – 3/48
FLT 1/39 – 3/39	GGJ 1/40 – 4/41 PO	GXU 8/43 – 2/44	HLT 5/46 – 11/48
FLU 2/39 – 3/39	GGK 3/40 – 7/40	GXV 3/44 – 4/47	HLU 6/46 – 5/47
FLW 2/39 – 4/39	GGN 7/40 – 11/40	GXW 3/44 – 2/47	HLW 2/46 – 1/49 C
FLX 2/39 – 4/39	GGO 5/40 – 7/40	GXX 4/44 – 2/46	HLX 3/46 – 8/48 C
FLY 2/39 – 5/39	GGP 7/40 – 11/40	GXY 4/44 – 4/47	HLY 3/46 – 9/49 C
(FUC not alloc.)	GGT 11/40 – 5/41	GYE 6/44 – 11/46	HUC 4/46 – 7/48 C
FUL 3/39 – 5/39	GGU 12/40 – 12/42	GYF 9/44 – 10/48	HUL 5/46 – 9/49 C
FUU 3/39 – 5/39	GGW 3/41 – 12/41	GYH 11/44 – 8/46	HUU 5/46 – 2/48 C
FUV 3/39 – 5/39	GGX 6/41 – 5/46	GYK 1/45 – 3/47	HUV 6/46 – 6/48 C
FUW 3/39 – 4/39	GGY 3/41 – 4/46 PO	GYL 3/45 – 3/47	HUW 8/46 – 11/47 C
FXA 3/39 – 6/39	GJJ 6/41 – 10/41	GYM 4/45 – 8/46	HXA 9/46 – 11/48 C
FXB 3/39 – 5/39	GLA 8/41 – 10/41	GYN 9/43 – 2/48	HXB 7/46 – 3/48
FXC 3/39 – 6/39	GLB 8/41 – 1/42	GYO 9/43 – 11/46	HXC 8/46 – 3/47
FXD 3/39 – 6/39	GLC 9/41 – 11/41 **	GYP 4/44 – 2/48	HXD 9/46 – 8/47
FXE 4/39 – 6/39	GLD 10/41 – 10/41	GYR 8/44 – 1/52	HXE 9/46 – 7/47
FXF 5/39 – 6/39	GLE 10/41 – 1/42	GYT 9/44 – 4/45 PO	HXF 9/46 – 9/47
FXH 4/39 – 6/39	GLF 12/41 – 4/42	GYU 9/44 – 4/45 PO	HXH 10/46 – 7/47
FXK 4/39 – 6/39	GLH 2/42 – 10/42	GYV 9/44 – 11/46 PO	HXK 10/46 – 11/47
FXL 4/39 – 6/39	GLK 5/42 – 3/43	GYW 7/45 – 7/47 PO	HKL 10/46 – 3/50
FXM 6/39 – 6/39	GLL 7/42 – 5/46	GYX 2/46 – 8/48 PO	HXM 11/46 – 6/51
FXN 5/39 – 6/39	GLM 10/41 – 2/42	GYY 2/46 – 8/48 PO	HXN 11/46 – 9/48
FXO 5/39 – 6/39	GLN 10/41 – 1/42 PO		HXO 11/46 – 2/48
FXP 5/39 – 6/39	GLO 12/41 – 2/42 PO	HGC 6/45 – 4/47	HXP 12/46 – 11/48
FXR 5/39 – 6/39	GLP 12/41 – 5/43 PO	HGF 8/45 – 9/49	HXR 12/46 – 10/47
FXT 5/39 – 6/39	GLR 12/41 – 8/42	HGH 9/45 – 2/47	HXT 12/46 – 9/47
FXU 5/39 – 6/39	GLT 12/41 – 1/43	HGJ 10/45 – 4/47	HXU 12/46 – 8/47
FXV 6/39 – 6/39	GLU 12/41 – 2/43	HGK 11/45 – 7/49	HXV 1/47 – 2/48
FXW 6/39 – 6/39	GLW 1/42 – 4/42	HGN 11/45 – 8/47	HXW 9/46 – 3/48 C
FXX 6/39 – 6/39	GLX 1/42 – 1/44	HGO 12/45 – 2/48	HXX 10/46 – 3/48 C
FXY 6/39 – 7/39	GLY 4/42 – 6/42	HGP 1/46 – 1/49	HXY 11/46 – 4/49 C
FYE 6/39 – 9/39	GUC 5/42 – 8/42	HGT 1/46 – 4/51	HYE 11/46 – 11/48 C
FYF 6/39 – 7/42	GUL 7/42 – 1/43 PO	HGU 1/46 – 4/49	HYF 12/46 – 1/50 C
FYH 6/39 – 6/39	GUU 8/42 – 11/42	HGW 12/45 – 7/46 PO	HYH 1/47 – 10/47 C
FYK 6/39 – 7/39	GUV 8/42 – 9/43 PO	HGX 12/45 – 7/46 PO	HYK 2/47 – 1/48 C
FYL 7/39 – 8/39	GUW 9/42 – 11/43 PO	HGY 12/45 – 7/46 PO	HYL 3/47 – 1/48 C
FYM 8/39 – 9/39	GXA 12/42 – 11/43	HJJ 2/46 – 1/47	HYM 4/47 – 5/49 C
FYN 7/39 – 7/39	GXB 12/42 – 5/44	HLA 2/46 – 12/48 PO	HYN 5/47 – 9/49 C
FYO 8/39 – 8/39	GXC 1/43 – 3/43	HLB 7/46 – 3/47	HYO 5/47 – 1/48 C
FYP 8/39 – 9/39	GXD 3/43 – 8/43	HLC 7/46 – 3/47	HYP 6/47 – 9/49 C
FYR 9/39 – 12/39	GXE 7/43 – 5/44	HLD 6/46 – 5/47	HYR 7/47 – 9/49 C
FYT 9/39 – 10/39	GXF 7/43 – 1/44	HLE 7/46 – 2/47	HYT 7/47 – 11/47 C
FYU 10/39 – 10/39	GXH 11/42 – 9/43	HLF 8/46 – 3/47	HYU 8/47 – 1/48 C
FYV 10/39 – 10/39	GXK 1/43 – 12/44 PO	HLH 2/46 – 10/47	HYV 1/47 – 8/47
FYW 10/39 – 12/39	GXL 1/43 – 3/45 PO	HLK 2/46 – 3/48	HYW 2/47 – 7/47
FYX 12/39 – 1/40	GXM 2/43 – 3/43	HLL 3/46 – 3/47	HYX 2/47 – 11/47
FYY 1/40 – 2/40	GXN 3/43 – 7/43	HLM 3/46 – 6/47	HYY 3/47 – 1/48
GXO 6/43 – 5/44	HLN 4/46 – 8/47		

GPO 2/37 (1 & 2 issued 1937, 3 issued 1961, 4-8 unused, rest issued 1946).

PO Post Office.
** 1 – 300 Post Office, rest other government departments.
C mainly commercial.

Mark	Period		Mark	Period		Mark	Period		Mark	Period	
JGC	3/47 - 12/47		JXP	6/48 - 9/49	C	KLO	2/49 - 6/49		LGC	3/50 - 5/50	
JGF	3/47 - 8/47		JXR	6/48 - 11/48	C	KLP	2/49 - 9/50		LGF	3/50 - 9/50	
JGH	4/47 - 7/47		JXT	7/48 - 5/50	C	KLR	3/49 - 5/49		LGH	3/50 - 5/51	
JGJ	4/47 - 12/47		JXU	8/48 - 10/49	C	KLT	3/49 - 5/50		LGJ	3/50 - 10/50	
JGK	4/47 - 10/47		JXV	9/48 - 3/49	C	KLU	3/49 - 5/50		LGK	4/50 - 9/51	
JGN	4/47 - 12/47		JXW	10/48 - 7/50	G*	KLW	4/49 - 2/50		LGN	4/50 - 12/51	
JGO	5/47 - 10/47		JXX	7/49 - 4/51	G*	KLX	4/49 - 6/49		LGO	4/50 - 7/50	
JGP	5/47 - 12/47		JXY	8/49 - //	PO	KLY	4/49 - 2/50		LGP	4/50 - 11/50	
JGT	5/47 - 11/47		JYE	4/48 - 9/49		KUC	5/49 - 11/50		LGT	5/50 - 9/51	
JGU	5/47 - 11/47		JYF	5/48 - 10/48		KUL	5/49 - 9/49		LGU	5/50 - 10/50	
JGW	6/47 - 11/47		JYH	5/48 - 9/48		KUU	5/49 - 4/50		LGW	5/50 - 10/50	
JGX	6/47 - 11/47		JYK	5/48 - 9/49		KUV	5/49 - 9/49		LGX	5/50 - 10/50	
JGY	6/47 - 12/47		JYL	6/48 - 4/49		KUW	6/49 - 7/50		LGY	5/50 - 9/51	
JJJ	6/47 - 12/48		JYM	6/48 - 4/49		KXA	6/49 - 2/50		LJJ	6/50 - 11/50	
JLA	7/47 - 6/48		JYN	6/48 - 3/49		KXB	6/49 - 1/50		LLA	4/50	L
JLB	7/47 - 2/48		JYO	6/48 - 11/48		KXC	7/49 - 2/50		LLB	6/50 - 9/51	
JLC	4/47 - 9/47	PO	JYP	7/48 - 11/48		KXD	7/49 - 10/49		LLC	6/50 - 11/50	
JLD	4/47 - 8/48	PO	JYR	7/48 - 10/49		KXE	7/49 - 2/50		LLD	6/50 - 5/51	
JLE	4/47 - 4/50	PO	JYT	7/48 - 1/49		KXF	8/49 - 1/50		LLE	7/50 - 7/51	
JLF	7/47 - 2/48		JYU	8/48 - 11/51		KXH	8/49 - 6/50		LLF	7/50 - 10/50	
JLH	8/47 - 9/49		JYV	8/48 - 3/49		KXK	8/49 - 2/50		LLH	7/50 - 1/51	
JLK	8/47 - 5/48		JYW	9/48 - 1/49		KXL	9/49 - 1/50		LLK	7/50 - 12/51	
JLL	9/47 - 10/48		JYX	7/48 - 9/48	PO	KXM	9/49 - 1/51		LLL	8/50 - 11/51	
JLM	9/47 - 3/48		JYY	7/48 - 7/50	PO	KXN	9/49 - 2/50		LLM	8/50 - 2/51	
JLN	10/47 - 3/48					KXO	10/49 - 1/50		LLN	9/50 - 11/50	
JLO	10/47 - 11/51		KGC	9/48 - 5/49		KXP	10/49 - 6/50		LLO	9/50 - 12/51	
JLP	11/47 - 12/48		KGF	9/48 - 4/49		KXR	10/49 - 1/51		LLP	9/50 - 7/52	
JLR	11/47 - 5/48		KGH	10/48 - 5/51	C	KXT	9/49 - 1/50	C	LLR	9/50 - 12/51	
JLT	12/47 - 8/48		KGJ	11/48 - 4/49	C	KXU	9/49 - 9/51	C	LLT	4/50 - 10/50	C
JLU	1/48 - 5/49		KGK	12/48 - 10/50	C	KXV	10/49 - 11/51	C	LLU	5/50 - 12/51	C
JLW	1/48 - 2/49		KGN	12/48 - 1/52	C	KXW	11/49 - 1/52	C	LLW	5/50 - 1/52	C
JLX	2/48 - 5/49		KGO	12/48 - 10/51	PO	KXX	11/49 - 5/50	C	LLX	7/50 - 11/51	C
JLY	3/48 - 4/49		KGP	2/49 - 9/49	C	KXY	12/49 - 11/50	C	LLY	8/50 - 12/51	C
JUC	3/48 - 12/48		KGT	2/49 - 6/50	C	KYE	1/50 - 11/51	C	LUC	8/50 - 1/52	C
JUL	4/48 - 6/49		KGU	3/49 - 6/50	C	KYF	1/50 - 12/51	C	LUL	8/50 - 9/50	PO
JUU	4/48 - 4/49		KGW	4/49 - 6/50	C	KYH	2/50 - 2/51	C	LUU	8/50 - 11/51	PO
JUV	9/47 - 12/52	C	KGX	4/49 - 9/49	C	KYK	3/50 - 9/51	C	LUV	10/50 - 12/51	C
JUW	9/47 - 10/51	PO	KGY	5/49 - 10/50	C	KYL	10/49 - 5/50		LUW	5/50 - 5/52	C
JXA	10/47 - 7/50	C	KJJ	6/49 - 1/52	C	KYM	11/49 - 5/50		LXA	10/50 - 12/51	
JXB	10/47 - 5/48	C	KLA	7/49 - 9/49	C	KYN	11/49 - 7/50		LXB	10/50 - 12/51	
JXC	10/47 - 2/51	C	KLB	7/49 - 1/52	C	KYO	12/49 - 11/50		LXC	10/50 - 11/51	
JXD	11/47 - 12/48	C	KLC	8/49 - 11/51	C	KYP	12/49 - 4/51		LXD	10/50 - 7/51	
JXE	12/47 - 3/50	C	KLD	10/48 - 1/51		KYR	1/50 - 4/50		LXE	11/48 - 7/51	
JXF	12/47 - 4/48	C	KLE	10/48 - 4/50		KYT	1/50 - 7/51	PO	LXF	11/48 - 11/51	
JXH	1/48 - 12/51	C	KLF	11/48 - 4/49		KYU	1/50 - 7/50		LXH	11/48 - 10/51	
JXK	3/48 - 11/48	C	KLH	11/48 - 1/50		KYV	2/50 - 11/51		LXK	12/50 - 12/51	
JXL	3/48 - 5/50	C	KLK	12/48 - 1/50		KYW	2/50 - 9/51	G*	LXL	12/50 - 12/51	
JXM	5/48 - 9/48	C	KLL	1/49 - 3/49		KYX	2/50 - 11/50		LXM	12/50 - 11/51	
JXN	5/48 - 10/49	C	KLM	1/49 - 12/51		KYY	2/50 - 12/51		LXN	1/51 - 12/51	
JXO	6/48 - 12/48	PO	KLN	1/49 - 9/49					LXO	1/51 - 12/51	

Date of completion not available.
C   Mainly commercial.
G   Government Departments.
G*   Partly Government Departments, (rest commercial).
L   Local Authority (series incomplete).

Code	Dates		Code	Dates		Code	Dates		Code	Dates	
LXP	1/51 – 11/51		MLO	9/51 – 5/52		NGC	8/52 – 12/52		NXP	5/53 – 5/54	
LXR	2/51 – 11/51		MLP	9/51 – 1/52		NGF	8/52 – 4/54	C	NXR	5/53 – 7/53	
LXT	2/51 – 10/51		MLR	10/51 – 7/52		NGH	8/52 – 1/53		NXT	5/53 – 5/54	
LXU	2/51 – 12/51		MLT	10/51 – 5/52		NGJ	9/52 //	PO	NXU	6/53 – 9/53	
LXV	2/51 – 10/51		MLU	10/51 – 5/52		NGK	9/52 – 10/52		NXV	6/53 – 10/53	
LXW	3/51 – 11/51		MLW	11/51 – 5/52		NGN	9/52 – 4/53		NXW	6/53 – 11/54	
LXX	3/51 – 12/51		MLX	11/51 – 5/52		NGO	9/52 – 2/53		NXX	6/53 – 12/53	
LXY	3/51 – 9/52		MLY	11/51 – 3/53		NGP	10/52 – 3/53		NXY	6/53 – 10/53	
LYE	12/50 – 9/51	C	MUC	12/51 – 5/52		NGT	10/52 – 6/53		NYE	7/53 – 11/54	
LYF	12/50 – 5/52	C	MUL	12/51 – 3/53		NGU	10/52 – 5/53		NYF	7/53 – 12/53	
LYH	12/50 – 7/52	C	MUU	12/51 – 5/52		NGW	10/52 – 4/53		NYH	7/53 – 5/55	PO
LYK	1/51 – 11/51	PO	MUV	1/52 – 7/52		NGX	10/52 – 9/53	C	NYK	7/53 – 4/54	
LYL	1/51 – 12/52	C	MUW	1/52 – 5/52		NGY	10/52 – //	G	NYL	7/53 – 12/53	
LYM	2/51 – 11/51	C	MXA	1/52 – 5/52		NJJ	11/52 – 3/53		NYM	7/53 – 12/53	
LYN	2/51 – //	G	MXB	1/52 – 2/53	C	NLA	11/52 – 12/52		NYN	7/53 – 11/54	
LYO	3/51 – //	G*	MXC	1/52 – 7/52		NLB	11/52 – 10/53	C	NYO	8/53 – 12/53	
LYP	4/51 – 5/52	C	MXD	1/52 – 5/52	C	NLC	11/52 – 5/53		NYP	8/53 – 5/54	
LYR	4/51 – 2/53	C	MXE	2/52 – 7/52		NLD	11/52 – 3/53		NYR	8/53 – //	G
LYT	3/51 – 9/51		MXF	2/52 – 9/52		NLE	12/52 – 4/54		NYT	8/53 – 3/54	
LYU	4/51 – 12/51		MXH	3/52 – 7/52		NLF	12/52 – 2/53		NYU	9/53 – 4/54	
LYV	4/51 – 1/52		MXK	2/52 – 5/52		NLH	12/52 – 7/53		NYV	9/53 – //	G
LYW	4/51 – 5/52		MXL	3/52 – 2/53	C	NLK	12/52 – 4/53		NYW	9/53 – 12/53	
LYX	5/51 – 12/51		MXM	3/52 – 7/52		NLL	12/52 – 6/54	C	NYX	9/53 – 5/54	
LYY	5/51 – 11/51		MXN	3/52 – 9/52		NLM	12/52 – 5/53		NYY	9/53 – 7/54	
			MXO	3/52 – 7/52		NLN	1/53 – 9/53				
MGC	5/51 – 1/52		MXP	4/52 – 7/52		NLO	1/53 – 9/53		OGC	5/53 – 9/53	HD
MGF	5/51 – 12/51		MXR	4/52 – 9/52		NLP	1/53 – 6/54		OGF	6/53 – 2/54	HD
MGH	5/51 – 11/51		MXT	4/52 – 3/53		NLR	2/53 – 11/54		OGH	6/53 – 2/54	HD
MGJ	6/51 – 1/52		MXU	4/52 – 8/52	C	NLT	2/53 – 5/53		OGJ	7/53 – 5/55	HD
MGK	6/51 – 1/52		MXV	4/52 – 12/53	C	NLU	2/53 – 9/53		OGK	7/53 – 5/55	HD
MGN	6/51 – 11/51		MXW	4/52 – 9/52		NLW	2/53 – 11/54	PO	OGN	9/53 – 7/54	HD
MGO	6/51 – 12/51		MXX	4/52 – 7/54	C	NLX	2/53 – 6/53		OGO	10/53 – 5/55	HD
MGP	7/51 – 1/52		MXY	5/52 – 8/52		NLY	3/53 – 7/53		OGP	1/54 – 7/54	HD
MGT	7/51 – 1/52		MYE	4/52 – //	PO	NUC	3/53 – 7/54		OGT	9/53 – 12/54	
MGU	7/51 – 1/52		MYF	4/52 – //	PO	NUL	3/53 – 7/53		OGU	10/53 – 7/54	
MGW	8/51 – 11/51		MYH	5/52 – 7/52		NUU	4/53 – 7/53		OGW	10/53 – 7/54	
MGX	8/51 – 1/52		MYK	5/52 – 9/52		NUV	4/53 – 9/53		OGX	10/53 – 12/53	
MGY	8/51 – 5/52		MYL	5/52 – 10/52		NUW	4/53 – 11/54		OGY	10/53 – 5/54	
MJJ	8/51 – 7/52		MYM	5/52 – 9/52		NXA	4/53 – 7/53		OJJ	10/53 – 4/54	
MLA	5/51 – 9/51	C	MYN	6/52 – 5/53		NXB	4/53 – 4/54		OLA	10/53 – 1/56	
MLB	5/51 – 5/52	PO	MYO	6/52 – 5/53		NXC	2/53 – 9/53	HD	OLB	10/53 – 8/56	
MLC	6/51 – 5/52	C	MYP	6/52 – 9/52		NXD	3/53 – 8/53	HD	OLC	11/53 – 7/54	
MLD	7/51 – 1/52	C	MYR	7/52 – 9/53		NXE	3/53 – 9/53	HD	OLD	11/53 – 12/55	
MLE	8/51 – 3/53	C	MYT	7/52 – 12/52		NXF	4/53 – 1/57	HD	OLE	11/53 – 7/54	
MLF	9/51 – 2/53	C	MYU	7/52 – 5/53		NXH	4/53 – 9/53		OLF	11/53 – 7/54	
MLH	10/51 – //	PO	MYV	7/52 – 12/52	C	NXK	5/53 – 9/53	HD	OLH	11/53 – 7/54	
MLK	11/51 – 5/52	C	MYW	7/52 – 6/53		NXL	5/53 – 9/53		OLK	12/53 – 7/54	
MLL	11/51 – 7/53	C	MYX	7/52 – 9/52		NXM	5/53 – 9/53		OLL	12/53 – 7/54	
MLM	11/51 – //	G	MYY	7/52 – 11/52		NXN	5/53 – 9/53		OLM	12/53 – 6/54	
MLN	9/51 – 1/52					NXO	5/53 – 5/54	PO	OLN	12/53 – 7/54	

C   Mainly commercial.

G   Government Departments. (NYR and NYV include "Green Goddess" fire tenders)

G*   Partly Government Departments, (rest commercial). (LYO 401-900 Government).

HD   Home Delivery Export Scheme.

PO   Post Office.

COUNTY COUNCIL OF LONDON (continued)

OLO 1/54 - 7/54	PGC 6/54 - 11/54	PXP 1/55 - 5/56	RLO 6/55 - 1/56
OLP 1/54 - 11/54	PGF 6/54 - 5/55 G*	PXR 1/55 - 11/55	RLP 6/55 - 1/56
OLR 1/54 - 12/54	PGH 7/54 - 12/54	PXT 1/55 - 11/55	RLR 6/55 - 1/56
OLT 1/54 - 7/54	PGJ 7/54 - 12/54	PXU 1/55 - 5/55	RLT 6/55 - 1/56
OLU 1/54 - 12/54	PGK 7/54 - 8/56	PXV 1/55 - 6/56	RLU 7/55 - 12/55
OLW 1/54 - 7/54	PGN 7/54 - 12/54	PXW 1/55 - 1/56	RLW 7/55 - 9/56
OLX 2/54 - 7/54	PGO 7/54 # PO	PXX 2/55 - 5/55 PO	RLX 7/55 - 1/56
OLY 2/54 - 7/54	PGP 7/54 - 12/54	PXY 2/55 - 10/55	RLY 7/55 - 1/56
OUC 2/54 - 5/55 HD	PGT 7/54 - 5/55	PYE 1/55 - 10/55	RUC 5/55 - 5/56 HD
OUL 3/54 - 5/55 HD	PGU 8/54 - 5/55	PYF 2/55 - 1/56	RUL 6/55 - 11/55 HD
OUU 4/54 - 5/55 HD	PGW 8/54 - 9/56 G*	PYH 2/55 - 10/55	RUU 6/55 - 5/56 HD
OUV 5/54 - 5/55 HD	PGX 8/54 - 12/54	PYK 2/55 - 5/55	RUV 7/55 - 5/57 HD
OUW 5/54 - 5/55 HD	PGY 8/54 - 12/54	PYL 2/55 - 10/55	RUW 8/55 - 5/56 HD
OXA 5/54 - 5/55 HD	PJJ 8/54 - 11/55	PYM 2/55 - 11/55	RXA 8/55 - 5/56 HD
OXB 6/54 - 5/55 HD	PLA 9/54 - 12/54	PYN 3/55 - 12/55	RXB 9/55 - 5/56 HD
OXC 6/54 - 5/55 HD	PLB 9/54 - 12/54	PYO 3/55 - 11/56	RXC 10/55 - 7/56 HD
OXD 7/54 - 5/55 HD	PLC 9/54 - 4/55	PYP 3/55 - 1/56	RXD 10/55 - 7/56 HD
OXE 8/54 - 5/55 HD	PLD 9/54 - 5/55	PYR 3/55 - 10/55	RXE 11/55 - 7/56 HD
OXF 9/54 - 5/55 HD	PLE 9/54 - 5/55	PYT 3/55 - 5/55	RXF 2/56 - 7/56 HD
OXH 10/54 - 5/55 HD	PLF 9/54 - 11/56 G*	PYU 3/55 - 12/55	RXH 2/56 - 7/56 HD
OXK 2/54 - 7/54	PLH 9/54 - 4/55	PYV 3/55 - 12/55	RXK 3/56 - 7/56 HD
OXL 2/54 - 11/54	PLK 10/54 - 4/55	PYW 3/55 - 10/55	RXL 4/56 - 5/57 HD
OXM 3/54 - 6/54	PLL 10/54 - 12/54	PYX 3/55 - 1/56	RXM 7/55 - 6/56
OXN 3/54 - 11/55 PO	PLM 6/54 - 5/55	PYY 4/55 - 12/55	RXN 7/55 - 11/55
OXO 11/53 - 12/54	PLN 12/54 - 5/55 HD		RXO 7/55 - 1/56
OXP 3/54 - 7/54	PLO 2/55 - 6/56 HD	RGC 4/55 - 5/57 G*	RXP 7/55 - 1/56 G*
OXR 3/54 - 7/54	PLP 2/55 - 11/55 HD	RGF 4/55 - 10/55	RXR 7/55 - 1/56
OXT 3/54 - 12/54	PLR 3/55 - 11/55 HD	RGH 4/55 - 11/55	RXT 7/55 # PO
OXU 3/54 - 7/54	PLT 3/55 - 11/55 HD	RGJ 4/55 - 11/55 PO	RXU 8/55 - 1/56
OXV 3/54 - 7/54	PLU 4/55 - 7/56 HD	RGK 4/55 - 5/57 PO	RXV 8/55 - 1/56
OXW 3/54 - 7/54	PLW 4/55 - 11/55 HD	RGN 4/55 - 12/55	RXW 8/55 - 6/56
OXX 3/54 - 7/54	PLX 5/55 - 7/56 HD	RGO 4/55 - 11/55	RXX 8/55 - 6/56
OXY 4/54 - 12/54	PLY 5/55 - 11/55 HD	RGP 4/55 - 1/56	RXY 8/55 - 6/56
OYE 4/54 - 11/54	PUC 10/54 - 11/55	RGT 4/55 - 6/56	RYE 8/55 - 7/57 **
OYF 4/54 - 11/55 PO	PUL 10/54 - 11/55 PO	RGU 4/55 - 1/56	RYF 8/55 - 12/55
OYH 4/54 - 7/54	PUU 10/54 - 5/55	RGW 5/55 - 1/56	RYH 8/55 - 6/56
OYK 4/54 - 7/54	PUV 11/54 - 11/55	RGX 5/55 - # G	RYK 8/55 - 6/56
OYL 4/54 - 5/55	PUW 11/54 - 11/55	RGY 5/55 - 12/55	RYL 9/55 - 12/55
OYM 4/54 - 11/55	PXA 11/54 - 11/56	RJJ 5/55 - 10/55	RYM 9/55 - 6/56
OYN 5/54 - 11/54	PXB 11/54 - 5/55	RLA 5/55 - 1/56	RYN 9/55 - 12/55
OYO 5/54 - 11/54	PXC 11/54 - 5/55	RLB 5/55 # PO	RYO 9/55 - 9/56
OYP 5/54 - 7/54	PXD 11/54 - 5/55	RLC 5/55 - 1/56	RYP 9/55 - 6/56
OYR 5/54 - 11/54	PXE 11/54 - 11/55	RLD 5/55 - 1/56	RYR 9/55 - 6/56
OYT 5/54 - 11/54	PXF 12/54 - 4/55	RLE 5/55 - 10/55	RYT 10/55 - 6/56
OYU 6/54 - 11/54	PXH 12/54 - 5/55	RLF 6/55 - 12/55	RYU 10/55 - 5/56
OYV 6/54 - 5/55	PXK 12/54 - 5/55	RLH 6/55 - 10/55	RYV 10/55 - 12/56
OYW 6/54 - 12/54	PXL 12/54 - 4/55	RLK 6/55 - 1/56	RYW 10/55 - 6/56
OYX 6/54 - 12/54	PXM 12/54 - 4/55	RLL 6/55 - 12/55	RYX 10/55 - 6/57 G*
OYY 6/54 - 12/54	PXN 12/54 - 5/55	RLM 6/55 - 6/56	RYY 10/55 - 1/56
	PXO 1/55 - 11/55	RLN 6/55 - 1/56	

    #   Date of completion not available.   G   Government Departments.

    G*   Partly Government Departments. (PGW 1-699, PLF 251-999, RGC 501-999, RXP 501-900, RYX 11-560).

    HD   Home Delivery Export Scheme.   PO   Post Office.

    **   Allocated (except 1-9) to Claude Rye, motorcycle dealer, London.

Special mark for Diplomatic Corps : QLD 1   /74

COUNTY COUNCIL OF LONDON (continued)

Code	Dates		Code	Dates		Code	Dates		Code	Dates	
SGC	10/55 - 10/56		SXP	5/56 - 12/56		TLO	1/57 - 11/57		UGC	7/57 - 4/58	HD
SGF	10/55 - 6/56		SXR	5/56 - 3/57		TLP	1/57 - 7/57		UGF	7/57 - 4/58	HD
SGH	11/55 - 5/57	PO	SXT	5/56 - 7/58		TLR	1/57 - 10/57		UGH	8/57 - 6/58	HD
SGJ	11/55 - 10/56		SXU	5/56 - 11/56		TLT	1/57 - 6/57		UGJ	9/57 - 4/58	HD
SGK	11/55 - 12/56		SXV	5/56 - 11/56		TLU	1/57 - 1/58		UGK	10/57 - 9/58	HD
SGN	11/55 - 8/56		SXW	5/56 - 11/56		TLW	2/57 - 7/58		UGN	10/57 - 6/58	HD
SGO	11/55 - 6/56		SXX	5/56 - 1/57		TLX	2/57 - 11/57		UGO	1/58 - 7/58	HD
SGP	11/55 - 5/56		SXY	6/56 - 7/58		TLY	2/57 - 7/57		UGP	2/58 - 7/58	HD
SGT	11/55 - 6/56		SYE	6/56 - 1/57		TUC	2/57 - 11/57		UGT	3/58 - 7/58	HD
SGU	11/55 - 6/56		SYF	6/56 - 12/56		TUL	2/57 - 10/57		UGU	3/58 - 7/58	HD
SGW	11/55 - 1/57		SYH	6/56 - 7/57	G*	TUU	2/57 - 10/57		UGW	4/58 - 10/58	HD
SGX	12/55 - 12/56		SYK	6/56 - 1/57		TUV	2/57 - #	PO	UGX	4/58 - 10/58	HD
SGY	12/55 - 12/56		SYL	6/56 - 1/57		TUW	2/57 - 11/57		UGY	4/58 - 10/58	HD
SJJ	12/55 - 1/57		SYM	7/56 - 1/57		TXA	12/56 - 9/57	HD	UJJ	6/57 - 1/58	
SLA	12/55 - 2/57		SYN	4/56 - 6/57	HD	TXB	1/57 - 10/57	HD	ULA	6/57 - 11/57	
SLB	1/56 - 12/56		SYO	5/56 - 12/56	HD	TXC	1/57 - 1/58	HD	ULB	6/57 - 4/58	
SLC	1/56 - 5/56		SYP	5/56 - 11/56	HD	TXD	3/57 - 11/57	HD	ULC	6/57 - 11/57	
SLD	1/56 - 12/56		SYR	9/56 - 9/56	HD	TXE	4/57 - 7/58	HD	ULD	7/57 - 7/58	
SLE	1/56 - 11/56		SYT	6/56 - 9/56	HD	TXF	5/57 - 11/57	HD	ULE	7/57 - 1/58	
SLF	1/56 - 5/56	PO	SYU	6/56 - 11/56	HD	TXH	5/57 - 10/57	HD	ULF	8/57 - 4/58	
SLH	1/56 - 11/56		SYV	7/56 - 5/57	HD	TXK	6/57 - 10/57	HD	ULH	7/57 - 1/58	
SLK	1/56 - 5/56		SYW	7/56 - 6/57	HD	TXL	6/57 - 11/57	HD	ULK	7/57 - 1/58	
SLL	1/56 - 11/56		SYX	7/56 - 5/58	HD	TXM	3/57 - 7/57		ULL	7/57 - 11/57	
SLM	1/56 - 5/56	PO	SYY	9/56 - 6/57	HD	TXN	3/57 - 11/57		ULM	7/57 - 7/58	
SLN	1/56 - 12/56					TXO	3/57 - 10/57		ULN	7/57 - 1/58	
SLO	1/56 - 5/57	PO	TGC	6/56 - #	PO	TXP	3/57 - 11/57		ULO	7/57 - 1/58	
SLP	1/56 - 12/56		TGF	7/56 - 12/56		TXR	3/57 - 10/57		ULP	8/57 - 1/58	
SLR	2/56 - 6/56		TGH	7/56 - 6/57		TXT	3/57 - 10/57		ULR	8/57 - 4/58	
SLT	1/56 - 3/57		TGJ	7/56 - 1/58		TXU	3/57 - 11/57		ULT	8/57 - 10/58	
SLU	2/56 - 12/56		TGK	7/56 - 10/57		TXV	3/57 - 1/59		ULU	8/57 - 1/58	
SLW	2/56 - 1/57		TGN	7/56 - 1/57		TXW	4/57 - 1/58		ULW	9/57 - 4/58	
SLX	3/56 - 1/57		TGO	8/56 - 1/57		TXX	4/57 - 11/57		ULX	9/57 - 10/58	
SLY	3/56 - 11/56		TGP	8/56 - 1/57		TYY	4/57 - 11/57		ULY	9/57 - 7/59	
SUC	3/56 - 11/56		TGT	8/56 - 1/57		TYE	4/57 - 1/58		UUC	9/57 - 4/58	
SUL	3/56 - 1/57		TGU	8/56 - 1/58		TYF	4/57 - 11/57		UUL	9/57 - 7/58	
SUU	3/56 - 3/57		TGW	9/56 - 7/57		TYH	4/57 - 1/59		UUU	9/57 - 4/58	
SUV	3/56 - 12/56		TGX	9/56 - 1/57		TYK	5/57 - 10/57		UUV	10/57 - 4/58	
SUW	3/56 - 12/56		TGY	9/56 - 7/57		TYL	5/57 - 11/57		UUW	10/57 - 4/58	
SXA	4/56 - 1/57		TJJ	9/56 - 1/59		TYM	5/57 - 10/57		UXA	10/57 - 10/58	
SXB	4/56 - 1/57		TLA	10/56 - 7/57		TYN	5/57 - 1/58		UXB	10/57 - 4/58	
SXC	4/56 - 2/57		TLB	10/56 - 6/57		TYO	5/57 - 1/59		UXC	10/57 - 9/58	
SXD	4/56 - 11/56		TLC	10/56 - 1/58		TYP	3/57 - 7/58		UXD	10/57 - 4/58	
SXE	4/56 - 1/57		TLD	10/56 - 4/58		TYR	5/57 - 7/58		UXE	10/57 - 7/58	
SXF	4/56 - #	G	TLE	10/56 - 6/57		TYT	5/57 - 11/57		UXF	11/57 - 4/58	
SXH	4/56 - #	PO	TLF	11/56 - 7/57		TYU	5/57 - 1/58		UXH	11/57 - #	PO
SXK	4/56 - 12/56		TLH	11/56 - 11/57		TYV	6/57 - 11/57		UXK	11/57 - 4/58	
SXL	4/56 - 1/57		TLK	11/56 - 5/57		TYW	6/57 - 11/57		UXL	11/57 - 4/58	
SXM	4/56 - 1/57		TLL	12/56 - 7/58		TYX	6/57 - 8/58		UXM	11/57 - 7/61	
SXN	4/56 - 1/57		TLM	12/56 - 7/58		TYY	6/57 - 8/58		UXN	11/57 - 7/58	
SXO	5/56 - 1/57		TLN	12/56 - 7/58					UXO	11/57 - 4/58	

| Date of completion not available.
G Government Departments.
G* Partly Government Departments, (SYH 101-550).
HD Home Delivery Export Scheme.
PO Post Office.

COUNTY COUNCIL OF LONDON (continued)

UXP 11/57 - 1/59	VLO 5/58 - 1/59	WGC 5/58 - 12/58 HD	WXP 4/59 - 7/60
UXR 12/57 - 9/58	VLP 5/58 - 1/59	WGF 5/58 - 12/58 HD	WXR 4/59 - 7/60
UXT 12/57 - 4/59	VLR 6/58 - 1/59	WGH 6/58 - 1/59 HD	WXT 4/59 - 12/59
UXU 12/57 - 10/58	VLT 6/58 - 2/62	WGJ 7/58 - 1/59 HD	WXU 4/59 - 12/59
UXV 12/57 ∥ PO	VLU 6/58 - 1/59	WGK 7/58 - 1/59 HD	WXV 4/59 - 12/59
UXW 12/57 - 1/59	VLW 6/58 - 5/59	WGN 7/58 - 1/59 HD	WXW 4/59 - 12/59
UXX 12/57 - 10/58	VLX 6/58 - 1/59	WGO 8/58 - 5/59 HD	WXX 4/59 - 12/59
UXY 12/57 - 10/58	VLY 6/58 - 1/59	WGP 8/58 - 5/59 HD	WXY 4/59 - 12/59
UYE 1/58 - 5/59	VUC 6/56 ∥ PO	WGT 9/58 - 12/59 HD	WYE 4/59 - 7/60
UYF 1/58 - 10/58	VUL 6/56 - 12/59	WGU 9/58 - 6/59 HD	WYF 4/59 - 10/59
UYH 1/58 - 1/59	VUU 7/58 - 1/59	WGW 9/58 - 6/59 HD	WYH 4/59 - 7/60
UYK 1/58 - 1/59	VUV 7/58 - 1/59	WGX 10/58 - 5/59 HD	WYK 4/59 - 10/59
UYL 1/58 - 7/59	VUW 7/58 - 7/59	WGY 11/58 - 7/59 HD	WYL 4/59 - 12/59
UYM 1/58 - 7/58	VXA 7/58 - 12/58	WJJ 12/58 - 11/59	WYM 4/59 - 11/59
UYN 1/58 - 9/58	VXB 7/58 - 1/59	WLA 12/58 ∥ PO	WYN 5/59 - 7/60
UYO 1/58 - 10/58	VXC 7/58 - 6/59	WLB 12/58 - 12/59	WYO 5/59 - 10/59
UYP 2/58 - 12/59	VXD 7/58 - 7/59	WLC 12/58 - 12/59	WYP 5/59 - 7/60
UYR 2/58 - 7/59	VXE 7/58 - 1/59	WLD 12/58 - 12/59	WYR 5/59 - 11/59
UYT 2/58 - 1/59	VXF 7/58 - 5/59	WLE 12/58 - 12/59	WYT 5/59 - 12/59
UYU 2/58 - 7/58	VXH 8/58 - 7/59	WLF 1/59 - 12/59	WYU 5/59 - 7/60
UYV 2/58 - 10/58	VXK 8/58 - 5/59	WLH 1/59 - 12/59	WYV 5/59 - 7/60
UYW 2/58 - 10/58	VXL 8/58 - 7/59	WLK 1/59 - 7/59	WYW 5/59 - 12/59
UYX 2/58 - 1/59	VXM 8/58 - 7/59	WLL 1/59 - 12/59	WYX 5/59 - 12/59
UYY 3/58 - 10/58	VXN 8/58 - 12/59	WLM 1/59 - 7/59	WYY 4/59 - 10/59
	VXO 9/58 - 6/59	WLN 1/59 - 7/61	
VGC 3/58 - 7/58	VXP 9/58 - 7/59	WLO 1/59 - 7/59	
VGF 3/58 - 7/59	VXR 9/58 - 12/59	WLP 1/59 - 12/60	
VGH 3/58 - 10/58	VXT 9/58 - 7/59	WLR 1/59 - 7/60	
VGJ 3/58 - 10/58	VXU 9/58 - 7/59	WLT 1/59 - 2/62	
VGK 3/58 - 1/59	VXV 9/58 - 4/59	WLU 2/59 - 12/59	
VGN 3/58 - 7/59	VXW 9/58 - 5/59	WLW 2/59 - 12/59	
VGO 3/58 - 10/58	VXX 10/58 - 11/59	WLX 2/59 - 7/59	
VGP 3/58 - 10/58	VXY 10/58 - 7/59	WLY 2/59 - 11/59	
VGT 3/58 - 9/58	VYE 10/58 - 5/59	WUC 2/59 - 7/60	
VGU 3/58 - 5/59	VYF 10/58 - 7/59	WUL 2/59 - 12/59	
VGW 4/58 - 10/58	VYH 10/58 - 7/59	WUU 2/59 - 9/60	
VGX 4/58 - 1/59	VYK 10/58 - 7/59	WUV 2/59 - 11/59	
VGY 4/58 - 7/59	VYL 10/58 - 7/59	WUW 2/59 - 7/60	
VJJ 4/58 - 10/58	VYM 11/58 - 11/59	WXA 3/59 - 11/59	
VLA 4/58 - 12/58	VYN 11/58 - 7/59	WXB 3/59 - 7/59	
VLB 4/58 - 1/59	VYO 11/58 - 12/59	WXC 3/59 - 7/60	
VLC 4/58 - 1/59	VYP 11/58 - 12/59	WXD 3/59 - 11/59	
VLD 5/58 - 10/58	VYR 11/58 - 6/59	WXE 3/59 - 8/60	
VLE 5/58 - 1/59	VYT 11/58 - 7/60	WXF 3/59 - 12/59	
VLF 5/58 - 1/59	VYU 11/58 - 6/59	WXH 3/59 - 7/60	
VLH 5/58 - 7/59	VYV 11/58 - 7/59	WXK 3/59 - 12/59	
VLK 5/58 - 7/59	VYW 11/58 - 7/59	WXL 3/59 - 12/59	
VLL 5/58 - 1/59	VYX 12/58 - 7/59	WXM 3/59 - 12/59	
VLM 5/58 - 1/59	VYY 12/58 - 7/59	WXN 3/59 - 11/59	
VLN 5/58 - 7/60		WXO 4/59 - 12/59	

∥ Date of completion not available.
G   Government Departments.
G* Partly Government Departments, (SYH 101-550).
HD Home Delivery Export Scheme.
PO Post Office.

XGC	2/59 - 7/59 HD	XUW	7/59 - 7/60	YGC	8/59 - 9/60 HD	YUW	1/60 - 7/60
XGF	3/59 - 11/59 HD	XXA	8/59 - 7/60	YGF	10/59 - 7/61 HD	YXA	1/60 - 11/60
XGH	4/59 - 11/59 HD	XXB	8/59 - 7/60	YGH	11/59 - 2/62 HD	YXB	1/60 - 11/60
XGJ	4/59 - 12/59 HD	XXC	8/59 - 7/60	YGJ	11/59 - 7/60 HD	YXC	2/60 - 7/61
XGK	5/59 - 12/59 HD	XXD	8/59 // PO	YGK	11/59 - 10/60 HD	YXD	2/60 - 11/60
XGN	5/59 - 12/59 HD	XXE	8/59 - 7/60	YGN	12/59 - 7/60 HD	YXE	2/60 - 11/60
XGO	5/59 - 7/60 HD	XXF	8/59 - 7/61	YGO	2/60 - 7/60 HD	YXF	2/60 // PO
XGP	6/59 - 12/59 HD	XXH	8/59 - 7/60	YGP	3/60 - 10/60 HD	YXH	2/60 - 7/61
XGT	6/59 - 7/60 HD	XXK	8/59 - 7/60	YGT	3/60 - 7/60 HD	YXK	2/60 - 11/60
XGU	7/59 - 7/60 HD	XXL	9/59 - 7/60	YGU	4/60 - 9/60 HD	YXL	2/60 - 11/60
XGW	7/59 - 7/60 HD	XXM	9/59 - 7/60	YGW	4/60 - 9/60 HD	YXM	2/60 - 12/60
XGX	8/59 - 7/60 HD	XXN	9/59 - 7/60	YGX	5/60 - 8/60 HD	YXN	2/60 - 7/61
XGY	8/59 - 7/60 HD	XXO	9/59 - 7/60	YGY	5/60 - 12/60 HD	YXO	2/60 - 11/60
XJJ	6/59 - 12/59	XXP	9/59 - 7/60	YJJ	11/59 - 7/60	YXP	2/60 - 7/61
XLA	6/59 - 12/59	XXR	9/59 - 7/60	YLA	11/59 - 7/60	YXR	2/60 - 11/60
XLB	6/59 - 12/59	XXT	9/59 - 7/60	YLB	12/59 - // PO	YXT	2/60 - 11/60
XLC	6/59 - 7/60	XXU	9/59 - 7/60	YLC	12/59 - 7/60	YXU	2/60 - 7/61
XLD	6/59 - 12/59	XXV	9/59 - 7/60	YLD	12/59 - 10/60	YXV	3/60 - 11/60
XLE	6/59 - 7/60	XXW	10/59 - 10/60	YLE	12/59 - 7/60	YXW	3/60 - 7/61
XLF	6/59 - 7/60	(XXX not issued)	YLF	12/59 - 7/60	YXX	3/60 - 11/60		
XLH	6/59 - 12/59	XXY	10/59 - 7/60	YLH	12/59 - // PO	YXY	3/60 - 11/60
XLK	6/59 - 7/60	XYE	10/59 - 7/60	YLK	12/59 - 7/60	YYE	3/60 - 11/60
XLL	6/59 - 12/59	XYF	10/59 - 7/60	YLL	12/59 - 7/60	YYF	3/60 - 11/60
XLM	6/59 - 12/59	XYH	10/59 - 7/60	YLM	12/59 - 11/60	YYH	3/60 - 12/60
XLN	7/59 - 7/60	XYK	10/59 - 7/60	YLN	12/59 - 7/60	YYK	3/60 - 7/61
XLO	7/59 - 7/60	XYL	10/59 - 7/60	YLO	12/59 - 11/60	YYL	3/60 - 7/61
XLP	7/59 - 7/60	XYM	10/59 - 7/60	YLP	1/60 - 7/60	YYM	3/60 - 7/61
XLR	7/59 - 12/59	XYN	10/59 - 7/60	YLR	1/60 - 7/60	YYN	3/60 - 11/60
XLT	7/59 - 7/60	XYO	10/59 - 7/60	YLT	1/60 - 7/60	YYO	3/60 - 11/60
XLU	7/59 - 12/59	XYP	10/59 - 1/62	YLU	1/60 - 7/61	YYP	3/60 - 11/60
XLW	7/59 - 7/60	XYR	11/59 - 7/60	YLW	1/60 - 7/60	YYR	3/60 - 10/60
XLX	7/59 - 12/59	XYT	11/59 - 7/60	YLX	1/60 - 11/60	YYT	3/60 - 10/60
XLY	7/59 - 7/60	XYU	11/59 - 7/60	YLY	1/60 - 11/60	YYU	4/60 - 11/60
XUC	7/59 - 7/60	XYV	11/59 - 7/60	YUC	1/60 - 11/60	YYV	4/60 - 11/60
XUL	7/59 - 12/59	XYW	11/59 - 7/60	YUL	1/60 - 11/60	YYW	4/60 - 11/60
XUU	7/59 - 7/60	XYX	11/59 - 7/60	YUU	1/60 - 11/60	YYX	4/60 - 1/62
XUV	7/59 - 7/60	XYY	11/59 - 6/62	YUV	1/60 - 11/60	(YYY not issued)	

//   Date of completion not available.
HD   Home Delivery Export Scheme.
PO   General Post Office.

Reverse format issues commenced simultaneously with *AJJ* and *AXA* in 4/60. In the *Axx* only, commercials were again segregated, but this time the commercial series somewhat curiously included motorcycles. Home Delivery Exports continued as before and there were therefore two sequences current after the *Axx*.

Special Series
General Post Office : *ALK, BLE, BXE, BXY, BYF, BYY, CLB, CXN, CXY, DLF, DXV, ELP, EXU, FLE, FUU, FXY, FYM, GPO, GXF (705-999 voided).*
Other Government Departments : *DYE*, including 601-999 for London Transport, of which 886-999 were voided, also BR/WR and Ministry of Supply (ex War Department); *ELM* (including MOD, Ministry of Aviation, Forestry Commission); *FUL, FUV* and the lower numbers of *FUW* were issued to the Ministry of Public Buildings and Works for vehicles transferred from the Armed Services, the higher numbers of *FUW* were used for other Government Departments; *GXE* (very few issued).
Commercial vehicles and motorcycles : *AJJ to ALH, ALL to AUW.*
Mainly motorcycles : *ELU, EYM, GLW*
Home Delivery Exports : *AGC to AGY, CGC to CGY, DGC to DGY, EGC to EGY, GGC to GGY* (not all issued), *HGC to HGY* (only odd issues). The following were exclusive to Fords : *AGH, CGH, CGO, CGU, CGX, DGH, EGF, EGX, GGH, GGN.*

Code	From	To	Note	Code	From	To	Note	Code	From	To	Note	Code	From	To	Note
AGC	5/60	11/60	HD	AXP	5/60	1/61		BLO	12/60	1/62		CGC	2/61	7/61	HD
AGF	5/60	1/62	HD	AXR	5/60	7/61		BLP	12/60	7/61		CGF	2/61	1/62	HD
AGH	6/60	9/60	HD	AXT	5/60	12/60		BLR	12/60	6/62		CGH	4/61	1/62	HD
AGJ	6/60	8/60	HD	AXU	6/60	7/61		BLT	1/61	1/62		CGJ	3/61	7/61	HD
AGK	6/60	7/61	HD	AXV	6/60	11/60		BLU	1/61	7/61		CGK	4/61	1/62	HD
AGN	6/60	11/60	HD	AXW	6/60	12/60		BLW	1/61	7/61		CGN	5/61	1/62	HD
AGO	6/60	8/60	HD	AXX	6/60	12/60		BLX	1/61	6/62		CGO	6/61	1/62	HD
AGP	6/60	7/61	HD	AXY	6/60	7/61		BLY	1/61	7/61		CGP	6/61	1/62	HD
AGT	6/60	12/60	HD	AYE	6/60	12/60		BUC	1/61	1/62		CGT	6/61	3/63	HD
AGU	7/60	7/61	HD	AYF	6/60	1/61		BUL	1/61	7/61		CGU	7/61	6/62	HD
AGW	7/60	7/61	HD	AYH	7/60	11/62		BUU	1/61	7/61		CGW	7/61	6/62	HD
AGX	12/60	7/61	HD	AYK	7/60	7/61		BUV	2/61	7/61		CGX	8/61	6/62	HD
AGY	1/61	1/62	HD	AYL	7/60	7/61		BUW	2/61	12/62		CGY	9/61	6/62	HD
AJJ	4/60	12/60	C	AYM	7/60	7/61		BXA	2/61	7/63		CJJ	4/61	6/62	
ALA	4/60	7/61	C	AYN	7/60	12/60		BXB	2/61	1/62		CLA	4/61	7/61	
ALB	4/60	7/61	C	AYO	7/60	7/61		BXC	2/61	7/61		CLB	5/61	//	PO
ALC	4/60	1/62	C	AYP	7/60	7/61		BXD	2/61	1/62		CLC	5/61	6/62	
ALD	4/60	7/61	C	AYR	7/60	6/62		BXE	2/61	//	PO	CLD	5/61	6/62	
ALE	5/60	1/63	C	AYT	8/60	1/62		BXF	2/61	1/62		CLE	5/61	1/62	
ALF	5/60	6/62	C	AYU	8/60	6/62		BXH	2/61	6/62		CLF	5/61	1/62	
ALH	5/60	7/61	C	AYV	8/60	1/61		BXK	2/61	1/62		CLH	5/61	6/62	
ALK	5/60	//	PO	AYW	8/60	12/60		BXL	2/61	7/61		CLK	5/61	1/62	
ALL	5/60	1/62	C	AYX	8/60	7/61		BXM	3/61	11/62		CLL	5/61	6/62	
ALM	6/60	2/63	C	AYY	9/60	6/62		BXN	3/61	1/62		CLM	5/61	1/62	
ALN	6/60	7/61	C					BXO	3/61	7/61		CLN	5/61	1/64	
ALO	6/60	7/61	C	BGC	9/60	1/62		BXP	3/61	1/62		CLO	5/61	1/62	
ALP	6/60	1/62	C	BGF	9/60	7/61		BXR	3/61	1/62		CLP	5/61	6/62	
ALR	6/60	1/62	C	BGH	9/60	7/61		BXT	3/61	7/61		CLR	5/61	6/62	
ALT	6/60	12/60	C	BGJ	9/60	1/62		BXU	3/61	7/61		CLT	5/61	11/62	
ALU	6/60	6/62	C	BGK	9/60	7/61		BXV	3/61	1/62		CLU	5/61	1/62	
ALW	7/60	7/61	C	BGN	10/60	7/61		BXW	3/61	7/61		CLW	6/61	7/63	
ALX	7/60	7/61	C	BGO	10/60	12/62		BXX	3/61	1/62		CLX	6/61	12/62	
ALY	7/60	7/61	C	BGP	10/60	7/61		BXY	3/61	//	PO	CLY	6/61	1/62	
AUC	8/60	7/61	C	BGT	10/60	7/61		BYE	3/61	1/62		CUC	6/61	1/62	
AUL	8/60	7/61	C	BGU	10/60	7/61		BYF	3/61	//	PO	CUL	6/61	6/62	
AUU	8/60	1/62	C	BGW	10/60	7/61		BYH	3/61	1/62		CUU	6/61	6/62	
AUV	9/60	7/61	C	BGX	10/60	1/62		BYK	3/61	1/62		CUV	6/61	1/62	
AUW	9/60	7/61	C	BGY	10/60	7/61		BYL	3/61	1/62		CUW	6/61	6/62	
AXA	4/60	11/60		BJJ	11/60	7/61		BYM	3/61	1/62		CXA	6/61	6/62	
AXB	4/60	11/60		BLA	11/60	1/62		BYN	4/61	7/63		CXB	6/61	6/62	
AXC	4/60	11/60		BLB	11/60	7/61		BYO	4/61	1/62		CXC	6/61	1/63	
AXD	4/60	11/60		BLC	11/60	7/61		BYP	4/61	7/61		CXD	6/61	12/62	
AXE	4/60	11/60		BLD	11/60	1/62		BYR	4/61	6/62		CXE	7/61	1/62	
AXF	5/60	11/60		BLE	11/60	//	PO	BYT	4/61	1/62		CXF	7/61	6/62	
AXH	5/60	11/60		BLF	11/60	7/61		BYU	4/61	1/62		CXH	7/61	6/62	
AXK	5/60	11/60		BLH	12/60	7/61		BYV	4/61	1/62		CXK	7/61	6/62	
AXL	5/60	11/60		BLK	12/60	6/62		BYW	4/61	7/61		CXL	7/61	1/62	
AXM	5/60	1/61		BLL	12/60	1/62		BYX	4/61	1/62		CXM	7/61	6/62	
AXN	5/60	6/62		BLM	12/60	7/63		BYY	4/61	//	PO	CXN	7/61	//	PO
AXO	5/60	6/62		BLN	12/60	1/62						CXO	7/61	7/63	

//   Date of completion not available.
C   Commercials and motorcycles.
HD   Home delivery Exports.
PO   General Post Office.

CXP	7/61	-	6/62		DLO	12/61	-	6/62		EGC	6/62	-	7/63	HD	EXP	9/62	-	7/63
CXR	7/61	-	6/62		DLP	12/61	-	1/63		EGF	9/62	-	7/63	HD	EXR	9/62	-	7/63
CXT	8/61	-	1/63		DLR	12/61	-	1/63		EGH	9/62	-	7/63	HD	EXT	9/62	-	7/63
CXU	8/61	-	6/62		DLT	12/61	-	6/62		EGJ	10/62	-	7/63	HD	EXU	10/62	//		PO
CXV	8/61	-	12/62		DLU	1/62	-	12/62		EGK	11/62	-	3/64	HD	EXV	9/62	-	7/63
CXW	8/61	-	1/62		DLW	1/62	-	1/63		EGN	1/63	-	7/63	HD	EXW	9/62	-	7/63
CXX	8/61	-	6/62		DLX	1/62	-	1/63		EGO	1/63	-	1/64	HD	EXX	10/62	-	7/63
CXY	9/61	//		PO	DLY	1/62	-	1/63		EGP	1/63	-	1/64	HD	EXY	10/62	-	7/63
CYE	8/61	-	12/62		DUC	1/62	-	1/63		EGT	3/63	-	1/64	HD	EYE	10/62	-	7/63
CYF	8/61	-	6/62		DUL	1/62	-	7/63		EGU	4/63	-	1/64	HD	EYF	10/62	-	7/63
CYH	8/61	-	6/62		DUU	1/62	-	1/63		EGW	5/63	-	1/64	HD	EYH	10/62	-	7/63
CYK	9/61	-	6/62		DUV	1/62	-	6/62		EGX	4/63	-	1/64	HD	EYK	10/62	-	7/63
CYL	9/61	-	6/62		(DUW not alloc.)					EGY	4/63	-	3/64	HD	EYL	10/62	-	7/63
CYM	9/61	-	6/62		DXA	1/62	-	6/62		EJJ	5/62	-	1/63		EYM	10/62	-	7/63	M
CYN	9/61	-	6/62		DXB	1/62	-	1/63		ELA	5/62	-	7/63		EYN	11/62	-	7/63
CYO	9/61	-	12/62		DXC	2/62	-	1/64		ELB	5/62	-	7/63		EYO	11/62	-	1/64
CYP	9/61	-	6/62		DXD	2/62	-	6/62		ELC	5/62	-	1/63		EYP	11/62	-	7/63
CYR	9/61	-	6/62		DXE	2/62	-	7/63		ELD	5/62	-	1/63		EYR	11/62	-	1/64
CYT	10/61	-	6/62		DXF	2/62	-	1/63		ELE	5/62	-	1/63		EYT	11/62	-	7/63
CYU	10/61	-	6/63		DXH	2/62	-	1/63		ELF	5/62	-	7/63		EYU	11/62	-	1/64
CYV	10/61	-	6/62		DXK	2/62	-	6/62		ELH	5/62	-	1/63		EYV	11/62	-	7/63
CYW	10/61	-	6/62		DXL	2/62	-	1/64		ELK	6/62	-	3/64		EYW	12/62	-	1/64
CYX	10/61	-	6/62		DXM	2/62	-	1/64		ELL	6/62	-	7/63		EYX	12/62	-	3/64
CYY	10/61	-	6/62		DXN	2/62	-	1/63		ELM	6/62	//		G	EYY	12/62	-	7/63
					DXO	3/62	-	1/63		ELN	6/62	-	1/63					
DGC	11/61	-	3/64	HD	DXP	3/62	-	7/63		ELO	6/62	-	7/63					
DGF	12/61	-	6/62	HD	DXR	3/62	-	6/62		ELP	6/62	//		PO				
DGH	12/61	-	6/62	HD	DXT	3/62	-	12/62		ELR	6/62	-	7/63					
DGJ	2/62	-	1/63	HD	DXU	3/62	-	1/63		ELT	6/62	-	1/63					
DGK	2/62	-	1/63	HD	DXV	3/62	//		PO	ELU	6/62	-	1/63	M				
DGN	4/62	-	1/63	HD	DXW	3/62	-	7/63		ELW	6/62	-	7/63					
DGO	3/62	-	1/63	HD	DXX	3/62	-	1/63		ELX	6/62	-	1/63					
DGP	4/62	-	7/63	HD	DXY	3/62	-	1/63		ELY	6/62	-	1/63					
DGT	5/62	-	1/63	HD	DYE	3/62	//		G	EUC	7/62	-	1/63					
DGU	5/62	-	1/63	HD	DYF	3/62	-	1/63		EUL	7/62	-	7/63					
DGW	6/62	-	7/63	HD	DYH	3/62	-	7/63		EUU	7/62	-	1/63					
DGX	6/62	-	7/63	HD	DYK	3/62	-	7/63		EUV	7/62	-	7/63					
DGY	6/62	-	7/63	HD	DYL	4/62	-	1/63		EUW	7/62	-	7/63					
DJJ	10/61	-	12/62		DYM	4/62	-	7/63		EXA	7/62	-	7/63					
DLA	10/61	-	6/62		DYN	4/62	-	6/63		EXB	7/62	-	1/63					
DLB	11/61	-	6/62		DYO	4/62	-	7/63		EXC	7/62	-	7/63					
DLC	11/61	-	6/62		DYP	4/62	-	1/63		EXD	7/62	-	7/63					
DLD	11/61	-	6/62		DYR	4/62	-	1/63		EXE	8/62	-	1/64					
DLE	11/61	-	6/62		DYT	4/62	-	1/63		EXF	8/62	-	7/63					
DLF	12/61	//		PO	DYU	4/62	-	1/63		EXH	8/62	-	3/64					
DLH	11/61	-	7/63		DYV	5/62	-	1/63		EXK	8/62	-	7/63					
DLK	12/61	-	7/63		DYW	5/62	-	1/63		EXL	8/62	-	7/63					
DLL	12/61	-	12/62		DYX	5/62	-	7/63		EXM	9/62	-	7/63					
DLM	12/61	-	12/62		DYY	5/62	-	1/63		EXN	9/62	-	7/63					
DLN	12/61	-	12/62							EXO	9/62	-	7/63					

// Date of completion not available.
G   Government Departments. (866-999 DYE unused).
HD Home delivery Exports.
M   Mainly motorcycles.
PO General Post Office.

Mark	Dates	Mark	Dates	Mark	Dates	Mark	Dates
FGC	12/62 - 7/63	FUW	4/63 // G	GGC	6/63 - 3/64 HD	GUW	8/63 - 3/64
FGF	12/62 - 7/63	FXA	3/63 - 7/63	GGF	6/63 - 1/64 HD	GXA	8/63 - 1/64
FGH	1/63 - 1/64	FXB	3/63 - 1/64	GGH	6/63 - 1/64 HD	GXB	9/63 - 3/64
FGJ	1/63 - 1/64	FXC	4/63 - 7/63	GGJ	7/63 - 3/64 HD	GXC	9/63 - 3/64
FGK	1/63 - 7/63	FXD	4/63 - 1/64	GGK	2/64 - 3/64 HD	GXD	9/63 - 3/64
FGN	1/63 - 1/64	FXE	3/63 - 1/64	GGN	7/63 - 3/64 HD	GXE	9/63 // G
FGO	1/63 - 7/63	FXF	4/63 - 1/64	GGO	8/63 - 3/64 HD	GXF	9/63 // PO
FGP	1/63 - 1/64	FXH	4/63 - 1/64	GGP	8/63 - 3/64 HD	GXH	9/63 - 3/64
FGT	1/63 - 7/63	FXK	4/63 - 1/64	GGT	9/63 - 3/64 HD	GXK	9/63 - 3/64
FGU	1/63 - 1/64	FXL	4/63 - 3/64	GGU	1/64 - 3/64 HD	GXL	9/63 - 3/64
FGW	1/63 - 7/63	FXM	4/63 - 1/64	(GGW not issued)		GXM	9/63 - 3/64
FGX	1/63 - 3/64	FXN	4/63 - 1/64	GGX	**	GXN	9/63 - 3/64
FGY	2/63 - 7/63	FXO	4/63 - 1/64	GGY	**	GXO	9/63 - 3/64
FJJ	2/63 - 3/64	FXP	4/63 - 3/64	GJJ	6/63 - 3/64	GXP	10/63 - 3/64
FLA	2/63 - 7/63	FXR	4/63 - 1/64	GLA	6/63 - 3/64	GXR	10/63 - 3/64
FLB	2/63 - 1/64	FXT	4/63 - 1/64	GLB	6/63 - 1/64	GXT	10/63 - 3/64
FLC	2/63 - 1/64	FXU	5/63 - 1/64	GLC	$	GXU	9/63 - 3/64
FLD	2/63 - 7/63	FXV	4/63 - 1/64	GLD	6/63 - 3/64	GXV	10/63 - 3/64
FLE	2/63 // PO	FXW	5/63 - 1/64	GLE	6/63 - 1/64	GXW	10/63 - 3/64
FLF	2/63 - 7/63	FXX	5/63 - 3/64	GLF	6/63 - 1/64	GXX	10/63 - 3/64
FLH	2/63 - 1/64	FXY	5/63 // PO	GLH	6/63 - 1/64	GXY	10/63 - 3/64
FLK	2/63 - 1/64	FYE	5/63 - 1/64	GLK	7/63 - 3/64	GYE	10/63 - 3/64
FLL	3/63 - 3/64	FYF	5/63 - 1/64	GLL	7/63 - 1/64	GYF	10/63 - 3/64
FLM	3/63 - 3/64	FYH	5/63 - 1/64	GLM	7/63 - 3/64	GYH	11/63 - 3/64
FLN	3/63 - 1/64	FYK	5/63 - 1/64	GLN	7/63 - 1/64	GYK	11/63 - 3/64
FLO	3/63 - 1/64	FYL	5/63 - 3/64	GLO	7/63 - 3/64	GYL	11/63 - 3/64
FLP	3/63 - 7/63	FYM	6/63 // PO	GLP	7/63 - 1/64	GYM	11/63 - 3/64
FLR	3/63 - 1/64	FYN	5/63 - 1/64	GLR	7/63 - 3/64	GYN	11/63 - 3/64
FLT	2/63 - 7/63	FYO	5/63 - 1/64	GLT	7/63 - 3/64	GYO	11/63 - 3/64
FLU	3/63 - 3/64	FYP	5/63 - 3/64	GLU	7/63 - 3/64	GYP	11/63 - 3/64
FLW	3/63 - 1/64	FYR	5/63 - 1/64	GLW	7/63 - 1/64 M	GYR	12/63 - 3/64
FLX	3/63 - 1/64	FYT	5/63 - 1/64	GLX	7/63 - 3/64	GYT	12/63 - 3/64
FLY	3/63 - 1/64	FYU	6/63 - 1/64	GLY	8/63 - 1/64	GYU	12/63 - 3/64
(FUC not alloc.)		FYV	6/63 - 1/64	GPO	8/63 // PO	GYV	12/63 - 3/64
FUL	4/63 // G	FYW	6/63 - 3/64	GUC	8/63 - 3/64	GYW	12/63 - 3/64
FUU	4/63 // PO	FYX	6/63 - 1/64	GUL	8/63 - 3/64	GYX	12/63 - 3/64
FUV	4/63 // G	FYY	6/63 - 1/64	GUU	8/63 - 1/64	GYY	12/63 - 3/64
				GUV	8/63 - 3/64		

2 HUV early issue for Diplomatic Corps 1/64.

**   Intended for HDES, but not so used, The only issues were 750 GGX and 57 GGY, (dates unknown, but before 4/64).

$ Intended for Greater London Council, but not taken up before commencement of suffix marks and remained unused except for 1 GLC on Chairman's Official Car.

G   Government Departments.   HD   Home Delivery Export Scheme.

PO   Post Office, (705-999 GXF unused).   M   Mainly motorcycles.

HGC to HGY were intended for Home Delivery Export Scheme, but not so used; there was one issue in each of HGJ and HGT only, (1 HGJ, 3 HGT - dates of issue unknown, but before 4/64). HXA to HXY inclusive were omitted.

Mark	Dates	Mark	Dates	Mark	Dates	Mark	Dates
HJJ	12/63 - 3/64	HLH	1/64 - 3/64	HLR	2/64 - 3/64	HUL	3/64 - 3/64
HLA	1/64 - 3/64	HLK	1/64 - 3/64	HLT	2/64 - 3/64	HUU	3/64 - 3/64
HLB	1/64 - 3/64	HLL	1/64 - 3/64	HLU	2/64 - 3/64	HUV	3/64 - 3/64
HLC	1/64 - 3/64	HLM	1/64 - 3/64	HLW	2/64 - 3/64	HUW	3/64 - 3/64
HLD	1/64 - 3/64	HLN	1/64 - 3/64	HLX	2/64 - 3/64	HYE	3/64 - 3/64
HLE	1/64 - 3/64	HLO	2/64 - 3/64	HLY	2/64 - 3/64	HYF	3/64 - 3/64
HLF	1/64 - 3/64	HLP	2/64 - 3/64	HUC	2/64 - 3/64	HYH	3/64 - 3/64

Suffix Marks commenced 1.4.64

COUNTY COUNCIL OF LONDON (continued)

HYK and *HYL* were re-registration series commenced by the LCC. On formation of the GLC five area offices were set up and further re-registration series from *HYM* onwards, issued by the GLC, were allocated to a specific office, although in practice Central and North West usually shared series.

Re-registration series :

HYK 6/64 LCC	HYP 3/66 C	HYW 3/71 C/NW	JGH 5/73 C/NW	JGP 5/74 C	JGY 7/74 C
HYL 1/65 LCC*	HYR 4/65 NW	HYX 10/71 C/NW	JGJ 7/73 C/NW	JGT 7/74 C/NW	(JJJ not iss.)
HYM 4/65 SE	HYT 8/67 C	HYY 7/71 C/NW	JGK 11/73 C/NW	JGU c1/76 C	JLA 10/74 C
HYN 4/65 SW	HYU 3/69 C *	JGC 12/72 C/NW	JGN 1/74 C/NW*	JGW c3/76 C	JLB c4/75 C
HYO 4/65 NE	HYV 5/70 C	JGF 3/73 C/NW	JGO 2/74 C	JGX 9/74 NW	JLC c9/75 C *

* The dates shown are those for the general introduction of the series. Odd numbers were often issued earlier, e.g.
  1 HYL 9/64, 1 HYU 11/65, 9 JGN 11/73, 1 JGY 5/74, 1 JLC 10/74.

Further re-registration series in the former LCC sequence were issued by three of the London LVLOs and are mentioned here for the sake of completeness. Very few numbers were issued in these series : *KYY* (Central), *KGC* (South West), *KGU* and *LGU* (South East). (North West used *KBY*, a mark inherited from Croydon by the GLC.)

Special marks for Diplomatic Corps : *1-6 KUW ca. 2/63; 1 KYR ca.3/98; 1 MLT ca.10/66; 1-3 MLW ca. 11/66; 1 MYN 7/93; 1 RUV ca. 10/63; 1 SGP ca. 8/66; 1 SLK ca. 10/93. 1 SLU 3/99.*

G.P.O. Registration Marks. The Post Office have decided not to retain registration marks with the letters GPO which they have had allocated to them for many years. These marks are not being surrendered en masse but will be gradually withdrawn as vehicles are disposed of. When the Post Office sell a vehicle, the GPO mark will not be transferred to another of their vehicles and they do not wish it to remain on the vehicle when sold. It has been agreed that, in these circumstances, the vehicle passing from the possesssion of the Post Office should be given a fresh registration mark, as nearly as possible appropriate to the vehicle's age when requested by the local post office manager. Councils are requested to comply with requests for a change of mark made by their local post office and to inform the G.L.C. when GPO marks become void. *M.o.T.Memo 106/69, 18.8.69*

COUNTY COUNCIL OF MERIONETH

Registration commenced January 1904.

FF 1/04

Registers commence with a single series of numbers issued in sequence for both cars and motorcycles, but by February 1904 some numbers had been issued to both cars and motorcycles, so a decision seems to have been taken to duplicate numbers thereafter, issuing earlier numbers somewhat randomly and out of sequence. The motorcycle sequence reached 561 by February 1921 between which date and October 1921 a separate motorcycle series FF 01 to FF 0112 was issued. From December 1921 to August 1922, (between FF 840 and FF 1043), cars received odd numbers and motorcycles even ones. Thereafter segregation was abandoned.

First issues each year :

	Cars	Cycles		Cars	Cycles		All Vehicles				
1905	*	37	1914	231	208	1922	852	1934	4002	1946	6203
1906	31	53	1915	303	258	1923	1130	1935	4229	1947	6497
1907	46	72	1916	378	327	1924	1422	1936	4525	1948	6890
1908	69	77	1917	414	343	1925	1704	1937	4849	1949	7299
1909	84 #	91	1918	420	348	1926	2042	1938	5204	1950	7693
1910	102	104	1919	434	361	1927	2343	1939	5479	1951	8036
1911	119	121	1920	523	429 **	1928	2653	1940	5725	1952	8357
1912	143	135	1921	701	552 ##	1929	2901	1941	5836	1953	8686
1913	180	162				1930	3147	1942	5925	1954	9170
						1931	3414	1943	5977	1955	9680
						1932	3621	1944	6047		
						1933	3821	1945	6122		

*   1904 issues were 1-30, 1905 : 8, 13, 14, 17-27; (29 issued 1906).
#   FF 100 & 102 early issues, 1908.
** FF 691 (isolated) issued 1920
Plus FF 01 to FF 0112

AFF	6/55	CFF	8/58	EFF	8/60	GFF	6/62
BFF	2/57	DFF	10/59	FFF	7/61	HFF	4/63

Commenced suffix marks 2.1.64

(KFF to YFF inclusive were allocated 10/93 to 12/94 by the DVLA to various VROs for "Age Related" marks.)

COUNTY COUNCIL OF MIDDLESEX

Incorporated in GREATER LONDON COUNCIL 1.4.65.

From 1926 onward the issues of Middlesex were more complicated than those of any other authority. The reasons for this included at different times, (a) reservation of blocks of numbers and whole series for War Department vehicles, (b) reservation of series for particular dealers or manufacturers, (c) reservation of certain series for specific classes of vehicle. Unfortunately no records of this authority have survived and certain of the information which follows has no official basis.

War Department

From 1920 to the outbreak of World War II practically all War Department vehicles were registered with Middlesex. Some of the very earliest received void numbers in H; later blocks of 200 or more numbers, usually at the end of a series, (as well as numerous scattered numbers), were allocated in various two-letter series, (including ME, MH, MK, ML, MT and HX. In MG the block was from 8001 to 9999). In the three-letter era complete series were allocated to the War Department. The first two nominally War Department series excluded the numbers 1 to 20 which were used for private cars, in the next eleven series it was just the number 1 which was similarly excluded. Then in late 1938, when normal issues had reached the Kxx block, the War Department were allocated marks in the Rxx series, followed by the Pxx series and SHX. Civilian registration of War Department vehicles ceased in 1939. From May 1952, when Middlesex were becoming hard pressed for available marks, the unused portions of certain War Department series were released for civilian issue, whilst those blocks which had been allocated to armoured vehicles were reissued for civilian purposes, since there was no likelihood of these vehicles returning to service with their pre-war registrations. (However, numerous vehicles of civilian types released by the War Department did resume their pre-war numbers.) No official dates are available for the start and end of War Department series; the issue dates shown in the tabulation are approximate, but believed to be accurate within a couple of months.

Manufacturers and Dealers

The first reservation of a complete mark for a motor dealer came with the issue of MM in May 1926, which was reserved for Stewart and Ardern Ltd., the largest distributors of Morris vehicles in the London area. This was followed in September 1929 by MU; thereafter three-letter combinations of MM and MU were, for some years, reserved for this dealer, with the exception of AMM, BMM and CMM. Stewart and Ardern first used AMU, BMU, CMU, DMU. EMU and then in 5/36 a separate series FMU was commenced for commercial vehicles; thereafter the 'MM' combinations were used for private cars, (DMM to JMM) and the 'MU' combinations for commercials (FMU to JMU). Then Stewart & Ardern's MM and MU monopoly ceased. Their marks had always lagged behind the normal sequence, so that by the time JMU had finished KMM, KMU, LMM, LMU, MMM and MMU had already been omitted from the normal sequence in the expectation that Stewart & Ardern would need them; they were eventually used for other purposes. Even in the War Department blocks RMM, RMU, PMM and PMU had been left for Stewart & Ardern. However, just as Stewart & Ardern bowed out another dealer or, rather, maufacturer, appeared on the Middlesex scene, and Vauxhall Motors had exclusive use of MMU, RMU, TMU, VMC, VML, VMV, WMV and XMU.

It is commonly believed that MG, (excluding 8001-9999), was reserved for issue by the M.G. Car Company or by University Motors Ltd., and although it is true that MG contained numerous MG cars, the allocation was not exclusive. The issue of this mark was spread over 19 years !

Vehicle Type Segregation

In the H series there were separate blocks for Heavy Motor Cars, including H 1901-2000. The first mark reserved exclusively for commercial vehicles, (apart from those in the Stewart and Ardern series), appears to be FMY in 4/37, whilst motorcycle segregation appears to have commenced with LMK in 5/42.

Because of the irregularities detailed above there were, after 5/26, two or more series in use simultaneously and in some cases issues extended over a long period; numbers were not always issued sequentially but "allocated in blocks". For these reasons both start and finish dates are given for each series and for ease of reference marks are not shown in strict chronological order.

Omissions

The three letter marks NMC to NMY inclusive were originally omitted from Middlesex's allocation, but following their authorisation in SI 962 of 1.6.61 they were issued, first in the reverse format and then in the forward, during and after the currency of reverse two-letter marks. (It is believed that they were orginally omitted at the request of the Metropolitan Police to obviate telephonic confusion).

H	12/03 - 7/12		ML	9/26 - 8/27		
MX	7/12 - 8/17		MP	8/27 - 8/28		
MC	8/17 - 8/20		MT	8/28 - 6/29		
MD	8/20 - 11/21		MY	6/29 - 5/33	(issued irregularly after 4000)	
ME	11/21 - 5/23		MU	9/29 - 12/34	Stewart & Ardern, issued irregularly	
MF	5/23 - 7/24		MG	3/30 - 3/49	(8001-9999 War Department)	
MH	7/24 - 8/25		HX	6/30 - 3/33	(issued irregularly after 4000)	
MK	8/25 - 9/26		MV	7/31 - 6/33	(issued irregularly in two series,	
MM	5/26 - 12/29	(Stewart & Ardern)			1 up and 9999 down simultaneously).	

AHX	12/32 - 2/33			CHX	10/35 - 12/35		
AMC	12/32 - 12/33			CMC	2/35 - 3/35		
AMD	3/33 - 6/33			CMD	5/35 - 9/35		
AME	3/33 - 3/34			CME	1/35 - 7/35		
AMF	4/33 - 3/34			CMF	5/35 - 9/35		
AMG	6/33 - 9/33			CMG	3/35 - 6/35		
AMH	6/33 - 2/34			CMH	3/35 - 6/35		
AMK	7/33 - 12/34			CMK	4/35 - 7/35		
AML	9/33 - 1/34			CML	3/35 - 11/35	(30-399, 471-999)	
AMM	10/33 - 1/34				/52 - 11/52	(400-470 only)	
AMP	c4/34	21-999 WD		CMM	c5/35	2-999 WD, of which	
AMT	10/33 - 5/34					800-999 armoured.	
AMU	9/34 11/35	Stewart & Ardern			7/52 - 1/53	800-999 reissued.	
AMV	1/34 - 3/34			CMP	5/35 - 10/35		
AMX	1/34 - 7/34			CMT	7/35 - 1/36		
AMY	10/32 - 4/34	(issued at this time to		CMU	6/35 - 2/36	Stewart & Ardern	
		commemorate Amy Johnson's		CMV	8/35 - 3/36		
		flight)		CMX	8/35 - 9/35		
				CMY	9/35 - 1/36		

BHX	11/34 - 1/35			DHX	1/36 - 3/36		
BMC	2/34 - 10/34	(1-500)		DMC	c10/35	2-999 WD	
	2/34 - 10/36	(501-999)		DMD	11/35 - 4/36		
BMD	3/34 - 3/35			DME	12/35 - 3/36		
BME	3/34 - 5/34			DMF	c3/36	2-999 WD	
BMF	4/34 - 11/34			DMG	12/35 - 3/36		
BMG	5/34 - 7/34			DMH	1/36 - 4/36		
BMH	5/34 - 12/34			DMK	3/36 - 6/36		
BMK	6/34 - 12/34			DML	3/36 - 8/36		
BML	7/34 - 11/34			DMM	8/36 - 3/37	Stewart & A. private	
BMM	c12/34	21-999 WD, of which		DMP	3/36 - 6/36		
		21-220, 800-999 armoured.		DMT	3/36 - 11/36		
	5/52 - 5/53	21-220 & 800-999 reissued.		DMU	11/35 - 3/36	Stewart & Ardern	
		(mainly or all m/cycles)		DMV	c8/36	2-999 WD, of which	
BMP	7/34 - 11/34					800-999 armoured	
BMT	9/34 - 3/35				11/52 - 3/53	800-999 reissued.	
BMU	3/35 - 12/35	Stewart & Ardern		DMX	4/36 - 6/36		
BMV	10/34 - 11/35			DMY	4/36 - 8/36		
BMX	12/34 - 4/35						
BMY	11/34 - 6/35						

Code	Dates	Notes	Code	Dates	Notes
EHX	c1/37	2-999 WD, of which 800-999 armoured	HHX	c10/37	WD
			HMC	c6/38	WD. All armoured.
	9/52 - 1/53	800-999 reissued		7/52 - 1/53	All reissued m/cycles
EMC	5/36 - 9/36		HMD	c3/38	WD
EMD	5/36 - 9/36		HME	4/38 - 9/38	Commercial
EME	c7/36	2-999 WD	HMF	12/37 - 3/38	
EMF	6/36 - 10/36		HMG	1/38 - 4/38	
EMG	c9/36	2-999 WD	HMH	c5/38	WD. All armoured
EMH	6/36 - 9/36			9/52 - 11/53	All reissued m/cycles
EMK	7/36 - 10/36		HMK	12/37 - 5/38	
EML	9/26 - 12/36		HML	c1/38	WD
EMM	2/37 - 10/37	Stewart & Ardern. Private	HMM	12/38 - 6/39	Stewart & A. Private
EMP	9/36 - 1/37		HMP	c1/38	WD
EMT	8/36 - 11/36		HMT	c4/38	WD
EMU	3/36 - 8/36	Stewart & Ardern	HMU	5/39 - 5/49	Stewart & A. Commer'l
EMV	c12/36	2-999 WD	HMV	12/36 - 12/38	Block 11-110 comm.
EMX	10/36 - 12/36				early for Gramophone Co.
EMY	11/36 - 1/37	1-499			and issued up to 1947
	1/37 - 7/50	500-999	HMX	3/38 - 5/38	
			HMY	c2/38	WD
FHX	c5/37	WD	JHX	3/38 - 5/38	Private
FMC	11/36 - 4/37		JMC	5/38 - 7/38	Private
FMD	12/36 - 4/37		JMD	4/38 - 8/38	
FME	c2/37	2-999 WD, of which 800-999 armoured	JME	c4/38	WD
			JMF	c8/38	WD
	12/52 - 3/53	800-999 reissued.	JMG	c5/38	WD
FMF	12/36 - 3/37		JMH	5/38 - 9/38	
FMG	c3/37	2-999 WD	JMK	c9/38	WD
FMH	12/36 - 6/37		JML	9/38 - 12/38	
FMK	1/37 - 4/37		JMM	9/45 - 6/47	Stewart & A. Private
FML	2/37 - 5/37		JMP	6/38 - 10/38	
FMM	10/37 - 4/38	Stewart & A. Private.	JMT	9/38 - 1/39	Commercial
FMP	3/37 - 4/37		JMU	3/49 - 8/52	Stewart & A. Commer'l
FMT	3/37 - 7/37		JMV	c7/38	WD
FMU	5/36 - 5/38	Stewart & A. Commercial	JMX	c4/38	WD
FMV	4/37 - 6/37		JMY	8/38 - 12/38	
FMX	c6/37	WD (799-999 armoured)			
	1/53 - 3/53	799-999 reissued.			
FMY	4/37 - 12/37	Commercial			
GHX	10/37 - 1/38	Private cars	KHX	9/38 - 12/38	Private
GMC	4/37 - 5/37		KMC	11/38 - 1/39	
GMD	6/37 - 7/37		KMD	12/38 - 4/39	
GME	6/37 - 9/37		KME	12/38 - 5/39	
GMF	c9/37	WD	KMF	1/39 - 6/39	
GMG	12/37 - 5/38	Commercial	KMG	3/39 - 5/39	
GMH	6/37 - 9/37		KMH	3/39 - 7/39	
GMK	8/37 - 1/38	Commercial	KMK	4/39 - 6/39	
GML	6/37 - 10/37		KML	2/39 - 5/39	
GMM	4/38 - 12/38	Stewart & Ardern. Private.	KMM	4/47 - 2/48	
GMP	8/37 - 10/37		KMP	5/39 - 7/39	
GMT	12/37 - 2/38		KMT	5/39 - 7/39	
GMU	5/38 - 11/49	Stewart & Ardern. Commercial.	KMU	7/50 - 1/51	Motorcycles, (except 1)
GMV	9/37 - 11/37		KMV	2/39 - 10/39	Commercial
GMX	9/37 - 12/37		KMX	7/39 - 2/40	Commercial
GMY	c8/37	WD	KMY	6/39 - 9/39	Commercial

COUNTY COUNCIL OF MIDDLESEX (continued)

Code	Period	Description
LHX	7/39 - 12/39	private
LMC	7/39 - 3/40	cars and m/cycles
LMD	11/39 - 12/41	private
LME	3/40 - 3/42	commercial
LMF	3/40 - 8/41	
LMG	9/41 - 1/46	
LMH	10/41 - 9/42	commercial
LMK	5/42 - 7/46	m/cycles
LML	7/42 - 9/43	
LMM	2/48 - 3/49	private
LMP	9/43 - 10/43	commercial
LMT	9/44 - 10/45	
LMU	3/51 - 1/53	
LMV	9/45 - 2/46	
LMX	12/45 - 5/46	
LMY	2/46 - 6/46	commercial
MHX	3/46 - 6/46	
MMC	2/46 - 6/46	m/cycles
MMD	5/46 - 9/46	m/cycles
MME	5/46 - 9/46	commerial
MMF	7/46 - 10/46	private
MMG	5/46 - 9/46	private
MMH	8/46 - 11/47	commercial
MMK	8/46 - 2/47	m/cycles
MML	9/46 - 2/49	private
MMM	5/49 - 4/50	private
MMP	9/46 - 11/47	commercial
MMT	10/46 - 12/48	
MMU	1/50 - 10/50	Vauxhall Motors
MMV	11/46 - 11/47	m/cycles
MMX	11/46 - 10/47	
MMY	11/46 - 2/49	commercial
NHX	12/46 - 2/48	private.

(See after reverse series for NMC to NMY)

Code	Period	Description
OHX	12/46 - 5/48	private
OMC	c2/46	G **
OMD	c2/46	G **
OME	c3/46 -	G **
OMF	c3/46	G **
OMG	c2/46	G **
OMH	c10/46	G **
OMK	2/47 - 11/47	commercial
OML	1/47 - 1/49	commercial
OMM	11/49 - 10/50	private
OMP	2/47 - 7/48	private
OMT	3/47 - 7/48	commercial
OMU	3/50 - 7/50	m/cycles
OMV	c8/46	G ** 1-609, 626-637, 876-999
	9/47 - 9/47	commer'l 610-625, 638-875
OMX	c3/47	G ** 1-250
	11/49 - 10/50	commercial 251-999
OMY	c10/46	G ** 1-374
	9/47 - 9/49	commercial 375-999

Code	Period	Description
PHX	c6/39	WD
PMC	c9/39	WD
PMD	c7/39	WD
PME	c7/39	WD
PMF	c7/39	WD
PMG	c8/39	WD
PMH	c9/39	WD
PMK	c9/39	WD
PML	/39	WD 1-330
	5/50 - 2/52	331-999
PMM	10/50 - 10/51	private
PMP	c10/39	WD
PMT	c9/39	WD
PMU	5/50 - 8/51	m/cycles
PMV	/39	WD (All armoured)
	10/52 - 5/53	Reissued
PMX	/39	WD ***
PMY	c10/39	WD 1-551
	1/51 - 6/51	552-999
RHX	c10/38	WD
RMC	c11/38	WD
RMD	c3/39	WD
RME	c2/39	WD
RMF	c3/39	WD
RMG	c3/39	WD
RMH	c8/39	WD
RMK	c3/39	WD
RML	c4/39	WD
RMM	10/50 - 8/51	m/cycles
RMP	c5/39	WD
RMT	c7/39	WD
RMU	7/50 - 7/51	Vauxhall Motors
RMV	/39	WD (All armoured)
	11/52 - 11/53	Reissued
RMX	c4/39	WD
RMY	c10/39	WD (All armoured)
	9/52 - 5/53	reissued.
SHX	c7/39	WD
SMC	4/47 - 7/49	private
SMD	5/47 - 11/47	ex WD vehicles only
SME	4/47 - 12/48	commercial
SMF	7/47 - 8/48	commercial
SMG	5/47 - 5/48	private
SMH	8/47 - 12/48	private
SMK	9/47 - 9/49	m/cycles
SML	11/47 - 10/49	commercial
SMM	4/51 - 8/51	m/cycles
SMP	5/47 - 9/49	m/cycles
SMT	6/47 - 4/48	private
SMU	1/51 - 5/52	commercial
SMV	10/47 - 9/49	private
SMX	1/48 - 9/49	private
SMY	1/48 - 9/49	commercial

G**   Government. Vehicles transferred from War Department to civilian ministries.

WD   War Department.   WD *** May not be complete, 1 to at least 476 armoured.

THX	3/48	-	7/49	private	WHX	2/51	-	9/51	private
TMC	6/48	-	3/49	m/cycles	WMC	2/50	-	4/51	private
TMD	8/48	-	9/49	m/cycles	WMD	9/50	-	10/51	private
TME	9/48	-	9/49	private	WME	6/50	-	1/51	private
TMF	11/48	-	4/49	m/cycles	WMF	12/50	-	8/51	
TMG	4/48	-	3/49	commercial	WMG	9/50	-	5/52	m/cycles
TMH	6/48	-	9/49	private	WMH	1/51	-	7/51	m/cycles
TMK	10/48	-	1/50	commercial	WMK	6/51	-	3/52	m/cycles
TML	1/49	-	10/49	private	WML	5/51	-	10/51	m/cycles
TMM	4/50	-	10/51	commercial	WMM	1/52	-	8/52	private
TMP	3/48	-	11/49	m/cycles	WMP	10/51	-	1/53	commercial
TMT	5/48	-	7/49	private	WMT	4/51	-	7/52	commercial
TMU	5/51	-	1/52	Vauxhall Motors Ltd.	WMU	3/52	-	7/53	commercial
TMV	6/48	-	9/49	commercial	WMV	10/51	-	1/54	Vauxhall Motors Ltd.
TMX	11/48	-	4/49	private	WMX	6/50	-	1/54	***
TMY	1/49	-	6/50	commercial	WMY	7/51	-	7/52	commercial
UHX	6/49	-	4/50	commercial	XHX	7/51	-	11/52	private
UMC	3/49	-	10/49	private	XMC	4/51	-	2/52	private
UMD	4/49	-	6/50	private	XMD	8/51	-	8/52	m/cycles
UME	7/49	-	2/50	m/cycles	XME	12/51	-	7/52	private
UMF	11/49	-	5/50	m/cycles	XMF	8/51	-	8/52	private
UMG	5/49	-	5/52	*	XMG	3/52	-	5/53	private
UMH	3/49	-	7/49	m/cycles	XMH	2/52	-	8/52	m/cycles
UMK	7/49	-	1/50	private	XMK	5/52	-	11/52	m/cycles
UML	6/48	-	1/53	**	XML	4/52	-	7/53	m/cycles
UMM	7/51	-	3/52	m/cycles	XMM	11/52	-	11/53	private & commercial
UMP	3/49	-	6/50	commercial	XMP	7/52	-	12/52	m/cycles
UMT	5/49	-	1/50	m/cycles	XMT	1/52	-	3/53	commerial
UMU	6/52	-	11/53	commercial	XMU	7/52	-	5/53	Vauxhall Motors Ltd.
UMV	6/49	-	6/50	private	XMV	3/52	-	7/53	m/cycles
UMX	9/49	-	10/50	private	XMX	10/51	-	8/52	private
UMY	8/49	-	10/50	commercial	XMY	2/52	-	11/52	private
VHX	1/50	-	8/50	private	YHX	5/52	-	11/52	private
VMC	5/49	-	2/50	Vauxhall Motors Ltd.	YMC	6/52	-	11/52	private
VMD	9/49	-	4/50	m/cycles	YMD	7/52	-	1/53	private
VME	1/50	-	9/51	commercial	YME	9/52	-	6/53	private
VMF	4/50	-	8/51	private	YMF	12/52	-	11/53	private
VMG	11/49	-	10/50	private	YMG	11/52	-	1/54	
VMH	4/50	-	8/51	m/cycles	YMH	1/53	-	9/53	
VMK	6/50	-	9/51	private	YMK	1/53	-	9/53	
VML	2/48	-	5/51	Vauxhall Motors Ltd.	YML	2/53	-	9/53	
VMM	10/51	-	3/52	m/cycles	YMM	2/53	-	8/53	
VMP	1/50	-	6/50	m/cycles	YMP	3/53	-	11/53	
VMT	6/50	-	1/51	m/cycles	YMT	3/53	-	11/53	
VMU	12/51	-	11/52	m/cycles	YMU	5/53	-	10/53	
VMV	11/49	-	7/52	Vauxhall Motors Ltd.	YMV	4/53	-	8/53	
VMX	10/50	-	9/51	commercial	YMX	5/53	-	8/53	
VMY	3/51	-	10/51	m/cycles	YMY	5/53	-	1/54	

*   UMG Early issues were all MG cars, later used as motorcycle series.

**   UML Early issues were for University Motors Ltd., later ordinary (mixed) issue.

***   WMX 1 issued early, (2/50), for mayoral car of Wembley, other low numbers Middlesex C.C.,
        general issue from 1953.

Reverse format marks commenced with H, then all three-letter marks were used before the two-letter ones. The regular segregation of vehicle categories came to an end and the issue of marks more closely followed alphabetical order. Most series, however, continued to remain in use for several months.

H   6/53 - 3/54   (issued in two blocks, 1000-4999 and 5000-5999).

Mark	Dates		Mark	Dates			Mark	Dates			Mark	Dates	
AHX	9/53 - 1/54		DHX	10/54 - 3/55			GHX	9/55 - 3/56			KHX	9/56 - 9/57	
AMC	9/53 - 5/54		DMC	10/54 - 10/55			GMC	10/55 - 2/56			KMC	12/56 - 8/57	
AMD	9/53 - 9/54		DMD	10/54 - 5/55			GMD	9/55 - 6/56			KMD	10/56 - 9/57	
AME	10/53 - 9/54		DME	11/54 - 3/55			GME	11/55 - 5/56			KME	1/57 - 9/57	
AMF	10/53 - 9/54		DMF	11/54 - 4/55			GMF	10/55 - 6/56			KMF	12/56 - 8/57	
AMG	10/53 - 9/54		DMG	11/54 - 5/55			GMG	11/55 - 5/56			KMG	2/57 - 7/57	
AMH	10/53 - 5/54		DMH	12/54 - 5/55			GMH	9/55 - 6/56			KMH	10/56 - 7/57	
AMK	11/53 - 9/54		DMK	12/54 - 10/55			GMK	10/55 - 5/56			KMK	1/57 - 8/57	
AML	11/53 - 9/54		DML	12/54 - 10/55	F		GML	12/55 - 5/56			KML	2/57 - 1/58	
AMM	11/53 - 9/54		DMM	12/54 - 8/55			GMM	9/55 - 3/56			KMM	11/56 - 7/57	
AMP	12/53 - 9/54		DMP	1/55 - 9/55			GMP	10/55 - 6/56			KMP	1/57 - 7/57	
AMT	12/53 - 9/54		DMT	1/55 - 7/55			GMT	12/55 - 5/56			KMT	2/57 - 8/57	
AMU	1/54 - 8/54		DMU	1/55 - 6/55			GMU	11/55 - 7/56			KMU	11/56 - 12/57	M
AMV	1/54 - 9/54		DMV	1/55 - 9/55			GMV	10/55 - 6/56			KMV	11/56 - 7/57	
AMX	1/54 - 12/54		DMX	2/55 - 8/55			GMX	11/55 - 4/56			KMX	12/56 - 8/57	
AMY	1/54 - 8/54		DMY	2/55 - 9/55			GMY	12/55 - 4/57	V		KMY	3/57 - 9/57	
BHX	2/54 - 9/54		EHX	2/55 - 7/55			HHX	12/55 - 4/56			LHX	3/57 - 11/57	
BMC	2/54 - 10/54		EMC	2/55 - 8/55			HMC	2/56 - 9/56			LMC	4/57 - 7/57	
BMD	3/54 - 12/54		EMD	3/55 - 9/55			HMD	1/56 - 10/56			LMD	3/57 - 10/57	
BME	3/54 - 10/54		EME	3/55 - 12/55			HME	3/56 - 10/56			LME	5/57 - 4/58	
BMF	3/54 - 9/54		EMF	3/55 - 9/55			HMF	3/56 - 9/56			LMF	4/57 - 11/57	
BMG	3/54 - 9/54		EMG	3/55 - 9/55			HMG	3/56 - 9/56			LMG	5/57 - 1/58	
BMH	3/54 - 3/55		EMH	3/55 - 2/56	V		HMH	1/56 - 9/56			LMH	3/57 - 10/57	
BMK	4/54 - 11/54		EMK	3/55 - 9/55			HMK	3/56 - 10/56			LMK	4/57 - 11/57	
BML	4/54 - 1/55		EML	4/55 - 9/55			HML	4/56 - 10/56			LML	5/57 - 2/58	
BMM	2/54 - 9/54		EMM	4/55 - 9/55			HMM	1/56 - 12/56			LMM	3/57 - 8/57	
BMP	4/54 - 11/54		EMP	4/55 - 9/55			HMP	1/56 - 9/56			LMP	5/57 - 12/57	
BMT	4/54 - 10/54		EMT	4/55 - 11/55			HMT	4/56 - 10/56			LMT	6/57 - 10/57	
BMU	3/54 - 11/54		EMU	5/55 - 12/55			HMU	2/56 - 9/56			LMU	6/57 - 6/58	
BMV	5/54 - 1/55		EMV	5/55 - 10/55			HMV	2/56 - 9/56			LMV	4/57 - 8/57	
BMX	5/54 - 11/54		EMX	5/55 - 10/55			HMX	2/56 - 9/56			LMX	5/57 - 10/57	
BMY	6/54 - 3/55		EMY	5/55 - 9/55			HMY	4/56 - 10/56			LMY	3/57 - 1/59	
CHX	6/54 - 3/55		FHX	5/55 - 3/56			JHX	4/56 - 1/57			MHX	6/57 - 3/58	
CMC	6/54 - 4/55		FMC	6/55 - 11/55			JMC	6/56 - 1/57			MMC	8/57 - 9/58	
CMD	6/54 - 3/55		FMD	5/55 - 1/56			JMD	5/56 - 11/56			MMD	6/57 - 1/58	
CME	7/54 - 2/55		FME	7/55 - 2/56			JME	7/56 - 4/57			MME	9/57 - 4/58	
CMF	7/54 - 6/55		FMF	6/55 - 1/56			JMF	6/56 - 2/57			MMF	9/57 - 6/58	
CMG	7/54 - 5/55		FMG	8/55 - 2/56			JMG	7/56 - 6/57			MMG	10/57 - 6/58	
CMH	8/54 - 3/55		FMH	5/55 - 2/56			JMH	5/56 - 1/57			MMH	7/57 - 2/58	
CMK	8/54 - 4/55		FMK	7/55 - 2/56			JMK	7/56 - 3/57			MMK	9/57 - 3/58	
CML	8/54 - 3/55		FML	7/55 - 2/56			JML	9/56 - 7/57			MML	10/57 - 1/59	
CMM	6/54 - 3/55		FMM	6/55 - 2/56			JMM	6/56 - 2/57	M		MMM	6/57 - 7/59	
CMP	9/54 - 3/55		FMP	7/55 - 2/56			JMP	6/56 - 2/57			MMP	9/57 - 6/58	
CMT	9/54 - 4/55		FMT	8/55 - 2/56			JMT	8/56 - 3/57			MMT	9/57 - 3/58	
CMU	9/54 - 3/55		FMU	8/55 - 3/56			JMU	8/56 - 5/57			MMU	8/57 - 4/58	
CMV	10/54 - 4/55		FMV	6/55 - 1/56			JMV	5/56 - 4/57			MMV	7/57 - 2/58	
CMX	10/54 - 6/57		FMX	7/55 - 1/56			JMX	7/56 - 3/57			MMX	7/57 - 12/58	
CMY	10/54 - 4/55		FMY	8/55 - 3/56			JMY	9/56 - 4/57			MMY	7/57 - 7/58	

F   Mainly or all Ford   M   All Morris   V   Mainly or all Vauxhall

COUNTY COUNCIL OF MIDDLESEX (continued)

NHX 10/57 - 6/58 (See after reverse two-letter marks for NMC to NMY)

PHX	1/58 - 9/58	THX	10/58 - 9/59	WHX	6/59 - 1/60	
PMC	10/57 - 9/58	TMC	11/58 - 9/59	WMC	7/59 - 6/60	
PMD	11/57 - 9/58	TMD	10/58 - 7/59	WMD	6/59 - 11/59	
PME	2/58 - 5/59	TME	11/58 - 6/59	WME	8/59 - 1/60	
PMF	1/58 - 6/58	TMF	12/58 - 10/59	WMF	7/59 - 1/60	
PMG	3/58 - 8/58	TMG	12/58 - 7/59	WMG	8/59 - 1/60	
PMH	11/57 - 12/58	TMH	10/58 - 6/59	WMH	9/59 - 4/60	
PMK	2/58 - 9/58	TMK	12/58 - 10/59	WMK	7/59 - 3/60	
PML	2/58 - 9/58	TML	11/58 - 10/59	WML	8/59 - 3/60	
PMM	1/58 - 6/58	TMM	10/58 - 10/59	WMM	7/59 - 5/60	
PMP	1/58 - 2/59	TMP	11/58 - 7/59	WMP	7/59 - 5/60	
PMT	2/58 - 9/58	TMT	12/58 - 7/59	WMT	9/59 - 4/60	
PMU	2/58 - 7/59	TMU	1/59 - 9/59	WMU	9/59 - 3/60	
PMV	12/57 - 7/58	TMV	10/58 - 5/59	WMV	7/59 - 3/60	
PMX	12/57 - 2/59	TMX	12/58 - 7/59	WMX	7/59 - 1/61	
PMY	12/57 - 9/59	TMY	1/59 - 9/59	WMY	8/59 - 10/59	
RHX	3/58 - 11/58	UHX	1/59 - 11/59	XHX	9/59 - 6/60	
RMC	3/58 - 1/59	UMC	2/59 - 10/59	XMC	10/59 - 6/60	
RMD	3/58 - 11/58	UMD	1/59 - 7/59	XMD	10/59 - 6/60	
RME	5/58 - 2/59	UME	3/59 - 10/59	XME	11/59 - 6/60	
RMF	4/58 - 11/58	UMF	2/59 - 9/59	XMF	10/59 - 6/60	
RMG	5/58 - 3/59	UMG	3/59 - 1/60	XMG	12/59 - 6/60	
RMH	3/58 - 10/58	UMH	1/59 - 9/59	XMH	10/59 - 6/60	
RMK	4/58 - 2/59	UMK	3/59 - 10/59	XMK	11/59 - 4/60	
RML	5/58 - 1/59	UML	3/59 - 9/59	XML	12/59 - 7/60	
RMM	3/58 - 10/58	UMM	3/59 - 12/59	XMM	10/59 - 5/60	
RMP	4/58 - 12/58	UMP	2/59 - 9/59	XMP	11/59 - 6/60	
RMT	5/58 - 11/58	UMT	3/59 - 9/59	XMT	12/59 - 11/60	
RMU	5/58 - 1/59	UMU	2/59 - 5/60	XMU	9/59 - 11/60	
RMV	3/58 - 12/58	UMV	2/59 - 7/59	XMV	10/59 - 6/60	
RMX	4/58 - 11/58	UMX	3/59 - 7/59	XMX	11/59 - 1/61	
RMY	6/58 - 1/59	UMY	4/59 - 10/59	XMY	12/59 - 5/60	
SHX	6/58 - 1/59	VHX	4/59 - 11/59	YHX	12/59 - 6/60	
SMC	7/58 - 4/59	VMC	4/59 - 11/59	YMC	1/60 - 7/60	
SMD	7/58 - 9/59	VMD	4/59 - 12/59	YMD	12/59 - 7/60	
SME	6/58 - 2/59	VME	5/59 - 10/59	YME	2/60 - 6/60	
SMF	7/58 - 7/59	VMF	5/59 - 12/59	YMF	1/60 - 7/60	
SMG	9/58 - 3/59	VMG	5/59 - 11/59	YMG	2/60 - 11/60	
SMH	6/58 - 5/59	VMH	4/59 - 1/60	YMH	1/60 - 11/60	
SMK	7/58 - 5/59	VMK	5/59 - 9/59	YMK	1/60 - 11/60	
SML	8/58 - 5/59	VML	6/59 - 11/59	YML	1/60 - 10/60	
SMM	7/58 - 5/59	VMM	5/59 - 1/60	YMM	3/60 - 11/60	■/cycles only
SMP	8/58 - 5/59	VMP	5/59 - 1/60	YMP	12/59 - 10/60	
SMT	9/58 - 4/59	VMT	5/59 - 9/59	YMT	2/60 - 10/60	
SMU	10/58 - 3/59	VMU	6/59 - 12/59	YMU	3/60 - 9/60	■/cycles only
SMV	6/58 - 5/59	VMV	4/59 - 10/59	YMV	12/59 - 11/60	
SMX	8/58 - 6/59	VMX	5/59 - 10/59	YMX	2/60 - 11/60	
SMY	9/58 - 2/59	VMY	6/59 - 11/59	YMY	2/60 - 10/60	■/cycles only

Two-letter marks commenced either at 1 or 1000, depending upon whether they were in use or earmarked for trade plates. They were issued in the order shown, numbers being allocated in blocks of 1000 or 2000 :

MK	2/60 - 11/61	1000	MM	1/61 - 5/62	1	MX	2/62 - 7/63	1000
HX	2/60 - 3/61	1	MC	1/61 - 7/62	1000	MD	2/62 - 4/63	1000
MV	3/60 - 1/62	1	MT	2/61 - 6/62	1	MG	3/62 - 7/63	1000
MP	3/60 - 9/61	1	MF	2/61 - 7/62	1000	MU	4/62 - 7/63	1000
ME	6/60 - 11/61	1000	MY	2/61 - 7/62	1			
MH	6/60 - 9/61	1000	ML	9/61 - 2/63	1			

The previously omitted marks NMC to NMY were issued firstly in reverse format, contemporaneously with the later two-letter reverse marks and then in forward format following the last of the two-letter marks - the forward marks were the last issues before suffix marks commenced. Both reverse and forward were issued in haphazard order.

NMC	10/61 - 7/62		NMM	3/62 - 9/62 M	NMC	8/62 - 4/63		NMM	1/63 - 7/63
NMD	12/61 - 7/62		NMP	2/62 - 6/62	NMD	5/62 - 10/62		NMP	2/63 - 5/63
NME	11/61 - 7/62		NMT	12/61 - 7/62	NME	11/62 - 5/63		NMT	12/62 - 5/63
NMF	2/62 - 9/62		NMU	12/61 - 4/63	NMF	1/63 - 6/63		NMU	12/62 - 2/63
NMG	12/61 - 7/62		NMV	1/62 - 7/62	NMG	2/63 - 5/63		NMV	9/62 - 5/63
NMH	1/62 - 7/62		NMX	10/61 - 7/62	NMH	12/62 - 6/63		NMX	7/62 - 4/63
NMK	5/62 - 10/62 M	NMY	12/61 - 6/62	NMK	1/63 - 4/63		NMY	2/63 - 12/63
NML	1/62 - 6/62				NML	1/63 - 9/63			

M   mainly or all motorcycles.

Suffix marks commenced 18/2/63.

Arrangements have been made whereby the undermentioned Government Departments will transfer their exempt vehicles, other than such vehicles as are domiciled in Ireland, to a central authority for bulk registration :

Department	Central Licensing Authority
Admiralty)	
Air Ministry)	Middlesex County Council
Ministry of Labour)	
War Office)	
General Post Office	London County Council

The existing identification marks will be retained.

Circular RF 147, 9.12.21

Tanks, Armoured Cars and other mechanically-propelled military vehicles forming part of the fighting equipment of the Army and which are obviously "engines of War" carry identification marks issued by the Middlesex County Council, but by special arrangement licences are not issued in respect of these vehicles. Vehicles of normal construction and appearance, i.e. touring cars, lorries and motor cycles, are supplied with exempt licences....

M.o.T.Handbook, 1925 edition

COUNTY COUNCIL OF MONMOUTH

AX 1/04   WO 3/27

It appears that the original intention was to allot separate blocks of numbers for motorcycles and motor cars and issues started from AX 1 for cycles and AX 50 for cars. However, having reached AX 49, motorcycles continued without a break and thereafter there were two parallel series until early 1921. AX 1-49 were also used for cars, being issued spasmodically between 1907 and 1911.

First issues each year :

	Cars	Cycles		Cars	Cycles			All Vehicles			
		AX			AX						
1905	104	187	1914	611	857	1922	AX	3865 **	1931	WO	4929 **
1906	147	227	1915	788	1070	1923	AX	4654 **	1932	WO	5965
1907	194 + 1-8	258	1916	997	1296	1924	AX	5674 **	1933	WO	6957
1908	257 + 9-40	293	1917	1119	1422	1925	AX	6967	1934	WO	7909
1909	282 + 41-5	337	1918	1173	1508	1926	AX	8567	1935	WO	9210
1910	314 + 46-8	405	1919	1209	1531	1927	AX	9790 **			
1911	349 + 49	475	1920	1483	1979	1928	WO	1181 **			
1912	404	564	1921	2095 *	2740 *	1929	WO	2347 **			
1913	474	684				1930	WO	3597			

*   Last in car series was AX 2096 and in cycle series AX 2746; common series from AX 2747.
**   Numbers shown are actually one above the highest issued in the previous year.
***   AX 9998 was early issue in 1926 and WO 6000, 7000 and 8000 in 1931, 1932 & 1933 respectively.

AAX	6/35	BAX	9/39	JAX	11/49	NAX	10/54	SAX	8/57	WAX	8/59
AWO	3/36	BWO	3/42	JWO	8/50	NWO	3/55	SWO	12/57	WWO	11/59
BAX	9/36	FAX	9/44	KAX	5/51	OAX	6/55	TAX	3/58	XAX	2/60
BWO	4/37	FWO	8/46	KWO	3/52	OWO	10/55	TWO	6/58	XWO	4/60
CAX	11/37	GAX	3/47	LAX	10/52	PAX	2/56	UAX	9/58	YAX	6/60
CWO	7/38	GWO	10/47	LWO	6/53	PWO	6/56	UWO	1/59	YWO	8/60
DAX	3/39	HAX	6/48	MAX	12/53	RAX	12/56	VAX	3/59		
DWO	omitted	HWO	3/49	MWO	4/54	RWO	4/57	VWO	5/59		

AAX	11/60	CAX	9/61	EAX	5/62	GAX	3/63	JAX	10/63
AWO	2/61	CWO	1/62	EWO	7/62	GWO	5/63	JWO	1/64
BAX	4/61	DAX	3/62	FAX	10/62	HAX	6/63	KAX	1/66 (re-registrations)
BWO	6/61	DWO	omitted	FWO	1/63	HWO	8/63		

No reason has ever been adduced for the non-issue of DWO.

Commenced suffix marks 27.2.64

COUNTY COUNCIL OF MONTGOMERY

A common sequence for all vehicles.

EP 12/03

First issues each year, (approximate) :

1904	10	1912	216	1920	1077	1928	3885	1936	6350	1944	8607
1905	46	1913	297	1921	1501	1929	4166	1937	6695	1945	8786
1906	71	1814	433	1922	1822	1930	4500	1938	7116	1946	8947
1907	92	1915	584	1923	2048	1931	4867	1939	7448	1947	9419
1908	106	1916	724	1924	2342	1932	5165	1940	7780		
1909	120	1917	793	1925	2741	1933	5436	1941	7960		
1910	135	1918	832	1926	3164	1934	5701	1942	8194		
1911	163	1919	858	1927	3537	1935	5993	1943	8408		

AEP	11/47	DEP	12/52	GEP	9/56	KEP	4/59	NEP	5/61	REP	6/63
BEP	3/49	EEP	5/54	HEP	11/57	LEP	2/60	OEP	2/62	SEP	1/64
CEP	1/51	FEP	7/55	JEP	8/58	MEP	10/60	PEP	10/62	TEP	7/64

Commenced suffix marks 1.1.65

COUNTY COUNCIL OF NORFOLK

AH 1/04   PW 1/23   VF 2/27   NG 12/30

Before 1921 there were three parallel sequences : AH 1 up for cars etc., AH 1 up for motorcycles; AH 01 up for Heavy Motor Cars. The latter series reached at least AH 0824, but no information is available on the extent of the motorcycle series.

No information is available to the writer on yearly issues, but some details may be available in Norfolk Record Office. The following are known ranges of numbers in the HMC series for certain years :

1906	AH 05-07	1911	AH 059	1916	AH 0297-0318
1907	AH 09	1912	AH 075-0108	1917	AH 0370
1908	AH 022-026	1913	AH 0117-0163		
		1914	AH 0171-0221	1919	AH 0499-0633
1910	AH 048-054	1915	AH 0240-0268	1920	AH 0750-0824

First issues :

1929	VF 4881	1931	NG 156	1933	NG 4084	1935	NG 8751
1930	VF 7571	1932	NG 2139	1934	NG 6191		

AAH	5/35	BAH	9/40	JAH	4/48	NAH	1/52	SAH	12/54	WAH	2/57
ANG	9/35	BNG	10/41	JNG	7/48	NNG	3/52	SNG	2/55	WNG	4/57
APW	1/36	BPW	8/42	JPW	10/48	NPW	6/52	SPW	3/55	WPW	5/57
AVF	4/36	BVF	5/43	JVF	1/49	NVF	8/52	SVF	5/55	WVF	7/57
BAH	8/36	FAH	5/44	KAH	4/49	OAH	10/52	TAH	6/55	XAH	8/57
BNG	11/36	FNG	5/45	KNG	7/49	ONG	1/53	TNG	8/55	XNG	10/57
BPW	3/37	FPW	1/46	KPW	9/49	OPW	3/53	TPW	9/55	XPW	12/57
BVF	5/37	FVF	5/46	KVF	11/49	OVF	6/53	TVF	10/55	XVF	2/58
CAH	9/37	GAH	8/46	LAH	3/50	PAH	8/53	UAH	12/55	YAH	3/58
CNG	1/38	GNG	11/46	LNG	5/50	PNG	10/53	UNG	2/56	YNG	5/58
CPW	4/38	GPW	1/47	LPW	8/50	PPW	12/53	UPW	3/56	YPW	6/58
CVF	8/38	GVF	4/47	LVF	10/50	PVF	2/54	UVF	5/56	YVF	7/58
DAH	12/38	HAH	6/47	MAH	2/51	RAH	4/54	VAH	7/56		
DNG	3/39	HNG	8/47	MNG	4/51	RNG	6/54	VNG	8/56		
DPW	7/39	HPW	11/47	MPW	7/51	RPW	8/54	VPW	10/56		
DVF	2/40	HVF	1/48	MVF	9/51	RVF	10/54	VVF	12/56		

In the reverse format the two-letter marks were used first; in *AH, NG and VF 1-999* were used mainly for motorcycles, other vehicles using *1000-9999*. After *999 VF* motorcycles used three-letter series commencing with *AAH*; cars used *1000-9999 PW* (*1-999* not used to avoid conflict with trade plates), then three-letter marks from *BNG* onwards. After motorcycles completed *BAH* a common series was used from *CPW* onwards.

Cycles			Cars			All Vehicles	
1-999 AH	*8/58*		*1000-9999 AH*	*8/58*		*CPW*	*4/63*
1-999 NG	*3/59*		*1000-9999 NG*	*9/59*		*CVF*	*5/63*
1-999 VF	*7/59*		*1000-9999 VF*	*10/60*		*DAH*	*6/63*
AAH	*1/60*		*1000-9999 PW*	*9/61*		*DNG*	*7/63*
ANG	*6/60*		*BNG*	*10/62*		*DPW*	*8/63*
APW	*2/61*		*BPW*	*11/62*		*DVF*	*9/63*
AVF	*7/61*		*BVF*	*1/63*		*EAH*	*10/63*
BAH	*4/62*		*CAH*	*2/63*		*ENG*	*11/63*
			CNG	*3/63*		*EPW*	*12/63*

(EVF was used solely on trade plates)

Special mark for Diplomatic Corps: *1 PNG   c. 8/77*

Commenced suffix marks 2.1.64

145

COUNTY COUNCIL OF NORTHAMPTON

BD 12/03   RP 10/24   NV 3/31

No information is available to the writer on yearly issues before 1929 but some details may be available in the Northamptonshire Record Office.

First issues each year, (no information available to the writer for 1922-1928, but for the earlier of these years some details may be available in the Northamptonshire Record Office) :

1904 c. BD 92	1909 c. BD 802	1914 c. BD 2115	1919 BD 3713
1905 c. BD 351	1910 c. BD 944	1915 c. BD 2637	1920 BD 3961
1906 c. BD 492	1911 c. BD 1120	1916 c. BD 3228	1921 BD 5243
1907 c. BD 598	1912 c. BD 1344	1917 BD 3495	
1908 c. BD 704	1913 BD 1682	1918 c. BD 3673	

1929 RP 6737	1932 NV 919	1935 NV 4805
1930 RP 8200	1933 NV 2057	1936 NV 6480
1931 RP 9724	1934 NV 3291	1937 NV 8302

ABD	10/37	EBD	12/47	JBD	2/53	NBD	2/56	SBD	8/58	WBD	5/60
ANV	4/38	ENV	5/48	JNV	6/63	NNV	4/56	SNV	10/58	WNV	6/60
ARP	12/38	ERP	11/48	JRP	9/53	NRP	7/56	SRP	12/58	WRP	7/60
BBD	6/39	FBD	5/49	KBD	1/54	OBD	10/56	TBD	3/59 *	XBD	9/60
BNV	4/40	FNV	9/49	KNV	4/54	ONV	1/57	TNV	4/59	XNV	11/60
BRP	10/41	FRP	3/50	KRP	7/54	ORP	4/57	TRP	6/59	XRP	2/61
CBD	2/43	GBD	8/50	LBD	10/54	PBD	6/57	UBD	7/59	YBD	3/61
CNV	1/45	GNV	1/51	LNV	1/55	PNV	8/57	UNV	9/59	YNV	4/61
CRP	3/46	GRP	6/51	LRP	4/55	PRP	10/57	URP	10/59	YRP	6/61
DBD	9/46	HBD	11/51	MBD	6/55	RBD	1/58	VBD	12/59		
DNV	2/47	HNV	4/52	MNV	8/55	RNV	4/58	VNV	2/60		
DRP	6/47	HRP	9/52	MRP	11/55	RRP	6/58	VRP	3/60		

* Some TBD issued early for bus company.

ABD	7/61 *	CBD	7/62	DBD	12/62	EBD	4/63	FBD	8/63	GBD	12/63
ANV	9/61	CNV	8/62	DNV	2/63	ENV	5/63	FNV	9/63	GNV	2/64
ARP	12/61	CRP	10/62	DRP	3/63	ERP	7/63	FRP	11/63	GRP	6/76 #
BBD	2/62										
BNV	3/62										
BRP	5/62										

* 1 ABD early issue (6/61)   # Re-registrations only, commencing at 214.

Special mark for Diplomatic Corps :   1 NBD ca. 2/87

Commenced suffix marks 2.3.64,

> The attention of the Ministry has been drawn to the fact that some Registration Authorities require that a person allotted an identification number of less than four figures shall, on the identification plates, prefix noughts so as to make four figures. In view of the Minister's proposals in connection with general identification marks, (details of which will be communicated later), it is requested that this practice may be discontinued in future cases.
> It is also understood that some Registration Authorities duplicate the identification numbers, e.g. the same number may be allotted both to a motor car and to a motor cycle. Under the new scheme such duplication may entail confusion and I am to ask that it may be discontinued in all future cases."
>
> *Circular RF 105 29.11.20*

COUNTY COUNCIL OF NORTHUMBERLAND

X 12/03   NL 1/21   TY 8/25   JR 11/32

It is possible that NL was issued from 1 up and 1000 up simultaneously.

First issues each year.
No information is available prior to 1922. Some of the following are approximate :

1922	NL 2869	1928	TY 3991 *	1934	JR 1344
1923	NL 4373	1929	TY 5344	1935	JR 2760
1924	NL 6403	1930	TY 6742	1936	JR 4242
1925	NL 8581	1931	TY 8063	1937	JR 5875
1926	TY 506	1932	TY 9171	1938	JR 7531
1927	TY 2341	1933	JR 101	1939	JR 9114

* TY 4000 early issue, 1927.

Three-letter marks were issued in the same sequence as their two-letter elements.

ANL	7/39	ENL	7/50	JNL	4/55	NNL	3/58	SNL	4/60	WNL	6/62
ATY	5/41	ETY	2/51	JTY	7/55	NTY	5/58	STY	6/60	WTY	8/62
AJR	8/42	EJR	9/51	JJR	10/55	NJR	7/58	SJR	8/60	WJR	10/62
BNL	6/44	FNL	4/52	KNL	1/56	ONL	10/58	TNL	11/60	XNL	12/62
BTY	4/46	FTY	10/52	KTY	4/56	OTY	12/58	TTY	2/61	XTY	3/63
BJR	7/46	FJR	2/53	KJR	6/56	OJR	3/59	TJR	3/61	XJR	4/63
CNL	5/47	GNL	7/53	LNL	9/56	PNL	5/59	UNL	5/61	YNL	5/63
CTY	10/47	GTY	11/53	LTY	2/57	PTY	6/59	UTY	7/61	YTY	6/63
CJR	5/48	GJR	3/54	LJR	4/57	PJR	9/59	UJR	9/61	YJR	8/63
DNL	1/49	HNL	6/54	MNL	6/57	RNL	11/59	VNL	1/62		
DTY	7/49	HTY	10/54	MTY	9/57	RTY	1/60	VTY	2/62		
DJR	1/50	HJR	1/55	MJR	12/57	RJR	3/60	VJR	4/62		

Suffix marks commenced 1.10.63.

147

COUNTY COUNCIL OF NOTTINGHAM

AL 12/03   NN 5/21   RR 3/25   VO 10/28

A single sequence for all vehicles.

First issues each year, (no information available for 1922-1928) :

1904	AL	129		1912	AL 1931		1920	AL 6823
1905	AL	412		1913	AL 2428		1921	AL 8975
1906	AL	588		1914	AL 3015			
1907	AL	762		1915	AL 3629		1929	VO 420 appx.
1908	AL	927		1916	AL 4410		1930	VO 2780 "
1909	AL 1102			1917	AL 4919		1931	VO 5060 "
1910	AL 1310			1918	AL 5203		1932	VO 7070 "
1911	AL 1577			1919	AL 5383		1933	VO 9040 "

AAL	3/33	EAL	3/38	JAL	7/47	NAL	3/52	SAL	12/54	WAL	12/56
ANN	11/33	ENN	5/38	JNN	10/47	NNN	6/52	SNN	2/55	WNN	2/57
ARR	3/34	ERR	9/38	JRR	2/48	NRR	8/52	SRR	3/55	WRR	3/57
AVO	7/34	BVO	1/39	JVO	5/48	NVO	11/52	SVO	4/55	WVO	5/57
BAL	11/34	FAL	3/39	KAL	9/48	OAL	2/53	TAL	5/55	XAL	6/57
BNN	3/35	FNN	7/39	KNN	1/49	ONN	4/53	TNN	7/55	XNN	7/57
BRR	6/35	FRR	1/40	KRR	4/49	ORR	6/53	TRR	8/55	XRR	9/57
BVO	10/35	FVO	6/41	KVO	7/49	OVO	8/53	TVO	9/55	XVO	10/57
CAL	2/36	GAL	8/42	LAL	1/50	PAL	10/53	UAL	11/55	YAL	12/57
CNN	5/36	GNN	4/44	LNN	3/50	PNN	12/53	UNN	12/55	YNN	1/58
CRR	8/36	GRR	8/45	LRR	6/50	PRR	3/54	URR	2/56	YRR	3/58
CVO	11/36	GVO	4/46	LVO	10/50	PVO	4/54	UVO	3/56	YVO	4/58
DAL	3/37	HAL	7/46	MAL	1/51	RAL	5/54	VAL	5/56		
DNN	5/37	HNN	10/46	MNN	4/51	RNN	7/54	VNN	6/56		
DRR	7/37	HRR	1/47	MRR	7/51	RRR	9/54	VRR	8/56		
DVO	11/37	HVO	5/47	MVO	11/51	RVO	10/54	VVO	10/56		

AAL	5/58	EAL	10/59	JAL	1/61	NAL	4/62	TAL	5/63	XAL	5/64
ANN	6/58	ENN	11/59	JNN	2/61	NNN	4/62	TNN	6/63	XNN	5/64
ARR	7/58	ERR	12/59	JRR	3/61	NRR	5/62	TRR	7/63	XRR	6/64
AVO	9/58	EVO	1/60	JVO	3/61	NVO	6/62	TVO	7/63	XVO	6/64
BAL	10/58	FAL	2/60	KAL	4/61	PAL	7/62	UAL	8/63	YAL	7/64
BNN	11/58	FNN	3/60	KNN	5/61	PNN	8/62	UNN	9/63	YNN	8/64
BRR	12/58	FRR	4/60	KRR	5/61	PRR	9/62	URR	10/63	YRR	c/75 *
BVO	2/59	FVO	4/60	KVO	6/61	PVO	10/62	UVO	11/63	YVO	c/75 *
CAL	3/59	GAL	5/60	LAL	7/61	RAL	11/62	VAL	11/63		
CNN	4/59	GNN	6/60	LNN	8/61	RNN	12/62	VNN	12/63		
CRR	4/59	GRR	6/60	LRR	9/61	RRR	1/63	VRR	1/64		
CVO	5/59	GVO	7/60	LVO	10/61	RVO	2/63	VVO	2/64		
DAL	6/59	HAL	8/60	MAL	12/61	SAL	3/63	WAL	3/64		
DNN	7/59	HNN	9/60	MNN	1/62	SNN	4/63	WNN	3/64		
DRR	8/59	HRR	10/60	MRR	2/62	SRR	4/63	WRR	4/64		
DVO	9/59	HVO	12/50	MVO	3/62	SVO	5/63	WVO	4/64		

* Re-registrations only, (both series incomplete).

Commenced suffix marks 1.9.64

COUNTY COUNCIL OF OXFORD

BW 12/03   UD 5/26

First issues each year, (no information available prior to 1929) :

1929	UD 2566		1932	UD 4791		1935	UD 6474		1938	UD 9201
1930	UD 3476		1933	UD 5285		1936	UD 7312			
1931	UD 4221		1934	UD 5802		1937	UD 8200			

ABW	10/38	EBW	8/49	JBW	1/55	NBW	6/58	SBW	9/60	WBW	8/62
AUD	10/39	EUD	6/50	JUD	6/55	NUD	10/58	SUD	12/60	WUD	11/62
BBW	4/42	FBW	3/51	KBW	11/55	OBW	3/59	TBW	3/61	XBW	3/63
BUD	12/44	FUD	1/52	KUD	4/56	OUD	5/59	TUD	5/61	XUD	5/63
CBW	8/46	GBW	9/52	LBW	10/56	PBW	9/59	UBW	8/61	YBW	7/63
CUD	4/47	GUD	5/53	LUD	4/57	PUD	12/59	UUD	12/61	YUD	9/63
DBW	1/48	HBW	12/53	MBW	8/57	RBW	3/60	VBW	3/62		
DUD	10/48	HUD	7/54	MUD	1/58	RUD	6/60	VUD	6/62		

Commenced suffix marks 6.11.63

COUNTY COUNCIL OF PEMBROKE

DE 12/03

A single sequence for all vehicles.

First issues each year, (no information available for 1922-1924) :

1904	13		1912	357		1920	1735		1930	7362
1905	54		1913	489		1921	2372		1931	8036
1906	82		1914	614					1932	8583
1907	108		1915	830		1925	ca. 4350		1933	9127
1908	142		1916	1142		1926	5128		1934	9651
1909	180		1917	1302		1927	5708			
1910	230		1918	1364		1928	6292			
1911	285		1919	1456		1929	6790			

ADE	7/34	EDE	5/39	JDE	7/47	NDE	11/50	SDE	3/54	WDE	4/56
BDE	12/35	FDE	7/41	KDE	4/48	ODE	12/51	TDE	9/54	XDE	9/56
CDE	2/37	GDE	6/44	LDE	2/49	PDE	11/52	UDE	4/55	YDE	5/57
DDE	3/38	HDE	9/46	MDE	11/49	RDE	7/53	VDE	9/55		

ADE	10/57	EDE	4/59	JDE	7/60	NDE	1/62	TDE	5/63	XDE	7/64
BDE	3/58	FDE	7/59	KDE	11/60	PDE	5/62	UDE	9/63	YDE	10/64
CDE	8/58	GDE	12/59	LDE	4/61	RDE	7/62	VDE	1/64		
DDE	12/58	HDE	4/60	MDE	7/61	SDE	3/63	WDE	4/64		

Suffix marks commenced 1.1.65

COUNTY COUNCIL OF THE SOKE OF PETERBOROUGH

FL 12/03   EG 7/31

A common sequence for all vehicles.

First issues each year :

1904	FL 10	1916	FL 1061	1928	FL 6603	1940	EG 5835
1905	FL 87	1917	FL 1190	1929	FL 7397	1941	EG 6042
1906	FL 130	1918	FL 1269	1930	FL 8512	1942	EG 6131
1907	FL 175	1919	FL 1331	1931	FL 9551	1943	EG 6240
1908	FL 213	1920	FL 1749	1932	EG 256	1944	EG 6333
1909	FL 254	1921	FL 2265	1933	EG 653	1945	EG 6428
1910	FL 297	1922	FL 2488	1934	EG 1149	1946	EG 6621
1911	FL 349	1923	FL 2958	1935	EG 1778	1947	EG 7409
1912	FL 403	1924	FL 3362	1936	EG 2596	1948	EG 8330
1913	FL 515	1925	FL 4109	1937	EG 3470	1949	EG 9120
1914	FL 666	1926	FL 4676	1938	EG 4398		
1915	FL 813	1927	FL 5712	1939	EG 5194		

AEG	11/49	EEG	7/55	JEG	2/59	NEG	2/61	SEG	4/63
AFL	10/50	EFL	1/56	JFL	5/59	NFL	5/61	SFL	6/63
BEG	9/51	FEG	6/56	KEG	8/59	OEG	7/61	TEG	9/63
BFL	9/52	FFL	1/57	KFL	11/59	OFL	11/61	TFL	11/63
CEG	6/53	GEG	6/57	LEG	3/60	PEG	4/62	UEG	2/64
CFL	1/54	GFL	1/58	LFL	4/60	PFL	6/62	UFL	4/64
DEG	8/54	HEG	5/58	MEG	7/60	REG	10/62		
DFL	3/55	HFL	10/58	MFL	10/60	RFL	12/62	YEG	c/75 *

* Issued by Huntingdon and Peterborough for re-registrations only, comencing at 301.

Commenced suffix marks 1.6.64

Amalgamated with the County Council of Huntingdon to form the County Council of Huntingdon and Peterborough as from 1 April 1965.

Under the new system all vehicles (other than tramcars) which do not come within the provisions of the Motor Car Act 1903, but are liable to duty under the Second Schedule of the Finance Act 1920 will be allotted identification marks and be required to carry number plates in precisely the same manner as vehicles at present coming within the provisions of that Act. The existing system of licensing of locomotives under the Locomotive Acts, (including the issue of plates and daily permits), will cease. Refunds will be made under regulations to be issued later.   *Circular RF 105 29.11.20*

COUNTY COUNCIL OF RADNOR

FO   12/03

Common sequence for all vehicles.

First issues each year :

1904	3	1918	668	1932	2774	1946	4516
1905	34	1919	684	1933	2905	1947	4798
1906	60	1920	788	1934	3003	1948	5144
1907	89	1921	970	1935	3148	1949	5518
1908	111	1922	1089	1936	3299	1950	5908
1909	135	1923	1199	1937	3461	1951	6217
1910	157	1924	1358	1938	3626	1952	6579
1911	185	1925	1545	1939	3767	1953	6933
1912	231	1926	1774	1940	3937	1954	7368
1913	286	1927	1963	1941	4021	1955	7857
1914	372	1928	2143	1942	4127	1956	8490
1915	479	1929	2318	1943	4252	1957	8983
1916	580	1930	2486	1944	4343	1958	9513
1917	631	1931	2638	1945	4444		

AFO	8/58	BFO	12/59	CFO	3/61	DFO	7/62	EFO	12/63

Commenced suffix marks 4.8.64

(GFO to YFO inclusive were allocated between 12/94 and 4/96 by the DVLA to various VROs for "Age Related" marks).

COUNTY COUNCIL OF RUTLAND

FP   12/03

A common sequence for all vehicles.

First issues each year :

1904	20	1919	748	1934	2667	1949	4953
1905	74	1920	853	1935	2822	1950	5153
1906	110	1921	1015	1936	2959	1951	5358
1907	133	1922	1174	1937	3119	1952	5546
1908	146	1923	1277 *	1938	3305	1953	5835
1909	164	1924	1401 *	1939	3434	1954	6144
1910	185	1925	1516 *	1940	3592	1955	6516
1911	217	1926	1667 *	1941	3682	1956	6964
1912	257	1927	1814	1942	3798	1957	7417
1913	330	1928	1950	1943	3915	1958	7873
1914	412	1929	2104	1944	3989	1959	8458
1915	494	1930	2249	1945	4074	1960	9290
1916	643	1931	2364	1946	4154		
1917	690	1932	2464	1947	4387		
1918	722	1933	2567	1948	4675		

* approximate.

AFP	8/60	BFP	10/61	CFP	12/62	DFP	10/63

Commenced suffix marks 2.1.64

COUNTY COUNCIL OF SALOP

Although usually referred to as Shropshire, the above was the official title of the Council until 31.3.74.

AW 12/03   NT 11/21   UX 3/27   UJ 4/32

First issues each year : (No information available to the writer on issues before 1929, but some details may exist in the Shropshire Archives).

1929	UX 3811	1932	UX 9573	1934	UJ 2553	1936	UJ 6444
1930	UX 5903	1933	UJ 1045	1935	UJ 4342	1937	UJ 8742
1931	UX 7976						

AAW	6/37	EAW	10/47	JAW	7/52	NAW	11/55	SAW	10/58	WAW	10/60
ANT	12/37	ENT	3/48	JNT	11/52	NNT	1/56	SNT	12/58	WNT	1/61
AUJ	6/38	EUJ	6/48	JUJ	3/53	NUJ	3/56	SUJ	2/59	WUJ	2/61
AUX	12/38	EUX	10/48	JUX	5/53	NUX	6/56	SUX	3/59	WUX	3/61
BAW	4/39	FAW	2/49	KAW	8/53	OAW	8/56	TAW	5/59	XAW	5/61
BNT	10/39	FNT	5/49	KNT	11/53	ONT	11/56	TNT	6/59	XNT	6/61
BUJ	10/40	FUJ	9/49	KUJ	2/54	OUJ	2/57	TUJ	7/59	XUJ	7/61
BUX	2/42	FUX not alloc.		KUX	4/54	OUX	4/57	TUX	9/59	XUX	9/61
CAW	3/43	GAW	1/50	LAW	6/54	PAW	6/57	UAW	11/59	YAW	11/61
CNT not iss.		GNT	4/50	LNT	9/54	PNT	9/57	UNT	1/60	YNT	1/62
CUX	12/44 *	GUJ	8/50	LUJ	11/54	PUJ	11/57	UUJ	2/60	YUJ	3/62
CUJ	2/46	GUX	1/51	LUX	1/55	PUX	1/58	UUX	3/60	YUX	4/62
DAW	7/46	HAW	4/51	MAW	3/55	RAW	3/58	VAW	4/60		
DNT	11/46	HNT	7/51	MNT	5/55	RNT	5/58	VNT	6/60		
DUJ	3/47	HUJ	12/51	MUJ	7/55	RUJ	6/58	VUJ	7/60		
DUX	7/47	HUX	4/52	MUX	9/55	RUX	8/58	VUX	9/60		

* CUX and CUJ issued in reverse order.

A common sequence for all vehicles in reversed format marks :

AW (from 501) 5/62   NT (from 501) 7/63.

Special Marks for Diplomatic Corps : 1 LUX ca. 7/69 1 ONT ca. 11/78

Suffix marks commenced 3.2.64

COUNTY COUNCIL OF SOMERSET

Registrations commenced 25.11.03. Motorcycles numbered in a separate sequence to Y 2043 in 6/14; thereafter common sequence with cars etc. from Y 2560.

Y 11/03   YA 2/21   YB 9/24   YC 6/27   YD 6/30

First issues each year :

Motorcycles		Cars			Common Series				
1904	Y 50	1904	Y 113		1915	Y 2963		1926	YB 4608
1905	Y 334	1905	Y 303		1916	Y 3956		1927	YB 8147
1906	Y 430	1906	Y 437		1917	Y 4533		1928	YC 1738
1907	Y 533	1907	Y 593		1918	Y 4796		1929	YC 4858
1908	Y 587	1908	Y 760		1919	Y 5092		1930	YC 8241
1909	Y 639	1909	Y 917		1920	Y 6818		1931	YD 1353
1910	Y 714	1910	Y 1068		1921	Y 9732		1932	YD 3844
1911	Y 828	1911	Y 1262		1922	YA 2331		1933	YD 6185
1912	Y 1045	1912	Y 1490		1923	YA 4609		1934	YD 8638
1913	Y 1384	1913	Y 1827		1924	YA 7479			
1914	Y 1733	1914	Y 2238		1925	YB 777			

AYA	7/34	EYA	12/38	JYA	6/47	NYA	4/51	SYA	6/54	WYA	4/56
AYB	11/34	EYB	3/39	JYB	9/47	NYB	7/51	SYB	7/54	WYB	5/56
AYC	2/35	EYC	6/39	JYC	12/47	NYC	11/51	SYC	9/54	WYC	7/56
AYD	5/35	EYD	10/39	JYD	3/48	NYD	2/52	SYD	11/54	WYD	9/56
BYA	9/35	FYA	5/40	KYA	6/48	OYA	4/52	TYA	12/54	XYA	11/56
BYB	1/36	FYB	5/41	KYB	9/48	OYB	7/52	TYB	2/55	XYB	1/57
BYC	4/36	FYC	3/42	KYC	12/48	OYC	9/52	TYC	3/55	XYC	3/57
BYD	7/36	FYD	10/42	KYD	3/49	OYD	12/52	TYD	4/55	XYD	4/57
CYA	10/36	GYA	10/43	LYA	5/49	PYA	3/53	UYA	5/55	YYA	5/57
CYB	1/37	GYB	1/45	LYB	8/49	PYB	4/53	UYB	6/55	YYB	6/57
CYC	4/37	GYC	1/46	LYC	11/49	PYC	7/53	UYC	8/55	YYC	8/57
CYD	7/37	GYD	5/46	LYD	3/50	PYD	9/53	UYD	9/55	YYD	9/57
DYA	10/37	HYA	8/46	MYA	5/50	RYA	11/53	VYA	10/55		
DYB	2/38	HYB	11/46	MYB	8/50	RYB	1/54	VYB	12/55		
DYC	5/38	HYC	1/47	MYC	11/50	RYC	3/54	VYC	1/56		
DYD	9/38	HYD	4/47	MYD	2/51	RYD	4/54	VYD	3/56		

AYA	10/57	EYA	5/59	JYA	6/60	NYA	10/61	SYA	11/62	WYA	1/64
AYB	12/57	EYB	6/59	JYB	7/60	NYB	11/61	SYB	12/62	WYB	1/64
AYC	2/58	EYC	6/59	JYC	8/60	NYC	12/61	SYC	2/63	WYC	2/64
AYD	3/58	EYD	7/59	JYD	9/60	NYD	2/62	SYD	2/63	WYD	3/64
BYA	4/58	FYA	9/59	KYA	11/60	OYA	3/62	TYA	3/63	XYA	3/64
BYB	5/58	FYB	9/59	KYB	12/60	OYB not iss.		TYB	4/63	XYB	4/64
BYC	6/58	FYC	10/59	KYC	1/61	OYC not iss.		TYC	5/63	XYC	5/64
BYD	7/58	FYD	11/59	KYD	2/61	OYD not iss.		TYD	5/63	XYD	5/64
CYA	9/58	GYA	12/59	LYA	3/61	PYA	4/62	UYA	6/63	YYA	6/64
CYB	10/58	GYB	1/60	LYB	4/61	PYB	4/62	UYB	7/63	YYB	7/64
CYC	11/58	GYC	2/60	LYC	4/61	PYC	5/62	UYC	7/63	YYC	7/64
CYD	12/58	GYD	3/60	LYD	5/61	PYD	6/62	UYD	8/63	YYD	7/73 *
DYA	1/59	HYA	4/60	MYA	6/61	RYA	7/62	VYA	9/63		
DYB	2/59	HYB	4/60	MYB	7/61	RYB	8/62	VYB	10/63		
DYC	3/59	HYC	5/60	MYC	7/61	RYC	9/62	VYC	11/63		
DYD	4/59	HYD	6/60	MYD	9/61	RYD	10/62	VYD	12/63		

* 1 YYD (only) issued for re-registration.

Suffix marks commenced 4.8.64

COUNTY COUNCIL OF SOUTHAMPTON

Although commonly known as Hampshire the above was the official title of the Council until it became the County Council of Hampshire with effect from 1 April 1959.

AA 12/03   HO 10/17   OR 10/22   OT 1/26   OU 11/28   CG 11/31

All vehicles were numbered in a common series, but heavy motor cars were segregated in the following blocks : AA 2001-2500; AA 5001-6000; HO 2001-3000 and HO 5501-6500. The second HO block continued in use after 1.1.21 for heavy commercial vehicles and was not completed until 1926, by which time other vehicles had exhausted not only HO but OR as well.

No information is available to the writer on annual issues before 1929, but some details of 1904-1913 and 1921-28 may be available at the Hampshire Record Office. However, the following details are available concerning (incomplete) ranges of numbers issued in the HMC series for the years shown :

1905	AA 2062	1913	AA 5086-5207	1921	HO 5556-
1906	AA 2124-2157	1914	AA 5253-5459	1922	HO 6037-6142
1907	AA 2167-2197	1915	AA 5639	1923	HO 6161-6260
1908	AA 2229-2254			1924	HO 6281-6354
1909	AA 2288-2299	1917	HO 2040	1925	HO 6360-6459
1910	AA 2356			1926	HO 6472-6496 (3/26)
1911	AA 2442	1919	HO 2285-2621		
1912	AA 2470-2500	1920	HO 2779-2930		
	& 5001-5056				

First issues each year, 1929-1934 :

1929	OU 501	1931	OU 7570	1933	CG 3224
1930	OU 4181	1932	CG 300	1934	CG 6421

In the three-letter sequence AHO and BHO (forward format only) were omitted to obviate confusion with surviving HMCs with AH 0xxx and BH 0xxx registrations.

AAA	12/34	KAA	5/40	JAA	6/50	NAA	10/54	SAA	6/57	WAA	5/59		
ACG	3/35	KCG	6/41	JCG	9/50	NCG	11/54	SCG	7/57	WCG	6/59		
AHO not iss.		KHO	6/42	JHO	12/50	NHO	1/55	SHO	8/57	WHO	7/59		
AOR	5/35	KOR	12/43	JOR	2/51	NOR	2/55	SOR	10/57	WOR	8/59 ##		
AOT	8/35	KOT	6/45	JOT	4/51	NOT	3/55	SOT not alloc		WOT	8/59		
AOU	11/35	KOU	2/46	JOU	7/51	NOU	4/55	SOU	11/57	WOU	9/59		
BAA	2/36	KAA	5/46	KAA	10/51	OAA	5/55	TAA	12/57	XAA	10/59		
BCG	4/36	FCG	8/46	KCG	1/52	OCG	7/55	TCG	1/58	XCG	11/59		
BHO not iss.		FHO	10/46	KHO	3/52	OHO	8/55	THO	3/58	XHO	12/59		
BOR	6/36	FOR	1/47	KOR	5/52	OOR	9/55	TOR	4/58	XOR	1/60		
BOT	9/36	FOT	4/47	KOT	7/52	OOT	10/55	TOT	5/58	XOT	1/60		
BOU	12/36	FOU	6/47	KOU	10/52	OOU	12/55	TOU	6/58	XOU	2/60		
CAA	2/37	GAA	8/47	LAA	1/53	PAA	1/56	UAA	7/58	YAA	3/60		
CCG	4/37	GCG	11/47	LCG	3/53	PCG	2/56	UCG	8/58	YCG	4/60		
CHO	7/37	GHO	2/48	LHO	5/53	PHO	3/56	UHO	9/58	YHO	4/60		
COR	10/37	GOR	5/48	LOR	7/53	POR	5/56	UOR	10/58	YOR	5/60		
COT	1/38	GOT	7/48	LOT	9/53	POT	6/56	UOT	11/58	YOT	6/60		
COU	4/38	GOU	10/48	LOU	11/53	POU	7/56	UOU	12/58	YOU	6/60		
DAA	7/38	HAA	1/49	MAA	1/54	RAA	9/56	VAA	1/59				
DCG	10/38	HCG	4/49	MCG	2/54	RCG	11/56	VCG	2/59				
DHO	1/39	HHO	7/49	MHO	4/54	RHO	1/57 *	VHO	2/59				
DOR	4/39	HOR	9/49	MOR	5/54	ROR	2/57	VOR	3/59				
DOT	6/39	HOT	12/49	MOT	7/54	ROT	3/57	VOT	4/59				
DOU	10/39	HOU	4/50	MOU	8/54	ROU	5/57	VOU	5/59				

*   RHO 1 special early issue for Diplomatic Corps, ca. 4/54.

WOR irregular, issued contemporaneously with WOT and completed 10/59.

COUNTY COUNCIL OF SOUTHAMPTON (continued)

AAA	7/60	DAA	7/61	GAA	12/62	KAA	11/63	NAA	9/64	
ACG	8/60	DCG	10/61	GCG	1/63	KCG	12/63	NCG	10/64	
AHO	9/60	DHO	11/61	GHO	2/63	KHO	1/64	NHO	10/64	
AOR	9/60	DOR	11/61	GOR	2/63	KOR	1/64	NOR	11/64	
AOT	10/60	DOT	1/62	GOT	3/63	KOT	2/64	NOT	12/64	
AOU	11/60	DOU	2/62	GOU	4/63	KOU	3/64	NOU	12/64 *	
BAA	12/60	EAA	3/62	HAA	4/63	LAA	3/64			
BCG	1/61	ECG	3/62	HCG	5/63	LCG	3/64	PAA	/76 **	
BHO	2/61	EHO	4/62	HHO	5/63	LHO	4/64			
BOR	3/61	EOR	5/62	HOR	6/63	LOR	5/64			
BOT	3/61	EOT	5/62	HOT	6/63	LOT	5/64			
BOU	4/61	EOU	6/62	HOU	6/63	LOU	6/64			
CAA	4/61	FAA	7/62	JAA	7/63	MAA	6/64			
CCG	5/61	FCG	8/62	JCG	8/63	MCG	6/64			
CHO	5/61	FHO	9/62	JHO	8/63	MHO	7/64			
COR	6/61	FOR	9/62	JOR	9/63	MOR	7/64			
COT	6/61	FOT	10/62	JOT	10/63	MOT	8/64			
COU	7/61	FOU	11/62	JOU	11/63	MOU	9/64			

* Only 2, 3 and 4 issued 12/64, then used for re-registrations from c 7/67.   ** Re-registrations only.

Special Marks for Diplomatic Corps : *1 POR* ca. 4/70   *1 ROU* 2/68

Suffix marks commenced 1.1.65.

COUNTY COUNCIL OF STAFFORD

E 1/04 - 1/25   RE 1/21 - 3/47   RF 12/24 - 7/32.

Until 12/20, when motorcycles reached E 9999, there were separate and parallel series in E for cars and motorcycles. Motorcycles outstripped cars which had reached E 5042 on 31.12.20. Motorcycles then commenced RE and cars completed E 5043-9999 before commencing RF in 1/25. RE was the only two-letter mark used solely for motorcycles.
Information on first issues each year prior to 1921 is not available.

	Cycles		Cars			Cycles			
1921	RE	1	E 5043	1933	RE 7713	1945	RE 9331		
1922	RE	906	E 6512	1934	RE 7871	1946	RE 9399		
1923	RE	1511	E 7495	1935	RE 8107	1947	RE 9949		
1924	RE	2218	E 8638	1936	RE 8285				
1925	RE	3024	RF 3 *	1937	RE 8504				
1926	RE	3902	RF 1363	1938	RE 8714				
1927	RE	4859	RF 2586	1939	RE 8871				
1928	RE	5666	RF 3946	1940	RE 9055				
1929	RE	6204	RF 5271	1941	RE 9201				
1930	RE	6724	RF 6658	1942	RE 9257				
1931	RE	7180	RF 8011	1943	RE 9289				
1932	RE	7443	RF 9239	1944	RE 9303				

* E 9998 = 31.12.24, E 9999 = 24.1.25, RF 1 & 2 = 31.12.24

Because RE was still in use Staffordshire commenced their three-letter issues with ARF, BRF and CRF. However, no further combinations were allocated in the 1932 SR&O, so CRF was followed by ARE, BRE and CRE. Thereafter issues followed alphabetical sequence. ARF was the first three-letter mark issued anywhere. After RE finished motorcycles joined the main series from ca NRE 7xx.

ARF	7/32	ERE	9/36	JRE	9/39	NRE	3/47	SRE	4/49	WRE	8/51	
BRF	5/33	ERF	1/37	JRF	8/40	NRF	6/47	SRF	8/49	WRF	12/51	
CRF	1/34	FRE	5/37	KRE	2/42	ORE	8/47	TRE	11/49	XRE	3/52	
ARE	7/34	FRF	10/37	KRF	2/43	ORF	11/47	TRF	3/50	XRF	7/52	
BRE	1/35	GRE	5/38	LRE	12/44	PRE	2/48	URE	6/50	YRE	10/52	
CRE	6/35	GRF	7/38	LRF	2/46	PRF	6/48	URF	9/50	YRF	1/53	
DRE	11/35	HRE	1/39	MRE	8/46	RRE	10/48	VRE	1/51			
DRF	4/36	HRF	4/39	MRF	11/46	RRF	2/49	VRF	4/51			

Staffordshire was the first authority to issue reverse format marks, commencing with *E*, (from 1000), on 22.4.53. During the currency of *E* it was announced that, owing to the unsuitability of four-figure numbers for the plates of current cars, three-letter issues would be used for the time being. Accordingly *E* was suspended at 2500 in 7/53. *ARE* onwards were then used for all vehicles up to *WRE*. *E* was then resumed for cars etc. from 2501 in 6/58, whilst motorcycles used the remaining three-letter marks. *E* was followed by *RE* (from 1000) for cars etc. and, following completion of *YRF*. motorcycles used *200-999 RE* from 1/60. *RF from 1000* followed (3/60), being used for all vehicles after motorcycles reached *999 RE* in the same month.

1000-2500 E   4/53

ARE	7/53	ERE	10/54	JRE	10/55	NRE	10/56	TRE	10/57
ARF	10/53	ERF	12/54	JRF	12/55	NRF	12/56	TRF	11/57
BRE	12/53	FRE	2/55	KRE	1/56	PRE	2/57	URE	1/58
BRF	2/54	FRF	3/55	KRF	3/56	PRF	3/57	URF	2/58
CRE	4/54	GRE	4/55	LRE	4/56	RRE	4/57	VRE	3/58
CRF	5/54	GRF	6/55	LRF	5/56	RRF	5/57	VRF	4/58
DRE	7/54	HRE	7/55	MRE	7/56	SRE	7/57	WRE	5/58
DRF	9/54	HRF	9/55	MRF	8/56	SRF	8/57		

Cars etc.

2501-9999 E   6/58

RE (from 1000) 5/59

Motorcycles

WRF	6/58
XRE	12/58
XRF	4/59
YRE	6/59
YRF	9/59
200-999 RE	1/60

All Vehicles

RF (from 1000) 3/60

Special Mark for Diplomatic Corps : *1 RF* ca. 11/93

Since Staffordshire were on the point of exhausting all their available marks, and pending the introduction of a new system, stop-gap measures were called for and took the form of SI 1155 dated 1.8.60 which allotted to Staffordshire the index mark BF, defunct since 1920, but only in three-letter combinations, omitting ABF, BBF and UBF. CBF was immediately commenced for cycles, cars joining this series rrom 544 after the completion of *RF* in 11/60. YBF was followed by *CBF to YBF* in reverse format.

CBF	8/60	GBF	2/61	LBF	5/61	PBF	8/61	VBF	1/62
DBF	11/60	HBF	3/61	MBF	5/61	RBF	9/61	WBF	2/62
EBF	12/60	JBF	3/61	NBF	6/61	SBF	10/61	XBF	3/62
FBF	1/61	KBF	4/61	OBF	7/61	TBF	12/61	YBF	3/62
CBF	4/62	GBF	7/62	LBF	11/62	RBF	3/63	WBF	5/63
DBF	5/62	HBF	8/62	MBF	1/63	SBF	4/63	XBF	6/63
EBF	6/62	JBF	9/62	NBF	2/63	TBF	4/63	YBF	6/63
FBF	6/62	KBF	10/62	PBF	2/63	VBF	5/63		

Commenced suffix marks 2.7.63

COUNTY COUNCIL OF EAST SUFFOLK

BJ 12/03   RT 5/25

A single sequence for all vehicles.

Dates of first issues each year. The figures shown for 1904 to 1914 are approximate, (but accurate to within + or - 10). No information is available for 1924 to 1928.

1904	BJ	100		1911	BJ	990		1918	BJ	3737		1929	RT	5101
1905	BJ	250		1912	BJ	1210		1919	BJ	4190		1930	RT	6236
1906	BJ	360		1913	BJ	1535		1920	BJ	4855		1931	RT	7365
1907	BJ	450		1914	BJ	1906		1921	BJ	5773		1932	RT	8336
1908	BJ	545		1915	BJ	2437		1922	BJ	6982		1933	RT	9209
1909	BJ	650		1916	BJ	2955		1923	BJ	7844			
1910	BJ	795		1917	BJ	3299						

ABJ	10/33	EBJ	7/39	JBJ	10/48	NBJ	7/52	SBJ	3/55	WBJ	4/57
ART	7/34	ERT	7/41	JRT	4/49	NRT	12/52	SRT	6/55	WRT	7/57
BBJ	4/35	FBJ	1/44	KBJ	10/49	OBJ	4/53	TBJ	8/55	XBJ	9/57
BRT	1/36	FRT	3/46	KRT	3/50	ORT	8/53	TRT	11/55	XRT	1/58
CBJ	9/36	GBJ	10/46	LBJ	9/50	PBJ	12/53	UBJ	2/56	YBJ	4/58
CRT	4/37	GRT	4/47	LRT	3/51	PRT	4/54	URT	5/56	YRT	6/58
DBJ	1/38	HBJ	9/47	MBJ	9/51	RBJ	8/54	VBJ	8/56		
DRT	10/38	HRT	3/48	MRT	2/52	RRT	12/54	VRT	12/56		

ABJ	*9/58*	*EBJ*	*2/60*	*JBJ*	*4/61*	*NBJ*	*8/62*	*TBJ*	*9/63*
ART	*11/58*	*ERT*	*4/60*	*JRT*	*6/61*	*NRT*	*9/62*	*TRT*	*11/63*
BBJ	*1/59*	*FBJ*	*6/60*	*KBJ*	*7/61*	*PBJ*	*11/62*	*UBJ*	*1/64*
BRT	*4/59*	*FRT*	*7/60*	*KRT*	*9/61*	*PRT*	*2/63*	*URT*	*2/64*
CBJ	*6/59*	*GBJ*	*9/60*	*LBJ*	*12/61*	*RBJ*	*3/63*	*VBJ*	*4/64*
CRT	*7/59*	*GRT*	*11/60*	*LRT*	*2/62*	*RRT*	*5/63*	*VRT*	*5/64*
DBJ	*10/59*	*HBJ*	*1/61*	*MBJ*	*4/62*	*SBJ*	*6/63*	*WBJ*	*6/64*
DRT	*12/59*	*HRT*	*3/61*	*MRT*	*6/62*	*SRT*	*8/63*		

Commenced suffix marks 1.7.64

COUNTY COUNCIL OF WEST SUFFOLK

CF 1/04   GV 7/30

First issues each year. No records survive earlier than 1921 and the figures shown for 1921-1928 are approximate only.

1921	CF	3170		1928	CF	8089		1935	GV	3047		1942	GV	8232
1922	CF	4050		1929	CF	8866		1936	GV	3951		1943	GV	8677
1923	CF	4430		1930	CF	9630		1937	GV	5004		1944	GV	9053
1924	CF	5000		1931	GV	300		1938	GV	6000		1945	GV	9316
1925	CF	572)		1932	GV	947		1939	GV	6713		1946	GV	9743
1926	CF	6480		1933	GV	1603		1940	GV	7530			
1927	CF	7247		1934	GV	2284		1941	GV	7950			

ACF	4/46	ECF	12/51	JCF	10/55	NCF	2/59	SCF	4/61	WCF	6/63
AGV	2/47	EGV	6/52	JGV	2/56	NGV	6/59	SGV	6/61	WGV	9/63
BCF	11/47	FCF	12/52	KCF	8/56	OCF	9/59	TCF	10/61	XCF	11/63
BGV	8/48	FGV	6/53	KGV	1/57	OGV	2/60	TGV	2/62	XGV	2/64
CCF	7/49	GCF	1/54	LCF	7/57	PCF	4/60	UCF	5/62	YCF	4/64
CGV	5/50	GGV	7/54	LGV	7/60	PGV	7/60	UGV	9/62	YGV	6/64
DCF	11/50	HCF	1/55	MCF	5/58	RCF	11/60	VCF	12/62		
DGV	6/51	HGV	6/55	MGV	10/58	RGV	1/61	VGV	3/63		

ACF   c 6/66 (re-registrations only)

Special mark for Diplomatic Corps : *1 CF* ca. 5/89

Suffix marks commenced, (ahead of original schedule), 4.8.64

COUNTY COUNCIL OF SURREY

A common sequence for all vehicles, but it is understood that prior to 1930 1-999 in each series were usually reserved for motorcycles.

P	12/03	PC	7/21	PF	3/26	PG	5/29
PA	11/13	PD	7/23	PH	5/27	PL	5/30
PB	8/19	PE	2/25	PK	5/28	PJ	8/31

No details are available of annual issues before 1929.

1929	PK 5501	1930	PG 5550	1931	PL 4601	1932	PJ 2750

Surrey's three-letter marks were not invariably issued in alphabetical sequence. Those issued ahead of their alphabetical position are marked * in the tabulation. Two or more marks were normally in use simultaneously and the issue of a mark might extend over several months.

APA	10/32	EPA	5/36	JPA	6/39	NPA	12/48 *	SPA	6/52	WPA	10/54
APB	12/32	EPB	5/36	JPB	6/39	NPB	3/49	SPB	7/52	WPB	11/54
APC	1/33	EPC	6/36	JPC	7/39	NPC	4/49	SPC	8/52	WPC	12/54
APD	3/33	EPD	7/36	JPD	8/39	NPD	4/49	SPD	9/52	WPD	12/54
APE	not alloc	EPE	8/36	JPE	10/39	NPE	6/49	SPE	10/52	WPE	12/54
APF	4/33	EPF	9/36	JPF	2/40	NPF	6/49	SPF	10/52	WPF	12/54
APG	5/33	EPG	10/36	JPG	7/40	NPG	8/49	SPG	11/52	WPG	12/54
APH	6/33	EPH	12/36	JPH	9/40	NPH	8/49	SPH	12/52	WPH	2/55
APJ	7/33	EPJ	11/36 *	JPJ	6/41	NPJ	10/49	SPJ	1/53	WPJ	2/55
APK	8/33	EPK	12/36	JPK	4/42	NPK	10/49	SPK	1/53	WPK	3/55
APL	11/33	EPL	1/37	JPL	4/43	NPL	11/49	SPL	2/53	WPL	3/55
BPA	11/33	FPA	2/37	KPA	9/44	OPA	1/50	TPA	4/53	XPA	4/55
BPB	12/33	FPB	3/37	KPB	9/45	OPB	2/50	TPB	4/53	XPB	4/55
BPC	1/34	FPC	3/37	KPC	1/46	OPC	3/50	TPC	4/53	XPC	4/55
BPD	3/34	FPD	4/37	KPD	3/46	OPD	4/50	TPD	5/53	XPD	5/55
BPE	3/34	FPE	4/37	KPE	3/46	OPE	5/50	TPE	5/53	XPE	5/55
BPF	4/34	FPF	4/37	KPF	6/46	OPF	5/50	TPF	7/53	XPF	5/55
BPG	5/34	FPG	6/37	KPG	8/46	OPG	6/50	TPG	7/53	XPG	6/55
BPH	6/34	FPH	6/37	KPH	8/46	OPH	7/50	TPH	8/53	XPH	6/55
BPJ	8/34	FPJ	7/37	KPJ	10/46	OPJ	7/50	TPJ	9/53	XPJ	6/55
BPK	7/34 *	FPK	9/37	KPK	10/46	OPK	9/50	TPK	9/53	XPK	7/55
BPL	11/34	FPL	9/37	KPL	11/46	OPL	5/50 *	TPL	10/53	XPL	7/55
CPA	10/34 *	GPA	10/37	LPA	12/46	PPA	10/50	UPA	11/53	YPA	8/55
CPB	11/34	GPB	11/37	LPB	1/47	PPB	11/50	UPB	11/53	YPB	8/55
CPC	12/34	GPC	12/37	LPC	1/47	PPC	1/51	UPC	12/53	YPC	9/55
CPD	1/35	GPD	1/38	LPD	1/47	PPD	11/50 *	UPD	12/53	YPD	9/55
CPE	3/35	GPE	2/38	LPE	4/47	PPE	2/51	UPE	1/54	YPE	9/55
CPF	3/35	GPF	3/38	LPF	5/47	PPF	3/51	UPF	2/54	YPF	10/55
CPG	3/35	GPG	4/38	LPG	6/47	PPG	4/51	UPG	2/54	YPG	11/55
CPH	5/35	GPH	4/38	LPH	6/47	PPH	4/51	UPH	2/54	YPH	11/55
CPJ	5/35	GPJ	5/38	LPJ	7/47	PPJ	5/51	UPJ	3/54	YPJ	10/55
CPK	6/35	GPK	6/38	LPK	10/47	PPK	7/51	UPK	3/54	YPK	11/55 *
CPL	7/35	GPL	7/38	LPL	9/47 *	PPL	7/51	UPL	3/54	YPL	12/55
DPA	9/35	HPA	8/38	MPA	12/47	RPA	8/51	VPA	5/54		
DPB	9/35	HPB	9/38	MPB	2/48	RPB	10/51	VPB	5/54		
DPC	10/35	HPC	10/38	MPC	3/48	RPC	10/51	VPC	6/54		
DPD	11/35	HPD	11/38	MPD	4/48	RPD	12/51	VPD	7/54		
DPE	12/35	HPE	12/38	MPE	5/48	RPE	12/51	VPE	6/54 *		
DPF	12/35	HPF	1/39	MPF	6/48	RPF	1/52	VPF	7/54		
DPG	1/36	HPG	2/39	MPG	8/48	RPG	1/52	VPG	8/54		
DPH	2/36	HPH	3/39	MPH	9/48	RPH	3/52	VPH	9/54		
DPJ	3/36	HPJ	3/39	MPJ	10/48	RPJ	4/52	VPJ	9/54		
DPK	4/36	HPK	3/39	MPK	12/48	RPK	5/52	VPK	9/54		
DPL	4/36	HPL	4/39	MPL	1/49	RPL	5/52	VPL	7/54 *@		

@ Some low numbers issued early for Vine Products Ltd.

158

COUNTY COUNCIL OF SURREY (continued)

APA	12/55	EPA	9/57	JPA	1/59	NPA	1/60	SPA	9/60	WPA	9/61
APB	1/56	EPB	9/57	JPB	1/59	NPB	1/60	SPB	9/60	WPB	9/61
APC	1/56	EPC	9/57	JPC	1/59	NPC	1/60	SPC	9/60	WPC	10/61
APD	2/56	EPD	10/57	JPD	2/59	NPD	1/60	SPD	10/60	WPD	10/61
APE	not alloc	EPE	10/57	JPE	2/59	NPE	2/60	SPE	10/60	WPE	11/61
APF	3/56	EPF	11/57	JPF	2/59	NPF	2/60	SPF	10/60	WPF	11/61
APG	3/56	EPG	11/57	JPG	3/59	NPG	2/60	SPG	8/60 *	WPG	9/61 *
APH	3/56	EPH	11/57	JPH	3/59	NPH	3/60	SPH	11/60	WPH	12/61
APJ	3/56	EPJ	12/57	JPJ	3/59	NPJ	3/60	SPJ	12/60	WPJ	12/61
APK	4/56	EPK	12/57	JPK	3/59	NPK	3/60	SPK	12/60	WPK	1/62
APL	5/56	EPL	1/58	JPL	4/59	NPL	3/60	SPL	12/60	WPL	1/62
BPA	5/56	FPA	1/58	KPA	4/59	OPA	3/60	TPA	12/60	XPA	1/62
BPB	5/56	FPB	2/58	KPB	4/59	OPB	3/60	TPB	1/61	XPB	2/62
BPC	6/56	FPC	2/58	KPC	4/59	OPC	4/60 //	TPC	1/61	XPC	2/62
BPD	6/56	FPD	3/58	KPD	5/59			TPD	1/61	XPD	2/62
BPE	6/56	FPE	3/58	KPE	5/59			TPE	2/61	XPE	3/62
BPF	7/56	FPF	3/58	KPF	5/59			TPF	2/61	XPF	3/62
BPG	8/56	FPG	4/58	KPG	5/59			TPG	2/61	XPG	3/62
BPH	9/56	FPH	4/58	KPH	5/59			TPH	3/61	XPH	3/62
BPJ	9/56	FPJ	5/58	KPJ	6/59			TPJ	3/61	XPJ	4/62
BPK	10/56	FPK	5/58	KPK	6/59			TPK	3/61	XPK	4/62
BPL	6/56 *	FPL	5/58	KPL	6/59			TPL	3/61	XPL	4/62
CPA	10/56	GPA	6/58	LPA	7/59	PPA	4/60	UPA	3/61	YPA	4/62
CPB	11/56	GPB	6/58	LPB	7/59	PPB	4/60	UPB	4/61	YPB	5/62
CPC	12/56	GPC	6/58	LPC	7/59	PPC	4/60	UPC	4/61	YPC	5/62
CPD	1/57	GPD	7/58	LPD	7/59	PPD	4/60	UPD	4/61	YPD	5/62
CPE	1/57	GPE	7/58	LPE	7/59	PPE	4/60	UPE	4/61	YPE	5/62
CPF	2/57	GPF	7/58	LPF	8/59	PPF	5/60	UPF	5/61	YPF	6/62
CPG	2/57	GPG	8/58	LPG	8/59	PPG	5/60	UPG	5/61	YPG	6/62
CPH	2/57	GPH	8/58	LPH	9/59	PPH	5/60	UPH	5/61	YPH	6/62
CPJ	3/57	GPJ	8/58	LPJ	9/59	PPJ	6/60	UPJ	5/61	YPJ	6/62
CPK	3/57	GPK	9/58	LPK	9/59	PPK	6/60	UPK	6/61	YPK	7/62
CPL	3/57	GPL	9/58	LPL	9/59	PPL	6/60	UPL	6/61	YPL	7/62
DPA	4/57	HPA	9/58	MPA	10/59	RPA	6/60	VPA	6/61	
DPB	4/57	HPB	10/58	MPB	10/59	RPB	6/60	VPB	6/61	
DPC	5/57	HPC	9/58 *	MPC	10/59	RPC	6/60	VPC	6/61	
DPD	5/57	HPD	10/58	MPD	10/59	RPD	7/60	VPD	7/61	
DPE	5/57	HPE	10/58	MPE	11/59	RPE	7/60	VPE	7/61	
DPF	6/57	HPF	11/58	MPF	11/59	RPF	7/60	VPF	7/61	
DPG	7/57	HPG	11/58	MPG	11/59	RPG	8/60	VPG	7/61	
DPH	7/57	HPH	11/58	MPH	12/59	RPH	8/60	VPH	8/61	
DPJ	7/57	HPJ	12/58	MPJ	12/59	RPJ	8/60	VPJ	8/61	
DPK	8/57	HPK	12/58	MPK	12/59	RPK	8/60	VPK	8/61	
DPL	8/57	HPL	1/59	MPL	12/59	RPL	9/60	VPL	7/61 *	

* OPC abandoned after only eight scattered numbers had been issued.

In each of the two-letter reverse format series there was a tendency for motorcycles to receive numbers below 1000, but segregation was not strictly observed. All series started from 1 and were issued in reverse alphabetical sequence.

PL	7/62	PJ	1/63	PH	4/63	PG	5/63	PF	8/63	PE	10/63
PK	10/62									

Suffix marks commenced 2.1.64

159

COUNTY COUNCIL OF EAST SUSSEX

AP 12/03   PM 2/22   PN 7/27   NJ 9/32

In AP and PM motorcycles were segregated from motor cars and HMCs. In AP the odd numbers were cars and the even numbers cycles. AP 9999 was reached by 2/22 and PM (odd numbers) commenced. Motorcycles did not reach AP 9998 until 6/24, when PM 2 up commenced. Cars reached PM 9999 in 12/25 and then used even numbers from PM 5002 up. Motorcycles reached PM 5000 in 7/27, a matter of only ten days before cars reached PM 9998. Motorcycles then used PN 1-21 (consecutive) and from PN 22 a common sequence was adopted.

First issues each year:

	Cars	Cycles
1904	AP 287	AP 166
1905	AP 623	AP 566
1906	AP 1001	AP 800
1907	no info	AP 946
1908	"	AP 1076

Cars reached AP 1163 by 6/07 and motorcycles AP 1130 by 4/08; no information is available thereafter until 1924.

	Cars	Cycles		Common Sequence		
1924	PM 4311		1928	PN 589	1933	NJ 543
1925	PM 7065	PM 764	1929	PN 2616	1934	NJ 2583
1926	PM 5036	PM 2458	1930	PN 4885	1935	NJ 4961
1927	PM 7896	PM 4006	1931	PN 6799	1936	NJ 7760
			1932	PN 8763		

AAP	10/36	EAP	4/48	JAP	4/54	NAP	12/57	SAP	3/60	WAP	12/61
ANJ	2/37	ENJ	9/48	JNJ	8/54	NNJ	3/58	SNJ	5/60	WNJ	2/62
APM	6/37	EPM	3/49	JPM	11/54	NPM	5/58	SPM	6/60	WPM	3/62
APN	10/37	EPN	7/49	JPN	2/55	NPN	6/58	SPN	7/60	WPN	4/62
BAP	4/38	FAP	11/49	KAP	4/55	OAP	8/58	TAP	8/60	XAP	5/62
BNJ	9/38	FNJ	4/50	KNJ	7/55	ONJ	10/58	TNJ	9/60	XNJ	7/62
BPM	2/39	FPM	8/50	KPM	9/55	OPM	12/58	TPM	11/60	XPM	8/62
BPN	7/39	FPN	2/51	KPN	12/55	OPN	2/59	TPN	12/60	XPN	10/62
CAP	5/40	GAP	7/51	LAP	3/56	PAP	4/59	UAP	2/61	YAP	11/62
CNJ	2/42	GNJ	12/51	LNJ	5/56	PNJ	5/59	UNJ	3/61	YNJ	12/62
CPM	8/44	GPM	5/52	LPM	7/56	PPM	7/59	UPM	4/61	YPM	2/63
CPN	5/46	GPN	10/52	LPN	11/56	PPN	9/59	UPN	5/61	YPN	3/63
DAP	10/46	HAP	2/53	MAP	2/57	RAP	10/59	VAP	6/61		
DNJ	2/47	HNJ	6/53	MNJ	4/57	RNJ	12/59	VNJ	7/61		
DPM	6/47	HPM	10/53	MPM	7/57	RPM	1/60	VPM	9/61		
DPN	11/47	HPN	1/54	MPN	9/57	RPN	2/60	VPN	11/61		

AP (from 1001 for all vehicles) 4/63

Suffix marks commenced 3.2.64

COUNTY COUNCIL OF WEST SUSSEX

BP 12/03   PX 4/23   PO 4/29

In BP, cars received odd numbers and motorcycles even numbers, but matters became complicated after the issue of BP 9999. The situation may be summarised as follows

        BP 1 - 9999 (odd numbers) Cars 12/03 to 4/23, BP 2 -7098 (evens) Cycles 12/03 to 5/23
        PX 1 - 181 (odd numbers) Cars 4/23 to 5/23
        BP 7100 - 9998 (evens) All vehicles 5/23 to 4/24
        PX 2 - 182 (evens) All vehicles 4/24 to 5/24
        PX 183 up (odds and evens) All vehicles 5/24 on

Heavy Motor Cars were numbered in a separate series BP 01 to BP 0163.

First issues each year:

	Cars (Odd Nos.)	Motorcycles (Even Nos.)		Cars (Odd Nos.)	Motorcycles (Even Nos.)	
1904	BP 121	BP 86	1914	BP 2361	BP 2148	(For 1923-1924
1905	BP 335	BP 450	1915	BP 3201	BP 2718	issues, see above)
1906	BP 519	BP 652	1916	BP 3671	BP 3180	
1907	BP 715	BP 780	1917	BP 3963	BP 3442	
1908	BP 893	BP 870	1918	none issued	BP 3514	
1909	BP 1089	BP 958	1919	BP 4079	BP 3516	
1910	BP 1269	BP 1074	1920	BP 4463	BP 4110	
1911	BP 1507	BP 1204	1921	BP 5443	BP 4978	
1912	BP 1743	BP 1422	1922	no info	BP 5940	
1913	BP 2169	BP 1728	1923	c. BP 6640	no info	

1925	c. PX 1200	1928	c. PX 7528	1931	PO 3368	1934	PO 8763
1926	c. PX 3290	1929	c. PX 9383	1932	PO 5038		
1927	c. PX 5361	1930	PO 1411	1933	PO 6799		

ABP	6/34	EBP	5/38	JBP	6/47	NBP	10/51	SBP	10/54	WBP	9/56
APO	12/34	EPO	10/38	JPO	11/47	NPO	2/52	SPO	1/55	WPO	12/56
APX	3/35	EPX	2/39	JPX	4/48	NPX	6/52	SPX	3/55	WPX	2/57
BBP	7/35	FBP	6/39	KBP	8/48	OBP	10/52	TBP	4/55	XBP	4/57
BPO	12/35	FPO	12/39	KPO	1/49	OPO	2/53	TPO	6/55	XPO	6/57
BPX	3/36	FPX	9/41	KPX	5/49	OPX	5/53	TPX	8/55	XPX	7/57
CBP	6/36	GBP	3/44	LBP	9/49	PBP	8/53	UBP	9/55	YBP	9/57
CPO	10/36	***		LPO	1/50	PPO	11/53	UPO	11/55	YPO	11/57
CPX	2/37	GPX	2/46	LPX	5/50	PPX	2/54	UPX	1/56	YPX	1/58
DBP	5/37	HBP	8/46	MBP	9/50	RBP	4/54	VBP	3/56		
DPO	9/37	HPO	11/46	MPO	1/51	RPO	6/54	VPO	5/56		
DPX	1/38	HPX	3/47	MPX	6/51	RPX	8/54	VPX	7/56		

In the reverse format series there was no segregation of cycles.

BP   1 - 99 and 1000 - 9999   3/58
PO   1 - 9999   3/59
PX   1 - 99 and 1000 - 9999   2/60

ABP	*11/60*	*DBP*	*8/61*	*GBP*	*7/62*	*KBP*	*4/63*	*NBP*	*11/63*
APO	*12/60*	*DPO*	*10/61*	****		*KPO*	*5/63*	*NPO*	*12/63*
APX	*2/61*	*DPX*	*11/61*	*GPX*	*8/62*	*KPX*	*5/63*	*NPX*	*1/64*
BBP	*3/61*	*EBP*	*1/62*	*HBP*	*10/62*	*LBP*	*6/63*	*OBP*	*2/64*
BPO	*3/61*	*EPO*	*2/62*	*HPO*	*11/62*	*LPO*	*7/63*	*OPO*	*3/64 (completed)*
BPX	*5/61*	*EPX*	*3/62*	*HPX*	*12/62*	*LPX*	*8/63*	*OPX*	*not issued*
CBP	*5/61*	*FBP*	*4/62*	*JBP*	*1/63*	*MBP*	*9/63*	*PBP*	*4/64*
CPO	*6/61*	*FPO*	*5/62*	*JPO*	*2/63*	*MPO*	*10/63*	*PPO*	*12/66 (re-registrations)*
CPX	*7/61*	*FPX*	*6/62*	*JPX*	*3/63*	*MPX*	*10/63*		

*** GPO transferred to London County Council.

Suffix marks commenced 1.5.64

COUNTY COUNCIL OF WARWICK

AC 12/03   NX 4/21   UE 12/25   WD 2/30

Before 1921 a common series for cars and cycles, but heavy motor cars were numbered in a duplicated and parallel series AC 1 - 100, commencing 4/05.

First issues each year:

	Main Series	Heavy Motor Cars			
1904	AC 124		1921	AC 9042
1905	AC 515		1922	NX 1214
1906	AC 719	AC 12	1923	NX 2958
1907	AC 944		1924	NX 4909
1908	AC 1176	AC 13	1925	NX 7372
1909	AC 1410		1926	UE 140
1910	AC 1684		1927	UE 2734
1911	AC 2072	AC 14	1928	UE 5395
1912	AC 2583	AC 16	1929	UE 7610
1913	AC 3248	AC 19	1930	UE 9798
1914	AC 3961	AC 24	1931	WD 1771
1915	AC 4789	AC 37	1932	WD 3244
1916	AC 5488	AC 43	1933	WD 4817
1917	AC 5832	AC 45	1934	WD 6601
1918	AC 6021	AC 52	1935	WD 8766
1919	AC 6162	AC 55		
1920	AC 7333	AC 61 (to AC 100)		

AAC	6/35	EAC	3/43	JAC	6/49	NAC	1/53	SAC	4/55	WAC	4/57
ANX	11/35	ENX	9/44	JNX	9/49	NNX	3/53	SNX	5/55	WNX	5/57
AUE	3/36	EUE	1/46	JUE	12/49	NUE	5/53	SUE	6/55	WUE	7/57
AWD	6/36	EWD	6/46	JWD	3/50	NWD	7/53	SWD	8/55	WWD	8/57
BAC	12/36	FAC	8/46	KAC	6/50	OAC	9/53	TAC	9/55	XAC	10/57
BNX	3/37	FNX	11/46	KNX	8/50	ONX	11/53	TNX	10/55	XNX	11/57
BUE	6/37	FUE	2/47	KUE	11/50	OUE	1/54	TUE	12/55	XUE	1/58
BWD	10/37	FWD	5/47	KWD	2/51	OWD	3/54	TWD	2/56	XWD	2/58
CAC	2/38	GAC	7/47	LAC	4/51	PAC	4/54	UAC	3/56	YAC	3/58
CNX	6/38	GNX	9/47	LNX	6/51	PNX	6/54	UNX	4/56	YNX	4/58
CUE	11/38	GUE	1/48	LUE	9/51	PUE	7/54	UUE	6/56	YUE	6/58
CWD	3/39	GWD	4/48	LWD	12/51	PWD	9/54	UWD	7/56	YWD	7/58
DAC	6/39	HAC	6/48	MAC	2/52	RAC	10/54	VAC	9/56		
DNX	12/39	HNX	9/48	MNX	5/52	RNX	12/54	VNX	11/56		
DUE	2/41	HUE	12/48	MUE	7/52	RUE	2/55	VUE	1/57		
DWD	2/42	HWD	3/49	MWD	10/52	RWD	3/55	VWD	3/57		

Special mark for Diplomatic Corps : QUE 1 ca. 1/78.

Reverse format marks commenced with two-letter marks, all commencing at 1001, for cars and three-letter marks for motorcycles. When cars completed *WD* in 3/62, they joined cycles from *441 CNX* up.

Cars etc					Cycles				
AC	8/58		AAC	8/58	BAC	12/59	CAC	6/61
NX	9/59		ANX	2/59	BNX	4/60	CNX	10/61
UE	6/60	.	AUE	5/59	BUE	7/60		
WD	4/61		AWD	8/59	BWD	1/61		

All Vehicles										
		EAC	8/62	GAC	4/63	JAC	10/63	LAC	3/64
		ENX	9/62	GNX	5/63	JNX	10/63	LNX	4/64
CUE	3/62	EUE	11/62	GUE	5/63	JUE	11/63	LUE	9/75 (re-registrations)
CWD	4/62	EWD	12/62	GWD	6/63	JWD	12/63		
DAC	5/62	FAC	1/63	HAC	7/63	KAC	1/64		
DNX	6/62	FNX	2/63	HNX	7/63	KNX	2/64		
DUE	6/62	FUE	3/63	HUE	8/63	KUE	2/64		
DWD	7/62	FWD	3/63	HWD	9/63	KWD	3/64		

Suffix marks commenced 1.5.64

COUNTY COUNCIL OF WESTMORLAND

EC 12/03   JM 12/31

A single sequence for all vehicles.

First issues each year. No information available for 1910 to 1928.

1905	ca. EC 153	1929	EC 8541	1937	JM 3007	1945	JM 5607
1906	ca. EC 213	1930	EC 9081	1938	JM 3678	1946	JM 5743
1907	ca. EC 270	1931	EC 9590	1939	JM 4201	1947	JM 6409
1908	ca. EC 330	1932	JM 47	1940	JM 4788	1948	JM 7205
1909	EC 420	1933	JM 504	1941	JM 4994	1949	JM 8062
		1934	JM 1051	1942	JM 5137	1950	JM 9141
		1935	JM 1631	1943	JM 5331		
		1936	JM 2340	1944	JM 5482		

AEC	11/50	CEC	7/54	EEC	5/57	GEC	9/59	JEC	6/61	LEC	5/63
AJM	1/52	CJM	4/55	EJM	1/58	GJM	3/60	JJM	1/62	LJM	10/63
BEC	1/53	DEC	11/55	FEC	7/58	HEC	7/60	KEC	6/62	MEC	3/64
BJM	11/53	DJM	7/56	FJM	3/59	HJM	1/61	KJM	12/62	MJM	6/64

Special mark for Diplomatic Corps :   *1 EC 5/79*

Commenced suffix marks 4.8.64

COUNTY COUNCIL OF THE ISLE OF WIGHT

DL 12/03

First numbers each year. No information is available prior to 1929.

1929	DL 6030	1931	DL 7324	1933	DL 8216	1935	DL 9387
1930	DL 6751	1932	DL 7756	1934	DL 8739		

ADL	10/35	EDL	3/46	JDL	3/52	NDL	3/56	SDL	1/59	WDL	3/61
BDL	1/37	FDL	7/47	KDL	7/53	ODL	1/57	TDL	7/59	XDL	8/61
CDL	4/38	GDL	3/49	LDL	7/54	PDL	9/57	UDL	2/60	YDL	4/62
DDL	9/39	HDL	8/50	MDL	5/55	RDL	5/58	VDL	7/60		

ADL	*11/62*	*BDL*	*5/63*	*CDL*	*10/63*

Suffix marks commenced 3.2.64

COUNTY COUNCIL OF WILTS

Registration commenced 12.12.03

A common sequence for all vehicles.

AM 12/03   HR 7/19   MR 1/24   MW 6/27   WV 8/31

First numbers issued each year :

1904	AM 180	1913	AM 2774	1922	HR 5839	1931	MW 8602		
1905	AM 561	1914	AM 3449	1923	HR 7632	1932	WV 424		
1906	AM 746	1915	AM 4420	1924	HR 9925	1933	WV 2593		
1907	AM 948	1916	AM 5809	1925	MR 2458	1934	WV 4475		
1908	AM 1120	1917	AM 7229	1926	MR 5613	1935	WV 6776		
1909	AM 1327	1918	AM 8298	1927	MR 8489	1936	WV 9565		
1910	AM 1545	1919	AM 9090	1928	MW 1047				
1911	AM 1826	1920	HR 908	1929	MW 3540				
1912	AM 2170	1921	HR 3222	1930	MW 6163				

AAM	2/36	EAM	9/46	JAM	6/52	NAM	9/55	SAM	7/58	WAM	5/60
AHR	5/36	EHR	12/46	JHR	9/52	NHR	11/55	SHR	9/58	WHR	5/60
AMR	9/36	EMR	3/47 #	JMR	11/52	NMR	1/56	SMR	10/58	WMR	7/60
AMW	1/37	EMW	6/47	JMW	2/53	NMW	3/56	SMW	11/58	WMW	7/60
AWV	5/37	EWV	10/47	JWV	5/53	NWV	4/56	SWV	1/59	WWV	9/60
BAM	8/37	FAM	1/48	KAM	7/53	OAM	6/56	TAM	2/59	XAM	10/60
BHR	1/38	FHR	4/48	KHR	9/53	OHR	8/56	THR	3/59	XHR	12/60
BMR	4/38	FMR	8/49	KMR	11/53	OMR	10/56	TMR	4/59	XMR	1/61
BMW	9/38	FMW	12/48	KMW	2/54	OMW	12/56	TMW	5/59	XMW	2/61
BWV	1/39	FWV	4/49	KWV	3/54	OWV	2/57	TWV	6/59	XWV	3/61
CAM	4/39	GAM	7/49	LAM	5/54	PAM	4/57	UAM	6/59	YAM	4/61
CHR	8/39	GHR	10/49	LHR	7/54	PHR	5/57	UHR	7/59	YHR	5/61
CMR	2/40	GMR	2/50	LMR	9/54	PMR	7/57	UMR	9/59	YMR	6/61
CMW	11/40	GMW	5/50	LMW	11/54	PMW	8/57	UMW	10/59	YMW	6/61
CWV	1/42	GWV	9/50	LWV	1/55	PWV	10/57	UWV	11/59	YWV	7/61
DAM	not alloc	HAM	1/51	MAM	3/55	RAM	12/57	VAM	12/59		
DHR	3/43	HHR	4/51	MHR	4/55	RHR	2/58 #	VHR	1/60		
DMR	10/44	HMR	7/51	MMR	5/55	RMR	3/58	VMR	2/60		
DMW	1/46	HMW	11/51	MMW	7/55	RMW	5/58	VMW	3/60		
DWV	5/46	HWV	3/52	MWV	8/55	RWV	6/58	VWV	4/60		

early issues : EMR 1 (1/47), RHR 1 (11/57)

Reverse format issues commenced concurrently with *MW (from 1)* and *AAM*, the three-letter marks being mainly used for motorcycles and agricultural tractors, though many cars also received numbers in these series. After completion of *MW (2/63)*, a common series from *ca 700 AMW* onwards.

Cars			Mainly Cycles	
MW	9/61		AAM	10/61
			AHR	3/62
			AMR	7/62
			AMW	10/62

All Vehicles

		BAM	3/63	CAM	7/63 #	DAM	not alloc	EAM	3/64	FAM	7/76 *
		BHR	4/63	CHR	7/63	DHR	11/63	EHR	3/64		
		BMR	4/63	CMR	8/63	DMR	1/64	EMR	4/64		
		BMW	5/63	CMW	9/63	DMW	1/64	EMW	5/64		
AWV	2/63	BWV	6/63	CWV	10/63	DWV	2/64	EWV	8/74 *		

1 CAM early for Diplomatic Corps (c. 5/63).

* Re-registrations only.

Special issues for Diplomatic Corps : ZAM 1 (6/69), 1 GAM (c.8/70), 1 JAM (c.1/63), 1 NAM (1/92).

Commenced suffix marks 1.6.64

COUNTY COUNCIL OF WORCESTER

AB 12/03   NP 8/21   UY 1/27 (UY 2 early, 11/26)   WP 4/31

A single sequence for all vehicles.

First issues each year :

1904	AB 101	1912	AB 2169	1920	AB 6691	1928	UY 2216
1905	AB 351	1913	AB 2747	1921	AB 8699	1929	UY 4578
1906	AB 524	1914	AB 3380	1922	NP 386	1930	UY 7068
1907	AB 716	1915	AB 4070	1923	NP 1845	1931	UY 9353
1908	AB 905	1916	AB 4706	1924	NP 3455	1932	WP 1228
1909	AB 1097	1917	AB 5092	1925	NP 5281	1933	WP 3101
1910	AB 1341	1918	AB 5311	1926	NP 7518	1934	WP 5159
1911	AB 1673	1919	AB 5517	1927	NP 9825	1935	WP 7770

AAB	10/35	EAB	6/42	JAB	1/50	NAB	5/54	SAB	9/56	WAB	12/58
ANP	2/36	ENP	10/43	JNP	5/50	NNP	7/54	SNP	12/56	WNP	2/59
AUY	5/36	EUY	6/45	JUY	9/50	NUY	9/54	SUY	2/57	WUY	3/59
AWP	9/36	EWP	3/46	JWP	1/51	NWP	11/54	SWP	4/57	WWP	4/59
BAB	12/36	FAB	7/46	KAB	5/51	OAB	1/55	TAB	5/57	XAB	5/59
BNP	3/37	FNP	10/46	KNP	9/51	ONP	3/55	TNP	7/57	XNP	6/59
BUY	6/37	FUY	2/47	KUY	1/52	OUY	5/55	TUY	8/57	XUY	7/59
BWP	10/37	FWP	5/47	KWP	5/52	OWP	6/55	TWP	10/57	XWP	8/59
CAB	2/38	GAB	7/47	LAB	8/52	PAB	7/55	UAB	12/57	YAB	10/59
CNP	5/38	GNP	10/47	LNP	12/52	PNP	8/55	UNP	2/58	YNP	11/59
CUY	9/38	GUY	2/48	LUY	3/53	PUY	10/55	UUY	3/58	YUY	12/59
CWP	1/39	GWP	6/48	LWP	6/53	PWP	11/55	UWP	5/58	YWP	1/60
DAB	4/39	HAB	10/48	MAB	8/53	RAB	1/56	VAB	6/58		
DNP	7/39	HNP	2/49	MNP	11/53	RNP	3/56	VNP	7/58		
DUY	3/40	HUY	6/49	MUY	1/54	RUY	5/56	VUY	9/58		
DWP	7/41	HWP	9/49	MWP	4/54	RWP	6/56	VWP	11/58		

AAB	2/60	DAB	2/61	GAB	3/62	KAB	4/63	NAB	8/63 **
ANP	3/60	DNP	3/61	GNP	4/62	KNP	4/63	NNP	c12/75 *
AUY	4/60	DUY	4/61	GUY	5/62	KUY	5/63		
AWP	5/60	DWP	5/61	GWP	6/62	KWP	5/63		
BAB	6/60	EAB	6/61	HAB	6/62	LAB	6/63		
BNP	6/60	ENP	6/61	HNP	8/62	LNP	7/63		
BUY	7/60	EUY	7/61	HUY	9/62	LUY	8/63		
BWP	8/60	EWP	8/61	HWP	10/62	LWP	9/63		
CAB	9/60	FAB	9/61	JAB	11/62	MAB	10/63		
CNP	10/60	FNP	11/61	JNP	1/63	MNP	11/63		
CUY	12/60	FUY	1/62	JUY	2/63	MUY	12/63		
CWP	1/61	FWP	2/62	JWP	3/63	MWP	c2/72 *		

* Re-registrations.
** 1 - 7 NAB only, special issues.

Commenced suffix marks 2.1.64

COUNTY COUNCIL OF THE EAST RIDING OF YORKSHIRE

BT 12/03   WF 8/26

In the early part of BT separate blocks were allocated to motor cars, motorcycles and heavy motor cars, as follows :

BT 1- 60 Cars and HMC	BT 251-260 HMC	BT 2301-2350 HMC	BT 3201-3300 cycles
BT 61-150 * cycles	BT 351-400 HMC	BT 2801-2829 HMC	BT 3401-3500 cycles
BT 201-220 HMC	BT 1501-1550 HMC	BT 2901-3099 cycles.	

* except 140.

Blocks not listed were motor cars.
A common sequence from BT 3501 up.

First issues each year. No information is available to the writer prior to 1929, but details for 1923 to 1928 may be found at the County Archives, Beverley.

1929	WF 2019		1932	WF 4633		1935	WF 7273
1930	WF 2966		1933	WF 5390		1936	WF 8457
1931	WF 3855		1934	WF 6214		1937	WF 9774

ABT	3/37	EBT	8/46	JBT	5/50	NBT	3/54	SBT	6/56	WBT	10/58
AWF	12/37	EWF	1/47	JWF	11/50	NWF	7/54	SWF	10/56	WWF	1/59
BBT	9/38	FBT	6/47	KBT	6/51	OBT	11/54	TBT	3/57	XBT	3/59
BWF	5/39	FWF	11/47	KWF	2/52	OWF	2/55	TWF	6/57	XWF	5/59
CBT	6/40	GBT	4/48	LBT	9/52	PBT	5/55	UBT	10/57	YBT	8/59
CWF	5/42	GWF	10/48	LWF	2/53	PWF	9/55	UWF	2/58	YWF	10/59
DBT	3/44	HBT	4/49	MBT	7/53	RBT	12/55	VBT	4/58		
DWF	1/46	HWF	10/49	MWF	11/53	RWF	3/56	VWF	7/58		

Reverse issues began with the simultaneous issue of *1000-9999 BT* mainly for cars and *1-999 WF* mainly for motorcycles. The former was followed by *1000-9999 WF* and the latter by *1-999 ABT*. 9999 WF was reached 9/63 and cars went into *AWF*, being joined one month later by cycles.

Mainly Cars			Mainly Cycles			All Vehicles		
1000-9999 BT	*1/60*		*1-999 WF*	*1/60*		AWF	*9/63*	
1000-9999 WF	*11/61*		ABT	*6/61*		BBT	*12/63*	
						BWF	*3/64*	
						CBT	*4/64*	
						CWF	*8/68* (re-registrations)	

Suffix issues commenced 1.6.64

War Department vehicles handed over to Slough Trading Company - cancellation of registration numbers. All War Department vehicles disposed of through the Slough Trading Company should be regarded as not having been previously registered, (even if by accident numbers remain on the vehicles)...... In cases where the registration marks and numbers have not been removed from vehicles prior to their arrival st the Slough Trading Company's deport, the Company will take steps to delete the registration marks and numbers....

Circular RF 155 4.8.22

COUNTY COUNCIL OF THE NORTH RIDING OF YORKSHIRE

Registration commenced 17.12.03

AJ 12/03   PY 7/23   VN 4/29

A common sequence for all vehicles.

First issues each year. No information available for 1913 to 1921.

1904	AJ 62	1922	AJ 7598	1930	VN 999
1905	AJ 252	1923	AJ 8924	1931	VN 2320
1906	AJ 382	1924	PY 534	1932	VN 3377
1907	AJ 501	1925	PY 2482	1933	VN 4364
1908	AJ 640	1926	PY 4497	1934	VN 5375
1909	AJ 755	1927	PY 6305	1935	VN 6648
1910	AJ 846	1928	PY 7991	1936	VN 8158
1911	AJ 899	1929	PY 9548	1937	VN 9796
1912	AJ 1132				

AAJ	2/37	EAJ	10/47	JAJ	9/52	NAJ	9/55	SAJ	4/58	WAJ	3/60
APY	10/37	EPY	3/48	JPY	1/53	NPY	11/55	SPY	5/58	WPY	4/60
AVN	4/38	EVN	7/48	JVN	5/53	NVN	2/56	SVN	7/58	WVN	5/60
BAJ	12/38	FAJ	1/49	KAJ	8/53	OAJ	4/56	TAJ	10/58	XAJ	7/60
BPY	7/39	FPY	5/49	KPY	12/53	OPY	6/56	TPY	12/58	XPY	9/60
BVN	1/41	FVN	10/49	KVN	3/54	OVN	10/56	TVN	2/59	XVN	11/60
CAJ	9/42	GAJ	3/50	LAJ	5/54	PAJ	1/57	UAJ	4/59	YAJ	1/61
CPY	3/44	GPY	7/50	LPY	9/54	PPY	4/57	UPY	5/59	YPY	3/61
CVN	1/46	GVN	12/50	LVN	12/54	PVN	6/57	UVN	7/59	YVN	4/61
DAJ	8/46	HAJ	5/51	MAJ	3/55	RAJ	8/57	VAJ	9/59		
DPY	1/47	HPY	11/51	MPY	4/55	RPY	11/57	VPY	11/59		
DVN	5/47	HVN	4/52	MVN	7/55	RVN	2/58	VVN	1/60		

AAJ	5/61	CAJ	4/62	EAJ	3/63	GAJ	12/63
APY	7/61	CPY	6/62	EPY	4/63	GPY	2/64
AVN	8/61	CVN	8/62	EVN	6/63	GVN	3/64
BAJ	11/61	DAJ	10/62	FAJ	7/63	HAJ	4/64
BPY	1/62	DPY	12/62	FPY	9/63	HPY	5/76 (re-registrations only)
BVN	3/62	DVN	2/63	FVN	10/63		

Special marks for Diplomatic Corps :   *1 PY* (9/95); *1 VN* (12/78)

Suffix Marks Commenced 1.5.64

COUNTY COUNCIL OF THE WEST RIDING OF YORKSHIRE

C 1/04	WY 7/21	WU 4/25	WX 4/29
WR 4/15	WT 7/23	WW 2/27	YG 3/32

First issues each year. No information is available before 1921.

1921	WR 6580 **	1925	WT 7697	1929	WW 8443	1933	YG 2584
1922	WY 1443	1926	WU 3929	1930	WX 2653	1934	YG 5908
1923	WY 6047	1927	WU 9484	1931	WX 6253	1935	YG 9870
1924	WT 1495	1928	no info.	1932	WX 9468		

** WR 9999 was reached 15.6.21, then C 2100 - 2999 (omitted previously) were issued before WY 1 commenced 28.7.21

AWR	1/35	EWR	5/42	JWR	9/49	NWR	2/54	SWR	5/56	WWR	7/58
AWT	4/35	EWT	12/42	JWT	11/49	NWT	3/54	SWT	6/56	WWT	8/58
AWU	6/35	EWU	8/43	JWU	1/50	NWU	4/54	SWU	7/56	WWU	9/58
AWW	9/35	EWW	6/44	JWW	3/50	NWW	6/54	SWW	9/56	WWW	10/58
AWX	11/35	EWX	6/45	JWX	5/50	NWX	7/54	SWX	10/56	WWX	11/58
AWY	2/36	EWY	12/45	JWY	6/50	NWY	7/54	SWY	11/56	WWY	12/58
AYG	4/36	EYG	3/46	JYG	9/50	NYG	9/54	SYG	1/57	WYG	12/58
BWR	6/36	FWR	6/46	KWR	11/50	OWR	10/54	TWR	2/57	XWR	1/59
BWT	8/36	FWT	8/46	KWT	1/51	OWT	11/54	TWT	3/57	XWT	2/59
BWU	11/36	FWU	10/46	KWU	3/51	OWU	12/54	TWU	4/57	XWU	3/59
BWW	1/37	FWW	11/46	KWW	5/51	OWW	1/55	TWW	5/57	XWW	3/59
BWX	3/37	FWX	1/47	KWX	7/51	OWX	2/55	TWX	5/57	XWX	4/59
BWY	5/37	FWY	3/47	KWY	9/51	OWY	3/55	TWY	6/57	XWY	4/59
BYG	7/37	FYG	4/47	KYG	12/51	OYG	4/55	TYG	7/57	XYG	5/59
CWR	9/37	GWR	6/47	LWR	2/52	PWR	5/55	UWR	8/57	YWR	5/59
CWT	12/37	GWT	7/47	LWT	5/52	PWT	6/55	UWT	9/57	YWT	6/59
CWU	2/38	GWU	9/47	LWU	7/52	PWU	7/55	UWU	10/57	YWU	6/59
CWW	4/38	GWW	11/47	LWW	9/52	PWW	8/55	UWW	11/57	YWW	7/59
CWX	6/38	GWX	1/48	LWX	11/52	PWX	9/55	UWX	12/57	YWX	7/59
CWY	10/38	GWY	3/48	LWY	1/53	PWY	9/55	UWY	1/58	YWY	8/59
CYG	12/38	GYG	5/48	LYG	2/53	PYG	10/55	UYG	2/58	YYG	9/59
DWR	2/39	HWR	7/48	MWR	4/53	RWR	11/55	VWR	3/58		
DWT	4/39	HWT	9/48	MWT	5/53	RWT	12/55	VWT	3/58		
DWU	6/39	HWU	11/48	MWU	7/53	RWU	1/56	VWU	4/58		
DWW	8/39	HWW	1/49	MWW	9/53	RWW	3/56	VWW	5/58		
DWX	1/40	HWX	3/49	MWX	10/53	RWX	3/56	VWX	5/58		
DWY	8/40	HWY	5/49	MWY	11/53	RWY	4/56	VWY	6/58		
DYG	11/41	HYG	7/49	MYG	12/53	RYG	5/56	VYG	7/58		

There was no segregation of motorcycles in the reverse format issues. All two-letter issues started from 1.

WU	10/59	WW	3/60	WX	8/60	WY	3/61	YG	7/61

AWR	2/62	CWR	9/62	EWR	5/63	GWR	11/63	
AWT	3/62	CWT	10/62	EWT	5/63	GWT	11/63	
AWU	3/62	CWU	11/62	EWU	5/63	GWU	12/63	
AWW	4/62	CWW	11/62	EWW	6/63	GWW	12/63	
AWX	4/62	CWX	12/62	EWX	6/63	GWX	1/64	
AWY	4/62	CWY	1/63	EWY	7/63	GWY	1/64	
AYG	5/62	CYG	1/63	EYG	7/63	GYG	2/64	
BWR	5/62	DWR	2/63	FWR	7/63	HWR	2/64	
BWT	6/62	DWT	3/63	FWT	8/63	HWT	c8/72 (re-registrations only)	
BWU	6/62	DWU	3/63	FWU	8/63			
BWW	7/62	DWW	3/63	FWW	9/63			
BWX	7/62	DWX	4/63	FWX	9/63			
BWY	8/62	DWY	4/63	FWY	10/63			
BYG	9/62	DYG	4/63	FYG	10/63			

Special mark for Diplomatic Corps : *1 NWY* (ca.11/76)

Suffix marks commenced 2.3.64

COUNTY BOROUGH COUNCIL OF BARNSLEY

Barnsley was created a County Borough with effect from 1.4.13

HE 4/13

A single sequence for all vehicles.

First issues each year, (no information available for 1922 - 1927) :

1914	HE	84	1928	HE 3689	1936	HE 7253	1944	HE 9855
1915	HE	222	1929	HE 4134	1937	HE 7829	1945	HE 9976
1916	HE	367	1930	HE 4673	1938	HE 8471		
1917	HE	454	1931	HE 5180	1939	HE 9098		
1918	HE	484	1932	HE 5538	1940	HE 9616		
1919	HE	503	1933	HE 5933	1941	HE 9685		
1920	HE	737	1934	HE 6295	1942	HE 9716		
1921	HE	1189	1935	HE 6714	1943	HE 9784		

AHE	3/45	EHE	6/51	JHE	4/55	NHE	10/57	SHE	10/59	WHE	6/61
BHE	6/47	FHE	11/52	KHE	11/56	OHE	4/58	THE	3/60	XHE	11/61
CHE	12/48	GHE	10/53	LHE	6/56	PHE	11/58	UHE	7/60	YHE	5/62
DHE	3/50	HHE	7/54	MHE	3/57	RHE	5/59	VHE	1/61		

There was no segregation of cycles in reverse format issues.

HE (from 1000)   9/62

Suffix marks commenced 1.7.64

COUNTY COUNCIL OF BARROW-IN-FURNESS

EO 1/04

A single sequence for all vehicles.

First numbers issued each year.

1905	EO	71	1917	EO 1475	1929	EO 4503	1941	EO 7802
1906	EO	104	1918	EO 1592	1930	EO 4753	1942	EO 7824
1907	EO	143	1919	EO 1639	1931	EO 4991	1943	EO 7904
1908	EO	171	1920	EO 2019	1932	EO 5209	1944	EO 7931
1909	EO	202	1921	EO 2586	1933	EO 5387	1945	EO 7956
1910	EO	223	1922	EO 2796	1934	EO 5576	1946	EO 8007
1911	EO	245	1923 ca.	EO 2920	1935	EO 5861	1947	EO 8292
1912	EO	318	1924 ca.	EO 3075	1936	EO 6230	1948	EO 8615
1913	EO	416	1925	EO 3280	1937	EO 6649	1949	EO 8888
1914	EO	576	1926	EO 3603	1938	EO 7037	1950	EO 9203
1915	EO	821	1927	EO 3893	1939	EO 7386	1951	EO 9490
1916	EO	1203	1928	EO 4238	1940	EO 7728	1952	EO 9753

AEO	9/52	CEO	5/56	EEO	3/59	GEO	9/60	JEO	4/62	LEO	11/63
BEO	11/54	DEO	2/58	FEO	1/60	HEO	6/61	KEO	3/63	MEO	7/64

Suffix Marks Commenced 1.9.64

COUNTY BOROUGH COUNCIL OF BATH

FB 11/03   GL 8/32

A single sequence for motor cars and motor cycles, but between 1905 and 1921 heavy motor cars were numbered in a separate series FB 01 to FB 0101. Some of these numbers were reissued to new vehicles as late as 1925.

First issues each year. Information not available before 1929, but a random selection of earlier issues is shown.

Main Series				Heavy Motor Cars		
FB 540	2/12	FB 5837	2/27	FB 01 to 07	8/05 - 12/05
FB 1047	6/14	FB 5890	4/27	FB 08 to 013	6/06 - 12/06
FB 1540	5/18	FB 6487	12/27	FB 023 to 029	4/12 - 8/12
FB 1977	1/20	FB 6571	1/38	FB 030	1/13
FB 2355	1/21	FB 6826	5/28	FB 032 to 037	3/13 - 5/13
FB 2616	3/21	FB 7070	8/28	FB 039 to 043	4/13 - 6/13
FB 3009	4/22			FB 045 to 050	7/14 - 9/14
FB 3890	4/24			FB 051	/16
FB 4000	7/24			FB 070 to 080	2/20 - 5/20
FB 4994	12/25			FB 098	1/21

1929	FB 7240	1934	GL 1060	1939	GL 6541	1944	GL 8188
1930	FB 8060	1935	GL 2000	1940	GL 7555	1945	GL 8239
1931	FB 8880	1936	GL 3035	1941	GL 7806	1946	GL 8387
1932	FB 9550	1937	GL 4131	1942	GL 7964	1947	GL 9440
1933	GL 230	1938	GL 5511	1943	GL 8117		

AFB	6/47	DFB	4/52	GFB	3/56	KFB	8/59	NFB	4/62		
AGL	5/48	DGL	3/53	GGL	11/56	KGL	1/60	NGL	9/62		
BFB	3/49	EFB	12/53	HFB	7/57	LFB	6/60	OFB	3/63		
BGL	1/50	EGL	8/54	HGL	2/58	LGL	11/60	OGL	7/63		
CFB	9/50	FFB	3/55	JFB	8/58	MFB	4/61	PFB	3/68	(re-registrations)
CGL	6/51	FGL	9/55	JGL	3/59	MGL	9/61	PGL	c1/78	(re-reg. PGL 1 only)

Suffix marks commenced 2.1.64

COUNTY BOROUGH COUNCIL OF BIRKENHEAD

CM 1/04   BG 1/31

Heavy motor cars had a reserved block from CM 501 up, (upper limit not known).

First issues each year. No information is available prior to 1929.

1929	CM 8468	1934	BG 2013	1939	BG 7283	1944	BG 8554
1930	CM 9244	1935	BG 3018	1940	BG 8197	1945	BG 8706
1931	CM 9994	1936	BG 4036	1941	BG 8337	1946	BG 8857
1932	BG 570	1937	BG 5194	1942	BG 8400	1947	BG 9385
1933	BG 1189	1938	BG 6383	1943	BG 8473		

In the three-letter sequence combinations of CM preceded those of BG.

ACM	1/48	DCM	6/54	GCM	11/57	KCM	5/60	NCM	7/62	RCM	12/63
ABG	9/49	DBG	2/55	GBG	6/58	KBG	9/60	NBG not alloc		RBG	3/64
BCM	12/50	ECM	7/55	HCM	1/59	LCM	2/61	OCM	12/62	SCM	5/64
BBG	4/52	EBG	3/56	HBG	5/59	LBG	6/61	OBG	4/63		
CCM	12/52	FCM	10/56	JCM	10/59	MCM	10/61	PCM	6/63		
CBG	9/53	FBG	5/57	JBG	3/60	MBG	3/62	PBG	8/63		

Suffix marks commenced 4.8.64

OI 251 Belfast CBC, c.1905. Humber

SL 166 Clackmannanshire CC, c.1910. Wolseley

D 5378 Kent CC, 1910. Ford; **LD 7707** London CC, 1910. Ford; **A 1203** London CC, 1904. Darracq

U 1467 Leeds CBC, 1910. Vauxhall; **N 6186** Manchester CBC, c.1910. Vauxhall

AH 602 Norfolk CC, 1908. Phoenix

(Photos: Bryan Goodman Collection)

AH 0140 Norfolk CC, 1913. Daimler. Heavy motor car (with zero prefix) *(John Banks Collection)*

AE 3350 Bristol CBC, Pre-1920. AC Sociable *(Bryan Goodman Collection)*

BY 1906 Croydon CBC, c.1911. Martinsyde *(Bryan Goodman Collection)*

CN 2542 Gateshead CBC, 1926. Hudson *(Bryan Goodman Collection)*

PF 7497 Surrey CC, 1926/7. Amilcar *(Bryan Goodman Collection)*

HD 2109 Dewsbury CBC, 1924. Leyland *(Bryan Goodman Collection)*

FMM 832, DMM 959, EMM 65, DMM 938   Middlesex CC, 1937/8. Morris *(Bryan Goodman Collection)*

CC 9424   Caernarvonshire CC, 1930. Dennis *(Peter Robson)*

THX 323   Middlesex CC, 1948. Allard *(Bryan Goodman Collection)*

OJ 6677   Birmingham CBC, 1933. Lagonda *(Bryan Goodman Collection)*

AYR 74   London CC, 1934. Morris *(Bryan Goodman Collection)*

GM 7110   Motherwell & Wishaw BC, 1955. MG *(Bryan Goodman Collection)*

RBT 548   Yorkshire (East Riding) CC, 1956. Ferguson *(Peter Robson)*

64 MOO   Essex CC, 1963. Ford *(Bryan Goodman Collection)*

1000 E   Staffordshire CC, 1953. Vauxhall. Cherished on newer car. The first reversed single-letter mark   *(Reg Wilson)*

PGR 231   Sunderland CBC, 1960/1. Ford *(Peter Robson)*

9600 HP   Coventry CBC, 1961. Jaguar *(Bryan Goodman Collection)*

ELB 851J   London CC, 1970. Morris *(John Harrison)*

C21 SEK   Liverpool LVLO, 1985. Vauxhall. A Warrington mark issued especially at the request of a Warrington resident after the closure of Warrington LVLO *(John Harrison)*

CK51 WZD   Cardiff LO, 2001/2. BMW *(Peter Robson)*

K130 EXP   June 1993. VAT-free export mark *(Reg Wilson)*

166 Q02   2002. Temporary import *(Vic Brumby Collection)*

QQ 8451   Temporary import. Mercedes-Benz. Photo taken 1929 *(Bryan Goodman Collection)*

Q781 DHN   Vehicle of indeterminate age. Middlesbrough VRO, c1997. AC Cobra replica *(Peter Robson)*

MJI 2465   Northern Ireland. Omagh LVLO, 1989. Ford *(Peter Robson)*

GLI 606   Irish Republic. Westmeath CC, 1966. Morris *(Gerry Costello)*

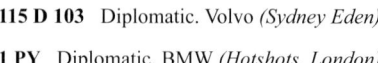

ZV 5681   Irish Republic. Wicklow CC. Morris. ZV marks are used for vehicles aged thirty years or more if the owner prefers an old-style registration *(John Harrison)*

103 DZM   Irish Republic. Galway CC, 1985. Volkswagen. Red rear plate *(Gerry Costello)*

00-KY-4204   Irish Republic. Kerry CC, 2000. Honda. Current format *(Peter Robson)*

115 D 103   Diplomatic. Volvo *(Sydney Eden)*

1 PY   Diplomatic. BMW *(Hotshots, London)*

CL-A 25 Norwich CBC, pre-1921. General Identification Mark (trade plate). Sunbeam
      (Bryan Goodman Collection)

0614 DU Coventry CBC. General trade plate (1923-1969). Standard *(Bryan Goodman Collection)*

057 LK London CC. Limited trade plate (1923-1969). This style still in use for all trade plates. Alfa Romeo
      (Bryan Goodman Collection)

PSJ 305 Middlesbrough VRO, 1998. Fordson (manufactured 1954). Age-related mark *(Peter Robson)*

FRE 3A Stoke-on-Trent LVLO. Replacement mark. Austin-Healey (first registered 1963) *(John Harrison)*

RH 14 AA Military, 1993 onwards. Unipower Carmichael *(Peter Robson)*

73 KK 33 Military, 1982-1993. Leyland Daf *(Peter Robson)*

SS 9191 East Lothian CC, 1954. Cherished on 1928 vehicle. Foden *(Peter Robson)*

CWR 1 Yorkshire (West Riding) CC, 1937. Cherished on newer car. Jaguar *(Peter Robson)*

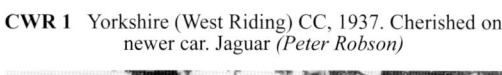

JUL 1A DVLA Auction, 1993. Mercedes-Benz *(John Harrison)*

WC 21 DVLA Auction, 2001. Ford. WC was allocated to Essex County Council in 1962 but two-letter WC marks were not issued *(John Harrison)*

JP51 MCP DVLA Select mark, 2001. Toyota *(Peter Robson)*

C3 KSM DVLA Select mark. Alfa-Romeo *(Peter Robson)*

COUNTY BOROUGH COUNCIL OF BIRMINGHAM

O	1/04	OH	5/20	ON	9/25	OF	5/29	OC	5/33
OA	2/13	OK	1/22	OP	8/26	OG	4/30		
OB	10/15	OL	7/23	OX	7/27	OV	4/31		
OE	5/19	OM	11/24	VP	7/28	OJ	5/32		

A single sequence for all vehicles during the two-letter era. No explanation has been found for the fact that, although allotted as early as 9/22, OC was not taken into use until 5/33. First issues each year. No information is available prior to 1929.

1929 VP 4574	1931 OG 7258	1933 OJ 5641
1930 OF 6368	1932 OV 6398	1934 OC 6375

AOA	3/34	BOA	5/35	COA	5/36	DOA	3/37
AOB	4/34	BOB	6/35	COB	5/36	DOB	3/37
AOC	5/34	BOC	7/35	COC	not alloc	DOC	4/37
AOE	6/34	BOE	8/35	COE	6/36	DOE	5/37
AOF	7/34	BOF	9/35	COF	7/36	DOF	5/37
AOG	8/34	BOG	not alloc	COG	7/36	DOG	6/37
AOH	9/34	BOH	10/35	COH	9/36	DOH	6/37
AOJ	10/34	BOJ	10/35	COJ	9/36	DOJ	7/37
AOK	11/34	BOK	11/35	COK	not alloc	DOK	8/37
AOL	12/34	BOL	12/35	COL	10/36		
AOM	1/35	BOM	1/36	COM	11/36		
AON	2/35	BON	2/36	CON	12/36		
AOP	3/35	BOP	3/36	COP	12/36		
AOV	3/35	BOV	3/36	COV	1/37		
AOX	4/35	BOX	3/36	COX	2/37		
AVP	4/35	BVP	4/36	CVP	3/37		

At this point it was decided to segregate commercial vehicles. Concurrently with DOL for other vehicles, DVP was commenced for commercials and thereafter issues did not appear in strict alphabetical sequence, but with a few exceptions, marks within each sequence were issued alphabetically. Note that FVP, FOX, FOV and FOP were issued in that order. (Some private car types which could be adapted to the carriage of goods, together with coaches, were included in the "Commercial" series, but stage carriage buses were not.) Later there were exclusive series for Birmingham City Transport, The Austin Motor Export Company and The Home Delivery Export Scheme.

Main Series				Commercial	Special
	FOB 3/39	HOB 3/47	KOB 9/49	DVP 9/37	JOJ 3/49
	FOC 4/39	HOC 4/47	KOC 10/49	EOA 1/38	(Birmingham
	FOE 5/39	HOE 5/47	KOE 11/49	EOJ 8/38	City
	FOF 6/39	HOF 6/47	KOF 1/50	EVP 2/39	Transport.
	FOG 6/39	HOG not alloc	KOH 3/50	FOA 6/39	Completed
	FOH 7/39	HOH 7/47	KOJ 4/50	FVP 2/40	8/53)
	FOJ 8/39	HOJ 8/47	KOK 5/50	FOX 10/41	
DOL 9/37	FOK 11/39	HOK 9/47	KOL 6/50	FOV 8/42	
DOM 10/37	FOL 4/40	HOL 9/47	KON 7/50	FOP 2/44	
DON 11/37	FOM 7/40	HOM 11/47	KOP 8/50	GOA 6/45	
DOP 12/37	FON 8/41	HON 2/48	KOV 9/50	GOG 4/46	
DOV 1/38		HOP 4/48	KOX 10/50	GOL 8/46	
DOX 2/38		HOV 5/48		GOX 10/46	
				GVP 1/47	
				HOA 5/47	
EOB 3/38	GOB 7/45	JOC 6/48	LOB 11/50	HOK 7/47	
EOC 4/38	GOC 2/46	JOE 8/48	LOC 1/51	HOX 11/47	
EOE 5/38	GOE 4/46	JOF 9/48	LOE 2/51	HVP 3/48	
EOF 5/38	GOF 5/46	JOH 11/48	LOF 3/51	JOA 7/48	
EOG 6/38	GOH 7/46	JOK 1/49	LOH 4/51	JOB 11/48	
EOH 7/38	GOJ 8/46	JOL 2/49	LOJ 5/51	JOG 2/49	
EOK 9/38	GOK 9/46	JOM 6/49	LOK 6/51	JVP 6/49	
EOL 10/38	GOM 10/46	JON 5/49	LOL 7/51	KOA 9/49	
EOM 11/38	GON 11/46	JOP 6/49	LON 8/51	KOG 1/50	
EON 12/38	GOP 12/46	JOV 7/49	LOP 10/51	KOM 4/50	
EOP 1/39	GOV 2/47	JOX 8/49	LOV 11/51	KVP 7/50	
EOV 2/39			LOX 12/51	LOA 11/50	
EOX 3/39				LOG 3/51	
				LOM 6/51	
				LVP 9/51	

Main Series												Commercial		Special
MOB	2/52	POB	6/54	TOB	2/56	WOB	2/58			MOA	1/52			Austin
MOC	2/52	POC	6/54	TOC	3/56	WOC	3/58			MOG	5/52			Motor
MOE	3/52	POE	not alloc	TOE	3/56	WOE	3/58			MOM	9/52			Export
MOF	4/52	POF	7/54	TOF	4/56	WOF	4/58			MVP	12/52			Co
MOH	5/52	POG	7/54	TOH	4/56	WOH	4/58			NOA	4/53			
MOK	6/52	POH	8/54	TOJ	5/56	WOJ	5/58			NOG	7/53			MOJ 4/52
MOL	7/52	POK	9/54	TOK	6/56	WOK	5/58			NVP	10/53			MOP 7/52
MON	9/52	POL	10/54	TOL	6/56	WOL	6/58			OOA	1/54			
MOV	10/52	POM	10/54	TON	7/56	WON	6/58			OVP	4/54			
MOX	10/52	PON	11/54	TOP	8/56	WOP	7/58			POA	7/54			
		POP	12/54	TOV	9/56	WOV	7/58			PVP	10/54			HDES
		POV	12/54	TOX	10/56					ROA	12/54			
		POX	not alloc							ROG	3/55			NOB 2/53
										ROM	4/55			NOP 6/53
NOC	11/52	ROB	1/55	UOB	11/56	XOB	8/58			RVP	6/55			OOG 4/54
NOE	1/53	ROC	2/55	UOC	12/56	XOC	9/58			SOA	7/55			POJ 9/54
NOF	2/53	ROE	2/55	UOE	1/57	XOE	10/58			SOG	10/55			ROP 7/55
NOH	3/53	ROF	3/55	UOF	2/57	XOF	10/58			SVP	11/55			
NOJ	4/53	ROH	3/55	UOH	3/57	XOH	11/58			TOA	1/56			
NOK	5/53	ROJ	4/55	UOJ	3/57	XOJ	11/58			TOG	3/56			
NOL	5/53	ROK	4/55	UOK	4/57	XOK	12/58			TOM	4/56			
NOM	6/53	ROL	4/55	UOL	4/57	XOL	1/59			TVP	6/56			
NON	7/53	RON	5/55	UON	5/57	XON	2/59			UOA	9/56			
NOV	7/53	ROV	5/55	UOP	5/57	XOP	2/59			UOG	11/56			
NOX	8/53	ROX	6/55	UOV	6/57	XOV	3/59			UOM	1/57			
				UOX	6/57	XOX	3/59			UVP	3/57			
										VOA	5/57			
OOB	9/53	SOB	6/55	VOB	7/57	YOB	3/59			VOG	7/57			
OOC	10/53	SOC	7/55	VOC	7/57	YOC	4/59			VOM	9/57			
OOE	10/53	SOE	7/55	VOE	8/57	YOE	4/59			VOX	11/57			
OOF	11/53	SOF	8/55	VOF	8/57	YOF	5/59			VVP	1/58			
OOH	12/53	SOH	8/55	VOH	9/57	YOJ	5/59			WOA	2/58			
OOJ	1/54	SOJ	9/55	VOJ	10/57	YOK	6/59			WOG	4/58			
OOK	2/54	SOK	9/55	VOK	11/57	YOL	6/59			WOM	5/58			
OOL	2/54	SOL	10/55	VOL	11/57	YOM	6/59			WOX	7/58			
OOM	3/54	SOM	10/55	VON	12/57	YON	7/59			WVP	9/58			
OON	3/54	SON	11/55	VOP	1/58	YOP	7/59			XOA	10/58			
OOP	4/54	SOP	11/55	VOV	2/58	YOV	7/59			XOG	12/58			
OOV	5/54	SOV	12/55			YOX	8/59			XOM	1/59			
OOX	5/54	SOX	1/56							XVP	3/59			
										YOA	4/59			
										YOG	5/59			
										YVP	7/59			

(A few cases are known of individual numbers, [mainly low ones], being issued ahead of the main series, notably a batch of buses in HOV, two months ahead of normal issues.)

YOX was completed 9/59 and YVP 8/59, whereafter the main series used reverse format three-letter combinations, while commercials used *VP*, commencing at 1. This was completed in 7/60 and commercials then used three-letter combinations, commencing with *AVP*. (*COM* followed *CVP*; *DOX* followed *DVP*; *EOL* followed *EOM*)

Main Series								Commercial	
AOA	9/59	BOA	3/60	COA	8/60	DOB	2/61	VP	8/59
AOB	9/59	BOB	3/60	COB	8/60	DOC	2/61	AVP	7/60
AOC	10/59	BOC	4/60	COC	not alloc	DOE	3/61	BVP	8/60
AOE	10/59	BOE	4/60	COE	9/60	DOF	3/61	COG	9/60
AOF	10/59	BOF	4/60	COF	9/60	DOH	3/61	CVP	11/60
AOG	11/59	BOG	not alloc	COH	10/60	DOJ	4/61	COM	11/60
AOH	11/59	BOH	5/60	COJ	10/60	DOK	4/61	DOA	1/61
AOJ	12/59	BOJ	5/60	COK	not alloc	DOL	5/61	DOG	1/61
AOK	12/59	BOK	5/60	COL	11/60	DON	5/61	DOM	3/61
AOL	1/60	BOL	5/60	CON	11/60	DOP	5/61	DVP	3/61
AOM	1/60	BOM	6/60	COP	12/60	DOV	6/61	DOX	4/61
AON	2/60	BON	6/60	COV	1/61				
AOP	2/60	BOP	6/60	COX	1/61				
AOV	2/60	BOV	7/60						
AOX	3/60	BOX	7/60						

COUNTY BOROUGH COUNCIL OF BIRMINGHAM (continued)

Main Series							Commercial			
EOB	6/61	HOB	11/62	LOB	11/63		EOA	5/61	KOA	7/63
EOC	6/61	HOC	11/62	LOC	12/63		EOG	6/61	KOG	7/63
EOE	7/61	HOE	12/62	LOE	12/63		EOM	6/61	KOM	9/53
EOF	7/61	HOF	1/63	LOF	12/63		EOL	7/61	KVP	10/63
EOH	7/61	HOH	1/63	LOH	1/64		EOX	8/61	LOA	11/63
EOJ	8/61	HOJ	2/63	LOJ	1/64		EVP	9/61	LOG	12/63
EOK	9/61	HOK	2/63	LOK	1/64		FOA	10/61	LOM	1/64
EON	10/61	HON	2/63	LOL	2/64		FOG	12/61	LVP	2/64
EOP	11/61	HOP	3/63	LON	2/64		FOL	1/62	MOA	3/64
EOV	11/61	HOV	3/63	LOP	2/64		FOM	2/62	MOG	4/64
				LOV	2/64		FOX	3/62	MVP	5/64
				LOX	3/64		FVP	4/62	NOA	6/64
							GOA	5/62	NOG	6/64
FOB	12/61	JOB	3/63	MOB	3/64		GOG	5/62		
FOC	1/62	JOC	4/63	MOC	3/64		GOM	6/62		
FOE	1/62	JOE	4/63	MOE	3/64		GOX	7/62		
FOF	2/62	JOF	4/63	MOF	4/64		GVP	8/62		
FOH	3/62	JOH	4/63	MOH	4/64		HOA	9/62		
FOJ	3/62	JOJ	5/63	MOJ	4/64		HOG not alloc			
FOK	3/62	JOK	5/63	MOK	4/64		HOL	10/62		
FON	4/62	JOM	5/63	MOL	4/64		HOM	11/62		
FOP	4/62	JON	5/63	MOM	5/64		HOX	1/63		
FOV	5/62	JOP	6/63	MON	5/64		HVP	3/63		
		JOV	6/63	MOP	5/64		JOA	3/63		
				MOV	5/64		JOG	4/63		
				MOX	6/64		JOL	5/63		
							JOX	6/63		
GOB	5/62	KOB	6/63	NOB	6/64		JVP	6/63		
GOC	5/62	KOC	7/63	NOC	6/64					
GOE	6/62	KOE	7/63	NOE	6/64					
GOF	6/62	KOF	7/63	NOF	7/64					
GOH	7/62	KOH	8/63	NOH	7/64					
GOJ	7/62	KOJ	8/63	NOJ	7/64					
GOK	8/62	KOK	9/63	NOK	c5/70 (re-registrations)					
GOL	8/62	KOL	9/63	NOL	c5/77 (re-registrations - very few issued)					
GON	9/62	KON	10/63							
GOP	9/62	KOP	10/63							
GOV	10/62	KOV	10/63							
		KOX	11/63							

Special issues for Diplomatic Corps : *1 POL* (2/79),   *1 ROA* (/96),   *1 ROK* (ca 4/71), *1 ROM* (ca 3/75),   *1 SOM* (ca /63),   *1 TOG* (ca 10/79),   *1 TON* (ca 10/71).

Suffix marks commenced 4.8.64

CHAPTER 36.

An Act to amend the Locomotives on Highways Act, 1896. A.D. 1903.
[14th August 1903.]

BE it enacted by the King's most Excellent Majesty, by and with the advice and consent of the Lords Spiritual and Temporal, and Commons, in this present Parliament assembled, and by the authority of the same, as follows :—

1.—(1) If any person drives a motor car on a public highway Reckless recklessly or negligently, or at a speed or in a manner which is driving. dangerous to the public, having regard to all the circumstances of the case, including the nature, condition, and use of the highway, and to the amount of traffic which actually is at the time, or which might reasonably be expected to be, on the highway, that person shall be guilty of an offence under this Act.

(2) Any police constable may apprehend without warrant the driver of any car who commits an offence under this section within his view, if he refuses to give his name and address or produce his licence on demand, or if the motor car does not bear the mark or marks of identification.

(3) If the driver of any car who commits an offence under this section refuses to give his name or address, or gives a false name or address, he shall be guilty of an offence under this Act, and it shall be the duty of the owner of the car, if required, to give any information which it is within his power to give, and which may lead to the identification and apprehension of the driver, and if the owner fails to do so he also shall be guilty of an offence under this Act.

2.—(1) Every motor car shall be registered with the council Registration of a county or county borough, and every such council shall assign of motor cars. a separate number to every car registered with them.

(2) A mark indicating the registered number of the car and the council with which the car is registered shall be fixed on the car or on a vehicle drawn by the car, or on both, in such manner as the council require in conformity with regulations of the Local Government Board made under this Act.

COUNTY BOROUGH COUNCIL OF BLACKBURN

CB 12/03   BV 6/30

Registration commenced 12/12/03; a common sequence for all vehicles.

First issues each year, (no information available for 1906-1928) :

1904	CB 23		1929	CB 8573		1933	BV 2010		1937	BV 6558
1905	CB 87		1930	CB 9615		1934	BV 2924		1938	BV 7900
			1931	BV 311		1935	BV 4008		1939	BV 9100
			1932	BV 1213		1936	BV 5211			

ABV	8/39	DBV	11/50	GBV	4/55	KBV	4/58	NBV	6/60	RBV	10/62
ACB	10/44	DCB	1/52	GCB	9/55	KCB	9/58	NCB	11/60	RCB	3/63
BBV	11/46	EBV	12/52	HBV	3/56	LBV	3/59	OBV	4/61	SBV	6/63
BCB	10/47	ECB	9/53	HCB	8/56	LCB	6/59	OCB	7/61	SCB	9/63
CBV	11/48	FBV	4/54	JBV	4/57	MBV	11/59	PBV	1/62		
CCB	10/49	FCB	9/54	JCB	9/57	MCB	3/60	PCB	5/62		

Suffix Marks commenced 28.1.64. Blackburn commenced suffix marks on this date because SCB was the last mark which had by then been allotted to them by Statutory Instrument.

COUNTY BOROUGH COUNCIL OF BLACKPOOL

Blackpool was created a County Borough with effect from 1.10.04.

FR 10/04   FV 4/29

Initially motorcycles were segregated from other vehicles, Up to FR 5250 the following blocks were cycles :   FR 49-96, 201-400, 701-1000, 1501-1700, 2300-2399, 3001-4260.   No information is available on segregation, if any, after FR 5250.

First issues each year, (no information available for 1905-1920 and 1924-1928):

1921	ca FR 2785		1929	FR 9729		1932	FV 2395		1935	FV 5481
1922	FR 4489		1930	FV 743		1933	FV 3184		1936	FV 6933
1923	FR 4960		1931	FV 1533		1934	FV 4237		1937	FV 8485

AFR	12/37	EFR	12/49	JFR	12/54	NFR	8/57	SFR	9/59	WFR	5/61
AFV	8/38	EFV	10/50	JFV	4/55	NFV	1/58	SFV	12/59	WFV	7/61
BFR	4/39	FFR	7/51	KFR	7/55	OFR	4/58	TFR	3/60	XFR	10/61
BFV	4/40	FFV	5/52	KFV	11/55	OFV	7/58	TFV	4/60	XFV	1/62
CFR	6/46	GFR	2/53	LFR	3/56	PFR	11/58	UFR	6/60	YFR	4/62
CFV	4/47	GFV	8/53	LFV	7/56	PFV	2/59	UFV	9/60	YFV	6/62
DFR	3/48	HFR	3/54	MFR	1/57	RFR	4/59	VFR	1/61		
DFV	3/49	HFV	7/54	MFV	5/57	RFV	7/59	VFV	3/61		

For a reason unknown, Blackpool issues only combinations of FR in the reverse format.

| AFR | 9/62 | CFR | 3/63 | EFR | 7/63 | GFR | 12/63 | JFR | 4/64 |
| BFR | 1/63 | DFR | 5/53 | FFR | 10/63 | HFR | 2/64 | | |

Suffix marks commenced 1.6.64

COUNTY BOROUGH COUNCIL OF BOLTON

BN 12/03   WH 5/27

First numbers issued each year. No information is available for 1922-1928.

1904	BN 53	1909	BN 475	1914	BN 1390	1919	BN 2562
1905	BN 160	1910	BN 531	1915	BN 1784	1920	c. BN 3422
1906	BN 253	1911	BN 630	1916	BN 2139	1921	c. BN 4850
1907	BN 327	1912	BN 805	1917	c. BN 2392		
1908	BN 413	1913	BN 1075	1918	BN 2503		

1929	WH 1400	1932	WH 3618	1935	WH 6060	1938	WH 9600
1930	WH 2244	1933	WH 4290	1936	WH 7100		
1931	WH 2952	1934	WH 5100	1937	WH 8300		

ABN	4/38	EBN	5/50	JBN	5/55	NBN	7/58	SBN	8/60	WBN	7/62
AWH	2/39	EWH	4/51	JWH	10/55	NWH	11/58	SWH	11/60	WWH	12/62
BBN	11/39	FBN	2/52	KBN	3/56	OBN	3/59	TBN	3/61	XBN	3/63
BWH	7/45	FWH	12/52	KWH	8/56	OWH	6/59	TWH	5/61	XWH	5/63
CBN	10/46	GBN	7/53	LBN	2/57	PBN	9/59	UBN	7/61	YBN	7/63
CWH	8/47	GWH	2/54	LWH	6/57	PWH	12/59	UWH	10/61	YWH	10/63
DBN	8/48	HBN	7/54	MBN	11/57	RBN	3/60	VBN	2/62		
DWH	6/49	HWH	1/55	MWH	3/58	RWH	5/60	VWH	5/62		

Commenced suffix marks 2.12.63

COUNTY BOROUGH COUNCIL OF BOOTLE

EM 12/03

First issues each year. No information is available prior to 1929, nor for 1941-1944.

1929	EM 2232	1936	EM 3127	1947	EM 3995	1954	EM 5647
1930	EM 2421	1937	EM 3261	1948	EM 4243	1955	EM 5942
1931	EM 2556	1938	EM 3403	1949	EM 4463	1956	EM 6362
1932	EM 2663	1939	EM 3530	1950	EM 4647	1957	EM 6794
1933	EM 2775	1940	EM 3624	1951	EM 5101	1958	EM 7529
1934	EM 2869	1945	EM 3776	1952	EM 5269	1959	EM 8270
1935	EM 3000	1946	EM 3825	1953	EM 5430	1960	EM 9535

AEM	4/60	BEM	6/61	CEM	9/62	DEM	3/63 (Special issues 1-11 only)

Special issues for Diplomatic Corps : LEM 1 5/84;   YEM 1 c. 7/73;   *1 CEM* c. /75;   *1 YEM* 12/90.

Commenced suffix issues 2.1.64

COUNTY BOROUGH COUNCIL OF BOURNEMOUTH

Registration commenced 1.12.03.

A single sequence for all vehicles.

EL 12/03   RU 11/24   LJ 7/29

First issues each year. (No information available for 1922-26)

1904	EL	114	1911	EL	973	1918	EL	3399	1927	RU 4428
1905	EL	251	1912	EL	1229	1919	EL	3514	1928	RU 6436 *
1906	EL	349	1913	EL	1551	1920	EL	4465	1929	RU 8562
1907	EL	441	1914	EL	1977	1921	EL	5805	1930	LJ 900 app.
1908	EL	531	1915	EL	2435				1931	LJ 3100 app.
1909	EL	663	1916	EL	2924				1932	LJ 4900 app.
1910	EL	782	1917	EL	3238				1933	LJ 6800 app.
									1934	LJ 8950 app.

* RU 6464, 6500, 6600 and 6666 all early issues, 1927.

In the 1970s numerous low numbered ELs, (mainly between EL 1000 & 1500) were reissued for vintage vehicles.

AEL	5/34	EEL	3/38	JEL	1/49	NEL	3/53	SEL	7/55	WEL	1/58
ALJ	9/34	ELJ	7/38	JLJ	5/49	NLJ	6/53	SLJ	9/55	WLJ	3/58
ARU	2/35	ERU	12/38	JRU	9/49	NRU	9/53	SRU	11/55	WRU	5/58
BEL	5/35	FEL	3/39	KEL	1/50	OEL	11/53	TEL	2/56	XEL	7/58
BLJ	9/35	FLJ	8/39	KLJ	5/50	OLJ	2/54	TLJ	4/56	XLJ	9/58
BRU	1/36	FRU	4/42	KRU	10/50	ORU	5/54	TRU	7/56	XRU	11/58
CEL	4/36	GEL	4/46	LEL	2/51	PEL	7/54	UEL	10/56	YEL	1/59
CLJ	8/36	GLJ	10/46	LLJ	6/51	PLJ	9/54	ULJ	1/57	YLJ	3/59
CRU	12/36	GRU	2/47	LRU	11/51	PRU	12/54	URU	4/57	YRU	4/59
DEL	3/37	HEL	7/47	MEL	3/52	REL	2/55	VEL	6/57		
DLJ	7/37	HLJ	1/48	MLJ	7/52	RLJ	4/55	VLJ	8/57		
DRU	11/37	HRU	7/48	MRU	11/52	RRU	5/55	VRU	10/57		

Reverse format marks commenced with *601 EL* up, but when *999 EL* was reached cycles went into three-letter marks. After *9999 EL* cars used *LJ* from 1 and *RU* from 1.
RU and *BLJ* finished almost simultaneously and *BRU* onwards were used for all vehicles.

All Vehicles
601 - 999 EL   6/59

Cars etc.
1000 - 9999 EL   6/59
1 - 9999 LJ   11/60
1 - 9999 RU   8/62

Motorcycles
AEL   6/59
ALJ   1/60
ARU   9/60
BEL   7/61
BLJ   9/62

All Vehicles
BRU   1/64
CEL   2/64
CLJ   4/64
CRU   12/72 (re-registrations)
DEL   7/76 (re-registrations)

Suffix marks commenced 1.5.64

175

COUNTY BOROUGH COUNCIL OF BRADFORD

AK 12/03   KU 3/22   KW 11/26   KY 3/31

Registration commenced 21.12.03

A common sequence for all vehicles.

First issues each year, (details for 1910-1928 not available to writer, but 1927/8 information available at West Yorkshire Archives.)

1904	AK 70		1908	AK 972		1929	KW 4927		1933	KY 3546
1905	AK 294		1909	AK 1150		1930	KW 7497		1934	KY 5966
1906	AK 472			approx.		1931	KW 9524		1935	KY 8690
1907	AK 763					1932	KY 1485			

AAK	5/35	BAK	2/46	JAK	9/52	NAK	7/56	SAK	7/59	WAK	6/61
AKU	9/35	BKU	9/46	JKU	1/53	NKU	11/56	SKU	8/59	WKU	7/61
AKW	1/36	BKW	12/46	JKW	5/53	NKW	3/57	SKW	10/59	WKW	9/61
AKY	4/36	BKY	5/47	JKY	8/53	NKY	5/57	SKY	11/59	WKY	12/61
BAK	8/36	FAK	10/47	KAK	12/53	OAK	7/57	TAK	1/60	XAK	2/62
BKU	12/36	FKU	5/48	KKU	3/54	OKU	9/57	TKU	3/60	XKU	3/62
BKW	3/37	FKW	10/48	KKW	5/54	OKW	12/57	TKW	3/60	XKW	5/62
BKY	6/37	FKY	3/49	KKY	9/54	OKY	3/58	TKY	4/60	XKY	6/62
CAK	10/37	GAK	8/49	LAK	12/54	PAK	4/58	UAK	5/60	YAK	8/62
CKU	3/38	GKU	12/49	LKU	3/55	PKU	6/58	UKU	7/60	YKU	10/62
CKW	6/38	GKW	4/50	LKW	5/55	PKW	8/58	UKW	9/60	YKW	12/62
CKY	11/38	GKY	9/50	LKY	7/55	PKY	11/58	UKY	10/60	YKY	2/63
DAK	3/39	HAK	2/51	MAK	9/55	RAK	1/59	VAK	1/61		
DKU	6/39	HKU	6/51	MKU	11/55	RKU	3/59	VKU	2/61		
DKW	1/40	HKW	12/51	MKW	3/56	RKW	4/59	VKW	3/62		
DKY	3/42	HKY	4/52	MKY	5/56	RKY	5/59	VKY	5/61		

PAK 1 was an early issue (ca. 1949) for the Diplomatic Corps. In order to regularise this issue the combination PAK was allotted early to Bradford by S.I. 1618 of 1949.

There was no segregation of motorcycles in reverse format issues.

KW (from 1)   4/63   *KY (from 1)   4/64*

Other special marks for Diplomatic Corps : *51 LAK* 2/79; *1 MAK* 5/94; *1 PAK* 4/91.

Suffix marks commenced 1.6.64

COUNTY BOROUGH COUNCIL OF BRIGHTON

CD 1/04   UF 7/25

First issues each year :

1905	CD 297	1913	CD 1872	1921 c. CD 6001	1929	UF 4151
1906	CD 420	1914	CD 2315	1922 c. CD 6801	1930	UF 5721
1907	CD 552	1915	CD 2902	1923 CD 7447	1931	UF 7093
1908	CD 699	1916	CD 3620	1924 CD 8266	1932	UF 8242
1909	CD 870	1917	CD 4017	1925 CD 9208	1933	UF 9512
1910	CD 1043	1918	CD 4246	1926 UF 384		
1911	CD 1258	1919	CD 4477	1927 UF 1440		
1912	CD 1529	1920 c. CD 5101		1928 UF 2780		

ACD	5/33	ECD	6/37	JCD	11/47	NCD	6/53	SCD	3/56	WCD	11/58
AUF	2/34	EUF	1/38	JUF	9/48	NUF	12/53	SUF	6/56	WUF	2/59
BCD	10/34	FCD	7/38	KCD	7/49	OCD	4/54	TCD	11/56	XCD	5/59
BUF	4/35	FUF	1/39	KUF	3/50	OUF	8/54	TUF	4/57	XUF	7/59
CCD	9/35	GCD	7/39	LCD	11/50	PCD	12/54	UCD	7/57	YCD	10/59
CUF	3/36	GUF	3/43	LUF	8/51	PUF	4/55	UUF	12/57	YUF	12/59
DCD	8/36	HCD	7/46	MCD	4/52	RCD	7/55	VCD	4/58		
DUF	1/37	HUF	3/47	MUF	12/52	RUF	11/55	VUF	7/58		

There was no segregation of motorcycles in reverse format issues.

CD (from 501)   3/60

(Note that *UF* was not issued, despite not being used on trade plates.)

ACD	*5/62*	*BCD*	*10/62*	*CCD*	*4/63*	*DCD*	*8/63*	*ECD*	*1/64*	*FCD*	*5/64*
AUF	*7/62*	*BUF*	*1/63*	*CUF*	*5/63*	*DUF*	*10/63*	*EUF*	*3/64*	*FUF*	*12/74 **

* Re-registrations only (from *101*)

Suffix marks commenced 1.7.64.

Mr Inverness Watts had better be content with plain English figures in place of the Roman numerals which have led to his appearance at the Hailsham Petty Sessions. On his identification plate he used the figures CCXXXIII instead of the regulation number 233. It was made clear by the Local Government Board that the figures were to be such as could be plainly seen and read by a policeman. The adoption of Roman numerals was certainly contrary to the Act.   *The Motor Car Journal, 12.3.04*

COUNTY BOROUGH COUNCIL OF BRISTOL

AE 1/04   HT 2/20   HU 7/24   HW 7/27   HY 7/30

No information is available to writer on first issues each year before 1929, except for 1926, but 1927/1928 information may be available at Bristol Record Office.

1926	HU 4847		1930	HW 7660		1932	HY 4484		1933	HY 7817
1929	HW 4144		1931	HY 1262						

AAE	7/33	EAE	7/37	JAE	12/44	NAE	3/50	SAE	11/53	WAE	11/55
AHT	12/33	EHT	9/37	JHT	11/45	NHT	6/50	SHT	1/54	WHT	12/55
AHU	3/34	EHU	11/37	JHU	3/46	NHU	8/50	SHU	3/54	WHU	1/56
AHW	6/34	EHW	1/38	JHW	6/46	NHW	11/50	SHW	4/54	WHW	3/56
AHY	8/34	EHY	3/38	JHY	9/46	NHY	1/51	SHY	5/54	WHY	3/56
BAE	11/34	FAE	5/38	KAE	12/46	OAE	4/51	TAE	6/54	XAE	4/56
BHT	2/35	FHT	7/38	KHT	2/47	OHT	6/51	THT	8/54	XHT	6/56
BHU	4/35	FHU	10/38	KHU	4/47	OHU	9/51	THU	9/54	XHU	7/56
BHW	6/35	FHW	12/38	KHW	7/47	OHW	12/51	THW	11/54	XHW	8/56
BHY	9/35	FHY	2/39	KHY	9/47	OHY	2/52	THY	12/54	XHY	10/56
CAE	11/35	GAE	3/39	LAE	12/47	PAE	4/52	UAE	1/55	YAE	12/56
CHT	1/36	GHT	5/39	LHT	3/48	PHT	6/52	UHT	2/55	YHT	1/57
CHU	3/36	GHU	7/39	LHU	6/48	PHU	9/52	UHU	3/55	YHU	3/57
CHW	5/36	GHW	10/39	LHW	10/48	PHW	11/52	UHW	4/55	YHW	4/57
CHY	7/36	GHY	4/40	LHY	1/49	PHY	1/53	UHY	5/55	YHY	5/57
DAE	10/36	HAE	12/40	MAE	3/49	RAE	3/53	VAE	6/55		
DHT	12/36	HHT	10/41	MHT	6/49	RHT	5/53	VHT	7/55		
DHU	1/37	HHU	5/42	MHU	8/49	RHU	6/53	VHU	8/55		
DHW	3/37	HHW	10/42	MHW	10/49	RHW	8/53	VHW	9/55		
DHY	5/37	HHY	5/43	MHY	1/50	RHY	10/53	VHY	10/55		

AAE	5/57	EAE	2/59	JAE	4/60	NAE	7/61	SAE	1/63	WAE	2/64
AHT	6/57	EHT	3/59	JHT	5/60	NHT	7/61	SHT	not iss.	WHT	3/64
AHU	7/57	EHU	4/59	JHU	5/60	NHU	9/61	SHU	2/63	WHU	4/64
AHW	8/57	EHW	4/59	JHW	6/60	NHW	10/61	SHW	3/63	WHW	4/64
AHY	10/57	EHY	5/59	JHY	7/60	NHY	11/61	SHY	3/63	WHY	5/64
BAE	11/57	FAE	6/59	KAE	7/60	OAE	12/61	TAE	4/63	XAE	5/64
BHT	12/57	FHT	6/59	KHT	8/60	OHT	1/62	THT	5/63	XHT	6/64
BHU	1/58	FHU	7/59	KHU	9/60	OHU	2/62	THU	5/63	XHU	6/64
BHW	3/58	FHW	8/59	KHW	10/60	OHW	3/62	THW	6/63	XHW	7/64
BHY	3/58	FHY	9/59	KHY	11/60	OHY	3/62	THY	6/63	XHY	7/64
CAE	4/58	GAE	10/59	LAE	12/60	PAE	4/62	UAE	7/63	YAE	8/64
CHT	5/58	GHT	10/59	LHT	1/61	PHT	5/62	UHT	8/63	YHT	c9/75 *
CHU	6/58	GHU	11/59	LHU	2/61	PHU	6/62	UHU	8/63		
CHW	7/58	GHW	12/59	LHW	3/61	PHW	6/62	UHW	9/63		
CHY	8/58	GHY	1/60	LHY	3/61	PHY	7/62	UHY	10/63		
DAE	9/58	HAE	1/60	MAE	4/61	RAE	8/62	VAE	11/63		
DHT	10/58	HHT	2/60	MHT	4/61	RHT	9/62	VHT	12/63		
DHU	11/58	HHU	3/60	MHU	5/61	RHU	10/62	VHU	1/64		
DHW	12/58	HHW	3/60	MHW	6/61	RHW	11/62	VHW	1/64		
DHY	1/59	HHY	4/60	MHY	6/61	RHY	12/62	VHY	2/64		

* re-registrations only.

Suffix marks commenced 1.9.64

COUNTY BOROUGH COUNCIL OF BURNLEY

A common sequence for all vehicles.

Registration commenced 1.1.04

CW 1/04   HG 3/30

Forst issues each year :

1905	CW	93	1916	CW 1515	1927	CW 7129	1938	HG 6178
1906	CW	156	1917	CW 1699	1928	CW 7944	1939	HG 6964
1907	CW	208	1918	CW 1789	1929	CW 8808	1940	HG 7716
1908	CW	251	1919	CW 1831	1930	CW 9770	1941	HG 7899
1909	CW	281	1920	CW 2520 *	1931	HG 535	1942	HG 7966
1910	CW	326 #	1921	CW 3575 *	1932	HG 1098	1943	HG 8027
1911	CW	397	1922	CW 4040 *	1933	HG 1725	1944	HG 8090
1912	CW	512	1923	CW 4510 *	1934	HG 2429	1945	HG 8147
1913	CW	701	1924	CW 4996	1935	HG 3174	1946	HG 8293
1914	CW	923	1925	CW 5545	1936	HG 4023	1947	HG 8917
1915	CW 1183		1926	CW 6346	1937	HG 5071	1948	HG 9603

* approximate.
# CW 382 issued out of sequence, 12/08.

ACW	9/48	DCW	11/54	GCW	11/57	KCW	2/60	NCW	1/62	RCW	1/64
AHG	2/50	DHG	5/55	GHG	4/58	KHG	5/60	NHG	5/62		
BCW	8/51	ECW	11/55	HCW	9/58	LCW	9/60	OCW	10/62		
BHG	1/53	EHG	4/56	HHG	2/59	LHG	1/61	OHG	3/63		
CCW	10/53	FCW	11/56	JCW	6/59	MCW	5/61	PCW	5/63		
CHG	4/54	FHG	5/57	JHG	10/59	MHG	8/61	PHG	9/63		

Suffix marks commenced 2.3.64

COUNTY BOROUGH COUNCIL OF BURTON-ON-TRENT

A common sequence for all vehicles.

FA 12/03

First issues each year, (no information is available for 1923-28)

1904	FA	2	1915	FA 401	1929	FA 3469	1940	FA 7813
1905	FA	66	1916	FA 480	1930	FA 3887	1941	FA 7882
1906	FA	98	1917	FA 515	1931	FA 4283	1942	FA 7897
1907	FA 119		1918	FA 548	1932	FA 4628	1943	FA 7924
1908	FA 155		1919	FA 561	1933	FA 4910	1944	FA 7947
1909			1920	FA 725	1934	FA 5213	1945	FA 7989
1910	FA 196		1921	FA 1018	1935	FA 5619	1946	FA 8081
1911	FA 216		1922	FA 1170	1936	FA 6099	1947	FA 8460
1912	FA 252				1937	FA 6587	1948	FA 8898
1913	FA 299				1938	FA 7033	1949	FA 9304
1914	FA 344				1939	FA 7424	1950	FA 9783

AFA	6/50	EFA	10/55	HFA	5/58	LFA	1/60	OFA	5/61	SFA	1/63
BFA	5/52	FFA	8/56	JFA	1/59	MFA	6/60	PFA	12/61	TFA	7/63
CFA	10/53	GFA	7/57	KFA	7/59	NFA	1/61	RFA	6/62	UFA	1/64
DFA	11/54										

Suffix marks commenced 1.5.64

COUNTY BOROUGH COUNCIL OF BURY

EN   12/03.

First issues each year, (no information available prior to 1929) :

1929	3909	1935	6070	1941	8328		1947	8851
1930	4377	1936	6479	1942	8367		1948	9207
1931	4758	1937	6935	1943	8395		1949	9565
1932	5058	1938	7420	1944	8416			
1933	5400	1939	7858	1945	8440			
1934	5733	1940	8230	1946	8509			

AEN	12/49	EEN	11/55	JEN	3/59	NEN	3/61	SEN	4/63 *
BEN	1/52	FEN	10/56	KEN	9/59	OEN	7/61	TEN	11/63
CEN	8/53	GEN	9/57	LEN	3/60	PEN	3/62	UEN	3/64
DEN	11/54	HEN	6/58	MEN	8/60	REN	9/62	VEN	7/64

* SEN 1, 2 & 3 early issues for Diplomatic Corps, c. /61

Special issues for Diplomatic Corps : *1 KEN* c. /63; *1 VEN* c.11/68..

Suffix issues commenced 1.9.64

COUNTY BOROUGH COUNCIL OF CANTERBURY

FN   1/04   JG   3/29

First issues each year. Information for 1904-1928 not known to writer but is available in Canterbury City & Cathedral Archives.

1929	FN 9717	1932	JG 2321	1935	JG 5325
1930	JG 580	1933	JG 3160	1936	JG 6851
1931	JG 1498	1934	JG 4170	1937	JG 8601

AFN	11/37	EFN	5/49	JFN	4/54	NFN	4/57	SFN	5/59	WFN	10/60
AJG	7/38	EJG	12/49	JJG	9/54	NJG	7/57	SJG	7/59	WJG	1/61
BFN	3/39	FFN	10/50	KFN	2/55	OFN	11/57	TFN	10/59	XFN	4/61
BJG	5/40	FJG	4/51	KJG	5/55	OJG	3/58	TJG	12/59	XJG	6/61
CFN	7/46	GFN	12/51	LFN	9/55	PFN	6/58	UFN	2/60	YFN	8/61
CJG	2/47	GJG	9/52	LJG	1/56	PJG	9/58	UJG	4/60	YJG	10/61
DFN	11/47	HFN	4/53	MFN	6/56	RFN	12/58	VFN	6/60		
DJG	7/48	HJG	10/53	MJG	11/56	RJG	3/59	VJG	8/60		

A common sequence for all vehicles in reverse issues.

FN (from 501)   1/62   JG (from 1)   9/63

Suffix issues commenced 2.1.64

COUNTY BOROUGH COUNCIL OF CARDIFF

BO   1/04   UH   8/25   KG   8/31

A separate and duplicated series for motorcycles prior to 1921, BO 1-3489.

First issues each year, (no information available prior to 1929) :

1929	UH 5551		1932	KG 391		1935	KG 5203
1930	UH 7264		1933	KG 1897		1936	KG 7461
1931	UH 9057		1934	KG 3376		1937	KG 9781

ABO	1/37	BBO	6/48	JBO	12/53	NBO	11/56	SBO	3/59	WBO	7/60
AKG	6/37	BKG	2/49	JKG	3/54	NKG	2/57	SKG	4/59	WKG	9/60
AUH	11/37	BUH	7/49	JUH	7/54	NUH	5/57	SUH	5/59	WUH	11/60
BBO	5/38	FBO	1/50	KBO	10/54	OBO	7/57	TBO	7/59	XBO	1/61
BKG	11/38	FKG	8/50	KKG	1/55	OKG	10/57	TKG	9/59	XKG	3/61
BUH	3/39	FUH	3/51	KUH	3/55	OUH	12/57	TUH	10/59	XUH	4/61
CBO	7/39	GBO	8/51	LBO	6/55	PBO	3/58	UBO	12/59	YBO	5/61
CKG	6/40	GKG	3/52	LKG	8/55	PKG	5/58	UKG	1/60	YKG	6/61
CUH	1/46	GUH	7/52	LUH	10/55	PUH	6/58	UUH	3/60	YUH	8/61
DBO	9/46	HBO	12/52	MBO	1/56	RBO	9/58	VBO	4/60		
DKG	3/47	HKG	5/53	MKG	4/56	RKG	11/58	VKG	5/60		
DUH	10/47	HUH	9/53	MUH	7/56	RUH	1/59	VUH	6/60		

ABO	*11/61*	*BBO*	*5/62*	*CBO*	*9/62*	*DBO*	*3/63*	*EBO*	*6/63*	*FBO*	*10/63*
AKG	*1/62*	*BKG*	*6/62*	*CKG*	*11/62*	*DKG*	*4/63*	*EKG*	*7/63*	*FKG*	*12/63*
AUH	*3/62*	*BUH*	*7/62*	*CUH*	*2/63*	*DUH*	*5/63*	*EUH*	*9/63*	*FUH*	*11/67* *

* Re-registrations only.

Suffix marks commenced 3.2.64.

COUNTY BOROUGH COUNCIL OF CARLISLE

Carlisle was created a county borough with effect from 1.4.14.

HH   4/14

A single sequence for all vehicles.

First numbers issued each year. No information is available prior to 1929, but a few random dates of issue are :

| HH 2050 | 12/23 | | HH 2569 | 2/35 | | HH 3460 | 12/26 | | HH 3850 | 6/27 |

1929	4578		1932	6011		1935	7741		1938	9833
1930	5112		1933	6529		1936	8410			
1931	5554		1934	7124		1937	9059			

AHH	3/38	EHH	8/50	JHH	9/55	NHH	11/58	SHH	10/60	WHH	9/62
BHH	7/39	FHH	8/52	KHH	7/56	OHH	6/59	THH	4/61	XHH	3/63
CHH	11/46	GHH	12/53	LHH	7/57	PHH	12/59	UHH	9/61	YHH	7/63
DHH	10/48	HHH	12/54	MHH	4/58	RHH	5/60	VHH	4/62		

Suffix marks commenced 2.1.64

COUNTY BOROUGH COUNCIL OF CHESTER

FM 12/03

A common sequence for all vehicles.

First issues each year :

1904	21	1912	439	1920	1475		1928	4781
1905	70	1913	535	1921	1936		1929	5324
1906	113	1914	638	1922	2206		1930	5844
1907	150	1915	830	1923	2472		1931	6505
1908	190	1916	977	1924	2850	*	1932	7077
1909	229	1917	1133	1925	3320	*	1933	7670
1910	282	1918	1231	1926	3771	*	1934	8300
1911	348	1919	1263	1927	4322		1935	9238

* approximate.

AFM	10/35	EFM	4/39	JFM	2/48	NFM	1/51	SFM	6/53	WFM	1/55
BFM	9/36	FFM	7/40	KFM	12/48	OFM	10/51	TFM	12/53	XFM	5/55
CFM	5/37	GFM	7/46	LFM	9/49	PFM	5/52	UFM	5/54	YFM	8/55
DFM	5/38	HFM	3/47	MFM	5/50 #	RFM	12/52	VFM	10/54		

MFM 1 was an early issue (1/50).

AFM	12/55	EFM	6/57	JFM	9/58	NFM	9/59	SFM	7/60	WFM	7/61
BFM	4/56	FFM	10/57	KFM	1/59	OFM	12/59	TFM	10/60	XFM	11/61
CFM	9/56	GFM	3/58	LFM	4/59	PFM	3/60	UFM	2/61	YFM	3/62
DFM	3/57	HFM	6/58	MFM	6/59	RFM	4/60	VFM	5/61		

It will be noticed that Chester was the first authority to overlook the instruction that reverse Oxx combinations should not be issued, but when it became necessary to use *FM*, (commencing from 301), all numbers ending in '0' were omitted in order to avoid duplication.

FM 6/62

Special issue for Diplomatic Corps : *1 FM ca. 5/59*

Suffix marks commenced 1.6.64.

COUNTY BOROUGH COUNCIL OF COVENTRY

DU 12/03   HP /19   RW /24   WK 12/26   VC 5/29   KV 11/31.
(Months of issue not available for HP and RW).

First issues each year, (no information available prior to 1929)

1929	WK 8429	1931	VC 7261	1933	KV 3691
1930	VC 2801	1932	KV 381	1934	KV 7330

In both forward and reverse formats marks were issued in the same sequence as the prime marks.

A common sequence for all vehicles applied until 2/53, when a separate series was commenced for vehicles under the Home Delivery Export Scheme. NDU to NKV and UDU to UKV were thus used.

											H.D.E.S.	
ADU	7/34	FDU	5/44	LDU	6/51	SDU	11/55	YDU	7/59	NDU	1/53
AHP	10/34	FHP	3/46	LHP	7/51	SHP	1/56	YHP	9/59	NHP	8/53
ARW	1/35	FRW	7/46	LRW	9/51	SRW	3/56	YRW	10/59	NRW	6/54
AWK	3/35	FWK	9/46	LWK	11/51	SWK	4/56	YWK	11/59	NWK	4/55
AVC	5/35	FVC	11/46	LVC	1/52	SVC	6/56	YVC	12/59	NVC	12/55
AKV	7/35	FKV	1/47	LKV	3/52	SKV	8/56	YKV	1/60	NKV	6/56
BDU	10/35	GDU	4/47	MDU	5/52	TDU	10/56			UDU	3/57
BHP	1/36	GHP	5/47	MHP	7/52	THP	12/56			UHP	8/57
BRW	3/36	GRW	7/47	MRW	9/52	TRW	2/57			URW	3/58
BWK	5/36	GWK	9/47	MWK	11/52	TWK	4/57			UWK	7/58
BVC	6/36	GVC	12/47	MVC	1/53	TVC	5/57			UVC	12/58
BKV	9/36	GKV	3/48	MKV	4/53	TKV	7/57			UKV	5/59
CDU	12/36	HDU	5/48	ODU	6/53	VDU	8/57				
CHP	2/37	HHP	7/48	OHP	8/53	VHP	10/57				
CRW	3/37	HRW	9/48	ORW	10/53	VRW	11/57				
CWK	5/37	HWK	12/48	OWK	12/53	VWK	1/58				
CVC	7/37	HVC	3/49	OVC	2/54	VVC	3/58				
CKV	9/37	HKV	5/49	OKV	4/54	VKV	4/58				
DDU	12/37	JDU	6/49	PDU	6/54	WDU	5/58				
DHP	3/38	JHP	8/49	PHP	7/54	WHP	6/58				
DRW	4/38	JRW	10/49	PRW	9/54	WRW	8/58				
DWK	6/38	JWK	1/50	PWK	11/54	WWK	9/58				
DVC	9/38	JVC	4/50	PVC	12/54	WVC	11/58				
DKV	12/38	JKV	6/50	PKV	2/55	WKV	12/58				
EDU	2/39	KDU	8/50	RDU	3/55	XDU	1/59				
EHP	3/39	KHP	10/50	RHP	4/55	XHP	3/59				
ERW	5/39	KRW	12/50	RRW	6/55	XRW	4/59				
EWK	7/39	KWK	1/51	RWK	7/55	XWK	5/59				
EVC	2/40	KVC	4/51	RVC	8/55	XVC	6/59				
EKV	3/41	KKV	5/51	RKV	10/55	XKV	6/59				

Further segregation took place upon the commencement of reverse issues. *3001-9999 DU* were allocated for Home Delivery Exports in 7/59 whilst other vehicles were still on the forward Yxx series. When the general series commenced reverse issues motorcycles received three-letter marks, whilst cars and commercials used the two-letter series. Finally, in 2/63 commercial vehicles were split off and used reverse *Cxx* combinations.

H.D.E.S		Cars & Commercials		Motorcycles		Commercials	
*DU from 3001 * 7/59*		*HP from 1*	*2/60*	ADU	*2/60*	*CDU*	*2/63*
WK from 1	*9/61*	*RW from 1*	*2/61*	*AHP*	*5/60*	*CHP*	*5/63*
		VC from 1	*4/62*	*ARW*	*9/60*	*CRW*	*10/63*
* 1501 DU up later		Cars only		*AWK*	*3/61*	*CWK*	*3/64*
used for re-regist-		*KV from 1*	*5/63*	*AVC*	*7/61*		
rations, comm /75				*AKV*	*2/62*		
				BDU	*7/62*		
				BHP	*3/63*		
				BRW	*8/63*		
				BWK	*2/64*		

Suffix marks commenced 1.6.64

COUNTY BOROUGH COUNCIL OF CROYDON

BY 12/03   RK 12/22   VB 6/27   OY 1/31

First issues each year, (no information available prior to 1929) :

1929	VB 4575			1933	OY 4629	
1930	VB 7346	1932	OY 2340	1934	OY 7572	

From at least FRK onwards it was commonplace for large users, especially Hall & Co. and the South Eastern Gas Board, to be allocated large blocks, (most commonly 901-999), and consequently numbers were not always issued sequentially.

ABY	9/34	EBY	1/39	JBY	8/50	NBY	10/54	SBY	5/57	WBY	6/59
AOY	12/34	EOY	4/39	JOY	11/50	NOY	11/54	SOY	7/57	WOY	7/59
ARK	3/35	ERK	8/39	JRK	2/51	NRK	1/55	SRK	9/57	WRK	8/59
AVB	6/35	EVB	11/41	JVB	6/51	NVB	4/55	SVB	12/57	WVB	9/59
BBY	10/35	FBY	1/46	KBY	11/51	OBY	6/55	TBY	2/58	XBY	11/59
BOY	1/36	FOY	7/46	KOY	3/52	OOY	7/55	TOY	3/58	XOY	12/59
BRK	4/36	FRK	11/46	KRK	7/52	ORK	9/55	TRK	5/58	XRK	2/60
BVB	7/36	FVB	1/47	KVB	11/52	OVB	10/55	TVB	6/58	XVB	4/60
CBY	11/36	GBY	5/47	LBY	1/53	PBY	1/56	UBY	8/58	YBY	5/60
COY	2/37	GOY	11/47	LOY	5/53	POY	3/56	UOY	9/58	YOY	5/60
CRK	4/37	GRK	5/48	LRK	8/53	PRK	5/56	URK	10/58	YRK	6/60
CVB	7/37	GVB	11/48	LVB	10/53	PVB	6/56	UVB	12/58	YVB	6/60
DBY	11/37	HBY	4/49	MBY	1/54	RBY	9/56	VBY	1/59		
DOY	2/38	HOY	6/49	MOY	3/54	ROY	11/56	VOY	3/59		
DRK	5/38	HRK	10/49	MRK	6/54	RRK	1/57	VRK	4/59		
DVB	10/38	HVB	3/50	MVB	8/54	RVB	4/57	VVB	5/59		

When YVB had reached about 250 cars etc. commenced reverse format marks, YVB ca. 250-900 being used for motorcycles only. (901-999 allocated to Hall & Co.)

Cars etc.			Motorcycles			
1000-9999 BY	*6/60*		*1-900 BY*	*2/61*	*(901-999 BY alloc. SEGB)*	
1000-9999 RK	*7/61*		*701-999 RK*	*10/61*	**	
1000-9999 VB	*7/62*		*501-999 VB*	*c.8/62*		

Special issues : *1 BY* (Civic car), *1 RK* and *1 VB* (Civic car).
** *999 RK* was reached ca. 3/62 and motorcycles joined cars in late *RK* before using ca. *550-999 VB* and when this block was completed motorcycles finally rejoined cars in *VB*.

ABY	*4/63*	*BBY*	*10/63*	*CBY*	*3/64*	*DBY*	*6/64*	*EBY*	*9/64*
AOY	*7/63*	*BOY*	*11/63*	*COY*	*3/64*	*DOY*	*6/64*	*EOY*	*11/64*
ARK	*8/63*	*BRK*	*1/64*	*CRK*	*4/64*	*DRK*	*7/64*		
AVB	*9/63*	*BVB*	*2/64*	*CVB*	*5/64*	*DVB*	*8/64*		

Commenced suffix marks 1.1.65.

(The County Borough of Croydon was absorbed into the Greater London Council with effect from 1.4.65).

COUNTY BOROUGH COUNCIL OF DARLINGTON

Darlington was created a county borough with effect from 1.4.15.

HN 4/15

Commenced with a common series for all vehicles up to HN 102; motorcycles were then allocated the block HN 500-1999. When this block was completed motorcycles joined the main series from HN 2993.

First numbers issued each year.

Cars etc.		Motorcycles
1915	Issued : 2-38, 103 - *	500
1916	Issued : 1, 39-98, * - 194	612
1917	Issued : 99, 100, 195-281	713
1918	Issued : 282-437	819
1919	Issued : 438-499, 2000-2133	939
1920	2134	1210
1921	2422	1517

* block 103-194 issued 1915/6, but year end dividing line not known.

No information available for 1922-1928, but following incomplete ranges are known for these years :

1922	- 2833	1926	4363 - 4954
1923	2858 - 3175	1927	4955 - 5656
1924	3229 - 3717	1928	5696 -
1925	3907 - 4359		

First numbers issued each year :

1929	6361	1931	7761	1933	8940
1930	7084	1932	8335	1934	9619

AHN	6/34	EHN	3/38	JHN	12/46	NHN	1/50	SHN	12/52	WHN	11/54
BHN	6/35	FHN	3/39	KHN	9/47	OHN	9/50	THN	6/53	XHN	3/55
CHN	6/36	GHN	7/40	LHN	7/48	PHN	6/51	UHN	12/53	YHN	6/55
DHN	4/37	HHN	1/46	MHN	4/49	RHN	3/52	VHN	6/54		

Reverse format issues commenced with *AHN (10/55)* for all vehicles and then in order to *NHN*.
Then *HN from 1000* for cars etc., concurrently with *PHN* for motorcycles (3/60).
HN finished 4/63 and cars then started *SHN*. Motorcycles completed *RHN 5/63* and rejoined cars in late *SHN*.

Common Series

AHN	10/55	DHN	1/57	GHN	2/58	KHN	2/59	NHN	11/59
BHN	3/56	EHN	5/57	HHN	5/58	LHN	5/59		
CHN	7/56	FHN	9/57	JHN	9/58	MHN	8/59		

Cars etc.		Motorcycles	
HN	3/60	PHN	3/60
SHN	4/63	RHN	6/61

Common Series

THN	5/63	UHN	9/63	VHN	1/64	WHN	3/64	XHN	5/64	YHN	8/64

Commenced suffix marks, (ahead of original schedule), 1.9.64

COUNTY BOROUGH COUNCIL OF DERBY

CH   12/03   RC   5/31

A common sequence for all vehicles.

First issues each year :

1904	CH	49		1915	CH	1143		1926	CH	5496		1937	RC	4671
1905	CH	149		1916	CH	1307		1927	CH	6266		1938	RC	5858
1906	CH	199		1917	CH	1421		1928	CH	7171		1939	RC	6890
1907	CH	260		1918	CH	1459		1929	CH	8032		1940	RC	7873
1908	CH	307		1919	CH	1503		1930	CH	8874		1941	RC	8086
1909	CH	355		1920	CH	1817		1931	CH	9664		1942	RC	8205
1910	CH	413		1921	CH	2286		1932	RC	384		1943	RC	8329
1911	CH	470		1922	CH	2834		1933	RC	1054		1944	RC	8414
1912	CH	572		1923	CH	3336		1934	RC	1656		1945	RC	8521
1913	CH	718		1924	CH	3889		1935	RC	2432		1946	RC	8735
1914	CH	884		1925	CH	4561		1936	RC	3501		1947	RC	9565

ACH	4/47	ECH	3/53	JCH	2/56	NCH	8/58	SCH	1/60	WCH	4/61
ARC	3/48	ERC	8/53	JRC	6/56	NRC	11/58	SRC	3/60	WRC	5/61
BCH	3/49	FCH	2/54	KCH	11/56	OCH	2/59	TCH	4/60	XCH	7/61
BRC	11/49	FRC	6/54	KRC	3/57	ORC	4/59	TRC	6/60	XRC	9/61
CCH	6/50	GCH	10/54	LCH	6/57	PCH	6/59	UCH	8/60	YCH	12/61
CRC	3/51	GRC	3/55	LRC	10/57	PRC	7/59	URC	10/60	YRC	3/62
DCH	12/51	HCH	6/55	MCH	2/58	RCH	9/59	VCH	1/61		
DRC	8/52	HRC	10/55	MRC	5/58	RRC	11/59	VRC	3/61		

ACH	*5/62*	*BCH*	*9/62*	*CCH*	*2/63*	*DCH*	*5/63*	*ECH*	*8/63*	*FCH*	*12/63*
ARC	*6/62*	*BRC*	*12/62*	*CRC*	*4/63*	*DRC*	*6/63*	*ERC*	*10/63*		

Special mark for Diplomatic Corps : *1 GRC* c. 8/97.

Suffix marks commenced 3.2.64

COUNTY BOROUGH COUNCIL OF DEVONPORT

DR   1/04

Devonport was absorbed into the enlarged County Borough of Plymouth with effect from 1.4.15, by which date it had issued DR 1-268. For further issues of DR see County Borough of Plymouth.

COUNTY BOROUGH COUNCIL OF DEWSBURY

Dewsbury was created a county borough and commenced issuing registrations on 1.4.13.

HD   4/13

First numbers each year before 1929 not known to writer, but information is available at West Yorkshire Archives, Wakefield.

1929	HD 3784		1936	HD 5892		1943	HD 7326	1950	HD 8827
1930	HD 4099		1937	HD 6234		1944	HD 7383	1951	HD 9096
1931	HD 4337		1938	HD 6569		1945	HD 7447	1952	HD 9322
1932	HD 4563		1939	HD 6890		1946	HD 7515	1953	HD 9654
1933	HD 4870		1940	HD 7147		1947	HD 7630		
1934	HD 5120		1941	HD 7262		1948	HD 8150		
1935	HD 5469		1942	HD 7286		1949	HD 8410		

AHD	11/53	CHD	8/56	EHD	4/59	GHD	11/60	JHD	8/62	LHD	3/64
BHD	5/55	DHD	2/58	FHD	3/60	HHD	8/61	KHD	7/63		

Suffix marks commenced 1.9.64

COUNTY BOROUGH COUNCIL OF DONCASTER

Doncaster was created a county borough and commenced issuing registrations with effect from 1.4.27 - this was the only county borough created between 1915 (Darlington) and 1964 (Luton & Solihull).

DT   4/27

First issues each year :

1928	DT 657 *		1931	DT 2804		1934	DT 4787	1937	DT 8236
1929	DT 1348		1932	DT 3457		1935	DT 5646	1938	DT 9547
1930	DT 2076		1933	DT 4097		1936	DT 6761		

* DT 666 early, 12/27.

ADT	4/38	EDT	2/47	JDT	5/50	NDT	5/53	SDT	4/55	WDT	1/57
BDT	3/39	FDT	1/48	KDT	2/51	ODT	11/53	TDT	8/55	XDT	5/57
CDT	9/41	GDT	10/48	LDT	1/52	PDT	5/54	UDT	2/56	YDT	9/57
DDT	4/46	HDT	8/49	MDT	10/52	RDT	10/54	VDT	6/56		

Reverse format issues commenced 3/58 with *DT* from 1001 for cars etc. concurrently with *ADT* for motorcycles. *DT* was completed 5/62 and cars joined motorcycles from *238 GDT*.

Cars etc.

DT	*3/58*

Motorcycles

ADT	*3/58*	*BDT*	*1/59*
CDT	*7/59*	*DDT*	*2/60*
EDT	*7/60*	*FDT*	*5/61*
GDT	*3/62*		

Common Series

HDT	*7/62*	*KDT*	*3/63*	*MDT*	*7/63*	*PDT*	*1/64*
JDT	*11/62*	*LDT*	*5/63*	*NDT*	*10/63*	*RDT*	*4/64*

Suffix marks commenced 1.5.64, (ahead of original schedule).

COUNTY BOROUGH COUNCIL OF DUDLEY

FD   12/03

Registration commenced 18.12.03. A common sequence for all vehicles.

First issues each year :

1904	FD	9	1912	FD	318	1920	FD	1198	1928	FD	4084
1905	FD	50	1913	FD	414	1921	FD	1672	1929	FD	4549
1906	FD	74	1914	FD	514	1922	FD	1874	1930	FD	5387
1907	FD	112	1915	FD	614	1923	FD	2056	1931	FD	6239
1908	FD	139	1916	FD	712	1924	FD	2321	1932	FD	6876
1909	FD	169	1917	FD	795	1925	FD	2705	1933	FD	7551
1910	FD	198	1918	FD	857	1926	FD	3111	1934	FD	8265
1911	FD	246	1919	FD	890	1927	FD	3560	1935	FD	9184

AFD	10/35	EFD	3/39	JFD	7/48	NFD	9/52	SFD	7/55	WFD	1/58
BFD	7/36	FFD	3/42	KFD	7/49	OFD	7/53	TFD	12/55	XFD	6/58
CFD	4/37	GFD	7/46	LFD	7/50	PFD	4/54	UFD	9/56	YFD	1/59
DFD	3/38	HFD	4/47	MFD	8/51	RFD	1/55	VFD	5/57		

The dates shown above are those when each series was taken into general use, but low numbers were frequently issued early, e.g. OFD 1 in 4/53, WFD 3 in 10/57.

Reverse format issues commenced with *AFD* on 4/6/59, but after only two weeks *FD* from 1001 up was commenced for cars etc., the remainder of *AFD* from 67 up being used mainly for motorcycles, with only rare exceptions. *AFD* was followed by *BFD* and *CFD*.
When cars finished *FD* in 12/63 they joined motorcycles from *452 CFD* on.

Cars etc.

FD	*6/59*	*(from 1001)* *

* Special issue for Mayoral car :
1 FD 17.3.59

Motorcycles

AFD	6/59
BFD	7/60
CFD	9/62

All Vehicles

DFD	2/64
EFD	5/64

Suffix marks commenced : 1.7.64.

COUNTY BOROUGH COUNCIL OF EASTBOURNE

Eastbourne was created a county borough and commenced issuing registrations with effect from 1.4.11.

HC 4/11   JK 12/28.

From the outset odd numbers were allocated to cars, commercials and buses, whilst even numbers were used for motorcycles.   Cars reached HC 9999 in 12/28 and commenced JK, using both odd and even numbers; meanwhile motorcycles continued using even numbers in HC. However, when JK 9999 was reached in 2/48, the remaining even numbers of HC, commencing at 8056, were used for all classes and there was no segregation thereafter.

First numbers each year, (no information is available prior to 1928) :

Cars etc.				Motorcycles			
1928	HC 8615	1939	JK 8163	1928	HC 5062	1939	HC 7434
1929	JK 63	1940	JK 8758	1929	HC 5408	1940	HC 7518
1930	JK 807	1941	JK 8843	1930	HC 5728	1941	HC 7554
1931	JK 1575	1942	JK 8858	1931	HC 6086	1942	HC 7568
1932	JK 2159	1943	JK 8873	1932	HC 6340	1943	HC 7578
1933	JK 2759	1944	JK 8897	1933	HC 6528	1944	HC 7592
1934	JK 3476	1945	JK 8918	1934	HC 6708	1945	HC 7604
1935	JK 4324	1946	JK 9007	1935	HC 6866	1946	HC 7650
1936	JK 5307	1947	JK 9496	1936	HC 7074	1947	HC 7844
1937	JK 6383	1948	JK 9937	1937	HC 7238	1948	HC 8028
1938	JK 7391			1938	HC 7366		

Common Series
1949 HC 9040

AHC	9/49	CHC	5/54	EHC	2/57	GHC	8/59	JHC	5/61	LHC	5/63
AJK	2/51	CJK	1/55	EJK	11/57	GJK	1/60	JJK	10/61	LJK	9/63
BHC	6/52	DHC	9/55	FHC	8/58	HHC	5/60	KHC	4/62	MHC	3/64
BJK	7/53	DJK	5/56	FJK	3/59	HJK	11/60	KJK	10/62	MJK	7/64

Commenced suffix marks 4.8.64

COUNTY BOROUGH COUNCIL OF EAST HAM

East Ham was created a county borough and commenced issuing registrations with effect from 1.4.15.

A single sequence for all classes of vehicle.

HM 4/15   HV 9/29

First issues each year, (No information available prior to 1929) :

1929	HM 9433	1932	HV 1705	1935	HV 4411	1938	HV 9229
1930	HV 134	1933	HV 2464	1936	HV 5648		
1931	HV 1001	1934	HV 3367	1937	HV 7406		

AHM	5/38	BHM	4/50	JHM	10/54	NHM	3/58	SHM	7/60	WHM	1/63
AHV	2/39	BHV	10/50	JHV	3/55	NHV	8/58	SHV	10/60	WHV	4/63
BHM	2/40	FHM	6/51	KHM	7/55	OHM	1/59	THM	3/61	XHM	6/63
BHV	4/46	FHV	3/52	KHV	11/55	OHV	5/59	THV	5/61	XHV	9/63
CHM	1/47	GHM	11/52 *	LHM	4/56	PHM	6/59	UHM	8/61	YHM	1/64
CHV	9/47	GHV	6/53	LHV	11/56	PHV	9/59	UHV	1/62	YHV	4/64
DHM	7/48	HHM	1/54	MHM	5/57	RHM	1/60	VHM	4/62		
DHV	6/49	HHV	5/54	MHV	10/57	RHV	4/60	VHV	7/62		

* GHM was issued irregularly, not finished until 9/53, whilst GHV commenced 6/53.

Suffix marks commenced 1.5.64.

COUNTY BOROUGH COUNCIL OF EXETER

Registration commenced 18.12.03

FJ 12/03

Although proof is lacking it is almost certain that motorcycles were numbered in a separate and parallel series until 1907; there was no segregation thereafter.

First numbers issued each year, (no information is available for the missing years) :

1904	10	1911	161 *	1919	900	1928	5357
1905	31	1912	229	1920	1109	1929	6022
1906	43			1921	1510	1930	6683
1907	54	1915	ca. 590			1931	7400
1908	73	1916	746	1925	3375	1932	8042
1909	100	1917	838	1926	4016	1933	8699
1910	125	1918	877	1927	4642	1934	9466

* FJ 173 early issue, 1910.

AFJ	8/34	EFJ	4/38	JFJ	2/48	NFJ	7/52	SFJ	7/55	WFJ	4/58
BFJ	8/35	FFJ	4/39	KFJ	5/49	OFJ	7/53	TFJ	2/56	XFJ	12/58
CFJ	7/36	GFJ	11/43	LFJ	6/50	PFJ	4/54	UFJ	11/56	YFJ	6/59
DFJ	5/37	HFJ	1/47	MFJ	7/51	RFJ	12/54	VFJ	8/57		

AFJ	12/59	CFJ	11/60	EFJ	12/61	GFJ	2/63	JFJ	12/63
BFJ	5/60	DFJ	5/61	FFJ	6/62	HFJ	6/63		

Suffix marks commenced 3.2.64

COUNTY BOROUGH COUNCIL OF GATESHEAD

CN 1/04

First issues each year, (no information available prior to 1929) :

1929	3788	1934	5836	1939	9061	1944	9739
1930	4229	1935	6383	1940	9537	1945	9763
1931	4624	1936	7010	1941	9656	1946	9855
1932	5080	1937	7720	1942	9664		
1933	5398	1938	8411	1943	9710		

Whilst ACN commenced 4/46, CN was not completed until 11/46.

ACN	4/46	DCN	1/53	GCN	11/56	KCN	7/59	NCN	6/61	RCN	11/63
BCN	7/48	ECN	6/54	HCN	11/57	LCN	4/60	OCN	4/62	SCN	6/64
CCN	10/50	FCN	10/55	JCN	11/58	MCN	11/60	PCN	3/63		

Suffix marks commenced 1.7.64

COUNTY BOROUGH COUNCIL OF GLOUCESTER

Registration commenced 19.12.03.

FH   12/03

The original allocation was from FH 1 up for cars etc. and FH 51 up for motorcycles, but after 51-60 had been issued motorcycles jumped to 101 up. Cars eventually duplicated 51-60 and surviving motorcycles 52, 53, 54 and 57 were renumbered to avoid clashing. By January 1910 cars reached 100, by which time motorcycles were at 215; a common series was adopted from 216 up.

First numbers issued each year, (no information is available for 1922-1928) :

Motor Cars   Motorcycles

1904	5		1908	70		1904	59, 60, 101 up	1908	181
1905	26		1909	83		1905	132	1909	204
1906	35		1910	99		1906	155		
1907	53					1907	166		

Common Series

1910	216		1916	1083		1929	5828		1935	9203
1911	270		1917	1176		1930	6498		1936	9879
1912	386		1918	ca. 1221		1931	7081			
1913	550		1919	1246		1932	7553			
1914	759		1920	1624		1933	8068			
1915	930		1921	2235		1934	8599			

AFH	1/36	EFH	3/46	JFH	3/51	NFH	10/54	SFH	3/57	WFH	2/59
BFH	4/37	FFH	5/47	KFH	5/52	OFH	4/55	TFH	9/57	XFH	5/59
CFH	5/38	GFH	7/48	LFH	5/53	PFH	10/55	UFH	4/58	YFH	9/59
DFH	5/39	HFH	11/49	MFH	2/54	RFH	6/56	VFH	9/58		

Reverse format issues commenced 1/60 with *FH* from 401 for cars etc. concurrently with *AFH* for motorcycles, which was followed by *BFH*.   *CFH* was reserved for T. Wall & Son Ltd., (but the numbers unused at 31.5.64, i.e. 375 up, were later used for re-registrations.)   Motorcycles commenced *DFH* 9/63, being joined by cars 11/63 on completion of *FH*.

Motor Cars   Motorcycles

FH (from 401)   *1/60*

Special Series

CFH   *3/63*

Common Series

EFH   *2/64*   *FFH*   *4/64*

AFH	*1/60*
BFH	*6/61*
DFH	*9/63*

Suffix marks commenced 1.6.64

COUNTY BOROUGH COUNCIL OF GREAT YARMOUTH

EX 1/04

First issues each year. Information prior to 1929 not known to writer, but 1921-9 details may be available at Norfolk Record Office.

A few random dates of issue are quoted :

| EX 270 | 10/16 | EX 1067 | 3/24 | EX 1266 | 3/25 | EX 1638 | 9/26 |
| EX 599 | 4/21 | EX 1114 | 6/24 | EX 1513 | 3/26 | | |

1929	2216	1936	3895	1943	5201	1950	6672
1930	2512	1937	4215	1944	5253	1951	7009
1931	2762	1938	4558	1945	5305	1952	7324
1932	2988	1939	4847	1946	5367	1953	7648
1933	3161	1940	5117	1947	5655	1954	8205
1934	3345	1941	5160	1948	6029	1955	8835
1935	3590	1942	5174	1949	6334	1956	9600

| AEX | 7/56 | CEX | 12/58 | EEX | 4/60 | GEX | 8/61 | JEX | 2/63 |
| BEX | 11/57 | DEX | 9/59 | FEX | 1/61 | HEX | 5/62 | KEX | 9/63 |

Special issue for Diplomatic Corps : MEX 1 8/80.

Suffix marks commenced 2.3.64.

COUNTY BOROUGH COUNCIL OF GRIMSBY

EE 1/04   JV 11/30

Motor cars and motorcycles in a common series but in EE blocks of numbers were reserved for motorcycles. The surviving records are incomplete, but it would appear that the following blocks were allocated to mtorcycles : EE 51-99, 151-299, 400-699, 700-799, 800-899, 1000-1099, 1200-1399, 1500-1599, 1700-1799, 1900-1999, 2300-2399 and thereafter alternate blocks of 100 to 4100-4199. No information thereafter.

Precise details of issues each year prior to 1929 are not available to the writer , but the following ranges of numbers are known for 1904-1923. Similar information for 1924-1928 may be available at Grimsby Record Office.

	Cars	Motorcycles		Cars	Motorcycles
1904		EE - 73	1914	EE 785- 973	EE 829-1057
1905	EE 100-109	EE 88-170	1915	EE 982-1169	EE 1059-1295
1906	EE 111-120	EE 175-214	1916	EE 1165-1434	EE 1296-1399
1907	EE 123-	EE 216-232	1917	EE 1431-1469	EE 1500-1534
1908	EE 309-317	EE 235-272	1918	EE 1470-1611	None issued ?
1909	EE 320-326	EE 275-409	1919	EE 1612-2166	EE 1537-1929
1910	EE 335-348	EE 412-451	1920	EE 2171-3002*	EE 1930-2704*
1911	EE 349-371	EE 454-508	1921	No info.	No info.
1912	EE 378-712	EE 513-611	1922	EE 3499-4044	EE 3500-3785
1913	EE 717-784	EE 614-827	1923	EE 4045-	EE 3786-

* Actual year-end figure considerable higher than this.

First issues each year.

1929	EE 8261	1934	JV 2391	1939	JV 7490	1944	JV 8642
1930	EE 9279	1935	JV 3216	1940	JV 8227	1945	JV 8765
1931	JV 146	1936	JV 4137	1941	JV 8362	1946	JV 8950
1932	JV 863	1937	JV 5349	1942	JV 8406	1947	JV 9988
1933	JV 1658	1938	JV 6449	1943	JV 8511		

AEE	1/47	EEE	10/53	JEE	4/57	NEE	11/59	SEE	9/61	WEE	7/63
AJV	12/47	EJV	5/54	JJV	9/57	NJV	2/60	SJV	1/62	WJV	10/63
BEE	2/49	FEE	10/54	KEE	2/58	OEE	4/60	TEE	4/62	XEE	12/63
BJV	2/50	FJV	4/55	KJV	6/58	OJV	7/60	TJV	7/62	XJV	2/64
CEE	9/50	GEE	7/55	LEE	10/58	PEE	10/60	UEE	10/62	YEE	4/64
CJV	8/51	GJV	12/55	LJV	3/59	PJV	2/61	UJV	1/63	YJV	6/64
DEE	6/52	HEE	5/56	MEE	5/59	REE	4/61	VEE	3/63		
DJV	3/53	HJV	11/56	MJV	8/59	RJV	7/61	VJV	5/63		

Special issue for Diplomatic Corps : *1 EE* 1/86.

Suffix marks commenced, (ahead of original schedule), 24.7.64.

192a

COUNTY BOROUGH COUNCIL OF HALIFAX

CP 12/03   JX 5/32

Separate and duplicated series for cars and motorcycles prior to 1921 : Cars CP 1-1855, motorcycles CP 1-1631; a common series CP 1856 up from 1/21.

First issues each year, (no information available for missing years) :

Motor cars :

1904	CP 13	1906	CP 76	1908	CP 108	1910	CP 156
1905	CP 48	1907	CP 91	1909	CP 127	1911	CP 195

1921	CP 1856	1929	CP 7188	1936	JX 3598	1943	JX 8415
1922	CP 2307	1930	CP 8150	1937	JX 4834	1944	JX 8468
1923	CP 2718	1931	CP 8936	1938	JX 6102	1945	JX 8523
1924	CP 3218	1932	CP 9625	1939	JX 7189	1946	JX 8677
1925	CP 3766	1933	JX 442	1940	JX 8067	1947	JX 9580
1926	ca CP 4400	1934	JX 1319	1941	JX 8319		
1927	ca CP 5200	1935	JX 2423	1942	JX 8358		

ACP	5/47	ECP	2/54	JCP	10/57	NCP	8/60	SCP	4/63
AJX	5/48	EJX	7/54	JJX	3/58	NJX	1/61	SJX	7/63
BCP	5/49	FCP	2/55	KCP	8/58	OCP	4/61	TCP	11/63
BJX	3/50	FJX	6/55	KJX	2/59	OJX	7/61	TJX	2/64
CCP	2/51	GCP	11/55	LCP	5/59	PCP	12/61	UCP	5/64
CJX	2/52	GJX	5/56	LJX	9/59	PJX	4/62		
DCP	11/52	HCP	11/56	MCP	2/60	RCP	8/62		
DJX	7/53	HJX	5/57	MJX	5/60	RJX	1/63		

Suffix marks commenced 1.6.64

COUNTY BOROUGH COUNCIL OF HANLEY

See COUNTY BOROUGH COUNCIL OF STOKE-ON-TRENT.

COUNTY BOROUGH COUNCIL OF HARTLEPOOL

See COUNTY BOROUGH COUNCIL OF WEST HARTLEPOOL.

COUNTY BOROUGH COUNCIL OF HASTINGS

Registration commenced 23.11.03, A single sequence for all vehicles.

DY 11/03

First numbers issued each year, (no details known to writer for 1922-1928 but some information may be available at East Sussex Record Office and/or Kithead Trust).

1904	49			1913	499							1929	5435
1905	120			1914	636							1930	6020
1906	155			1915	802							1931	6462
1907	182			1916	941							1932	6869
1908	208			1917	1008							1933	7311
1909	236			1918	1044							1934	7851
1910	273			1919	1104							1935	8444
1911	327			1920	1291							1936	9134
1912	388			1921	1703							1937	9845

ADY	2/37	EDY	12/49	JDY	6/55	NDY	3/59	SDY	12/61
BDY	7/38	FDY	12/51	KDY	5/56	ODY	10/59	TDY	9/62
CDY	3/45	GDY	8/53	LDY	6/57	PDY	5/60	UDY	6/63
DDY	12/47	HDY	9/54	MDY	5/58	RDY	3/61	VDY	2/64

Special mark for Diplomatic Corps : *1 PDY* c. 1/79.

Suffix marks commenced 1.6.64

COUNTY BOROUGH COUNCIL OF HUDDERSFIELD

CX 12/03   VH 10/27.

VH 1-999 for mtorcycles issued concurrently with VH 1000 up for cars etc., but after VH 999 cycles joined the main series from VH 4347. It is not known whether there was similar segregation in CX.

First issues each year, (no information available prior to 1929) :

1929	VH 1907	1931	VH 3459	1933	VH 4956	1935	VH 7275
1930	VH 2744	1932	VH 4100	1934	VH 5990	1936	VH 8607

ACX	1/37	ECX	10/48	JCX	9/54	NCX	11/57	SCX	4/60	WCX	5/62
AVH	7/37	EVH	8/49	JVH	3/55	NVH	3/58	SVH	6/60	WVH	7/62
BCX	3/38	FCX	6/50	KCX	6/55	OCX	7/58	TCX	9/60	XCX	10/62
BVH	1/39	FVH	5/51	KVH	10/55	OVH	12/58	TVH	1/61	XVH	2/63
CCX	12/39	GCX	5/52	LCX	3/56	PCX	4/59	UCX	4/61	YCX	4/63
CVH	2/46	GVH	2/53	LVH	8/56	PVH	6/59	UVH	6/61	YVH	6/63
DCX	12/46	HCX	10/53	MCX	2/57	RCX	10/59	VCX	9/61		
DVH	10/47	HVH	4/54	MVH	6/57	RVH	1/60	VVH	2/62		

Suffix marks commenced 28.8.63

The only reverse format mark issued by Huddersfield was *CX* (from 1000) for re-registrations only, 3/67, This was the only reverse format two-letter mark commenced by any authority after 1964.

COUNTY BOROUGH COUNCIL OF IPSWICH

DX 1/04   PV 7/32

A common sequence for all vehicles.

First issues each year, (no information available for 1923-1928) :

1905	DX	112	1916	DX 1590	1929	DX 7686	1940	PV 6452
1906	DX	175	1917	DX 1755	1930	DX 8415	1941	PV 6677
1907	DX	253	1918	DX 1837	1931	DX 9048	1942	PV 6712
1908	DX	304	1919	DX 1889	1932	DX 9625	1943	PV 6769
1909	DX	345	1920	DX 2265	1933	PV 280	1944	PV 6800
1910	DX	383	1921	DX 3020	1934	PV 970	1945	PV 6909
1911	DX	469	1922	DX 3319	1935	PV 1774	1946	PV 7032
1912	DX	599			1936	PV 2765	1947	PV 7697
1913	DX	798			1937	PV 3750	1948	PV 8412
1914	DX 1011				1938	PV 4703	1949	PV 9115
1915	DX 1281				1939	PV 5669	1950	PV 9944

ADX	1/50	EDX	11/55	JDX	3/59	NDX	3/61	SDX	5/63
APV	2/51	EPV	4/56	JPV	6/59	NPV	6/61	SPV	7/63
BDX	2/52	FDX	10/56	KDX	9/59	ODX	9/61	TDX	10/63
BPV	1/53	FPV	4/57	KPV	12/59	OPV	1/62	TPV	1/64
CDX	10/53	GDX	10/57	LDX	3/60	PDX	4/62	UDX	3/64
CPV	6/54	GPV	2/58	LPV	5/60	PPV	7/62	UPV	5/64
DDX	1/55	HDX	6/58	MDX	8/60	RDX	11/62	VDX	10/70 *
DPV	6/55	HPV	11/58	MPV	12/60	RPV	3/63		

* Re-registrations only.

Suffix marks commenced 4.8.64

COUNTY BOROUGH COUNCIL OF KINGSTON-UPON-HULL

AT 1/04   KH 1/25   RH 12/29

First issues each year. No information available to writer prior to 1929, but details for 1904-1918 available at Hull Transport Museum.

| 1929 | KH 7886 | | 1931 | RH 2383 | | 1933 | RH 6738 |
| 1930 | RH 50 | | 1932 | RH 4624 | | 1934 | RH 8700 |

AAT	6/34	EAT	11/37	JAT	5/47	NAT	2/52	SAT	11/34	WAT	1/57
AKH	10/34	EKH	2/38	JKH	10/47	NKH	6/52	SKH	1/55	WKH	3/57
ARH	3/35	ERH	5/38	JRH	4/48	NRH	9/52	SRH	3/55	WRH	5/57
BAT	5/35	FAT	9/38	KAT	10/48	OAT	1/53	TAT	4/55	XAT	6/57
BKH	9/35	FKH	1/39	KKH	3/49	OKH	4/53	TKH	6/55	XKH	8/57
BRH	1/36	FRH	3/39	KRH	8/49	ORH	7/53	TRH	8/55	XRH	10/57
CAT	3/36	GAT	7/39	LAT	1/50	PAT	9/53	UAT	10/55	YAT	1/58
CKH	6/36	GKH	5/40	LKH	5/50	PKH	12/53	UKH	1/56	YKH	3/58
CRH	10/36	GRH	9/43	LRH	9/50	PRH	3/54	URH	3/56	YRH	5/58
DAT	2/37	HAT	1/46	MAT	1/51	RAT	5/54	VAT	5/56		
DKH	4/37	HKH	8/46	MKH	5/51	RKH	7/54	VKH	7/56		
DRH	6/37	HRH	12/46	MRH	10/51	RRH	8/54	VRH	10/56		

Reverse issues commenced with *KH*, from 1 mainly for motorcycles and 1000 for cars etc. concurrently, 7/58. *999 KH* was reached 11/58 and followed by *AAT* and successive three-letter marks for motorcycles; after *9999 KH* cars etc. used *AT* from 1001 and *RH* from 1. *GAT* was the last all motorcycle series and, when *RH* was completed, *GKH* onwards were used for all classes.

Cars etc			Motorcycles					All Vehicles		
1000-9999 KH	7/58		1-999 KH 7/58		DAT	7/60		GKH	11/63	
1001-9999 AT	6/60		AAT	11/58	DKH	11/60		GRH	1/64	
2-9999 RH	3/62		AKH	2/59	DRH	3/61		HAT	3/64	
			ARH	4/59	EAT	5/61		HKH	3/64	
			BAT	6/59	EKH	8/61		HRH	/66 *	
			BKH	7/59	ERH	2/62				
			BRH	9/59	FAT	6/62				
			CAT	11/59	FKH	1/63				
			CKH	3/60	FRH	5/63				
			CRH	4/60	GAT	8/63 (completed 1/64)				

* Re-registrations only.

Suffix marks commenced 1.5.64.

195

COUNTY BOROUGH COUNCIL OF LEEDS

U 1/04   NW 10/21   UM 1/25   UA 7/27   UB 10/29   UG 1/32

Prior to 1921 a separate and duplicating series was used for motorcycles, U 1 to U 5794.

An M.o.T Circular dated 4.8.22 contained the following, "The Index Mark UM has been allotted to certain vehicles by the Leeds City Council under a misapprehension. In view of the inconvenience and expense involved it has been decided that the identification marks already allotted should be allowed to stand, and that in the next Order relating to Index Marks the mark UM will be appropriated to the Leeds authority." The Order in question was dated 27.9.22, but UM was not brought into general use until 1/25. The reason for the Circular would appear to lie in the fact that Leeds' pre-1921 G.I.M. marks consisted of the letters U-M followed by a number and it seems probable that some vehicles bearing such numbers were erroneously registered with them as normal marks after 1.1.21.

No information on annual issues before 1929 is known to the writer, but some details may be available at the West Yorkshire Archives.

The following ranges of numbers are known for the car series for the years shown :

1905 : U 388 (12/05)		1915 : U 3287 (6/15)	- U 3541 (9/15)
1907 : U 587 (1/07)	- U 720	1916 : U 3965	- U 4013
1908 : U 785 (1/08)	- U 827 (4/08)	1917 : U 4212	- U 4416
1910 : U 1103		1918 : U 4662 (6/18)	- U 4729
1911 : U 1520		1919 : U 4868	- U 5896
1912 : U 1745	- U 1769 (3/12)	1920 : U 5933	- U 7660 (11/20)
1913 : U 2059 (1/13) - U 2384		1921 : U 7729	
1914 : U 2573 (3/14) - U 2896			

First issues each year :

1929	UA 5780		1931	UB 4493		1933	UG 3142
1930	UB 926		1932	UB 9033		1934	UG 7356

ANW	5/34	BNW	1/37	JNW	3/40	NNW	10/49	SNW	9/53	WNW	10/55
AUA	7/34	BUA	2/37	JUA	11/40	NUA	12/49	SUA	11/53	WUA	11/55
AUB	10/34	BUB	3/37	JUB	1/44	NUB	3/50	SUB	1/54	WUB	1/56
AUG	12/34	BUG	5/37	JUG	12/45	NUG	5/50	SUG	2/54	WUG	2/56
AUM	2/35	BUM	6/37	JUM	5/46	NUM	7/50	SUM	3/54	WUM	3/56
BNW	3/35	FNW	7/37	KNW	8/46	ONW	10/50	TNW	4/54	XNW	4/56
BUA	5/35	FUA	10/37	KUA	10/46	OUA	12/50	TUA	5/54	XUA	5/56
BUB not alloc.		FUB	12/37	KUB	12/46	OUB	2/51	TUB	7/54	XUB	6/56
BUG not alloc.		FUG	1/38	KUG	3/47	OUG	5/51	TUG	9/54	XUG	8/56
BUM not alloc.		FUM	3/38	KUM	5/47	OUM	8/51	TUM	10/54	XUM	10/56
CNW	7/35	GNW	4/38	LNW	7/47	PNW	11/51	UNW	11/54	YNW	11/56
CUA	10/35	GUA	5/38	LUA	9/47	PUA	2/52	UUA	1/55	YUA	1/57
CUB	11/35	GUB	7/38	LUB	12/47	PUB	5/52	UUB	2/55	YUB	2/57
CUG	1/36	GUG	10/38	LUG	3/48	PUG	7/52	UUG	3/55	YUG	3/57
CUM	3/36	GUM	12/38	LUM	6/48	PUM	10/52	UUM	4/55	YUM	4/57
DNW	4/36	HNW	1/39	MNW	9/48	RNW	12/52	VNW	5/55		
DUA	6/36	HUA	3/39	MUA	11/48	RUA	2/53	VUA	6/55		
DUB	7/36	HUB	4/39	MUB	2/49	RUB	4/53	VUB	7/55		
DUG	9/36	HUG	6/39	MUG	5/49	RUG	6/53	VUG	8/55		
DUM	11/36	HUM	8/39	MUM	7/49	RUM	7/53	VUM	9/55		

continued.....

COUNTY BOROUGH COUNCIL OF LEEDS (continued)

Reverse issues commenced 16.5.57 with *U*, issued simultaneously from ·1 up for motorcycles and 1000 up for cars. Motorcycles reached 999 before cars reached 9999, but instead of going into the next series motorcycles were assimilated into the main series pending the issue of the next mark. *NW, UA, UB, UG* and *UM* were issued similarly, then *ANW* on for all vehicles.

U	5/57	NW	4/58	UA	2/59	UB	10/59	UG	5/60	UM	2/61
ANW	9/61	CNW	4/62	ENW	1/63	GNW	8/63	JNW	3/64	LNW	9/64
AUA	10/61	CUA	5/62	EUA	2/63	GUA	9/63	JUA	4/64	LUA	10/64
AUB	11/61	CUB	5/62	EUB	3/63	GUB	10/63	JUB	4/64	LUB	11/64
AUG	1/62	CUG	6/62	EUG	3/63	GUG	11/63	JUG	5/64	LUG	12/64
AUM	2/62	CUM	7/62	EUM	4/63	GUM	11/63	JUM	5/64	LUM	/74 *
BNW	3/62	DNW	8/62	FNW	4/63	HNW	12/63	KNW	6/64		
BUA	3/62	DUA	9/62	FUA	5/63	HUA	1/64	KUA	6/64		
BUB not alloc.		DUB	10/62	FUB	6/63	HUB	2/64	KUB	7/64		
BUG not alloc.		DUG	11/62	FUG	6/63	HUG	2/64	KUG	8/64		
BUM not alloc.		DUM	12/62	FUM	7/63	HUM	3/64	KUM	8/64		

* re-registrations only.

Suffix marks commenced 1.1.65.

COUNTY BOROUGH COUNCIL OF LEICESTER

BC 12/03   RY 1/25   JF 3/30

First issues each year, (no information available prior to 1929) :

1929 RY 7521	1931 JF 1064	1933 JF 4205	1935 JF 7477
1930 RY 9384	1932 JF 2498	1934 JF 5610	

In the forward three-letter sequence marks were allotted in the same order as the basic marks.

ABC	1/36	EBC	6/46	JBC	5/52	NBC	4/55	SBC	7/57	WBC	8/59
ARY	4/36	ERY	11/46	JRY	9/52	NRY	6/55	SRY	10/57	WRY	10/59
AJF	9/36	EJF	5/47	JJF	1/53	NJF	8/55	SJF	12/57	WJF	11/59
BBC	2/37	FBC	12/47	KBC	5/53	OBC	10/55	TBC	3/58	XBC	1/60
BRY	6/37	FRY	6/48	KRY	7/53	ORY	1/56	TRY	5/58	XRY	2/60
BJF	11/37	FJF	2/49	KJF	11/53	OJF	3/56	TJF	7/58	XJF	4/60
CBC	4/38	GBC	7/49	LBC	2/54	PBC	5/56	UBC	9/58	YBC	5/50
CRY	10/38	GRY	1/50	LRY	4/54	PRY	7/56	URY	11/58	YRY	6/60
CJF	3/39	GJF	6/50	LJF	7/54	PJF	10/56	UJF	2/59	YJF	7/60
DBC	7/39	HBC	12/50	MBC	9/54	RBC	1/57	VBC	4/59		
DRY	7/40	HRY	6/51	MRY	12/54	RRY	3/57	VRY	5/59		
DJF	5/45	HJF	11/51	MJF	2/55	RJF	5/57	VJF	6/59		

Reverse marks were issued in alphabetical order.

ABC	9/60	CBC	7/61	EBC	6/62	GBC	5/63	JBC c. 3/72 *
AJF	11/60	CJF	8/61	EJF	8/62	GJF	7/63	
ARY	1/61	CRY	11/61	ERY	11/62	GRY	8/63	
BBC	3/61	DBC	1/62	FBC	1/63	HBC	10/63	
BJF	4/61	DJF	3/62	FJF	3/63	HJF	12/63	
BRY	5/61	DRY	5/62	FRY	4/63	HRY	1/64	

* re-registrations only.

Special mark for Diplomatic Corps : *1 BC* c. 11/78

Suffix marks commmenced 2.3.64.

COUNTY BOROUGH COUNCIL OF LINCOLN

FE 12/03   VL 3/28

A single sequence for all vehicles.

No information on annual issues before 1929 is known to the writer, but details are available at the Lincolnshire Archives.

The following ranges of numbers are known for the years shown :

1905 : FE	159		- FE	206 (11/05)	1916 : FE 1889 (1/16) - FE 2205 (11/16)
1906 : FE	247				1918 : FE 2375 (10/18)
1907 : FE	298 (10/07)				1919 : FE 2660 (7/19) - FE 2870 (10/19)
1908 : FE	416 (4/08)				1920 : FE 3041 (1/20) - FE 3970 (12/20)
1909 : FE	592				1924 : FE 5736 (1/24)
1910 : FE	669 (10/10)				1925 : FE 7855 (11/25)
1913 : FE	985 (2/13) - FE 1206 (12/13)				1926 : FE 8111 (4/26)
1914 : FE 1351 (6/14)					1927 : FE 8898 (4/27) - FE 9590 (9/27)
1915 : FE 1589 (4/15) - FE 1866 (12/15)					1928 : VL 388 (6/28)

First issues each year :

1929	VL 850	1932	VL 3700	1935	VL 6355
1930	VL 2000	1933	VL 4492	1936	VL 7565
1931	VL 2901	1934	VL 5312	1937	VL 8975

AFE	9/37	EFE	3/50	JFE	4/55	NFE	1/59	SFE	6/61	WFE	11/63
AVL	8/38	EVL	12/50	JVL	8/55	NVL	5/59	SVL	9/61	WVL	2/64
BFE	6/39	FFE	9/51	KFE	2/56	OFE	8/59	TFE	2/62	XFE	5/64
BVL	11/43	FVL	7/52	KVL	8/56	OVL	12/59	TVL	5/62	XVL	7/64
CFE	8/46	GFE	4/53	LFE	3/57	PFE	4/60	UFE	9/62		
CVL	6/47	GVL	10/53	LVL	9/57	PVL	7/60	UVL	2/63		
DFE	6/48	HFE	5/54	MFE	3/58	RFE	11/60	VFE	5/63		
DVL	6/49	HVL	10/54	MVL	7/58	RVL	3/61	VVL	7/63		

Suffix marks commenced 1.9.64

Town Council of Aberdeen - Index Mark. The attention of the Minister has been drawn to the fact that, prior to December 1920, a series of identification marks, R.S.-X-1 to R.S.-X-152 inclusive, were allotted to heavy motor cars registered with the Town Council of Aberdeen. Although the interpolation of the letter X and the use of a duplicate series of numbers are irregular it is considered that, in the "special" circumstances of the case, it is not necessary that the licensees should be allotted new numbers in respect of these vehicles and consequently put to trouble and expense. It should therefore be noted that the vehicles to which these identification marks have been allotted should be regarded as properly bearing an Aberdeen Town Council identification mark.   *Circular RF 147, 9.12.21*

COUNTY BOROUGH COUNCIL OF LIVERPOOL

K 12/03   KB 6/14   KC 3/20   KA 6/25   KD 12/27   KF 3/30   LV 7/32

A single sequence for all vehicles, but there appear to have been block allocations for heavy motor cars, e.g. K 1501-1700.

Liverpool's pre-1921 G.I.M.s were in the format K-A and a number and it is thought that this is the reason why KB and KC were allocated and used before KA for normal issues.

First issues each year, (no information available prior to 1929) :

| 1929 | KD 4160 | 1931 | KF 3590 | 1933 | LV 1950 |
| 1930 | KD 8520 | 1932 | KF 7630 | 1934 | LV 6470 |

AKA	8/34	BKA	3/38	JKA	8/47	NKA	2/52	SKA	11/54	WKA	12/56
AKB	10/34	BKB	5/38	JKB	11/47	NKB	4/52	SKB	12/54	WKB	1/57
AKC	12/34	BKC	6/38	JKC	2/48	NKC	6/52	SKC	2/55	WKC	2/57
AKD	2/35	BKD	8/38	JKD	5/48	NKD	8/52	SKD	3/55	WKD	3/57
AKF	4/35	BKF	10/38	JKF	7/48	NKF	9/52	SKF	3/55	WKF	4/57
ALV	6/35	BLV	12/38	JLV	10/48	NLV	11/52	SLV	4/55	WLV	5/57
BKA	8/35	FKA	1/39	KKA	12/48	OKA	1/53	TKA	5/55	XKA	5/57
BKB	10/35	FKB	3/39	KKB	3/49	OKB	2/53	TKB	6/55	XKB	6/57
BKC	12/35	FKC	4/39	KKC	5/49	OKC	4/53	TKC	7/55	XKC	7/57
BKD	1/36	FKD	5/39	KKD	7/49	OKD	6/53	TKD	7/55	XKD	8/57
BKF	3/36	FKF	6/39	KKF	9/49	OKF	7/53	TKF	8/55	XKF	9/57
BLV	4/36	FLV	8/39	KLV	12/49	OLV	8/53	TLV	9/55	XLV	10/57
CKA	5/36	GKA	1/40	LKA	2/50	PKA	9/53	UKA	10/55	YKA	11/57
CKB	7/36	GKB	9/40	LKB	4/50	PKB	11/53	UKB	11/55	YKB	12/57
CKC	10/36	GKC	3/42	LKC	6/50	PKC	12/53	UKC	12/55	YKC	2/58
CKD	12/36	GKD	2/45	LKD	8/50	PKD	1/54	UKD	1/56	YKD	2/58
CKF	1/37	GKF	1/46	LKF	10/50	PKF	3/54	UKF	3/56	YKF	3/58
CLV	3/37	GLV	3/46	LLV	12/50	PLV	4/54	ULV	3/56	YLV	4/58
DKA	4/37	HKA	7/46	MKA	2/51	RKA	5/54	VKA	4/56		
DKB	6/37	HKB	9/46	MKB	4/51	RKB	6/54	VKB	5/56		
DKC	7/37	HKC	11/46	MKC	5/51	RKC	7/54	VKC	6/56		
DKD	9/37	HKD	2/47	MKD	7/51	RKD	8/54	VKD	7/56		
DKF	12/37	HKF	4/47	MKF	9/51	RKF	10/54	VKF	9/56		
DLV	1/38	HLV	6/47	MLV	12/51	RLV	10/54	VLV	10/56		

Reverse format marks commenced with *AKA* for all vehicles, followed by three-letter marks to *FLV*. When this finished *K* was commenced for cars etc. amd *GKA* for motorcycles simultaneously as from 4/60. Cars then used two-letter series until *LV* was completed, when they rejoined motocycles in *HLV* onwards.

				All Vehicles							
AKA	5/58	BKA	10/58	CKA	3/59	DKA	6/59	EKA	9/59	FKA	1/60
AKB	6/58	BKB	11/58	CKB	3/59	DKB	6/59	EKB	10/59	FKB	2/60
AKC	7/58	BKC	11/58	CKC	4/59	DKC	7/59	EKC	10/59	FKC	2/60
AKD	7/58	BKD	12/58	CKD	4/59	DKD	7/59	EKD	11/59	FKD	3/60
AKF	8/58	BKF	1/59	CKF	5/59	DKF	8/59	EKF	12/59	FKF	3/60
ALV	9/58	BLV	2/59	CLV	5/59	DLV	9/59	ELV	12/59	FLV	4/60

Cars				Motorcycles		
K	(from 1) 4/60		GKA	4/60	HKA	1/62
KB	(from 1) 1/61		GKB	6/60	HKB	5/62
KC	(from 1) 9/61		GKC	9/60	HKC	11/62
KD	(from 1) 6/62		GKD	3/61	HKD	4/63
KF	(from 1) 3/63		GKF	5/61	HKF	7/63
LV	(from 1001) 10/63		GLV	8/61	HLV	10/63

All vehicles
JKA   *3/64*
JKB   *4/64*
JKC   *c. 3/75 re-registrations only*

Suffix marks commenced 1.5.64.

COUNTY BOROUGH COUNCIL OF MANCHESTER

N	1/04	NB	5/19	ND	3/23	NF	8/26	VR	5/29	XJ	3/32
NA	10/13	NC	8/20	NE	3/25	VM	2/28	VU	7/30		

A single sequence for all vehicles.

First issues each year, (no information available prior to 1929) :

1929	VM 6394	1931	VU 2271	1933	XJ 5162
1930	VR 4876	1932	VU 8586		

ANA	9/33	ENA	11/37	JNA	10/47	NNA	9/52	SNA	9/55	WNA	5/58
ANB	11/33	ENB	12/37	JNB	12/47	NNB	10/52	SNB	10/55	WNB	6/58
ANC	12/33	ENC	2/38	JNC	2/48	NNC	11/52	SNC	10/55	WNC	7/58
AND	2/34	END	3/38	JND	4/48	NND	12/52	SND	11/55	WND	7/58
ANE	3/34	ENE	4/38	JNE	5/48	NNE	1/53	SNE	12/55	WNE	8/58
ANF	4/34	ENF	5/38	JNF	7/48	NNF	3/53	SNF	1/56	WNF	9/58
AVM	6/34	EVM	6/38	JVM	8/48	NVM	4/53	SVM	2/56	WVM	10/58
AVR	7/34	EVR	7/38	JVR	10/48	NVR	5/53	SVR	3/56	WVR	10/58
AVU	9/34	EVU	9/38	JVU	11/48	NVU	6/53	SVU	3/56	WVU	11/58
AXJ	10/34	EXJ	10/38	JXJ	1/49	NXJ	7/53	SXJ	4/56	WXJ	12/58
BNA	12/34	FNA	11/38	KNA	3/49	ONA	8/53	TNA	5/56	XNA	12/58
BNB	1/35	FNB	12/38	KNB	4/49	ONB	9/53	TNB	6/56	XNB	1/59
BNC	3/35	FNC	2/39	KNC	5/49	ONC	10/53	TNC	6/56	XNC	2/59
BND	4/35	FND	3/39	KND	7/49	OND	11/53	TND	7/56	XND	3/59
BNE	5/35	FNE	3/39	KNE	8/49	ONE	12/53	TNE	9/56	XNE	3/59
BNF	6/35	FNF	4/39	KNF	9/49	ONF	1/54	TNF	10/56	XNF	4/59
BVM	7/35	FVM	5/39	KVM	11/49	OVM	2/54	TVM	11/56	XVM	4/59
BVR	9/35	FVR	6/39	KVR	1/50	OVR	3/54	TVR	12/56	XVR	5/59
BVU	10/35	FVU	7/39	KVU	2/50	OVU	4/54	TVU	1/57	XVU	5/59
BXJ	12/35	FXJ	8/39	KXJ	4/50	OXJ	5/54	TXJ	2/57	XXJ	5/59
CNA	1/36	GNA	12/39	LNA	5/50	PNA	6/54	UNA	3/57		
CNB	2/36	GNB	3/40	LNB	6/50	PNB	7/54	UNB	4/57		
CNC	3/36	GNC	6/40	LNC	7/50	PNC	7/54	UNC	4/57		
CND	4/36	GND	5/41	LND	9/50	PND	8/54	UND	5/57		
CNE	5/36	GNE	4/43	LNE	10/50	PNE	9/54	UNE	6/57		
CNF	6/36	GNF	9/45	LNF	12/50	PNF	10/54	UNF	6/57		
CVM	7/36	GVM	2/46	LVM	1/51	PVM	11/54	UVM	7/57		
CVR	9/36	GVR	4/46	LVR	2/51	PVR	12/54	UVR	7/57		
CVU	10/36	GVU	5/46	LVU	4/51	PVU	1/55	UVU	8/57		
CXJ	11/36	GXJ	6/46	LXJ	5/51	PXJ	1/55	UXJ	9/57		
DNA	12/36	HNA	8/46	MNA	7/51	RNA	2/55	VNA	10/57		
DNB	2/37	HNB	9/46	MNB	8/51	RNB	3/55	VNB	11/57		
DNC	3/37	HNC	10/46	MNC	9/51	RNC	3/55	VNC	12/57		
DND	4/37	HND	12/46	MND	11/51	RND	4/55	VND	1/58		
DNE	5/37	HNE	1/47	MNE	1/52	RNE	5/55	VNE	1/58		
DNF	6/37	HNF	3/47	MNF	2/52	RNF	5/55	VNF	2/58		
DVM	6/37	HVM	4/47	MVM	4/52	RVM	6/55	VVM	3/58		
DVR	7/37	HVR	5/47	MVR	5/52	RVR	7/55	VVR	3/58		
DVU	9/37	HVU	6/47	MVU	6/52	RVU	7/55	VVU	4/58		
DXJ	10/37	HXJ	8/47	MXJ	8/52	RXJ	8/55	VXJ	5/58		

When XXJ was completed cars etc. went into reverse marks, commencing with *N* in 6/59, then two-letter marks, whilst motorcycles used up YNA to YXJ. When the latter was completed, motorcycles also went into reverse (two-letter) marks. (Cars in motorcycle series were not uncommon.)

Cars etc.				Motorcycles			
1000-9999 *N*	*6/59*			YNA	*6/59*	100-999 *NB*	*5/63*
1000-9999 *NA*	*12/59*			YNB	*8/59*	101-999 *NE*	*8/63*
1000-9999 *NB*	*5/60*			YNC	*11/59*	100-999 *NF*	*1/64*
100-9999 *NC*	*10/60*			YND	*3/60*	100-767 *VM*	*5/64*
100-9999 *ND*	*5/61*			YNE	*5/60*		
1000-9999 *NE*	*12/61*			YNF	*10/60*		
1000-9999 *NF*	*6/62*			YVM	*4/61*		
1000-9999 *VM*	*1/63*			YVR	*8/61*		
1000-9999 *VR*	*5/63*			YVU	*3/62*		
100-9999 *VU*	*11/63*			YXJ	*9/62*		
1 up	*XJ*	*4/64*					

Special marks for Diplomatic Corps : IND 1 (ca. 7/59); *1 VNA* /96.

Suffix marks commenced 1.7.64

200

COUNTY BOROUGH COUNCIL OF MERTHYR TYDFIL

Merthyr Tydfil was created a County Borough and commenced issuing registrations as from 1.4.08.

HB 4/08

A single sequence for all vehicles, First issues each year :

1909	15	1922	1746	1935	4697	1948	6525
1910	37	1923	1866	1936	4917	1949	6737
1911	72	1924	2068	1937	5199	1950	6912
1912	97	1925	2377	1938	5458	1951	7054
1913	124	1926	2710	1939	5692	1952	7197
1914	212	1927	2909	1940	5912	1953	7414
1915	395	1928	3170	1941	5929	1954	7736
1916	536	1929	3344	1942	5934	1955	8142
1917	611	1930	3557	1943	5965	1956	8637
1918	639	1931	3844	1944	5983	1957	9100
1919	655	1932	4063	1945	6033	1958	9621
1920	993	1933	4276	1946	6095		
1921	1622	1934	4454	1947	6316		

AHB 8/58   BHB 2/60   CHB 5/61   DHB 10/62   EHB 11/63

Commenced suffix marks 1.4.64

COUNTY BOROUGH COUNCIL OF MIDDLESBROUGH

DC 12/03   XG 4/30

Separate and duplicated series for cars, (including HMCs), and motorcycles prior to 1921. The final figure for each sequence is not known but the cycle series had reached DC 732 by 4/15 and the cars DC 823 by 9/19.

First issues each year. No information available for the years not shown.

Motor Cars		Motorcycles		Motor Cars		Motorcycles	
1904	DC 2	DC 1		1912	DC 312	DC 322	
1905	DC 58	DC 58		1913	DC 350	DC 381	
1906	DC 83	DC 80		1914	DC 432	DC 514	
1907	DC 117	DC 117		1915	DC 539	DC 676	
1908	DC 152	DC 148		1916	DC 617		
1909	DC 187	DC 182		1917	DC 687		
1910	DC 241	DC 228		1918	DC 715		
1911	DC 260	DC 256					

		All Vehicles					
1929	DC 8700	1934	XG 2350	1939	XG 6501	1944	XG 7946
1930	DC 9700	1935	XG 3000	1940	XG 7427	1945	XG 7988
1931	XG 570	1936	XG 3800	1941	XG 7745	1946	XG 8124
1932	XG 1100	1937	XG 4600	1942	XG 7830	1947	XG 8968
1933	XG 1850	1938	XG 5600	1943	XG 7900	1948	XG 9759

ADC	5/48	DDC	11/53	GDC	10/56	KDC	3/59	NDC	10/60	RDC	10/62
AXG	7/49	DXG	6/54	GXG	3/57	KXG	6/59	NXG	3/61	RXG	4/63
BDC	7/50	EDC	12/54	HDC	7/57	LDC	9/59	ODC	5/61	SDC	7/63
BXG	5/51	EXG	5/55	HXG	1/58	LXG	1/60	OXG	8/61	SXG	11/63
CDC	5/52	FDC	10/55	JDC	6/58	MDC	4/60	PDC	2/62	TDC	ca./76*
CXG	3/53	FXG	3/56	JXG	11/58	MXG	7/60	PXG	6/62	* Re-registrations only

Suffix marks commenced 2.3.64.

The County Borough of Middlesbrough was amalgamated with the Borough of Stockton-on-Tees and the Urban District of Eston to form the new County Borough of Teesside as from 1.4.68

BB 12/03   TN 1/25   VK 5/29

First issues each year, (no information available prior to 1929) :

1929	TN 8987	1931	VK 3801	1933	VK 8440
1930	VK 1263	1932	VK 6100		

ABB	7/33	BBB	1/37	JBB	10/39	NBB	5/49	SBB	3/53	WBB	4/55
ATN	12/33	BTN	3/37	JTN	6/41	NTN	9/49	STN	5/53	WTN	6/55
AVK	3/34	BVK	6/37	JVK	7/44	NVK	12/49	SVK	7/53	WVK	7/55
BBB	7/34	FBB	9/37	KBB	2/46	OBB	4/50	TBB	10/53	XBB	9/55
BTN	11/34	FTN	12/37	KTN	7/46	OTN	7/50	TTN	12/53	XTN	11/55
BVK	3/35	FVK	3/38	KVK	11/46	OVK	11/50	TVK	3/54	XVK	1/56
CBB	5/35	GBB	5/38	LBB	3/47	PBB	3/51	UBB	5/54	YBB	3/56
CTN	9/35	GTN	7/38	LTN	7/47	PTN	7/51	UTN	7/54	YTN	4/56
CVK	1/36	GVK	11/38	LVK	12/47	PVK	12/51	UVK	9/54	YVK	6/56
DBB	3/36	HBB	1/39	MBB	5/48	RBB	4/52	VBB	11/54		
DTN	6/36	HTN	4/39	MTN	9/48	RTN	8/52	VTN	1/55		
DVK	10/36	HVK	6/39	MVK	2/49	RVK	12/52	VVK	3/55		

ABB	8/56	EBB	6/58	JBB	10/59	NBB	10/60	TBB	4/62
ATN	10/56	ETN	7/58	JTN	11/59	NTN	12/60	TTN	5/62
AVK	1/57	EVK	9/58	JVK	11/59 *	NVK	2/61	TVK	6/62
BBB	3/57	FBB	11/58	KBB	12/59	PBB	3/61	UBB	7/62
BTN	5/57	FTN	1/59	KTN	2/60	PTN	4/61	UTN	9/62
BVK	6/57	FVK	2/59	KVK	3/60	PVK	5/61	UVK	10/62
CBB	7/57	GBB	3/59	LBB	3/60	RBB	6/61	VBB	12/62
CTN	9/57	GTN	4/59	LTN	4/60	RTN	7/61	VTN	2/63
CVK	11/57	GVK	5/59	LVK	5/60	RVK	8/61	VVK	3/63
DBB	1/58	HBB	6/59	MBB	6/60	SBB	10/61		
DTN	3/58	HTN	7/59	MTN	7/60	STN	1/62		
DVK	4/58	HVK	8/59	MVK	8/60	SVK	2/62		

On completion of *VVK* in 4/63, *BB* was issued simultaneously with *WBB to XBB* until 12/63. Motorcycles were not especially segregated and it was largely left to the choice of an individual motorist whether he received a *BB* mark or a three-letter one.

BB (from 1001) 4/63		WBB	4/63
		WTN	6/63
		WVK	8/63
		XBB	10/63

* *JVK* was reserved for Newcastle Corporation Transport buses and other municipal vehicles and remained in use until 12/63.

Suffix marks commenced 2.1.64.

COUNTY BOROUGH COUNCIL OF NEWPORT

DW 1/04

A single sequence for all vehicles.

No information is available on first issues each year before 1913, but the following random issue dates are known :

1907 DW 68 (5/07)   1909 DW 188 (4/08)   1909 DW 216 (1/09)   1911 DW 281 (3/11).

Figures for 1912-1918 are approximate, but accurate within + or - 5.

1912	DW 356		1919	DW 1166		1926	DW 4681	1933	DW 8091
1913	DW 470		1920	DW 1381		1927	DW 5211	1934	DW 8508
1914	DW 608		1921	DW 2098		1928	DW 5789	1935	DW 9060
1915	DW 780		1922	DW 2532		1929	DW 6290	1936	DW 9741
1916	DW 942		1923	DW 2924		1930	DW 6843		
1917	DW 1066		1924	DW 3364		1931	DW 7306		
1918	DW 1150		1925	DW 3933		1932	DW 7677		

ADW	4/36	EDW	3/47	JDW	4/53	NDW	7/56	SDW	6/59	WDW	9/60
BDW	7/37	FDW	9/48	KDW	4/54	ODW	7/57	TDW	10/59	XDW	3/61
CDW	11/38	GDW	3/50	LDW	2/55	PDW	4/58	UDW	2/60	YDW	7/61
DDW	4/42	HDW	9/51	MDW	10/55	RDW	12/58	VDW	5/60		

Reverse issues commenced 2/62 with *DW* from 501 for all vehicles, but when this series reached 999 a separate series, *ADW*, followed by *BDW*, was used for cycles. *DW* continuing for other vehicles until the commencement of year-letter marks.

DW from 501 2/62

ADW 5/62 Cycles only
BDW 3/64 Cycles only

Commenced suffix marks 1.7.64

COUNTY BOROUGH COUNCIL OF NORTHAMPTON

DF 1/04   NH 7/05   VV 6/30

A single sequence for all vehicles.

Following representations from motorists objecting to the initial allocation of DF, the Council made a request to the Local Government Board for a change of index mark. The Board originally proposed FY, but eventually acceded to the Council's request for the allocation of NH. As in the case of Dorset, the substitution was optional, but no records as to the extent of issues in DF, or of substitutions, have survived.
(DF was subsequently reallocated to Gloucester C.C.)

No information is available on first issues each year prior to 1929.

1929	NH 8804		1934	VV 2462		1939	VV 7579	1944	VV 8849
1930	NH 9591		1935	VV 3390		1940	VV 8418	1945	VV 8900
1931	VV 358		1936	VV 4446		1941	VV 8646	1946	VV 9057
1932	VV 1040		1937	VV 5584		1942	VV 8725	1947	VV 9868
1933	VV 1676		1938	VV 6685		1943	VV 8806		

ANH	2/47	DNH	12/52	GNH	6/56	KNH	2/59	NNH	1/61	RNH	12/62
AVV	2/48	DVV	10/53	GVV	2/57	KVV	6/59	NVV	3/61	RVV	4/63
BNH	4/49	ENH	6/54	HNH	6/57	LNH	9/59	ONH	7/61	SNH	7/63
BVV	3/50	EVV	12/54	HVV	11/57	LVV	1/60	OVV	12/61	SVV	10/63
CNH	2/51	FNH	7/55	JNH	5/58	MNH	4/60	PNH	3/62	TNH	1/64
CVV	2/52	FVV	12/55	JVV	10/58	MVV	7/60	PVV	8/62	TVV	4/64

Commenced suffix marks 1.7.64

COUNTY BOROUGH COUNCIL OF NORWICH

CL 1/04   VG 8/27

No information is available on first issues each year prior to 1929. The following random dates of issue are known :

1906 : CL 206 2/06		1924 : CL 6405 2/24	
1908 : CL 410 6/08		1927 : CL 9779 4/27 – VG 140 11/27	
1919 : CL 2889 3/19		1928 : VG 259 1/28	

First issues each year :

1929	VG 1190	1932	VG 4234	1935	VG 7175
1930	VG 2268	1933	VG 5137	1936	VG 8376
1931	VG 3300	1934	VG 6123	1937	VG 9646

ACL	4/37	ECL	7/50	JCL	11/55	NCL	6/59	SCL	6/61	WCL	10/63
AVG	1/38	EVG	7/51	JVG	5/56	NVG	9/59	SVG	10/61	WVG	1/64
BCL	12/38	FCL	6/52	KCL	12/56	OCL	12/59	TCL	3/62	XCL	4/64
BVG	2/40	FVG	4/53	KVG	7/57	OVG	4/60	TVG	6/62	XVG	6/64
CCL	5/46	GCL	10/53	LCL	1/58	PCL	6/60	UCL	9/62	YCL	9/64
CVG	4/47	GVG	5/54	LVG	6/58	PVG	10/60	UVG	2/63	YVG	11/64
DCL	6/48	HCL	12/54	MCL	11/58	RCL	2/61	VCL	4/63		
DVG	8/49	HVG	6/55	MVG	3/59	RVG	4/61	VVG	7/63		

Commenced suffix marks 1.1.65   Special mark for Diplomatic Corps: 2 SVG 12/98

COUNTY BOROUGH COUNCIL OF NOTTINGHAM

AU 12/03   TO 4/24   TV 5/29

First issues each year, (no information available prior to 1929).

1929	TO 9073	1931	TV 3464	1933	TV 7643	
1930	TV 1320	1932	TO 5606	1934	TV 9956	

AAU	1/34	EAU	9/37	JAU	11/46	NAU	10/50	SAU	1/54	WAU	12/55
ATO	5/34	ETO	12/37	JTO	3/47	NTO	2/51	STO	3/54	WTO	2/56
ATV	10/34	ETV	4/38	JTV	6/47	NTV	7/51 *	STV	5/54	WTV	3/56
BAU	2/35	FAU	8/36	KAU	10/47	OAU	11/51	TAU	7/54	XAU	5/56
BTO	7/35	FTO	12/38	KTO	2/48	OTO	4/52	TTO	10/54	XTO	7/56
BTV	11/35	FTV	3/39	KTV	6/48	OTV	7/52	TTV	11/54	XTV	10/56
CAU	3/36	GAU	6/39	LAU	9/48	PAU	10/52	UAU	2/55	YAU	1/57
CTO	5/36	GTO	11/39	LTO	2/49	PTO	1/53	UTO	3/55	YTO	3/57
CTV	8/36	GTV	1/42	LTV	6/49	PTV	3/53	UTV	5/55	YTV	5/57
DAU	12/36	HAU	4/45	MAU	10/49	RAU	6/53	VAU	6/55		
DTO	3/37	HTO	5/46	MTO	2/50	RTO	9/53	VTO	8/55		
DTV	6/37	HTV	8/46	MTV	6/50	RTV	11/53	VTV	10/55		

* NTV 1 was an early issue 5/51 for Lord Mayoral Car.

AAU	7/57	EAU	4/59	JAU	6/60	NAU	12/61	TAU	7/63
ATO	9/57	ETO	5/59	JTO	7/60	NTO	2/62	TTO	8/63
ATV	11/57	ETV	6/59	JTV	8/60	NTV	3/62	TTV	9/63
BAU	2/58	FAU	7/59	KAU	10/60	PAU	5/62	UAU	11/63
BTO	3/58	FTO	8/59	KTO	12/60	PTO	6/62	UTO	12/63
BTV	5/58	FTV	10/59	KTV	2/61	PTV	7/62		
CAU	6/58	GAU	11/59	LAU	3/61	RAU	10/62		
CTO	8/58	GTO	12/59	LTO	4/61	RTO	12/62	VTO	1/64 #
CTV	10/58	GTV	2/60	LTV	5/61	RTV	2/63		
DAU	11/58	HAU	3/60	MAU	6/61	SAU	3/63		
DTO	1/59	HTO	4/60	MTO	8/61	STO	4/63		
DTV	3/59	HTV	5/60	MTV	10/61	STV	5/63		

1 VTO only - special issue for pilot of first vertical take-off aeroplane.

Commenced suffix marks 3.2.64

COUNTY BOROUGH COUNCIL OF OLDHAM

BU 12/03

There were originally three parallel and duplicate series, each commencing at BU 1. Motorcycles reached BU 1258 by the end of 1920, after which they joined the main series from BU 1848. Heavy Motor Cars used BU 1 to BU 166 before the separate series was abandoned.

First issues each year. No information available to writer prior to 1929, but details for 1903 to 1920 may be available at Oldham Library. The following dates are known for individual numbers or ranges within the main series :

1906	BU 67	1913	BU 421-464	1917	BU 813- 829		
1908	BU 143-152	1914	BU 573-579	1918	BU 853- 892		
1909	BU 191	1915	BU 599-709	1919	BU 956-1174		
1910	BU 225-247	1916	BU 717-782	1920	BU 1182-1313		
1929	BU 5730	1932	BU 7040	1935	BU 8400		
1930	BU 6300	1933	BU 7400	1936	BU 9049		
1931	BU 6690	1934	BY 7830	1937	BU 9877		

ABU	2/37	EBU	5/47	JBU	4/53	NBU	6/56	SBU	12/58	WBU	6/60
BBU	3/38	FBU	10/48	KBU	4/54	OBU	4/57	TBU	5/59	XBU	11/60
CBU	5/39	GBU	3/50	LBU	4/55	PBU	11/57	UBU	10/59	YBU	4/61
DBU	4/46	HBU	9/51	MBU	10/55	RBU	5/58	VBU	3/60		

ABU	7/61	CBU	5/62	EBU	3/63	GBU	10/63	JBU	4/64		
BBU	1/62	DBU	10/62	FBU	6/63	HBU	2/64	KBU	7/64		

Commenced suffix marks 4.8.64.

Vehicle and Driver Licensing - Isles of Scilly.

1. Councils will wish to know that as from 1 April 1971 vehicles used or kept on public roads in the Isles of Scilly will require to be registered and licensed in the same way as vehicles in the rest of Great Britain.

2. It has been arranged that Cornwall County Council will act as the Secretary of State's agent for the Isles of Scilly in this and driving licensing matters and records will be retained by that Council in their offices at Truro.

3. New vehicles registered and licensed by or on behalf of an applicant who is resident in the Isles of Scilly will be assigned a registration mark in the SCY series. This mark was previously held for use by Swansea County Borough Council and Councils should amend copies of VE 182 accordingly.

M.o.T. Memo 31/71, 19.3.71

COUNTY BOROUGH COUNCIL OF OXFORD

FC 12/03   WL 12/25   JO 6/30

First issues each year. No information is available prior to 1923 and all figures shown are approximate :

1923	FC 5009	1926	FC 9853 *	1929	WL 6238	1932	JO 3600
1924	FC 6134	1927	WL 1858 **	1930	WL 8700	1933	JO 6100
1925	FC 7631	1928	WL 4008	1931	JO 800	1934	JO 8650

* Early issues in WL were irregular : WL 2 isolated issue in 10/25; WL 3-15 in 12/25 and became general issue, (including WL 1), when FC was completed in 3/26. FC 9999 late issue 6/26.

** WL 1900 early issue in 1926.

Three-letter marks were issued in the same sequence as the basic two-letter marks.

AFC	5/34	EFC	1/37	JFC	8/39	NFC	2/48	SFC	1/52	WFC	9/54
AWL	7/34	EWL	4/37	JWL	7/44	NWL	7/48	SWL	4/52	WWL	11/54
AJO	12/34	EJO	5/37	JJO	9/44	NJO	1/49	SJO	8/52	WJO	2/55
BFC	3/35	FFC	7/37	KFC	2/46	OFC	5/49	TFC	10/52	XFC	3/55
BWL	5/35	FWL	11/37	KWL	4/46	OWL	9/49	TWL	2/53	XWL	5/55
BJO	7/35	FJO	3/38	KJO	7/46	OJO	12/49	TJO	4/53	XJO	6/55
CFC	10/35	GFC	4/38	LFC	8/46	PFC	4/50	UFC	6/53	YFC	8/55
CWL	1/36	GWL	7/38	LWL	11/46	PWL	7/50	UWL	9/53	YWL	10/55
CJO	4/36	GJO	11/38	LJO	1/47	PJO	10/50	UJO	12/53	YJO	1/56
DFC	5/36	HFC	2/39	MFC	5/47	RFC	2/51	VFC	3/54		
DWL	8/36	HWL	4/39	MWL	7/47	RWL	6/51	VWL	5/54		
DJO	11/36	HJO	6/39	MJO	10/47	RJO	9/51	VJO	7/54		

AFC	3/56	EFC	9/58	JFC	4/60	NFC	3/62	TFC	1/64
AWL	6/56	EWL	11/58	JWL	6/60	NWL	4/62	TWL	2/64
AJO	9/56	EJO	1/59	JJO	7/60	NJO	5/62	TJO	3/64
BFC	1/57	FFC	3/59	KFC	8/60	PFC	7/62	UFC	4/64
BWL	3/57	FWL	4/59	KWL	10/60	PWL	10/62	UWL	6/64
BJO	5/57	FJO	6/59	KJO	1/61	PJO	12/62	UJO	7/64
CFC	7/57	GFC	7/59	LFC	3/61	RFC	3/63	VFC	9/64
CWL	9/57	GWL	9/59	LWL	4/61	RWL	5/63	VWL	10/64
CJO	12/57	GJO	10/59	LJO	5/61	RJO	6/63	VJO	6/72 Re-registrations only
DFC	3/58	HFC	12/59	MFC	7/61	SFC	7/63		
DWL	5/58	HWL	2/60	MWL	10/61	SWL	9/63		
DJO	7/58	HJO	3/60	MJO	11/61	SJO	10/63		

Commenced suffix marks 1.1.65.

COUNTY BOROUGH COUNCIL OF PLYMOUTH

CO 1/04   DR 6/26 *   JY 3/32

A single sequence for all vehicles.   * DR 1-268 were issued by the County Borough of Devonport between 1/04 and 3/15. On 1.4.15 Devonport was absorbed into the enlarged County Borough of Plymouth, who issued DR 269 up from 6/26.

First issues each year. No information prior to 1921, and figures for 1921-1928 are approximate :

1921	CO 3750	1927	DR 1184	1933	JY 1136
1922	CO 4425	1928	DR 2835	1934	JY 2781
1923	CO 5293	1929	DR 4540	1935	JY 4828
1924	CO 6308	1930	DR 6165	1936	JY 7273
1925	CO 7515	1931	DR 7856	1937	JY 9546
1926	CO 9000	1932	DR 9521		

ACO	2/37	ECO	11/47	JCO	10/53	NCO	4/57	SCO	9/59	WCO	10/61
ADR	6/37	EDR	6/48	JDR	2/54	NDR	7/57	SDR	11/59	WDR	2/62
AJY	12/37	EJY	1/49	JJY	6/54	NJY	10/57	SJY	2/60	WJY	4/62
BCO	5/38	FCO	7/49	KCO	10/54	OCO	1/58	TCO	3/60	XCO	6/62
BDR	10/38	FDR	1/50	KDR	1/55	ODR	4/58	TDR	5/60	XDR	9/62
BJY	3/39	FJY	6/50	KJY	4/55	OJY	6/58	TJY	7/60	XJY	12/62
CCO	7/39	GCO	12/50	LCO	7/55	PCO	9/58	UCO	9/60	YCO	3/63
CDR	7/40	GDR	6/51	LDR	10/55	PDR	12/58	UDR	11/60	YDR	5/63
CJY	4/45	GJY	1/52	LJY	1/56	PJY	2/59	UJY	2/61	YJY	7/63
DCO	5/46	HCO	7/52	MCO	5/56	RCO	4/59	VCO	4/61		
DDR	11/46	HDR	1/53	MDR	9/56	RDR	6/59	VDR	6/61		
DJY	5/47	HJY	6/53	MJY	1/57	RJY	7/59	VJY	7/61		

Special Mark for Diplomatic Corps : *1 MCO* ca. 8/77   *1 CDR* 1999

Commenced suffix marks 12.9.63

COUNTY BOROUGH COUNCIL OF PORTSMOUTH

BK 12/03   TP 4/24   RV 2/31

A single sequence for all vehicles but motorcycles numbered in blocks in BK and TP :
BK 1000 - 1999, 3001 - 3999, 5000 - 5999, 7001 - 7999, 9001 - 9999; TP 1000 - 1999, 3001 - 3999, 5001 - 5998.

First issues each year, (no information available prior to 1929) :

1929	TP 7362	1931	TP 9827	1933	RV 2940	1935	RV 6040
1930	TP 8544	1932	RV 1372	1934	RV 4401	1936	RV 8002

Three-letter marks were issued in the same sequence as the basic two-letter marks.

ABK	11/36	EBK	7/48	JBK	11/53	NBK	8/56	SBK	1/59	WBK	9/60
ATP	4/37	ETP	3/49	JTP	2/54	NTP	11/56	STP	3/59	WTP	11/60
ARV	8/37	ERV	9/49	JRV	5/54	NRV	3/57	SRV	5/59	WRV	1/61
BBK	2/38	FBK	2/50	KBK	8/54	OBK	5/57	TBK	6/59	XBK	3/61
BTP	8/38	FTP	8/50	KTP	11/54	OTP	7/57	TTP	8/59	XTP	5/61
BRV	3/39	FRV	1/51	KRV	2/55	ORV	9/57	TRV	9/59	XRV	6/61
CBK	7/39	GBK	7/51	LBK	5/55	PBK	12/57	UBK	11/59	YBK	8/61
CTP	9/42	GTP	1/52	LTP	7/55	PTP	3/58	UTP	1/60	YTP	11/61
CRV	4/46	GRV	6/52	LRV	9/55	PRV	5/58	URV	3/60	YRV	1/62
DBK	10/46	HBK	11/52	MBK	11/55	RBK	7/58	VBK	4/60		
DTP	5/47	HTP	4/53	MTP	3/56	RTP	10/58	VTP	5/60		
DRV	12/47	HRV	7/53	MRV	5/56	RRV	11/58	VRV	7/60		

ABK	*4/62*	*BBK*	*9/62*	*CBK*	*4/63*	*DBK*	*9/63*	*EBK*	*2/66 *
ATP	*5/62*	*BTP*	*12/62*	*CTP*	*6/63*	*DTP*	*11/63*	*Re-registrations only*
ARV	*7/62*	*BRV*	*2/63*	*CRV*	*7/63*	*DRV*	*1/64*	

Special mark for Diplomatic Corps : *1 HRV* ca 3/98

Suffix marks commenced 2.3.64

COUNTY BOROUGH COUNCIL OF PRESTON

CK 1/04   RN 10/28

A single sequence for all vehicles, but separate blocks of numbers for motor cars, motorcycles and heavy motor cars. This segregation persisted until the completion of RN, the heavy motor car series being perpetuated after 1920 for all commercial vehicles.

The following table shows the blocks allocated to each category, the commencing date of each block and the first issues each year :

Motor Cars		Motorcycles		HMC/Commercials	
CK 1- 49	1/04	CK 50- 400	1/04	CK 401- 500	3/05
CK 501-1000	5/05	CK 1001-1999	5/11		
CK 2000-2999*	2/18	CK 5001-7999	7/20	CK 3001-5000	8/16
CK 8001-9999	3/23				
RN 1#-7500	10/28	RN 9001-9650	7/35	RN 7501-9000	9/34
RN 9651-9999	4/39				

* CK 3000 unused.

\# Normal issues of RN commenced at RN 101; RN 1 to RN 100 were issued individually and at random between 1/29 and 5/38. Although RN commenced 10/28 the CK car block was not completed until 12/28.

1905	CK 44	CK 138	CK 401		
1906	CK 523	CK 184	CK 428		
1907	CK 546	CK 229	CK 441		
1908	CK 571	CK 264	none issued		
1909	CK 588	CK 302	CK 445		
1910	CK 608	CK 325	CK 448		
1911	CK 629	CK 369	CK 452		
1912	CK 655	CK 1036	CK 455		
1913	CK 688	CK 1126	CK 464		
1914	CK 744	CK 1248	CK 474		
1915	CK 809	CK 1374	CK 482		
1916	CK 889	CK 1457 *	CK 490		
1917	CK 966	CK 1494	CK 3009		
1918	CK 997	CK 1513	CK 3038		
1919	CK 2018	CK 1521	CK 3074		
1920	CK 2149	CK 1715	CK 3172		
1921	CK 2518	CK 5103	CK 3386		
1922	CK 2780	CK 5291	CK 3444		
1923	CK 2963	CK 5437	CK 3493		
1924	CK 8202	CK 5675	CK 3545		
1925	CK 8500	CK 5954	CK 3629		
1926	CK 8836	CK 6221	CK 3713		
1927	CK 9182	CK 6523	CK 3806		
1928	CK 9601	CK 6749	CK 3913		
1929	RN 198	CK 6900	CK 4119		
1930	RN 777	CK 7108	CK 4255		
1931	RN 1233	CK 7285	CK 4561		
1932	RN 1775	CK 7423	CK 4617		
1933	RN 2324	CK 7579	CK 4701		
1934	RN 3080	CK 7749	CK 4843		
1935	RN 3925	CK 7923	RN 7544		
1936	RN 4749	RN 9050	RN 7844		
1937	RN 5576	RN 9211	RN 8129		
1938	RN 6406	RN 9366	RN 8475		
1939	RN 7204	RN 9512	RN 8846		
1940			RN 8949		

* CK 1550/1 issued 10/15 in error for 1450/1.

RN 9000 reached 2/40 and RN 9650 7/39; normal issues in car block finished 12/39.

ACK	12/39	BCK	3/51	JCK	9/55	NCK	6/59	SCK	4/62
ARN	10/45	BRN	12/51	JRN	3/56	NRN	11/59	SRN	9/62
BCK	10/46	FCK	9/52	KCK	10/56	OCK	3/60	TCK	2/63
BRN	6/47	FRN	5/53	KRN	4/57	ORN	6/60	TRN	5/63
CCK	4/48	GCK	11/53	LCK	9/57	PCK	11/60	UCK	9/63
CRN	1/49	GRN	5/54	LRN	3/58	PRN	3/61	URN	1/64
DCK	10/49	HCK	11/54	MCK	8/58	RCK	6/61	VCK	5/64
DRN	7/50	HRN	4/55	MRN	3/59	RRN	11/61		

Special issues for Diplomatic Corps : WRN 1 ca. 9/56; *1 ERN* ca. 8/57; *1 GRN* ca. 8/75.

Commenced suffix marks 1.7.64.

COUNTY BOROUGH COUNCIL OF READING

DP 12/03   RD 9/28

First issues each year, (no information available prior to 1929) :

1929	RD 260		1932	RD 3150		1935	RD 6345
1930	RD 1290		1933	RD 3990		1936	RD 7700
1931	RD 2300		1934	RD 5050		1937	RD 9151

ADP	7/37	EDP	5/49	JDP	12/53	NDP	1/57	SDP	4/59	WDP	9/60
ARD	4/38	ERD	2/50	JRD	5/54	NRD	5/57	SRD	6/59	WRD	12/60
BDP	1/39	FDP	10/50	KDP	9/54	ODP	8/57	TDP	8/59	XDP	3/61
BRD	9/39	FRD	5/51	KRD	3/55	ORD	1/58	TRD	10/59	XRD	5/61
CDP	7/45	GDP	11/51	LDP	6/55	PDP	4/58	UDP	12/59	YDP	8/61
CRD	11/46	GRD	6/52	LRD	10/55	PRD	7/58	URD	3/60	YRD	11/61
DDP	8/47	HDP	1/53	MDP	3/56	RDP	11/58	VDP	4/60		
DRD	6/48	HRD	8/53	MRD	7/56	RRD	2/59	VRD	7/60		

A single sequence for all vehicles in reverse format marks.

DP (from 1)   2/62   *RD (from 701)   3/64*

Commenced suffix marks 1.6.64

COUNTY BOROUGH COUNCIL OF ROCHDALE

DK 12/03

A single sequence for all vehicles.

First issues each year. No information available for 1922 to 1928, but 1927 and 1928 details may be available at Greater Manchester Record Office.   Figures for 1904 to 1919 are approximate.

1904	4		1913	331				1929	5401
1905	45		1914	437				1930	6301
1906	65		1915	585				1931	7051
1907	97		1916	768				1932	7612
1908	125		1917	880				1933	8281
1909	150		1918	905				1934	8884
1910	177		1919	928				1935	9691
1911	225		1920	1217					
1912	276		1921	1472					

ADK	4/35	EDK	3/39	JDK	6/51	NDK	5/55	SDK	10/57	WDK	1/60
BDK	4/36	FDK	1/46	KDK	2/53	ODK	11/55	TDK	5/58	XDK	5/60
CDK	3/37	GDK	1/48	LDK	1/54	PDK	6/56	UDK	1/59	YDK	10/60
DDK	3/38	HDK	9/49	MDK	10/54	RDK	3/57	VDK	7/59		

Reverse format marks commenced with *DK*, from 201 for motorcycles and 1000 for cars simultaneously 5/4/61. After *999 DK* motorcycles used *ADK*.

DK   4/61   *ADK   9/63*

Commenced suffix marks 1.6.64.

COUNTY BOROUGH COUNCIL OF ROTHERHAM

ET   12/03

A common sequence for all vehicles.

First issues each year. No information available for 1922, 1926-1928.

1904	ET	11	1912	ET	406	1920	ET	1468	1929 ET 5391
1905	ET	54	1913	ET	515	1921	ET	1937	1930 ET 6006
1906	ET	89	1914	ET	646				1931 ET 6503
1907	ET	117	1915	ET	823	1923	ET	2491	1932 ET 6980
1908	ET	147	1916	ET	1012	1924	ET	2846	1933 ET 7447
1909	ET	199	1917	ET	1121	1925	ET	3283	1934 ET 7973
1910	ET	249	1918	ET	1180				1935 ET 8660
1911	ET	318	1919	ET	1210				1936 ET 9307

AET	10/36	EET	12/47	JET	3/53	NET	10/55	SET	3/58	WET	4/60
BET	12/37	FET	5/49	KET	12/53	OET	5/56	TET	11/58	XET	8/60
CET	4/39	GET	9/50	LET	8/54	PET	1/57	UET	5/59	YET	3/61
DET	3/46	HET	1/52	MET	4/55	RET	6/57	VET	11/59		

Reverse format issues commenced with *ET* from 1000 for cars and *AET* for motorcycles. *AET* was followed by *BET*.

ET	*7/61*		*AET*	*7/61*
			BET	*2/64*

Suffix marks commenced 1.1.65

COUNTY BOROUGH COUNCIL OF ST. HELENS

DJ   1/04

Registration commenced 1.1.04.

A single sequence for all vehicles.

First issues each year.

1905	DJ	51	1916	DJ	533	*	1927	DJ 3008	1938	DJ 7917
1906	DJ	81	1917	DJ	590	*	1928	DJ 3435	1939	DJ 8400
1907	DJ	109	1918	DJ	624		1929	DJ 3853	1940	DJ 8834
1908	DJ	138	1919	DJ	637		1930	DJ 4367	1941	DJ 8938
1909	DJ	162	1920	DJ	846	*	1931	DJ 4871	1942	DJ 8989
1910	DJ	171	1921	DJ	1125	*	1932	DJ 5247	1943	DJ 9080
1911	DJ	181	1922	DJ	1381		1933	DJ 5552	1944	DJ 9104
1912	DJ	223	1923	DJ	1598		1934	DJ 5919	1945	DJ 9149
1913	DJ	282	1924	DJ	1876		1935	DJ 6363	1946	DJ 9289
1914	DJ	318	1925	DJ	2173		1936	DJ 6812	1947	DJ 9699
1915	DJ	416	1926	DJ	2584		1937	DJ 7351		

* approximate, (accurate to + or - 5)

ADJ	9/47	EDJ	1/55	JDJ	7/58	NDJ	8/60	SDJ	5/62	WDJ	10/63
BDJ	2/50	FDJ	12/55	KDJ	3/59	ODJ	2/61	TDJ	10/62	XDJ	2/64
CDJ	6/52	GDJ	12/56	LDJ	9/59	PDJ	6/61	UDJ	3/63		
DDJ	11/53	HDJ	10/57	MDJ	3/60	RDJ	11/61	VDJ	7/63		

Suffix marks commenced 1.4.64

COUNTY BOROUGH COUNCIL OF SALFORD

BA 1/04   RJ 6/31

A single sequence for all vehicles.

First issues each year :

1905	BA 141	1908	BA 373	1911	BA 598
1906	BA 194	1909	BA 446	1912	BA 726
1907	BA 266	1910	BA 509	1913	BA 872

Up to this point numbers had been issued in sequence, but in 1914, when the main series had reached just over 1000, a special block, BA 2000 up, was commenced for the Salford Fire Brigade. Further "specials" followed in 1915 (BA 1500 and 1881), whilst BA 1600 commenced a block of HMCs. Between 1916 and 1920 the issue sequence became quite chaotic, (BA 3000 was another "special" in 1917), and it was not until BA 2300 that something like an orderly progression was resumed. Hence it would be meaningless to quote first issues each year for 1914 to 1920 and instead the table shows all numbers issued in each of those years :

```
1914 : BA 1009-1217, 2000-2002
1915 : BA 1218-1391, 1500, 1600-5, 1881, 2003
1916 : BA 1392-1499, 1501-26, 1606-18/94/5, 1800, 2020/30-3
1917 : BA 1527-86/8, 1620-7/62, 1711/20/1, 2021/2/42, 3000
1918 : BA 1587/89-99, 1628-35/50/60/1/75, 1717-9/22-56/8-60, 1801/50-3, 1903/4, 2004/5/23
1919 : BA 1636-49/51-9/63-74/6-93/6-9, 1700-10/2-6/57/61-99, 1803-49/54-80/2-92, 1905/10-98,
         2006/11-9/24-8/34-41/3-95/7-9, 2100-41/3-77/9-99, 2200-30/2-9/41-8/54-89/91/3-9
1920 : BA 1893/4, 1906-9, 2007/96, 2137/42/78, 2231/40/9-53/90/2/7, 2300-2965
```

First issues each year :

1921	BA 2966	1926	BA 5628 *	1931	BA 9574	1936	RJ 5343
1922	BA 3545	1927	BA 6277	1932	RJ 366	1937	RJ 7164
1923	BA 3950	1928	BA 6874	1933	RJ 1207	1938	RJ 9439
1924	BA 4405	1929	BA 7634	1934	RJ 2218		
1925	BA 4921	1930	BA 8664	1935	RJ 3741		

* BA 6331-6344 issued in error for 6231-6244 in 1926; the latter being omitted.

ABA	4/38	EBA	9/49	JBA	2/55	NBA	6/58	SBA	6/60	WBA	6/62
ARJ	9/38	ERJ	8/50	JRJ	6/55	NRJ	10/58	SRJ	8/60	WRJ	9/62
BBA	4/39	FBA	7/51	KBA	12/55	OBA	2/59	TBA	11/60	XBA	2/63
BRJ	10/39	FRJ	7/52 *	KRJ	4/56	ORJ	5/59	TRJ	3/61	XRJ	3/63
CBA	10/46	GBA	3/53 #	LBA	9/56	PBA	8/59	UBA	5/61	YBA	5/63
CRJ	1/47	GRJ	9/53	LRJ	4/57	PRJ	11/59	URJ	7/61	YRJ	8/63
DBA	11/47	HBA	3/54	MBA	8/57	RBA	2/60	VBA	12/61		
DRJ	11/48	HRJ	9/54	MRJ	1/58	RRJ	4/60	VRJ	3/62		

* A batch of FRJ early for Salford City Transport buses (4/51)
# GBA 3 early for Salford City Transport service van (1/53).

Suffix marks commenced 1.11.63

COUNTY BOROUGH COUNCIL OF SHEFFIELD

W 1/04   WA 10/19   WB 4/24   WE 7/27   WJ 12/30

First issues each year. No information available prior to 1929, except 1905/6:

1905	W 138	1906	W 362				

| 1929 | WE 3763 | 1931 | WJ 242 | 1933 | WJ 5687 |
| 1930 | WE 6974 | 1932 | WJ 2953 | 1934 | WJ 8701 |

AWA	4/34	EWA	9/37	JWA	9/46	NWA	10/50	SWA	3/54	WWA	11/55
AWB	7/34	EWB	11/37	JWB	11/46	NWB	1/51	SWB	4/54	WWB	1/56
AWE	11/34	EWE	2/38	JWE	2/47	NWE	4/51	SWE	5/54	WWE	3/56
AWJ	2/35	EWJ	3/38	JWJ	4/47	NWJ	7/51	SWJ	7/54	WWJ	3/56
BWA	4/35	FWA	5/38	KWA	7/47	OWA	10/51	TWA	9/54	XWA	5/56
BWB	7/35	FWB	8/38	KWB	10/47	OWB	1/52	TWB	10/54	XWB	6/56
BWE	11/35	FWE	11/38	KWE	1/48	OWE	3/52	TWE	11/54	XWE	7/56
BWJ	1/36	FWJ	1/39	KWJ	5/48	OWJ	7/52	TWJ	1/55	XWJ	9/56
CWA	3/36	GWA	3/39	LWA	8/48	PWA	10/52	UWA	2/55	YWA	11/56
CWB	5/36	GWB	5/39	LWB	11/48	PWB	1/53	UWB	3/55	YWB	1/57
CWE	7/36	GWE	7/39	LWE	3/49	PWE	3/53	UWE	4/55	YWE	2/57
CWJ	10/36	GWJ	2/40	LWJ	6/49	PWJ	5/53	UWJ	6/55	YWJ	4/57
DWA	12/36	HWA	11/41	MWA	9/49	RWA	7/53	VWA	7/55		
DWB	3/37	HWB	4/44	MWB	12/49	RWB	9/53	VWB	8/55		
DWE	4/37	HWE	1/46	MWE	4/50	RWE	11/53	VWE	9/55		
DWJ	6/37	HWJ	5/46	MWJ	6/50	RWJ	1/54	VWJ	10/55		

Reverse format issues commenced with *WB* from 1 for all vehicles, followed by *WE* from 1, *WJ* from 1 and *W* from 1001. It was then decided to segregate motorcycles in *AWA*, followed by *AWB*. After *9999 W* cars used *WA* from 1001, then rejoined motorcycles from *492 AWB* up.

Cars etc.			Motorcycles	
WB from 1	5/57		**AWA**	6/60
WE from 1	5/58		**AWB**	3/61
WJ from 1	5/59			
W from 1001	3/60			
WA from 1001	10/60			

All Vehicles

		CWA	2/62	**EWA**	10/62	**GWA**	5/63	**JWA**	12/63
		CWB	3/62	**EWB**	11/62	**GWB**	5/63	**JWB**	1/64
AWE	7/61	**CWE**	4/62	**EWE**	12/62	**GWE**	6/63	**JWE**	ca. 8/75 re-registrations only.
AWJ	8/61	**CWJ**	5/62	**EWJ**	1/63	**GWJ**	7/63		
BWA	10/61	**DWA**	6/62	**FWA**	2/63	**HWA**	8/63		
BWB	11/61	**DWB**	7/62	**FWB**	3/63	**HWB**	9/63		
BWE	12/61	**DWE**	8/62	**FWE**	4/63	**HWE**	10/63		
BWJ	1/62	**DWJ**	9/62	**FWJ**	4/63	**HWJ**	11/63		

Commenced suffix marks 3.2.64.

COUNTY BOROUGH COUNCIL OF SMETHWICK

SMETHWICK was created a county borough and commenced issuing registrations from 1.4.07. On 1.4.66 it was incorporated into the new County Borough of WARLEY, who continued the issue of 'HA' marks.

HA   4/07

First issues each year, (no information is available prior to 1929).

1929	HA 5300	1931	HA 7120	1933	HA 8500
1930	HA 6140	1932	HA 7660	1934	HA 9200

AHA	8/34	EHA	9/37	JHA	8/46	NHA	7/49	SHA	6/52	WHA	7/54
BHA	5/35	FHA	7/38	KHA	4/47	OHA	3/50	THA	1/53	XHA	1/55
CHA	4/36	GHA	5/39	LHA	2/48	PHA	10/50	UHA	9/53	YHA	5/55
DHA	1/37	HHA	1/45 *	MHA	12/48	RHA	7/51	VHA	3/54		

* A batch of HHA early for Birmingham & Midland Motor Omnibus Co. Ltd., 3/1944.

Reverse format marks commenced with *AHA* in 9/55 for all vehicles and three-letter marks in order to *MHA*. Then *HA* from 501 for cars etc. and *NHA* for motorcycles simultaneously, 4/60, followed by *PHA, RHA* and *SHA*. A few *THA* were issued for re-registrations when *HA* was completed.

All Vehicles

AHA	9/55	CHA	6/56	EHA	5/57	GHA	4/58	JHA	1/59	LHA	8/59
BHA	2/56	DHA	1/57	FHA	10/57	HHA	8/58	KHA	5/59	MHA	1/60

Cars etc.

*HA (from 501 *)   4/60*

Motorcycles

NHA	4/60
PHA	3/61
RHA	5/62
SHA	10/63

* *1 HA and 2 HA special issues for civic cars.*

Re-registrations only

THA   ca. 6/76.

Commenced suffix issues 4.8.64

COUNTY BOROUGH COUNCIL OF SOUTHAMPTON

CR 12/03   TR 2/25   OW 2/31

Registration commenced 3.12.03

A single sequence for all vehicles.

First issues each year : (No information available for 1920-1928 and figures for 1914/16/17/18 are approximate) :

1904	CR	81	1912	CR	1227	1929	TR	6130
1905	CR	257	1913	CR	1513	1930	TR	7970
1906	CR	349	1914	CR	1850	1931	TR	9770
1907	CR	444	1915	CR	2308	1932	OW	1238
1908	CR	552	1916	CR	2850	1933	OW	2549
1909	CR	681	1917	CR	3250	1934	OW	4148
1910	CR	825	1918	CR	3450	1935	OW	6055
1911	CR	994	1919	CR	3725	1936	OW	8300

Three-letter marks were issued in the same sequence as the basic two-letter marks.

ACR	8/36	BCR	9/46	JCR	5/51	NCR	7/54	SCR	9/56	WCR	9/58
ATR	1/37	BTR	1/47	JTR	10/51	NTR	9/54	STR	12/56	WTR	10/58
AOW	6/37	BOW	6/47	JOW	2/52	NOW	12/54	SOW	3/57	WOW	12/58
BCR	10/37	FCR	11/47	KCR	5/52	OCR	2/55	TCR	4/57	XCR	2/59
BTR	3/38	FTR	5/48	KTR	8/52	OTR	4/55	TTR	6/57	XTR	4/59
BOW	6/38	FOW	12/48	KOW	12/52	OOW	5/55	TOW	8/57	XOW	5/59
CCR	11/38	GCR	5/49	LCR	3/53	PCR	7/55	UCR	10/57	YCR	6/59
CTR	2/39	GTR	9/49	LTR	6/53	PTR	10/55	UTR	11/57	YTR	7/59
COW	6/39	GOW	1/50	LOW	9/53	POW	1/56	UOW	2/58	YOW	8/59
DCR	2/40	HCR	6/50	MCR	12/53	RCR	3/56	VCR	4/58		
DTR	2/44	HTR	10/50	MTR	3/54	RTR	5/56	VTR	5/58		
DOW	4/46	HOW	3/51	MOW	6/54	ROW	7/56	VOW	7/58		

Reverse format issues commenced with *CR*, issued simultaneously from 201 up for motorcycles and 1000 up for cars from 9/59. After *999 CR* motorcycles briefly joined main *CR* series before commencing *ACR* in 6/60. After *9999 CR* cars used *1001 - 9999 TR* whilst after *ACR* was completed motorcycles used *201-999 TR*, then *ATR*. After *9999 TR* cars joined motorcycles from *776 ATR*.

Cars etc.

*1000-9999 CR *	9/59
1001-9999 TR #	10/60

Motorcycles

201-999 CR	9/59
ACR	6/60
201-999 TR	2/61
ATR	6/61 **

* Contains motorcycles in ca. *4xxx to 7xxx*.
** Mixed series from *776 ATR*.
# *1000 TR* apparently omitted.

All Vehicles

		CCR	7/62	BCR	5/63	GCR	2/64
		CTR	9/62	ETR	6/63	GTR	3/64
AOW	2/62	COW	10/62	EOW	7/63	GOW	4/64
BCR	3/62	DCR	1/63	FCR	9/63	HCR	5/64
BTR	5/62	DTR	2/63	FTR	10/63	HTR	6/64
BOW	6/52	DOW	4/63	FOW	12/63	HOW	12/64 Re-registrations only.

Special mark for Diplomatic Corps : QTR 1 ca. 7/75.

Suffix marks commenced 1.7.64

Mr David Napier
NHS Number: 6108481366
DoB: 23/10/1944
141 The Grove
Christchurch
Dorset
BH23 2EZ

The Grove Surgery
- Fairmile Road Fairmile
Christchurch
Dorset
BH23 2FQ

Prescription Start Date: 21/08/2020
Prescription Expiry Date: 21/02/2021

Patient Medication History

[ ] Co-codamol 8mg/500mg capsules, 32 capsule, take 1
or 2 4 times/day, Last Issued: Monday 20 Jul 2020, Next
Issue Due: Tue 21 Jul 2020

[ ] Pregabalin 100mg capsules, 56 capsule, take one
twice daily, Last Issued: Monday 03 Aug 2020, Next
Issue Due: Mon 31 Aug 2020

[ ] Omeprazole 20mg gastro-resistant capsules, 112
capsule, 1 -2 DAY, Last Issued: Monday 20 Jul 2020,
Next Issue Due: Mon 14 Sep 2020

[ ] Atorvastatin 40mg tablets, 56 tablet, 1on, Last
Issued: Monday 20 Jul 2020, Next Issue Due: Mon 14 Sep
2020

[ ] Bisoprolol 5mg tablets, 56 tablet, take one daily,
Last Issued: Monday 20 Jul 2020, Next Issue Due: Mon 14
Sep 2020

[ ] Metformin 500mg modified-release tablets, 28
tablet, 1 tablet a day, Last Issued: Monday 20 Jul
2020, Next Issue Due: Mon 14 Sep 2020

[ ] Tamsulosin 400microgram modified-release capsules,
60 capsule, ONE TO BE TAKEN DAILY, Last Issued: Monday
20 Jul 2020, Next Issue Due: Fri 18 Sep 2020

[ ] Aspirin 75mg dispersible tablets, 56 tablet, take
one daily, Last Issued: Monday 18 May 2020, Next Issue

When should I pay?

You must pay if none of the statements apply to you on the day you were asked to pay. These are the only accepted reasons for not paying.

I'm not sure if I should pay

Pay and ask for a **prescription refund form (FP57).** You can't get one later. If you find you didn't need to pay, you can claim a refund up to 3 months later.

What if I don't pay when I should?

We check claims made for free prescriptions. If we can't confirm that you are entitled to exemption from prescription charges, you may be issued a Penalty Charge Notice and you may have to pay up to £100 as well as your prescription charge(s), and you could be prosecuted.

Can I get help to pay?

Help with costs may be available. You could also save money by buying a prescription prepayment certificate.

Check at **www.nhsbsa.nhs.uk/check**

Is my exemption certificate still valid?

Visit www.nhsbsa.nhs.uk/exemption to see what help is available or ask at your GP surgery or pharmacy.

I am unable to collect my prescription

If you are unable to collect your prescription someone can do so on your behalf. Your representative should complete the 'If you paid' box and sign the form, or you or your representative should complete the 'If you didn't pay' box, and your representative should sign the form. Your representative will need to put a cross in the 'on behalf of patient' box next to their signature.

Why did the pharmacy ask to see evidence?

We need to check your exemption is valid.

The NHS Business Services Authority is responsible for this service. We will use your information to check your exemption is valid, pay the dispenser and help plan and improve NHS services. Find out more at www.nhsbsa.nhs.uk/yourinformation

Mr David Napier
NHS Number: 6108481366
DoB: 23/10/1944
141 The Grove
Christchurch
Dorset
BH23 2EZ

The Grove Surgery
- Fairmile Road Fairmile
Christchurch
Dorset
BH23 2FQ

Due: Mon 13 Jul 2020

[ ] Fexofenadine 120mg tablets, 60 tablet, ONE TO BE
TAKEN EACH MORNING, Last Issued: Tuesday 21 Jul 2020,
Next Issue Due: Sat 19 Sep 2020

[ ] Perindopril erbumine 2mg tablets, 56 tablet, take
one daily, Last Issued: Tuesday 21 Jul 2020, Next Issue
Due: Tue 15 Sep 2020

When should I pay?

You must pay if none of the statements apply to you on the day you were asked to pay. These are the only accepted reasons for not paying.

I'm not sure if I should pay

Pay and ask for a **prescription refund form (FP57).** You can't get one later. If you find you didn't need to pay, you can claim a refund up to 3 months later.

What if I don't pay when I should?

We check claims made for free prescriptions. If we can't confirm that you are entitled to exemption from prescription charges, you may be issued a Penalty Charge Notice and you may have to pay up to £100 as well as your prescription charge(s), and you could be prosecuted.

Can I get help to pay?

Help with costs may be available. You could also save money by buying a prescription prepayment certificate.

Check at **www.nhsbsa.nhs.uk/check**

Is my exemption certificate still valid?

Visit www.nhsbsa.nhs.uk/exemption to see what help is available or ask at your GP surgery or pharmacy.

I am unable to collect my prescription

If you are unable to collect your prescription someone can do so on your behalf. Your representative should complete the 'If you paid' box and sign the form, or you or your representative should complete the 'If you didn't pay' box, and your representative should sign the form. Your representative will need to put a cross in the 'on behalf of patient' box next to their signature.

Why did the pharmacy ask to see evidence?

We need to check your exemption is valid.

The NHS Business Services Authority is responsible for this service. We will use your information to check your exemption is valid, pay the dispenser and help plan and improve NHS services. Find out more at www.nhsbsa.nhs.uk/yourinformation

COUNTY BOROUGH COUNCIL OF SOUTHEND-ON-SEA

HJ 4/14   JN 5/30

SOUTHEND was created a county borough and commenced issuing registrations from 1.4.14.

First issues each year. No information known to writer for 1921-1928, but details are available at Essex Record Office, Southend branch.

1915	HJ	152	1917	HJ	403		1919	HJ	514
1916	HJ	316	1918	HJ	466		1920	HJ	962

1929	HJ	8435	1932	JN	1722	1935	JN 5100
1930	HJ	9568	1933	JN	2672	1936	JN 6608
1931	JN	740	1934	JN	3760	1937	JN 8400

AHJ	12/37	EHJ	2/50	JHJ	6/54	NHJ	9/56	SHJ	1/59	WHJ	4/60
AJN	8/38	EJN	8/50	JJN	11/54	NJN	3/57	SJN	3/59	WJN	6/60
BHJ	4/39	FHJ	4/51	KHJ	2/55	OHJ	6/57	THJ	5/59	XHJ	8/60
BJN	2/46	FJN	2/52	KJN	5/55	OJN	9/57	TJN	6/59	XJN	11/60
CHJ	12/46	GHJ	10/52	LHJ	8/55	PHJ	1/58	UHJ	8/59	YHJ	1/61
CJN	9/47	GJN	5/53	LJN	10/55	PJN	5/58	UJN	10/59	YJN	3/61
DHJ	8/48	HHJ	10/53	MHJ	2/56	RHJ	7/58	VHJ	1/60		
DJN	7/49	HJN	2/54	MJN	5/56	RJN	10/58	VJN	3/60		

Reverse format issues commenced with *HJ* from 1000 for cars etc. concurrently with *AHJ* for motorcycles, 15/5/61. *JN* from 1000 followed for cars and *AJN & BJN* for motorcycles.

Cars etc.			Motorcycles	
HJ from 1000	*5/61*		*AHJ*	*5/61*
JN from 1000	*7/63*		*AJN*	*6/62*
			BHJ	*8/63*

Commenced suffix marks 1.5.64

COUNTY BOROUGH COUNCIL OF SOUTHPORT

SOUTHPORT was created a county borough and commenced issuing registrations from 1.10.05

FY 10/05   WM 1/27

First issues each year, (no information is available prior to 1929).

1929	WM 2980	1931	WM 5912	1933	WM 8357
1930	WM 4489	1932	WM 7115	1934	WM 9713

AFY	2/34	EFY	2/39	JFY	3/53	NFY	3/57	SFY	12/59	WFY	5/62
AWM	9/34	EWM	1/40	JWM	10/53	NWM	7/57	SWM	3/60	WWM	9/62
BFY	4/35	FFY	10/46	KFY	4/54	OFY	1/58	TFY	6/60	XFY	1/63
BWM	12/35	FWM	11/47	KWM	11/54	OWM	5/58	TWM	10/60	XWM	4/63
CFY	6/36	GFY	2/49	LFY	4/55	PFY	9/58	UFY	2/61	YFY	7/63
CWM	2/37	GWM	2/50	LWM	9/55	PWM	2/59	UWM	5/61	YWM	10/63
DFY	9/37	HFY	3/51	MFY	2/56	RFY	5/59	VFY	8/61		
DWM	6/38	HWM	4/52	MWM	9/56	RWM	9/59	VWM	1/62		

Commenced suffix marks 3.2.64.

Reverse format mark issued only for re-registrations :

AFY   10/75   Re-registrations only.

COUNTY BOROUGH COUNCIL OF SOUTH SHIELDS

CU 12/03

First issues each year, (no information available prior to 1929) :

1929	CU 2412		1937	CU 3631		1945	CU 4575		1953	CU 6290
1930	CU 2592		1938	CU 3915		1946	CU 4625		1954	CU 6693
1931	CU 2786		1939	CU 4242		1947	CU 4783		1955	CU 7376
1932	CU 2902		1940	CU 4470		1948	CU 5000		1956	CU 8320
1933	CU 3005		1941	CU 4530		1949	CU 5161		1957	CU 9157
1934	CU 3122		1942	No inc.		1950	CU 5332			
1935	CU 3246		1943	CU 4533		1951	CU 5552			
1936	CU 3440		1944	CU 4566		1952	CU 5794			

ACU	11/57	DCU	1/60	GCU	8/61	KCU	6/63	NCU	11/64
BCU	9/58	ECU	6/60	HCU	5/62	LCU	1/64		
CCU	5/59	FCU	2/61	JCU	1/63	MCU	6/64		

Special mark for Diplomatic Corps : *1 ECU* ca 3/75

Commenced suffix marks 1.1.65.

COUNTY BOROUGH COUNCIL OF STOCKPORT

DB 1/04 JA 6/29

Originally separate and duplicate series for cars and motorcycles, each commencing at DB 1. The motorcycle series was abandoned after DB 1320 (6/21) and the first motorcycle in the main series was DB 2810.

First issues each year :

Motorcycles						Cars etc.					
1905	DB 44		1914	DB 456*		1905	DB 30?		1914	DB 799
1906	DB 68		1916	DB 610*		1907	DB 130*		1916	DB 1125*
1908	DB 125*		1917	DB 639*		1908	DB 185		1917	DB 1213*
1909	DB 150*		1918	DB 668*		1909	DB 250*		1918	DB 1322*
1910	DB 200*		1919	DB 696*		1910	DB 330*		1919	DB 1373*
1911	DB 245*		1920	DB 929		1911	DB 425*		1920	DB 1778
1912	DB 320*		1921	DB 1226		1912	DB 544		1921	DB 2665
1913	DB 393*					1913	DB 665*			

* These figures are approximate, but believed accurate to + or - 10.

All Vehicles

1922	DB 3153		1926	DB 6575		1930	JA 647		1934	JA 4170
1923	DB 3761		1927	DB 7551		1931	JA 1392		1935	JA 5288
1924	DB 4500 *		1928	DB 8573 **		1932	JA 2092		1936	JA 6543
1925	DB 5575		1929	DB 9720		1933	JA 3166		1937	JA 8404

* DB 5000-5299 allocated to North Western Road Car Co. Ltd. and issued over a period, 2/24-3/29.
** DB 9301-9500   "   "   "   "   "   "   "   "   "   "   " , 3/29-3/32.

ADB	1/38	EDB	3/50	JDB	5/55	NDB	4/58	SDB	4/60	WDB	4/62
AJA	9/38	EJA	1/51	JJA	7/55	NJA	7/58	SJA	5/60	WJA	6/62
BDB	4/39	FDB	10/51	KDB	12/55	ODB	11/58	TDB	8/60	XDB	10/62
BJA	11/41	FJA	7/52	KJA	5/56	OJA	3/59	TJA	12/80	XJA	2/63
CDB	10/46	GDB	5/53	LDB	11/56	PDB	6/59	UDB	3/61	YDB	5/63
CJA	7/47	GJA	12/53	LJA	3/57	PJA	8/59	UJA	5/61	YJA	7/63
DDB	5/48	HDB	5/54	MDB	7/57	RDB	11/59	VDB	8/61		
DJA	5/49	HJA	12/54	MJA	11/57	RJA	2/60	VJA	12/61		

Commenced suffix marks 4.11.63

COUNTY BOROUGH COUNCIL OF STOKE-ON-TRENT

The County Borough of Stoke-on-Trent came into existence with effect from 1.4.10, incorporating the existing county borough of Hanley and the districts of Burslem, Fenton, Longton, Stoke and Tunstall. The new county borough took over the existing Hanley mark, EH, which had been commenced in 1/04. (The SR&O authorising the transfer was issued retrospectively, being dated 25.6.10.)

EH   1/04 (by Hanley)   VT   7/27

EH was originally issued in three separate and parallel series, each starting at EH 1, for motor cars, motorcycles and heavy motor cars respectively. The HMC series was abandoned at EH 21 in 1912 and HMCs joined car series from EH 293. The motorcycle series reached EH 2230 at the end of 1920 and from 1/1/21 the car series was used for all vehicles from EH 2396 onwards.

First numbers issued each year, (no information available for 1922-1928) :

	Cars etc	Motorcycles	HMC
1905	EH 31	EH 46	EH 1
1906	EH 45	EH 82	EH 5
1907	EH 66	EH 105	EH 6
1908	EH 102	EH 127	EH 7
1909	EH 127	EH 145	EH 8
1910	EH 156	EH 168	EH 9
1911	EH 208	EH 183	EH 17
1912	EH 272	EH 267	EH 21
1913	EH 347	EH 396	
1914	EH 520	EH 545	
1915	EH 762	EH 761	
1916	EH 967	EH 1003	
1917	EH 1126	EH 1100	
1918	EH 1202	EH 1145	
1919	EH 1237	EH 1168	
1920	EH 1580	EH 1601	
1921	EH 2396		

All Vehicles

1929	VT 2250	1931	VT 5734	1933	VT 8882
1930	VT 4011	1932	VT 7317		

AEH	9/33	EEH	1/37	JEH	2/42	NEH	4/49	SEH	3/53	WEH	4/55
AVT	3/34	EVT	5/37	JVT	4/45	NVT	10/49	SVT	6/53	WVT	6/55
BEH	9/34	FEH	9/37	KEH	6/46	OEH	4/50	TEH	10/53	XEH	8/55
BVT	3/35	FVT	2/38	KVT	11/46	OVT	11/50	TVT	2/54	XVT	11/55
CEH	7/35	GEH	6/38	LEH	4/47	PEH	4/51	UEH	5/54	YEH	2/56
CVT	12/35	GVT	12/38	LVT	10/47	PVT	11/51	UVT	7/54	YVT	4/56
DEH	4/36	HEH	4/39	MEH	4/48	REH	4/52	VEH	11/54		
DVT	9/36	HVT	9/39	MVT	10/48	RVT	10/52	VVT	1/55		

AEH	6/56	EEH	4/58	JEH	7/59	NEH	6/60	TEH	6/61	XEH	8/62
AVT	10/56	EVT	6/58	JVT	8/59	NVT	7/60	TVT	7/61	XVT	10/62
BEH	2/57	FEH	8/58	KEH	10/59	PEH	9/60	UEH	9/61	YEH	11/62
BVT	4/57	FVT	10/58	KVT	12/59	PVT	11/60	UVT	12/61	YVT	1/63
CEH	6/57	GEH	1/59	LEH	1/60	REH	1/61	VEH	2/62		
CVT	8/57	GVT	3/59	LVT	3/60	RVT	3/61	VVT	3/62		
DEH	11/57	HEH	4/59	MEH	4/60	SEH	4/61	WEH	5/62		
DVT	2/58	HVT	5/59	MVT	5/60	SVT	5/61	WVT	6/62		

After the completion of *YVT* motorcycles commenced *2-999 VT*, whilst cars used *1000-9999 VT*. (*1 VT* was a special early issue for the mayoral car in 9/59.) *999 VT* was reached 1/64 and motorcycles then joined main series. *VT* was followed by *1000 EH* up for all vehicles,

VT   3/63   (*1 VT* early for mayoral car, 9/59)   EH   3/64

Commenced suffix marks 1.1.65

COUNTY BOROUGH COUNCIL OF SUNDERLAND

BR 12/03   GR 3/33

Figures for first issues each year prior 1929 not known to writer, but information may be available at Durham County Record Office. The following incomplete blocks are known for the years 1919-1928 :

1919	BR 773- 791			
1921	ca BR 1400-1857		1925	BR 3750-4500
1922	BR 1896-2330		1926	BR 4612-5277
1923	BR 2474-2914		1927	BR 5450-6106
1924	BR 2949-3559		1928	BR 6250-

First issues each year :

1929	BR 6983	1934	GR 572	1939	GR 6370	1944	GR 7764
1930	BR 7833	1935	GR 1494	1940	GR 7416	1945	GR 7834
1931	BR 8573	1936	GR 2545	1941	GR 7564	1946	GR 8065
1932	BR 9209	1937	GR 3659	1942	GR 7623	1947	GR 8855
1933	BR 9857	1938	GR 5048	1943	GR 7702	1948	GR 9671

ABR	6/48	EBR	6/54	JBR	7/57	NBR	10/59	SBR	7/61	WBR	10/63
AGR	7/49	EGR	11/54	JGR	12/57	NGR	1/60	SGR	12/61	WGR	1/64
BBR	5/50	FBR	4/55	KBR	4/58	OBR	3/60	TBR	4/62	XBR	3/64
BGR	3/51	FGR	8/55	KGR	7/58	OGR	5/60	TGR	7/62	XGR	5/64
CBR	3/52	GBR	12/55	LBR	11/58	PBR	7/60	UBR	10/62	YBR	7/64
CGR	12/52	GGR	5/56	LGR	3/59	PGR	11/60	UGR	3/63		
DBR	6/53	HBR	11/56	MBR	5/59	RBR	3/61	VBR	5/63		
DGR	12/53	HGR	4/57	MGR	7/59	RGR	5/61	VGR	7/63		

Commenced suffix marks 4.8.64

COUNTY BOROUGH COUNCIL OF SWANSEA

CY 1/04   WN 5/27

A single sequence for all vehicles, but in CY prior to 1921 separate blocks were allocated for cars, (including HMCs) and motorcycles. No details of the blocks are available. The reissue of void numbers persisted as late as 1925.

First issues each year, (no information available prior to 1929) :

1929	WN 1622	1931	WN 3503	1933	WN 5218	1935	WN 7552
1930	WN 2606	1932	WN 4324	1934	WN 6200	1936	WN 9188

ACY	6/36	ECY	6/46	JCY	8/52	NCY	1/56	SCY	5/58	WCY	1/60
AWN	1/37	EWN	4/47	JWN	4/53	NWN	4/56	SWN	8/58	WWN	3/60
BCY	7/37	FCY	1/48	KCY	11/53	OCY	7/56	TCY	11/58	XCY	5/60
BWN	1/38	FWN	11/48	KWN	4/54	OWN	1/57	TWN	2/59	XWN	7/60
CCY	6/38	GCY	8/49	LCY	9/54	PCY	5/57	UCY	4/59	YCY	10/60
CWN	1/39	GWN	4/50	LWN	2/55	PWN	7/57	UWN	6/59	YWN	1/61
DCY	6/39	HCY	1/51	MCY	6/55	RCY	11/57	VCY	9/59		
DWN	6/40	HWN	11/51	MWN	9/55	RWN	2/58	VWN	11/59		

ACY	4/61	CCY	3/62	ECY	1/63	GCY	7/63	JCY	3/64
AWN	6/61	CWN	5/62	EWN	3/63	GWN	10/63	JWN	3/65 Re-registrations only
BCY	8/61	DCY	8/62	FCY	4/63	HCY	12/63		
BWN	12/61	DWN	10/62	FWN	6/63	HWN	2/64		

Special mark for Diplomatic Corps : 1 CY 10/82.

Commenced suffix marks 1.5.64

COUNTY BOROUGH COUNCIL OF TEESSIDE

See COUNTY BOROUGH OF MIDDLESBROUGH

COUNTY BOROUGH COUNCIL OF TYNEMOUTH

Tynemouth was created a county borough and commenced issuing registrations as from 1.10.04.

FT   10/04

First issues each year, (no information available prior to 1929) :

1929	FT 1928	1937	FT 4070	1945	FT 5589	1953	FT 7725
1930	FT 2148	1938	FT 4479	1946	FT 5665	1954	FT 8167
1931	FT 2379	1939	FT 4871	1947	FT 5953	1955	FT 8660
1932	FT 2609	1940	FT 5241	1948	FT 6276	1956	FT 9318
1933	FT 2826	1941	FT 5328	1949	FT 6577	1957	FT 9970
1934	FT 3059	1942	FT 5391	1950	FT 6882		
1935	FT 3377	1943	FT 5486	1951	FT 7158		
1936	FT 3640	1944	FT 5549	1952	FT 7443		

AFT	2/57	CFT	5/59	EFT	9/60	GFT	4/62	JFT	10/63
BFT	4/58	DFT	1/60	FFT	6/61	HFT	2/63	KFT	6/64

Commenced suffix marks 4.8.64.

COUNTY BOROUGH COUNCIL OF WAKEFIELD

Wakefield was created a county borough and commenced to issue registrations as from 1.4.15

HL   4/15

First issues each year, (no information available prior to 1929) :

1929	HL 4178	1933	HL 5560	1937	HL 7873	1941	HL 9915
1930	HL 4535	1934	HL 5955	1938	HL 8580	1942	HL 9937
1931	HL 4861	1935	HL 6550	1939	HL 9220	1943	HL 9980
1932	HL 5188	1936	HL 7164	1940	HL 9804		

AHL	4/43	EHL	1/52	JHL	3/56	NHL	3/59	SHL	7/60	WHL	4/62
BHL	5/47	FHL	5/53	KHL	2/57	OHL	7/59	THL	1/61	XHL	9/62
CHL	1/49	GHL	6/54	LHL	11/57	PHL	12/59	UHL	5/61	YHL	3/63
DHL	5/50	HHL	5/55	MHL	7/58	RHL	4/60	VHL	10/61		

The only reverse format issue was *HL* from 1001 for all vehicles.

HL (from 1001)   7/63

Commenced suffix marks 4.8.64

COUNTY BOROUGH COUNCIL OF WALLASEY

Wallasey was created a county borough and commenced issuing registrations from 1.4.13.

HF 4/13

A common sequence for all vehicles, but odd numbers were issued to cars etc. and even numbers to motorcycles. Cars reached HF 9999 in 10/34, by which time motorcycles had reached HF 4400. Even numbers HF 4402-9998 were used for all classes.

First issues each year, (no information available for cars 1916-1928, nor for motorcycles after 1915)

Cars etc.					Motorcycles				
1914	HF 89				HF 100				
1915	HF 191				HF 226				

				Cars etc.					
1929	HF 5943	1931	HF 7181		1933	HF 8591			
1930	HF 6561	1932	HF 7921		1934	HF 9331			

				All Vehicles					
1935	HF 4628	1938	HF 7724		1941	HF 9242	1944	HF 9346
1936	HF 5598	1939	HF 8450		1942	HF 9264	1945	HF 9390
1937	HF 6660	1940	HF 9142		1943	HF 9298	1946	HF 9520

AHF	10/46 *	DHF	6/55	GHF	3/59	KHF	6/61	NHF	11/63
BHF	2/51	EHF	11/56	HHF	12/59	LHF	5/62	OHF	6/64
CHF	1/54	FHF	3/58	JHF	7/60	MHF	4/63		

* AHF 1 was a special early issue in 1935.

Commenced suffix marks 1.1.65.

The Act came into operation on the 1st. inst. and within four days one motorist had cancelled the registration of his car. Mr S.J.Langridge of Epsom registered his automobile in two places, receiving in East Sussex the identification mark A.P. 26 and in the other district a number he liked better. Thereupon he decided to cancel A.P.26 and thus achieve the distinction of being the first motorist to cancel a registration.

The Motor Car Journal, 9.1.04.

COUNTY BOROUGH COUNCIL OF WALSALL

Registration commenced 1.1.04

DH 1/04

A single sequence for all vehicles. First issues each year.

1905	DH 96	1913	DH 471	1921	DH 2448		1929	DH 6908
1906	DH 122	1914	DH 608	1922	DH 2811		1930	DH 7710
1907	DH 141	1915	DH 806	1923	DH 3190		1931	DH 8442
1908	DH 168	1916	DH 1048	1924	DH 3624		1932	DH 9142
1909	DH 196	1917	DH 1218	1925	DH 4105		1933	DH 9754
1910	DH 222	1918	DH 1322	1926	DH 4727			
1911	DH 284	1919	DH 1377	1927	DH 5496			
1912	DH 365	1920	DH 1820	1928	DH 6291			

ADH	5/33	EDH	2/37	JDH	3/43	NDH	8/49	SDH	8/53	WDH	9/55
BDH	7/34	FDH	12/37	KDH	7/46	ODH	10/50	TDH	3/54	XDH	3/56
CDH	7/35	GDH	10/38	LDH	6/47	PDH	11/51	UDH	10/54	YDH	7/56
DDH	4/36	HDH	8/39	MDH	7/48	RDH	12/52	VDH	4/55		

ADH	*3/57*	*EDH*	*11/58*	*JDH*	*2/60*	*NDH*	*3/61*	*TDH*	*5/62*
BDH	*7/57*	*FDH*	*4/59*	*KDH*	*4/60*	*PDH*	*5/61*	*UDH*	*9/62*
CDH	*2/58*	*GDH*	*7/59*	*LDH*	*7/60*	*RDH*	*8/61*	*VDH*	*1/63*
DDH	*6/58*	*HDH*	*11/59*	*MDH*	*11/60*	*SDH*	*2/62*		

After *VDH* was completed *DH* (from 1001) was used for cars etc. and *WDH* for motorcycles.

DH (from 1001)   4/63 (Cars etc.)   *WDH   5/63* (Motorcycles)

XDH was commenced for re-registrations only ca. 8/75.

Commenced suffix marks 1.9.64

COUNTY BOROUGH COUNCIL OF WARLEY

SEE COUNTY BOROUGH COUNCIL OF SMETHWICK

COUNTY BOROUGH COUNCIL OF WARRINGTON

ED 12/03

First issues each year. No details prior to 1929 known to writer but information for 1922-1928 available at Cheshire Record Office.

1929	ED 5275	1931	ED 6238	1933	ED 7393	1935	ED 8756
1930	ED 5734	1932	ED 6795	1934	ED 8010	1936	ED 9646

AED	5/36	EED	5/46	JED	9/51	NED	2/55	SED	10/57	WED	9/59
BED	5/37	FED	11/47	KED	9/52	OED	10/55	TED	5/58	XED	2/60
CED	6/38	GED	7/49	LED	7/53	PED	5/56	UED	12/58	YED	5/60
DED	8/39	HED	10/50	MED	6/54	RED	3/57	VED	5/59		

Reverse format issues commenced with *ED* 10/60, issued simultaneously from 101 up for motorcycles and 1000 up for cars etc. *999 ED* was followed by *AED* for motorcycles, 3/62, but when this was completed in 4/64 motorcycles joined main series from *7585 ED*..

ED   10/60   *AED   3/62   (Motorcycles only).*

Suffix marks commenced 1.9.64

COUNTY BOROUGH COUNCIL OF WEST BROMWICH

EA 1/04

First issues for each year. No information is available prior to 1929, except for the approximate figures shown for 1926 & 1927.

1926   ca EA 2500   1927   ca EA 2900

1929	EA 3820		1932	EA 5100		1935	EA 6550		1938	EA 9151
1930	EA 4313		1933	EA 5450		1936	EA 7288			
1931	EA 4753		1934	EA 5900		1937	EA 8176			

AEA	12/38	EEA	8/48	JEA	7/53	NEA	10/55	SEA	10/57
BEA	11/39	FEA	1/50	KEA	3/54	OEA	4/56	TEA	4/58
CEA	6/46	GEA	5/51	LEA	11/54	PEA	11/56	UEA	9/58
DEA	4/47	HEA	9/52	MEA	5/55	REA	5/57	VEA	2/59

On completion of VEA it was decided to segregate motorcycles from other vehicles. Cars etc. used WEA and motorcycles XEA. WEA was followed by YEA and then *AEA* (from 201), *CEA* and *DEA*. At this stage *BEA* was reserved for cycles but not commenced until XEA finished in 3/61. Subseqeuent issues are shown below. *1 EA* was a special issue for the mayoral car, 1/5/59.

Cars etc.				Motorcycles	
WEA	6/59	YEA	11/59	XEA	6/59

1 EA only, 5/59, special issue for mayoral car.

AEA (from 201) *	3/60	KEA	3/63	BEA	3/61
CEA	6/60	MEA	6/63	LEA	4/63
DEA	10/60	NEA	10/63	SEA	7/64
EEA	3/61	PEA	3/64		
FEA	7/61	REA	5/64		
GEA	1/62	TEA	8/64		
HEA	5/62	UEA	12/64		
JEA	10/62				

* This is the only three-letter mark which started at a number other than 1, the reason being that, exceptionally, *AEA* was also used for trade plates.

Commenced suffix marks 1.1.65.

Cases have been brought to the notice of the Ministry in which owners of vehicles which have been stolen have been allowed to retain the old identification numbers when registering substituting vehicles. This increases the difficulties of the Police in tracing the stolen vehicle, and the owner of the substituting vehicle is liable to be constantly stopped by the Police. In such cases, therefore, a new number should invariably be issued.

Circular RF 134, 19.7,21

COUNTY BOROUGH COUNCIL OF WEST HAM

AN 1/04   JD 12/29

First issues each year, (no information available prior to 1929) :

1929	AN 9142	1932	JD 2090	1935	JD 4896	1938	JD 8881
1930	JD 103	1933	JD 2896	1936	JD 6193	1939	JD 9938
1931	JD 1011	1934	JD 3760	1937	JD 7520		

AAN	1/39	EAN	1/51	JAN	6/55	NAN	2/58	SAN	2/60	WAN	4/62
AJD	11/39	EJD	10/51	JJD	10/55	NJD	6/58	SJD	4/60	WJD	6/62
BAN	9/45	FAN	7/52	KAN	3/56	OAN	10/58	TAN	7/60	XAN	10/62
BJD	9/46	FJD	5/53	KJD	8/56	OJD	1/59	TJD	11/60	XJD	1/63
CAN	6/47	GAN	11/53	LAN	1/57	PAN	4/59	UAN	3/61	YAN	4/63
CJD	5/48	GJD	5/54	LJD	5/57	PJD	6/59	UJD	5/61	YJD	6/63
DAN	5/49	HAN	10/54	MAN not alloc*		RAN	8/59	VAN	8/61		
DJD	4/50	HJD	3/55	MJD	9/57	RJD	11/59	VJD	12/61		

* to avoid confusion with Isle of Man marks.

AAN not alloc*	BAN	10/63	CAN	3/64	DAN	6/64	EAN	11/64
AJD 8/63	BJD	1/64	CJD	4/64	DJD	8/64		

* According to official information omitted "to avoid any confusion with the issue of Trade
Plate numbers, which were issued as AN in reverse".

Special mark for Diplomatic Corps : *1 TAN* ca.2/78

Commenced suffix marks 1.1.65

WEST HAM was absorbed into the GREATER LONDON COUNCIL with effect from 1 April 1965.

COUNTY BOROUGH COUNCIL OF WEST HARTLEPOOL

EF 12/03

A single sequence for all vehicles. First issues each year :

1904	EF 30	1908	EF 204	1912	EF 338	1916	EF 710*
1905	EF 88	1909	EF 229	1913	EF 375		
1906	EF 128	1910	EF 253	1914	EF 470		
1907	EF 166	1911	EF 293	1915	EF 600*	* approximate.	

No information available for 1917 to 1923, but the following random issue dates are known :

EF 758	11/16	EF 857	3/19	EF 2015	7/23
EF 768	1/17	EF 965	12/19	EF 2102	10/23

1924	EF 2149	1931	EF 4618	1938	EF 6608	1945	EF 7486
1925	EF 2594	1932	EF 4808	1939	EF 6983	1946	EF 7555
1926	EF 3025*	1933	EF 5029	1940	EF 7318	1947	EF 7911
1927	EF 3347	1934	EF 5257	1941	EF 7368	1948	EF 8337
1928	EF 3653	1935	EF 5600*	1942	EF 7387	1949	EF 8701
1929	EF 3977	1936	EF 5924	1943	EF 7423	1950	EF 9265
1930	EF 4348	1937	EF 6259	1944	EF 7448	1951	EF 9752
* approximate							

AEF	7/51	DEF	1/56	GEF	11/58	KEF	9/60	NEF	10/62	REF	6/64
BEF	7/53	EEF	2/57	HEF	6/59	LEF	5/61	OEF	6/63		
CEF	1/55	FEF	1/58	JEF	3/60	MEF	2/62	PEF	1/64		

Commenced suffix marks 1.9.64

WEST HARTLEPOOL was amalgamated with the borough of HARTLEPOOL to form the new
County Borough of HARTLEPOOL as from 1.4.67. EF was transferred to the new authority.

COUNTY BOROUGH COUNCIL OF WIGAN

EK 1/04   JP 4/34

A single sequence for all vehicles, but blocks of numbers were allocated to motorcycles. Details of any such blocks prior to EK 5000, if any, are unknown, but thereafter the following blocks were allocated to motorcycles : EK 5000-5699, 6100-6199, 6500-6599, 7000-7099, 7600-7699, 7920-7999, 8500-8599, 9100-9199, 9850-9899.   JP 300-399 was a further motorcycle block, but although blocking continued as late as FJP, blocks after JP 399 were generally much smaller and only the following exceeded 100 : AEK 675-799, BJP 450-566, EEK 428-559, EJP 619-750, FEK 131-351, FJP 191-299, FJP 860-999.

First issues each year.   No information is available prior to 1929, but the following random issue dates are known :

Cars etc.		Motorcycles	
EK 2096	11/22	EK 5002	4/23
EK 2131	1/23	EK 5697	5/27
EK 3000	4/24	EK 6199	8/28
EK 5996	9/26		

Note that motorcycles were receiving numbers in EK 5xxx when cars were only in EK 2xxx.

1929	EK 6740		1935	JP 550		1941	JP 4854		1947	JP 6039
1930	EK 7342		1936	JP 1272		1942	JP 4992		1948	JP 6785
1931	EK 8083		1937	JP 2170		1943	JP 5030		1949	JP 7422
1932	EK 8633		1938	JP 3020		1944	JP 5092		1950	JP 8136
1933	EK 9062		1939	JP 3861		1945	JP 5123		1951	JP 8856
1934	EK 9792		1940	JP 4573		1946	JP 5268		1952	JP 9524

AEK	8/52	CEK	9/55	EEK	6/58	GEK	4/60	JEK	2/62	LEK	1/64
AJP	8/53	CJP	5/56	EJP	2/59	GJP	9/60	JJP	8/62	LJP	5/64
BEK	6/54	DEK	3/57	FEK	7/59	HEK	3/61	KEK	3/63		
BJP	2/55	DJP	12/57	FJP	1/60	HJP	7/61	KJP	8/63		

Commenced suffix marks 4.8.64

COUNTY BOROUGH COUNCIL OF WOLVERHAMPTON

DA 12/03   UK 6/25   JW 3/31

Originally duplicate series for cars and motorcycles, but motorcycle series abandoned after DA 215 and thereafter a common sequence for all vehicles.

First numbers issued each year, (no information available prior to 1926 nor for 1928 and figures for 1926 and 1927 are approximate only.)

1926	UK 980	1929	UK 6344	1932	JW 1007	1935	JW 6100
1927	UK 2810	1930	UK 8092	1933	JW 2469	1936	JW 8600
		1931	UK 9636	1934	JW 4033		

ADA	7/36	EDA	5/46	JDA	11/50	NDA	5/54	SDA	5/56	WDA	5/58
AJW	12/36	EJW	9/46	JJW	5/51	NJW	7/54	SJW	7/56	WJW	6/58
AUK	4/37	EUK	1/47	JUK	10/51	NUK	10/54	SUK	10/56	WUK	8/58
BDA	7/37	FDA	7/47	KDA	3/52	ODA	12/54	TDA	1/57	XDA	10/58
BJW	1/38	FJW	12/47	KJW	7/52	OJW	3/55	TJW	3/57	XJW	12/58
BUK	4/38	FUK not alloc.		KUK	11/52	OUK	4/55	TUK	4/57	XUK	2/59
CDA	10/38	GDA	4/48	LDA	3/53	PDA	6/55	UDA	6/57	YDA	3/59
CJW	2/39	GJW	10/48 #	LJW	6/53	PJW	7/55	UJW	7/57	YJW	4/59
CUK	5/39	GUK	3/49	LUK	9/53	PUK	8/55	UUK	9/57	YUK	5/59 *
DDA	10/39	HDA	7/49	MDA	12/53	RDA	11/55	VDA	11/57		
DJW	9/41	HJW	1/50	MJW	3/54	RJW	1/56	VJW	2/58		
DUK	11/44	HUK	6/50	MUK not iss.		RUK	3/56	VUK	3/58		

\# GJW 1 early issue (8/48)

* After YJW cars used *DA* from 1000, 5/59, leaving YUK for motorcycles. Motorcycles then used *301-999 DA*, followed by *ADA* to *BUK* inclusive. After *9999 DA* cars used *301-9999 JW* and *301-9999 UK*, then *CDA* onwards.

<table>
<tr><td colspan="2"><u>Cars etc.</u></td><td colspan="2"><u>Motorcycles</u></td></tr>
<tr><td>1000-9999 DA</td><td>5/59</td><td>301-999 DA</td><td>9/59</td></tr>
<tr><td>301-9999 JW</td><td>8/60</td><td>ADA</td><td>2/60</td></tr>
<tr><td>301-9999 UK</td><td>1/62</td><td>AJW</td><td>6/60</td></tr>
<tr><td>CDA</td><td>3/63</td><td>AUK</td><td>3/61</td></tr>
<tr><td>CJW</td><td>5/63</td><td>BDA</td><td>9/61</td></tr>
<tr><td>CUK</td><td>6/63</td><td>BJW</td><td>8/62</td></tr>
<tr><td>DDA</td><td>7/63</td><td>BUK</td><td>8/63</td></tr>
<tr><td>DJW</td><td>8/63</td><td></td><td></td></tr>
<tr><td>DUK</td><td>9/63</td><td></td><td></td></tr>
<tr><td>EDA</td><td>11/63</td><td></td><td></td></tr>
<tr><td>EJW</td><td>12/63</td><td></td><td></td></tr>
<tr><td>EUK</td><td>1/64</td><td></td><td></td></tr>
<tr><td>FDA</td><td>2/64</td><td></td><td></td></tr>
<tr><td>FJW</td><td>3/64</td><td></td><td></td></tr>
<tr><td>FUK not alloc.</td><td></td><td></td><td></td></tr>
<tr><td>GDA</td><td>4/64</td><td></td><td></td></tr>
</table>

Commenced suffix marks 1.5.64.

COUNTY BOROUGH COUNCIL OF WORCESTER

FK 12/03

Registration commenced 23.12.03.
A common sequence for all vehicles.

First numbers issued each year :

1904	FK 5	1914	FK 449	1924	FK 1950	1934	FK 5905
1905	FK 72	1915	FK 574	1925	FK 2323	1935	FK 6495
1906	FK 95	1916	FK 670	1926	FK 2773	1936	FK 7089
1907	FK 123	1917	FK 705	1927	FK 3180	1937	FK 7780
1908	FK 146	1918	*	1928	FK 3571	1938	FK 8524
1909	FK 164	1919	FK 707	1929	FK 3934	1939	FK 9162
1910	FK 193	1920	FK 812	1930	FK 4341	1940	FK 9695
1911	FK 238	1921	FK 1086	1931	FK 4718	1941	FK 9840
1912	FK 313	1922	FK 1355	1932	FK 5093	1942	FK 9968
1913	FK 387	1923	FK 1621	1933	FK 5447		

* No new numbers issued in 1918

AFK	2/42	BFK	5/50	JFK	3/54	NFK	1/56	SFK	10/57	WFK	3/59
BFK	7/46	FFK	7/51	KFK	9/54	OFK	6/56	TFK	4/58	XFK	6/59
CFK	8/47	GFK	7/52	LFK	2/55	PFK	12/56	UFK	7/58	YFK	8/59
DFK	2/49	HFK	6/53	MFK	7/55	RFK	6/57	VFK	11/58		

Reverse issue marks for normal series used *AFK* to *YFK* in order, but in 4/63 the series *FK* (from 1001) was reserved for vehicles belonging to Great Universal Stores. Numbers from *5001 FK* up were later used for re-registrations.

AFK	11/59	EFK	7/60	JFK	4/61	NFK	12/61	TFK	12/62	XFK	12/63
BFK	1/60	FFK	10/60	KFK	6/61	PFK	4/62	UFK	2/63	YFK	3/64
CFK	4/60	GFK	12/60	LFK	7/61	RFK	6/62	VFK	5/63		
DFK	6/60	HFK	2/61	MFK	9/61	SFK	8/62	WFK	8/63		

*FK (from 1001) 4/63 *

Reserved for Great Universal Stores; re-registrations from 5001 up.

Suffix marks were originally scheduled to commence 1.5.64, but in fact commenced 9.6.64.

COUNTY BOROUGH COUNCIL OF YORK

DN 1/04   VY 5/28

There were originally three separate series for motor cars, motorcycles and heavy motor cars respectively, each commencing at DN 1. The HMC series was abandoned after DN 35 (8/16) and joined the normal series from DN 932. The normal motor car series jumped from DN 1317 to 2318 in 5/19 to avoid further duplication with cycles, but DN 2000-2005 & 2010 were also issued in 1919; the motorcycle series ceased at DN 1999 in 3/20. Motorcycles then jumped to DN 3000 and subsequently a single sequence was used for all vehicles, but the following blocks of numbers were reserved for motorcycles : DN 3000-3999, 5000-5999, 7000-7999. After DN 7999 cycles joined main series from DN 9762 in 3/28. Segregation was thereafter abandoned until the commencement of reverse format issues.

First issues each year :

Motor Cars		Motorcycles	HMCs	
1905	DN 36	DN 91	DN 1	
1906	DN 61	DN 132	DN 3	
1907	DN 103	DN 161	None issued	
1908	DN 145	DN 188	DN 4	
1909	DN 181	DN 208	None issued	
1910	DN 213	DN 237	DN 5	
1911	DN 261	DN 277	DN 6	
1912	DN 342	DN 336	DN 7	
1913	DN 452	DN 419	DN 8	
1914	DN 550	DN 539	DN 11	
1915	DN 674	DN 710	DN 12	
1916	DN 872	DN 887	DN 22	
1917	DN 977	DN 1063		
1918	DN 1141	DN 1235		
1919	DN 1246	DN 1492		
1920	DN 2487	DN 1891		
1921	DN 2942	DN 3305		
1922	DN 4315	DN 3570		
1923	DN 4657	DN 3847		
1924	DN 6083	DN 5127		
1925	DN 6658	DN 5507		
1926	DN 8281	DN 5967		
1927	DN 8947	DN 7420		
1928	DN 9576	DN 7901		

All Vehicles					
1929	VY 521	1932	VY 3172	1935	VY 6088
1930	VY 1540	1933	VY 3961	1936	VY 7363
1931	VY 2445	1934	VY 4877	1937	VY 8872

ADN	8/37	EDN	2/49	JDN	10/53	NDN	7/56	SDN	2/59	WDN	9/60
AVY	4/38	EVY	11/49	JVY	3/54	NVY	1/57	SVY	4/59	WVY	12/60
BDN	1/39	FDN	7/50	KDN	7/54	ODN	5/57	TDN	7/59	XDN	3/61
BVY	10/39	FVY	1/51	KVY	1/55	OVY	8/57	TVY	9/59	XVY	4/61
CDN	2/46	GDN	8/51	LDN	3/55	PDN	1/58	UDN	12/59	YDN	6/61
CVY	11/46	GVY	4/52	LVY	7/55	PVY	4/58	UVY	3/60	YVY	9/61
DDN	9/47	HDN	12/52	MDN	11/55	RDN	7/58	VDN	4/60		
DVY	7/48	HVY	5/53	MVY	4/56	RVY	11/58	VVY	6/60		

The number 1 and/or other low numbers were not infrequently issued one or two months ahead of the main series, e.g. BVY 1 8/39, CDN 1 1/46, DDN 2 8/47.

Reverse format issues commenced with *DN* from 2001 for cars etc. and *ADN* for motorcycles simultaneously. *DN* was followed by *VY* from 1; motorcycle series continued to *BVY*.

Cars etc.		Motorcycles	
DN from 2001	*1/62*	*ADN*	*1/62*
VY from 1	*1/64*	*AVY*	*3/63*
		BDN	*10/63*
		BVY	*5/64*

Commenced suffix marks 4.8.64

COUNTY COUNCIL OF ABERDEEN

SA 1/04   AV 9/26

First issues each year, (no information available prior to 1929) :

1929	AV 2450		1932	AV 4980		1935	AV 7027		1938	AV 9965
1930	AV 3440		1933	AV 5600		1936	AV 7887			
1931	AV 4330		1934	AV 6250		1937	AV 8950			

AAV	1/38	EAV	12/47	JAV	1/53	NAV	4/56	SAV	7/59	WAV	3/62
ASA	1/39	ESA	6/48	JSA	8/53	NSA	11/56	SSA	12/59	WSA	6/62
BAV	11/39	FAV	1/49	KAV	2/54	OAV	5/57	TAV	4/60	XAV	10/62
BSA	7/41	FSA	8/49	KSA	8/54	OSA	9/57	TSA	7/60	XSA	2/63
CAV	7/43	GAV	4/50	LAV	not alloc	PAV	3/58	UAV	11/60	YAV	5/63
CSA	8/45	GSA	1/51	LSA	1/55	PSA	6/58	USA	4/61 *	YSA	8/63
DAV	8/46	HAV	8/51	MAV	6/55	RAV	11/58	VAV	7/61		
DSA	5/47	HSA	6/52	MSA	11/55	RSA	4/59	VSA	11/61		

* USA 1 special early issue for Diplomatic Corps, ca. 9/59.

Special issue for Diplomatic Corps : *1 RSA* ca 3/92.

Commenced suffix marks 2.12.63

COUNTY COUNCIL OF ANGUS

The official name of the county was the COUNTY COUNCIL OF FORFARSHIRE until it was changed to the COUNTY COUNCIL OF ANGUS by resolution of the County Council in May 1928.

SR 12/03

A single sequence for all vehicles.

First issues each year, (no information is available for 1916-1919) :

1904	SR	18		1913	SR	658		1922	SR 2739		1931	SR 7813
1905	SR	90		1914	SR	831		1923	SR 3252		1932	SR 8128
1906	SR	138		1915	SR 1006		1924	SR 3853		1933	SR 8437
1907	SR	183				1925	SR 4415		1934	SR 8775
1908	SR	227				1926	SR 5162		1935	SR 9210
1909	SR	262				1927	SR 5899		1936	SR 9714
1910	SR	316				1928	SR 6484			
1911	SR	393		1920	SR 1629		1929	SR 6976			
1912	SR	489		1921	SR 2155		1930	SR 7459			

ASR	6/36	BSR	5/47	JSR	5/52	NSR	7/55	SSR	1/58	WSR	11/59
BSR	3/38	FSR	7/48	KSR	6/53	OSR	2/56	TSR	6/58	XSR	4/60
CSR	3/40	GSR	11/49	LSR	3/54	PSR	10/56	USR	12/58	YSR	8/60 *
DSR	2/45	HSR	3/51	MSR	11/54	RSR	6/57	VSR	6/59		

* Motorcycles only.

Special mark for Diplomatic Corps : ISR 1   2/68

Reverse format issues commenced for cars with *SR* from 501 in 8/60, on completion of XSR, leaving YSR for motorcycles only. YSR was followed by *BSR*, leaving *ASR* unused.

SR (from 501) 8/60 Cars etc.   *BSR   5/62*   Motorcycles only.

Commenced suffix marks 1.7.64

COUNTY COUNCIL OF ARGYLL

SB 1/04

First issues each year, (no information available prior to 1929) :

1929	SB 3226		1936	SB 4893		1943	SB 6422		1950	SB 8046
1930	SB 3521		1937	SB 5246		1944	SB 6489		1951	SB 8378
1931	SB 3747		1938	SB 5605		1945	SB 6541		1952	SB 8743
1932	SB 3948		1939	SB 5924		1946	SB 6615		1953	SB 9149
1933	SB 4161		1940	SB 6233		1947	SB 6870		1954	SB 9712
1934	SB 4371		1941	SB 6274		1948	SB 7220			
1935	SB 4602		1943	SB 6338		1949	SB 7587			

ASB	8/54	DSB	4/58	GSB	11/60	KSB	3/63	NSB	12/64
BSB	9/55	ESB	3/59	HSB	8/61	LSB	10/63		
CSB	3/57	FSB	2/60	JSB	5/62	MSB	5/64		

Commenced suffix marks 1.1.65

COUNTY COUNCIL OF AYR

SD 1/04   AG 11/25   CS 5/34

First issues each year, (no information available prior to 1929) :

1929	AG 3701		1932	AG 7140		1935	CS 1109		1938	CS 7040
1930	AG 4955		1933	AG 8401		1936	CS 2902		1939	CS 9103
1931	AG 6170		1934	AG 9536		1937	CS 4988			

AAG	5/39	EAG	9/51	JAG	1/56	NAG	1/59	SAG	4/61	WAG	4/63
ACS	1/40	ECS	5/52	JCS	4/56	NCS	4/59	SCS	6/61	WCS	6/63
ASD	8/42	ESD	11/52	JSD	7/56	NSD	6/59	SSD	7/61	WSD	7/63
BAG	1/46	FAG	5/53	KAG	11/56	OAG	9/59	TAG	10/61	XAG	9/63
BCS	10/46	FCS	9/53	KCS	4/57	OCS	11/59	TCS	1/62	XCS	11/63
BSD	5/47	FSD	1/54	KSD	6/57	OSD	1/60	TSD	3/62	XSD	1/64
CAG	11/47	GAG	5/54	LAG	9/57	PAG	3/60	UAG	5/62	YAG	2/64
CCS	7/48	GCS	10/54	LCS	12/57	PCS	5/60	UCS	6/62	YCS	4/64
CSD	3/49	GSD	1/55	LSD	3/58	PSD	7/60	USD	8/62	YSD	5/64
DAG	10/49	HAG	4/55	MAG	5/58	RAG	9/60	VAG	11/62		
DCS	5/50	HCS	7/55	MCS	8/58	RCS	12/60	VCS	1/63		
DSD	1/51	HSD	10/55	MSD	11/58	RSD	1/61	VSD	3/63		

Special marks for Diplomatic Corps : *1 AG* 3/83   *1 MAG* 3/86

Commenced suffix marks, (ahead of original schedule), 1.6.64.

COUNTY COUNCIL OF BANFF

SE 1/04

First issues each year, (no information available prior to 1922) :

1922	SE 1273	1931	SE 3473	1940	SE 5195	1949	SE 6846
1923	SE 1523	1932	SE 3641	1941	SE 5322	1950	SE 7245
1924	SE 1772	1933	SE 3814	1942	SE 5419	1951	SE 7560
1925	SE 2052	1934	SE 3949	1943	SE 5531	1952	SE 7838
1926	SE 2378	1935	SE 4091	1944	SE 5618	1953	SE 8162
1927	SE 2633	1936	SE 4305	1945	SE 5709	1954	SE 8660
1928	SE 2843	1937	SE 4510	1946	SE 5819	1955	SE 9170
1929	SE 3062	1938	SE 4749	1947	SE 6026	1956	SE 9778
1930	SE 3275	1939	SE 4961	1948	SE 6456		

ASE	5/56	CSE	12/58	ESE	12/60	GSE	10/62	JSE by 5/84 re-registrations only *
BSE	10/57	DSE	1/60	FSE	12/61	HSE	8/63	

* only JSE 1 is known.

Suffix marks commenced 1.5.64

COUNTY COUNCIL OF BERWICK

SH 12/03

First issues each year, (no information available prior to 1936) :

1936	SH 4963	1941	SH 6406	1946	SH 7250	1951	SH 9270
1937	SH 5303	1942	SH 6579	1947	SH 7614	1952	SH 9630
1938	SH 5645	1943	SH 6797	1948	SH 8076		
1939	SH 5922	1944	SH 6938	1949	SH 8485		
1940	no info.	1945	SH 7107	1950	SH 8890		

ASH	11/52	CSH	2/56	ESH	9/58	GSH	11/60	JSH	12/62
BSH	8/54	DSH	7/57	FSH	11/59	HSH	11/61	KSH	11/63

Suffix marks commenced 1.7.64

COUNTY COUNCIL OF BUTE

SJ 12/03

Registration commenced 18.12.03

A single sequence for all vehicles.

First issues each year :

1904	SJ	2	1919	SJ 189	1934	SJ 772	1949	SJ 1245
1905	SJ	21	1920	SJ 234	1935	SJ 802	1950	SJ 1311
1906	SJ	35	1921	SJ 279	1936	SJ 845	1951	SJ 1353
1907	SJ	49	1922	SJ 320	1937	SJ 881	1952	SJ 1405
1908	SJ	66	1923	SJ 370	1938	SJ 914	1953	SJ 1447
1909	SJ	78	1924	SJ 422	1939	SJ 950	1954	SJ 1520
1910	SJ	93	1925	SJ 457	1940	SJ 979	1955	SJ 1604
1911	SJ 108		1926	SJ 501	1941	SJ 992	1956	SJ 1726
1912	SJ 117		1927	SJ 543	1942	SJ 995	1957	SJ 1829
1913	SJ 125		1928	SJ 580	1943	SJ 1001	1958	SJ 1913
1914	SJ 138		1929	SJ 605	1944	SJ 1017	1959	SJ 2038
1915	SJ 151		1930	SJ 633	1945	SJ 1029	1960	SJ 2167
1916	SJ 160		1931	SJ 673	1946	SJ 1042	1961	SJ 2353
1917	SJ 172		1932	SJ 707	1947	SJ 1112	1962	SJ 2519
1918	SJ 186		1933	SJ 738	1948	SJ 1180	1963	SJ 2683 *

* Last normal issue SJ 2860, re-registrations to SJ 2877.

Commenced suffix marks 2.1.64

ASJ to YSJ allocated by DVLA to various VROs for "age-related" marks from 2/97.

COUNTY COUNCIL OF CAITHNESS

SK 12/03

Registration commenced 29.12.03.

A single sequence for all vehicles.

First issues each year, (no information available for 1922-1928) :

1904	SK	4	1909	SK	69	1914	SK 231	1919	SK 348
1905	SK	24	1910	SK 100	1915	SK 285	1920	SK 413
1906	SK	30	1911	SK 117	1916	SK 316	1921	SK 630
1907	SK	41	1912	SK 146	1917	SK 332		
1908	SK	53	1913	SK 187	1918	SK 341		

1929	SK 1505	1938	SK 2332	1947	SK 3040	1956	SK 5086
1930	SK 1591	1939	SK 2456	1948	SK 3166	1957	SK 5522
1931	SK 1700	1940	SK 2577	1949	SK 3412	1958	SK 5990
1932	SK 1792	1941	SK 2643	1950	SK 3617	1959	SK 6668
1933	SK 1855	1942	SK 2689	1951	SK 3792	1960	SK 7254
1934	SK 1913	1943	SK 2749	1952	SK 3949	1961	SK 7971
1935	SK 1990	1944	SK 2814	1953	SK 4128	1962	SK 8712
1936	SK 2100	1945	SK 2885	1954	SK 4395	1963	SK 9455
1937	SK 2225	1947	SK 2939	1955	SK 4664		

ASK   8/63

Suffix marks commenced 4.8.64

BSK to YSK allotted by DVLA to various VROs for "Age-Related" marks between 3/90 and 3/92.

COUNTY COUNCIL OF CLACKMANNAN

SL 12/03

A separate series for Heavy Motor Cars, commencing at SL 01. Unusually this series remained in use until at least 5/25, by which time it had reached SL 082. Known dates of issue are : 051 - 1921; 057 - 10/22; 064 - 11/23; 069 - 5/24; 082 - 5/25.

First issues each year, (normal series). No information is available prior to 1929.

1929	SL 1377	1938	SL 2388	1947	SL 3011	1956	SL 5031
1930	SL 1464	1939	SL 2580	1948	SL 3154	1957	SL 5404
1931	SL 1540	1940	SL 2713	1949	SL 3258	1958	SL 5828
1932	SL 1625	1941	SL 2745	1950	SL 3395	1959	SL 6340
1933	SL 1705	1942	SL 2764	1951	SL 3552	1960	SL 6983
1934	SL 1792	1943	SL 2799	1952	SL 3714	1961	SL 7612
1935	SL 1904	1944	SL 2821	1953	SL 3918	1962	SL 8081
1936	SL 2043	1945	SL 2843	1954	SL 4191	1963	SL 8602
1937	SL 2210	1946	SL 2882	1955	SL 4600	1964	SL 9179 *

* Last normal issue SL 9602. Higher numbers issued for re-registrations and from 9737 up by DVLA for "Age-Related" marks.

Special marks for Diplomatic Corps : HSL 1 ca. 2/62; *1 SL* 7/90.

Suffix marks commenced 1.7.64

ASL to YSL allocated by DVLA to various VROs for "age-related" marks from 1/99.

COUNTY COUNCIL OF DUMFRIES

SM 12/03

Registration commenced 14.12.03.

A single sequence for all vehicles.

First issues each year :

1904	SM 36	1912	SM 589	1920	SM 2018	1928	SM 6759
1905	SM 91	1913	SM 742	1921	SM 2629	1929	SM 7386
1906	SM 135	1914	SM 920	1922	SM 3128	1930	SM 8007
1907	SM 207	1915	SM 1190	1923	SM 3570	1931	SM 8664
1908	SM 272	1916	SM 1394	1924	SM 4185	1932	SM 9201
1909	SM 346	1917	SM 1573	1925	SM 4810	1933	SM 9754
1910	SM 405	1918	SM 1663	1926	SM 5495		
1911	SM 491	1919	SM 1720	1927	SM 6105		

ASM	6/33	ESM	1/39	JSM	6/48	NSM	10/52	SSM	6/55	WSM	11/57
BSM	3/35	FSM	6/40	KSM	7/49	OSM	8/53	TSM	1/56	XSM	5/58
CSM	6/36	GSM	11/45	LSM	8/50	PSM	4/54	USM	8/56	YSM	11/58
DSM	7/37	HSM	6/47	MSM	10/51	RSM	12/54	VSM	5/57		

Reverse format issues commenced with *SM* from 1 to 99 and 1000 up for cars etc., concurrently with *ASM* for motorcycles, followed by *BSM*. After completing *SM* cars etc. used *CSM* and *DSM*. *ESM* and *FSM* were used for all classes.

Cars etc.				Motorcycles	
SM (1-99 and 1000-9999 *)		*4/59*		*ASM*	*4/59*
* Special issue 777 SM later.				*BSM*	*3/61*
CSM	*5/63*	*ESM*	*2/64*		
DSM	*10/63*	*FSM*	*5/64*		

Suffix marks commenced 1.7.64.

COUNTY COUNCIL OF DUNBARTON

(The name of this Council was officially DUNBARTON from its formation in 1889, but was mis-spelt DUMBARTON in SR&O 999 of 1903.)

SN 12/03

First issues each year, (no information available prior to 1929) :

1929	SN 4553	1934	SN 6176	1939	SN 8860	1944	SN 9659
1930	SN 4914	1935	SN 6600	1940	SN 9337	1945	SN 9723
1931	SN 5221	1936	SN 7098	1941	SN 9469	1946	SN 9773
1932	SN 5508	1937	SN 7715	1942	SN 9539		
1933	SN 5806	1938	SN 8325	1943	SN 9603		

ASN	11/46	ESN	3/55	JSN	10/58	NSN	3/61	SSN	6/63	WSN	ca. /74 *
BSN	4/49	FSN	1/56	KSN	6/59	OSN	8/61	TSN	1/64		
CSN	3/52	GSN	2/57	LSN	2/60	PSN	5/62	USN	not allocated #		
DSN	12/53	HSN	1/58	MSN	6/60	RSN	12/62	VSN	5/64		

* Re-registrations only.

Specially allocated to London County Council for United States Navy vehicles, but never used for civilian registrations.

Special issue for Diplomatic Corps : *1 KSN* /96.

Commenced suffix marks 4.8.64

COUNTY COUNCIL OF EAST LOTHIAN

Until 9.5.21 the official name of the county was the COUNTY COUNCIL OF HADDINGTON.

SS 1/04

First issues each year, (no information available prior to 1929) :

1929	SS 2918	1936	SS 4299	1943	SS 5851	1950	SS 7458
1930	SS 3102	1937	SS 4562	1944	SS 5944	1951	SS 7771
1931	SS 3266	1938	SS 4868	1945	SS 6035	1952	SS 8085
1932	SS 3429	1939	SS 5207	1946	SS 6127	1953	SS 8505
1933	SS 3621	1940	SS 5456	1947	SS 6390	1954	SS 8927
1934	SS 3827	1941	SS 5608	1948	SS 6758	1955	SS 9414
1935	SS 4067	1942	SS 5710	1949	SS 7105		

ASS	not iss.	CSS	8/57	ESS	5/60	GSS	8/62	JSS	ca. /74 re-registrations
BSS	11/55	DSS	3/59	FSS	6/61	HSS	8/63		only

Suffix marks commenced 2.3.64

COUNTY COUNCIL OF ELGIN

See COUNTY COUNCIL OF MORAY

COUNTY COUNCIL OF FIFE

SP 12/03   FG 4/25

First issues each year. No information available prior to 1929, but the following random dates are known :

SP 5402   /21   SP 8063   6/23   SP 9228   7/24

| 1929 | FG 4610 | | 1931 | FG 6589 | | 1933 | FG 8251 |
| 1930 | FG 5664 | | 1932 | FG 7389 | | 1934 | FG 9082 |

AFG	10/34	EFG	11/41	JFG	6/50	NFG	8/54	SFG	4/57	WFG	5/59
ASP	7/35	ESP	8/45	JSP	2/51	NSP	12/54	SSP	7/57	WSP	7/59
BFG	4/36	FFG	9/46	KFG	10/51	OFG	4/55	TFG	11/57	XFG	10/59
BSP	1/37	FSP	5/47	KSP	6/52	OSP	8/55	TSP	3/58	XSP	1/60
CFG	10/37	GFG	2/48	LFG	1/53	PFG	12/55	UFG	5/58	YFG	3/60
CSP	3/38	GSP	9/48	LSP	5/53	PSP	4/56	USP	8/58	YSP	5/60
DFG	12/38	HFG	4/49	MFG	10/53	RFG	7/56	VFG	11/58		
DSP	6/39	HSP	11/49	MSP	3/54	RSP	12/56	VSP	3/59		

Reverse format issues commenced with *SP* from 301 for all vehicles, 7/60; followed by *FG* from 1 for motorcycles and 2001 for cars etc.

SP (from 301)   7/60   *FG (from 1)   10/62.*

Special mark for Diplomatic Corps : *1 AFG* ca 6/78

Commenced suffix marks 1.5.64.

COUNTY COUNCIL OF FORFAR

See COUNTY COUNCIL OF ANGUS

COUNTY COUNCIL OF INVERNESS

ST 12/03

Registration commenced 28/12/03. A single sequence for all vehicles.

First issues each year :

1904	ST 10		1913	ST 467		1922	unknown		1931	ST 6412
1905	ST 48		1914	ST 610		1923	ST 2278		1932	ST 6825
1906	ST 69		1915	ST 805		1924	ST 2681		1933	ST 7181
1907	ST 104		1916	ST 1005		1925	ST 3117		1934	ST 7517
1908	ST 136		1917	ST 1118		1926	ST 3752		1935	ST 7959
1909	ST 160		1918	ST 1153		1927	ST 4304		1936	ST 8446
1910	ST 203		1919	ST 1194		1928	ST 4868		1937	ST 8947
1911	ST 259		1920	ST 1360		1929	ST 5407		1938	ST 9489
1912	ST 346		1921	ST 1678		1930	ST 5933			

AST	1/39	EST	6/50	JST	6/55	NST	1/59	SST	7/61	WST	11/63
BST	8/44	FST	1/52	KST	5/56	OST	10/59	TST	3/62	XST	5/64
CST	7/47	GST	6/53	LST	6/57	PST	5/60	UST	10/62	YST	11/64
DST	2/49	HST	7/54	MST	4/58	RST	12/60	VST	5/63		

Special Mark for Diplomatic Corps : *1 EST* 9/94

Commenced suffix marks 1.1.65

COUNTY COUNCIL OF KINCARDINE

SU 1/04

First issues each year, (no information available prior to 1929) :

1929	SU 2450	1938	SU 3456	1947	SU 4639	1956	SU 7535
1930	SU 2570	1939	SU 3628	1948	SU 4998	1957	SU 7866
1931	SU 2682	1940	SU 3781	1949	SU 5295	1958	SU 8273
1932	SU 2769	1941	SU 3834	1950	SU 5570	1959	SU 8732
1933	SU 2846	1942	SU 3963	1951	SU 5839	1960	SU 9182
1934	SU 2932	1943	SU 4062	1952	SU 6108	1961	SU 9670
1935	SU 3027	1944	SU 4171	1953	SU 6453		
1936	SU 3139	1945	SU 4268	1954	SU 6770		
1937	SU 3305	1946	SU 4372	1955	SU 7152		

ASU   8/61   BSU   5/63

Special issue for Diplomatic Corps : *1 SU* ca /66.

Commenced suffx marks 1.6.64

CSU to YSU issued by DVLA to various VROs for "Age-Related" marks, 7/86 - 1/90.

COUNTY COUNCIL OF KINROSS

SV 1/04

A common sequence for all vehicles.

First issues each year, (no information available 1922-1928) :

1905	SV 22	1918	SV 251	1937	SV 1130	1950	SV 1695
1906	SV 48	1919	SV 255	1938	SV 1192	1951	SV 1762
1907	SV 95	1920	SV 315	1939	SV 1239	1952	SV 1829
1908	SV 104	1921	SV 400	1940	SV 1281	1953	SV 1898
1909	SV 112			1941	SV 1310	1954	SV 1983
1910	SV 119	1929	SV 842	1942	SV 1336	1955	SV 2093
1911	SV 134	1930	SV 872	1943	SV 1370	1956	SV 2241
1912	SV 147	1931	SV 908	1944	SV 1379	1957	SV 2362
1913	SV 159	1932	SV 944	1945	SV 1404	1958	SV 2481
1914	SV 180	1933	SV 971	1946	SV 1435	1959	SV 2655
1915	SV 198	1934	SV 1004	1947	SV 1487	1960	SV 2845
1916	SV 222	1935	SV 1034	1948	SV 1558	1961	SV 3046
1917	SV 242	1936	SV 1080	1949	SV 1621	1962	SV 3248
						1963	SV 3486 *

* Last normal issue SV 3722. Higher numbers used for re-registrations and from 4001 up issued by DVLA for "Age-Related" marks.

Commenced suffix marks 2.1.64

ASV to YSV and *ASV, BSV* allotted by DVLA to various VROs for "Age-Related" marks, 8/83 to 7/86 (except XSV, 1/90)

COUNTY COUNCIL OF KIRKCUDBRIGHT

SW 12/03

Registration commenced 19.12.03

Until 1921 separate and duplicate series for cars, motorcycles and Heavy Motor Cars.

First issues each year :

Cars etc.		Motorcycles		HMCs	
1904	SW 16	SW 9			
1905	SW 31	SW 28			
1906	SW 41	SW 35		SW 1	
1907	SW 53	SW 43			
1908	SW 70	SW 45		SW 2	
1909	SW 94	SW 48			
1910	SW 112	SW 53			
1911	SW 141	SW 57			
1912	SW 157	SW 77			
1913	SW 197	SW 109			
1914	SW 264	SW 138			
1915	SW 329	SW 180			
1916	SW 413	SW 206			
1917	SW 450	SW 226		SW 3	
1918	SW 463	SW 239			
1919	SW 478	SW 246			
1920	SW 541	SW 306		SW 6	

Last issues at the end of 1920 were SW 687, SW 386 and SW 6 respectively; a common series from SW 688 1.1.21.

ALL Vehicles

1921	SW 688	1930	SW 3432	1939	SW 6035	1948	SW 7410
1922	SW 961	1931	SW 3694	1940	SW 6292	1949	SW 7705
1923	SW 1199	1932	SW 3897	1941	SW 6397	1950	SW 8078
1924	SW 1462	1933	SW 4113	1942	SW 6468	1951	SW 8356
1925	SW 1731	1934	SW 4331	1943	SW 6564	1952	SW 8651
1926	SW 2079	1935	SW 4622	1944	SW 6656	1953	SW 8995
1927	SW 2412	1936	SW 4989	1945	SW 6752	1954	SW 9446
1928	SW 2713	1937	SW 5364	1946	SW 6823	1955	SW 9997
1929	SW 3079	1938	SW 5718	1947	SW 7087		

ASW	1/55	CSW	6/58	ESW	3/61	GSW	10/63
BSW	9/56	DSW	12/59	FSW	6/62		

Special mark for Diplomatic Corps : NSW 1 ca. 10/57

Commenced suffix marks 1.5.64

COUNTY COUNCIL OF LANARK

V 1/04   VA 7/22   VD 7/30

Dates of first issue each year not available prior to 1929, but the following ranges of numbers are known for the years shown :

1906	V 306 -	433		1911	V 1069 - 1279
1907	V 434 -	534		1912	V 1288 - 1692
1908	V 545 -	695		1913	V 1754 - 2286
1909	V 708 -	829		1914	V 2373 - 2744
1910	V 833 -	1026		1915	V 3128 - 3671

1921   V 7839 - 9234

First issues each year :

1929	VA 8346		1932	VD 1304		1935	VD 4250		1938	VD 8898
1930	VA 9374		1933	VD 2226		1936	VD 5631			
1931	VD 348		1934	VD 3027		1937	VD 7276			

AVA	8/38	EVA	6/48	JVA	7/53	NVA	3/56	SVA	5/58	WVA	2/60
AVD	3/39	EVD	2/49	JVD	1/54	NVD	5/56	SVD	8/58	WVD	4/60
BVA	11/39	FVA	10/49	KVA	6/54	OVA	10/56	TVA	11/58	XVA	6/60
BVD	11/42	FVD	7/50	KVD	10/54	OVD	3/57	TVD	2/59	XVD	8/60
CVA	2/46	GVA	3/51	LVA	2/55	PVA	6/57	UVA	4/59	YVA	10/60
CVD	11/46	GVD	1/52	LVD	5/55	PVD	9/57	UVD	6/59	YVD	1/61
DVA	5/47	HVA	9/52	MVA	8/55	RVA	12/57	VVA	9/59		
DVD	12/47	HVD	3/53	MVD	12/55	RVD	3/58	VVD	12/59		

AVA	3/61	CVA	12/61	EVA	10/62	GVA	8/63	JVA	2/64
AVD	5/61	CVD	3/62	EVD	12/62	GVD	8/63	JVD	4/64
BVA	7/61	DVA	5/62	FVA	3/63	HVA	10/63	KVA	5/64
BVD	9/61	DVD	7/62	FVD	4/63	HVD	1/64	KVD	ca. 6/76 *

* Re-registrations only.

Suffix marks commenced 1.6.64

COUNTY COUNCIL OF MIDLOTHIAN

SY 12/03

First issues each year, (no information available prior to 1929) :

1929	SY 3745		1935	SY 5369		1941	SY 7113		1947	SY 8080
1930	SY 4067		1936	SY 5697		1942	SY 7218		1948	SY 8524
1931	SY 4376		1937	SY 6018		1943	SY 7337		1950	SY 9001
1932	SY 4620		1938	SY 6384		1944	SY 7435		1951	SY 9413
1933	SY 4842		1939	SY 6720		1945	SY 7540		1952	SY 9783
1934	SY 5076		1940	SY 7017		1946	SY 7655			

ASY	5/51	DSY	7/56	GSY	11/59	KSY	4/62	NSY	6/64
BSY	9/53	ESY	11/57	HSY	7/60	LSY	2/63		
CSY	4/55	FSY	12/58	JSY	6/61	MSY	11/63		

Commenced suffix marks 4.8.64

PSY to YSY allotted by DVLA to various VROs for "Age-Related" marks, 5/96 - 2/97

COUNTY COUNCIL OF MORAY

Until 7.5.19 the official name of the county was the COUNTY COUNCIL OF ELGIN.

SO 12/03

First issues each year, (no information available prior to 1922) :

1922	SO 1279	1930	SO 3773	1938	SO 6126	1946	SO 7402
1923	SO 1500	1931	SO 4058	1939	SO 6469	1947	SO 7755
1924	SO 1811	1932	SO 4333	1940	SO 6841	1948	SO 8225
1925	SO 2143	1933	SO 4578	1941	SO 6979	1949	SO 8616
1926	SO 2535	1934	SO 4823	1942	SO 7099	1950	SO 9091
1927	SO 2879	1935	SO 5097	1943	SO 7163	1951	SO 9493
1928	not known	1936	SO 5417	1944	SO 7227	1952	SO 9916
1929	SO 3466	1937	SO 5742	1945	SO 7310		

ASO	2/52	DSO	10/56	GSO	3/60	KSO	9/62	NSO /73 re-regs. only.
BSO	12/53	ESO	3/58	HSO	2/61	LSO	6/63	
CSO	5/55	FSO	3/59	JSO	11/61	MSO	3/64	

Commenced suffix marks 1.9.64

COUNTY COUNCIL OF NAIRN

AS 12/03

First issues each year, (no information available prior to 1929) :

1929	AS 1182	1938	AS 1513	1947	AS 1746	1956	AS 2614
1930	AS 1213	1939	AS 1559	1948	AS 1833	1957	AS 2719
1931	AS 1237	1940	AS 1604	1949	AS 1903	1958	AS 2816
1932	AS 1260	1941	AS 1625	1950	AS 1990	1959	AS 2964
1933	AS 1286	1942	AS 1647	1951	AS 2062	1960	AS 3125
1934	AS 1327	1943	AS 1659	1952	AS 2154	1961	AS 3286
1935	AS 1370	1944	AS 1671	1953	AS 2235	1962	AS 3485
1936	AS 1416	1945	AS 1689	1954	AS 2370	1963	AS 3646
1937	AS 1465	1946	AS 1708	1955	AS 2477	1964	AS 3867 *

* Last normal issue AS 4097; higher numbers are re-registrations.

Special mark for Diplomatic Corps : TAS 1 ca. /71

Suffix marks commenced 1.1.65

COUNTY COUNCIL OF ORKNEY

BS 1/04

A single sequence for all vehicles.

First issues each year :

1905 BS 21	1909 BS 76	1913 BS 167	1917 BS 447	1921 BS 646
1906 BS 35	1910 BS 88	1914 BS 209	1918 BS 470	1922 BS 716
1907 BS 51	1911 BS 101	1915 BS 265	1919 BS 517	
1908 BS 62	1912 BS 118	1916 BS 374	1920 BS 582	

No information on first numbers each year is available for 1923-1928, but the following ranges of numbers are known for the years shown :

1923	BS 781 - 823	1925	BS 937 - 952	1927	BS 1105 - 1114
1924	BS 851 - 860	1926	BS 1015 - 1024	1928	BS 1151 - 1160

First issue each year :

1929 BS 1168	1937 BS 1623	1945 BS 2176	1953 BS 4195	1961 BS 6230
1930 BS 1238	1938 BS 1692	1946 BS 2229	1954 BS 4419	1962 BS 6593
1931 BS 1287	1939 BS 1769	1947 BS 2380	1955 BS 4629	1963 BS 6955
1932 BS 1345	1940 BS 1868	1948 BS 2720	1956 BS 4887	1964 BS 7353
1933 BS 1381	1941 BS 1942	1949 BS 3070	1957 BS 5110	
1934 BS 1427	1942 BS 2023	1950 BS 3436	1958 BS 5291	
1935 BS 1468	1943 BS 2085	1951 BS 3701	1959 BS 5551	
1936 BS 1528	1944 BS 2132	1952 BS 3977	1960 BS 5856	

Last normal issue BS 7778; higher numbers used for re-registrations and from 8000 up by DVLA for "Age-Related" marks.

Commenced suffix marks 1.1.65

COUNTY COUNCIL OF PEEBLES

DS 12/03

First issues each year, (no information available prior to 1929) :

1929 DS 1464	1937 DS 2067	1945 DS 2428	1953 DS 3280	1961 DS 5040
1930 DS 1572	1938 DS 2147	1946 DS 2448	1954 DS 3407	1962 DS 5354
1931 DS 1668	1939 DS 2231	1947 DS 2546	1955 DS 3576	1963 DS 5687
1932 DS 1734	1940 DS 2297	1948 DS 2667	1956 DS 3775	1964 DS 6061
1933 DS 1795	1941 DS 2330	1949 DS 2752	1957 DS 3965	
1934 DS 1854	1942 DS 2362	1950 DS 2904	1958 DS 4198	
1935 DS 1920	1943 DS 2397	1951 DS 3000	1959 DS 4438	
1936 DS 1991	1944 DS 2417	1952 DS 3126	1960 DS 4690	

Last normal issue DS 6396; higher numbers re-registrations and from 6574 up issued by DVLA for "Age-Related" marks.

Special mark for Diplomatic Corps : BDS 1 ca. 1/71

Commenced suffix marks 1.1.65

COUNTY COUNCIL OF PERTH

ES 12/03   GS 1/28

First issues each year not available prior to 1929, except for 1910 & 1911 (see below), but the following ranges or random numbers are known for the years shown :

1904	ES 126 (7/04)	1920	ES 3089 (7/20)-3090 (8/20)
1905	ES 180 (6/05)	1921	ES 3549 -4243 (4/21)
1906	ES 210 (1/06)	1922	ES 4685 (6/22)
1907	ES 381 (9/07)	1923	ES 5303 (2/23)-5859 (8/23)
		1924	ES 6292 (4/24)-6969 (11/24)
1909	ES 499 (2/09)-582 (12/09)	1925	ES 7337 (5/25)-7547 (6/25)
1910	ES 583 (1/10)-700 (12/10)	1926	ES 8244 (3/26)-8400 (4/26)
1911	ES 701 (1/11)-736 (3/11)	1927	ES 9796 (11/27)
		1928	GS 307 (5/28)
1914	ES 1230 (2/14)-1460 (6/14)		
1915	ES 1622 (3/15)		
1916	ES 1993 (3/16)		

1929	GS 795	1933	GS 3526	1937	GS 6670	1941	GS 9821
1930	GS 1589	1934	GS 4193	1938	GS 7729		
1931	GS 2342	1935	GS 4880	1939	GS 8616		
1932	GS 2954	1936	GS 5728	1940	GS 9444		

AES	9/41	EES	10/51	JES	6/56	NES	10/59	SES	1/62
AGS	3/45	EGS	9/52	JGS	1/57	NGS	2/60	SGS	4/62
BES	11/46	FES	4/53	KES	6/57	OES	5/60	TES	7/62
BGS	7/47	FGS	12/53	KGS	12/57	OGS	7/60	TGS	11/62
CES	5/48	GES	7/54	LES	4/58	PES	11/60	UES	3/63
CGS	3/49	GGS	2/55	LGS	9/58	PGS	3/61	UGS	5/63
DES	1/50	HES	7/55	MES	2/59	RES	6/61	VES	8/63
DGS	12/50	HGS	1/56	MGS	5/59	RGS	9/61	VGS	11/63

Special marks for Diplomatic Corps : *1 LES* ca. 3/67; *1 OES* 2/68

Commenced suffix marks 3.2.64.

COUNTY COUNCIL OF RENFREW

HS 12/03

Registration commenced 22.12.03

A single sequence for all vehicles.

First issues each year :

1904	HS 27	1913	HS 503	1922	HS 2401 *	1931	HS 6194
1905	HS 75	1914	HS 625	1923	HS 2760 *	1932	HS 6505
1906	HS 118	1915	HS 760	1924	HS 3179	1933	HS 6927
1907	HS 165	1916	HS 884	1925	HS 3655	1934	HS 7419
1908	HS 202	1917	HS 979	1926	HS 4111 *	1935	HS 8090
1909	HS 241	1918	HS 1049	1927	HS 4537	1936	HS 8809
1910	HS 303	1919	HS 1112	1928	HS 4923	1937	HS 9591
1911	HS 352	1920	HS 1455	1929	HS 5346		
1912	HS 407	1921	HS 1908	1930	HS 5780		

* approximate.

AHS	6/37	EHS	5/49	JHS	4/55	NHS	6/58	SHS	11/60	WHS	12/62
BHS	11/38	FHS	7/51	KHS	1/56	OHS	2/59	THS	5/61	XHS	5/63
CHS	7/40	GHS	4/53	LHS	11/56	PHS	10/59	UHS	12/61	YHS	10/63
DHS	5/47	HHS	5/54	MHS	9/57	RHS	4/60	VHS	5/62		

Suffix marks commenced 2.3.64

240

COUNTY COUNCIL OF ROSS & CROMARTY

JS 12/03

First issues each year, (no information available prior to 1929) :

1929	JS 3381	1935	JS 4781	1941	JS 6464	1947	JS 7223
1930	JS 3652	1936	JS 5030	1942	JS 6552	1948	JS 7750
1931	JS 3887	1937	JS 5390	1943	JS 6621	1949	JS 8201
1932	JS 4103	1938	JS 5714	1944	JS 6712	1950	JS 8780
1933	JS 4287	1939	JS 6052	1945	JS 6838	1951	JS 9200
1934	JS 4552	1940	JS 6372	1946	JS 6924	1952	JS 9644

AJS	9/52	DJS	6/56	GJS	6/59	KJS	10/61	NJS	11/63
BJS	3/54	EJS	8/57	HJS	4/60	LJS	7/62		
CJS	6/55	FJS	8/58	JJS	2/61	MJS	4/63		

Commenced suffix marks 2.3.64

COUNTY COUNCIL OF ROXBURGH

KS 11/03

Registration commenced 28.11.03

A common sequence for all vehicles.

First numbers issued each year :

1904	KS 14	1915	KS 725	1926	KS 3186	1937	KS 7380
1905	KS 58	1916	KS 853	1927	KS 3519	1938	KS 7895
1906	KS 88	1917	KS 863	1928	unknown	1939	KS 8294
1907	KS 119	1918	KS 875	1929	KS 4183	1940	KS 8713
1908	KS 151	1919	KS 887	1930	KS 4603	1941	KS 8882
1909	KS 179	1920	KS 1014	1931	KS 5024	1942	KS 8991
1910	KS 213	1921	KS 1361	1932	KS 5342	1943	KS 9118
1911	KS 276	1922	KS 1699	1933	KS 5661	1944	KS 9229
1912	KS 352	1923	KS 2015	1934	KS 6041	1945	KS 9353
1913	KS 460	1924	KS 2395	1935	KS 6462	1946	KS 9434
1914	KS 571	1925	KS 2774	1936	KS 6945	1947	KS 9831

AKS	4/47	DKS	4/53	GKS	12/56	KKS	6/59	NKS	7/61	RKS	9/63
BKS	4/49	EKS	9/54	HKS	11/57	LKS	3/60	OKS	4/62	SKS	5/64
CKS	5/51	FKS	9/55	JKS	8/58	MKS	10/60	PKS	2/63		

Commenced suffix marks 1.6.64

COUNTY COUNCIL OF SELKIRK

LS 12/03

First issues each year, (no information available prior to 1930) :

1930	LS 2443	1939	LS 4242	1948	LS 4890	1957	LS 6864
1931	LS 2630	1940	unknown	1949	LS 5016	1958	LS 7177
1932	LS 2819	1941	LS 4456	1950	LS 5196	1959	LS 7473
1933	LS 2961	1942	LS 4471	1951	LS 5350	1960	LS 7860
1934	LS 3125	1943	LS 4486	1952	LS 5509	1961	LS 8288
1935	LS 3371	1944	LS 4502	1953	LS 5680	1962	LS 8642
1936	LS 3603	1945	LS 4532	1954	LS 5916	1963	LS 9006
1937	LS 3832	1946	LS 4569	1955	LS 6200	1964	LS 9449
1938	LS 4060	1947	LS 4713	1956	LS 6553		

Last normal issue LS 9584; higher numbers on re-registrations.

Special marks for Diplomatic Corps : ELS 1 ca. 3/67; *1 BLS* 7/95

Commenced suffix marks 1.4.64.

COUNTY COUNCIL OF STIRLING

MS 12/03   WG 11/30

A single sequence for all vehicles.

First numbers issued each year :

1904	MS 44	1909	MS 356	1914	MS 1044	1919	MS 1948
1905	MS 126	1910	MS 430	1915	MS 1351	1920	MS 2353
1906	MS 189	1911	MS 542	1916	MS 1659	1921	MS 3014
1907	MS 226	1912	MS 663	1917	MS 1806		
1908	MS 287	1913	MS 827	1918	MS 1890		

No details available for 1922-1928, but the following ranges of numbers are known :

1921		3480 (8/21)	1925	MS 5678 (5/25)
1922	MS 3793 (3/22)-4018 (11/22)		1926	MS 6284 (3/26)-6926 (11/26)
1923	MS 4157 (2/23)-4260 (4/23)		1927	MS 7022 (1/27)-7471 (5/27)
1924	MS 4830 (3/24)-5216 (9/24)		1928	MS 8206 (4/28)

1929	MS 8530	1933	WG 1540	1937	WG 5560	1941	WG 9554
1930	MS 9400	1934	WG 2245	1938	WG 7005	1942	WG 9654
1931	WG 107	1935	WG 3210	1939	WG 8183	1943	WG 9876
1932	WG 824	1936	WG 4300	1940	WG 9278		

AMS	7/43	BMS	8/52	JMS	5/56	NMS	4/59	SMS	3/61	WMS	3/63
AWG	9/46	BWG	3/53	JWG	11/56	NWG	6/59	SWG	5/61	WWG	5/63
BMS	6/47	FMS	10/53	KMS	4/57	OMS	10/59	TMS	7/61	XMS	7/63
BWG	3/48	FWG	4/54	KWG	9/57	OWG	1/60	TWG	11/61	XWG	10/63
CMS	2/49	GMS	10/54	LMS	1/58	PMS	3/60	UMS	3/62	YMS	12/65 *
CWG	11/49	GWG	2/55	LWG	5/58	PWG	5/60	UWG	5/62		
DMS	10/50	HMS	8/55	MMS	9/58	RMS	8/60	VMS	8/62		
DWG	9/51	HWG	12/55	MWG	1/59	RWG	12/60	VWG	12/62		

* re-registrations only.

Special mark for Diplomatic Corps : *1 BMS* 6/88

Suffix marks commenced 3.2.64.

COUNTY COUNCIL OF SUTHERLAND

NS 1/04

A single sequence for all vehicles. First issues each year, (no information available for 1922-1928) :

1905	NS 18	1919	NS 297	1939	NS 1747	1953	NS 2587
1906	NS 38	1920	NS 319	1940	NS 1827	1954	NS 2738
1907	NS 65	1921	NS 365*	1941	NS 1844	1955	NS 2924
1908	NS 84			1942	NS 1862	1956	NS 3147
1909	NS 102	1929	NS 1052	1943	NS 1888	1957	NS 3362
1910	NS 116	1930	NS 1140	1944	NS 1905	1958	NS 3613
1911	NS 135	1931	NS 1233	1945	NS 1931	1959	NS 3937
1912	NS 158	1932	NS 1290	1946	NS 1955	1960	NS 4245
1913	NS 178	1933	NS 1343	1947	NS 2016	1961	NS 4520
1914	NS 209	1934	NS 1384	1948	NS 2111	1962	NS 4817
1915	NS 252	1935	NS 1454	1949	NS 2231	1963	NS 5107
1916	NS 277	1936	NS 1510	1950	NS 2332	1964	NS 5501
1917	NS 289	1937	NS 1589	1951	NS 2422		
1918	NS 292	1938	NS 1680	1952	NS 2505		

* approximate.

Last normal issue NS 5683, higher numbers on re-registrations.

Commenced suffix issues 1.7.64

COUNTY COUNCIL OF WEST LOTHIAN

Until 1921 the official name of the county was the COUNTY COUNCIL OF LINLITHGOW.

SX 1/04

Until at least 1921 motor cars and motorcycles were numbered in separate blocks and there was some duplication. The blocks were :
Motor cars (and HMCs) : SX 1-50, 101-149, 251-299, 400-950, 1135-1199, 1251-1299.
Motorcycles : SX 51-100, 150-250, 350-399, 500-1134, 1200-1250, 1300-1350.
Note that 300-349 were omitted and 500-950 were duplicated. No information is available on later blocks, if any.

First issues each year : (No information available for 1922-1928)

Motor Cars				Motorcycles			
1905	SX 22	1914	SX 419	1905	SX 63	1914	SX 521
1906	SX 34	1915	SX 452	1906	SX 69	1915	SX 609
1907	SX 38	1916	SX 494	1907	SX 80	1916	SX 673
1908	SX 47	1917	SX 539	1908	SX 88	1917	SX 715
1909	SX 113	1918	SX 564	1909	SX 96	1918	SX 747
1910	SX 129	1919	SX 583	1910	SX 154	1919	SX 770
1911	SX 142	1920	SX 665	1911	SX 181	1920	SX 926
1912	SX 255	1921	SX 887	1912	SX 218	1921	SX 1130
1913	SX 273			1913	SX 357		

All Vehicles							
1929	SX 2819	1936	SX 4190	1943	SX 5391	1950	SX 6860
1930	SX 2991	1937	SX 4449	1944	SX 5450	1951	SX 7181 **
1931	SX 3184	1938	SX 4749	1945	SX 5525	1952	SX 7432
1932	SX 3350	1939	SX 4971	1946	SX 5610	1953	SX 8029
1933	SX 3513	1940	SX 5182	1947	SX 5886	1954	SX 8618
1934	SX 3703	1941	SX 5240	1948	SX 6244	1955	SX 9160
1935	SX 3914	1942	SX 5328	1949	SX 6518	1956	SX 9854

** SX 7501-7600 allocated to British Road Services 8/51.

ASX	2/56	CSX	5/58	ESX	1/60	GSX	6/61	JSX	4/63
BSX	4/57	DSX	4/59	FSX	9/60	HSX	5/62	KSX	11/63

Commenced suffix marks 1.4.64

COUNTY COUNCIL OF WIGTOWN

OS 1/04

A common sequence for all vehicles.

First numbers issued each year (no information available 1923-1928) :

1905 OS 12	1917 OS 362	1932 OS 3197	1944 OS 5997
1906 OS 24	1918 OS 393	1933 OS 3438	1945 OS 6103
1907 OS 36	1919 OS 425	1934 OS 3609	1946 OS 6183
1908 OS 46	1920 OS 508	1935 OS 3848	1947 OS 6423
1909 OS 59	1921 OS 739	1936 OS 4226	1948 OS 6777
1910 OS 65	1922 OS 835	1937 OS 4581	1949 OS 7083
1911 OS 81		1938 OS 4933	1950 OS 7446
1912 OS 97		1939 OS 5260	1951 OS 7761
1913 OS 131		1940 OS 5588	1952 OS 8079
1914 OS 174	1929 OS 2448	1941 OS 5682	1953 OS 8425
1915 OS 243	1930 OS 2723	1942 OS 5765	1954 OS 8981
1916 OS 316	1931 OS 3007	1943 OS 5895	1955 OS 9628

AOS	7/55	COS	6/58	EOS	10/60	GOS	12/62
BOS	3/57	DOS	8/59	FOS	11/61	HOS	1/64

Special issue for Diplomatic Corps : *1 COS* 6/79

Commenced suffix marks 1.9.64

COUNTY COUNCIL OF ZETLAND

PS 1/04

A single sequence for all vehicles.

First issues each year:

1905	PS 21	1920	PS 347	1935	PS 1053	1950	PS 1938
1906	PS 34	1921	PS 393	1936	PS 1100	1951	PS 2052
1907	PS 46	1922	PS 413	1937	PS 1160	1952	PS 2161
1908	PS 56	1923	PS 435	1938	PS 1215	1953	PS 2248
1909	PS 69	1924	PS 479	1939	PS 1271	1954	PS 2332
1910	PS 88	1925	PS 535	1940	PS 1305	1955	PS 2454
1911	PS 104	1926	PS 622	1941	PS 1315	1956	PS 2611
1912	PS 130	1927	PS 684	1942	PS 1320	1957	PS 2726
1913	PS 161	1928	PS 726	1943	PS 1349	1958	PS 2877
1914	PS 191	1929	PS 770	1944	PS 1370	1959	PS 3027
1915	PS 231	1930	PS 824	1945	PS 1378	1960	PS 3216
1916	PS 264	1931	PS 877	1946	PS 1396	1961	PS 3417
1917	PS 282	1932	PS 924	1947	PS 1501	1962	PS 3613
1918	PS 288	1933	PS 959	1948	PS 1643	1963	PS 3787
1919	PS 308	1934	PS 994	1949	PS 1767	1964	PS 3922

Last normal issue PS 4080, higher numbers used for re-registrations.

Commenced suffix marks 1.1.65

BURGH COUNCIL OF ABERDEEN

RS 12/03   RG 11/28

Prior to 1921 the Heavy Motor Car series was composed of the letters RS, a hyphen, a letter X and a serial number, e.g. RS-X 123. Unusually some numbers in this series were perpetuated after 1920 and allowed to stand. The series reached RS-X 152. Sometimes the hyphen was omitted on plates, giving the appearance of a three-letter prefix !

First numbers issued each year, (no information available prior to 1929) :

1929	RG 38	1932	RG 2558	1935	RG 5032	1938	RG 8814
1930	RG 878	1933	RG 3276	1936	RG 6243		
1931	RG 1775	1934	RG 4122	1937	RG 7613		

ARG	12/38	ERG	8/50	JRG	11/55	NRG	4/59	SRG	8/61	WRG	1/64
ARS	not alloc	ERS	7/51	JRS	4/56	NRS	7/59	SRS	1/62	WRS	4/64
BRG	8/39	FRG	8/52	KRG	10/56	ORG	11/59	TRG	4/62		
BRS	12/44	FRS	5/53	KRS	5/57	ORS	3/60	TRS	7/62		
CRG	9/46	GRG	1/54	LRG	10/57	PRG	5/60	URG	12/62		
CRS	8/47	GRS	7/54	LRS	3/58	PRS	9/60	URS	4/63		
DRG	9/48	HRG	2/55	MRG	7/58	RRG	2/61	VRG	6/63		
DRS	9/49	HRS	6/55	MRS	12/58	RRS	5/61	VRS	9/63		

Special issues for Diplomatic Corps : *1 ARG* ca. 9/74; *1 GRG* ca. 12/95

Commenced suffix marks 1.5.64

BURGH COUNCIL OF DUNDEE

TS 1/04   YJ 6/32

A single sequence for all vehicles.

Until 1907 numbers appear to have been issued in a haphazard sequence; first issues each year thereafter :

1907	TS 197	1918	TS 1661	1929	TS 7709	1940	YJ 7476
1908	TS 274	1919	TS 1716	1930	TS 8449	1941	YJ 7695
1909	TS 333	1920	TS 2102	1931	TS 9033	1942	YJ 7781
1910	TS 386	1921	TS 2910	1932	TS 9628	1943	YJ 7880
1911	TS 460	1922	TS 3407	1933	YJ 349	1944	YJ 7973
1912	TS 557	1923	TS 3837	1934	YJ 1120	1945	YJ 8041
1913	TS 738	1924	TS 4314	1935	YJ 2045	1946	YJ 8203
1914	TS 976	1925	TS 4808	1936	YJ 3197	1947	YJ 9017
1915	TS 1214	1926	TS 5480	1937	YJ 4401	1948	YJ 9931
1916	TS 1455	1927	TS 6278	1938	YJ 5513		
1917	TS 1582	1928	TS 7015	1939	YJ 6512		

ATS	1/48	DTS	1/54	GTS	5/57	KTS	12/59	NTS	2/62	RTS	2/64
AYJ	5/49	DYJ	8/54	GYJ	11/57	KYJ	4/60	NYJ	5/62	RYJ	4/64
BTS	6/50	ETS	2/55	HTS	5/58	LTS	7/60	OTS	10/62	STS	7/64
BYJ	6/51	EYJ	8/55	HYJ	10/58	LYJ	12/60	OYJ	3/63		
CTS	7/52	FTS	3/56	JTS	4/59	MTS	5/61	PTS	6/63		
CYJ	5/53	FYJ	9/56	JYJ	7/59	MYJ	8/61	PYJ	10/63		

Commenced suffix marks 4.8.64.

TYJ to YYJ allocated by DVLA to various VROs for "Age-Related" marks 4/93 to 10/93.

BURGH COUNCIL OF EDINBURGH

S 12/03   SG 12/20   SF 6/24   SC 10/27   FS 4/31   WS 6/34 *

* WS was taken over from BURGH COUNCIL OF LEITH (q.v.) who had issued WS 1 - 520; Edinburgh issues commenced at WS 521

First issues each year, (no information available prior to 1929) :

| 1929 | SC 3103 | | 1931 | SC 9177 | | 1933 | FS 4688 | | 1935 | WS 2402 |
| 1930 | SC 6150 | | 1932 | FS 1824 | | 1934 | FS 7771 | | 1936 | WS 7259 |

AFS	7/36	EFS	7/44	JFS	3/51	NFS	5/55	SFS	5/58	WFS	7/60
ASC	10/36	ESC	10/45	JSC	6/51	NSC	7/55	SSC	6/58	WSC	7/60
ASF	12/36	ESF	4/46	JSF	11/51	NSF	9/55	SSF	8/58	WSF	9/60
ASG	3/37	ESG	7/46	JSG	3/52	NSG	10/55	SSG	10/58	WSG	10/60
AWS	4/37	EWS	9/46	JWS	5/52	NWS	12/55	SWS	12/58	WWS	12/60
BFS	7/37	FFS	11/46	KFS	9/52	OFS	2/56	TFS	1/59	XFS	1/61
BSC	10/37	FSC	2/47	KSC	12/52	OSC	3/56	TSC	3/59	XSC	3/61
BSF	1/38	FSF	5/47	KSF	4/53	OSF	5/56	TSF	4/59	XSF	3/61
BSG	3/38	FSG	7/47	KSG	6/53	OSG	7/56	TSG	5/59	XSG	4/61
BWS	5/38	FWS	11/47	KWS	8/53	OWS	10/56	TWS	6/59	XWS	5/61
CFS	7/38	GFS	3/48	LFS	10/53	PFS	12/56	UFS	7/59	YFS	6/61
CSC	11/38	GSC	6/48	LSC	12/53	PSC	2/57	USC	9/59	YSC	7/61
CSF	1/39	GSF	11/48	LSF	3/54	PSF	4/57	USF	10/59	YSF	8/61
CSG	3/39	GSG	2/49	LSG	5/54	PSG	6/57	USG	12/59	YSG	10/61
CWS	5/39	GWS	5/49	LWS	7/54	PWS	7/57	UWS	1/60	YWS	12/61
DFS	7/39	HFS	8/49	MFS	9/54	RFS	9/57	VFS	2/60		
DSC	2/40	HSC	12/49	MSC	11/54	RSC	11/57	VSC	3/60		
DSF	8/40	HSF	4/50	MSF	12/54	RSF	1/58	VSF	4/60		
DSG	12/41	HSG	7/50	MSG	3/55	RSG	3/58	VSG	5/60		
DWS	12/42	HWS	11/50	MWS	4/55	RWS	4/58	VWS	6/60		

There was no segregation of motorcycles in reverse format issues. Each series commenced at 1.

SF   1/62   SC   2/63   FS   1/64 .

Commenced suffix marks 3.2.64.

BURGH COUNCIL OF GLASGOW

G 12/03   GA /18   GB 12/21   GD 7/25   GE 3/28   GG 7/30   US * 3/33   YS * 1/35

* US taken over from BURGH COUNCIL OF GOVAN (q.v.), who issued US 1-529;
  Glasgow issues commenced US 530.
* YS taken over from BURGH COUNCIL OF PARTICK (q.v.), who issued YS 1-39;
  Glasgow issues commenced YS 40.

First numbers issued each year, (no information available prior to 1929) :

1929	GE 3599		1931	GG 2055		1933	GG 9205		1935	US 8800
1930	GE 7945		1932	GG 5631		1934	US 4130		1936	YS 5000

AGA	9/36	EGA	2/46	JGA	12/50	NGA	7/54	SGA	11/56	WGA	12/58
AGB	11/36	EGB	5/46	JGB	2/51	NGB	8/54	SGB	12/56	WGB	1/59
AGD	12/36	EGD	7/46	JGD	4/51	NGD	10/54	SGD	1/57 *	WGD	2/59
AGE	1/37	EGE	9/46	JGE	6/51	NGE	11/54	SGE	2/57	WGE	3/59
AGG	3/37	EGG	11/46	JGG	8/51	NGG	12/54	SGG	3/57	WGG	4/59
AUS	4/37	EUS	1/47	JUS	10/51	NUS	1/55	SUS	4/57	WUS	4/59
AYS	6/37	EYS	4/47	JYS	12/51	NYS	2/55	SYS	4/57	WYS	5/59
BGA	7/37	FGA	5/47	KGA	2/52	OGA	3/55	TGA	5/57	XGA	5/59
BGB	9/37	FGB	7/47	KGB	4/52	OGB	3/55	TGB	6/57	XGB	6/59
BGD	11/37	FGD	9/47	KGD	6/52	OGD	4/55	TGD	7/57	XGD	6/59
BGE	12/37	FGE	12/47	KGE	8/52	OGE	5/55	TGE	7/57	XGE	7/59
BGG	3/38	FGG	2/48	KGG	10/52	OGG	6/55	TGG	9/57	XGG	7/59
BUS	4/38	FUS	5/48	KUS	11/52	OUS	7/55	TUS	10/57	XUS	8/59
BYS	5/38	FYS	6/48 *	KYS	1/53	OYS	7/55	TYS	11/57	XYS	9/59
CGA	8/38	GGA	7/48	LGA	3/53	PGA	9/55	UGA	12/57	YGA	10/59
CGB	10/38	GGB	9/48	LGB	4/53	PGB	10/55	UGB	1/58	YGB	11/59
CGD	11/38	GGD	11/48	LGD	5/53	PGD	10/55	UGD	2/58	YGD	12/59
CGE	1/39	GGE	2/49	LGE	7/53	PGE	11/55	UGE	3/58	YGE	12/59
CGG	2/39	GGG	4/49	LGG	8/53	PGG	12/55	UGG	3/58	YGG	1/60
CUS	4/39	GUS	5/49	LUS	9/53	PUS	2/56	UUS	4/58	YUS	2/60
CYS	5/39	GYS	7/49	LYS	11/53	PYS	3/56	UYS	5/58	YYS	2/60
DGA	7/39	HGA	9/49	MGA	12/53	RGA	3/56	VGA	5/58		
DGB	10/39	HGB	11/49	MGB	1/54	RGB	4/56	VGB	6/58		
DGD	3/40	HGD	1/50	MGD	2/54	RGD	5/56	VGD	7/58		
DGE	9/40	HGE	3/50	MGE	3/54	RGE	6/56	VGE	8/58		
DGG	3/42	HGG	5/50	MGG	4/54	RGG	7/56	VGG	9/58		
DUS	8/43	HUS	7/50	MUS	5/54	RUS	8/56	VUS	10/58		
DYS	3/45	HYS	10/50	MYS	6/54	RYS	10/56	VYS	11/58		

* FYS and SGD reserved for Glasgow City Transport.

AGA	3/60	CGA	12/60	EGA	8/61	GGA	7/62	JGA	5/63
AGB	3/60	CGB	1/61	EGB	9/61	GGB	7/62	JGB	5/63
AGD	4/60	CGD	2/61	EGD	10/61	GGD	8/62	JGD	6/63
AGE	4/60	CGE	2/61	EGE	11/61	GGE	9/62	JGE	7/63
AGG	5/60	CGG	3/61	EGG	12/61	GGG	10/62	JGG	7/63
AUS	5/60	CUS	3/61	EUS	1/62	GUS	11/62	JUS	8/63
AYS	6/60	CYS	4/61	EYS	2/62	GYS	12/62	JYS	9/63
BGA	6/60	DGA	4/61	FGA	3/62	HGA	1/63	KGA	9/63
BGB	7/60	DGB	5/61	FGB	3/62	HGB	2/63	KGB	10/63
BGD	7/60	DGD	5/61	FGD	4/62	HGD	2/63	KGD	11/63
BGE	8/60	DGE	6/61	FGE	4/62	HGE	3/63	KGE	12/63
BGG	9/60	DGG	6/61	FGG	5/62	HGG	4/63	KGG	/75 *
BUS	10/60	DUS	7/61	FUS	5/62	HUS	4/63		
BYS	11/60	DYS	7/61	FYS	6/62	HYS	4/63		

* re-registrations only.

Special issue for Diplomatic Corps : *1 UGA* 4/64

Commenced suffix marks 2.1.64.

BURGH COUNCIL OF GOVAN

US 1/04

Issued US 1 - 529 before being absorbed into the BURGH OF GLASGOW, as from 1.11.12.

GLASGOW issued US 530 up.

BURGH COUNCIL OF GREENOCK

VS 12/03

First issues each year, (no information available prior to 1929) :

1929	VS 1443	1937	VS 3336	1945	VS 4319	1953	VS 5780
1930	VS 1817	1938	VS 3682	1946	VS 4421	1954	VS 6081
1931	VS 2008	1939	VS 3931	1947	VS 4624	1955	VS 6536
1932	VS 2154	1940	VS 4159	1948	VS 4829	1956	VS 7179
1933	VS 2293	1941	VS 4190	1949	VS 4974	1957	VS 7760
1934	VS 2496	1942	VS 4209	1950	VS 5168	1958	VS 8379
1935	VS 2751	1943	VS 4262	1951	VS 5317	1959	VS 9156
1936	VS 3021	1944	VS 4275	1952	VS 5545		

AVS   12/59   BVS   11/60   CVS   10/61   DVS   8/62   EVS 7/63 *   FVS **

* Later numbers in this series issued with B suffix.
** Re-registrations only

Commenced suffix marks 1.4.64

GVS to YVS allocated by DVLA to various VROs for "Age-Related" marks, 3/92 to 4/93.

BURGH COUNCIL OF LEITH

WS 12/03

Registration commenced 19.12.03.

Separate and duplicated series for motor cars (including HMCs) and motorcycles.

First issues each year :

	Motor Cars				Motorcycles		
1904	WS 11	1913	WS 161	1904	WS 6	1913	WS 119
1905	WS 27	1914	WS 190	1905	WS 25	1914	WS 136
1906	WS 43	1915	WS 222	1906	WS 34	1915	WS 158
1907	WS 59	1916	WS 241	1907	WS 42	1916	WS 182
1908	WS 77	1917	WS 267	1908	WS 47	1917	WS 201
1909	WS 90	1918	WS 280	1909	WS 59	1918	WS 219
1910	WS 104	1919	WS 291	1910	WS 67	1919	WS 233
1911	WS 121	1920	WS 386	1911	WS 86	1920	WS 307
1912	WS 139			1912	WS 98		

LEITH issues ended at WS 520 and WS 395 respectively.

The BURGH OF LEITH was absorbed into the BURGH OF EDINBURGH as from 1.11.20 and further issues of WS were made by the latter council from 6/34.

BURGH COUNCIL OF MOTHERWELL & WISHAW

The previously separate burghs of MOTHERWELL and WISHAW were amalgamated with
effect from 1.1.21. The new authority had a combined population exceeding 50,000 and thus
became a registration authority.

GM 1/21

First issues each year, (no information available prior to 1929) :

1929	GM 1348	1937	GM 2698	1945	GM 3691	1953	GM 5781
1930	GM 1541	1938	GM 3000	1946	GM 3725	1954	GM 6316
1931	GM 1660	1939	GM 3294	1947	GM 4006	1955	GM 6930
1932	GM 1813	1940	GM 3553	1948	GM 4302	1956	GM 7807
1933	GM 1923	1941	GM 3592	1949	GM 4530	1957	GM 8507
1934	GM 2090	1942	GM 3614	1950	GM 4896	1958	GM 9172
1935	GM 2262	1943	GM 3635	1951	GM 5163	1959	GM 9924
1936	GM 2485	1944	GM 3666	1952	GM 5434		

AGM	1/59	CGM	1/61	EGM	6/62	GGM	**
BGM	2/60	DGM	8/61	FGM	4/63		

** Re-registration; only GGM 1 known.

Commenced suffix marks 10/63. This date was determined by the fact that FGM, which was
then completed, was the last mark allotted in the current regulations.

BURGH COUNCIL OF PAISLEY

XS 1/04

Prior to 1921 there were separate and duplicate series for motor cars, motorcycles and HMCs.

First issues each year, (no information available prior to 1929) :

1929	XS 2218	1937	XS 4276	1945	XS 5624	1953	XS 7978
1930	XS 2434	1938	XS 4662	1946	XS 5687	1954	XS 8419
1931	XS 2618	1939	XS 5031	1947	XS 6017	1955	XS 8976
1932	XS 2808	1940	XS 5361	1948	XS 6280	1956	XS 9616
1933	XS 3017	1941	XS 5449	1949	XS 6570		
1934	XS 3271	1942	XS 5473	1950	XS 6920		
1935	XS 3571	1943	XS 5515	1951	XS 7207		
1936	XS 3908	1944	XS 5556	1952	XS 7602		

AXS	7/56	CXS	3/59	EXS	3/61	GXS	10/62	JXS	4/64
BXS	1/58	DXS	3/60	FXS	12/61	HXS	7/63		

Commenced suffix marks 1.9.64

BURGH COUNCIL OF PARTICK

YS 1/04

The BURGH OF PARTICK issued YS 1 to 39 before being absorbed by the BURGH OF
GLASGOW as from 1.11.12.

YS 40 up were issued by GLASGOW commencing 1/35.

NOTE.—In addition to the fee payable to the Registering Authority (County Council, &c.) on the registration of a Motor Car or Motor Cycle, under the provisions of the Motor Car Act, 1903, an Excise License is required to be taken out *annually* in respect of every such vehicle, unless the person keeping it is entitled to exemption (13970 Ex. 1905).

YOUR ATTENTION IS DIRECTED TO THE INFORMATION ON THE BACK HEREOF.

COUNTY BOROUGH OF STOCKPORT.

Copy of Register of Heavy Motor Cars.

1. Index Mark and Number on Identification Plates.	2. Full Name of Owner and Postal Address of his usual Residence.	3. Description or Type of Car.	4. Type and Colour of Body of Car.	5. Weight unladen.	6. Axle-weight of each Axle.	7. Diameter of each Wheel.	8. Width and Material of Tyres.	9. Maximum Speed permissible.	10. Whether intended for—			11. Date of Registration.	12. If Cancelled, Date of Cancellation.
									(a) Private use.	(b) Use for Trade Purposes.	(c) Use as a Public Conveyance.		
D.B. Dennis Bros, Ltd 142 Onslow St, Guildford.		Dennis 30 cwt Van.	Covered Box Van, dark green	2 5 0	Front 2 c 9 3.10.0 Back 2 c 9 3.10.0	34"	Iron 4", Iron rubber, Back 8" rubber	12 miles per hour		Trade Purposes		3/9/07	

Entered by ___R. Lindall___

Examined _____
Chief Clerk.

Signed, ___Frederick Brindley___
Chief Constable.

250

APPENDIX 4

REGISTRATION MARKS BY
AUTHORITY & DATE
NORTHERN IRELAND

In both parts of Ireland the sequence of use of the various formats of letters and numerals followed a different pattern from that of Great Britain. In Northern Ireland, as each authority exhausted its allocation of two-letter marks, (followed by a number), it used its two-letter allocation in reverse format, commencing January 1958. As on the mainland, marks which were already in use or earmarked for trade plates commenced at numbers other than 1 and, where known, this information is shown in the tables. As and when the reverse format marks were exhausted, the format changed to three letters followed by up to four numerals, commencing January 1966. As in Great Britain, the last two letters of the trio were the basic index mark identifying the issuing authority. However, whereas in Great Britain each mark of an authority was used with the letter A before moving on the Bxx multiples and so on, (e.g. AEL, ALJ, ARU, BEL, BLJ, BRU etc.), in Northern Ireland the sequence was and is, e.g. AIA, BIA, CIA to YIA, before commencing ADZ, BDZ, CDZ etc. Again, unlike the mainland, I (but not Z) was used as a first letter in three-letter combinations.

When computerisation commenced in October 1986 the series in use in each authority was terminated and a new series begun. The tabulation shows the last normal issue before computerisation, but further issues were subsequently made above the numbers shown for re-registrations.

From November 1985 the first 100 numbers of each series were withheld from normal issues and since April 1989 the first 999 numbers are withheld. Even 1000s and "three-of-a-kind" are also withheld, but all these omitted numbers may be offered for sale in auctions. Each series ends normally at 9500 and the remaining numbers are used mostly for security type re-registrations.

The tabulation shows all marks commenced by 31 December 1998, but the series for each VRO are continuing. In general there was no gap or overlap between the completion of a mark and the commencement of its successor; exceptions are noted in the tables, but discrepancies of one month are ignored. Reverse format marks are shown in *italic* script.

COUNTY COUNCIL OF ANTRIM

IA	12/03		DZ	3/32		KZ	1/47		RZ	2/54

IA (from 1)	1/58	DZ (from 301)	6/60	KZ (from 1) 9/62		RZ (from 501)	6/64

AIA	1/66	CIA	9/68	EIA	3/71	GIA	1/73 (to 8976)
BIA	5/67	DIA	2/70	FIA	4/72		

BALLYMENA LVLO/VRO

GIA*	1/74	JIA	9/75	MIA	11/77	PIA	9/79	TIA	1/82	WIA	12/83
HIA	2/74	KIA	5/76	NIA	6/78	RIA	5/80	UIA	9/82	XIA	5/84
IIA	12/74	LIA	2/77	OIA	3/79	SIA	3/81	VIA	4/83	YIA	1/85
* from 8977.											

ADZ	7/85	EDZ	2/88	IDZ	3/90	MDZ	4/92	RDZ	4/94	VDZ	3/96
BDZ	3/86 #	FDZ	8/88	JDZ	9/90	NDZ	10/92	SDZ	9/94	WDZ	10/96
CDZ	10/86	GDZ	3/89	KDZ	3/91	ODZ	4/93	TDZ	3/95	XDZ	5/97
DDZ	6/87	HDZ	9/89	LDZ	9/91	PDZ	10/93	UDZ	8/95	YDZ	11/97
# last normal 7458.											

AKZ 5/98

COUNTY COUNCIL OF ARMAGH

IB	12/03		LZ	1/47*		XZ	11/57

* Although LZ commenced 1/47, IB was not completed until 8/47.

IB	4/62 (from 301)	LZ	11/65 (from 1)	XZ	3/69 (from 1)

AIB 3/72 (to 7785)

ARMAGH LVLO/VRO

AIB*	1/74	EIB	4/79	IIB	2/85	MIB	11/88	RIB	8/91	VIB	3/94
BIB	7/74	FIB	12/80	JIB	2/86 #	NIB	8/89	SIB	4/92	WIB	11/94
CIB	5/76	GIB	7/82	KIB	10/86	OIB	5/90	TIB	11/92	XIB	6/95
DIB	12/77	HIB	12/83	LIB	1/88	PIB	1/91	UIB	8/93	YIB	3/96
* from 7786				# last normal 4400							

ALZ	11/96	BLZ	6/97	CLZ	2/98	DLZ	8/98

COUNTY COUNCIL OF DOWN

IJ 1-100 were mixed, but thereafter there was a period when motorcycles were segregated in blocks. The following were the motorcycle blocks : IJ 101-150, 201-249, 301-350, 451-500, 551-600, 651-700, 751-800, 851-950, 1001-1100, 1151-1200 and 1251 up, (no information thereafter). Other vehicles took the remaining numbers, but 1001-1050 were, in fact, duplicated.

IJ	12/03	BZ	4/30	JZ	10/46	SZ	8/54		

IJ (from 101)	10/58	BZ (from 201)	5/61	JZ (from 201 ?)	11/63	SZ (from 1 ?)	7/65.

AIJ	5/67	BIJ	1/69	CIJ	6/70	DIJ	10/71	EIJ	11/72	FIJ	11/73 (to 1239)

DOWNPATRICK LVLO/VRO

FIJ*	1/74	JIJ	5/77	NIJ	5/80	SIJ	6/83	WIJ	12/85	
GIJ	11/74	KIJ	3/78	OIJ	1/81	TIJ	2/84	XIJ	6/86 (last normal 3439)
HIJ	10/75	LIJ	11/78	PIJ	2/82	UIJ	8/84	YIJ	10/86	
IIJ	8/76	MIJ	6/79	RIJ	10/82	VIJ	4/85			

* from 1240

ABZ	5/87	EBZ	11/89	IBZ	4/92	MBZ	11/94	RBZ	1/97
BBZ	1/88	FBZ	5/90	JBZ	1/93	NBZ	5/95	SBZ	6/97
CBZ	8/88	GBZ	1/91	KBZ	8/93	OBZ	12/95	TBZ	1/98
DBZ	3/89	HBZ	8/91	LBZ	4/94	PBZ	6/96	UBZ	6/98

COUNTY COUNCIL OF FERMANAGH

IL	1/04	IL (from 51)	2/58	AIL	8/66 (to 9400)

ENNISKILLEN LVLO/VRO

AIL*	1/74	DIL	9/82	GIL	7/89	JIL	11/93	MIL	11/95	PIL	2/98
BIL	4/74	EIL#	12/85	HIL	1/91	KIL	not iss.	NIL	10/96		
CIL	8/78	FIL	10/86	IIL	2/92	LIL	11/94	OIL	9/97		

* from 9401   # last normal 2423

COUNTY COUNCIL OF LONDONDERRY

IW	12/03	NZ	1/49	YZ	12/57

IW (from 1)	9/62	NZ (from 1 ?)	10/66	YZ (from 1 ?)	11/70

AIW 10/73 (to 687)

COLERAINE LVLO/VRO

AIW*	1/74	EIW	4/81	IIW	10/86	MIW	6/91	RIW	1/95	VIW	12/97
BIW	1/76	FIW	1/83	JIW	5/88	NIW	4/92	SIW	9/95	WIW	7/98
CIW	9/77	GIW	5/84	KIW	6/89	OIW	3/93	TIW	5/96		
DIW	5/79	HIW#	9/85	LIW	6/90	PIW	3/94	UIW	2/97		

* from 688   # incomplete, but last normal unknown.

COUNTY COUNCIL OF TYRONE

JI	12/03			HZ	2/44			VZ	4/56	
JI (from 100)	4/61			HZ (from 200)	10/64			VZ (from 200)	3/68	
AJI	6/71			BJI	10/73 (to 799)					

OMAGH LVLO/VRO

BJI*	1/74	FJI	3/80	JJI#	2/86	NJI	4/90	SJI	2/94	WJI	8/97
CJI	11/75	GJI	3/82	KJI	10/86	OJI	3/91	TJI	12/94	XJI	6/98
DJI	4/77	HJI	10/83	LJI	3/88	PJI	4/92	UJI	9/95		
EJI	9/78	IJI	11/84	MJI	5/89	RJI	4/93	VJI	10/96		

* from 800   # to 4700

COUNTY BOROUGH COUNCIL OF BELFAST

OI	1/04	CZ	11/32	GZ	5/42	PZ	1/53	WZ	3/57
XI	1/21	EZ	10/35	MZ	12/47	TZ	8/54		
AZ	2/28	FZ	10/38	OZ	6/50	UZ	10/55		

OI*	6/58	CZ	3/61	GZ	1/64	PZ	3/66	WZ	6/68
XI*	6/59	EZ	4/62	MZ	9/64	TZ	1/67		
AZ	4/60	FZ	4/63	OZ	5/65	UZ#	10/67		

* commenced at 1000, all other series from 1.
# batch early for City Transport 7/67.

AOI	4/69	COI	12/70	BOI	4/72	GOI	6/73 (to 8300)
BOI	3/70	DOI	8/71	FOI	12/72		

BELFAST LVLO/VRO

GOI*	1/74	JOI	9/74	MOI	5/76	POI	6/77	TOI	1/79	WOI	6/80
HOI	2/74	KOI	4/75	NOI	12/76	ROI	1/78	UOI	6/79	XOI	2/81
IOI unalloc.		LOI	11/75	OOI	unalloc.	SOI	6/78	VOI	1/80	YOI	9/81

* from 8301.

AXI	4/82	EXI	4/84	IXI	5/86	MXI	3/88	RXI	12/89	VXI	6/91
BXI	10/82	FXI	9/84	JXI	10/86	NXI	8/88	SXI	4/90	WXI	11/91
CXI	4/83	GXI	3/85	KXI	3/87	OXI	2/89	TXI	8/90	XXI	4/92
DXI	10/83	HXI	8/85	LXI	9/87	PXI	7/89	UXI	1/91	YXI	8/92

AAZ	2/93	EAZ	6/94	IAZ	8/95	MAZ	9/96	RAZ	5/97	VAZ	4/98
BAZ	7/93	FAZ	9/94	JAZ	12/95	NAZ not iss.		SAZ	8/97	WAZ	6/98
CAZ	10/93	GAZ	1/95	KAZ	2/96	OAZ	11/96	TAZ	11/97		
DAZ	3/94	HAZ	4/95	LAZ	5/96	PAZ	3/97	UAZ	1/98		

Computerisation occurred early in Belfast - on 19.3.86, during currency of HXI.

COUNTY BOROUGH COUNCIL OF LONDONDERRY

UI	1/04	UI (from 100 ?)	8/63	AUI	4/73 (to 1109)

LONDONDERRY LVLO/VRO

AUI*	1/74	CUI	7/83 (to 7388)	EUI	6/90	GUI	1/93	IUI	11/96
BUI	7/78	DUI	10/86	FUI not iss.		HUI	2/95	JUI	5/98

* from 1110

APPENDIX 5

REGISTRATION MARKS BY
AUTHORITY & DATE
REPUBLIC OF IRELAND

In the Republic of Ireland the sequence of issue of the various formats was [1] single and two-letter marks preceding up to four numerals, [2] three-letter marks preceding up to three numerals, (commencing May 1954), [3] reverse of [1], (commencing February 1970), and [4] reverse of [2] (commencing July 1974). As in Great Britain, the last two letters of the trio were the basic index mark identifying the issuing authority. However, whereas in Great Britain each mark of an authority was used with the letter A before moving on the Bxx multiples and so on, (e.g. AEL, ALJ, ARU, BEL, BLJ, BRU etc.), in the Republic of Ireland, (as in Northern Ireland) the sequence was e.g. AIH, BIH, CIH etc. to ZIH, before commencing AZP, BZP, CZP etc. In the first three-letter sequence issued, GRI, IRI, SRI and VRI were omitted and other early sequences omitted certain of these first letters, but eventually all letters except Q were used as the first in a three-letter trio, except that ZZx combinations were not issued, (ZZP slipped through by mistake.) As on the mainland, reverse format marks which were already in use or earmarked for trade plates commenced at numbers other than 1 and, where known, this information is shown in the tables.
By June 1981 Dublin CC & CBC and three other counties were running out of available marks and the previously unused combinations of GI, IS, IV, SI, ZG, ZS and ZV were allocated, but only in three-letter combinations. Subsequently, in January 1986 SI, ZG, ZS and ZV were allotted as two-letter marks to Dublin, (but in the event ZV was unused before the new system was introduced). Combinations of IG, II and VI remained unused.

In general there was no gap or overlap between the completion of a mark and the commencement of its successor; exceptions are noted in the tables, but discrepancies of one month are ignored. Reverse format marks are shown in *italic* script.

On 1st January 1987 a completely new system was introduced. The format was now (1) two numerals indicating the last two digits of the year of first registration, (2) one or two letters indicating the issuing authority, (3) a serial number, commencing at 1 for each year. Existing vehicles retained their old format marks. Imported second-hand vehicles and other vehicles previously unregistered in the republic were given a year prefix conforming to their date of manufacture or first registration abroad. New plates were introduced, black on reflective white at front and rear, with a blue "Euroband" at the left and the Irish language version of the name of the issuing authority superimposed in small print above the registration number. The index mark ZV followed by a number in the old format, (allocated in blocks to the various authorities), was retained for vehicles over 30 years old.

A tabulation of the index letters allocated under the new system will be found on page 267

COUNTY COUNCIL OF CARLOW

A duplicate series for cars and motorcycles prior to 1921.

IC   12/03

AIC	4/64	FIC	12/70	KIC	1/76	PIC	2/79	VIC	10/82	
BIC	9/65	GIC	3/72	LIC	8/76	RIC	10/79	WIC	9/83	
CIC	6/67	HIC	2/73	MIC	5/77	SIC	5/80	XIC	10/84	
DIC	10/68	IIC	1/74	NIC	1/78	TIC	2/81	YIC	11/85	Last issue YIC 994.
EIC	11/69	JIC	1/75	OIC	7/78	UIC	11/81			

COUNTY COUNCIL OF CAVAN

ID   1/04

AID	7/58	FID	8/63	KID	7/67	PID	2/71	VID	2/74	
BID	7/59	GID	6/64	LID	5/68	RID	10/71	WID	9/74	
CID	7/60	HID	4/65	MID	3/69	SID	5/72	XID	6/75	
DID	9/61	IID	1/66	NID	10/69	TID	1/73	YID	2/76	
EID	10/62	JID	10/66	OID	6/70	UID	7/73	ZID	5/76	

ID   *12/76*

AID	*2/81*	*CID*	*1/82*	*EID*	*2/83*	*GID*	*9/84*	*IID*	*3/86*	*Last issue 906 IID.*
BID	*7/81*	*DID*	*7/82*	*FID*	*1/84*	*HID*	*6/85*			

COUNTY COUNCIL OF CLARE

A duplicate series for cars and motorcycles prior to 1921.

IE   12/03

AIE	3/59	FIE	12/63	KIE	3/67	PIE	3/70	VIE	9/72
BIE	4/60	GIE	6/64	LIE	12/67	RIE	8/70	WIE	2/73
CIE	6/61	HIE	2/65	MIE	7/68	SIE	3/71	XIE	6/73
DIR	5/62	IIE	7/65	NIE	2/69	TIE	9/71	YIE	12/73
EIE	4/63	JIE	5/66	OIE	8/69	UIE	4/72	ZIE	5/74

IE   *11/74*

AIE	*9/78*	*FIE*	*2/80*	*KIE*	*8/81*	*PIE*	*9/83*	*VIE*	*1/86*	
BIE	*1/79*	*GIE*	*5/80*	*LIE*	*1/82*	*RIE*	*3/84*	*WIE*	*5/86*	
CIE	*3/79*	*HIE*	*10/80*	*MIE*	*5/82*	*SIE*	*7/84*	*XIE*	*11/86*	*Last issue 107 XIE.*
DIE	*6/79*	*IIE*	*2/81*	*NIE*	*10/82*	*TIE*	*2/85*			
EIE	*10/79*	*JIE*	*5/81*	*OIE*	*3/83*	*UIE*	*6/85*			

COUNTY COUNCIL OF CORK

IF	12/03	ZB	4/35	ZK	4/49	ZT	5/53			

AIF	12/55	FIF	9/57	KIF	1/59	PIF	4/60	VIF	5/61
BIF	3/56	GIF	1/58	LIF	4/59	RIF	7/60	WIF	7/61
CIF	6/56	HIF	4/58	MIF	7/59	SIF	9/60	XIF	10/61
DIF	12/56	IIF	6/58	NIF	10/59	TIF	1/61	YIF	1/62
EIF	5/57	JIF	10/58	OIF	1/60	UIF	3/61	ZIF	3/62

AZB	5/62	EZB	2/63	IZB	10/63	MZB	6/64	RZB	1/65	VZB	8/65
BZB	7/62	FZB	4/63	JZB	1/64	NZB	7/64	SZB	3/65	WZB	12/65
CZB	9/62	GZB	6/63	KZB	2/64	OZB	9/64	TZB	5/65	XZB	3/66
DZB	12/62	HZB	8/63	LZB	4/64	PZB	11/64	UZB	6/65	YZB	6/66

AZK	7/66	EZK	6/67	IZK	4/68	MZK	11/68	RZK	6/69	VZK	2/70
BZK	10/66	FZK	8/67	JZK	5/68	NZK	1/69	SZK	8/69	WZK	4/70
CZK	1/67	GZK	11/67	KZK	7/68	OZK	3/69	TZK	10/69	XZK	5/70
DZK	4/67	HZK	1/68	LZK	9/68	PZK	5/69	UZK	1/70	YZK	7/70

AZT	8/70	EZT	4/71	IZT	11/71	MZT	6/72	RZT	1/73	VZT	5/73
BZT	10/70	FZT	5/71	JZT	1/72	NZT	7/72	SZT	2/73	WZT	7/73
CZT	12/70	GZT	7/71	KZT	3/72	OZT	9/72	TZT	3/73	XZT	8/73
DZT	2/71	HZT	9/71	LZT	4/72	PZT	10/72	UZT	5/73	YZT	9/73

IF	11/73	ZB	5/75	ZK	7/76	ZT	8/77			

AIF	6/78	FIF	11/78	KIF	3/79	PIF	8/79	VIF	2/80
BIF	7/78	GIF	1/79	LIF	4/79	RIF	9/79	WIF	3/80
CIF	8/78	HIF	1/79	MIF	5/79	SIF	11/79	XIF	4/80
DIF	9/78	IIF	2/79	NIF	6/79	TIF	1/80	YIF	5/80
EIF	10/78	JIF	2/79	OIF	7/79	UIF	1/80	ZIF	7/80

AZB	8/80	EZB	1/81	IZB	5/81	MZB	9/81	RZB	3/82	VZB	10/82
BZB	9/80	FZB	2/81	JZB	6/81	NZB	12/81	SZB	4/82	WZB	1/83
CZB	11/80	GZB	3/81	KZB	7/81	OZB	1/82	TZB	6/82	XZB	1/83
DZB	1/81	HZB	4/81	LZB	8/81	PZB	2/82	UZB	8/82	YZB	2/83

AZK	3/83	DZK	9/83	GZK	3/84	JZK	8/84	MZK	2/85	PZK	6/85
BZK	5/83	EZK	1/84	HZK	4/84	KZK	10/84	NZK	3/85	
CZK	7/83	FZK	1/84	IZK	6/84	LZK	1/85	OZK	5/85	

In June 1974 Cork County Council and Cork County Borough Council set up a joint motor taxation authority, administered by the County Council. However separate registers continued in use for the county and the county borough until August 1985. Subsequent issues by the Joint Office are shown on page 264.

COUNTY COUNCIL OF DONEGAL

IH	12/03	ZP	5/52	A duplicate series for cars and motorcycles prior to 1921.

AIH	11/61	FIH	12/64	KIH	6/68	PIH	5/71	VIH	1/74
BIH	6/62	GIH	7/65	LIH	1/69	RIH	1/72	WIH	7/74
CIH	3/63	HIH	3/66	MIH	8/69	SIH	7/72	XIH	2/75
DIH	10/63	IIH	1/67	NIH	3/70	TIH	1/73	YIH	8/75
EIH	6/64	JIH	10/67	OIH	11/70	UIH	6/73	ZIH	2/76

AZP	4/76	FZP	1/77	KZP	4/78	PZP	7/79	VZP	12/80
BZP	5/76	GZP	3/77	LZP	7/78	RZP	10/79	WZP	2/81
CZP	6/76	HZP	6/77	MZP	9/78	SZP	2/80	XZP	5/81
DZP	7/76	IZP	10/77	NZP	1/79	TZP	5/80	YZP	8/81
EZP	10/76	JZP	1/78	OZP	4/79	UZP	8/80	ZZP	1/82 *

* ZZP was not authorised by SR&O and was issued in error - no retrospective SR&O was issued to legitimise its issue. When the error was discovered ZZP was terminated at 407; in consequence the next series, *IH*, commenced at 408.

IH	2/82	ZP	4/85	Final issue *4853 ZP*

COUNTY COUNCIL OF DUBLIN

IK   12/03   Z   3/27   ZE   1/40 (completed 2/52)

A duplicate series for cars and motorcycles prior to 1921.
In February 1952 Dublin County Council and Dublin County Borough Council set up a joint motor taxation authority. The joint office was administered by Dublin County Borough Council, q.v. for subsequent issues.

COUNTY COUNCIL OF GALWAY

IM	1/04	ZM	10/50								
AIM	11/59	FIM	11/62	KIM	2/65	PIM	4/67	VIM	12/68		
BIM	6/60	GIM	5/63	LIM	6/65	RIM	8/67	WIM	3/69		
CIM	2/61	HIM	10/63	MIM	12/65	SIM	1/68	XIM	6/69		
DIM	9/61	IIM	4/64	NIM	5/66	TIM	4/68	YIM	10/69		
EIM	4/62	JIM	9/64	OIM	10/66	UIM	8/68	ZIM	2/70		
AZM	5/70	EZM	8/71	IZM	9/72	MZM	7/73	RZM	7/74	VZM	9/75
BZM	9/70	FZM	12/71	JZM	12/72	NZM	10/73	SZM	11/74	WZM	1/76
CZM	1/71	GZM	3/72	KZM	3/73	OZM	2/74	TZM	3/75	XZM	3/76
DZM	4/71	HZM	6/72	LZM	5/73	PZM	4/74	UZM	6/75	YZM	5/76
IM	8/76	ZM	4/78								
AIM	10/79	FIM	8/80	KIM	7/81	PIM	6/82	VIM	9/83		
BIM	1/80	GIM	11/80	LIM	8/81	RIM	9/82	WIM	1/84		
CIM	2/80	HIM	1/81	MIM	11/81	SIM	1/83	XIM	4/84		
DIM	4/80	IIM	3/81	NIM	2/82	TIM	2/83	YIM	7/84		
EIM	6/80	JIM	5/81	OIM	4/82	UIM	5/83	ZIM	10/84		
AZM	2/85	CZM	7/85	EZM	3/86	GZM	8/86 Last issue 797 GZM				
BZM	5/85	DZM	12/85	FZM	5/86						

COUNTY COUNCIL OF KERRY

IN	12/03	ZX	1/54								
AIN	1/62	FIN	7/64	KIN	1/67	PIN	5/69	VIN	3/71		
BIN	7/62	GIN	1/65	LIN	8/67	RIN	10/69	WIN	8/71		
CIN	2/63	HIN	5/65	MIN	2/68	SIN	3/70	XIN	1/72		
DIN	7/63	IIN	10/65	NIN	7/68	TIN	7/70	YIN	5/72		
EIN	2/64	JIN	6/66	OIN	1/69	UIN	10/70	ZIN	9/72		
AZX	1/73	EZX	2/74	IZX	6/75	MZX	8/76	RZX	10/77	VZX	8/78
BZX	4/73	FZX	5/74	JZX	11/75	NZX	1/77	SZX	1/78	WZX	10/78
CZX	6/73	GZX	9/74	KZX	2/76	OZX	4/77	TZX	3/78	XZX	1/79
DZX	10/73	HZX	2/75	LZX	5/76	PZX	7/77	UZX	6/78	YZX	3/79
IN	6/79	ZX	1/82								
AIN	1/86	BIN	5/86	CIN	10/86	Last issue 375 CIN.					

COUNTY COUNCIL OF KILDARE

IO	12/03	ZW	6/53								
AIO	4/63	FIO	10/66	KIO	4/69	PIO	6/71	VIO	10/73		
BIO	1/64	GIO	6/67	LIO	11/69	RIO	1/72	WIO	4/74		
CIO	8/64	HIO	2/68	MIO	6/70	SIO	7/72	XIO	9/74		
DIO	4/65	IIO	unalloc.	NIO	11/70	TIO	1/73	YIO	3/75		
EIO	1/66	JIO	9/68	OIO	unalloc.	UIO	6/73	ZIO	10/75		
AZW	3/76	EZW	8/77	IZW	9/78	MZW	10/79	RZW	1/81	VZW	1/82
BZW	7/76	FZW	1/78	JZW	1/79	NZW	2/80	SZW	3/81	WZW	4/82
CZW	1/77	GZW	3/78	KZW	4/79	OZW	5/80	TZW	5/81	XZW	8/82
DZW	4/77	HZW	6/78	LZW	6/79	PZW	8/80	UZW	8/81	YZW	1/83
ZW	5/83	Last issue 9343 ZW									

COUNTY COUNCIL OF KILKENNY

IP   1/04

AIP	2/55	FIP	1/61	KIP	unalloc.	PIP	2/68	VIP	8/71
BIP	1/56	GIP	unalloc.	LIP	9/64	RIP	10/68	WIP	4/72
CIP	6/57	HIP	1/62	MIP	6/65	SIP	6/69	XIP	10/72
DIP	8/58	IIP	1/63	NIP	5/66	TIP	3/70	YIP	5/73
EIP	10/59	JIP	12/63	OIP	4/67	UIP	11/70	ZIP	11/73

IP   7/74

AIP	10/78	EIP	3/80	IIP	5/81	MIP	12/82	RIP	not iss.		
BIP	2/79	FIP	7/80	JIP	10/81	NIP	5/83	SIP	5/85		
CIP	6/79	GIP	unalloc.	KIP	unalloc.	OIP	2/84	TIP	2/86		
DIP	10/79	HIP	1/81	LIP	4/82	PIP	10/84	UIP	10/86	Last issue	235 UIP.

COUNTY COUNCIL OF KING'S COUNTY

County was renamed County Council of Offaly in June 1922, q.v.

COUNTY COUNCIL OF LAOIGHIS

Named Queen's County until June 1922. Alternative spellings Laois and Leix.

CI   12/03

ACI	7/60	FCI	6/67	KCI	4/72	PCI	3/76	VCI	10/78
BCI	1/62	GCI	7/68	LCI	1/73	RCI	10/76	WCI	3/79
CCI	6/63	HCI	6/69	MCI	9/73	SCI	5/77	XCI	10/79
DCI	9/64	ICI	5/70	NCI	7/74	TCI	1/78	YCI	4/80
ECI	1/66	JCI	4/71	OCI	5/75	UCI	5/78	ZCI	11/80

CI   4/81   Last issue   7342 CI

COUNTY COUNCIL OF LEITRIM

Duplicated series for cars and motorcycles prior to 1921.

IT   12/03

AIT	5/72	DIT	6/76	GIT	10/79	JIT	9/83		
BIT	6/73	EIT	8/77	HIT	1/81	KIT	7/85	Last issue KIT 780
CIT	3/75	FIT	8/78	IIT	2/82				

COUNTY COUNCIL OF LIMERICK

IU   12/03

AIU	11/54	FIU	11/59	KIU	1/63	PIU	1/66	VIU	3/69
BIU	7/55	GIU	unalloc.	LIU	8/63	RIU	10/66	WIU	8/69
CIU	5/56	HIU	10/60	MIU	4/64	SIU	6/67	XIU	3/70
DIU	12/57	IIU	6/61	NIU	10/64	TIU	3/68	YIU	8/70
EIU	12/58	JIU	4/62*	OIU	5/65	UIU	8/68	ZIU	3/71
		* JIU 111 early (12/61)							

IU   9/71

AIU	5/75	FIU	3/77	KIU	4/78	PIU	5/79	VIU	9/80
BIU	10/75	GIU	unalloc.	LIU	6/78	RIU	8/79	WIU	1/81
CIU	2/76	HIU	6/77	MIU	9/78	SIU	1/80	XIU	4/81
DIU	6/76	IIU	9/77	NIU	1/79	TIU	3/80	YIU	7/81
EIU	10/76	JIU	1/78	OIU	2/79	UIU	6/80	ZIU	8/81

AIV	2/82	DIV	2/83	GIV	4/84	JIV	3/85	MIV	unalloc.
BIV	5/83	EIV	6/83	HIV	9/84	KIV	7/85	NIV	4/86
CIV	10/82	FIV	1/84	IIV	unalloc.	LIV	1/86	OIV	9/86 Last issue OIV 520

COUNTY COUNCIL OF LONGFORD

IX	12/03									
AIX	2/70	DIX	9/73	GIX	1/77	JIX	5/79	MIX	1/82	PIX 1/86
BIX	6/71	EIX	1/75	HIX	10/77	KIX	3/80	NIX	2/83	Last issue
CIX	9/72	FIX	2/76	IIX	7/78	LIX	2/81	OIX	7/84	PIX 710

COUNTY COUNCIL OF LOUTH

IY	12/03	ZY	10/54								
AIY	1/64	FIY	3/67	KIY	2/70	PIY	9/72	VIY	7/74		
BIY	7/64	GIY	10/67	LIY	7/70	RIY	2/73	WIY	1/75		
CIY	3/65	HIY	6/68	MIY	3/71	SIY	6/73	XIY	7/75		
DIY	10/65	IIY	12/68	NIY	10/71	TIY	11/73	YIY	2/76		
EIY	7/66	JIY	6/69	OIY	4/72	UIY	4/74	ZIY	6/76		
AZY	11/76	EZY	3/78	IZY	5/79	MZY	9/80	RZY	1/82	VZY	10/83
BZY	3/77	FZY	6/78	JZY	9/79	NZY	1/81	SZY	4/82	WZY	4/84
CZY	7/77	GZY	10/78	KZY	2/80	OZY	5/81	TZY	10/82	XZY	10/84
DZY	1/78	HZY	2/79	LZY	5/80	PZY	7/81	UZY	3/83	YZY	4/85

ZY   *9/85*   Last issue *2507 ZY*

COUNTY COUNCIL OF MAYO

IZ	1/04									
AIZ	10/54	FIZ	10/59	KIZ	8/62	PIZ	9/65	VIZ	11/68	
BIZ	7/55	GIZ	unalloc.	LIZ	5/63	RIZ	6/66	WIZ	5/69	
CIZ	8/56	HIZ	6/60	MIZ	1/64	SIZ	2/67	XIZ	11/69	
DIZ	2/58	IIZ	4/61	NIZ	7/64	TIZ	9/67	YIZ	5/70	
EIZ	1/59	JIZ	1/62	OIZ	3/65	UIZ	4/68	ZIZ	10/70	

IZ   *5/71*

AIZ	*2/76*	*FIZ*	*6/77*	*KIZ*	*7/78*	*PIZ*	*2/80*	*VIZ*	*8/81*
BIZ	*3/76*	*GIZ*	*unalloc.*	*LIZ*	*11/78*	*RIZ*	*5/80*	*WIZ*	*12/81*
CIZ	*6/76*	*HIZ*	*10/77*	*MIZ*	*2/79*	*SIZ*	*9/80*	*XIZ*	*3/82*
DIZ	*11/76*	*IIZ*	*2/78*	*NIZ*	*6/79*	*TIZ*	*1/81*	*YIZ*	*9/82*
EIZ	*3/77*	*JIZ*	*5/78*	*OIZ*	*9/79*	*UIZ*	*4/81*	*ZIZ*	*1/83*

AIS	4/83	CIS	3/84	EIS	3/85	GIS	1/86	
BIS	10/83	DIS	8/84	FIS	7/85	HIS	8/86	Last issue HIS 990.

COUNTY COUNCIL OF MEATH

AI	12/03	ZN	12/51								
AAI	2/62	FAI	5/65	KAI	6/68	PAI	2/71	VAI	4/73		
BAI	11/62	GAI	1/66	LAI	12/68	RAI	8/71	WAI	8/73		
CAI	7/63	HAI	8/66	MAI	6/69	SAI	2/72	XAI	1/74		
DAI	3/64	IAI	4/67	NAI	1/70	TAI	7/72	YAI	6/74		
EAI	9/64	JAI	11/67	OAI	7/70	UAI	12/72	ZAI	12/74		
AZN	6/75	EZN	1/77	IZN	3/78	MZN	2/79	RZN	4/80	VZN	6/81
BZN	1/76	FZN	4/77	JZN	5/78	NZN	5/79	SZN	8/80	WZN	9/81
CZN	4/76	GZN	8/77	KZN	8/78	OZN	7/79	TZN	11/80	XZN	1/82
DZN	7/76	HZN	11/77	LZN	11/78	PZN	1/80	UZN	3/81	YZN	5/82

AI   *10/82*   *ZN*   *12/86*   Last issue *88 ZN*

COUNTY COUNCIL OF MONAGHAN

BI   12/03

ABI	3/61	FBI	10/67	KBI	11/72	PBI	7/76	VBI	2/79
BBI	8/62	GBI	12/68	LBI	6/73	RBI	2/77	WBI	7/79
CBI	2/64	HBI	12/69	MBI	3/74	SBI	8/77	XBI	3/80
DBI	4/65	IBI	11/70	NBI	4/75	TBI	2/78	YBI	9/80
EBI	7/66	JBI	1/72	OBI	2/76	UBI	6/79	ZBI	4/81

BI   10/81   Last issue 6540 BI

COUNTY COUNCIL OF OFFALY

Named King's County until June 1922

IR   12/03

AIR	5/60	FIR	6/66	KIR	8/71	PIR	6/75	VIR	7/78
BIR	8/61	GIR	9/67	LIR	6/72	RIR	3/76	WIR	1/79
CIR	2/63	HIR	10/68	MIR	3/73	SIR	1/77	XIR	8/79
DIR	4/64	IIR	9/69	NIR	10/73	TIR	8/77	YIR	2/80
EIR	3/65	JIR	9/70	OIR	8/74	UIR	2/78	ZIR	8/80

IR   3/81   Last issue 7834 IR

COUNTY COUNCIL OF QUEEN'S COUNTY

Renamed County Council of Laoghis June 1922, q.v.

COUNTY COUNCIL OF ROSCOMMON

A duplicated series for cars and motorcycles prior to 1921

DI   12/03

ADI	1/63	FDI	7/68	KDI	7/72	PDI	10/75	VDI	3/78
BDI	3/64	GDI	6/69	LDI	3/73	RDI	4/76	WDI	7/78
CDI	4/65	HDI	4/70	MDI	8/73	SDI	10/76	XDI	1/79
DDI	6/66	IDI	2/71	NDI	6/74	TDI	4/77	YDI	5/79
EDI	6/67	JDI	11/71	ODI	1/75	UDI	9/77	ZDI	10/79

DI   4/80

ADI   2/86   BDI   9/86   Last issue   292 BDI

COUNTY COUNCIL OF SLIGO

EI   12/03

AEI	11/59	FEI	12/65	KEI	10/70	PEI	6/74	VEI	8/77
BEI	5/61	GEI	2/67	LEI	9/71	REI	4/75	WEI	3/78
CEI	7/62	HEI	3/68	MEI	6/72	SEI	2/76	XEI	8/78
DEI	11/63	IEI	1/69	NEI	2/73	TEI	6/76	YEI	2/79
EEI	12/64	JEI	12/69	OEI	8/73	UEI	2/77	ZEI	7/79

EI   2/80

AEI   4/86   Last issue 835 AEI

COUNTY COUNCIL OF TIPPERARY (NORTH RIDING)

Issued FI 1-50 for cars only; then duplicated series for cars and motorcycles from FI 51 up, (until 1920)

FI   12/03

AFI	1/58	FFI	1/64	KFI	9/67	PFI	5/71	VFI	5/74
BFI	5/59	GFI	11/64	LFI	6/68	RFI	3/72	WFI	2/75
CFI	7/60	HFI	9/65	MFI	3/69	SFI	10/72	XFI	10/75
DFI	1/62	IFI	10/66	NFI	11/69	TFI	4/73	YFI	4/76
EFI	2/63	JFI	not iss.	OFI	7/70	UFI	10/73	ZFI*12/76

* ZFI issued despite lack of authorisation in SR&O.

FI   5/77

AFI	1/80	DFI	10/82	GFI	7/84	JFI	7/86	Last issue 418 JFI
BFI	8/81	EFI	3/83	HFI	3/85			
CFI	3/82	FFI	1/84	IFI	12/85			

COUNTY COUNCIL OF TIPPERARY (SOUTH RIDING)

HI   12/03

AHI	9/54	FHI	9/59	KHI	4/62	PHI	10/65	VHI	3/69
BHI	5/55	GHI	unalloc.	LHI	2/63	RHI	8/66	WHI	9/69
CHI	3/56	HHI	8/60	MHI	10/63	SHI	5/67	XHI	4/70
DHI	9/57	IHI	unalloc.	NHI	6/64	THI	2/68	YHI	9/70
EHI	9/58	JHI	7/61	OHI	2/65	UHI	8/68	ZHI	4/71

HI   11/71

AHI	5/76	FHI	3/78	KHI	1/79	PHI	9/80	VHI	10/82
BHI	10/76	GHI	unalloc.	LHI	4/79	RHI	2/81	WHI	2/83
CHI	3/77	HHI	6/78	MHI	8/79	SHI	6/81	XHI	8/83
DHI	7/77	IHI	unalloc.	NHI	1/80	THI	9/81	YHI	4/84
EHI	12/77	JHI	9/78	OHI	4/80	UHI	3/82	ZHI	11/84

AGI	5/85	BGI	1/86	CGI	6/86	Last issue CGI 871

COUNTY COUNCIL OF WATERFORD

KI   1/04

AKI	3/61	FKI	3/66	KKI	7/70	PKI	11/73	VKI	5/77
BKI	4/62	GKI	4/67	LKI	4/71	RKI	8/74	WKI	11/77
CKI	5/63	HKI	3/68	MKI	2/72	SKI	7/75	XKI	4/78
DKI	5/64	IKI	12/68	NKI	9/72	TKI	3/76	YKI	8/78
EKI	3/65	JKI	9/69	OKI	5/73	UKI	10/76	ZKI	2/79

KI   7/79

AKI   6/86   Last issue 586 AKI

COUNTY COUNCIL OF WESTMEATH

LI   12/03

ALI	6/59	FLI	1/65	KLI	1/70	PLI	7/73	VLI	7/76
BLI	8/60	GLI	1/66	LLI	10/70	RLI	2/74	WLI	2/77
CLI	9/61	HLI	4/67	MLI	8/71	SLI	9/74	XLI	7/77
DLI	12/62	ILI	4/68	NLI	5/72	TLI	7/75	YLI	1/78
ELI	2/64	JLI	2/69	OLI	12/72	ULI	2/76	ZLI	5/78

LI   8/78

ALI	2/83	CLI	3/84	ELI	4/85	GLI	4/86	Last issue 869 GLI
BLI	7/83	DLI	10/84	FLI	9/85			

COUNTY COUNCIL OF WEXFORD

MI   1/04   ZR   6/52

MI 9923-9999 were issued by the Police in 1921 as a consequence of The Road Vehicles (Defaulting Councils) (Ireland) Order, 1921.

AMI	5/61	FMI	7/64	KMI	4/67	PMI	7/69	VMI	12/71
BMI	1/62	GMI	1/65	LMI	10/67	RMI	2/70	WMI	5/72
CMI	9/62	HMI	7/65	MMI	4/68	SMI	6/70	XMI	10/72
DMI	5/63	IMI	3/66	NMI	9/68	TMI	11/70	YMI	3/73
EMI	1/64	JMI	9/66	OMI	3/69	UMI	6/71	ZMI	unalloc.

AZR	7/73	EZR	2/75	IZR	6/76	MZR	8/77	RZR	7/78	VZR	6/79
BZR	10/73	FZR	7/75	JZR	9/76	NZR	11/77	SZR	9/78	WZR	9/79
CZR	4/74	GZR	1/76	KZR	2/77	OZR	2/78	TZR	1/79	XZR	1/80
DZR	8/74	HZR	4/76	LZR	5/77	PZR	4/78	UZR	3/79	YZR	3/80

MI   *6/80*   *ZR*   *10/83*   Last issue *8071 ZR*

COUNTY COUNCIL OF WICKLOW

NI   1/04

ANI	5/57	FNI	2/63	KNI	9/66	PNI	1/70	VNI	10/72
BNI	11/58	GNI	11/63	LNI	6/67	RNI	8/70	WNI	4/73
CNI	2/60	HNI	7/64	MNI	3/68	SNI	3/71	XNI	9/73
DNI	3/61	INI	4/65	NNI	10/68	TNI	10/71	YNI	3/74
ENI	2/62	JNI	1/66	ONI	5/69	UNI	4/72	ZNI	9/74

NI   *5/75*

ANI	*3/79*	*ENI*	*7/80*	*INI*	*11/81*	*MNI*	*9/83*	*RNI*	*9/85*
BNI	*6/79*	*FNI*	*1/81*	*JNI*	*4/82*	*NNI*	*3/84*	*SNI*	*3/86*
CNI	*11/79*	*GNI*	*3/81*	*KNI*	*10/82*	*ONI*	*9/84*	*TNI*	*8/86* Last issue *426 TNI*
DNI	*2/80*	*HNI*	*7/81*	*LNI*	*3/83*	*PNI*	*3/85*		

COUNTY BOROUGH COUNCIL OF CORK

PI   12/03   ZF   8/46

API	12/58	FPI	7/62	KPI	4/65	PPI	2/67	VPI	8/68
BPI	11/59	GPI	4/63	LPI	7/65	RPI	6/67	WPI	12/68
CPI	7/60	HPI	10/63	MPI	1/66	SPI	10/67	XPI	3/69
DPI	4/61	IPI	5/64	NPI	5/66	TPI	2/68	YPI	6/69
EPI	1/62	JPI	10/64	OPI	9/66	UPI	5/68	ZPI	9/69

AZF	2/70	EZF	2/71	IZF	2/72	MZF	2/73	RZF	12/73	VZF	1/75
BZF	4/70	FZF	4/71	JZF	5/72	NZF	4/73	SZF	4/74	WZF	5/75
CZF	7/70	GZF	7/71	KZF	7/72	OZF	6/73	TZF	6/74	XZF	8/75
DZF	10/70	HZF	10/71	LZF	10/72	PZF	8/73	UZF	9/74	YZF	1/76

PI   *3/76*   *ZF*   *6/78*

API	*2/80*	*FPI*	*2/81*	*KPI*	*1/82*	*PPI*	*1/83*	*VPI*	*5/84*
BPI	*4/80*	*GPI*	*3/81*	*LPI*	*2/82*	*RPI*	*3/83*	*WPI*	*7/84*
CPI	*6/80*	*HPI*	*5/81*	*MPI*	*4/82*	*SPI*	*7/83*	*XPI*	*1/85*
DPI	*8/80*	*IPI*	*7/81*	*NPI*	*6/82*	*TPI*	*10/83*	*YPI*	*3/85*
EPI	*12/80*	*JPI*	*8/81*	*OPI*	*10/82*	*UPI*	*1/84*	*ZPI*	*5/85*

In June 1974 Cork County Council and Cork County Borough Council set up a joint motor taxation authority. However separate registers continued in use for the county and the county borough until the expiry of *ZPI* in August 1985. Subsequent issues are shown on the following page.

CORK COUNTY & COUNTY BOROUGH JOINT OFFICE

In June 1974 Cork County Council and Cork County Borough Council set up a joint motor taxation authority, administered by the County Council. However separate registers continued in use for the county and the county borough until August 1985. The following were subsequently issued covering both areas.

RZK	8/85	TZK	11/85	VZK	1/86	XZK	3/86
SZK	9/85	UZK	1/86	WZK	2/86	YZK	4/86

AZF	5/86	CZF	7/86	EZF	9/86		
BZF	6/86	DZF	8/86	FZF	11/86	Last issue 542 FZF

COUNTY BOROUGH COUNCIL OF DUBLIN

Up to RI 3000 duplicated series for cars and motorcycles.

RI	12/03	ZI	3/27	ZC	3/37	ZH	6/47	ZL	7/50
YI	4/21	ZA	5/33	ZD	1/40	ZJ	1/49		

In February 1952 the Dublin County Council and the Dublin County Borough Council set up a Joint Local Taxation Office and the two registers were combined. The joint office was administered by the County Borough Council.

DUBLIN COUNTY AND COUNTY BOROUGH JOINT OFFICE

ZO	2/52	ZU	5/53						

ARI	5/54	FRI	9/54	KRI	12/54	PRI	4/55	VRI	unalloc.
BRI	6/54	GRI	unalloc.	LRI	1/55	RRI	5/55	WRI	6/55
CRI	6/54	HRI	10/54	MRI	2/55	SRI	unalloc.	XRI	7/55
DRI	7/54	IRI	unalloc.	NRI	3/55	TRI	5/55	YRI	7/55
ERI	8/54	JRI	11/54	ORI	3/55	URI	6/55	ZRI	unalloc.

AIK	9/55	FIK	1/56	KIK	4/56	PIK	11/56	VIK	unalloc.
BIK	10/55	GIK	unalloc.	LIK	5/56	RIK	2/57	WIK	5/57
CIK	10/55	HIK	2/56	MIK	6/56	SIK	unalloc.	XIK	6/57
DIK	11/55	IIK	3/56	NIK	7/56	TIK	4/57	YIK	7/57
EIK	12/55	JIK	3/56	OIK	9/56	UIK	5/57	ZIK	9/57

AYI	10/57	FYI	4/58	KYI	9/58	PYI	3/59	VYI	6/59
BYI	12/57	GYI	5/58	LYI	10/58	RYI	3/59	WYI	7/59
CYI	1/58	HYI	6/58	MYI	11/58	SYI	4/59	XYI	7/59
DYI	2/58	IYI	6/58	NYI	1/59	TYI	5/59	YYI	8/59
EYI	3/58	JYI	7/58	OYI	1/59	UYI	6/59	ZYI	unalloc.

AZA	9/59	EZA	1/60	IZA	3/60	MZA	5/60	RZA	7/60	VZA	10/60
BZA	10/59	FZA	1/60	JZA	4/60	NZA	6/60	SZA	8/60	WZA	11/60
CZA	11/59	GZA	2/60	KZA	4/60	OZA	6/60	TZA	9/60	XZA	12/60
DZA	12/59	HZA	3/60	LZA	5/60	PZA	7/70	UZA	9/60	YZA	1/61

AZC	2/61	EZC	4/61	IZC	6/61	MZC	9/61	RZC	12/61	VZC	3/62
BZC	2/61	FZC	4/61	JZC	6/61	NZC	9/61	SZC	1/62	WZC	3/62
CZC	3/61	GZC	5/61	KZC	7/61	OZC	10/61	TZC	1/62	XZC	4/62
DZC	3/61	HZC	5/61	LZC	8/61	PZC	11/61	UZC	2/62	YZC	4/62

AZD	4/62	EZD	6/62	IZD	9/62	MZD	12/62	RZD	2/63	VZD	4/63
BZD	5/62	FZD	7/62	JZD	10/62	NZD	12/62	SZD	3/63	WZD	5/63
CZD	5/62	GZD	7/62	KZD	10/62	OZD	1/63	TZD	3/63	XZD	5/63
DZD	6/62	HZD	8/62	LZD	11/62	PZD	2/63	UZD	4/63	YZD	5/63

AZE	6/63	EZE	8/63	IZE	10/63	MZE	1/64	RZE	3/64	VZE	5/64
BZE	6/63	FZE	9/63	JZE	11/63	NZE	2/64	SZE	4/64	WZE	5/64
CZE	7/63	GZE	9/63	KZE	12/63	OZE	2/64	TZE	4/64	XZE	6/64
DZE	7/63	HZE	10/63	LZE	1/64	PZE	3/64	UZE	4/64	YZE	6/64

AZH	6/64	EZH	9/64	IZH	11/64	MZH	1/65	RZH	3/65	VZH	4/65
BZH	7/64	FZH	9/64	JZH	11/64	NZH	1/65	SZH	3/65	WZH	5/65
CZH	7/64	GZH	10/64	KZH	12/64	OZH	2/65	TZH	4/65	XZH	5/65
DZH	8/64	HZH	10/64	LZH	12/64	PZH	2/65	UZH	4/65	YZH	6/65
AZI	6/65	EZI	7/65	IZI	10/65	MZI	1/66	RZI	3/66	VZI	5/66
BZI	6/65	FZI	8/65	JZI	11/65	NZI	2/66	SZI	3/66	WZI	5/66
CZI	7/65	GZI	9/65	KZI	12/65	OZI	2/66	TZI	4/66	XZI	6/66
DZI	7/65	HZI	9/65	LZI	1/66	PZI	3/66	UZI	5/66	YZI	6/66
AZJ	7/66	EZJ	9/66	IZJ	11/66	MZJ	2/67	RZJ	3/67	VZJ	5/67
BZJ	7/66	FZJ	9/66	JZJ	12/66	NZJ	2/67	SZJ	4/67	WZJ	5/67
CZJ	8/66	GZJ	10/66	KZJ	1/67	OZJ	3/67	TZJ	4/67	XZJ	6/67
DZJ	8/66	HZJ	10/66	LZJ	1/67	PZJ	3/67	UZJ	5/67	YZJ	6/67
AZL	6/67	EZL	9/67	IZL	11/67	MZL	1/68	RZL	3/68	VZL	4/68
BZL	7/67	FZL	9/67	JZL	12/67	NZL	2/68	SZL	3/68	WZL	5/68
CZL	7/67	GZL	10/67	KZL	12/67	OZL	2/68	TZL	4/68	XZL	5/68
DZL	8/67	HZL	10/67	LZL	1/68	PZL	3/68	UZL	4/68	YZL	5/68
AZO	6/68	EZO	7/68	IZO	9/68	MZO	11/68	RZO	1/69	VZO	2/69
BZO	6/68	FZO	7/68	JZO	10/68	NZO	12/68	SZO	1/69	WZO	3/69
CZO	6/68	GZO	8/68	KZO	10/68	OZO	12/68	TZO	1/69	XZO	3/69
DZO	7/68	HZO	9/68	LZO	11/68	PZO	12/68	UZO	2/69	YZO	4/69
AZU	4/69	EZU	5/69	IZU	6/69	MZU	8/69	RZU	10/69	VZU	12/69
BZU	4/69	FZU	5/69	JZU	7/69	NZU	9/69	SZU	10/69	WZU	1/70
CZU	5/69	GZU	6/69	KZU	7/69	OZU	9/69	TZU	11/69	XZU	1/70
DZU	5/69	HZU	6/69	LZU	7/69	PZU	10/69	UZU	12/69	YZU	2/70
RI	2/70	Z	2/71	ZD	3/72	ZI	2/73	ZO	12/73		
IK	5/70	ZA	6/71	ZE	6/72	ZJ	5/73	ZU	4/74		
YI	9/70	ZC	10/71	ZH	10/72	ZL	8/73				
ARI	7/74	FRI	9/74	KRI	11/74	PRI	1/75	VRI	unalloc.		
BRI	8/74	GRI	unalloc.	LRI	11/74	RRI	2/75	WRI	3/75		
CRI	8/74	HRI	10/74	MRI	12/74	SRI	unalloc.	XRI	4/75		
DRI	8/74	IRI	unalloc.	NRI	1/75	TRI	2/75	YRI	4/75		
ERI	9/74	JRI	10/74	ORI	1/75	URI	3/75	ZRI	unalloc.		
AIK	5/75	FIK	7/75	KIK	9/75	PIK	12/75	VIK	unalloc.		
BIK	5/75	GIK	unalloc.	LIK	9/75	RIK	12/75	WIK	1/76		
CIK	5/75	HIK	7/75	MIK	10/75	SIK	unalloc.	XIK	2/76		
DIK	6/75	IIK	8/75	NIK	11/75	TIK	1/76	YIK	2/76		
EIK	6/75	JIK	8/75	OIK	11/75	UIK	1/76	ZIK	2/76		
AYI	3/76	FYI	4/76	KYI	6/76	PYI	8/76	VYI	10/76		
BYI	3/76	GYI	5/76	LYI	6/76	RYI	9/76	WYI	11/76		
CYI	4/76	HYI	5/76	MYI	7/76	SYI	9/76	XYI	11/76		
DYI	4/76	IYI	6/76	NYI	7/76	TYI	9/76	YYI	12/76		
EYI	4/76	JYI	6/76	OYI	8/76	UYI	10/76	ZYI	unalloc.		
AZA	1/77	EZA	2/77	IZA	3/77	MZA	4/77	RZA	5/77	VZA	6/77
BZA	1/77	FZA	2/77	JZA	3/77	NZA	4/77	SZA	6/77	WZA	7/77
CZA	1/77	GZA	2/77	KZA	4/77	OZA	5/77	TZA	6/77	XZA	7/77
DZA	1/77	HZA	3/77	LZA	4/77	PZA	5/77	UZA	6/77	YZA	7/77
AZC	8/77	EZC	9/77	IZC	11/77	MZC	12/77	RZC	1/78	VZC	2/78
BZC	8/77	FZC	9/77	JZC	11/77	NZC	1/78	SZC	2/78	WZC	3/78
CZC	9/77	GZC	10/77	KZC	11/77	OZC	1/78	TZC	2/78	XZC	3/78
DZC	9/77	HZC	10/77	LZC	12/77	PZC	1/78	UZC	2/78	YZC	3/78
AZD	3/78	EZD	4/78	IZD	5/78	MZD	6/78	RZD	7/78	VZD	8/78
BZD	4/78	FZD	5/78	JZD	5/78	NZD	6/78	SZD	7/78	WZD	8/78
CZD	4/78	GZD	5/78	KZD	5/78	OZD	6/78	TZD	7/78	XZD	8/78
DZD	4/78	HZD	5/78	LZD	6/78	PZD	6/78	UZD	7/78	YZD	9/78

DUBLIN COUNTY AND COUNTY BOROUGH JOINT OFFICE (Continued)

AZE	9/78	EZE	10/78	IZE	12/78	MZE	1/79	RZE	2/79	VZE	3/79
BZE	9/78	FZE	10/78	JZE	1/79	NZE	1/79	SZE	2/79	WZE	3/79
CZE	9/78	GZE	11/78	KZE	1/79	OZE	1/79	TZE	2/79	XZE	3/79
DZE	10/78	HZE	11/78	LZE	1/79	PZE	2/79	UZE	3/79	YZE	3/79
AZH	4/79	EZH	5/79	IZH	5/79	MZH	6/79	RZH	7/79	VZH	9/79
BZH	4/79	FZH	5/79	JZH	5/79	NZH	7/79	SZH	8/79	WZH	9/79
CZH	4/79	GZH	5/79	KZH	6/79	OZH	7/79	TZH	8/79	XZH	10/79
DZH	4/79	HZH	5/79	LZH	6/79	PZH	7/79	UZH	8/79	YZH	10/79
AZI	10/79	EZI	1/80	IZI	1/80	MZI	2/80	RZI	3/80	VZI	4/80
BZI	10/79	FZI	1/80	JZI	1/80	NZI	2/80	SZI	3/80	WZI	4/80
CZI	11/79	GZI	1/80	KZI	1/80	OZI	2/80	TZI	3/80	XZI	4/80
DZI	11/79	HZI	1/80	LZI	2/80	PZI	2/80	UZI	3/80	YZI	4/80
AZJ	4/80	EZJ	5/80	IZJ	6/80	MZJ	7/80	RZJ	9/80	VZJ	11/80
BZJ	5/80	FZJ	6/80	JZJ	7/80	NZJ	8/80	SZJ	9/80	WZJ	11/80
CZJ	5/80	GZJ	6/80	KZJ	7/80	OZJ	8/80	TZJ	10/80	XZJ	12/80
DZJ	5/80	HZJ	6/80	LZJ	7/80	PZJ	9/80	UZJ	10/80	YZJ	1/81
AZL	1/81	EZL	1/81	IZL	2/81	MZL	3/81	RZL	4/81	VZL	4/81
BZL	1/81	FZL	1/81	JZL	2/81	NZL	3/81	SZL	4/81	WZL	5/81
CZL	1/81	GZL	1/81	KZL	2/81	OZL	3/81	TZL	4/81	XZL	5/81
DZL	1/81	HZL	2/81	LZL	3/81	PZL	3/81	UZL	4/81	YZL	5/81
AZO	5/81	EZO	6/81	IZO	7/81	MZO	8/81	RZO	9/81	VZO	11/81
BZO	6/81	FZO	7/81	JZO	7/81	NZO	8/81	SZO	10/81	WZO	12/81
CZO	6/81	GZO	7/81	KZO	7/81	OZO	8/81	TZO	10/81	XZO	1/82
DZO	6/81	HZO	7/81	LZO	8/81	PZO	9/81	UZO	11/81	YZO	1/82
AZU	1/82	EZU	2/82	IZU	3/82	MZU	4/82	RZU	5/82	VZU	6/82
BZU	1/82	FZU	2/82	JZU	3/82	NZU	4/82	SZU	5/82	WZU	7/82
CZU	1/82	GZU	2/82	KZU	3/82	OZU	4/82	TZU	6/82	XZU	7/82
DZU	2/82	HZU	3/82	LZU	4/82	PZU	4/82	UZU	6/82	YZU	8/82
ASI	8/82	FSI	10/82	KSI	1/83	PSI	2/83	VSI	4/83	
BSI	9/82	GSI	11/82	LSI	1/83	RSI	2/83	WSI	4/83	
CSI	9/82	HSI	12/82	MSI	2/83	SSI	3/83	XSI	5/83	
DSI	9/82	ISI	1/83	NSI	2/83	TSI	3/83	YSI	5/83	
ESI	10/82	JSI	1/83	OSI	2/83	USI	3/83	ZSI	5/83	
AZG	6/83	EZG	8/83	IZG	10/83	MZG	1/84	RZG	2/84	VZG	3/84
BZG	6/83	FZG	8/83	JZG	10/83	NZG	1/84	SZG	2/84	WZG	4/84
CZG	7/83	GZG	9/83	KZG	11/83	OZG	1/84	TZG	2/84	XZG	4/84
DZG	7/83	HZG	9/83	LZG	12/83	PZG	1/84	UZG	3/84	YZG	4/84
AZS	5/84	EZS	6/84	IZS	8/84	MZS	10/84	RZS	1/85	VZS	2/85
BZS	5/84	FZS	6/84	JZS	8/84	NZS	10/84	SZS	1/85	WZS	2/85
CZS	5/84	GZS	7/84	KZS	9/84	OZS	11/84	TZS	1/85	XZS	3/85
DZS	5/84	HZS	7/84	LZS	9/84	PZS	12/84	UZS	1/85	YZS	3/85
AZV	3/85	EZV	4/85	IZV	5/85	MZV	7/85	RZV	9/85	VZV	11/85
BZV	3/85	FZV	5/85	JZV	6/85	NZV	7/85	SZV	9/85	WZV	11/85
CZV	4/85	GZV	5/85	KZV	6/85	OZV	8/85	TZV	10/85	XZV	1/86
DZV	4/85	HZV	5/85	LZV	6/85	PZV	8/85	UZV	10/85	YZV	1/86
SI	1/86	ZG	4/86	ZS	7/86	Last issue ZS 8709						

International Circulation

ZZ   4/25 (1-9999)   ZZ   3/83   ZZ ca. 3/89 (10000 up)

Some reserved number blocks issued out of sequence with main series.

COUNTY BOROUGH COUNCIL OF LIMERICK

TI	1/04									
ATI	10/59	FTI	9/64	KTI	7/68	PTI	7/71	VTI	4/74
BTI	12/60	GTI	5/65	LTI	4/69	RTI	4/72	WTI	9/74
CTI	2/62	HTI	4/66	MTI	12/69	STI	9/72	XTI	6/75
DTI	2/63	ITI	3/67	NTI	5/70	TTI	4/73	YTI	2/76
ETI	1/64	JTI	1/68	OTI	2/71	UTI	8/73	ZTI	7/76

TI	3/77					
ATI	1/82	CTI	4/83	ETI	3/85	
BTI	8/82	DTI	4/84	FTI	2/86	Last Issue 929 FTI

COUNTY BOROUGH COUNCIL OF WATERFORD

Duplicated series for cars and motorcycles prior to 1921.

WI	1/04										
AWI	1/66	FWI	4/72	KWI	8/77	PWI	7/81	VWI	9/85
BWI	7/67	GWI	4/73	LWI	5/78	RWI	4/82	WWI	10/86	Last issue WWI 80
CWI	11/68	HWI	4/74	MWI	3/79	SWI	5/83	
DWI	2/70	IWI	7/75	NWI	2/80	TWI	7/84	
EWI	4/71	JWI	8/76	OWI	10/80	UWI	not issued	

NEW SYSTEM - 1987

The following is the allocation of index marks under the current system :

C	Cork County & City	L	Limerick City	RN	Roscommon County
CE	Clare County	LD	Longford County	SO	Sligo County
CN	Cavan County	LH	Louth County	TN	Tipperary (N.R.) County
CW	Carlow County	LK	Limerick County	TS	Tipperary (S.R.) County
D	Dublin City & County	LM	Leitrim County	W	Waterford City
DL	Donegal County	LS	Laoighis County	WD	Waterford County
G	Galway County & City	MH	Meath County	WH	Westmeath County
KE	Kildare County	MN	Monaghan County	WW	Wicklow County
KK	Kilkenny County	MO	Mayo County	WX	Wexford County
KY	Kerry County	OY	Offaly County		

APPENDIX 6

ORDERS & REGULATIONS DEALING WITH INDEX MARKS

AND REGISTRATION PLATES

ORDERS AND REGULATIONS DEALING WITH THE ALLOTMENT OF INDEX MARKS

1. REGULATIONS ISSUED UNDER AUTHORITY OF MOTOR CAR ACT, 1903

ORDERS MAKING THE INITIAL ALLOTMENT OF INDEX MARKS

Year	SR&O No.	Date	Title	Index Marks Allotted
1903	998	19.11.03	The Motor Car (Registration & Licensing) Order, 1903	A, B, C, D, E, F, H, J, K, L, M, N, O, P, R, T, U, W, X, Y, AA, AB, AC, AD, AE, AF, AH, AJ, AK, AL, AM, AN, AO, AP, AR, AT, AU, AW, AX, AY, BA, BB, BC, BD, BE, BF, BH, BJ, BK, BL, BM, BN, BO, BP, BR, BT, BU, BW, BX, BY, CA, CB, CC, CD, CE, CF, CH, CJ, CK, CL, CM, CN, CO, CP, CR, CT, CU, CW, CX, CY, DA, DB, DC, DE, DF, DH, DJ, DK, DL, DM, DN, DO, DP, DR, DU, DW, DX, DY, EA, EB, EC, ED, EE, EF, EH, EJ, EK, EL, EM, EN, EO, EP, ET, EU, EW, EX, EY, FA, FB, FC, FD, FE, FF, FH, FJ, FK, FL, FM, FN, FO, FP.
1903	1001	20.11.03	The Motor Car Registration & Licensing (Scotland) Order 1903	G, S, V, AS, BS, DS, ES, HS, JS, KS, LS, MS, NS, OS, PS, RS, SA, SB, SD, SE, SH, SJ, SK, SL, SM, SN, SO, SP, SR, SS, ST, SU, SV, SW, SX, SY, TS, US, VS, WS, XS, YS.
1903	1002	23.11.03	The Motor Car (Registration & Licensing) (Ireland) Order, 1903	AI, BI, CI, DI, EI, FI, HI, IA, IB, IC, ID, IE, IF, IH, IJ, IK, IL, IM, IN, IO, IP, IR, IT, IU, IW, IX, IY, IZ, JI, KI, LI, MI, NI, OI, PI, RI, TI, UI, WI.

Index Marks Allotted

ORDERS OF THE LOCAL GOVERNMENT BOARD, OR THE SECRETARY FOR SCOTLAND (marked *), AMENDING THE ABOVE REGULATIONS BY THE ALTERATION OF INDEX MARKS, THE ALLOTMENT OF ADDITIONAL INDEX MARKS AND THE ASSIGNMENT OF INDEX MARKS TO NEWLY CREATED COUNTY BOROUGHS AND REGISTERING BURGHS. (Orders are addressed to the Council or Councils named "and to all others whom it may concern").

Year	SR&O No.	Date	Council or Councils	Index Marks Allotted
1904	1571	26. 9.04	Blackpool and Tynemouth C.B.C.s	FR, FT
1904	1811	27.12.04	Dorset C.C.	FX (substituted for BF)
1905	494	17. 4.05	London C.C.	LC
1905	841	14. 7.05	Northampton C.B.C.	NH (substituted for DF)
1905	975	12. 8.05	Southport C.B.C.	FY
1906	673	31. 8.06	London C.C.	LN
1907	183	22. 2.07	Smethwick C.B.C.	HA
1907	662	13. 8.07	London C.C.	LB
1908	47	1. 1.08	Merthyr Tydfil C.B.C.	HB
1909	119	5. 2.09	London C.C.	LD
1910	388	8. 4.10	London C.C.	LA
1910	676	25. 6.10	Stoke-on-Trent C.B.C.	(EH transferred from Hanley C.B.C.)
1910	1128	22.10.10	Eastbourne C.B.C.	HC
1911	477	18. 5.11	London C.C.	LE
1912	405	29. 3.12	London C.C.	LF
1912	406	4. 4.12	Middlesex C.C.	MX
1912	1154	31. 7.12	Birmingham C.B.C.	OA
1912	1447	25. 9.12	London C.C.	LH
1912	1856	18.12.12	Barnsley, Dewsbury and Wallasey C.B.C.s	HD, HE, HF
1913	188	15. 2.13	Surrey C.C.	PA
1913	526	6. 5.13	Kent C.C.	KT
1913	784	19. 7.13	London C.C.	LK
1913	999	18. 9.13	Manchester C.B.C.	NA
1914	42	14. 1.14	Carlisle and Southend-on-Sea C.B.C.s	HH, HJ
1914	306	27. 2.14	London C.C.	LL
1914	564	20. 4.14	Liverpool C.B.C.	KB
1914	1081	15. 7.14	Essex C.C.	HK
1914	1082	15. 7.14	London C.C.	LM
1914	1840	22.12.14	London C.C.	LO
1914	1841	22.12.14	Plymouth C.B.C.	(DR transferred from Devonport C.B.C.)
1915	116	8. 2.15	East Ham and Wakefield C.B.C.s	HL, HM
1915	293	26. 3.15	Darlington C.B.C.	HN
1915	758	27. 7.15	Birmingham C.B.C.	OB
1915	759	27. 7.15	London C.C.	LP

Year	SR&O No.		Date			Index Marks Allotted
1915	892		8.	9.15	West Riding of Yorkshire C.C.	WR
1916	215		24.	3.16	London C.C.	LR
1916	216		24.	3.16	Southampton C.C.	HO
1916	365		1.	6.16	Middlesex C.C.	MC
1917	771		24.	7.17	Kent C.C., London C.C.	KN, LT
1917	* 960		19.	9.17	Glasgow B.C.	GA
1918	694		25.	4.18	London C.C.	LU
1918	1185		6.	9.18	Chester C.C.	MA
1919	48		16.	1.19	Middlesex C.C.	MD
1919	218		24.	2.19	London C.C.	LW
1919	599		8.	5.19	Lancaster, London and Surrey C.C.s, Birmingham and Manchester C.B.C.s	LX, NB, OE, PB, TB

ORDERS OF THE MINISTER OF HEALTH, OR THE SECRETARY FOR SCOTLAND (marked *). (The powers of the Local Government Board were transferred to the Minister of Health w.e.f. 1.7.19, by SR&O 1919, No. 850).

Year	SR&O No.		Date			Index Marks Allotted
1919	888		7.	7.19	Wilts C.C., Coventry C.B.C.	HP, HR
1919	* 1008		9.	8.19	Edinburgh B.C.	SG
1919	1069		7.	8.19	London C.C.	LY
1919	1257		16.	9.19	Sheffield C.B.C.	WA

ORDERS OF THE MINISTER OF TRANSPORT, OR THE SECRETARY FOR SCOTLAND (marked *). (The Ministry of Transport came into effect from 1.1.20)

Year	SR&O No.		Date			Index Marks Allotted
1920	146		2.	1.20	Bristol and Liverpool C.B.C.s	HT, KC
1920	153		22.	1.20	London C.C.	XA
1920	517		29.	3.20	London C.C.	XB, XC, XD
1920	784		20.	5.20	Devon, Hertford and Middlesex C.C.s, Birmingham C.B.C.	ME, NK, OH, TA
1920	1024		30.	6.20	Kent and Northumberland C.C.s, Manchester C.B.C.	KE, NC, NL
1920	***		12.	7.20	London C.C.	XE, XF, XH
1920	***		13.	9.20	Bedford C.C.	NM
1920	***		9.10.20		Nottingham C.C.	NN
1920	***		17.11.20		Essex C.C.	NO
1920	* 2432		17.12.20		Motherwell & Wishaw B.C.	GM
1921	64		11.	1.21	Belfast C.B.C.	XI
1921	127		20.	1.21	Derby, Glamorgan, Leicester, Salop, Somerset, Stafford, Warwick and Worcester C.C.s	NP, NR, NT, NU, NX, NY, RE, YA
1921	181		4.	2.21	Leeds C.B.C.	NW

*** These four orders do not appear to have been allotted SR&O numbers.

2. REGULATIONS ISSUED UNDER AUTHORITY OF ROADS ACT, 1920

Year	SR&O No.	Date		Index Marks Allotted or Other Effects of Order
1921	None	9. 3.21	ROAD VEHICLES (REGISTRATION & LICENSING) REGULATIONS, 1921. (Provisional Rules and Orders)	Substantive Regulations QQ and YI the only new marks.

(Allocations of Irish index marks after 1921 are shown in separate tabulations)

ORDERS OF THE MINISTER OF TRANSPORT AMENDING SCHEDULE 3 OF THE ABOVE REGULATIONS :
(Orders are addressed similarly to those of the Local Government Board)

Year	SR&O No.	Date		Index Marks Allotted or Other Effects of Order
1921	793	28. 4.21	Surrey C.C.	PC
1921	983	2. 6.21	London C.C.	XK, XL, XM
1921	1138	23. 6.21	Birmingham C.B.C.	OK
1921	1275	30. 7.21	West Riding of Yorkshire C.C.	WY
1921	1748	10.11.21	Berks, Cambridge, Chester, Gloucester, Kent, Lancaster, Lincoln (Parts of Lindsey), London, Southampton and Wilts C.C.s; Bradford, Bristol, Manchester and Sheffield C.B.Cs; Lanark C.C. and Glasgow B.C.	DD, ER, FU, GB, HU, KK, KU, MB, MO, MR, ND, OR, TC, VA, WB, XN, XO, XP
1922	24	2. 1.22	East Sussex C.C.	PM
1922	1084	27. 9.22	Bucks, Dorset, Durham, Essex, Middlesex, Norfolk, Surrey, West Sussex, North Riding of Yorkshire, West Riding of Yorkshire C.C.s; Birmingham, Croydon, Leeds and Liverpool C.B.C.s	KA, MF, OC, PD, PP, PR, PT, PU, PW, PX, PY, RK, UM, WT
1923	631	30. 5.23	Birmingham C.B.C.	OL
1923	1153	24. 9.23	Cornwall, Cumberland, Devon, Hertford, Kent, Lancaster, London, Middlesex, Northampton, Nottingham, Somerset, East Suffolk, Surrey, West Riding of Yorkshire C.C.s; Birmingham, Bournemouth, Coventry, Kingston-upon-Hull, Leeds, Leicester, Manchester, Newcastle-upon-Tyne, Nottingham, Portsmouth, Southampton C.B.C.s; Fife C.C.; Edinburgh B.C.	FG, KH, KL, MH, NE, OM, PE, RL, RM, RO, RP, RR, RT, RU, RW, RY, SF, TD, TN, TO, TP, TR, TT, UA, WU, XR, XT, XU, YB
1924	1074	19. 9.24	Chester, Essex, Glamorgan, Kent, London, Middlesex, Northumberland, Oxford, Southampton, Stafford, Surrey, and Warwick C.C.s; Birmingham, Brighton, Cardiff and Wolverhampton C.B.C.s; Ayr C.C.; Glasgow B.C.	AG, GD, KM, MK, ON, OT, PF, RF, TU, TW, TX, TY, UD, UE, UF, UH, UK, XW, XX, XY, YK

Year	SR&O No.	Date		Index Marks Allotted or Other Effects of Order
			Hereafter, the Regulations have specific titles and are not addressed to any particular authority.	
1924	1462	23.12.24	THE ROAD VEHICLES (REGISTRATION & LICENSING) REGULATIONS, 1924	Substantive regulations, also allotting new index marks : AV, DF, GS, KO, KW, ML, MM, NF, OP, PH, RA, TE, TM, UN, UO, UP, UR, UT, UX, UY, WF, WH, WK, WL, WM, WN, WO, WW, YC, YL, YM, YN, YO, YP, YR.
AMENDING THE REGULATIONS OF 1924 :				
1926	1405	11.11.26	THE ROAD VEHICLES (INDEX MARKS) REGULATIONS, 1926	FW, GE, HW, KD, KP, KX, MP, MT, MW, MY, OX, PK, PN, PO, RD, RG, RX, SC, TH, TK, TL, UC, UL, UU, UV, UW, VB, VC, VE, VF, VG, VH, VJ, VK, VL, VM, VN, VO, VP, VT, VW, VX, VY, WE, WX, XV, YE, YF, YH, YT, YU, YV, YW, YX, YY
1927	none	1. 4.27	THE ROAD VEHICLES (INDEX MARKS) (COUNTY BOROUGH OF DONCASTER) PROVISIONAL REGULATIONS, 1927	DT
1928	680	22. 9.28	THE ROAD VEHICLES (INDEX MARKS) REGULATIONS, 1928	BG, BV, CV, DG, DV, EV, FS, FV, GC, GF, GG, GH, GJ, GK, GN, GO, GP, GT, GU, GV, GW, GX, GY, HG, HV, HX, HY, JA, JB, JC, JD, JE, JF, JG, JH, JK, JL, JM, JN, JO, JP, JR, JT, JU, JV, JW, JX, JY, KF, KG, KR, KV, KY, LG, LJ, MG, MJ, MU, MV, NG, NV, OF, OG, OU, OV, OW, OY, PG, PL, PV, RB, RC, RH, RN, RV, TF, TG, TV, UB, VD, VR, VU, VV, WD, WG, WJ, WP, WV, XG, YD, YG
1930	745	10. 9.30	THE ROAD VEHICLES (INDEX MARKS) REGULATIONS, 1930	CG, EG, GL, GR, KJ, LV, NJ, OD, OJ, PJ, QA, QC, QS, RJ, TJ, UG, UJ, XJ, YJ
1932	332	29. 4.32	THE ROAD VEHICLES (INDEX MARKS) REGULATIONS, 1932	The Schedule consolidated all previous allocations and added : CS, JJ. Also the first allotment of three-letter index marks as in the tabulation
1935	581	14. 6.35	THE ROAD VEHICLES (INDEX MARKS) REGULATIONS, 1935	Consolidated all previous allocations and allotted further three-letter index marks as in tabulation.
1936	1015	18. 9.36	THE ROAD VEHICLES (INDEX MARKS) (COUNTY COUNCIL OF LONDON) REGULATIONS, 1936	Special allocation of GPO to London C.C.

Year	SR&O No.	Date		Index Marks Allotted or Other Effects of Order
1938	6	3. 1.38	THE ROAD VEHICLES (INDEX MARKS) REGULATIONS, 1938	Consolidated all previous allocations and allotted further three-letter index marks as in tabulation.
1941	1149	28. 7.41	THE ROAD VEHICLES (REGISTRATION & LICENSING) REGULATIONS, 1941	Consolidated regulations. No new marks allotted but GMR corrected to GMA (see tabulation).

AMENDING THE REGULATIONS OF 1941 :

Year	SR&O No.	Date		Index Marks Allotted or Other Effects of Order
1942	1441	23. 7.42	THE ROAD VEHICLES (REGISTRATION & LICENSING) (AMENDMENT) REGULATIONS, 1942	Three-letter marks as in tabulation.
1946	None	17. 7.46	THE ROAD VEHICLES (REGISTRATION & LICENSING) (AMENDMENT) PROVISIONAL REGULATIONS, 1946 – superseded by :	
1946	1557	24. 9.46	THE ROAD VEHICLES (REGISTRATION & LICENSING) (AMENDMENT) (No. 3) REGULATIONS, 1946	QB, QD and QE and three-letter marks as in tabulation.

Subsequent regulations are STATUTORY INSTRUMENTS: (This change of title took effect from 1.1.48)

Year	SR&O No.	Date		Index Marks Allotted or Other Effects of Order
1949	1618	1.10.49	THE ROAD VEHICLES (REGISTRATION & LICENSING) REGULATIONS, 1949	Consolidated regulations. PAK the only new index mark; FUX deleted
1951	1380	15. 8.51	THE ROAD VEHICLES (INDEX MARKS) REGULATIONS, 1951	Consolidated regulations, superseding above. QF, QG, QH, QJ, QK, QL, QM, QN and QP plus 3-letter marks as in tabulation.

AMENDING THE REGULATIONS OF 1951 :

Year	SR&O No.	Date		Index Marks Allotted or Other Effects of Order
1955	1666	17.11.55	THE ROAD VEHICLES (INDEX MARKS) (AMENDMENT) REGULATIONS, 1955	Three-letter marks as in tabulation.
1959	86	26. 1.59	THE ROAD VEHICLES (INDEX MARKS) (AMENDMENT) REGULATIONS, 1959	" " " "
1960	1155	1. 8.60	THE ROAD VEHICLES (INDEX MARKS) (AMENDMENT) REGULATIONS, 1960	CBF to YBF, (except UBF) only.
1961	962	1. 6.61	THE ROAD VEHICLES (INDEX MARKS) (AMENDMENT) REGULATIONS, 1961	OO, three-letter combinations of OO and WC and further three-letter marks as in tabulation.
1963	494	1. 4.63	THE ROAD VEHICLES (INDEX MARKS) (AMENDMENT) REGULATIONS, 1963	Three-letter marks as in tabulation, including allocation of AXA to CXA to Kirkcaldy, with consequential proviso that specified London marks are not to be used with a year letter.

Year	SR&O No.	Date		Index Marks Allotted or Other Effects of Order
1964	404	1. 4.64	THE ROAD VEHICLES (INDEX MARKS) REGULATIONS, 1964	Consolidated regulations. These regulations allotted all remaining three-letter marks, and included allocations to Coatbridge, Luton and Solihull.

AMENDING THE REGULATIONS OF 1964 :

Year	SR&O No.	Date		Index Marks Allotted or Other Effects of Order
1965	237	1. 4.65	THE ROAD VEHICLES (INDEX MARKS) (AMENDMENT) REGULATIONS, 1965	Reallocations following local government reorganisation : Cambridgeshire & Isle of Ely, Greater London Council, Huntingdon & Peterborough. Also corrections of errors in 1964/404 – see tabulation.
1966	250	1. 4.66	THE ROAD VEHICLES (INDEX MARKS) (AMENDMENT) REGULATIONS, 1966	Transfer Smethwick marks to Warley. Also correction of error in 1965/237 – see tabulation.
1967	315	1. 4.67	THE ROAD VEHICLES (INDEX MARKS) (AMENDMENT) REGULATIONS, 1967	Transfer West Hartlepool marks to Hartlepool C.B.C.
1968	355	1. 4.68	THE ROAD VEHICLES (INDEX MARKS) (AMENDMENT) REGULATIONS, 1968	Allocation of marks to Torbay C.B.C. Transfer of Middlesbrough marks to Teesside C.B.C. Record official name change for Berkshire.

Except for the following International Circulation Regulations there were no further Statutory Instruments covering the allocation of Index Marks; with the introduction of centralisation this became a matter for adminstrative arrangement.

Year	SR&O No.	Date		Index Marks Allotted or Other Effects of Order
1971	937	14. 6.71	THE MOTOR VEHICLES (INTERNATIONAL CIRCULATION) REGULATIONS, 1971	QR, QT, QU, QV, QW, QX, QY

NEW INDEX MARKS ALLOTTED BY NORTHERN IRELAND SR&Os

Year	SR&O No.	Date	Index Marks Allotted or Other Effects of Order
1927	114	28. 9.27	AZ
1929	169	20.12.29	BZ
1932	24	21. 3.32	CZ, DZ
1935	82	16. 7.35	EZ
1937	90	8.10.37	FZ
1942	56	21. 4.42	GZ
1943	125	10.11.43	HZ
1946	110	25. 6.46	JZ
1946	215	28.11.46	KZ, LZ
1947	167	9.10.47	MZ
1948	317	4.12.48	NZ
1950	68	24. 4.50	OZ
1952	211	12.11.52	PZ
1954	9	28. 1.54	RZ, SZ, TZ
1955	132	16. 8.55	UZ
1956	37	22. 3.56	VZ, WZ
1957	152	1. 8.57	XZ, YZ
1958	3	9. 1.58	All reverse format issues.
1963	79	15. 4.63	QI, QZ
1965	259	7.12.65	AIA-DIA, AIB-DIB, AIJ-DIJ, AIL-BIL, AIW-DIW, AJI-DJI, AOI-HOI, AUI-BUI
1970	290	10.11.70	EIA-NIA, EIJ-IIJ, JOI-NOI, POI, ROI.
1973	490	11.12.73	Revoked all previous regulations authorising allotment of index marks to Councils and gave the Department of Transport powers to decide on any future allocation.

NEW INDEX MARKS ALLOTTED BY IRISH FREE STATE & REPUBLIC OF IRELAND SR&Os and S.I.s

Year	SR&O No.	Date	Index Marks Allotted
1925	1	5.25	ZZ
1926	13	11.26	Z, ZI
1932	9	2.32	ZA
1935	5	4.35	ZB
1937	11	1.37	ZC
1939	20	9.39	ZD, ZE
1946	7	5.46	ZF
1947	1	1.47	ZH

N.B. No serial numbers were allotted to SR&Os before 1948.

Year	SR&O No.	Date	Index Marks Allotted
1948	282	18. 8.48	ZJ
1949	42	18. 2.49	ZK
1950	121	10. 5.50	ZL, ZM
1951	229	2. 8.51	ZN
1951	370	20.12.51	ZO, ZP, ZR
1953	171	27. 5.53	ZT, ZU, ZW
1953	411	22.12.53	ZX
1954	95	7. 5.54	ZY, ARI-FRI, HRI, JRI-PRI, RRI, TRI, URI, WRI-YRI
1954	178	16. 8.54	AIP-FIP, HIP-JIP, LIP, AIU-FIU, HIU-KIU, AIZ-FIZ, HIZ-KIZ, AHI-FHI, HHI, JHI-LHI
1955	154	9. 8.55	AIK-FIK, HIK-PIK, RIK, TIK, UIK, WIK-ZIK
1955	249	9.12.55	AIF-PIF, RIF-ZIF
1956	254	27. 9.56	ANI-JNI
1956	265	23.10.56	AFI-JFI
1957	165	1. 8.57	AYI-PYI, RYI-YYI
1958	14		Consolidated schedule; no new marks allotted.
1958	132	6. 6.58	AID-HID, JID
1958	248	5.12.58	API-JPI
1959	8	21. 1.59	AIE-JIE
1959	107	20. 6.59	AZA-PZA, RZA-YZA, ALI-JLI
1959	136	8. 8.59	ATI-JTI, AIM-JIM, AEI-JEI
1960	46	4. 3.60	ACI-JCI, AIR-JIR, ABI-JBI
1960	244	30.11.60	AZC-PZC, RZC-YZC, AKI-JKI, AMI-PMI, RMI-YMI
1961	283	8.12.61	AZD-PZD, RZD-YZD, AZB-PZB, RZB-YZB, AIH-NIH, AIO-HIO, JIO-NIO, LIU-PIU, RIU-ZIU, LIZ-PIZ, RIZ-ZIZ, AAI-NAI, ADI-LDI, MHI-PHI, RHI-ZHI
1963	69	26. 4.63	AZE-PZE, RZE-YZE, RPI-ZPI, AIC-LIC, AIY-LIY
1964	8	14. 1.64	AZH-PZH, RZH-YZH, KPI-PPI,
1965	30	15. 2.65	AZI-PZI, RZI-YZI, RZJ-PZJ, RZJ-YZJ, AWI-JWI, IID, KID-PID, RID-ZID, KIE-PIE, RIE-ZIE, AZK-PZK, RZK-YZK, KIM-PIM, RIM-ZIM, MIP-PIP, RIP-ZIP, KNI-PNI, RNI-ZNI
1967	128	18. 5.67	KFI-PFI, RFI-YFI, AZL-PZL, RZL-YZL, KTI-PTI, RTI-ZTI, OIN, PIN, RIN-ZIN, KLI-PLI, RLI-ZLI
1968	121	4. 6.68	AZU-PZU, RZU-YZU, AZF-LZF, AZT-PZT, RZT-YZT, OIH, PIH, RIH-ZIH, AZP-PZP, RZP-YZP, AZM-PZM,
1970	101	11. 5.70	MIC-PIC, RIC-ZIC, AZX-PZX, RZX-YZX, PIO, RIO-ZIO, AZW-PZW, RZW-YZW, KCI-PCI, RCI-ZCI, AIT-PIT, RZM-YZM, AZX-PZX, RIX-ZIX, MIY-PIY, RIY-ZIY, AZY-PZY, RZY-YZY, OAI, PAI, RAI-ZAI, RIT-ZIT, AIX-PIX, RIX-ZIX, KBI-PBI, RBI-ZBI, KIR-PIR, RIR-ZIR, MDI-PDI, RDI-ZDI, KEI-PEI, AZN-PZN, RZN-YZN, KBI-PBI, RKI-ZKI, AZR-PZR, RZR-YZR, MZF-PZF, RZF-YZF, KWI-PWI, RWI-ZWI, REI-ZEI, KKI-PKI, RKI-ZKI,
1981	231	26. 6.81	ASI-PSI, RSI-ZSI, AZG-PZG, RZG-YZG, AZS-PZS, RZS-YZS, AZV-PZV, RZV-YZV, AIV-HIV, JIV-LIV, NIV-PIV, RIV-ZIV, AIS-HIS, JIS-OIS, RIS-XIS, ZIS, AGI-PGI, RGI-ZGI
1986	6	9. 1.86	SI, ZG, ZS, ZV

REGULATIONS DEALING WITH MAJOR ASPECTS OF REGISTRATION PLATES OTHER THAN INDEX MARKS

(Dates shown are dates of coming into operation)

The Road Vehicles (Registration & Licensing) (Amendment) Regulations, 1950. (S.I. 1950 No. 2063, 1.1.51).
Exempted vehicles used for naval, military and air force purposes from civilian registration.

The Road Vehicle (Registration & Licensing) Regulations, 1953. (S.I. 1953, No. 231, 28.2.53)
Authorised the issue of reverse format registrations.

The Road Vehicles (Registration & Licensing (Amendment) Regulations, 1953. (S.I. 1953 No. 1753, 11.12.53)
Authorise silver or light grey characters, as well as white, on registration plates.

The Road Vehicles (Registration & Licensing) (Amendment) Regulations, 1962. (S.I. 1962 No. 1610 14.8.62).
Introduction of year-letter marks, together with reduced dimensions for plates. (Height of characters on plates for cars etc. had been unchanged at 3½" since 1903, now reduced optionally to 3¹/₈".)

The Road Vehicles (Registration & Licensing) (Amendment No. 2) Regulations, 1967. (S.I. 1967, No. 1844, 20.12.67)
Permitted optional use of reflective plates.

The Road Vehicles (Registration & Licensing) Regulations, 1971. (S.I. 1971 No. 450 1.4.71).
Transfer of registration and licensing functions to Secretary of State for the Environment as from 1 April 1971; local authorities thereafter act as agents for Secretary of State.
Revocation of all regulations relating to the allocation of Index Marks to Councils.
Replaced by Regulation 9 (5) ".......the expression "index mark" means such a letter of the alphabet or combination of such letters as fall to be assigned to a vehicle in pursuance of arrangements in that behalf made by the Secretary of State".

The Road Vehicles (Registration & Licensing) (Amendment) Regulations, 1972. (S.I. 1972 No. 1865, 29.12.72).
Compulsory use of reflective plates for all vehicles, (except certain exempted categories), first registered on and after 1 January 1973.

The Road Vehicles (Registration & Licensing) (Amendment) Regulations, 1975. (S.I. 1975, No. 1809, 1.8.75)
Deletion of requirement for motorcycles to carry front plates.

The Sale of Registration Marks Regulations, 1989, (S.I. 1989, No. 1938, 30.11.89)
Authorised the sale of registration marks by the Secretary of State for Transport.
(Amended by Sale of Marks (Amendment) Regulations 1993, [S.I. 986] and 1996 [S.I. 2977])
Replaced by Sale of Marks Regulations 1995, (S.I. 1993 No. 2880, 18.12.95).

LATEST INDEX MARK (ALPHABETICALLY) ALLOTTED TO EACH AUTHORITY BY SUCCESSIVE REGULATIONS

(N.B. Where no Index Mark is shown there were no additions to the existing allocation for that authority.)

Year and number of Order	1932 / 332	1935 / 581	1938 / 6	1942 / 1441	1946 / 1557	1951 / 1380	1955 / 1666	1959 / 86	1961 / 962	1963 / 494	1964 / 404
County Councils											
Anglesey							JEY	REY	TEY		YEY
Bedford	AMJ	CTM	FTM		OTM	TTM	YTM				
Berks	AJB	BRX	ERX		HRX	ORX	YRX				
Brecon					AEU	GEU	KEU	SEU			YEU
Buckingham	BPP	GPP	KPP		SPP	YPP					
Caernarvon					CJC	EJC	KJC	SJC			YJC
Cambridge	BVE	DVE	GVE		LVE	RVE	YVE				
Cardigan				BEJ	CEJ	JEJ	NEJ	YEJ			
Carmarthen		ATH	DTH	ETH	JTH	PTH	YTH				
Chester	DTU (1)	FTU (2)	KTU (3)		TTU	YTU					
Cornwall	CRL	FRL	LRL		SRL (4)	YRL (5)					
Cumberland	BRM	DRM	GRM		NRM	URM	YRM				
Denbigh	AUN	CCA	FUN		KUN	PUN	YUN				
Derby	CRB	FRB	LRB		VRB	YRB					
Devon	BUO	EUO	KUO (6)		PUO	YUO (7)					
Dorset		ATK	BTK		GTK	MTK	UTK	YTK			
Durham	BUP	EUP	GUP		OUP	TUP	YUP				
Isle of Ely					CJE	FJE	LJE	RJE	(8)		YJE
Essex	DVX	GVX	MVX		XVX	YVX					
Flint	ADM	CDM	DDM		LDM	PDM	YDM				
Glamorgan	ATX	DTX	HTX		STX	UTX	YTX				
Gloucester	ADG	DDG	GDG		NDG	TDG	YDG				
Hereford		AVJ	DVJ		KVJ	PVJ	YVJ				
Hertford	BUR	EUR	JUR		UUR	YUR					
Huntingdon		BEW	CEW	FEW	REW (9)		YEW				
Kent	CKT	FKT	KKT	LKT	UKT	YKT					
Lancaster	CTJ	DTJ	HTJ		RTJ	YTJ					
Leicester		BUT	DUT	EUT	MUT	PUT	YUT				
Lincs., Holland				AJL	FJL	LJL	RJL	YJL			
Lincs., Kesteven			BTL		FTL	OTL	UTL	YTL			
Lincs., Lindsey		AFW	CFW	DFW	KFW	UFW	YFW				

279

Year and number of Order	1932 / 332	1935 / 581	1938 / 6	1942 / 1441	1946 / 1557	1951 / 1380	1955 / 1666	1959 / 86	1961 / 962	1963 / 494	1964 / 404
London	CYY	FYY (10)	JYY (11)	USN only	SYY (12)		YYY				YFF
Merioneth						DFF	LFF	SFF			YFF
Middlesex	CMY	HMY	SMY (13)		XMY	YMY			(14)		
Monmouth	BWO	DWO	GWO		PWO	TWO	YWO				
Montgomery					CEP	MEP		TEP			YEP
Norfolk	AVF	DAH	GVF		NVF	UVF	YVF				
Northampton		BBD	CRP	FRP	HRP	NRP	YRP				
Northumberland		ATY	BTY		FTY	JTY	RTY	YTY			
Nottingham	CRR	EVO	JVO		SVO	WVO	YVO				
Oxford		AUD	BUD	CUD	JUD	MUD	SUD	YUD			
Pembroke	CDE	EDE	GDE	HDE	PDE	YDE					
Peterborough					CFL	GFL	NFL	TFL		XFL	YFL
Radnor							BFO	GFO			YFO
Rutland								EFP			YFP
Salop		AUX	CUX	DUX	HUX (15)	PUX	TUX	YUX			
Somerset	CYD	EYA	JYD		PYD	VYD	YYD				
Southampton	BOU	DOU	FOU		MOU	ROU	YOU (16)				
Stafford	CRF	GRF	MRF	NRF	WRF	YRF					
Suffolk, East	CRT	ERT	GRT		ORT	VRT	YRT				
Suffolk, West				AGV	EGV	JGV	YGV		1960/1155 : (17)		
Surrey	CPL (18)	KPL	NPL		UPL	YPL					
Sussex, East		CAP	DPN		KPN	MPN	SPN	YPN			
Sussex, West	BPX	EPX	HPX (19)		SPX	YPX					
Warwick	AWD	CWD	DWD	FWD	MWD	TWD	YWD				
Westmorland					BJM	DJM	JJM	PJM			YJM
Isle of Wight	BDL	DDL	FDL		MDL	PDL	YDL				
Wilts	AWV	CHR	DWV (20)	EWV	LWV	OWV	YWV				
Worcester	AWP	CWP	FWP		NWP	SWP	YWP				
Yorks., E.R.		BBT	DWF		LWF	SWF	YWF				
Yorks., N.R.	AVN	BAJ	CVN		KVN	OVN	YVN				
Yorks., W.R.	BYG	DWR	FYG		MYG	SYG	YYG				

County Boroughs :

Year and number of Order	1932 / 332	1935 / 581	1938 / 6	1942 / 1441	1946 / 1557	1951 / 1380	1955 / 1666	1959 / 86	1961 / 962	1963 / 494	1964 / 404
Barnsley			AHE		GHE	NHE	YHE				
Barrow					CEO		JEO	REO			YEO
Bath			AGL		EGL	HGL	NGL	TGL			YGL
Birkenhead			ACM		ECM	FCM	MCM	RCM (21)	SCM		YCM
Birmingham	BVP (22)	FOJ (23)	JVP (24)		OVP	TVP (25)	YVP				
Blackburn		ACB	BCB		HCB		NCB	SCB			YCB
Blackpool		AFV	DFV		MFV		YFV				
Bolton		AWH	CWH		JWH		PWH	YWH			
Bootle								CEM	EEM		YEM
Bournemouth	BRU	FRU	JRU		SRU	URU	YRU				
Bradford	AKY	EAK	FKY		MKY (26)	PKY	YKY				
Brighton	BUF	GUF	KUF		SUF		YUF				
Bristol	CHY	FHY	KHY		WHY	YHY					
Burnley					EHG		LHG	RHG		THG	YHG
Burton-on-T.					DFA	GFA	TFA	YFA			
Bury					CEN	FEN	TEN	YEN			
Canterbury		AJG	DJG		MJG		YJG				
Cardiff		BUH	DUH		NUH		TUH	YUH			
Carlisle		BHH	CHH		JHH	MHH	UHH	YHH (27)	(XHH only)		
Chester	BFM	EFM	HFM		RFM	YFM					
Coventry	BWK	EWK	HWK		PWK	VWK	YWK				
Croydon	BVB	EVB	HVB		PVB		YVB				
Darlington	CHN	FHN	GHN	JHN	SHN	YHN					
Derby			ARC		FRC	JRC	URC	YRC			
Dewsbury					BHD		GHD	NHD			YHD
Doncaster		BDT	EDT		SDT	WDT	YDT				
Dudley	BFD	EFD	KFD		RFD	UFD	YFD				
Eastbourne					EJK		KJK	RJK			YJK
East Ham		AHV	DHV		HHV	MHV	UHV	YHV			
Exeter	BFJ	FFJ	JFJ		RFJ	UFJ	YFJ				
Gateshead			ACN		FCN	GCN	LCN	SCN		TCN	YCN
Gloucester	AFH	CFH	FFH		OFH	RFH	YFH				
Gt. Yarmouth					BEX	DEX	GEX	MEX			YEX (28)
Grimsby			AJV		EJV	GJV	PJV	UJV	YJV		
Halifax			AJX		FJX	HJX	PJX	TJX	VJX		YJX
Hastings		BDY	DDY		MDY		TDY	YDY			
Huddersfield		BVH	DVH		KVH	NVH	UVH	YVH			

Year and number of Order	1932/332	1935/581	1938/6	1942/1441	1946/1557	1951/1380	1955/1666	1959/86	1961/962	1963/494	1964/404
Ipswich					DPV	HPV	RPV	UPV			YPV
Kingston on Hull	BRH	FAT	KRH		SRH	WRH	YRH				
Leeds	CUM (29)	JUM	NUM		XUM		YUM				
Leicester	ARY	CRY	FRY		ORY		YRY				
Lincoln		BFE	CVL		HVL	LVL	YVL				
Liverpool	CLV	ELV	JLV		ULV		YLV				
Luton											YXE
Manchester	BXJ	GXJ	JXJ		UXJ		YXJ				
Merthyr T.		AHB					CHB	HHB			YHB
Middlesbrough					EXG	HXG	PXG	TXG	VXG		YXG
Newcastle	BVK	HVK	MVK		XVK		YVK				
Newport (Mon.)	ADW	FDW			MDW		TDW	YDW			(30)
Northampton			AVV		EVV	JVV	PVV	YVV			
Norwich		BVG	CVG		HVG	KVG	RVG	YVG			
Nottingham	BTV	FTV	LTV		STV	YTV					
Oldham		DBU	EBU		NBU		YBU				
Oxford	BWL	GWL	NWL		XWL	YWL					
Plymouth		BJY	EJY		NJY	SJY	VJY	YJY			
Portsmouth	ATP	BTP	ETP		KTP	NTP	YTP				
Preston			BRN		HRN	LRN	YRN				
Reading		CRD	DRD		NRD	SRD	YRD				
Rochdale	BDK	HDK			PDK		YDK				
Rotherham	AET	BET	FET		JET	OET	YET				
St. Helens					FDJ		NDJ	TDJ	XDJ		YDJ
Salford		ARJ	DRJ		MRJ		TRJ	YRJ			
Sheffield	BWJ	FWJ	LWJ		XWJ		YWJ				
Smethwick	BHA	FHA	LHA		VHA	YHA					
Solihull											YXC
Southampton	ATR	DTR	GTR		OTR	WTR	YTR				
Southend		BJN	DJN		KJN	NJN	YJN				
Southport	BWM	FFY	GWM		PWM		YWM				
S. Shields							ECU	LCU	NCU	OCU	YCU
Stockport		BJA	DJA		KJA		TJA	YJA			
Stoke	BVT	GVT	NVT		XVT	YVT					
Sunderland					FGR		OGR	TGR	YGR		
Swansea		CWN	FWN	JWN	UWN		YWN				
Torbay											YXF
Tynemouth					FFT			MFT			YFT

Year and number of Order	1932/332	1935/581	1938/6	1942/1441	1946/1557	1951/1380	1955/1666	1959/86	1961/962	1963/494	1964/404
Wakefield			CHL		HHL	LHL	UHL	YHL			YHF
Wallasey		BHF			FHF		NHF	THF			
Walsall	CDH	HDH	LDH		WDH	YDH					
Warrington		EED	FED		OED	SED	YED				
West Bromwich		BEA	CEA	DEA	MEA	PEA	YEA				
West Ham		AJD	CJD		HJD	LJD	YJD (31)				
W. Hartlepool					BEF	EEF	KEF	REF			YEF (32)
Wigan					FJP		LJP	RJP			YJP
Wolverhampton		CJW	FJW		PUK (33)	SUK	YUK				
Worcester			BFK		HFK	MFK	YFK				
York		AVY	DVY		JVY	OVY	YVY				
County Councils, Scotland :											
Aberdeen		ASA	BSA	DSA	KSA	RSA (34)	YSA				(35)
Angus		BSR	CSR	DSR	KSR	PSR	YSR				
Argyll			BSD			DSB	LSB			OSB	YSB
Ayr					HSD		PSD	TSD	YSD		
Banff						BSE	GSE		LSE		YSE
Berwick					BSH	DSH	LSH				YSH
Bute								BSJ			YSJ
Caithness								BSK			YSK
Clackmannan							ASL	DSL			YSL
Dumfries	BSM	ESM	GSM		RSM	TSM	YSM				
Dunbarton			FSN			HSN	OSN	YSN (36)			
East Lothian						CSS	JSS	PSS			YSS
Fife	BSP	DSP	FSP		PSP	SSP	YSP				
Inverness		AST	BST		GST	MST	YST				
Kincardine							BSU	ESU			YSU
Kinross								CSV			YSV
Kirkcudbright					ASW	CSW	GSW (37) & NSW	HSW to MSW			YSW
Lanark		AVD	CVD	DVD	MVD		TVD	YVD			
Midlothian					FSY		HSY	OSY			YSY
Moray					CSO	ESO	LSO	SSO			YSO
Nairn											YAS
Orkney											YBS
Peebles											YDS
Perth			AGS	BGS	FGS	KGS	RGS	YGS			

283

Year and number of Order	1932 / 332	1935 / 581	1938 / 6	1942 / 1441	1946 / 1557	1951 / 1380	1955 / 1666	1959 / 86	1961 / 962	1963 / 494	1964 / 404
Renfrew		CHS	DHS		KHS		YHS				
Ross & Cromarty						FJS	JJS	OJS		RJS	YJS
Roxburgh					EKS	GKS	OKS	UKS			YKS
Selkirk							BLS	ELS			YLS
Stirling			BWG		GWG	JWG	OWG	SWG	YWG		
Sutherland								BNS			YNS
West Lothian							CSX	GSX	PSX		YSX
Wigtown					AOS	COS		GOS		HOS	YOS
Zetland											YPS

Burgh Councils, Scotland :

	1932 / 332	1935 / 581	1938 / 6	1942 / 1441	1946 / 1557	1951 / 1380	1955 / 1666	1959 / 86	1961 / 962	1963 / 494	1964 / 404
Aberdeen		ARS	CRS (38)		JRS		ORS	TRS	YRS		(39)
Coatbridge											YXB (40)
Dundee					FYJ		LVJ	PYJ		SYJ	YYJ
Edinburgh	BWS	DWS	FWS		PWS	VWS	YWS				
Glasgow		DYS	FYS		OYS	SYS	YYS				
Greenock							CVS	FVS			YVS
Kirkcaldy										CXA	YXA
Motherwell							BGM	EGM	FGM		YGM
Paisley							HXS	NXS			YXS

KEY TO NOTES

(1) BTU and DMA omitted in error.
(2) BTU and DMA included.
(3) GMA misprinted as GMR in 1938/6; corrected in 1941/1149.
(4) RAF omitted.
(5) RAF included.
(6) GOD omitted.
(7) SOD omitted.
(8) AOO-HOO, JOO-POO, ROO-YOO, BWC-HWC, JWC-PWC, RWC-TWC, VWC-YWC allotted.
(9) JEW omitted.
(10) DUW included; FUC omitted.
(11) DUW omitted. Including GPO allotted by 1936/1015.
(12) Plus USN.

284

(13) NMC, NMD, NME, NMF, NMG, NMH, NMK, NML, NMM, NMP, NMT, NMU, NMV, NMX and NMY omitted.

(14) NMC, NMD, NME, NMF, NMG, NMH, NMK, NML, NMM, NMP, NMT, NMU, NMV, NMX and NMY allotted.

(15) FUX included in 1946/1557, but omitted in 1949/1618.

(16) SOT omitted.

(17) CBF-HBF, JBF-PBF, RBF-TBF, VBF-YBF allotted.

(18) APE omitted.

(19) Excluding GPO.

(20) DAM omitted.

(21) NBG omitted.

(22) BOG omitted.

(23) COC and COK omitted.

(24) HOG omitted.

(25) POE and POX omitted.

(26) PAK added in 1949/1618. (Probably allotted at this time to permit isue of PAK 1 to Pakistan High Commissioner.)

(27) Excluding XHH, omitted in error. (Included in 1961/962).

(28) SEX omitted.

(29) BUB, BUG and BUM omitted.

(30) WDW omitted in error from 1964/404; corrected in 1965/237.

(31) Excluding MAN.

(32) OEF omitted in error from 1964/404; corrected in 1965/237.

(33) FUK omitted.

(34) LAV omitted.

(35) SAV and SSA omitted in error from 1964/404; allotted in error to Aberdeen B.C. in 1965/237; finally corrected in 1966/250.

(36) Excluding USN.

(37) NSW apparently misprinted for HSW in 1955/1666; HSW to MSW inclusive allotted by 1959/86.

(38) ARS omitted.

(39) SAV and SSA allotted in error in 1965/237; correctly allotted to Aberdeen B.C. in 1966/250.

(40) HXB misprinted as HXR in 1964/404, corrected in 1965/237.

285

SUMMARY OF OMISSIONS, ERRORS AND EXCEPTIONS

Never allotted

GOD, SOD, AWC, UWC, SOT, JEW, FUC, ABF, BBF, UBF, APE, DAM, NBG, BOG, COC, COK, HOG, POE, POX, SEX, BUB, BUG, BUM, MAN, FUK, LAV.
(Although the Isle of Man is not under the jurisdiction of the Ministry of Transport, MAN was not allotted to West Ham in order to avoid confusion with Manx vehicles.)

Initially allotted, but later withdrawn

DUW (allotted 1935, withdrawn 1938),   FUX (allotted 1946, withdrawn 1949),   ARS (allotted 1935, withdrawn 1938).

Initially omitted but later allotted

RAF was omitted from 1946/1557 and 1949/1380, but allotted in 1951/1380. (By the latter date the new series of registrations for Ministry of Defence vehicles was in use, hence there was no longer any risk of confusion between R.A.F. and civilian vehicles).
NMC to NMY were omitted in 1938 and not allotted until 1961.

Allotted, but never used without year letters.

VDG, XXX, YYY, DWO, CNT, MUK, ASS. (AHO and BHO were omitted in the forward format, but used in the reverse; SHT used in the forward format, omitted in reverse).

(See note on next page for marks omitted in year-letter sequences.)

Errors subsequently corrected

See notes 1, 2, 3, 27, 30, 32, 35, 37, 39 and 40 above.

Exception to rule.

GPO to London, (1936/1015), USN to London (1942/1441).
(USN was allotted to London at this time for issue to vehicles of the United States Navy. However, while such vehicles did bear registrations with a USN prefix they were never subject to civilian registration, so for the purpose of this study the combination remained unused.)

<u>Marks omitted in year-letter sequences.</u>

The marks omitted from the list of allocations to LVLOs/VROs (publication V382) show some differences from former practice. The following which were allocated to Local Taxation Offices were not allocated to VROs: KOC, KOK, DWO, ASS, BAS. (KOC and KOK were issued in both forward and reverse sequences and with suffix 'E'; the other three have never been issued). On the other hand, the following "banned" in LTO days were allotted to VROs: POE (omitted from V382 in 1975/6 but allotted in 1979/87 – although not then authorised had been used with G, M and R suffix). APE (omitted from 1975/6/9, but allotted in 1987 – although not then authorised had been used with T suffix). GPO and USN are no longer shown as allocated to London, but still are omitted from the allocations of Portsmouth and Dundee respectively. Finally it may be noted that all combinations ending –VD are now withdrawn from issue. (Last use was WVD-S).

The following, although not "censored", were omitted in certain sequences:

VDG First use VDG-J.
YYY First use YYY-G.
CNT First use CNT-B.
WOG Used in forward non-suffix sequence but not since.
SHT Used in forward non-suffix sequence, but then omitted until SHT-S.
PEE Used in forward non-suffix sequence, but then omitted until PEE-S.
MUK First use MUK-P.

Later, numerous other combinations were proscribed, despite their appearance in V382 allocations. On the other hand, commencing 15.2.96 certain trios previously suppressed were released for use on "Classic" and "Select" registrations, namely ABF, APE, AWC, BAS, BBF, BOG, BUB, BUG, DWO, GPO, HOG, LAV, NBG, SOT and UBF. Commencing in January 1997 certain of these were also released for normal registrations, being first issued as follows: P-BUG, P-UBF, R-BUB, R-DWO, R-NBG, S-ABF and S-BBF.

To the end of 1999 the following have never been issued in any normal sequence, forward, reverse, with year suffix or year prefix: EBS, FBS, WPS, YTK, SXS to YXS and XXX.

As there is little to distinguish a figure '1' from the letter 'I' or the number '10' from the letters 'IO', some registration marks will have the appearance of five or six letter words, for example RAP 1D, BUN 10N, D1 RTY etc. Those which a Council feel would cause embarrassment should not be used.
                    MoT "Handbook", (1965 issue)
(It is indicative of changing attitudes that such registrations are now auctioned by the DVLA !).

APPENDIX 7

LOCAL GOVERNMENT ORGANISATION AND NOMENCLATURE

LOCAL GOVERNMENT ORGANISATION AND NOMENCLATURE

ENGLAND & WALES

Registration authorities were the administrative counties and county boroughs set up under the Local Government Act of 1886. Several geographical counties were broken up for administration purposes into two or more parts, i.e. Yorkshire, (the three Ridings); Lincolnshire, (the three Parts); Suffolk and Sussex, (East and West); Cambridgeshire (the Soke of Peterborough and the Isle of Ely were separate administrative counties). County Boroughs were unitary authorities, completely independent of the geographical county within which they lay. Statutory Instruments always quoted the full official name of the authority. In the 1903 Regulations these are shown as "The County Council of ......" (except that the London County Council is shown as such), or "The Council of the County Borough of ......". These names often differed from the version of the name in common use. The following are the official titles used in the 1903 Regulations and the order in which they are listed in the alphabetical order section :

County Council of :

Anglesey	Gloucester	Pembroke
Bedford	Hereford	The Soke of Peterborough
Berks	Hertford	Radnor
Brecknock	Huntingdon	Rutland
Bucks	Kent	Salop
Cambridge	Lancaster	Somerset
Cardigan	Leicester	Southampton
Carmarthen	Lincolnshire :	Stafford
Carnarvon	The Parts of Holland	East Suffolk
Chester	The Parts of Kesteven	West Suffolk
Cornwall	The Parts of Lindsey	Surrey
Cumberland	London	East Sussex
Denbigh	Merioneth	West Sussex
Derby	Middlesex	Warwick
Devon	Monmouth	Westmorland
Dorset	Montgomery	The Isle of Wight
Durham	Norfolk	Wilts
The Isle of Ely	Northampton	Worcester
Essex	Northumberland	The East Riding of Yorkshire
Flint	Nottingham	The North Riding of Yorkshire
Glamorgan	Oxford	The West Riding of Yorkshire

County Borough Council of :

Barrow-in-Furness	Croydon	Liverpool	Sheffield
Bath	Derby	Manchester	Southampton
Birkenhead	Devonport	Middlesbrough	South Shields
Birmingham	Dudley	Newcastle-upon-Tyne	Stockport
Blackburn	Exeter	Newport (Monmouth)	Sunderland
Bolton	Gateshead	Northampton	Swansea
Bootle	Gloucester	Norwich	Walsall
Bournemouth	Great Yarmouth	Nottingham	Warrington
Bradford (Yorkshire)	Grimsby	Oldham	West Bromwich
Brighton	Halifax	Oxford	West Ham
Bristol	Hanley	Plymouth	West Hartlepool
Burnley	Hastings	Portsmouth	Wigan
Burton-upon-Trent	Huddersfield	Preston	Wolverhampton
Bury	Ipswich	Reading	Worcester
Canterbury	Kingston upon Hull	Rochdale	York
Cardiff	Leeds	Rotherham	
Chester	Leicester	St. Helens	
Coventry	Lincoln	Salford	

Supplementing the Statutory Rules and Orders and Statutory Instruments the Ministry of Transport issued the publication RF 182, (later VE 182), listing registration authorities and marks allotted thereto. This was revised periodically as more index marks were allocated. The publication consisted of three lists. List A showed registration authorities, in alphabetical order in each of the following groupings, with the index marks allocated to each, (note that Irish authorities, not covered by SR&Os or SIs since 1920, were nevertheless shown in this publication) : England & Wales, County Councils; England & Wales, County Borough Councils; Scotland, County Councils; Scotland, Burgh Councils; Northern Ireland, County Councils; Northern Ireland, County Borough Councils; Eire (later Republic of Ireland), County Councils; ditto, County Borough Councils. List B showed one and two-letter index marks in alphabetical order, together with the name of the authority to which they were allocated, whilst List C gave the addresses of the local taxation offices, in the same sequence as in List A.

Over the course of time changes in the original allocation resulted from :

1. Changes in nomenclature.
2 The creation of new county boroughs.
3. Statutory amalgamations of two or more councils and absorptions of one county council or county borough council by another.
4. Voluntary arrangements for the amalgamation of local taxation offices.
5. Local Government Reorganisation, 1974.

CHANGES IN NOMENCLATURE

1. "Carnarvon" was altered to "Caernarvon" in 1925.
2. "Berks" was officially altered to "Berkshire" by SI 1968 No. 355.
3. Although colloquially known as "Hampshire" the regulations continued to show "County Council of Southampton"; however, from 1955 it was shown as "....Southampton (Hampshire)" and the 1961 edition of RF 182 the name was shown simply as "Hampshire". Nevertheless, it was still shown as the County Council of Southampton in the 1964 S.I., but this also included an additional entry "Hampshire - see Southampton County Council". The name change was never recorded on a SI, as was that of Berkshire.
4. A minor change was the dropping of "Yorkshire" after Bradford in 1949. An ambivalent attitude was adopted, both in SR&Os and RF 182, concerning the inclusion or otherwise of hyphens in Kingston-upon-Hull.

Up to and including the 1946 edition of RF 182, (and perhaps later), both Lists A and C used exactly the same nomenclature as the SR&Os and SIs. However, by the 1961 edition the names in List A were those more commonly in use, in many cases including the suffix "shire" - even for Dorsetshire, where in fact it is rarely used, (but not Devonshire), - and see above for Hampshire.

CHANGES IN COUNTY BOROUGH STATUS

14 new and two reorganised county boroughs were created between 1904 and 1915. There was then a long period of stability, only one more county borough being created before 1964, (i.e. Doncaster in 1927); there were several more changes in the period 1964-1968.

	New County Boroughs	Alterations
1904	Blackpool, Tynemouth	
1905	Southport	
1907	Smethwick	
1908	Merthyr Tydfil	
1910		New C.B. of Stoke-on-Trent absorbed Hanley.
1911	Eastbourne	
1913	Barnsley, Dewsbury, Wallasey	
1914	Carlisle, Southend-on-Sea	Plymouth absorbed Devonport.
1915	East Ham, Wakefield, Darlington	
1927	Doncaster	
1964	Luton, Solihull	
1966		New C.B. of Warley incorporated Smethwick.
1967		New C.B. of Hartlepool incorporated West Hartlepool.
1968	Torbay	New C.B. of Teesside incorporated Middlesbrough.

CHANGES IN COUNTY COUNCIL STATUS

There was complete stability in the county council set-up between 1903 and 1965, in which year three amalgamations took place :

New Council	Incorporating
Greater London Council	London County Council, Middlesex, Croydon, East Ham, West Ham.
C.C. of Cambridge and The Isle of Ely	Cambridge, Isle of Ely
C.C. of Huntingdon and Peterborough	Huntingdon, Soke of Peterborough.

In all cases of amalgamations it was enacted that the new authority would take over the index marks of its constituents.

ISLES OF SCILLY

Motorists in the Isles of Scilly were exempt from registration and licensing provisions until 1 April 1971. From that date vehicles on the islands required registration and the combination SCY was transferred from Swansea, where it had already been issued without suffix and with G suffix. The Isles of Scilly registrations commenced with SCY and J suffix, being issued by Cornwall County Council and after centralisation by Truro LVLO.

VOLUNTARY AMALGAMATIONS OF LOCAL TAXATION OFFICES

1 April 1971	Ipswich and East Suffolk *
1 April 1972	Oxford C.C.* and Oxford C.B.C.
22 May 1972	Lancashire * and Preston
24 July 1972	Devon * and Exeter
1 April 1973	Glamorgan and Cardiff *
30 April 1973	Berkshire * and Reading
12 January 1974	Lindsey * and Lincoln C.B.C.

* indicates the council administering the LTO following the merger.

AMALGAMATION RESULTING FROM LOCAL GOVERNMENT REORGANISATION

1 April 1974   Birkenhead and Wallasey became part of Wirral Metropolitan Borough Council and the Birkenhead office was closed.

(Further amalgamations, following Local Government Reorganisation, are detailed in the tabulation which follows, but the above is the only one which occurred whilst the LTOs were still responsible for handling new registrations).

OTHER CHANGES RESULTING FROM LOCAL GOVERNMENT REORGANISATION, 1974

Under this reorganisation county boroughs were abolished. In seven areas (Greater London, the West Midlands, Greater Manchester, Merseyside, South Yorkshire, West Yorkshire and Tyne and Wear) Metropolitan Counties were created, being divided into Metropolitan Districts or Boroughs. The remainder of England and Wales was covered by "shire" counties, (not always coinciding with the old county council areas) which were divided into District Councils or Borough Councils. The following tabulation lists the new names of LTOs following reorganisation and their dates of closure, (after 1.10.74 LTOs remained responsible for several matters other than the first registration of vehicles, including the handling of cherished mark transfers and trade plate issues. The last of the LTOs were finally closed on 17 March 1978).

The nomenclature used in the first and second columns of this tabulation is that used in the 1968 and 1975 issues of RF 182/VE 182 respectively.

Old Name	Name from 1.4.74	Date Closed *	Amalgamations
* Where no date is shown in this column, closure occurred on 17 March 1978.			

County Councils

Old Name	Name from 1.4.74	Date Closed *	Amalgamations
Anglesey	Gwynedd CC (Llangefni office)	31.12.77	Absorbed by Caernarvon office
Bedfordshire	Bedfordshire CC		
Berkshire	Royal County of Berkshire		
Breconshire	Borough of Brecknock		
Buckinghamshire	Buckinghamshire CC		
Caernarvonshire	Gwynedd CC (Caernarvon office)		
Cambridgeshire & Isle of Ely	Cambridgeshire CC (Cambridge office)		

Old Name	Name from 1.4.74	Date Closed *	Amalgamations

* Where no date is shown in this column, closure occurred on 17 March 1978.

County Councils (continued)

Old Name	Name from 1.4.74	Date Closed *	Amalgamations
Cardiganshire	Dyfed CC (Aberystwyth office)		
Carmarthenshire	Dyfed CC (Carmarthen office)		
Cheshire	Cheshire CC		
Cornwall	Cornwall CC		
Cumberland	Cumbria (Carlisle office)		
Denbighshire	Clwyd CC (Ruthin office)		
Derbyshire	Derbyshire CC		
Devon	Devon CC		
Dorsetshire	Dorset CC		
Durham	Durham CC		
Essex	Essex CC		
Flintshire	Clwyd CC (Mold office)		
Gloucestershire	Gloucestershire CC		
Greater London	Greater London Council (5 offices)		
Hampshire	Hampshire CC		
Herefordshire	CC of Hereford & Worcester (Hereford office)		
Hertfordshire	Hertfordshire CC		
Huntingdon & Peterborough	Cambridgeshire CC (Peterborough office)		
Kent	Kent CC		
Lancashire	Lancashire CC		
Leicestershire	Leicestershire CC		
Lincolnshire-			
Parts of Holland	Lincolnshire CC (Boston office)		
Parts of Kesteven	" (Sleaford office)		
Parts of Lindsey	" (Lincoln office)		
Merionethshire	Gwynedd CC (Dolgellau office)		
Monmouthshire	Gwent CC		
Montgomeryshire	Montgomery DC		
Norfolk	Norfolk CC		
Northamptonshire	Northamptonshire CC		
Northumberland	Northumberland CC		
Nottinghamshire	Nottinghamshire CC		
Oxfordshire	Oxfordshire CC		
Pembrokeshire	Dyfed CC (Haverfordwest office)		
Radnorshire	Radnor DC		
Rutland	Rutland DC	30.9.77	Absorbed by Leicestershire
Salop	Salop CC		
Somerset	Somerset CC		
Staffordshire	Staffordshire CC		
East Suffolk	Suffolk CC (Ipswich office)		
West Suffolk	Suffolk CC (Bury St. Edmunds office)		
Surrey	Surrey CC		
East Sussex	East Sussex CC		
West Sussex	West Sussex CC		
Warwickshire	Warwickshire CC		
Westmorland	Cumbria CC (Kendal office)		
Isle of Wight	Isle of Wight CC		
Wiltshire	Wiltshire CC		
Worcestershire	CC of Hereford & Worcester (Worcester office)		
Yorkshire-			
East Riding	Humberside CC		
North Riding	North Yorkshire CC		
West Riding	West Yorkshire MCC		

Old Name	Name from 1.4.74	Date Closed *	Amalgamations
* Where no date is shown in this column, closure occurred on 17 March 1978.			

COUNTY BOROUGHS

Old Name	Name from 1.4.74	Date Closed *	Amalgamations
Barnsley	Barnsley MBC	16.12.77	Absorbed by Sheffield
Barrow-in-Furness	Borough of Barrow-in-Furness		
Bath	Bath City Council	1.9.77	Absorbed by Bristol
Birmingham	Birmingham DC		
Blackburn	Borough of Blackburn	16.12.77	Absorbed by Lancashire
Blackpool	Blackpool BC		
Bolton	Bolton MBC		
Bootle	MB of Sefton (Bootle office)	18.7.77	Absorbed by Liverpool
Bournemouth	Bournemouth DC		
Bradford	City of Bradford Met. Council	30.12.77	Absorbed by Leeds
Brighton	Brighton DC		
Bristol	The City Council of Bristol		
Burnley	Burnley BC		
Burton-upon-Trent	East Staffordshire DC	30.6.77	Absorbed by Staffordshire
Bury	Metropolitan Borough of Bury	30.9.77	Absorbed by Bolton
Canterbury	Canterbury City Council		
Cardiff	Cardiff City Council		
Carlisle	City of Carlisle	28.10.77	Absorbed by Cumbria
Chester	Chester City Council		
Coventry	Coventry City Council		
Darlington	Borough of Darlington		
Derby	Derby BC		
Dewsbury	Kirklees MBC (Dewsbury office)	15.3.77	Absorbed by Huddersfield office
Doncaster	Doncaster MBC		
Dudley	Dudley MBC		
Eastbourne	Eastbourne BC	18.7.77	Absorbed by Hastings
Gateshead	Gateshead MBC	15.8.77	Absorbed by Newcastle
Gloucester	Gloucester DC		
Great Yarmouth	The Borough of Great Yarmouth		
Grimsby	Grimsby BC		
Halifax	Calderdale MBC	2.1.78	Absorbed by Kirklees
Hartlepool	Hartlepool BC		
Hastings	Hastings BC		
Huddersfield	Kirklees MBC (Huddersfield office)		
Kingston-upon-Hull	Kingston-upon-Hull City Council		
Leeds	Leeds City Council		
Leicester	Leicester City Council		
Liverpool	Liverpool City Council		
Luton	Borough of Luton	21.10.77	Absorbed by Bedfordshire
Manchester	Manchester City Council		
Merthyr Tydfil	Merthyr Tydfil Borough Council		
Newcastle-u-Tyne	Newcastle-upon-Tyne MDC		
Newport (Mon.)	Newport BC		
Northampton	Northampton BC	1.11.76	Absorbed by Northamptonshire
Norwich	Norwich City Council		
Nottingham	Nottingham City Council	26.9.77	Absorbed by Nottinghamshire
Oldham	Metropolitan Boough of Oldham	31.7.77	Absorbed by Manchester
Plymouth	Plymouth City Council		
Portsmouth	Portsmouth City Council		
Rochdale	Rochdale MBC		
Rotherham	Rotherham BC		
St. Helens	St. Helens BC		

Old Name	Name from 1.4.74	Date Closed*	Amalgamations
*Where no date is shown in this column, closure occurred on 17 March 1978.

County Boroughs (continued)

Old Name	Name from 1.4.74	Date Closed*	Amalgamations
Salford	Salford City Council	31.7.77	Absorbed by Manchester
Sheffield	Sheffield City Council		
Solihull	Metropolitan Borough of Solihull	1.7.77	Absorbed by Birmingham
Southampton	City of Southampton		
Southend-on Sea	Southend-on-Sea BC		
Southport	MB of Sefton (Southport office)	18.7.77	Absorbed by Liverpool
South Shields	Borough of South Tyneside	1.8.77	Absorbed by Newcastle
Stockport	MB of Stockport	17.9.77	Absorbed by Manchester
Stoke-on-Trent	City of Stoke-upon-Trent		
Sunderland	Borough of Sunderland	22.8.77	Absorbed by Durham CC
Swansea	Swansea DC		
Teesside	Middlesbrough BC		
Torbay	Borough of Torbay		
Tynemouth	North Tyneside MBC	8.8.77	Absorbed by Newcastle
Wakefield	City of Wakefield MDC	17.12.76	Absorbed by West Yorkshire
Wallasey	Wirral MBC		
Walsall	Walsall MBC	30.1.78	Absorbed by Birmingham
Warley	Sandwell MBC (Warley office)		
Warrington	Warrington MBC		
West Bromwich	Sandwell MBC (West Bromwich office)	20.12.76	Absorbed by Warley Office
Wigan	Wigan MBC	30.12.77	Absorbed by Bolton
Wolverhampton	MB of Wolverhampton		
Worcester	Worcester City Council		
York	York District Council		

BC = Borough Council   CC= County Council   DC = District Council   MBC = Metropolitan Borough Council
MCC = Metropolitan County Council   MDC = Metropolitan District Council

SCOTLAND

Whereas in England and Wales the initial allocation was made on a population basis, in Scotland (and Ireland), the basis was alphabetical. The three largest authorities, Glasgow, Edinburgh and Lanarkshire received the single letter marks G, S and V respectively. The remaining authorities were arranged in alphabetical order in two groups, county councils and burgh councils.

The allocation commenced with SA, SB etc. to SY, then AS, BS etc. to YS. The alphabetical sequence was later broken when four counties changed their official names. As in England and Wales other alterations took place over the years.

The following are the official names used in the 1903 Regulations :

County Councils

Aberdeen	Dumbarton *	Lanark	Roxburgh
Argyll	Elgin	Linlithgow	Selkirk
Ayr	Fife	Midlothian	Stirling
Banff	Forfar	Nairn	Sutherland
Berwick	Haddington	Orkney	Wigtown
Bute	Inverness	Peebles	Zetland
Caithness	Kincardine	Perth	
Clackmannan	Kinross	Renfrew	
Dumfries	Kirkcudbright	Ross & Cromarty	

Burgh Councils

Aberdeen	Glasgow	Leith
Dundee	Govan	Paisley
Edinburgh	Greenock	Partick

CHANGES IN NOMENCLATURE

* Whilst "Dumbarton" was shown in the 1903 Regulations, this was incorrect, since the official name of the county was Dunbarton, from its inception in 1888 until re-organisation of Local Government, (notwithstanding the spelling Dumbarton for the county town).

The following counties changed their official names :

1919	Elgin CC became Moray CC.
1921	Haddington CC became East Lothian CC
1921	Linlithgow CC became West Lothian CC
1928	Forfar CC became Angus CC.

CHANGES IN BURGH STATUS

It will be recalled that in the case of Burgh Councils the qualification to become a registration authority was a population of or exceeding 50,000. Only three further burghs qualified before centralisation of licensing :

1920	Motherwell & Wishaw
1963	Kirkcaldy
1964	Coatbridge

Three of the original 1903 burghs were absorbed by their larger neighbours :

1912	Govan and Partick absorbed by Glasgow
1920	Leith absorbed by Edinburgh.

VOLUNTARY AMALGAMATION OF LOCAL TAXATION OFFICES

13.7.73   Inverness CC absorbed the Ross & Cromarty CC office.

CHANGES RESULTING FROM LOCAL GOVERNMENT REORGANISATION

Local Government reorganisation in Scotland took place on 16 May 1975, one year later than in England & Wales. In this case the top tier unit was the Regional Council, divided into District Councils.The LTOs of four old counties were closed immediately upon re-organisation and their functions taken over by the offices of their former neighbours, i.e. Kirkcudbright by Dumfries; Peebles and Selkirk by Roxburgh; West Lothian by Edinburgh. The tabulation shows the reorganisation and closure of the remaining counties and registering burghs. The nomenclature used in the first and second columns of the tabulation is that used in the 1968 and 1975 issues of RF 182/VE 182 respectively.

Old Name	Name from 16.5.75	Date Closed *	Absorbed by

* Where no date is shown in this column, closure occurred on 17 March 1978.

County Councils

Old Name	Name from 16.5.75	Date Closed *	Absorbed by
Aberdeen	Grampian RC		
Angus	Tayside RC (Forfar office)		
Argyll	Strathclyde RC (Lochgilphead office)		
Ayr	Strathclyde RC (Ayr office)		
Banff	Banff & Buchan DC	30.9.77	Moray DC
Berwick	Berwickshire DC	20.5.77	Borders RC
Bute	Strathclyde RC (Rothesay office)		
Caithness	Caithness DC		
Clackmannan	Central RC (Alloa office)	28.10.77	Stirling office
Dumfries	Dumfries & Galloway RC		
Dunbarton	Strathclyde RC (Dumbarton office)		
East Lothian	East Lothian DC	28.10.77	Lothian RC (Edinburgh)
Fife	Fife RC		
Inverness	Inverness DC		
Kincardine	Kincardine & Deeside DC	22.12.75	Grampian RC
Kinross	Tayside CC (Kinross office)	30.11.76	Perth office
Lanark	Strathcylde RC (Hamilton office)		
Midlothian	Lothian RC (ex Midlothian office)	1.9.76	Edinburgh office
Moray	Moray DC		
Nairn	Nairn DC	31.1.77	Inverness DC
Orkney	Orkney IC		
Perth	Tayside RC (Perth office)		
Renfrew	Strathclyde CC (Paisley office)		
Roxburgh	Borders RC		
Stirling	Central RC (Stirling office)		
Sutherland	Sutherland DC	30.9.77	Caithness
Wigtown	Wigtown DC		
Zetland	Shetland IC		

BURGH COUNCILS

Old Name	Name from 16.5.75	Date Closed *	Absorbed by
Aberdeen	City of Aberdeen DC	22.12.75	Grampian DC
Coatbridge	Monklands DC	16.4.77	Strathclyde (Hamilton office)
Dundee	Dundee DC		
Edinburgh	Lothian RC (former Edinburgh BC office)		
Glasgow	City of Glasgow DC		
Greenock	Inverclyde DC	29.7.77	Strathclyde (Paisley office)
Kirkcaldy	Kirkcaldy DC	28.10.77	Fife RC
Motherwell & Wishaw	Motherwell DC	2.5.77	Strathclyde (Hamilton office)
Paisley	Renfrew DC	14.11.77	Strathclyde (Paisley off.)

DC = District Council   IC = Island Council   RC = Regional Council

IRELAND

In 1903 the whole of Ireland was part of the United Kingdom. As in England & Wales county councils and county borough councils were the registration authorities. However, the allocation pattern was alphabetical, as in Scotland, using firstly IA to IZ, then AI to WI. In 1903 the authorities were as follows :

County Councils

Antrim	Fermanagh	Longford	Tipperary, South Riding
Armagh	Galway	Louth	Tyrone
Carlow	Kerry	Mayo	Waterford
Cavan	Kildare	Meath	West Meath
Clare	Kilkenny	Monaghan	Wexford
Cork	King's County	Queen's County	Wicklow
Donegal	Leitrim	Roscommon	
Down	Limerick	Sligo	
Dublin	Londonderry	Tipperary, North Riding	

County Borough Councils

Belfast	Dublin	Londonderry
Cork	Limerick	Waterford

There were no changes until after the partition of Ireland in 1921.

NORTHERN IRELAND

There were no changes in the Local Government set-up prior to the centralisation of vehicle and driver licensing in January 1974.
The existing LTOs all then became LVLOs as shown below :

Antrim CC	Ballymena LVLO	Londonderry CC	Coleraine LVLO
Armagh CC	Armagh LVLO	Tyrone CC	Omagh LVLO
Down CC	Downpatrick LVLO	Belfast CBC	Belfast LVLO
Fermanagh CC	Enniskillen LVLO	Londonderry CBC	Londonderry LVLO

IRISH FREE STATE (1921-1937)/EIRE (1937-1949)/REPUBLIC OF IRELAND (1949-date)

CHANGES IN NOMENCLATURE
In what is now the Republic of Ireland, two counties were renamed immediately after partition :
King's County became Offaly; Queen's County became Laoighis, later rendered as Laois, (and sometimes as Leix)..
A minor change is that Westmeath, spelt as two words in the 1903 Regulations, was later rendered as one word.

VOLUNTARY AMALGAMATIONS OF LOCAL TAXATION OFFICES
Joint offices were set up by Dublin County and County Borough Councils in February 1952 and Cork County and County Borough Councils in June 1974. Whereas in the case of Dublin the Joint Office immediately adopted a common series of registrations for the whole of the area, Cork retained separate series for the former county and county borough areas until August 1985, when they were combined.

Despite the fact that Southern Ireland was no longer part of the United Kingdom, the registration systems of the two countries remained compatible and there was no duplication of registration numbers. There was voluntary provision, but no compulsion, for a vehicle permanently exported from the United Kindom to Ireland, and vice-versa, to be re-registered with a local registration. This remained the situation until the Republic of Ireland adopted a completely new format as from 1 January 1987.

It should be mentioned that during the "troubles" which preceded the partition of Ireland, the Ministry of Transport issued SR&O 1921, No.272, dated March 1921, which stated that "whereas, in the opinion of the Minister, the county councils of the respective counties in Ireland named in the Schedule to this Order have neglected or refused to perform their functions under the Act, (i.e. the Roads Act of 1920) and the Motor Car Acts, 1896 and 1903....the functions.....of each of the counties named in the Schedule shall..... be discharged by the police authority instead of by the county council...." The Schedule listed the counties and county boroughs which later formed the Irish Free State. The Order was repealed by SR&O 1922, No. 355 dated 1st April 1922.

APPENDIX 8

THE NEW SYSTEM 2001

On 30th March 2000 new regulations were announced which introduced a mandatory typeface for use on number plates and provided for a new British Standard for the manufacture of plates. The new typeface is permitted from 1st March 2001 and compulsory in respect of new registrations from 1st September 2001. The main features are:

1. The overall width of individual characters, except on motorcycle plates, to be 50mm instead of 57mm.
2. Vehicles constructed but not first registered before 1st January 1973 to be allowed to display plates with white, silver or grey characters on a black background.
3. Removal of the variable spacing permitted between characters "1" or "I" and other characters.
4. The optional use of plates bearing the EU symbol will be permitted.

Note that the standardised EU style plates became compulsory on 1st January 1991 for all new vehicles registered in the Republic of Ireland, except for those bearing ZV or ZZ plates.

Also on 30th March 2000 final details of the new system of index marks were announced. The format will comprise firstly two letters, of which the first will indicate the region and the second the Local Office in whose area the first registration occurs. (Vehicle Registration Offices were renamed Local Offices from 1st January 2001.) The second element will be a two-digit number indicating the half-year of issue. 51 will commence in September 2001, 02 in March 2002, 52 in September 2002, 03 in March 2003, 53 in September 2003 and so on. It was stated that the final three letters will be allocated randomly. Letters I and Q will not be used in either the first or third elements but Z will be used in the third element.

A table of the allocation of initial letters appears on the opposite page.

ALLOCATION OF INITIAL LETTERS 2001 SYSTEM

In the initial announcement, the North region comprised NA-NM (Newcastle), NN-NT (Stockton) and NU-NY (Beverley) and Yorkshire was to be YA-YO (Leeds) and YP-YY (Sheffield). Following representations from inhabitants of the East Riding that they, too, were in Yorkshire, the allocations were changed to that below. In addition XA-XY did not appear in the first list.

A – ANGLIA
AA-AN Peterborough
AO-AU Norwich
AV-AY Ipswich

B – BIRMINGHAM
BA-BY Birmingham

C – CYMRU
CA-CO Cardiff
CP-CV Swansea
CW-CY Bangor

D – DEESIDE AND SHREWSBURY
DA-DK Chester
DL-DY Shrewsbury

E – ESSEX
EA-EY Chelmsford

F – FOREST & FENS
FA-FP Nottingham
FR-FY Lincoln

G – GARDEN OF ENGLAND
GA-GO Maidstone
GP-GY Brighton

H – HAMPSHIRE AND DORSET
HA-HJ Bournemouth
HK-HY (except HW) Portsmouth
HW Isle of Wight

K – LUTON
KA-KL Luton
KM-KY Northampton

L – LONDON
LA-LJ Wimbledon
LK-LT Stanmore
LU-LY Sidcup

M – MANCHESTER & MERSEYSIDE
MA-MY Manchester

NORTH
NA-NO Newcastle
NP-NY Stockton

O – OXFORD
OA-OY Oxford

P – PRESTON
PA-PT Preston
PU-PY Carlisle

R – READING
RA-RY Reading

S – SCOTLAND
SA-SJ Glasgow
SK-SO Edinburgh
SP-ST Dundee
SU-SW Aberdeen
SX-SY Inverness

V – SEVERN VALLEY
VA-VY Worcester

W – WEST COUNTRY
WA-WJ Exeter
WK-WL Truro
WM-WY Bristol

X – EXPORTS
XA-XF Tax Free Exports

Y - YORKSHIRE
YA-YK Leeds
YL-YU Sheffield
YV-YY Beverley

2006 update. This list differs in two respects from that published in the second edition of this book, which itself differed from that in the first edition. Two further changes were made to the new system before it was introduced in September 2001 and these are set out above. Firstly, the codes for the West Country were reallocated so that Truro could have WK, the "K" standing for Kernow, the name for Cornwall in the Cornish language. Secondly, just XA to XF of the "X" range are used for VAT-free exports to EC countries; cars registered in the first month of each six-month period are given XA marks, those in the second XB, etc. At the bottom of the list in the second edition was a comment that a newspaper had reported that BO would be omitted from Birmingham's allocation. This has not happened, though NF is not used.

A POSTSCRIPT – THE "NEW" SYSTEM
Edited by John Harrison

In producing the third edition of this book and this reprint of it we have for the most part left the text unaltered. There are elements of the book which could be updated, e.g. further series have been used for age-related re-registrations, but this updating has not been attempted. When the second edition of the book was published, the "new" (now, of course, "current") system was about to be introduced. The original Appendix 8 was updated to reflect the changes that occurred before the system's final introduction in September 2001. The purpose of this section is to explain more about the current system and how it has worked out in practice and also some other changes to the United Kingdom registration system that have occurred subsequently.

To understand the current system, it is first of all important to know what marks are available for sale under the "Select" scheme (It should be noted that the term "Select" was introduced as a marketing term by DVLA, but is now no longer used by them. Nevertheless, registration hobbyists still use the term for convenience. "Online sales" is a possible alternative, but as sales were originally by phone, this term would not be strictly correct if used to refer to early sales). There are five categories:

1. For around a month all available marks (apart from any held back for sale at auction or for reasons of censorship) are put on sale before being issued as normal marks. The "have anything you like" period is usually around December for March to August issues, i.e. 02s, 03s, 04s, etc., and June for September to February issues, i.e. 51s, 52s, 53s etc. Thereafter the following categories are reserved for sale:

2. "His 'n' hers" pairs. These are combinations where the last letter of the letter pair is the same as the last letter of the letter trio, e.g. AC51 ABC, DE06 FGE. These are aimed primarily at married couples, but someone with a name such as Arthur Brian Cox could choose a mark such as AC51 ABC.

3. Reserved pairs. These are letter pairs which are potentially attractive. They are held back for sale rather than being issued as regional identifiers. Most combinations have been available since 2001 as they are clearly attractive, e.g. AL, DR, MR, VW. At the commencement of the "03" period a review resulted in the combinations GB, MG, OO, TT and XX being added to the list available for each period. Also, note that some combinations have been available for specific periods because when combined with the year identifier they form words, etc., e.g. WH05 (WHO'S), BO55 (BOSS) and all *OO7 combinations.

4. Reserved trios. These are virtually all trios that spell a word, e.g. BUS, CAT, RUN, a name, e.g. BOB, SUE, YEO or a car make, e.g. BMW, JAG and TVR, plus "all of a kinds", i.e. AAA, BBB, etc. These trios are held back for sale rather than issued normally.

5. Others. Sometimes a row of characters within a mark can make it attractive. Some examples which have been held back for sale are CO57 A** (COSTA), **10 TUS, (LOTUS), HE11 EN* (HELEN), *S11 NGH (SINGH), *W11 OW* (WILLOW) and BR14 N** (BRIAN). Other similar such combinations are not issued as normal marks but put on sale instead.

Spotting a "Select", especially one issued in the "have anything you like" period, may not always be easy, but if you see a mark beginning with J, T (apart from T*07), U or XG to XY it is clearly a "Select" as these combinations are not used for normal issues.

Obviously, letter pairs reserved for sale under the "Select" scheme cannot be issued as normal series. What area codes are actually used is determined by, as far as possible, avoiding the most attractive combinations, i.e. those ending in popular surname initials such as B, J and R. Generally area codes follow the same sequence of issue for each six-month period and the table on p303 sets out this sequence. It must be emphasised that this is a guide only and the sequence may be varied as necessary, e.g. if a letter pair is withheld for sale under the "Select" scheme or censored.

There are in fact two "parallel" series for each set of area codes, one for Automated First Registration and Licensing (AFRL) and non-AFRL issues. AFRL is a system whereby the work of registering and (until recently) issuing a tax disc for a new vehicle is carried out by the supplying dealer, rather than by applying to DVLA. The AFRL system is now used by the dealers of all major car manufacturers and importers, and some motorcycle firms and lorry firms.

By no means are all letter trios used. Obviously, as explained above, some are reserved trios kept back for sale under the "Select" scheme. In addition, however, others are withheld, as with the letter pairs generally those likely to be more attractive. Thus, instead of the trios running right through the alphabetical sequence many combinations are omitted. In some instances when area codes have gone through the alphabet in a period, they have commenced a second cycle for some letter pairs, i.e. gone back to the beginning of the alphabet and used most of the combinations omitted on the first cycle. To demonstrate this, a first cycle will commence with AAE, but a second cycle will use AAB, AAC and AAD. AAA is, of course, reserved for sale under the "Select" scheme.

The end of the "51" period saw a reallocation of the Yorkshire Y* codes. YA and YO had been reserved for sale as "Selects" but, perhaps not surprisingly, were not popular. They were therefore removed as "Selects" so they could be issued normally. YL was transferred from Sheffield to Leeds. Leeds now had YA to YL therefore. Beverley originally had YV to YY, but YV was transferred to Sheffield so Sheffield now had YM to YV and Beverley had YW to YY. Whilst considering Yorkshire, it should be noted that in the 06 period all *W06 combinations were withdrawn. This meant that Beverley would have had insufficient marks with just YX and YY available, so Beverley issued YU which normally would have been issued by Sheffield. For similar reasons, Aberdeen issued SU, a combination usually reserved for sale as a "Select".

The "07" period saw another temporary change to the code allocation. More Scottish 07 codes than usual were held back for use as "Selects" or for censorship reasons, so some Scottish Local Offices were more likely to run out of marks. Therefore, the T* letter pairs were made available to the Scottish offices with their allocation "paralleling" that of the S* codes, e.g. TA to TJ were potentially available to Glasgow in addition to SA to SJ. Only Glasgow and Edinburgh actually used the additional T*07 codes, Glasgow issuing just TF and TJ and Edinburgh just TN and TK.

It should be noted that September 2001 saw the introduction of a new series for international circulation purposes to replace that described on page 39 in addition to the then new series for general issues. This took the format 123 Q 51, the last two numbers indicating the age identifier and the first three numbers being serial. It should also be noted that the Q-series for vehicles of indeterminate age, i.e. the Q123 ABC format, and also trade plates, did not change, so still used the pre-2001 codes.

In the autumn of 2013 the DVLA Local Offices were closed with their functions being passed to DVLA at Swansea gradually over the year. Increased use of computer systems such as the one that facilitated the AFRL system for registering new cars online meant that the Local Offices were no longer considered to be needed and their closure would bring about cost savings. This was part of the government's "digital by default" programme under which the presumption was that normally administrative processes would be carried out online as much as possible. The closure of the Local Offices did not result in the abolition of the local identifier on number plates, however. When a new vehicle is first registered now, the local identifier is determined on the basis of the postcode of the supplying garage or first keeper. Thus, with one exception, this major change in the system of vehicle registration did not result in readily noticeable changes to number plates. The one exception was trade plates which ceased to be issued on an area basis with a serial number followed by an area code. The new format for these is a five-digit number using lead zeros if necessary, e.g. 01234. These new trade plates are being introduced as new ones are issued; old style trade plates remain in circulation.

In July 2014 the Driver and Vehicle Agency (DVA), formerly known as Driver and Vehicle Licensing Northern Ireland, the Northern Ireland equivalent of the DVLA, was merged into the DVLA with the functions previously carried out by the DVA in Coleraine being transferred to the DVLA at Swansea. Some facilities available to motorists in Great Britain had not been available in Northern Ireland such as the ability to retax vehicles at Post Offices and the option of putting a number a car owner wanted to keep onto a retention certificate when buying a new car. The merger resulted in a rationalisation of such inconsistencies. There were some problems transferring data between the two sets of computers as the data was kept in slightly different formats, but these were eventually resolved. As part of this process the DVA Local Offices were closed in a similar way to the British ones by the end of 2014.

On 1 October 2014 the requirement for vehicles to display a tax disc was abolished, though vehicle tax still needs to be paid. This is mentioned because a chapter of this book is devoted to tax discs but also because abolishing the disc resulted in one change to number plates, new trade plates no longer having a licence holder.

...AND FINALLY

Whilst several books have been written on the British registration system, Les Newall's "History of Motor Vehicle Registration in the United Kingdom" is without doubt the most scholarly and detailed. Les published the first edition, and a second edition was produced by his family after his death. For a number of reasons, particularly the popularity of cherished numbers, interest in vehicle registrations is growing. Not surprisingly, this has resulted in a further demand for this book and those within the registration hobby are grateful to the Newall family for permitting this third edition. I would also like to thank Adrian Young for permission to use the table opposite which he compiled, Peter Robson whose publishing expertise has been very helpful to me in compiling this third edition, and various other hobbyists who have pointed out mistakes in the original book which have needed correction, and made helpful comments on the updates.

...And very finally, I personally would like to pay tribute to Les who not only was a great help to me in pursuing this hobby of vehicle registrations, but also a great friend. Les was a man of many aspects. He worked in the passenger transport industry ending up as Acting General Manager for St Helens Corporation; he was a family man, a supporter of charities, an authority

Use of two-letter codes by Local Offices

LO	Standard Issue	Overflow Issue	Occasional Issue
Peterborough	AE AF AK AJ AD	AG	AM AC AA AB AN
Norwich	AU AO AP	AR	AT
Ipswich	AY AV	AX AW	
Birmingham	BX BU BV BF BN BK BJ BG BD BT BL	BP BW BC	BA BM
Cardiff	CN CE CK CA	CF	CJ
Swansea	CU CV CP	CT	CR
Bangor	CX CW - then CY from 06		
Chester	DK DG DE DA	DF DC	DH
Shrewsbury	DX DU DY DV DN	DS DL	DP DT DW
Chelmsford	EU EY EX EO EK EA EJ EF	EN ET EG EP	EW
Nottingham	FJ FN FE FL FG FP FD FH	FM FA FB	FC FF
Lincoln	FX FY FV	FT	FR FW
Maidstone	GN GK GJ GF GL	GD GM	GC GH
Brighton	GX GU GY GV GP	GR	GW
Bournemouth	HF HJ HG	HD	HC
Portsmouth	HX HY HV HN HK	HT HS	HL
Isle of Wight	HW		
Luton %	KE KF KJ KL KG KD KC KH	KB KA	KK
Northampton	KX KY KU KV KN KP KM KR KS KW	KT KO	
Northampton – from 08 onwards	KX KY KU KV KN KP KM KR KS KW	KT KO	KJ KK
London Wimbledon	LJ LF LG LD LC LB	LA LE	LH
London Stanmore/ Borehamwood *	LK LN LT LR LS LM	LL LO	LP
London Borehamwood – from 08 onwards	LK LN LT LR LS LM	LL LO	LP KE KF KD KC
London Sidcup	LX LV LY	LW	LU
Manchester	MX MV MK MF MA ML MJ MT MW	MM MD MC	MH MP MB ME
Newcastle	NK NJ NL NA ND NG NC	NH NM	NB NE
Stockton	NX NU NV NY	NT	NR
Oxford	OU OY OV OE	OW	OX
Preston	PO PN PE PK PJ PF	PL PG	PA PM
Carlisle	PX PY		PV
Reading/Theale #	RX RK RV RO RE RJ RF RA	RY RN RL RD RG	
Glasgow	SF SJ SG SA SD SH SB SC	SE	
Edinburgh	SN SK SL SM SO		
Dundee	SP ST	SR	SS
Aberdeen	SV SW		SU – specially issued in 06
Inverness	SY	SX	
Worcester	VX VU VO VK VN VE VA	VF	VT
Exeter	WA WJ WF WG	WD	WH
Truro	WK	WL	
Bristol	WX WU WV WN WR WP	WM	WO WT
Leeds	YJ YK YD YG YH YC YE YF YB	YA YL	
Sheffield	YN YT YR YP YS	YM YO YU	YV
Beverley	YX YY	YW	YU – specially issued in 06

% In 2010 the Luton office was closed and its codes passed to Borehamwood and Northampton.
* In 2006 this office was relocated to Borehamwood and renamed.
# In 2007 this office was relocated to Theale and renamed.

Explanation of columns:

Standard issue	Codes which appear every season without fail except when deliberately withdrawn
Overflow issue	Codes which appear in average or good seasons but not in bad ones
Occasional issue	Codes appearing very rarely, or when regular issue codes are withdrawn. In some instances this code may have only been used for re-registrations, i.e. marks issued after the end of the relevant six-month period.

These combinations are regularly reserved for sale as "Selects" and are not issued regularly, AH, AL, BY, DJ (from 57), DR, ED, EH, GB (from 03), GO, HO, JO, MG (from 03), MO, MR, MS, MY, NO, OH, OK, ON, OO (from 03), OR, OS, RU, SU, TO, TT (from 03), UK, UM, UP, UR, VW, XK, XS and XX (from 03). Combinations not listed here or in the table above have generally not been used so far, but may appear if increased car ownership necessitates their issue.

on steam engines, both traction engines and railway locomotives, as well as vehicle registrations and much more. Above all, he was a true gentleman and a thoroughly nice person to know. He was more than happy to help me with many queries about the registration system.

Since his death others in the hobby have continued to research the British system. I have carried out further research on the pre-1921 General Identification Marks (GIMs) described on pages 47 and 48. Les queried the significance of the additional letter used on these plates by authorities such as Westmorland, Newcastle and Essex. As a result of my researches I have established a pattern from other authorities' GIMs and can say this letter is generally the initial of the authority. Les and I often shared many such little discoveries, but this is one I will never have the chance to share. I can, however, picture the smile on his face and the pleasure it would have given him had I been given this opportunity. Les will always be missed by those within the registration hobby.

INDEX